A DICTIONARY
OF THE EUROPEAN UNION

A DICTIONARY
OF THE EUROPEAN UNION

DAVID PHINNEMORE AND LEE McGOWAN

THIRD EDITION

Routledge
Taylor & Francis Group

LONDON AND NEW YORK

First published 2002
Third Edition 2006

© **Routledge 2006**
Haines House, 21 John Street, London, WC1N 2BP, United Kingdom
(Routledge is an imprint of the Taylor & Francis Group, an **informa** business)

ISBN-10: 1-85743-373-4
ISBN-13: 978-1-85743-373-9

Editor: Susan Leckey
Proofreader: John Bailie
Senior Editor, European Directories: Michael Salzman
Editorial Director: Paul Kelly

Typeset in 10.5 on 12 point Bembo

Typeset by Taylor & Francis Books
Printed and bound in Great Britain by MPG Books, Bodmin, Cornwall

Foreword

A DICTIONARY OF THE EUROPEAN UNION aims to give a comprehensive overview of the development and current status of the European Union. The journey from European Communities to European Union has been a long one; there have been many arguments and difficulties, but also co-operation and enlargement. Information on a variety of European issues is here brought together to give the reader a wide range of facts and background knowledge on the European Union. Thus, this Dictionary includes entries on the history of the European Union and the issues and personalities of importance to its development, as well as on current achievements, debates, concepts, programmes and people.

Most entries in the Dictionary will point the reader towards other relevant entries by means of cross-references. These cross-references within entries will be found in bold type, to denote the existence of a separate entry. However, it should be noted that the potential number of highlights precludes putting in bold those terms that are used in almost every entry. Thus, European Communities, European Union, the names of current Member States, etc. are not highlighted, unless the authors deem it necessary to further understanding for the reader to be pointed towards such entries. For the purposes of alphabetization, words such as 'and', 'of', 'the', etc. have been ignored.

The reader should be aware of the difference between the terms European Union, European Community and European Communities. The European Communities were established by three separate treaties, with, from 1967, common institutions. The name of one community, the European Economic Community, was formally changed to the European Community from 1993; thus, when referring to the Treaty of Rome alone after 1993, European Community (EC) is used in the singular. Referring to the three communities from their conception onwards, the Dictionary uses European Communities (EC) in the plural. The European Union, consisting of three inter-related pillars, came into existence in 1993. Thus, the supranational pillar of the European Union continues to be known in this book as the European Communities (EC), while references to the European Union as a whole, which includes the two inter-governmental pillars, use European Union (EU).

March 2006

The Authors

Lee McGowan is currently a Senior Lecturer in European Studies at the School of Politics, International Studies and Philosophy, Queen's University Belfast, where his teaching and research interests centre on three strands. These are: politics and policy-making in the European Union, and particularly the role of the European Commission as a quasi-judicial actor in the area of competition policy; the EU dimension of the devolution arrangements in Northern Ireland; and political extremism in Germany. He has published widely. Among his publications are articles in the *Journal of Common Market Studies, Journal of European Public Policy, Governance, European Journal of Political Research, Public Administration,* and *Regional and Federal Studies.* He has co-authored a book (with Michelle Cini) on *Competition Policy in the European Union* (Macmillan, 1998) and has written *The Radical Right in Germany: 1870 to the present* (Longman, 2003).

David Phinnemore is at present Senior Lecturer in European Integration at the School of Politics, International Studies and Philosophy, Queen's University Belfast, where he teaches courses on contemporary Europe, EU institutions, the enlargement of the EU, and EU external relations. His research interests also include treaty reform and the position of Romania within European integration processes. Among his most recent publications are *Understanding the European Constitution* (Routledge, 2006) and *The Penguin Guide to the European Treaties* (Penguin, 2002), both co-authored with Clive Church. Among his other publications are articles in *European Foreign Affairs Review, Journal of Common Market Studies, Journal of Southern Europe and the Balkans, Journal of Southeast European and Black Sea Studies* and *Revue d'études comparatives est-ouest.*

Abbreviations

AIDS	acquired immunodeficiency syndrome
bn	billion
e.g.	exempli gratia (for example)
etc.	et cetera
i.e.	id est (that is to say)
m.	million
UK	United Kingdom
US	United States
USA	United States of America
USSR	Union of Soviet Socialist Republics
v	versus

Acknowledgements

The authors and editors of this book gratefully acknowledge work previously carried out by Professor Derek Urwin and, subsequently, by Professor Urwin assisted by Linda M. Stevenson. These contributors provided the A–Z section for early editions of *The European Union Encyclopedia and Directory*, and their text has subsequently been extensively updated and expanded by the current authors.

A

À LA CARTE **EUROPE** is a term related to concepts of differentiated integration. Basically it suggests that European Union (EU) Member States should be able to pick and choose which programmes and policies they wish to adopt and participate in. Opponents of the concept argue that the reality of any such development would create a considerable amount of disarray and confusion, undermine solidarity and almost certainly make the EU unmanageable. Nevertheless, the idea is not infrequently espoused by some Member States as a means of showing their opposition towards certain priorities. The **opt-out** secured by the **United Kingdom** at the **Maastricht Summit of the European Council** in December 1991 on **economic and monetary union** is an example of an *à la carte* approach towards EU integration.

ABATEMENT is the term used to describe the annually calculated 'rebate', which the **United Kingdom** receives from the European Communities **budget** following an agreement reached in 1984 at the **Fontainebleau Summit** of the **European Council**. In recent years, the United Kingdom has come under increasing pressure to accept a reduction in the 'rebate', as the European Union seeks to meet the challenges of financing **enlargement**. There was a growing demand from other Member States, most notably **France**, for an end to the United Kingdom's rebate as part of the new multi-annual financial package for 2006–13. The entire issue rose to the top of European Council deliberations in June 2005, when the UK government refused to consider contemplating the rebate issue unless France agreed to review the financing of the **Common Agricultural Policy**. The meeting was reportedly one of the most acrimonious in the EU's history, and the UK government rejected the efforts of the Luxembourg presidency to broker an agreement. After several months a deal was finally reached at a meeting of the European Council in mid-December 2005, whereby the UK agreed to a reduction in the rebate. This deal will see £1 billion a year cut from the UK's rebate in order to invest in the future prosperity of Eastern Europe. The role of the new German Chancellor, **Angela Merkel**, was critical in securing overall agreement, especially from **Poland**.

ABSTENTION: See **Constructive Abstention**

ACCESSION CRITERIA, often referred to as the **Copenhagen criteria**, were adopted by the **Copenhagen Summit** of the **European Council** in June 1993, when the European Community committed itself to admitting the countries of **Central and Eastern Europe** (CEE). Accession was, however, to depend on the **candidate countries** meeting the following criteria: having stable institutions guaranteeing democracy, the rule of law, **human rights** and protection of minorities; possessing a functioning market economy and the capacity to cope with the competitive pressures of the **internal market**; and having the ability to take on the obligations of membership, including adherence to the aims of the European Union (EU), notably political, economic and monetary union. In 1995 the Madrid Summit of the European Council added a further criterion: that the countries seeking membership should possess the administrative capacity to implement the *acquis communautaire*. Formally, countries in the **Western Balkans** also have to pursue regional co-operation before they can be admitted to the EU. States are also required to have made every effort to resolve any outstanding border disputes and other related issues. This was agreed in 1999, with a particular view to the division of **Cyprus** being resolved before **Turkey** can join the EU.

ACCESSION NEGOTIATIONS need to be completed before **applicant countries** can join the European Union (EU). They are conducted on a bilateral basis, with the **European Commission** co-ordinating the position of the EU's Member States. Accession negotiations with **Cyprus** and five Central and Eastern European countries (the **Czech Republic**, **Estonia**, **Hungary**, **Poland** and **Slovenia**), often referred to as the 'Luxembourg group', were opened in 1998. Two years later, in 2000, the EU opened accession negotiations with the so-called **'Helsinki group'** (**Bulgaria**, **Latvia**, **Lithuania**, **Malta**, **Romania** and **Slovakia**). Negotiations with those applicant countries meeting the **accession criteria** – the Luxembourg group plus Latvia, Lithuania, Malta and Slovakia – were concluded at the **Copenhagen Summit** of the **European Council** held on 12–13 December 2002. The **Accession Treaty** was then signed on 16 April 2003. Following **ratification** of the Accession Treaty, the 10 countries joined the EU on 1 May 2004. The following month, Bulgaria concluded its accession negotiations with the EU. Romania followed suit in December 2004 and an Accession Treaty was signed on 25 April 2005. Bulgaria and Romania were scheduled to join the EU on 1 January 2007, although there was a possibility that accession might be delayed by one year. Accession negotiations with **Croatia** and **Turkey** were opened on 4 October 2005.

ACCESSION PARTNERSHIPS were first concluded with **applicant countries** from **Central and Eastern Europe** in 1998 and are designed to assist them in meeting the **accession criteria** and preparing themselves for membership of the European Union (EU). They list priority areas for legal adaptation and administrative reform in the countries concerned, and for EU financial assistance through the **Instrument for Structural Policies for Pre-Accession**, **PHARE** and **SAPARD** programmes. An Accession Partnership has since been concluded with **Turkey**. Similar in purpose and content, **European Partnerships** have been developed for countries of the **Western Balkans** seeking membership of the EU.

An **ACCESSION TREATY** contains the legal instruments governing the accession of a state to the European Union (EU). Accession treaties have to be ratified by all existing Member States as well as the acceding state or states. **Ratification** normally involves a referendum in the acceding country. Since the **Single European Act**, the approval of the **European Parliament** via the **assent procedure** has also been necessary. The most significant accession treaty of recent years was signed in Athens, **Greece**, on 16 April 2003 between the EU's Member States and 10 applicant states, mainly from **Central and Eastern Europe**: **Cyprus**, the **Czech Republic**, **Estonia**, **Hungary**, **Latvia**, **Lithuania**, **Malta**, **Poland**, **Slovakia** and **Slovenia**. With the exception of Cyprus, each of the applicant states held a referendum during 2003 on whether the country should join the EU. In each case, a majority of those voting voted in favour of membership. Successful ratification of the Accession Treaty in the Member States ensured that **enlargement** took place, as planned, on 1 May 2004. The most recent Accession Treaty was signed in Luxembourg on 25 April 2005 and governs the accession of **Bulgaria** and **Romania** to the EU. Neither country opted to hold a referendum to ratify the Accession Treaty.

ACCOUNTABILITY has been a major concern of the European Union (EU) since the early 1990s, as the EU's institutions have become perceived to be increasingly remote from the people. Although the EU has a democratically elected **European Parliament**, which has seen its powers increased, it continues to suffer from an increasing **democratic deficit**, with citizens feeling that decision-makers in Brussels are unaccountable. In response, the EU has sought to promote greater **transparency** and **openness**. It has also sought to increase monitoring of the activities of the **European Commission** and to ensure tighter financial control over the **budget**.

ACP STATES is the collective title of those African, Caribbean and Pacific developing countries which have entered into an **association agreement** with the European Communities (EC) under Articles 182–188 of the **Treaty of Rome** 'to further the interests and prosperity of the inhabitants of these countries and territories in order to lead them to the economic, social and cultural development to which they aspire'. The provisions were originally directed towards the colonies and ex-colonies of the **Six**, and were finalized in the **Yaoundé Convention** of 1963 and 1969. With the successive rounds of **enlargement**, ex-colonies of new Member States have joined the arrangement, which from 1975 was regulated by the **Lomé Convention**; this was replaced in 2000 by the **Cotonou Agreement**. The original 18 participants were known collectively as the Associated African States and Madagascar. The present title was adopted in 1975, and 77 countries currently belong to the agreement. ACP States are allowed duty-free entry to the European Union market for most of their products on a non-reciprocal basis, and are also eligible to receive both grants from the **European Development Fund** and low-interest loans from the **European Investment Bank**. Preferential treatment for ACP States has caused friction between the EC and members of the **World Trade Organization**, especially the **USA**, which has long objected to the preferential treatment given to **banana** producers in Caribbean states. (See also **Development Aid** and **OCTs**.)

ACQUIS COMMUNAUTAIRE is a phrase that collectively describes all the secondary **legislation** of the European Community (EC) passed under the provisions of the **founding treaties** and their subsequent amendments. It covers all the **directives**, **decisions** and **regulations** adopted by the EC. States that apply for EU membership have to accept the *acquis communautaire*.

ACQUIS POLITIQUE is a phrase describing all the **decisions** and **resolutions** adopted by the Member States of the European Union in the field of foreign policy. It is also used in a broader sense to describe the principles and goals underpinning the activities of the EU.

The **ACTION COMMITTEE FOR A UNITED STATES OF EUROPE** was an interest group established by **Jean Monnet** in 1955 following the failure of the **European Defence Community**. Monnet created it as a selective group of political and trade union leaders that would work for closer European unity, and it contributed to the ideas and pressures that led to the formation of the **European Economic Community**. After 1958, it continued to argue for more intensive integration that would include as many European countries as possible. It was led by Monnet until 1975, but after the 1960s it became a less prominent organization.

ACTS was a programme set up to develop Advanced Communications Technologies and Services, and to encourage the development of advanced **Trans-European Networks** and services that would further assist economic and social cohesion in the European Union. It superseded the **RACE** programme, and was itself superseded by the **Information Society Technologies** programme.

The *AD HOC* **GROUP ON IMMIGRATION** was a specialized sub-element of **TREVI** established in 1986. It was made responsible for increasing the stringency of the controls at external borders of the European Communities, co-ordinating national **visa policies**, harmonizing national asylum rights, and consolidating the exchange of information between Member States on immigration.

ADAPT is the abbreviation for Adaptation of the Workforce to Industrial Change, a programme established in 1994, which continued as ADAPT Bis (Building the Information Society) after 1996. Several thousand projects and partnerships were funded by the programme to assist in the transition to an information society.

ADDITIONALITY is a principle applied to the allocation of money from the **European Regional Development Fund** (ERDF). It means that ERDF funding is additional to that provided by local and national authorities. The principle is designed to ensure that Member States contribute to the financing of infrastructural projects.

KONRAD ADENAUER (1876–1967) was the first Chancellor (1949–63) of the Federal Republic of **Germany** (FRG, West Germany). He believed strongly in European co-operation and integration, based in particular upon reconciliation between **France** and Germany. In 1945 he emerged from retirement, eventually to become the leader of the Christian Democratic Union (CDU). He led the German delegation to the **Congress of Europe** at The Hague in 1948. As Chancellor, he also directed the FRG's foreign affairs. His foreign policy, known as a 'policy of strength', had two main objectives: the rehabilitation and the reunification of Germany. For Adenauer, the FRG had to work hard to be accepted by its Western neighbours as an equal, responsible and trustworthy partner in both Western co-operative endeavours and security measures in an alliance against the **USSR**. The recovery of the FRG and the policy of strength were aimed in the longer term at German reunification. Adenauer believed that West German participation in European integration was an essential element of rehabilitation that would remove fears of a renewed German militarism. He supported all European co-operative developments from the Congress of Europe through to the establishment of the **European Economic Community**. After 1958, he formed a close relationship with President **Charles de Gaulle** of France, with whom he was an architect of the 1963 **Treaty of Friendship** (Elysée Treaty) between the two countries. This treaty established much closer cultural, economic and political ties between both states and became the basis of the Franco-German axis that later came to dominate many of the developments and activities of the European Communities.

ADONNINO REPORTS: See **Committee for a People's Europe**

ADVISORY COMMITTEE FOR THE CO-ORDINATION OF FRAUD PREVENTION (COCOLAF) has responsibility for co-ordinating action by the Member States and the **European Commission** to combat fraud affecting the financial interests of the European Community.

ADVISORY COMMITTEES are bodies that advise the **European Commission** on problems and issues in specific areas. They are part of the world of **comitology**. More than 200 such committees exist and include advisory committees on food, consumer products, health and environmental risks, and equal opportunities. The membership is drawn from experts and professionals in the relevant area.

ADVOCATES GENERAL: See **Court of Justice**

The *AETR* **JUDGMENT**, sometimes referred to by its English equivalent – the *ERTA* Judgment – was a 1971 ruling by the **Court of Justice**, which established the important principle that, where the European Communities (EC) have an explicit internal competence, they also have a parallel external competence. Its implication was that in such areas of competence, Member States could not act independently of the EC. Where a Member State has entered into an international agreement that conflicts with EC law, the latter takes precedence over any obligation arising from the agreement.

AFRICAN, CARIBBEAN AND PACIFIC STATES: See **ACP States**

AGENDA 2000 was an **enlargement** strategy developed by the **European Commission** in 1997 following a request from the **European Council**. Its objectives were to strengthen growth, competitiveness and employment; to reform agriculture and structural policies; and to expand the membership of the European Union (EU) eastwards, to include 10 countries from **Central and Eastern Europe** (CEE). It recognized the need for further institutional reform prior to enlargement, and for a new financial framework to enable the EU to expand and integrate in the 21st century. The report comprised three sections: the first covered measures to strengthen and reform policies, in particular the **Common Agricultural Policy** and economic and social cohesion (see **cohesion policy**); the second contained recommendations for preparing the EU for enlargement; and the third proposed a new financial framework, covering the period 2000–06. Also published as part of Agenda 2000 were the Commission's *avis* on the membership applications from the 10 CEE countries. In these, the Commission assessed the extent to which the applicants had met the **accession criteria**. A report on the status of **Cyprus** was also included.

AGRICULTURAL POLICY: See **Common Agricultural Policy**

BERTIE AHERN (1951–) was elected as the youngest Prime Minister (Taoiseach) in the history of the **Irish Republic** in June 1997. He was born and educated in Dublin and took a degree in accountancy at University College Dublin. His activities in the political sphere commenced when he became involved with, and later joined, Fianna Fáil. His rise in the party was rapid and he became its leader in 1994. One of Ahern's greatest achievements as Taoiseach has been the ongoing Northern Ireland Peace Process and especially the 1998 Good Friday Agreement. The agreement was endorsed by the political parties, the British and Irish governments and the people of the Republic of Ireland and Northern Ireland. Ahern also presided over an unprecedented economic boom in Ireland in the later 1990s and this helped his party's re-election with an even bigger parliamentary (Dáil) majority in 2002. Ahern has also made a significant contribution to EU affairs, and the Irish presidency during the first half of 2004 was hailed as a major success. Ahern's efforts and Irish diplomacy ensured agreement on the both the **Treaty establishing a Constitution for Europe** and the selection of **José Manuel Barroso** as the new **European Commission** president in June 2004.

AIR TRANSPORT POLICY has been slow to develop towards a level that meets the **competition policy** requirements of the European Communities (EC). The airline industry has been dominated by an international cartel, the International Air Transport Association (IATA), and by a series of intergovernmental agreements. The emphasis of these was upon the mutual protection by governments of state-owned airlines, their pricing arrangements and access to scheduled routes. The result was an absence of competition, and some of the highest air fares in the world, in terms of cost per kilometre. Before 1986, **European Commission** initiatives were restricted to technical matters relating to, for example, co-operation on accident procedures and noise emissions. Challenges to the government-supported IATA structure were largely left to small, independent airlines.

In April 1986 the **Court of Justice** ruled in the *Nouvelles Frontières* case that EC competition policy also applied to air transport. The European Commission immediately threatened legal action against 10 European airlines unless they substantially modified their price-fixing arrangements. Simultaneously, it sought to persuade the Member States to opt for more liberal policies. In April 1987 the airlines indicated that they would comply with the Commission's demands. Subsequently, progress was positive, but slow. A number of Commission proposals relating to discount fares, competition on established routes, the rights of prospective new competitors and the establishment of new scheduled routes were implemented in January 1988. These measures also gave the Commission substantial investigatory powers.

In anticipation of the introduction of the **internal market**, and partly because many state-owned airlines were substantial money-losers, governments began to accept a greater degree of private ownership and capital, and also to urge the consolidation of their national companies as a way of warding off foreign competition in a more competitive market. Matters were complicated by the fact that the major carriers, to meet the conditions of the internal market and world developments in air transport, began to seek closer and more formal collaboration, which in turn threatened the survival of smaller, independent airlines. However, airline agreements and co-operative arrangements are subject to Commission approval and the EC's **merger policy**. The acceptance of liberalization also varied from one country to another. The **United Kingdom** and the **Netherlands** led the movement for change, while **France** and some of the Mediterranean states were more resistant. Full liberalization of the market did not occur until 1997, when restrictions on European airlines within the European Union (EU) were removed, with the result that airlines were able to operate domestic air services in EU countries other than their own. In 2000 the Commission proposed the creation of a European Aviation Safety Agency (EASA), which would be an independent organization within the EC; the proposal was adopted in 2002 and the EASA began operating in September 2003. The Commission has also tried to initiate policies in order to create 'Single Skies' within the EU, replacing each state's airspace with a single European zone, which would mean the creation of a unified supervisory structure for air traffic control.

In March 2003 the European Commission, in a communication to the **European Council** and the **European Parliament**, expressed its first reactions to the potential consequences of the US-led war in Iraq on energy and the air transport industry. This formed part of the Task Force established by the Directorate-General (DG) for Energy and Transport in December 2002, which is briefed to provide information on the dangers to both the security of energy supplies and the transport infrastructure in the EU and the **candidate countries**. The Task Force forwards this information to the DG RELEX's Crisis Room and to the DG Environment's Alert Centre. With reference to air transport policy, this communication maintained that civil aviation was likely to be affected by the war in three ways: the closure of air space in the region of the conflict; more congested air space; and finally, and most importantly, a reduction in demand for flights. This last consequence was expected adversely to affect operational costs and, indeed, very quickly resulted in demands for the provision of help to the air transport sector through some form of financial assistance, such as the relaxation of the rules on state aid (see **subsidies**) to airlines for a limited period only, as occurred immediately after the terrorist attacks in the **USA** on 11 September 2001.

AIRBUS is one of the success stories of European industrial co-operation. Founded in 1967 as a consortium of European aircraft manufacturers, Airbus aimed to design and build large passenger aircraft that could compete with Boeing, the large US corporation. Since 1992, Airbus' share of the large civil aircraft market has grown steadily, from over 30% to more than half by 2004, and its future successes seemed assured with the launch of the new double-decker-style aircraft (Airbus A380) in 2005. This new plane has been specifically designed to carry 500 passengers and has been marketed to fly to a series of hub international airports. It is set to revolutionize the nature of air travel in much the same way that the jumbo jet did some 50 years previously. However, Boeing has met the challenge by building a smaller plane, which will be able to land in smaller airports. Consumers, and their preferred choice of hub plus further plane connection to smaller airport or direct flight to their destination, will play a significant role in determining the success of both ventures. Airbus comprises four partners: British Aerospace, Construcciones Aeronáuticas SA (CASA) of **Spain**, Daimler-Benz Aerospace of **Germany** and Aérospatiale of **France**. Each of the four partners specializes in producing different parts of the aircraft. Airbus has grown considerably in terms of market share and by the 1990s had almost a 45% share of the market for large passenger aircraft. Boeing, however, has complained about the massive government subsidies being channelled into Airbus in order to make it viable, and has labelled such activity as constituting nothing less than unfair competition. Tension was particularly acute in the 1980s, until a bilateral agreement on civil aircraft, which capped government support for new aircraft, was reached in June 1992. Nevertheless, relations were still tense, as was evident in the European Union's (EU) total opposition to the planned merger between Boeing and McDonnell Douglas in 1997. This merger aimed to create the world's largest aerospace and defence company. Airbus would be the only other major competitor. The **European Commission** raised its concerns about the potential dominance in the world market of this new company, and threatened to oppose the merger and to impound Boeing aircraft if they landed on EU soil. The **USA** saw EU **competition policy** as another unfair means to protect Airbus. Rumours of a trade war between the EU and the USA grew, and the sensitivity of the issue also led to intervention by the US President, Bill Clinton. The issue was only resolved when the Commission sanctioned a merger, providing that many of the clauses that would have tied Boeing customers to the new company for 20 years were removed. In an effort to make Airbus more competitive and more efficient, it was transformed in 1999 into a limited company; it became a single integrated operating company in 2001. There remains a consistent rivalry between Airbus and Boeing, and the former overtook Boeing in terms of orders in 2002 after securing a huge 120-aircraft deal from the British low-cost carrier EasyJet in October of that year. In terms of production, Airbus delivered 303 aircraft in 2002, worth some US $19,500m., which constituted the third consecutive year that the company had delivered more than 300 aircraft. Tensions between Airbus and Boeing over the degree of subsidies supporting the activities of both companies have become almost a permanent feature of the EU/US trade discussions. In October 2004 both companies launched the largest trade dispute in the short history of the **World Trade Organization** (WTO). However, aware of the economic repercussions of any damaging ruling against them, both parties agreed in January 2005 to return to the negotiating table in an effort to consider how to cut subsidies. The ongoing bilateral negotiations certainly proved intense and a renewed bitter row erupted between both companies in May 2005. The difficulties centre on the failure of both Airbus and Boeing to agree on the level of subsidies and led to both sides reviving their charges before the WTO. EU Trade Commissioner Peter Mandelson placed responsibility for this latest problem with Boeing. The Europeans resent what they see as illegal subsidies that centre on the way in which Boeing is facilitated through a number of military contracts and tax breaks, while the Americans resent the aid being given in the construction of the new A380. It seems highly unlikely that subsidies will ever disappear altogether and both sides are certain to complain about unfair competitive advantages for some time to come. Indeed, in February 2006, the United States government raised its objections to a £5.2m. grant from the Welsh Assembly to train new workers at the Airbus factory in Broughton, near Chester. This factory is the largest manufacturing plant in Wales and employs some 6,000 people. It makes wings for the A380 and the new A350. The US authorities claimed that this subsidy breached WTO rules of fair competition.

Both parties are also certain to clash over assistance in the construction of new middle-sized aircraft (the 787 or 'dreamliner' and the A350). Airbus confirmed the development of the A350 in October 2005 and stated that it had deliberately turned down contentious state support for one year in an attempt to calm the ongoing row with Boeing and, of course, bearing in mind the case before the WTO. Airbus continues to mount a serious challenge to Boeing. It claimed that it won 51% of new orders in 2005 (1,055 compared to Boeing's tally of 1,002) and stated that it had constructed more planes (378 in comparison to Boeing's 290). These figures and the company's strong performance surprised many analysts, but closer examination of the figures reveals that Boeing maintains its lead in the larget jet market. Airbus announced in February 2006 that it was building 43 passenger planes (worth £1.4 billion) for India's state-owned airline; the company claimed to have more than a full order book and is on a major recruitment drive. In the meantime the WTO is investigating tit-for-tat accusations that the US and EU each unfairly support Boeing and Airbus respectively – with both sides claiming that the aid gives the other an unfair market advantage. The current case will prove highly expensive and it is unlikely that either side will achieve a clear victory.

ALBANIA concluded a trade and co-operation agreement with the European Community in 1992 that held out the prospect of negotiating an **association agreement**. Progress towards such a goal was hampered in the 1990s by domestic political and economic instability in Albania. In 1999, however, the country became part of the **Stabilization and Association Process** that the European Union (EU) launched in the aftermath of the Kosovo crisis. This led to assistance under the **CARDS** programme, and the possibility of opening negotiations on a **Stabilization and Association Agreement** (SAA). Albania is keen to become a member of the EU, a point recognized at the Feira summit of the **European Council** in 2000 when Albania, along with the other countries in the **Western Balkans**, was confirmed as a **potential candidate state**. In 2003 EU membership clearly remained a priority for the Albanian government. Although negotiations on an SAA were opened in February 2003, effectively representing Albania's first step towards eventual EU membership, the Commission President, **Romano Prodi**, asserted that substantial problems remained which required serious consideration by the authorities in Tirana before any real progress could be made by Albania towards the acquisition of full EU membership. These included suppressing criminal activities and showing evidence of solid economic progress. In July 2003 an 'Annual Programme for Albania', detailing how €46.5m. of CARDS funds would be spent in assisting Albania in its reform and modernization efforts, was adopted by the Commission. Negotiations on the SAA were eventually concluded in February 2006.

The SAA is currently awaiting **ratification** by Albania and the EU's 25 **Member States**.

ALDE: See **Group of the Alliance of Liberals and Democrats for Europe** (ALDE)

ALE: See **European Free Alliance**

ALGERIA: See **Maghreb States**

ALLIANCE OF LIBERALS AND DEMOCRATS FOR EUROPE (ALDE): See **Group of the Alliance of Liberals and Democrats for Europe** (ALDE)

ALTENER stands for Alternative Energy, an initiative relating to the development of new and renewable energy resources (RES) (see **electricity**). It was established in 1993 and its objectives were to make such resources competitive, to eliminate barriers to their marketability, and to develop public awareness about their availability and virtues. The 1997 White Paper laid down a clear strategy of doubling the proportion of RES in the European Union's gross domestic energy consumption from 6% in 1997 to 12% in 2010. The ALTENER II programme was renewed in 1998, but little progress had been made towards the objective by 2001. The **European Commission** has remained optimistic, however, and in September 2001 a directive was adopted by the **European Council** and the **European Parliament** on the production of electricity and RES. This aimed to increase a reliance on RES by advocating greater use of 'green' electricity, which it hoped to see rise to 22% by 2010 (it stood at 14% in 1997).

AMS is the acronym for Aggregate Measure of Support, the calculation of the costs to taxpayers and consumers of both the domestic farm support and the export subsidies provided by the **Common Agricultural Policy** (CAP).

AMSTERDAM TREATY: See **Treaty of Amsterdam**

The **ANDEAN COMMUNITY OF NATIONS** (CAN), formerly the Andean Pact, comprises five South American countries: Bolivia, Colombia, Ecuador, Peru and Venezuela. The community is based on a customs union, and formal ties with the European Community date back to agreements on bilateral trade and aid signed in 1983 and 1986. Since then, co-operation has developed both on a European Union (EU)–Andean Community basis and within the context of the EU's developing relations with **South and Central America**. Following a series of declarations in 1996, a new institutional framework for relations was developed, with dialogue focusing particularly on drugs. Funds amounting to more than €400m. have since been allocated by the EU to co-operation with the Andean Community for the period 2002–06. In December 2002, the EU and CAN signed a Political Dialogue and Cooperation Agreement, which, it is hoped, will be followed by a further agreement on free trade.

ANIMAL WELFARE is not formally a competence of the European Union, although concerns, notably from the **United Kingdom**, over the transportation of live animals within the **internal market**, have led to tighter controls being introduced. The **European Commission** established a computerized network (ANIMO) linking national veterinary authorities dealing with such transportation. According to a **Protocol** on the protection and welfare of animals adopted as part of the **Treaty of Amsterdam**, the European Community is obliged to pay full regard to the welfare requirements of animals when formulating and implementing agriculture, transport, internal market and research policies.

The **ANNUAL REPORT** is a general report on the activities of the European Communities and the Member States. It is published annually in all European Union languages and is submitted to the **European Parliament**.

ANTICI GROUP is the name given to the personal assistants of the Permanent Representatives (see **Permanent Representation**) in Brussels. It has no formal status, but functions as an integral and important part of the structure of the **Committee of Permanent Representatives**, and is consulted by the presidency on work programmes and procedures.

ANTI-DUMPING: See **Dumping**

The **ANTI-FRAUD OFFICE** (OLAF), an independent office within the **European Commission**, has been responsible for combating fraud against the European Union (EU) **budget**, as well as transnational organized crime and any fraud or illegal activity prejudicial to the budget, since June 1999. OLAF was established in April 1999 and replaced UCLAF (Task Force for the Co-ordination of Fraud Prevention), created in 1988. In contrast to its predecessor, OLAF is empowered to examine the management and the financing of all of the EU's institutions (not just the European Commission). The Director of OLAF is appointed by agreement between the **European Parliament**, the Commission and the **Council of the European Union**, and OLAF can bring cases before the Courts and can also authorize any investigation that it deems necessary.

ANTI-TRUST: See **Competition Policy**

The **APPLICANT COUNTRIES**, in order of application for membership of the European Union, are: **Turkey** (14 April 1987), **Romania** (22 June 1995), **Bulgaria** (14 December 1995), **Croatia** (21 February 2003) and **Macedonia** (22 March 2004). Other countries have also signalled their intention to apply for EU membership at some point in the future. These include **Albania** and **Ukraine**. **Switzerland** has applied for membership, but its application was frozen by the Swiss government following popular rejection of Swiss participation in the **European Economic Area** in 1992.

Of the current applicant countries, all are now formally **candidate countries**, Macedonia having had the status conferred on it most recently by the European Council in December 2005. Bulgaria and Romania have signed an **Accession Treaty,** and Turkey and Croatia opened **accession negotiations** in October 2005. Macedonia is awaiting the opening accession negotiations. Prior to **enlargement** in 2004, the list of applicant countries was much longer, comprising a further 10 countries: **Cyprus** (3 July 1990), **Malta** (16 July 1990), **Hungary** (31 March 1994), **Poland** (5 April 1994), **Slovakia** (27 June 1995), **Latvia** (13 October 1995), **Estonia** (24 November 1995), **Lithuania** (8 December 1995), the **Czech Republic** (17 January 1996) and **Slovenia** (10 June 1996).

APPROXIMATION is a term used to describe the process of removing undesired or unwarranted differences in national **legislation** within the context of the **internal market**. Proposals for approximation come from the **European Commission**, but must be approved by the **Council of the European Union**. Approximation can involve not only Member States, but also non-member countries.

ARC: See **Rainbow Group**

Creating an **AREA OF FREEDOM, SECURITY AND JUSTICE** was a goal inserted into the **Treaty of Rome** by the **Treaty of Amsterdam**. It involves co-operation in many of the areas previously dealt with under Pillar III of the European Union, the **pillar** covering **justice and home affairs**. Hence, an emphasis on assuring the **freedom of movement** of persons is accompanied by measures governing external border controls, asylum, immigration and the prevention and combating of crime. How to realize the area of freedom, security and justice was the key focus of the **Tampere Summit** in 1999.

ARIANE is the name of the French-designed rocket-launcher adopted by the European Launcher Development Organization (ELDO) after its own efforts to sponsor a collaborative European venture failed. The Ariane project was partly funded by loans from the **European Investment Bank**, and the first test flight was successfully concluded in 1979. In 1980 the **European Space Agency** (ESA) established the Ariane space company (Arianespace) to market the launcher commercially. Its facilities were made available to all, and a regular programme of launches has been sustained since it became commercially available. It has been used by the European Communities in joint ventures with other bodies such as the ESA. Arianespace launched its most powerful rocket to date in February 2005, when the new 50m-high (160ft) Ariane 5-ECA vehicle blasted off from the Kourou spaceport in French Guyana. Meanwhile in August 2005 Ariane 5 was responsible for placing the heaviest yet commercial communications satellite into orbit. The Thaicom 4 (Ipstar) craft, which is operated by Thailand's Shin Satellite, will provide net access across the Asia-Pacific region.

ARIANE was a five-year programme introduced in 1997 to promote knowledge through the dissemination of literary works and the history of the European peoples, and European artistic literary creation. It was later subsumed into the **Culture 2000** programme. (See also **Kaleidoscope; Raphael**.)

An **ARTICLE** is the basic clause or unit of a European treaty. It may be subdivided into paragraphs.

ARTICLE 36 COMMITTEE, formerly the K.4 Committee, was established by the **Treaty on European Union**. Its role is primarily to co-ordinate European Union activities under Pillar III on **police and judicial co-operation in criminal matters**. In addition, the Committee is expected to provide the **Council of the European Union** with opinions and assist in the preparation of the Council's discussions, along with the **Committee of Permanent Representatives**.

ARTICLE 133 COMMITTEE, formerly known as the Article 113 Committee, consists of representatives of European Union Member States. It assists the **European Commission** in trade negotiations with non-member states and within the **World Trade Organization.**

ARTICLE 308 is the so-called 'catch-all' clause in the **Treaty of Rome** which allows the European Union, in the absence of any explicit powers and acting by **unanimity**, to take 'appropriate measures' to achieve a particular Treaty objective. Use of the article is subject to the principle of **subsidiarity**. Prior to the **Treaty of Amsterdam**, Article 308 was Article 235.

ASEAN: See **Association of South East Asian Nations**

ASIA has not been the subject of a co-ordinated regional policy by the European Communities (EC), although most Asian countries participate in the EC **Generalized System of Preferences**, and the EU has developed links with the **Association of South East Asian Nations** (ASEAN). In addition, there are **Co-operation Agreements** with several Asian countries, while others have been the subjects of separate economic and development agreements. India is the largest single recipient of EC aid among developing countries.

ASIA-PACIFIC ECONOMIC CO-OPERATION (APEC): See **Association of South East Asian Nations**

The **ASSENT PROCEDURE**, introduced by the **Single European Act**, and extended to further policy areas by the **Treaty on European Union** and the **Treaty of Amsterdam**, is a decision-making procedure whereby specified decisions of the Council of Ministers (see **Council of the European Union**) must gain the assent of the **European Parliament** (EP) before they can enter into force. Among the decisions over which the EP therefore has a veto are those concerning the accession of new states to the European Union.

ASSIZES (or Conferences of the Parliaments) are consultative meetings of representatives of **national parliaments** designed to improve awareness of and support for the integration process.

ASSOCIATION AGREEMENTS have been concluded by the European Communities (EC) with numerous countries both within Europe and beyond.

Agreements concluded with the latter include the **Lomé Convention** and the **Cotonou Agreement**. Within Europe, Association Agreements were initially only concluded with countries aspiring to but as yet insufficiently developed economically for membership. Hence, those with **Greece** (1961) and **Turkey** (1963) envisaged the creation of a customs union with the EC as well as co-operation in a wide variety of areas. Later agreements with **Malta** (1971) and **Cyprus** (1972) were, by contrast, far less ambitious, restricting themselves to little more than the creation of a free-trade area, although they too involved the creation of a series of bodies (e.g. an Association Council and an Association Committee) to oversee the operation of the Association. Since the early 1990s an increasing number of Association Agreements have been concluded with European countries. These include the formation of a **European Economic Area** with the member states of the **European Free Trade Association** (EFTA), **Europe Agreements** with the countries of **Central and Eastern Europe**, and the **Stabilization and Association Agreements** with countries in the **Western Balkans.**

The **ASSOCIATION OF SOUTH EAST ASIAN NATIONS** (ASEAN), when formed in 1967, comprised Indonesia, Malaysia, the Philippines, Singapore and Thailand. Brunei and Viet Nam joined in 1984 and 1995 respectively, with Myanmar and Laos joining in 1997. Cambodia became a member of ASEAN in 1999. The Association's main purpose today is to promote free trade between its member states and other members of the Asia-Pacific Economic Co-operation (APEC) organization, which includes Australia, **Japan**, Russia and the People's Republic of China among its 21 members. Relations with the European Union (EU) date back to the early 1970s and include a **Co-operation Agreement** signed in 1980, although at times development of relations has been hampered by concerns over alleged **human rights** abuses in certain ASEAN countries, notably Indonesia. In 1997, a 'new dynamic' to EU–ASEAN relations was launched with a view to increasing co-operation and encouraging increased collaboration in business and trade.

An **ASYLUM POLICY** did not exist for the European Communities (EC) before 1989, although matters relating to asylum had been discussed more informally within the **TREVI** process. The collapse of communism in **Central and Eastern Europe** and fears, which were especially pronounced in **Germany**, that there would be a dramatic increase in the number of immigrants to the EC from the east, combined with increased immigration pressures from non-European sources, led to demands for more formal arrangements. The Member States, except **Denmark**, signed the **Dublin Convention on Asylum** in June 1990. Partly in response to growing unrest in the **USSR** and

Yugoslavia, the Member States agreed in June 1991 to establish a Quick Reaction Consultation Centre to deal with sudden and large-scale immigration pressures. After 1991 asylum procedures were generally tightened, and grants of asylum more restricted. More recently, the **Treaty of Amsterdam** established a timetable within which Member States had to establish common rules relating to both their **asylum** and **immigration policies**. Asylum and immigration policies were key issues raised at the **Tampere summit** of the **European Council** in 1999.

ATLANTIC ALLIANCE is a popular alternative name for the **North Atlantic Treaty Organization** (NATO).

The **ATLANTIC ARC COMMISSION** is an intergovernmental association of regional authorities from those regions of the European Union (EU) that border the Atlantic, including islands located in this ocean and any other regions with close economic and cultural ties with areas bordering the Atlantic. It was founded in 1989 and has as its main objective securing EU funding for infrastructural developments for the poorer, more peripheral areas of the EU.

ATMOSPHERIC POLLUTION has been a central element of European Communities initiatives in the field of **environment policy** since the mid-1980s. Regulations governing automobile emissions were introduced in 1985 and 1987, though the extent of improvement was hindered by disagreements between the Member States. There was also a series of **directives** on industrial pollution, especially the discharge of sulphur dioxide and chlorofluorocarbons (CFCs) into the atmosphere, with CFCs due to be totally banned by 1997. From 1990 the **European Commission** urged the introduction of a **carbon tax** as a way of reducing pollution further and paying for the rectification of its consequences. The European Union agreed in 1997 to curb emissions of six 'greenhouse' gases by 8% in comparison to 1990 levels by 2008–12. The Clean Air for Europe (CAFE) programme began in 2001, aiming to co-ordinate the collection of scientific and technical data necessary for policy-making in this area.

AUDIO-VISUAL POLICY dates from the 1980s and activity in the audio-visual sector comprises two broad aspects. The first focuses on mainly industry sector considerations that centre on efforts to ensure the standardization of the systems used in the Member States to broadcast programmes by satellite and cable. The first directive on this specific issue was approved in 1986. Later, in 1989, objectives were defined for the development of high-definition television

(HDTV). Then, in 1991, a single standard for high-definition television production and financial support for a programme of co-operation between the businesses concerned were introduced. There is also a legal dimension to audio-visual policy and this has centred on the controversial 'Television without Frontiers Directive', which was adopted in 1989 and amended in 1997. This directive seeks to provide a harmonized framework in order to promote the free movement, production and distribution of European television programmes. To this end common rules were agreed on advertising, sponsorship, the protection of minors and the right of reply. Interestingly, this directive also introduced distribution quotas, thus requiring TV channels to reserve, whenever possible, more than half their transmission time for European productions.

The European audio-visual market continues to face a series of hurdles that can be identified as continuing language barriers which prevent the free movement of programmes; an unwieldy decision-making process which generally requires unanimity; and the need to make considerable investment to anticipate technological developments, which requires international alliances and/or mergers. With regard to the last point, it is important to stress that the development of EU audio-visual policy must respect certain interests and priorities, such as competition rules (especially regarding state aid – see **subsidies**), the rules on intellectual property and the principles of public service.

Furthermore, since 1991, the Community MEDIA programme (measures to promote the development of the audio-visual industry – see **Media Policy**) has been supporting the European audio-visual industry by encouraging the development and distribution of European works. It also finances schemes to improve the training of professionals in the sector. The **MEDIA Plus** Programme (2000–05), which followed on from MEDIA II (1996–2000), had a budget of €4m.

AUSTRIA for many years felt unable to consider European Communities (EC) membership because of its neutral status and the terms of the Austrian State Treaty of 1955, which ended the Allied military occupation of the country. It did, however, become a founder member of the **European Free Trade Association** (EFTA) in 1960, despite the disapproval of the **USSR**, which had been a party to the 1955 Treaty. Austria requested a special arrangement with the EC, and exploratory talks began in 1964. Subsequent negotiations were vetoed in 1967 by the Italian government. Hence, it was not until **enlargement** was included on the agenda of the EC that Austria concluded a **Free Trade Agreement** with the EC, in 1972. Given its large volume of trade with the EC, especially with the Federal Republic of **Germany**, in the late 1980s Austria began to fear that its economy would suffer from the establishment of the **internal market**, unless it was party to the process. It supported the attempt by

EFTA to reach a general agreement with the EC, but soon broke ranks with its EFTA partners to apply formally for EC membership in July 1989, arguing that membership was not, in fact, precluded by the 1955 State Treaty. While the EC indicated that action on the application was unlikely until after 1992, the collapse of communism in **Central and Eastern Europe**, the successful completion of the **European Economic Area** talks and the decision by most of the other EFTA states to seek EC membership led to early progress being made. Negotiations on terms of entry began in 1993 and the terms were endorsed by a popular referendum in June 1994. Austria's membership of the European Union was effective from 1 January 1995 (**Finland** and **Sweden** also joined on the same date). Adapting to membership has been a relatively smooth process, although Austria was forced to endure a period of diplomatic isolation in 2000 when the far-right Freedom Party led by Jörg Haider entered briefly into coalition government. Austria became the eighth Member State of the European Union to ratify the **Treaty establishing a Constitution for Europe** in May 2005, when the upper house of parliament approved the treaty with almost unanimous support. The Austrian government found itself isolated in the summer of 2005 when it strongly resisted the opening of accession negotiations with Turkey. After much cajoling and persuading under the UK presidency the Austrians finally agreed to give the green light to Ankara so long as accession negotiations could commence with **Croatia**. Austria assumed the presidency of the European Union in January 2006 and made a lukewarm effort to re-activate a debate on the **Constitution** for Europe.

AVIS is the term applied to the opinion issued by the **European Commission** on the acceptability of a country's formal application for membership of the European Union.

B

BALKANS: See **Western Balkans**

BALTIC STATES: See **Estonia**; **Latvia**; **Lithuania**

BANANAS were the cause of a trade dispute between the European Union (EU) and the **USA** throughout the 1990s. The EU's banana regime had always been strongly contested as it granted preferential access to British and French markets to banana producers from their former colonies among the **African, Caribbean and Pacific** (ACP) **States**. The EU banana trade regime (BTR) antagonized the government of the USA as it restricted access for US producers such as Dole and Chiquita. With the support of several Central American producers, an appeal was made by the USA to the **World Trade Organization** (WTO) disputes settlement panel against this apparent discrimination. The WTO backed the US complaint and forced the EU to reconsider its BTR. Although a majority of EU Member States wanted to abolish the BTR, a minority, including **France** and the **United Kingdom**, wished to defend it. Efforts to enlarge the quota for Central American producers were rejected by the USA in 1999 and heralded the imposition of substantial tariffs on a range of British and French goods entering the US market. This trade war was only resolved in April 2001 when a resolution was reached between the EU and the USA which agreed a transition to a tariff-only system by 2006.

The **BANK FOR INTERNATIONAL SETTLEMENTS** (BIS) is a joint venture, originally of European national central banks, established in 1930 as an aid to the resolution of the problem of German reparations. After 1945 it extended its activities and membership to include, among others, Canada, **Japan** and the **USA**. In 2000 it held deposits for some 120 international financial institutions and central banks world-wide, managing some 7% of the world's foreign exchange reserves. Based in Basel, **Switzerland**, it has served as the headquarters of the **Committee of the Governors of the Central Banks**, and has acted on behalf of the European Communities as their agent for the

European Monetary Co-operation Fund (EMCF). By working closely with the International Monetary Fund (IMF), BIS provides a forum for the co-ordination of international monetary policy.

BARBER PROTOCOL is the name given informally to a **protocol** introduced by the **Treaty on European Union** intended to clarify the remuneration criteria contained within Article 141 of the **Treaty of Rome** regarding equal pay for equal work by men and women. It restricts the definition of remuneration by largely excluding benefits under occupational social security schemes, and has been interpreted as meaning that the **Court of Justice** has a more limited ability to clarify its own judgments. The Protocol results from political pressures and financial expediency.

The **BARCELONA DECLARATION** of November 1995 launched the **Euro-Mediterranean Partnership** and, in doing so, committed the signatories to the establishment of a **Euro-Mediterranean Economic Area** (EMEA) by 2010. The signatories were the European Union and the so-called MED-12 states: Algeria, **Cyprus**, Egypt, Israel, Jordan, Lebanon, **Malta**, Morocco, Palestinian Authority (now Palestinian Autonomous Areas), Syria, Tunisia and **Turkey**. (See also **Barcelona Process.**)

The **BARCELONA PROCESS**, initiated in 1995, is designed to promote closer ties between the European Union and the so-called MED-12 states of the Mediterranean (Algeria, **Cyprus**, Egypt, Israel, Jordan, Lebanon, **Malta**, Morocco, Palestinian Authority – now Palestinian Autonomous Areas – , Syria, Tunisia and **Turkey**). It was initiated by the **Barcelona Declaration** of 1995.

The **BARRE PLAN** was one of the alternative strategies for **economic and monetary union** that was advanced after the 1969 **Hague Summit**. Prepared by Raymond Barre, who was the French Minister of Economy and Finance in 1976–78, and written at the request of the **European Commission**, it was supported by **Belgium** as well as **France**. It favoured a monetarist approach to union with the immediate introduction of fixed exchange rates. This tactic, it argued, would enforce a **convergence** and **harmonization** of the economic policies of the Member States. The alternative argument, an economic approach, was expounded in the Schiller Plan. (See also **Optimum Currency Area**; **Werner Report**.)

JOSÉ MANUEL DURÃO BARROSO (1956–) was chosen as the new Commission President-designate by the **European Council** on 29 June 2004.

Barroso's background is steeped in European affairs. After taking a law degree in Lisbon he went on to take a diploma in European Studies and a Master's degree, both at the University of Geneva. Barroso initially took up academic posts before moving directly into politics. He was elected (and re-elected five times) as a member of the Portuguese parliament in 1985 as a member of the Social Democratic Party. He served as chairman of the parliament's Foreign Affairs Committee in 1995 and went on to act as both State Secretary for Foreign Affairs and Minister for Foreign Affairs before becoming Prime Minister of **Portugal** in April 2002. His nomination as **European Commission** President was universally endorsed by his peers in the European Council and his candidacy was endorsed by the **European Parliament** on 22 July 2004. Barroso's appointment was confirmed with a majority of 413 out of 711 votes cast. There were 251 votes against, 44 abstentions and three spoiled ballots. He had firm support from the centre-right groups and liberals, but was opposed by many members of the Socialist group as well as the Greens, the far left and the **Eurosceptics**. It should be noted that the **Socialist Group in the European Parliament** (PSE) voted by a large majority to reject Barroso's nomination, largely as a result of his neo-liberal views. Barroso took up his posting as the new Commission President on 1 November 2004 and spent much of the summer of 2004 'picking' his team of Commissioners. Barroso was determined from the outset to take charge of the **Lisbon agenda** and is committed to making economic reform the hallmark of his presidency. To this end he carefully and skilfully distributed Commission portfolios and placed responsibility for the key economic reforms (trade, competition and the **internal market**) in the hands of reform-minded countries (the **United Kingdom – Peter Mandelson**, the **Netherlands – Neelie Kroes** and **Ireland – Charlie McCreevy**). Nevertheless, his aspirations were dented almost immediately by a series of events that encompassed the watering down of the Lisbon agenda, the rejection of the **Treaty establishing a Constitution for Europe** in both **France** and the Netherlands, increased concerns in some national capitals over the economic direction in which the EU was heading and the heated debate on EU funding in the summer of 2005. On a more personal level he survived a no-confidence vote in the European Parliament in June 2005 by 589 votes to 35, with 35 abstentions, following an attempt by a number of Eurosceptic MEPs (including the UK Independence Party – UKIP) to censure the Commission President over a holiday he had taken on a Greek billionaire's yacht. The **Eurosceptics** had suggested that this holiday raised issues of conflict of interest, given that Mr Barroso's friend and host, the shipping magnate Spiros Latsis, had recently won Commission approval for a €10m (£6.9m) package of state aid (see **subsidies**). Barroso condemned the censure motion as 'gutter politics' and an attempt to undermine public confidence in the EU institutions prior to the referenda on the constitutional treaty in France and the Netherlands. After a somewhat shaky start to his term of office Barroso has been able to emerge as a more competent and media-savvy president than his two immediate predecessors. These abilities may in part explain why he was voted most powerful man in a poll for Britain's BBC Radio 4 in December 2005.

BASIC PRICE: See **target price**

BASKET OF CURRENCIES is a term used to describe those currencies that determined the value of the European Currency Unit (**ECU**). Each currency received a different 'weight' in the basket, based upon its issuing country's gross national product (GNP), trade and short-term credit quotas. The weights were reviewed every five years, or upon request if the weight of one currency changed by 25% or more. While the weight of the currencies in the basket was fixed, the latter provision covered the situation where changes in market exchange rates added weight to an appreciating currency or reduced that of a depreciating one. The **United Kingdom** allowed sterling to become part of the basket, but refused, until October 1990, to become a full member of the **European Monetary System** (EMS), of which the ECU was part. **Spain** and **Portugal** joined the basket for the first time in September 1989. The basket, which was heavily influenced by the Deutsche Mark, was to be a provisional step on the way to **economic and monetary union**, after which the establishment of a single European currency would eliminate the need for a basket. With the entry into force of the **Treaty on European Union** on 1 November 1993, the composition of the basket of currencies was 'frozen' and 1999 was set as the deadline for the establishment of a single currency. The composition of the basket was unaffected by the accession to the European Union (EU) in January 1995 of **Austria**, **Finland** and **Sweden**, whose currencies were not represented. The ECU was, from 1 January 1999, replaced on a one for one basis by the **euro** (€), the single currency introduced in 12 EU Member States in January 2002 (i.e. in all Member States with the exception of **Denmark**, Sweden and the United Kingdom).

BELGIUM was one of the pioneers of European integration after 1945. It is part of the **Benelux** Economic Union, and a founder member of the European Communities (EC). Belgian governments have been consistent supporters of the European Union (EU) integration process and all have regarded economic integration as only a step towards a political union. In the 1960s Belgium was strongly in favour of **enlargement**, especially the admission of the **United Kingdom**. After the mid-1980s it believed that neither the **Single European Act** nor the **Treaty on European Union** (TEU) had been sufficiently far-reaching, and was critical of states such as the **United Kingdom** and **Denmark** that were reluctant to accept fully the political implications of integration. However, it has at times been wary of a too forceful Franco-German leadership in the EC; this was a further reason for it to favour a strengthening of the EC's supranational institutions. Belgium was one of the first Member States to ratify the TEU. It has, overall, been a net beneficiary of EC membership, not least perhaps in terms of the employment possibilities which membership has created in **Brussels**: the fact that the city is the institutional heart of the EU means that Belgium has developed almost a proprietorial interest in the organization. However, the formal decentralization of the state on linguistic lines, which was concluded in 1993, along with an expensive social security system, imposed heavy public-sector costs and raised initial doubts as to whether the country could meet the **convergence criteria** set by the TEU for **economic and monetary union** (EMU). In the end, the criteria were relaxed sufficiently for Belgium to be declared eligible for EMU membership, and the country entered as one of the first wave of 11 states in January 1999. Belgium remains one of the EU's most enthusiastic members and maintains that a more flexible approach to EU integration should be adopted so as to enable a central core of states to integrate faster than others, if they so desire.

The **BELGO-LUXEMBOURG ECONOMIC UNION** (BLEU) is primarily a **customs union**, but in many ways a complete economic union, between **Belgium** and **Luxembourg**. The BLEU agreement dates from 1921 and led to the removal of frontier controls between the two states from May 1922. Although originally scheduled to last for some 50 years, the agreement has been renewed every 10 years since 1971. In 1944 the customs union element was extended with the creation of **Benelux**, although BLEU still exists within Benelux. As a result of the BLEU agreement, both countries hold their gold and foreign exchange reserves in common, while many financial, trade and other statistics for Belgium and Luxembourg are recorded together.

BENCHMARKING is an increasingly familiar part of current European Union (EU) vocabulary. It involves the use of comparison (from the perspective of a Member State or an EU institution) with other states or organizations (for example, with regard to issues such as pension reform or employment practices) with the aim of improving one's own performance by learning from the experience of others.

BENELUX is the commonly used shortened name of the Benelux Economic Union, an economic grouping of **Belgium**, the **Netherlands** and **Luxembourg** that exists within the broader economic structure of the European Communities

(EC). It was formed by the exiled governments of the three states in 1944, and a Benelux Customs Union was formally established in January 1948. Ten years later a new treaty of economic union was signed in The Hague and came into operation in January 1960. Benelux survives within the EC because the **Treaty of Rome** permits the existence of internal regional groupings of states, as long as these conform to its own stipulated goals. (See also **Belgo–Luxembourg Economic Union – BLEU.**)

BEP: See **BIOTECH**

BERLAYMONT is the name of the large 13-storey building in **Brussels** that was purpose-built in 1969 to house the **European Commission** and its administrative personnel, although not all Commission employees based in the city worked in the building. Berlaymont became a shorthand term often used to describe the Commission and the administrative structures of the European Communities, and has sometimes been employed in a derogatory sense to refer to bureaucratization, rigidity and red tape. In 1991 the building had to be evacuated for substantial renovations lasting for over a decade because large quantities of asbestos had been used in the original construction. The staff was relocated to a number of adjacent buildings, with the Commissioners moving initially into the Breydel building. The renovation and futuristic makeover of this vast star-shaped building, measuring 230,000 sq m (which critics have dubbed the 'Berlaymonster') took 13 years to complete. The building has been effectively gutted from top to bottom and now even includes a small sub-terranean sauna. It opened again for business in November 2004. After renovation, the Commission opted in 2002 to buy the building from the Belgian State for €553m. by means of an annuity over 27 years.

SILVIO BERLUSCONI (1936–) was sworn in for a second term as Italian Prime Minister in May 2001 after his Forza Italia party secured agreement on a centre-right coalition government with parties including the National Alliance and the Northern League. Berlusconi also assumed the position of Minister of Foreign Affairs and quickly antagonized fellow European Union (EU) leaders with the adoption of a much more sceptical position towards European integration, which ran contrary to the position adopted by all 59 Italian governments since 1945. This was manifest in Italy's initial decision to thwart the **European arrest warrant** in November 2001, and in Berlusconi's demand, made at the Laeken Summit, for the location of an EU institution in Italy. Berlusconi, who controls a huge media empire and owns AC Milan football club, remains Italy's richest man and one of the country's most colourful personalities.

His premiership has continued to prove controversial and he has repeatedly denied all accusations of Mafia links. In mid-2003 Berlusconi faced bribery charges, although he insisted that these were part of a conspiracy against him by what he described as a left-wing judiciary. His trial was halted in June 2003 by the introduction of controversial immunity laws and he was cleared of all allegations by the Italian courts in December 2004. Berlusconi had always dismissed the charges and asserted that he was simply the victim of a witch-hunt by a politically motivated judiciary. In the second half of 2003 Italy assumed the presidency of the EU and, accordingly, Berlusconi became responsible for representing the EU on the world stage and, importantly, for chairing the **European Council** when it met in Rome in December 2003. Berlusconi's reputation and authority as an international statesman were questioned from the outset of the Italian presidency as he made a number of gaffes (in relation to both **Germany** and **Russia**) and he did not escape criticism when the 15 Member States and the 10 candidate states failed to reach an agreement on a constitutional treaty for the EU. Indeed, some were quick to lambast his style of negotiation and claimed that he was responsible for one of the least prepared European Council meetings in recent EU history. Facing turmoil and dissent within his government coalition following disappointing results in a number of local elections, Berlusconi tendered his resignation to Italian President Carlo Ciampi on 20 April 2005. Ciampi resisted this move and asked Berlusconi just two days later to form a new government rather than opt to hold new elections. Berlusconi agreed and formed a new coalition government (the 60th in the history of the modern Italian republic) on 21 April. Berlusconi's political fortunes did not improve and he found himself facing mounting criticism and growing pressure prior to the national elections in April 2006. His personal standing had been damaged by a number of scandals, including his participation in several court cases where it was alleged that he had been involved with corrupt business practices, as well as claims of illegal party funding and even attempts to bribe judges. Italy's involvement in Iraq had further tarnished his image, as had some of his more infamous public pronouncements, but it was the sluggish Italian economy that really damaged his popularity.

Italy's national elections of April 2006 proved to be a very close contest. **Romano Prodi**'s centre-left coalition claimed a narrow victory, but Berlusconi demanded further scrutiny of ballot papers before he would consider conceding defeat.

BICs: See **Business and Innovation Centres**

BIOTECH: Biotechnology is an area in which the EU has been promoting research and developing policy since the mid-1980s. In 1985, the Biotechnology

Action Programme (BAP) was established as part of the new emphasis on the importance of **research and technological development** (RTD) **policy**. BAP succeeded the 1982–86 Biomolecular Engineering Programme (BEP), sponsoring collaborative research and training between industry and research institutions across the whole field of biotechnology. The original programme was concluded in 1989, but its work and objectives were incorporated into the subsequent BRIDGE programme of 1990, which also later changed its name to BIOTECH. This was superseded by the **Quality of Life and Management of Living Resources Programme** in 1999. A Life Patent directive on biotechnology was adopted in 1997 in an attempt to harmonize rules on gene patenting.

In the context of the Lisbon strategy (see **Lisbon agenda**), the Commission announced in March 2001 its intention to present a Communication setting out a strategic vision for life sciences and biotechnology up to 2010, and proposing how to address ethical issues. In preparing this Communication and in line with its policy on governance, the Commission launched on 4 September 2001 a broad public consultation based on a document entitled "Life Sciences and Biotechnology – Towards a Strategic Vision".

The **European Commission** then tabled a strategy paper and action plan on life sciences and biotechnology in Europe, as a contribution to the Barcelona **European Council** in March 2002. Based on consultations with a wide range of stakeholders, it paved the way for Europe to take its first decisive step towards agreeing a common biotechnology policy.

This paper sets out recommendations to help Europe master the frontier technologies it needs to become the world's most competitive economy by 2010. At the same time, its co-operative and consistent approach to fostering sustainable development is designed to address complex ethical and societal concerns and stimulate public debate.

Around 320 contributions were received and fed directly into the Commission's adoption of its first ever report on the progress made on the implementation of the strategy on life sciences and biotechnology in March 2003. It sets out what has been achieved in policy development and on the ground, and anticipates emerging issues. Where further action is needed, this report contains future orientations, makes appropriate recommendations or announces new initiatives.

Europe has around 1,570 dedicated biotechnology companies, compared with America's 1,273. But they are smaller, employ fewer people (61,000 as against 162,000), are much less well capitalized, and have far fewer biotechnology products in the pipeline.

BLACK MONDAY has become synonymous with a meeting of European Communities ministers of foreign affairs on 30 September 1991. At this meeting an ambitious draft of a potential treaty on political union, submitted by the Dutch presidency as part of the deliberations of the **intergovernmental conference** charged with drawing up the **Treaty on European Union** (TEU), was rejected by almost all other national delegations. Only **Belgium** accepted the draft. This was an embarrassing rebuke to the **Netherlands** and to the most enthusiastic supporters of deeper integration. The dismissal of this Dutch text and of its efforts to promote a unitary structure for the European Union essentially paved the way for the **pillar** structure that was enshrined in the TEU at Maastricht in December 1991.

BLACK WEDNESDAY is a popular term used to describe the international speculation against currencies in the **exchange-rate mechanism** (ERM) in September 1992. The ensuing crisis, largely fuelled by uncertainty over the fate of the **Treaty on European Union**, saw the suspension of the UK pound sterling and the Italian lira from the ERM. The speculation, which returned the following year, almost causing the collapse of the ERM, exposed weaknesses in the ERM and threatened the intentions of the European Union to establish **economic and monetary union** by 1999. Several countries were forced to devalue their currencies, and hence the fluctuation rules in the **European Monetary System** were made more flexible.

ANTHONY (TONY) BLAIR (1953–) became Labour Prime Minister of the **United Kingdom** in 1997, following almost two decades of Conservative government in that country, and was re-elected to a second term of office in June 2001 and to a third in May 2005. In terms of European policy, he proved much more favourably disposed towards the European Union (EU) than his two immediate predecessors, **Margaret Thatcher** and **John Major**. He agreed to subscribe to the content of the **social protocol**, and by implication the Charter of Fundamental Social Rights (see **Social Charter**). He was also instrumental in the final deliberations of the **intergovernmental conference** that led to the **Treaty of Nice** in December 2000. While promoting the completion of the **internal market** and **enlargement** of the EU, Blair has insisted that the United Kingdom remain outside full **economic and monetary union** until the country has met the UK Treasury's five economic tests. These tests owe more to political expediency than to any substantial economic rationale. Although Blair favours UK membership of the **euro**, this can only occur if the idea is endorsed by the British public in a referendum. Apparent early enthusiasm for a referendum has evaporated and there is now little likelihood of a referendum in the foreseeable future. Blair's decision in March 2003 actively to participate in the US-led war against Iraq, with the aim of bringing down the regime of the Iraqi President, Saddam Hussain, opened up fissures in relations with EU heads of government (most notably with **Jacques Chirac** of **France**) and ensured that moves towards a **common defence policy** became more problematic than ever. Crucially, the decision to send UK troops into Iraq also weakened Blair's reputation on the Continent. Given mounting criticism over EU governance, Blair announced in late spring 2004 that the UK would hold a referendum on the **Treaty establishing a Constitution for Europe**. This poll was expected to take place in early 2006 following the UK presidency of the **European Council** (July–December 2005). However, plans to introduce the legislation paving the way for a referendum were effectively shelved in June 2005 following the rejection of the Treaty establishing a Constitution for Europe in France and the **Netherlands** and, arguably, much to the relief of the UK government. Interestingly, and in line with his immediate predecessors, today Blair increasingly finds himself at odds with his European counterparts and especially President Jacques Chirac of France, as was very evident over the drawn-out issue of the UK rebate. The UK, once again, found itself in a minority of one. The UK presidency in the latter half of 2005 offered the potential for Blair to reassert a vision for the development of the EU, but it proved a rather lacklustre affair. Positively, it secured the opening of accession negotiations with **Turkey** and reached a deal on the future funding of the EU. However, this agreement was labelled at home by all of Blair's opponents as either a surrender or a disappointment. Blair's relationships with his fellow leaders had clearly deteriorated significantly since the UK had last held the presidency in 1998. Blair opted to leave the thornier issue of what to do about the Constitution for Europe to the succeeding Austrian presidency.

BLEU: See **Belgo-Luxembourg Economic Union**

BLOCK EXEMPTIONS is a term that refers to those categories of agreements under European Community (EC) **competition policy** between the European Communities and other states that, as stipulated by the **European Commission**, are exempted from the general prohibition of restrictive trade agreements. Under these, specific economic sectors are exempted from the general provisions relating to competition policy for a period of up to 10 years, after which time they need to be renewed or they lapse. Although such exemptions were initially designed as a means to allow the EC competition authorities greater time to investigate more pressing cases, the Commission is rather cautious about allowing too many block exemptions, and they are granted only rarely. The first, covering exclusive dealing agreements, came into force in 1967 and the second in 1972. They have been applied, for example, to patent licences, specialization agreements, research and development agreements and motor vehicle distribution (an exemption not renewed in 2002) and servicing agreements.

The **BLUE FLAG** is awarded annually to European Communities (EC) bathing beaches that reach certain standards of water quality, as part of the EC's **environment policy**. The information is published annually, and is also available on the Internet.

The **BOLKESTEIN DIRECTIVE** or, to give it its proper name, the Directive on Services in the Internal Market, sparked huge debate and controversy in various EU countries and especially **Belgium, France, Germany** and **Italy** in the first half of 2005. The directive was put together by Frits Bolkestein, the former Commissioner for the Internal Market, and aimed to establish a single market for services within the EU. Services are a rapidly growing sector and account for around 70% of EU economic activity. The directive contained changes to the EU services market, which can be summarized under two key principles. The first principle centred on the 'freedom of establishment' and sought to ensure that any company or individual who provided a service in one EU Member State should be allowed to provide it in all EU Member States. The second was the 'country of origin' principle. This sought to establish that if goods were produced in one EU Member State, then it was legitimate and acceptable to sell such goods in other EU Member States. In short, the Services Directive sought to remove the administrative and legal barriers that prevented firms from offering their services in other countries. The directive presented a radical vision and certainly could have had a wide-reaching impact in the EU services sector. Services that were covered included, for example, car hire, estate agencies, advice from architects, social care and environmental services. Trade unions argued vociferously that such changes would culminate in **social dumping** practices, as rules in Eastern European countries are often less rigid than in Western Europe. The Commission maintained that the directive would create 600,000 jobs, boost economic growth and provide greater choice for consumers. Critics feared however that the directive would unleash unwelcome competition between workers in different parts of the EU, push down income levels and lower standards of social and environmental protection. These fears, combined with concerns about the dangers of companies opting to relocate to low-cost economies, led to a series of mass protests that culminated in a 100,000-strong march through Brussels in opposition to this directive in March 2005. The pressure of public opinion led the **European Council** (and especially France) effectively to postpone the directive in late March 2005 by calling for alterations before it could be considered. There can be little doubt that this example of liberalization fed into the discussions on the **constitutional treaty** in France. The new German government of **Angela Merkel** has not yet adopted a position on the directive, but is not opposed in principle as was the Schröder administration which it replaced. The governments of the Czech Republic, Hungary, the Netherlands, Poland, Spain and the UK are the main supporters of the directive. The Services Directive was approved by the **European Parliament** (EP) at its first reading in February 2006. However, in effect the directive had been watered down and now excluded a number of services such as broadcasting, postal services, gambling and audio-visual services. The Commission pledged to take the EP's views into account before producing an amended proposal in April 2006 which would serve as a basis for a second reading in the parliament.

JOSEP BORRELL (1947–) was easily elected as the new President of the **European Parliament** (EP) on 20 July 2004. In total, 388 MEPs voted for him in a first round of voting that saw him surpass the absolute majority threshold (367), while his two challengers attracted 208 votes (Bronisław Geremek) and 51 votes (Francis Wurtz). Borrell is currently leader of the Spanish Socialist delegation in the EP and is a member of the **Group of the Party of European Socialists** (PSE) of the European Parliament. Borrell has a long association with, and interest in, European integration and trade union politics. He was born in the Catalonian Pyrenees and took degrees in aeronautical engineering, mathematics and economics. He worked in the USA before returning to **Spain** and joining the Spanish Socialist Party in 1974. He has held public office at local, national and now European levels. For example, he served in several Spanish administrations under **Felipe González** and more recently acted as the chair of the Parliamentary Committee on European affairs. He was a member of the **European Convention** and displayed a particular interest in issues relating to economic and social issues. At the recent elections he headed the Spanish Socialist Party's list when it secured its best ever result, polling 43% of the vote and securing 25 seats. Borrell launched an initiative in March 2006 to ensure that more MEPs attend key votes in the parliament, in an effort to raise the credibility of an institution that has long suffered a reputation among the EU public as a mere talking shop and a gravy train. It looks however as if Borrell's well-intentioned plans will be resisted fiercely by many MEPs, and they seem certain to fail.

BOSNIA-HERZEGOVINA declared its independence from **Yugoslavia** in 1992 only to become the focus of a ferocious civil war which lasted until 1995, when the Dayton Peace Accords, marking an agreement to end the war, were signed. Since then the government of the country has been overseen by the Office of the High Representative (which was created under the agreement), with initially a NATO-led force (IFOR) and since December 2004 a European Union (EU) peacekeeping force (EUFOR) seeking to maintain peace and stability. Relations with the EU since 1999 have developed, albeit slowly, in the context of the **Stabilization and Association Process (SAP)**. A Road Map initially detailed a catalogue of essential measures that would have to be adopted in the country before the feasibility of concluding a **Stabilization and Association Agreement (SAA)** could be explored. Appropriate steps were eventually taken, allowing the EU in November 2005 to announce the opening of negotiations on an SAA. In the meantime, Bosnia-Herzegovina had been granted the status of **potential candidate state** in 2000.

BOVINE SPONGIFORM ENCEPHALOPATHY (BSE), or, as it is more widely known, 'mad cow disease', became an issue for the European Union (EU) in early 1996 following a public announcement made by the **United Kingdom** government about the possible connection between BSE and a new variant of Creutzfeldt-Jakob disease (a degenerative and ultimately deadly brain disease) in humans. Several UK scientists had long believed that there was a link between the two diseases that originated in feeding offal (the remains of sheep and cattle) to cattle, and that the disease was now being passed to humans following their consumption of BSE-infected beef. The UK government had long denied the link, and its belated recognition of that possibility sparked public alarm about the safety of eating diseased beef across both the UK and Europe. The fact that **John Major's** government had not consulted its EU partners prior to its announcement only made matters worse. The **European Commission** responded by banning the import of all British beef into the EU, as did the governments of both the **USA** and Australia. The UK agricultural community was plunged into crisis as its export markets suddenly disappeared and the sale of beef in the UK fell dramatically. Major responded by introducing a 'no co-operation agreement' with the EU that effectively meant blocking all proposals (even those supported by the UK government) that were subject to unanimity in the **Council of the European Union**. At the same time many cattle herds were slaughtered on suspicion of infection. The crisis came to an end in June 1996 when the **European Council** approved a plan to have the ban on British beef gradually lifted once each sector was given the all-clear by the Commission's Scientific Veterinary Committee. The episode was investigated by the **European Parliament**, which in a 1997 report was openly critical of the Commission's handling of the crisis, and in particular accused the Commission of placing farmers' interests above those of consumers. The ban on British beef was gradually lifted, but some states, notably **France**, still refused to import British beef, which led to legal action being brought against the French government before the European Courts.

WILLY BRANDT (1913–92) was Chancellor of the Federal Republic of **Germany** (FRG – West Germany) from 1969 to 1974. His major interest was foreign policy, and his greatest achievement as Chancellor was the series of agreements, known collectively as **Ostpolitik**, negotiated between the FRG and the states of Eastern Europe, as well as with the **USSR**. All sought to develop closer economic, political and humanitarian links between West Germany and the countries of **Central and Eastern Europe**. In reorientating West German foreign policy away from Westpolitik and the 'policy of strength' pursued by **Konrad Adenauer** and his successors, Brandt was concerned to emphasize that this in no way represented a diminution of the FRG's commitment to the European Communities (EC) and to other Western organizations, such as the **North Atlantic Treaty Organization** (NATO). Nevertheless, Brandt's policy aroused extreme hostility among the leadership of the Christian Democratic opposition in West Germany. While Brandt was not averse to EC plans for further economic and political integration, he tended to think of Europe on a broader scale, an attitude instilled by his long exile in Scandinavia after 1933, which, he said, had taught him to think of himself as a European. Hence he supported the principle of **enlargement**, and argued with President Georges Pompidou of **France** that the French position on enlargement, or specifically on the membership of the **United Kingdom**, should be reversed. Equally, while supporting further integration, he was sceptical towards proposals that were either too expensive or had not been costed properly, and was highly critical of assumptions by other Member States that the extra costs would be borne by the FRG. For example, he opposed the creation of the **European Regional Development Fund** and was particularly concerned with the budget and spending patterns of the **Common Agricultural Policy**, a position that was resented by France and other EC states. In early 1974 Brandt resigned from office following the political scandal that surrounded one of his personal assistants who was discovered to be a spy working for the East German regime.

BRETTON WOODS in New Hampshire, **USA**, was the location and name of an agreement, made in 1944 by several Western countries, on the introduction of a new international monetary system based upon fixed exchange rates, and backed by two reserve currencies, the US dollar and UK pound sterling. The intention was to make currencies convertible on current account, so facilitating multilateral trade and reducing the need for disruptive devaluations. The system experienced a number of problems in the late 1940s, and did not become fully operational until 1958. In the 1960s the fixed exchange-rate system, especially the two reserve currencies, came under increasing pressure. The agreement effectively disintegrated in 1971, when the USA unilaterally suspended dollar convertibility against gold. The Smithsonian Agreement and the European

Snake were efforts to salvage some advantage from the failure of the Bretton Woods agreement since, despite the benefits that floating currencies may have held for governments, the consequent currency fluctuations adversely affected international monetary stability. The **European Monetary System** (EMS) of 1979 was an attempt by the European Communities to stabilize currency fluctuations by introducing a modified exchange-rate system that would replicate what were believed to have been the virtues of Bretton Woods.

BRITAIN: See **United Kingdom**

BRITE-EURAM was a composite initiative, launched in 1989 and lasting until 1998, in the fields of advanced industrial materials technology, design methodology and the application of quality assurance to both processes and products. It continued the work of two earlier programmes: Basic Research in Industrial Technologies in Europe (BRITE) and European Research in Advanced Materials (EURAM). The programme focused on encouraging **small and medium-sized enterprises** (SMEs) to undertake or commission new research into new design and manufacturing processes.

LEON BRITTAN (1939–), now Baron Brittan of Spennithorne, has perhaps been one of the most influential Commissioners in the history of the European Union. Prior to joining the **European Commission**, Brittan had enjoyed senior positions in Conservative governments of the **United Kingdom** during 1979–86. He was appointed to the European Commission as one of two British nominees in 1989. He was made one of the six Vice-Presidents of the Commission, and given the two important portfolios of **Competition Policy** and Financial Institutions. He therefore had a large part of the responsibility for ensuring that the European Communities (EC) reached their target of completing and implementing the **internal market**. His vigorous enforcement of EC competition policy made him a highly successful and much respected Commissioner, but his command of the competition brief along with his ultra-liberal credentials and commitment to free trade led to disagreements with his colleagues, and in particular with the President of the Commission, **Jacques Delors**. However, he also had policy disagreements with his former party leader, **Margaret Thatcher**, on several occasions. In particular, he believed that the United Kingdom should become a full member of the **European Monetary System** (EMS). In 1993–94, no longer a Vice-President of the Commission, he held the portfolios of Trade Policy and External Economic Relations, with responsibility for territories that included Eastern Europe and the **Commonwealth of Independent States** (CIS). Brittan was keen to succeed **Delors** as President, but the timing was neither right for a British incumbent nor was there a desire among several Member States for a formidable personality at the helm of the Commission. When a new Commission took office under the presidency of **Jacques Santer** in 1995, Brittan was once again appointed as one of the Vice-Presidents, now numbering only two; however, his responsibilities were reduced to Multilateral Trade and Relations with the Developed World. His final term in the Commission ended prematurely following the mass resignation of the Santer team in 1999. He remains a staunch supporter of the United Kingdom's entry into the **eurozone**.

BROADCASTING: See **Cultural Policy**; **European Broadcasting Union**; **Media Policy**

BRUGES GROUP is the name of a group of anti-European Union British Conservative Party politicians who formed the Campaign for a Europe of Sovereign States in 1988. The campaign was inspired by a speech made by the British Prime Minister, **Margaret Thatcher**, at the College of Europe in Bruges, **Belgium**, in September 1988, in which she attacked the **European Commission** and its efforts to impose what she regarded as a bureaucratic and unrepresentative centralization upon the European Communities at the expense of national **sovereignty**. The Group's major concern was primarily domestic British party politics and helped fuel the growing force of Euroscepticism (– see **Eurosceptics**). Its members were particularly vocal at the time of the **ratification** of the **Treaty on European Union** in the early 1990s, but thereafter the group has made little effort, and has had no effect, within and outside the **United Kingdom**.

BRUSSELS is the capital city of **Belgium** with a population of some one million people. Brussels is also home to the executive and administrative branches of the European Communities (EC). In addition to being the location of the **European Commission** and the Secretariat of the **Council of the European Union**, it also houses the offices of both the **Committee of the Regions** and the **European Economic and Social Committee**. The **European Parliament** has much of its staff in this city and the majority of its committee meetings take place in its new Brussels headquarters. In addition, all the national representations of the Member States reside in Brussels, as do representations of many regions (e.g. the German Länder) and sub-national authorities (e.g. the Northern Ireland Executive Office in Brussels and Scotland Europa), which have premises near the European Union (EU) institutions. Moreover, Brussels has attracted the attention of a variety of public, private and voluntary organizations that either own or rent offices in the city in the hope of being able to influence policy development and EU **decision-making**. Finally, Brussels has also been the home of the **North Atlantic Treaty Organization** (NATO) since 1967. The concentration of EC institutions in the city has meant that the name 'Brussels' has often been used as a term to describe the EC and their decision-making bodies. Suggestions have been made that Brussels, as it functions in many ways as a capital-elect of the EU, should be given a special status similar to that accorded to Canberra (Australian Capital Territory) or Washington (District of Columbia, **USA**).

BRUSSELS, TREATY OF: See **Treaty of Brussels**

'BRUSSELSIZATION' is a term that is associated with the evolution of the European Union's (EU) **Common Foreign and Security Policy** established under Pillar II of the **Treaty on European Union** in 1993. Although the EU's supranational powers are highly marginalized in this policy area, there is a growing sense that this policy's development is being determined to a greater extent than ever in Brussels by a number of Pillar II working groups. Since the days of **European political co-operation** in the 1970s and the 1980s, working groups have played an instrumental role in EU foreign policy business. There are an estimated 20 in existence and they exchange information on issues ranging from landmines to the **Organization for Security and Co-operation in Europe** (OSCE). Foreign policy may still remain firmly under the control of the national governments, but since the **Maastricht Summit** it has become increasingly apparent that more authority and expertise on Pillar II questions has shifted from Member States to their national delegations (**Permanent Representations**) in Brussels, which collaborate with the working groups. In other words, the process of 'Brusselsization' ensures that a substantial amount of information on foreign policy is exchanged between the national delegations, and more so than between any other sovereign states in any other international organization.

BSE: See **Bovine Spongiform Encephalopathy**

The **BUDGET** has always proved to be a source of controversy for the European Communities (EC), and then for the European Union (EU). When the **European Economic Community** was established in 1957, it was agreed that its budget would be financed by national contributions from the Member States, the contribution of each state to be determined by its gross national product (GNP). This was the standard means for financing international organizations such as the **United Nations**. The **European Commission** regarded the EC as being a different type of organization, however, and since the mid-1960s has sought access to its own revenue sources. In 1970 the original **six** Member States in the **Treaty of Luxembourg** decided that national contributions would be progressively phased out by 1975, to be replaced by a system of EC **own resources**, that is, funds that originate in the Member States but are the property of the EC.

EC **revenue** now comes from four main sources. Firstly, the EC receive the levies on imports of food from outside the EU to bring the price of the imports up to the EC level determined by the **Common Agricultural Policy** (CAP); there are also levies on agricultural products that are in surplus supply. The second source of revenue is the **customs duties** on non-agricultural imports from outside the EU. Both these sources are declining in importance, and they accounted for some 13% of the revenue stream in the 2005 budget. The third element, which is the second most important, is a proportion of the **value-added tax** (VAT) imposed at national level by the Member States. The ceiling for the VAT contribution has altered over the last two decades and has been declining since 1999 – firstly to 1% and subsequently to its current level of 0.5%. The fourth, and increasingly most important, revenue source was added in 1988 as part of the **Delors I** package. It consists of contributions from the Member States adjusted to their share of the total GNP (at 1.24%) of EU states. This fourth resource is the most important revenue stream and accounted for 65% of the EU budget's composition in 2005. In addition, fines imposed by the Commission for infringements of EC **competition policy** are added to the budget, and in recent years have accounted for approximately 2% of the entire budget. Also the now defunct **European Coal and Steel Community** (ECSC) retained its own budget, which was financed by a direct levy upon coal and steel enterprises within the EU. The **Treaty on European Union** formally recognized that the EC have their own sources of revenue, stipulating that there must be sufficient own resources to cover all agreed **expenditure**.

The general EU budget for 2006 was adopted in December 2005. It totalled some €121 billion. The budget is rather small in terms of the budgets of national governments, and accounts for around 1% of the total output of the Member States. Budget expenditure falls under six specific headings in 2006: Natural Resources, Citizenship, Competitiveness, Cohesion, a Global Partner and Administration. The most important expenditure item traditionally has been the CAP. Agriculture and efforts to modernize production and ensure high quality as well as to foster rural development are to be found under the Natural Resources heading. Agriculture used to account for around two-thirds of the budget. Its escalating costs, which were defined as **compulsory expenditure**, had increasingly limited possibilities of funding programmes in other policy areas. After years of disagreement, it was accepted in 1988 that future increases in agricultural spending would be limited to a maximum of 74% of the annual growth of GNP in the EC. As a result, by 2006 agricultural support spending had fallen to some 47% of the budget. The other major area of expenditure for 2006 is directed towards **cohesion policy** and initiatives to make the EU more competitive, and accounts for 39% of the 2006 budget. That left some 5% going to internal policies; 6% towards funding the EU administration; 7% going towards external policy priorities; and 1% being earmarked for **citizenship** initiatives. The budget does not distinguish between capital and recurrent expenditure, in part because the EC has little of the former: it does not, for example, own most of the buildings which it occupies in **Brussels**.

The budget process consists of five stages. A preliminary draft budget is prepared by the Commission for presentation to the **Council of the European Union** no later than 1 September of the year before the one during which the budget is to be implemented. The Council can then accept or amend the draft: it has tended invariably to reduce the total amount of proposed expenditure. By 5 October the Council must have agreed, by a qualified majority (see **Qualified Majority Voting**), upon a draft budget and have sent it to the **European Parliament** (EP). The EP enjoys 'power of the purse' with regard to the budget and has 45 days in which to consider the draft. On those items that are compulsory expenditure, the EP may only suggest modifications to the Council's proposals. On **non-compulsory expenditure**, it is free to amend the draft budget, albeit only within a general limit previously defined by the Council. Once its deliberations are complete, the revised budget returns to the Council, which may reject the EP's changes. When the proposed modifications to compulsory expenditure do not entail an overall increase in expenditure, a qualified majority vote is needed in the Council; when an increase is involved, a positive majority in the Council is required for rejection.

In cases where the Council decides to reject EP amendments to non-compulsory expenditure, the two institutions are obliged to enter into a conciliation procedure to seek a compromise. The final revised document is then returned to the EP for adoption. For the budget to be rejected by the EP a two-thirds' majority of the recorded votes must be against adoption, and this qualified majority must also constitute an overall majority of the total EP membership. If the EP votes against adoption, the net effect is that the EC do not have a budget for the new calendar year, and expenditure is restricted each month to one-twelfth of the budget approved for the previous year. This restriction remains in force until a new budget can be approved. The EP rejected the budget in 1979 and 1984, but each time it ultimately accepted a version that was only marginally different from the one it refused to adopt. Since 1993 the budget has been the subject of an inter-institutional agreement that seeks to inject greater budgetary discipline and to improve budgetary procedures between the Council, the Commission and the EP. This 1993 agreement was judged a success and was renewed in 1998.

Fraud remains a significant problem and it is estimated that between 2% and 10% of the budget becomes subject to fraudulent financial claims, primarily from the operation of the CAP. The **Treaty of Amsterdam** introduced measures to protect against fraud and misuse of EU finances. It also provided for greater scrutiny of expenditure within the CAP and the EAGGF. The **Court of Auditors** was to have an enhanced role in ensuring that the budget was not being misspent.

As part of the **Agenda 2000** reforms proposed by the Commission in July 1997, a new **financial perspective** was put forward, and adopted by the Council in 1999. This was scheduled to run from 2000 until 2006. This financial perspective designated appropriations for the enlargement of the EU, so that new Member States could be accepted without jeopardizing the EU's current main priorities, which was never going to be an easy task. The budget remains controversial and there are increasing signs of unease within Member States over its funding. Both **Germany** (traditionally the largest contributor) and the **Netherlands** have hinted strongly in recent years that they would like to receive a rebate in a similar manner to the one agreed for the **United Kingdom** at the **Fontainebleau Summit** in 1984. The existence of this rebate itself is controversial.

Discussions for the next financial perspective (running from 2007 to 2013) began in earnest at the end of 2004 and proved to be heavily contentious. The difficulties centred on the overall level of spending and the breakdown between the various headings of expenditure. Basically the Commission, with the support of some of the smaller EU states, had been keen to maintain the existing level of 1.24% of GNP to determine the overall size of the budget (amounting to £668 billion for the next seven years). However, the net contributors to the budget (Germany**, Sweden**, the Netherlands and the United Kingdom) wanted to limit spending to 1% of GNP (amounting to £545 billion). The final agreement will be determined by the Member State governments and is likely to fall somewhere in between these two desired levels. For example the **Luxembourg** presidency (January–June 2005) suggested 1.06%. The UK rebate and reform of the CAP remain very much part of the negotiations and discussions, but both are extremely contentious. The issue of EU financing is more controversial now than at any time since the early 1980s. Discussions between the EU Member States stalled in June 2005 at a meeting of the **European Council**. This meeting ended in considerable disarray, as the UK refused to give way on its rebate unless the French government showed willingness to engage in serious CAP reforms. With both sides unable to reach an agreement, the issue of the budget was postponed.

The ramifications of this frosty meeting endured for the remainder of 2005, with the French and UK governments in particular at loggerheads over how best to finance the 2004 enlargement to the advantage of the new entrants. President

Chirac insisted on an end to the UK rebate while **Blair** resisted and tried to make a direct link with the future reform of the CAP. The UK came under increasing pressure from all the other Member States to get an agreement on the budget and to recognize that the UK was no longer in a position to need the maintenance of the rebate. EU leaders finally secured an agreement for the new financial perspective (2007-13) of €862.4 billion. This figure corresponds to 1.045% of EU GNP, and although it represents an increase from an earlier proposal of 1.03%, falls far below the Commission's hopes (1.24%). Incidentally, the overall figure was also lower than the amount (€883 billion) that the European Parliament had requested. As part of the overall agreement the UK agreed to relinquish approximately €10.5 billion over this period in return for serious consideration of a farm subsidy reduction in 2008. The leaders of the Member States praised Blair for his decision on the rebate, which it was generally agreed had prevented another major crisis for the EU. The leaders of the states from Central and Eastern Europe expressed their satisfaction at the outcome, particularly the Polish Prime Minister, Kazimierz Marcinkiewicz, who secured an additional €4 billion in aid. Overall aid to the new Member States was capped at €157 billion. Farm and rural development remains the biggest item of expenditure and accounts for €292 billion. Time will tell how Member States come to view the revised budget agreement.

BULGARIA is one of the 10 Central and Eastern European **applicant countries** to the European Union (EU) that applied for membership in the 1990s, submitting its formal application in 1995. Prior to this it had signed a **Europe Agreement** with the European Communities in 1993, which entered into force in 1995. The **European Commission's** report on the applicant countries of July 1997, entitled **Agenda 2000,** proposed that **accession negotiations** with Bulgaria should be deferred, owing to the limited measures undertaken with regard to economic reform and the degree of political instability experienced in the early to mid-1990s. Although the country had almost fulfilled the political criteria for membership, the report stated that investment was still needed in the areas of environment, transport, energy, home affairs, justice and agriculture. Bulgaria was thus not a participant in the first round of accession negotiations that began in March 1998. However, greater political stability under Prime Minister Ivan Kostov (elected in 1997) helped Bulgaria's image, and the country was included in the second round of negotiations that commenced in 2000. The country continued to make steady progress under Prime Minister Simeon Saxe-Coburg Gotha (formerly King Simeon II), although difficulties still persisted over specific economic targets and the EU's demands for the early closure of the obsolete reactors at the controversial Kozloduy nuclear plant. The Bulgarian government made a decisive move towards achieving the latter in December 2002 when it closed two of the reactors and announced its intention to close a further two by the end of 2006. The final negotiating chapters were then closed in June 2004 and in April 2005 an **Accession Treaty** was signed. This was ratified by the Bulgarian parliament on 11 May 2005, with 230 MPs voting in favour and two against. It is envisaged that Bulgaria will join the EU on 1 January 2007 alongside **Romania**, although accession may be delayed by a unanimous decision of the EU's 25 **Member States** if there is 'a serious risk' of Bulgaria being 'manifestly unprepared to meet the requirements of membership'.

The **BUNDESBANK** is the central bank of the Federal Republic of **Germany**, and was established in 1957. It is unusual as a national central bank because of its substantial autonomy from government. Because of the importance of the German economy and the strength of its currency, the Bank has had a substantial influence upon Western European economic policy and activity, and was the core of the **European Monetary System**. The Bundesbank's central policy concern was to fight inflation in West Germany. However, this obsession with price stability as the core policy objective in turn affected other European economies, which experienced rising unemployment and weaker economic growth. This was particularly the case in **France** by the late 1980s, and was a prime motivating factor behind the French Prime Minister Edouard Balladur's pursuit of **economic and monetary union** (EMU). By the early 1990s, the heavy financial strains of the German reunification process only fortified the Bundesbank's priorities of controlling domestic inflation and maintaining high interest rates, and led to further political controversy in 1992–93, when these domestic objectives took precedence over policies that other Member States believed the Bank should have adopted in order to preserve the **exchange-rate mechanism** (ERM). The problem with the Bundesbank's policy was external, in that other countries, with weaker currencies, had to match the level of German interest rates if they wished to stay in the ERM. This adversely affected their own economies, while exposing them to market speculation on the grounds that their currency values were artificially high. The Bundesbank and a majority of the German electorate remained unenthusiastic about the notion of EMU and feared that any new currency would be less stable than the Deutsche Mark. The decision for Germany to embark on the EMU project was, however, politically driven and decided. With the establishment of the **euro** and the **European Central Bank** (ECB), the direct influence of the Bundesbank over European finance policy was certain to decline.

The **BUREAU** or Executive Committee is an essential part of the organization of the **European Parliament**. The Bureau comprises the President, Vice-Presidents,

Quaestors and potentially others, and focuses its activities on both political and administrative matters.

BUSINESS AND INNOVATION CENTRES (BICs) were launched by the **European Commission** in 1984 to encourage diversification of activity by small enterprises, and to help establish new small companies in innovative areas of activity and production. Their role today is very much to promote regional development. (See also **European Business and Innovation Centre Network**.)

BUTTER MOUNTAIN is a term that has become part of European Union (EU) folklore. It is a phrase, usually of derision, popularly employed to symbolize one of the consequences of the price guarantee scheme of the **Common Agricultural Policy** (CAP), the intervention purchasing by the European Community (EC) of agricultural produce, when either the market price falls below the predetermined EC level, or when over-production occurs. EC practice has been to store the surplus for an indefinite period, until either price levels rise or, more commonly, a decision is taken to sell the surplus at discounted prices to non-EC countries. CAP over-production had been most pronounced in dairy farming, and the butter surplus was one of the first to come to popular attention. Limits were placed upon production subsidies in dairy farming in 1984 with the introduction of milk quotas, after which the demand upon CAP financial resources made by milk products fell by one-third. Further restrictions were imposed in 1988 with the introduction of **stabilizers**. These measures have substantially reduced, but not totally eliminated, phenomena like the butter mountain. (See also **Wine Lake**.)

ROCCO BUTTIGLIONE was nominated by the Italian government to serve as a member of the **Barroso** Commission, where he was to be handed responsibility for justice and discrimination issues. His nomination as Commissioner-designate unexpectedly plunged the Commission and the EU into a state of crisis in the autumn of 2004 over Buttiglione's remarks on homosexuality and women to a panel of MEPs. Buttiglione, who is close to the Vatican and a member of the Christian Democrat UDC party, said that he considered homosexuality 'a sin' and went on to say the aim of marriage was 'to allow women to have children and to have the protection of a male'. This incident unleashed a torrent of controversy and debate. Although Buttiglione maintained that such personal views would not influence his work as a Commissioner, and in spite of strong support from the Vatican, large sections of the Italian media and the Berlusconi government, it rapidly became clear that a majority existed within the **European Parliament** (EP) to effectively block the appointment of the entire Barroso team of Commissioners unless Buttiglione was removed. The episode was certainly embarrassing and a clear example of the EP seeking to flex its muscles. The crisis lasted almost three weeks and was only finally resolved when Buttiglione withdrew his candidature and was duly replaced by the then Italian foreign minister, Franco Frattini. Only then was the Commission team approved by the EP.

C

CABINET is the name given to the group of personal advisers and aides attached to each Commissioner within the **European Commission**. Its purpose is to provide the Commissioner with political and policy advice, as well as liaising with other groups within the European Union and speaking for the Commissioner in meetings of officials.

CABOTAGE is the system whereby transport providers may offer services in the domestic market of another Member State. As part of the European Communities' (EC) **road transport** policy, the Council of Ministers (see **Council of the European Union**) agreed in 1993 on measures including a common tax system for heavy goods vehicles using EC roads, which led to full liberalization of road *cabotage* by 1998. Since then efforts have focused on promoting *cabotage* on the rail network and within shipping.

DAVID CAMERON (1966-) was elected as the leader of the UK Conservative Party in December 2005. He first entered Westminister in 2001 and his rise has been meteoric. He comes from the growing Eurosceptic wing of the party and since his election has been very critical of Blair and the prime minister's handling of the UK rebate issue. During Cameron's campaign hustings for the leadership he promised to withdraw the party's MEPs from the ranks of the **European People's Party** (EPP) within the European Parliament. He has repeatedly expressed his views on this issue since his election in the face of strong opposition from the UK's conservative MEPs, who argue that such a move will reduce the party's influence in the European Parliament.

CANDIDATE COUNTRIES was the term adopted by the Helsinki Summit of the **European Council** in December 1999 to refer to those countries involved in **accession negotiations** launched in February 2000. At the time, the term covered the 10 **applicant countries** from **Central and Eastern Europe**, **Cyprus**, **Malta** and **Turkey**. With the **enlargement** of the EU on 1 May 2004, the number was temporarily reduced to three: **Bulgaria**, **Romania**

and Turkey, although **Croatia** was granted the status in June 2004 and **Macedonia** in December 2005. In addition to adopting the term 'candidate countries', the European Council in 2000 also introduced the term **potential candidate state** to describe countries in the **Western Balkans** that aspire to membership.

CAP: See **Common Agricultural Policy**

CARBON TAX is the name of a proposed **energy tax** that has been under consideration by the **European Commission** since 1991. Part of the campaign to reduce **atmospheric pollution**, it was a key element of the European Communities' (EC) efforts to develop an **energy policy** that would be closely linked to EC **environment policy**. The tax would involve a levy on petroleum produced within the European Union (EU) as well as upon the fuel and carbon content of all non-renewable fuel. The tax is seen as part of the EU's acceptance of the agreement at the **United Nations** Framework Convention on Climate Change, held in Rio de Janeiro, Brazil, in 1992, to stabilize carbon dioxide emissions at 1990 levels by the end of the century. The proposal has been contentious within the EU, however. It finds support among the traditional 'leader' Member States on environmental policy (the **Netherlands**, **Germany** and **Denmark**), which sought EU-wide measures to match taxes already in place at the national level, but it has provoked strong opposition from the poorer Member States, as well as from energy-intensive industries which fear a loss of international competitiveness unless other major industrial states introduce a similar levy. The Commission published details of its proposal for a carbon tax in 1992. The **United Kingdom** strongly opposed any extension of taxation powers to the EU, and the supporters of the carbon tax ultimately gave way to their opponents at the 1994 **Essen Summit**. Instead of a tax the **European Council** agreed to move towards a far more modest position, whereby individual Member States could choose whether or not to adopt their own taxes. The issue did not disappear, however, and continues to resurface, particularly as some Member States have since adopted such a tax at the domestic level (**Austria**, Denmark, **Finland**, the Netherlands and **Sweden**), while the former Social Democratic Party (SPD) and Alliance 90/Greens coalition government in Germany, led by Gerhard Schröder, pursued adoption at EU level.

CARDS (Community Assistance for Reconstruction, Development and Stabilization) is the financial assistance programme dedicated to the **Western Balkans** as part of the **Stabilization and Association Process** launched in 1999. It replaces the OBNOVA programme and involved total funding to the region of €4,560m. for the period 2000–06.

CARTELS: See **Competition Policy**; **Industrial Policy**; **Transport Policy**; **Air Transport Policy**

CARTOON is another name for the European Association of Animated Films. It is based in Brussels and is linked to the MEDIA programme (see **Media policy**).

CASE-LAW: See **Court of Justice**; **Legislation**; **Law**

CASSIS DE DIJON is the popular name of an important ruling (*Rewe-Zentral AG v Bundesmonopolverwaltung für Branntwein*) by the **Court of Justice**. The Court ruled in 1979 that, where a product is manufactured and legally on sale in one Member State, another Member State cannot prohibit its import and sale, except on grounds of its constituting a risk to public health. The product in question was a French fruit liqueur, whose importer into the Federal Republic of **Germany** (West Germany) had appealed to the Court of Justice against a decision by the German courts to ban its import. The West German case rested on the argument that, under the national spirits monopoly, potable spirits had to contain at least 25% by volume of wine spirits to be marketable in the country: the product in question, *Cassis de Dijon*, had less than 20% by volume of wine spirits. In rejecting the West German argument, the Court delivered a decisive legal precedent for the European Communities (EC) in its affirmation of the unconstitutionality of national legislation and technical regulations in relation to intra-EC trade. It enabled the **European Commission** to develop the principle of **mutual recognition** as an important instrument of **harmonization** and the development of the **internal market**. The ruling was subsequently applied to a wide range of products, and its essence was formally incorporated into the **Treaty of Rome**.

CATCH-ALL CLAUSE: See **Article 308**

CCBE: See **Council of the Bars and Law Societies of the European Community**

CCP: See **Common Commercial Policy**

CCT: See **Common External Tariff**

CDP: See **Common Defence Policy**

The **CECCHINI REPORT** of 1988 gave the **European Commission** powerful ammunition in its quest to introduce a range of practical measures that would ensure the effective operation of the **internal market** by 1992. Requested by the Commission, the report was compiled by a committee of experts under the chairmanship of Paolo Cecchini, and published in 16 large volumes, with a summary presentation also published as *The European Challenge 1992 – The Benefits of a Single Community*. The committee consulted both economic and financial data collections and analyses, as well as other official and academic studies. It also interviewed some 11,000 companies across the European Communities (EC). The result was an extensive listing and costing of the obstacles – national practices, regulations and standards – that prevented the realization of the objective of **freedom of movement** contained in the **Treaty of Rome**. The report concluded that the cost of these obstacles was about €200,000m., or some 5% of the EC gross domestic product (GDP). Although it was accepted by the EC, not all authorities agreed with its findings.

CEDEFOP: See **European Centre for the Development of Vocational Training**

CEE: See **Central and Eastern Europe**

CELAD: See **European Committee to Combat Drugs**

CELEX stands for *Communitatis Europae Lex*, an inter-institutional database for European Union law, compiled by the Legal Service of the **European Commission**. Established in 1971, it contains details of, and provides an information service on, treaties, legal agreements resulting from the external relationships of the EU, all secondary **legislation**, case law and **Court of Justice** rulings, and questions and answers in the **European Parliament**.

CEN is the acronym of the European Committee for Standardization, a body of experts based in Brussels that was established to assist in the advancement of the **industrial policy** and research and development policy of the European Communities. Funded by the **European Commission**, it was given a general remit to prepare European standards across a whole range of products, processes and appliances, as well as in the field of **information technology**. The variety of systems of national standards employed by the Member States was believed to be a barrier to the effective implementation of the **internal market**. Some of the smaller states were concerned that the process of integrating the national standards would be dominated by **France**, **Germany** and the **United Kingdom**, which collectively produced some 85% of the national standards. Some 2,000 subjects have been covered by CEN. The field of electrotechnical standardization is the brief of a parallel committee, the European Committee for Electrotechnical Standardization (**CENELEC**).

CENELEC, the European Committee for Electrotechnical Standardization, is an expert body based in Brussels and funded by the **European Commission** whose role is to prepare European technical standards across a range of products and appliances as well as in the field of **information technology**. Its work is regarded as important for both the research and development policy and the **industrial policy** of the European Communities. Its work is similar to that of the European Committee for Standardization (**CEN**).

CENTRAL AMERICA: See **South and Central America**

CENTRAL AND EASTERN EUROPE (CEE), as far as the European Union is concerned, comprises 10 countries: **Bulgaria**, the **Czech Republic**, **Estonia**, **Hungary**, **Latvia**, **Lithuania**, **Poland**, **Romania**, **Slovakia** and **Slovenia**.

The **CENTRAL EUROPEAN FREE TRADE AREA** (CEFTA) agreement entered into force in 1993, agreed on by the so-called **Visegrad group** of countries (Czechoslovakia – now the **Czech Republic** and **Slovakia** – along with **Hungary** and **Poland**), with **Slovenia** and **Romania** joining them in 1996 and 1997 respectively. **Bulgaria** joined the association in 1999, followed by **Croatia** in 2003. The agreement has led to the establishment of free trade in industrial goods between the eight countries. While free trade is an important goal in itself, the main purpose behind CEFTA has always been to facilitate integration with the European Union (EU) and enhance the prospects of the participant countries obtaining EU membership. Indeed, five of CEFTA's members joined the EU on 1 May 2004, thus reducing the membership of CEFTA to just three countries: Bulgaria, Croatia and Romania.

CERIF stands for Common European Research Project Information Format. It is a facility established in 1991 to enable the Member States to exchange information on research projects as a prelude to a planned network of European research databases.

CERN is the acronym of the European Organization for Nuclear Research, a transnational research institution founded in 1954 and based in Geneva, **Switzerland**. CERN is a pure, as opposed to an applied, research institute, focusing upon the theoretical basis of nuclear and particle physics. Nineteen European nations, including most Member States of the European Union, are members, and the **European Commission** acts as an observer. CERN maintains links with the **European Atomic Energy Community**.

CESDP: Common European Security and Defence Policy. See **European Security and Defence Policy**

CET: See **Common External Tariff**

CFP: See **Common Fisheries Policy**

CFR: See **Charter of Fundamental Rights**

CFSP: See **Common Foreign and Security Policy**

CG: Coalition des Gauches – See **Left Unity**

The **CHANNEL TUNNEL** rail link between **France** and the **United Kingdom** was not a European Communities project. However, funding for the road and rail links to the tunnel was provided by the **European Regional Development Fund** because the project was widely regarded as an important contribution to an integrated European transport system (see **transport policy**). Some assistance for the tunnel itself came in the form of a loan from the **European Investment Bank**. The Channel Tunnel Treaty was signed in February 1986, and completion was scheduled for June 1993. Although the first engine to pass completely through the tunnel did so on schedule, technical problems and rising costs prevented the tunnel from becoming fully operational until late 1994. The tunnel has made a significant impact as a means of facilitating the shipment of goods, but in recent years has become a major source of controversy between the United Kingdom and France over the latter's policing of entry points to the tunnel, which have become some of the principal means by which immigrants gain illegal entry into the United Kingdom. The tunnel may have been a technical feat of modern engineering, but its operating company, Eurotunnel, has not yet managed to emerge as a profit maker. Indeed, it continues to face difficulties with breaking even. Its 2004 revenues were down 7% on 2003, while its losses stood at £540m. In response, Eurotunnel has been forced to reduce its prices in an attempt to win back car passengers who have been lost both to cheaper ferries and, more importantly, to the budget airlines.

CHAPTER is the term denoting a subdivision of a **Title** in a European Treaty. A Chapter may in turn be subdivided into **Sections**.

CHARLEMAGNE BUILDING: See **Council of the European Union**

CHARTER FOR A NEW EUROPE: See **Charter of Paris for a New Europe**

The **CHARTER OF FUNDAMENTAL RIGHTS** (CFR) was proclaimed by the presidents of the **European Commission**, the **Council of the European Union** and the **European Parliament** at the Nice Summit of the **European Council** in December 2000. Since then it has been adopted as Part II of the **Treaty establishing a Constitution for Europe**. It should not be confused with either the **European Convention on Human Rights** (ECHR) adopted by the **Council of Europe** in 1950 or the **Charter of Fundamental Social Rights of Workers**, otherwise known as the Social Charter, adopted in 1989. These two documents did, however, inspire some of the content of the CFR. Its existence owes much to the increased awareness of fundamental rights within the European Union (EU) and the desire of the EU to promote such, whether internally through, for example, **citizenship**, or externally through the **common foreign and security policy**.

The text of the CFR comprises seven chapters covering Dignity, Freedoms, Equality, Solidarity, Citizen's Rights, Justice and General Provisions. These contain a total of 54 **articles** setting out individual rights such as those to life, liberty and freedom, education, non-discrimination, good administration, and to a fair trial. As such, therefore, it presents in a single document the existing rights and freedoms enjoyed by EU citizens whether through the **European treaties** or through the ECHR or the Social Charter. Indeed, no new rights are created. All the same, the Member States were not willing at the time to make the CFR a legally binding document. However, they accepted the proposal of the **European Convention** to include it in the Treaty establishing a Constitution for Europe. This was only possible, however, after a number of additional clauses had been inserted clarifying the interpretation and application of the rights contained in the CFR.

CHARTER OF FUNDAMENTAL SOCIAL RIGHTS OF WORKERS is the official title of the original document that later became known as the Social Charter. It originated in the review of progress towards the target of completing the **internal market** by the end of 1992, in which the **European Council** referred to the equal importance of developing the social aspects of the single market. The **European Commission** then drew up a set of proposals for the introduction of a European Communities (EC) charter of fundamental social rights. A modified version of these proposals was then approved by the European Council at its Strasbourg Summit in December 1989, although UK opposition meant that only 11 of the 12 Member States signed the document. Subsequently, the Social Charter figured prominently in the discussions leading up to the **Treaty on European Union**, but persistent UK opposition prevented it from being included in the Treaty. Instead a Social Chapter, complete with an **opt-out** arrangement for the United Kingdom, was agreed allowing the 11 to proceed with measures, notably on health and safety and worker consultation, to implement the Charter. The Labour government elected to power in the **United Kingdom** in May 1997 agreed to sign the Charter shortly after taking office. Following this, the **Treaty of Amsterdam** removed the opt-out clause and incorporated the Social Chapter in the revised **Treaty of Rome**.

Essentially, the Charter set out to codify in general terms what the EC had already begun to do in the social sector, as well as introducing some new proposals. In emphasizing that the single internal market must benefit workers as well as employers, the Charter set out a code of practice that dealt with living and working conditions, **freedom of movement** of labour, collective bargaining, training, **equal opportunities**, gender equality, measures to protect underprivileged groups and safety and health protection. Much of this was already the subject of EC **directives** and **regulations**. The Commission wanted a further **harmonization** of practices that would bring them to the level of the best national practices currently in existence, and stressed the appropriateness of EC action where the desired goals could be more easily achieved at the EC, rather than the national, level. Since the Charter's adoption, many of the rights of workers contained in it have been incorporated into the **Charter of Fundamental Rights** proclaimed in 2000.

The **CHARTER OF PARIS FOR A NEW EUROPE**, often referred to simply as the Charter of Paris, was a document signed at the meeting of the Conference on Security and Co-operation in Europe (see **Organization for Security and Co-operation in Europe**) in Paris in November 1990. The signatories, including the European Communities Member States, declared that 'the era of confrontation and division in Europe has ended', and committed themselves to the promotion and defence of democracy, **human rights** and a free market economy. The Charter has often been held to mark the formal end of the **Cold War**.

CHASSE GARDÉE is a phrase ('protected competition') that has been employed within the European Union (EU) by opponents of too great a movement towards free trade. It refers to a belief that the EU's ability to survive economically in the context of international competition depends upon the provision of a protected domestic market for EU companies.

JACQUES CHIRAC (1932–) became the President of **France** in 1995 and embarked on his second term of office in May 2002 after a resounding victory over Jean-Marie Le Pen, the leader of the extreme right-wing Front National. Chirac studied administration and graduated from the elite Ecole Nationale d'Administration (ENA) prior to working in the Cour des Comptes (the highly prestigious French audit office) before entering politics. Thereafter he rapidly emerged as one of France's most prominent political figures on the Gaullist right in the late 20th century, serving as mayor of Paris from 1977 to 1995 and Prime Minister, firstly under **Valéry Giscard d'Estaing** from 1974 until his resignation in 1976, and later under **François Mitterrand** from 1986 to 1988. The latter marked the first period of *cohabitation,* where a socialist president was compelled to work with a right-of-centre prime minister following separate presidential and parliamentary elections. Chirac's election to the presidency in 1995 raised some concerns in **Germany** with respect to his more cavalier approach to European Union affairs, but Chirac quickly fell into line with the approach adopted by his immediate predecessors in the Elysée Palace. Chirac's strong opposition to a war with Iraq in 2003 fortified his popularity at home and transformed him into one of Europe's most respected leaders. His popularity has declined more recently, however, owing to the trial of his protégé and former Prime Minister, Alain Juppé. Juppé was found guilty of allowing party employees from Chirac's Rassemblement pour la République to be placed on the payroll of Paris City Hall when Chirac was mayor (1976–95) and Juppé was its finance director. Juppé received an 18-month suspended sentence and was banned from holding public office for 10 years. Chirac has stood loyally behind Juppé, but some have begun to question his own involvement in the affair. As President, Chirac is immune from any indictment or sentencing and has not ruled out standing for the presidency again in 2007. Chirac's decision to stage a referendum on the **Treaty establishing a Constitution for Europe** in May 2005 was not necessary and in retrospect, a major miscalculation. The outcome of the French 'non' has clearly undermined his authority and his subsequent skirmishes with Blair over the EU **budget** throughout 2005 undermined Chirac's position both at home and abroad. However, arguably more lasting damage was inflicted upon Chirac in relation to Paris' bid to host the Olympic Games in 2012. Chirac made several comments on the eve of the International Olympic Committee's vote that almost certainly torpedoed the Paris campaign. In the first he stated that the only food that is worse than British food is Finnish, and, more damningly, blamed the UK for mad cow disease. Paris lost the bid to London.

CHRISTIAN DEMOCRATIC GROUP: See **Group of the European People's Party (Christian Democrats) and European Democrats**

WINSTON CHURCHILL (1874–1965) made an important contribution to European developments after 1945. Before the Second World War, he had on several occasions expressed a belief in the value and necessity of European unity. As the charismatic Prime Minister of the **United Kingdom** during the war, he became a symbol to all those who sought the post-war construction of an integrated Europe, in part because of his offer to **France** in 1940 of a Franco-British Union. Churchill returned to the theme of a united Europe throughout the war. Although his premiership ended in 1945, he continued to urge integration. While delivering a major speech in Zürich, **Switzerland**, in 1946, he argued that it was imperative to establish a United States of Europe. He supported the **International Committee of the Movements for European Unity**, and acted as General President of the sessions of the 1948 **Congress of Europe**. After the Congress he became one of the patrons of the **European Movement**. However, notwithstanding his offer to France in 1940, Churchill did not see the United Kingdom as being part of an integrated Europe. That was to be a continental integration, built around reconciliation between France and **Germany**, which, he said in 1946, 'must take the lead together'. Upon his return as Prime Minister in 1951, his European policy did not differ from that of the previous Labour government. He believed that the United Kingdom should act as a transatlantic link between Europe and the **USA**. He was not willing to consider British involvement in anything other than limited intergovernmental co-operation, and during his premiership the United Kingdom refrained from participation in the developments being pursued by the Europe of the **Six**.

CIS: See **Commonwealth of Independent States**

CITIZENS' RIGHTS are determined and guaranteed by the provisions of the **Treaty of Rome** and others of the **European treaties**. However, the treaties only deal with rights in terms of general principles and in specific, mainly economic, areas. A second source of citizens' rights, again only in specific areas, has been the rulings of the **Court of Justice** in the context of its interpretation of the treaties. These cases have been concerned primarily with the principle of equality between citizens within one Member State, especially for minority groups. In the 1980s the European Communities (EC) began to emphasize citizens' rights as part of its promotion of awareness of, and loyalty to, the EC at the level of the individual. This was one of the objectives of the 1984 **Committee for a People's Europe**, but implementation of its proposals was slow. The **Treaty on European Union** attempted to expand the rights already enjoyed by individuals into a broader notion of **citizenship**. The **Treaty of Amsterdam** continued to build on this idea, and focused further attention on the citizen's rights. A new **Article** permits the **Council of the European Union** to take action, by unanimity, in cases of discrimination based on sex, race, ethnic origin, religion or belief, disability, age or sexual orientation. Member States signing the Treaty also agreed to eliminate inequalities between men and women; to protect citizens against misuse of data held by EC institutions; and to maintain and establish co-operation in areas of public health, the environment and sustainability, and development and consumer protection. The Treaty of Amsterdam, moreover, incorporated the **protocol** on social policy (see **Charter of Fundamental Social Rights of Workers**) into the revised Treaty of Rome. At Nice, in December 2000, the rights of citizens were once again on the agenda with the proclamation of the **Charter of Fundamental Rights**, which contains a section dedicated to citizens' rights.

CITIZENSHIP is a concept that remained undeveloped within the European Communities (EC) until the **intergovernmental conferences** of 1991 that preceded the **Maastricht Summit**. While certain individual rights were provided by the **Treaty of Rome**, they were based essentially upon the economic objectives set by the Treaty. While these rights were strengthened by rulings of the **Court of Justice**, they were limited in number and scope, and did not in any way provide a condition of citizenship. This lacuna in EC thinking was directly addressed by the **Treaty on European Union** (TEU), which attempted to formalize and develop the concept of citizenship beyond the economic rights of workers. The aim of introducing and defining European Union (EU) citizenship was part of the ambition to make the EU more democratic and to instil identity with, and commitment to, the EU in its inhabitants. However, it is not totally clear what citizenship is or involves. There are no references to the duties of citizens and, since the EU does not have a **legal personality**, citizenship would seem to lie within the EC **pillar**, which is the only part of the EU in which the Court of Justice, as the guarantor of rights, has jurisdiction. In addition, the TEU reaffirmed that **sovereignty** rested with the

Member States, so accepting that questions of nationality and citizenship should be decided at the national level. Even though EU citizenship is therefore indirect, its establishment was not accepted unanimously. There were fears, particularly among **Eurosceptics**, that the introduction of a formalized citizenship would be used by the European institutions to reduce further the freedom of the states, with the long-term aim of EU citizenship superseding national citizenship. Under the 2006 **budget** citizenship emerges as a new, albeit very small, category of expenditure. Initiatives under this heading include efforts to combat health threats from animal diseases such as bird flu, **BSE** and foot and mouth disease. The 2006 budget established an emergency fund of €48m. to help farmers who have been forced to cull their animals and also provides financial assistance for the destruction of carcasses, vaccination costs and the disinfecting of contaminated land and buildings.

CIVIL PROTECTION is a new area of European Union (EU) competence contained in the **Treaty establishing a Constitution for Europe**. It envisages the EU encouraging co-operation between Member States to improve the effectiveness of systems for preventing and protecting against natural or man-made disasters within the EU.

CMEA: See **Council for Mutual Economic Assistance**

CN: See **Combined Nomenclature**

COAL: See **ECSC**

COALITION DES GAUCHES: See **Left Unity**

COCOLAF: See **Advisory Committee for the Co-ordination of Fraud Prevention**

COCOM: See **Co-ordination Committee for Multilateral Export Controls**

The **CO-DECISION PROCEDURE** is the European Communities' main decision-making procedure. It was introduced by the **Treaty on European Union** (TEU), being later simplified by the **Treaty of Amsterdam**, and requires all **legislation** adopted under the procedure to be approved by both the

Council of the European Union and the **European Parliament**. Where the two institutions are initially unable to approve legislation, a **Conciliation Committee** is held. The co-decision procedure is used to adopt legislation in an increasing number of policy areas (e.g. the **internal market, social policy, transport policy** and **environmental policy**), although it does not apply to certain key areas, such as the **Common Agricultural Policy**, which is still governed by the **consultation procedure**, and matters of **economic and monetary union**, which are decided by the **co-operation procedure** introduced by the **Single European Act** of 1987. The **Treaty establishing a Constitution for Europe** envisaged the co-decision procedure being renamed the 'ordinary legislative procedure'.

The **COHESION FUND** was established by the **Treaty on European Union (TEU)** in 1993 as part of the European Communities' cohesion policy. It is a financial instrument available to finance transport infrastructure and environmental programmes in Member States with a gross national product (GNP) per head of less than 90% of the European Union average. The Fund is not designated as a structural fund, but is linked directly to the move towards **economic and monetary union (EMU)** and was designed to ease the fiscal problems faced by the poorer Member States as they tried to meet the excessive deficit criteria for EMU membership. Originally, only the four poorest countries in the EU-15 – Spain, Greece, Portugal and Ireland – were eligible for support from the Fund. The current period of funding runs from 2000 to 2006. Member State governments agreed to support this fund with annual commitment appropriations amounting to €2,615m. for each of the first four years, €2,515m. for 2004 and 2005, and finally, €2,510m. for 2006. If a Member State becomes ineligible it was always intended that the available resources would be reduced accordingly. Exactly how the overall resources of the Fund are allocated among the Member States is determined by a series of criteria that takes into account Member State population and area, overall per capita GNP and socio-economic factors. The existing financial allocation provides Spain with 61–63.5% of the fund; Greece with 16–18%; Ireland with 2–6%; and Portugal with 16–18% of the total. It should be noted that the total amount that Member States can receive from the Cohesion Fund each year (including any monies under structural funds) should not exceed 4% of their GDP. In 2006 the Cohesion Fund was substantially boosted and will provide €6 billion for some 200 environment and transport projects to assist the regions in the less prosperous Member States to meet and comply with environmental standards. EU Member States whose gross national product (GNP) per capita is below 90% of the EU-average are eligible for financial assistance from the Cohesion Fund. This calculation applies (as at 2005) to **Greece, Portugal, Spain, Cyprus, the Czech Republic,**

Estonia, Hungary, Latvia, Lithuania, Malta, Poland, Slovakia and **Slovenia**). The projects where financial assistance will be provided include waste water treatment plants and the construction of access roads that link the regions concerned into **Trans-European Networks**.

COHESION POLICY seeks to reduce the socio-economic gap between the richest and poorest Member States, and between rich and poor regions within states, through a coherent redistribution of financial resources. The strategy of reducing regional disparities has always been central to the European Communities (EC) because such disparities clearly undermine the integrity of the single market and also run contrary to the aims of solidarity and assistance advocated by the European integration project. The **Treaty of Rome** explicitly, although briefly, referred to regional disparities; however, the initial assumption was that the operation of the free market would help reduce these. Attention was originally focused upon southern **Italy**, and has since widened to cover other Mediterranean regions as well as **Ireland**. The decision to create an **internal market** made resolution of the disparities more urgent, and the term cohesion was first employed in the **Single European Act**. The inclusion of this paragraph (title V) owed much to the efforts of the four poorest states (**Greece**, Ireland, **Portugal** and **Spain**) but also was promoted by richer states (notably **Germany**) as a means of presenting financial support and inducements to those regions that would not necessarily or immediately reap benefits from the prompt completion of the single market. The term cohesion encompassed notions of solidarity and harmonious economic development that could not be secured by the free market alone, and four **structural funds** were established; these were the **European Regional Development Fund** (ERDF), the **European Social Fund** (ESF), the Guidance Section of the **European Agricultural Guidance and Guarantee Fund** (EAGGF) and the **Financial Instrument for Fisheries Guidance** (FIFG). The term 'cohesion' was further elaborated in the negotiations on the **European Economic Area** (EEA) and in the **Treaty on European Union**, which established a new structural fund, known as the **Cohesion Fund**, through which monies from the richer Member States and the other members of the EEA would be directed to aid infrastructural developments in the poorer countries of the European Union (EU). The latter, in return, agreed to accept the provisions in the Treaty relating to **economic and monetary union**. The financial assistance provided to counter regional disparities increased rapidly, from some 5% of the budget in 1975 to approximately one-third of the entire EU **budget** by 2000. Spending in these areas has now more or less stabilized, and stood at some €33,968m. in 2003. Although politically successful, the funds themselves lack sufficient scope and scale to reduce the disparities completely. At a **European Council** meeting in Berlin in

March 1999, although the Member States agreed to maintain their levels of spending on these funds, a general consensus emerged that such spending should be regarded as promoting short- and medium-term solutions, and that, in the longer term, market mechanisms would have to reduce the inequalities. The 2006 budget was heralded by the Commission as a decisive step towards reforming EU spending, in that it places emphasis on investment in growth and the necessity to create more and better jobs. As part of this objective the funds for cohesion policy have been linked to a new drive for competitiveness. Together the initiatives that fall under these two headings amount to 39% of the planned budgetary expenditure. The bulk of this remains earmarked for regional development. Some €11.6m. were directed towards the **European Social Fund** in the 2006 budget to promote better jobs and working conditions.

COLD WAR is a term that was first used in the late 1940s to describe the competition and tension that arose soon after the end of the Second World War, especially in Europe, between the **USSR** and the **USA** and its Western associates. Relations between the two sides were definitely frozen by 1948, with the imposition of Soviet hegemony over Eastern Europe being matched by a series of US commitments to Western Europe through the Truman Doctrine, the **Marshall Plan** and the **North Atlantic Treaty Organization** (NATO). The Cold War made impossible the pan-European alliance envisaged by some in the immediate aftermath of the Second World War, and ensured that any movement towards integration would be confined to Western Europe. It further strengthened US support for European integration. The fear of Soviet intentions also gave a powerful impetus within Western Europe to efforts at collaboration and integration as a wish for self-preservation, and to the feeling that the Federal Republic of **Germany** (West Germany), itself a product of the Cold War, must be thoroughly integrated with the rest of Western Europe. The US military protection guaranteed by NATO allowed the European Communities (EC) to develop without having to be overly concerned with political and defence requirements. On the other hand, the EC's later attempts, in the 1970s, to develop **European political co-operation** (EPC) were in part a response to the bipolarity engendered by the Cold War and the result of a wish to secure a distinctive Western European voice within it. While the necessity of preserving the US commitment limited the extent of EPC to the political and economic aspects of security, the end of the Cold War (as marked by the signing of the **Charter of Paris** in 1990) meant that the EC could feel less reliant upon US views, and less obliged to take account of them, and begin to consider developing their own **common foreign and security policy**.

COLUMBUS is the **European Space Agency**'s research laboratory that will form part of the international space station. Originally linked to the Hermes space shuttle project, the project to produce Columbus began in 1988.

COM DOCUMENTS are part of the official working documents of the **European Commission**. They are documents prepared by the **Directorates-General** and submitted to the **Secretariat-General** for placement on the agenda of Commission meetings. They consist of proposals for **legislation**, policy discussion papers, and reports on the implementation of policies.

COMBINED NOMENCLATURE (CN) is the goods nomenclature created by the European Communities. Established in 1988, it replaced two previous systems: the **common external tariff** (CET) nomenclature and the Nomenclature of Goods for the External Trade Statistics of the Community and Statistics of Trade between Member States (NIMEXE). The CN is published in the *Official Journal of the European Communities* (OJ), and is updated annually.

COMECON: See **Council for Mutual Economic Assistance**

COMENIUS is a support initiative that seeks European Co-operation on School Education. To this end it supports the first phase of education, from pre-school and primary to secondary school, and it is addressed to all members of the education community in the broad sense – pupils, teachers, other education staff, but also local authorities, parents' associations and non-government organizations. Comenius encourages school partnerships and projects that develop teacher training. It thus aims to enhance the quality of teaching, strengthen its European dimension and promote language learning and mobility. As part of its ethos, COMENIUS also emphasizes issues such as multi-cultural education, support for disadvantaged groups, countering under-achievement at school and preventing exclusion. See **Socrates**.

COMETT: See **Community Programme for Education and Training in Technology**

COMEXT is a databank of external trade statistics produced by the Statistical Office of the European Communities (**Eurostat**).

COMITEXTIL: The Co-ordinating Committee for the Textile Industries in the EEC.

COMITOLOGY, more commonly referred to as the 'committee procedure', is a name given to the process of decision-making and its scrutiny within committees of the **European Commission**. Basically, it describes a process whereby the Commission consults with a series of specialist advisory and other committees when seeking to draft and implement European Union (EU) law. The nature of the committees, which are made up of national bureaucrats, technical experts and representatives of interest groups, varies: some are management committees, with executive powers, while others are only advisory. The latter do, however, allow access to decision-making and can be highly influential.

There are three types of committees, namely the **advisory committees**, the management committees and the regulatory committees. All have different powers when it comes to decision-making. All are chaired by the Commission and enable the Commission to establish a dialogue with national administrations before adopting implementing measures. The Commission ensures that they reflect as far as possible the situation in each country in question.

Procedures which govern relations between the Commission and the committees are based on models set out in a Council Decision (Comitology Decision) of 13 July 1987. However, this initial decision has since been modernized by the Council Decision of 28 June 1999, to take into account treaty changes, the enhanced powers of the **European Parliament**s under **co-decision**, and also to respond to increasing criticism that the system was just too complex and too opaque.

The new Decision ensures that Parliament can watch over the implementation of legislative instruments adopted under the co-decision procedure. In cases where **legislation** comes under this procedure, Parliament can express its disapproval of measures proposed by the Commission or, where appropriate, by the Council, which, in Parliament's opinion, go beyond the implementing powers provided for in the legislation.

Lastly, several innovations in the new comitology Decision enhance the **transparency** of the committee system to the benefit of Parliament and the general public: committee documents will be more readily accessible to the citizen (the arrangements are the same as those applying to Commission documents). Committee documents will also be registered in a public register and, since 2000, the Commission has published an annual report giving a summary of committee activities during the previous year.

COMMISSION: See **European Commission**

COMMISSION OF THE EUROPEAN COMMUNITIES is the official title of the **European Commission**.

COMMISSION PRESIDENT: See **European Commission**

COMMISSIONER: See **European Commission**

COMMITTEE FOR A PEOPLE'S EUROPE is the name of a committee established by the **European Council** at the June 1984 **Fontainebleau Summit** 'to suggest ways of strengthening the identity of the Community at the individual level and of improving the image of the Community among the national populations'. The Committee was composed of personal representatives of the heads of government, and was chaired by Pietro Adonnino, a **Member of the European Parliament** (MEP) for Italy. The Committee produced two reports, often referred to as the **Adonnino Reports**. Both contained a series of recommendations based on the Committee's brief, as well as proposals for measures to improve the rights and freedoms of European Communities (EC) citizens, and both were approved in principle by the European Council.

The first report was submitted in March 1985. It recommended the immediate implementation of a number of specific measures relating to the simplification of border crossing formalities, duty-free allowances, tax exemption for books and magazines, the taxation of trans-frontier workers, rights of residence, and the reciprocal recognition of equivalent diplomas and other forms of professional qualifications. Several of these proposals were incorporated into the longer second report presented in June 1985. This report listed longer-term targets relating to **citizens' rights, cultural policy**, youth exchange schemes and education policy, **sport** and strengthening the image of Europe. It called, for example, for more use to be made of the **European Anthem, European Flag** and **European Passport**, as well as the introduction of special postage stamps. Legislative proposals on most of the Committee's recommendations were drafted by the **European Commission** in 1986 and 1987. Although progress was slow, the objective was to ensure that the bulk of the People's Europe programme was implemented by the target date of 1992. Some of the proposals with direct relevance to the **internal market** were incorporated into the **Single European Act**, which also referred to social justice. The more political and general rights were eventually to be incorporated into those provisions of the **Treaty on European Union** that related to **citizenship**; others have been the theme of specific EC programmes. While there has been much activity, People's Europe has been not so much a programme as a set of essentially unco-ordinated initiatives. The fact that over one-half of EU citizens surveyed claim never to have considered themselves European indicates that in some ways the People's Europe concept is superficial, and has little effect upon national identity. The **Treaty of Amsterdam** has further highlighted the desire of the EU to move closer to the people by introducing many new social measures. These include:

measures to combat unemployment; to extend **citizens' rights**; to expand the role of the **European Parliament**; and to encourage greater involvement of **national parliaments**; measures that emphasize the principle of subsidiarity; and measures that make public access to information relating to the European institutions easier, with a view to ensuring greater **openness** and **account-ability** within the EU.

COMMITTEE FOR THE CREATION OF EUROPEAN MONETARY UNION is the name of an interest group of politicians, financiers and indus-trialists established in February 1988 by **Valéry Giscard d'Estaing** and **Helmut Schmidt**, the former heads of government of, respectively, **France** and the Federal Republic of **Germany**. In a review of the successes and failures of the **European Monetary System** (EMS), the Committee argued that it was appropriate and necessary to advance the EMS to a second stage. It produced an Action Programme which listed the changes that would need to be made to the EMS, including the establishment of a **European Central Bank** and a common monetary policy, the adoption of the **European Currency Unit** as the single European currency, and control over budgetary policy to be trans-ferred from the Member States to the Council of Ministers (see **Council of the European Union**). The programme presaged many points in the **European Commission**'s 1989 proposals for **economic and monetary union**.

The **COMMITTEE OF AGRICULTURAL ORGANIZATIONS IN THE EUROPEAN UNION** (COPA) is based in Brussels and is a transnational fed-eration of farming unions and associations, which supplements the activities of the national agricultural unions by lobbying in the various institutions of the European Communities for farming interests. Its influence has been far in excess of the importance of farmers in European society and to the economy. The nature of the **Common Agricultural Policy** (CAP) has meant that in lobbying the **European Commission** and the national governments, COPA has effectively engaged in annual wage negotiations for the farming sector, and has opposed proposals for limiting the CAP.

COMMITTEE OF THE GOVERNORS OF THE CENTRAL BANKS was a body established in 1964. It was essentially a consultative body, charged with overseeing and commenting on monetary developments. However, because it consisted of the heads of the central banks of the Member States, its opinions had considerable influence. It provided technical and managerial advice and assistance for the operation of the **European Monetary System**, and was central to the planning and institutional development of **economic and**

monetary union (EMU) from January 1999. The Committee elected its own president on an annual basis, without any principle of rotation by state. It met on a monthly basis at the headquarters of the **Bank for International Settlements** in Basel, **Switzerland**. The Committee ceased to exist on the establishment of the **European Monetary Institute** in January 1994 (the start of stage two of EMU), although the governors of the central banks of the Member States were to play an important role in the Governing Council of the **European Central Bank** and in the **European System of Central Banks**.

The **COMMITTEE OF PERMANENT REPRESENTATIVES** (COREPER) consists formally of the heads of the delegation, or **Permanent Representation**, that each Member State maintains in Brussels, but the term COREPER is also used to refer to the totality of the delegations and their various committees and subcommittees. The members of COREPER, the Permanent Representatives, have senior ambassadorial status. COREPER's task, which expanded enormously as the European Communities (EC) extended the range and volume of their activities, is to act as both service agent and 'gatekeeper' for the **Council of the European Union**. Supported by diplomatic and bureaucratic personnel, it prepares the agenda for Council meetings. If the members of COREPER, who receive their instructions from their own national capitals, are able to reach unanimous agreement on a particular issue, the proposal is given an 'A' category on the Council agenda. This means that the proposal is approved by the Council without discussion. Where COREPER finds it impossible to reach a consensus, the issue is referred back for discussion and possible resolution. More generally, COREPER holds frequent meetings to review and consider the details of all proposals for EC **legislation**, in order to seek a common position acceptable to all national governments, and upon which it could make recommendations to the Council of the European Union.

The workload of COREPER has increased so much that the Permanent Representatives do not always attend its meetings. Much of the agenda evaluation is now handled by deputies, who meet as COREPER I, while the ambassadors' committee is known as COREPER II. By tradition, COREPER does not discuss agricultural questions: these are the province of the **Special Committee on Agriculture**. The centrality of COREPER to the decision-making process of the EC has been the subject of much criticism, notably from the **European Parliament**, particularly on the grounds that it both reinforces the role of national governments, and lacks **accountability** within the EC institutional framework. However, its existence was given formal recognition in the **Treaty on European Union**: previously, its authority was based only on the Rules of Procedure of the Council of the European Union.

The **COMMITTEE OF THE REGIONS** (CoR) was established by the **Treaty on European Union** (TEU), thereby formalizing a grouping that had emerged in the late 1980s. It was recognition of the fact that many regional political authorities in the European Communities (EC) had established their own liaison offices in **Brussels**. It was intended, in keeping with the principle of **subsidiarity**, to involve representatives of elected local and regional authorities in EC decision-making in an advisory capacity. Since the European Union (EU) was enlarged to 25 member states on 1 May 2004, the Committee has comprised 317 members appointed by the Council to four-year terms on the proposals of Member State governments and an equal number of alternates; it elects its own officers. The **European Commission** and the **Council of the European Union** must consult it as directed by the treaties or where they believe an opinion from it would be useful. The areas upon which the Committee must, according to the treaties, be consulted are: economic and social **cohesion**; **Trans-European Networks** in the areas of transport, telecommunications and energy; public health; education and youth; and culture. It was also given the right to issue opinions on matters which have been referred to the **European Economic and Social Committee** (ECOSOC), where it feels regional issues are involved. Its inauguration was delayed until 1994, but its potential impact could be considerable because of the importance of regionalism to the **structural funds**. The regions represented by the Committee's members do not correspond rigidly to any single level of **Nomenclature of Territorial Units for Statistics** (NUTS) regions.

Under the terms of the **Treaty of Amsterdam** the range of areas on which the Committee must be consulted was extended to include aspects of employment policy, **social policy, environmental policy** and vocational training. In fact CoR's impact has been modest, although it may yet emerge as a more formidable force. It has proved difficult to maintain a common purpose in a committee with such a disparate membership (ranging in depth and significance from local councillors in the **United Kingdom** to the premiers of the German Länder) and with such modest powers. Instead, many regions have opted to utilize CoR as merely another avenue to pursue their particular interests and gain access to the European Communities' decision-makers. Prior to the signing of the **Treaty of Nice** in February 2001 there had been suggestions that the size of CoR should be capped immediately. However, this proposal was rejected at Nice and an overall ceiling of 350 was established. Significantly, the Treaty of Nice linked membership of CoR to holding a regional or local authority mandate, with membership of CoR lapsing simultaneously with the ending of an elected mandate. The final declaration of a Committee conference convened in Salamanca in September 2001 included a proposal that the Committee be given the status of an institution in its own right, with the power to bring cases of alleged infringement of subsidiarity before the **Court of Justice**.

COMMITTEE OF THREE WISE MEN is the popular title of a body established in 1978 by the **European Council**, following a proposal by President **Valéry Giscard d'Estaing** of **France** that the Council should launch a further review of the operation of the institutional machinery of the European Communities (EC), even though the Council had not yet discussed the **Tindemans Report** of 1976, which covered the same theme. The proposal was for the appointment of a 'number of eminent persons' to investigate the EC institutions with a view to suggesting amendments to procedures and organization that would augment their effectiveness, and also to consider the possibility of progress towards European union. The group consisted of three senior politicians: Barend Biesheuvel of the **Netherlands**, Edmund Dell of the **United Kingdom** and Robert Marjolin of France. The group reported back to the European Council in 1979, identifying the cumbersome nature of policy-making as the major source of weakness and delay in the EC. They commented adversely on the negative role of the Council of Ministers (see **Council of the European Union**), concluding that the **European Commission** should be reorganized and endowed with more authority, and that **qualified majority voting** should be more widely applied in the Council of Ministers. While the European Council welcomed the report as a 'rich source of ideas and suggestions', it was not discussed in detail, and no action was taken on its recommendations.

The **COMMON AGRICULTURAL POLICY** (CAP) is one of the obligations made upon the European Communities (EC) by the **Treaty of Rome**. It represents one of the oldest and most established EU policy responsibilities. Agriculture has long been deemed a special area of economic activity. Rural areas make up over 90% of the EU's territory and account for approximately 50% of its population. Enlargement has brought an extra 4 million farmers into the EU and brings the total farming population to some 7 million. The enlargement process has also added a further 38 million hectares of land to the 130 million hectares that existed in the **EU15.** Agriculture and forestry are the main land users and play a key role in the management of natural resources in rural areas and in determining the rural landscape. The Commission argues that agriculture makes an important contribution to the EU's overall prosperity and estimates that the agri-food sector (including beverages) accounts for 14.2 % of total EU manufacturing output. Yet, the CAP remains an issue of controversy and its future is one that clearly divides the Member States. To understand the current calls for reform it is necessary to appreciate the reasons why agriculture became an EU competence and also the way in which this system was put into operation.

After much disagreement and protracted bargaining, the original **Six** members of the EC agreed, in January 1962, on the principles of a common market for agriculture based upon five objectives set down in Article 33 of the Treaty of Rome: an increase in agricultural productivity; a fair standard of living for the agricultural community; stabilized markets; guaranteed regular supplies of agricultural products; and a guarantee of reasonable prices to consumers. The 1962 agreement was an interim arrangement due to expire at the end of 1965, and the need for the EC to finalize the financial arrangements concerning the reform of agriculture in the various Member States was one factor which contributed to the **empty chair crisis**. In 1968 the framework for the CAP was described in detail in the **Mansholt Plan**. However, only a diluted version of the Plan was finally adopted by the Council of Ministers (see **Council of the European Union**) in 1972.

The CAP was established with three main components: a single market for agricultural products, with common prices; a **common external tariff** (CET), with levies on agricultural imports from outside the EC; and common financial responsibility. A further element, the development of which has remained at a very basic stage, was the restructuring of European agriculture.

Common prices for agricultural products were introduced between 1962 and 1967. The increasing volatility of exchange rates in the late 1960s that heralded the breakdown of the **Bretton Woods** agreement made it increasingly difficult to maintain a common price structure, except by artificial means. The solution was the adoption of artificial **green currencies**, with the difference in value between green rates (the original common prices) and real rates prevailing on the money markets being covered by **Monetary Compensatory Amounts** (MCAs). In the 1980s the **European Commission** came to favour the abolition of green currencies, but this was resisted by several Member States. It was agreed that MCAs were to be eliminated by 1989, but continued resistance preserved them until 1993.

The core of the CAP is the guaranteed price system, which is administered through the **European Agricultural Guidance and Guarantee Fund** (EAGGF). Prices are determined each year by the European Union (EU) agricultural ministers who, because of pressure from national interests and bodies such as the **Committee of Agricultural Organizations in the European Union** (COPA), have tended to set the common prices at high levels which, in the last resort, have been determined more by political pressure and compromise than by any form of rational economic calculation. Two basic prices are set each year. The first is a **target price** for each product covered by the price support mechanism; the other, set at a slightly lower level, is the **intervention price** below which the market price is not allowed to fall. EC prices fixed under the CAP have invariably been higher than those prevailing on world markets.

The guaranteed price system stimulated over-production. This did not affect farmers since, until the system was modified, under the guarantee system their income rose the more they produced, with over-production incurring no penalty. The surplus produce was bought at the fixed prices, and stored. This is the origin of the accumulation of huge stocks of produce, such as the **butter mountain** and the **wine lake**, the storage of which also came to consume large amounts of EC expenditure. The highest levels of over-production occurred in dairy farming, which, although producing only one-fifth of EC total agricultural produce, had by 1980 come to absorb some two-fifths of CAP financial support. Cereal and sugar cultivators were other major over-producers. After 1985, these products were treated more severely in the annual reviews of guaranteed prices, in an attempt to reduce the levels of production.

In addition to protecting farmers within the EU, the CAP helps European agriculture to compete on world markets. It guarantees the payment of export subsidies or **restitutions**, whereby exporters of EU agricultural produce receive refunds to cover the difference between the lower prices at which they must sell on the world markets, and the high EU prices at which they must purchase produce.

The price support mechanism is administered through the Guarantee Section of the EAGGF. This operates in four different ways, which together cover almost the whole of the EU agricultural output. The majority of produce has enjoyed full CAP protection, with guaranteed support and sale prices, and with intervention buying if market prices fall below the levels fixed in the annual review. Some 25% of production, including eggs, poultry, pork, quality wines and some minor cereals, fruit and vegetables, is protected only against lower-priced imports. Most remaining products have enjoyed direct subsidies to strike a balance between consumer prices and adequate income for the affected EU farmers. In the case of oilseed, where variable import duties apply, the CAP has operated a system of **deficiency payments** to cover the difference between the guaranteed price for the EU producer and the world price. Finally, a very small amount of produce, mainly cottonseed, flax, hemp and hops, is covered by a flat rate of aid based upon the quantity produced or the number of hectares planted.

The domination of the guaranteed price system has meant that, of the original aims of the Treaty of Rome, the CAP has greatly improved agricultural production, self-sufficiency and prosperity. This, however, has been at the expense of the fifth aim. The fact that the farm support prices of the CAP have invariably been higher than world market prices has led to higher costs for the consumer, not only directly through higher prices, but also indirectly, because of the demands made by the CAP on the EC **budget**. The CAP consumes almost one-half of the annual budget, and of this amount some 95% has been taken up by the guarantee system, leaving little for modernization, structural improvements and rationalization, under the control of the Guidance Section of the EAGGF.

The CAP has been unpopular with non-EU countries. The **USA** and other efficient and traditional exporters of food have been critical of its protectionist nature, as well as of the practice of **dumping** its stored surplus produce at reduced prices, which, they argue, distorts world trade. There is also a widespread opinion among developing countries that EU agricultural policy is detrimental to an effective development of their own agriculture. Internal criticism of the CAP has been less marked, except in the **United Kingdom**, where the costs of the CAP are seen as being directly related to the level of its own net budget contribution; this has been due in part to its own agricultural structure and its policy of importing large quantities of food from outside the EU.

By the early 1980s the European Commission had accepted the need for restraints on agricultural expenditure, firstly because it was rising at a much faster rate than the **own resources** of the EC could bear, and secondly because its financial appetite, consuming over two-thirds of the EC budget, effectively prevented the development of other EC policies. In the mid 1980s the cost of the CAP was spiralling out of control, which was one of the reasons why Member State governments were compelled to consider CAP reform. After much argument, it was agreed at the 1984 **Fontainebleau Summit** that CAP expenditure should increase at a lower rate than that of the budget as a whole. International currency instability over the next few years frustrated this objective, although **guarantee thresholds** and **quota restrictions** were introduced for some products in 1984 and 1986, and in 1988 it was agreed to introduce **stabilizers** for most products. It was also agreed in 1988 that the future annual growth of agricultural expenditure should not exceed 74% of the increase in total gross national product (GNP) of the EC Member States. While these measures contributed to a reduction in the share of the budget consumed by the CAP, in the early 1990s the problem intensified again with the re-emergence of surpluses and because CAP protectionism had become a major issue which threatened to prevent a satisfactory conclusion to the **Uruguay Round** negotiations on international trade. In June 1992 the Commission made a real political breakthrough when it agreed on a new programme of reforms which involved a further reduction of guaranteed prices for some products, a shift from subsidies for production to income support for producers, a considerable extension of **set–aside schemes**, the encouragement of less intensive and more environmentally friendly farming methods, and opportunities for early retirement. These were reflected in the Commission's forward budget planning for 1993–99, which anticipated the CAP share of the budget falling from 54% to 46%.

Moreover, in March 1999 reforms to the CAP were agreed by EU ministers of agriculture. Certain intervention prices (for example, for cereals and beef) were to be lowered in stages, although intervention prices for dairy produce were not to be lowered until 2005. The aim of the reforms had been to limit spending on the CAP while supporting farmers with direct income support. However, the accord reached did not go as far as the pro-reform Member States (which included **Denmark**, **Sweden** and the United Kingdom) wished, and exceeded budgetary stabilization limits. Moreover, the CAP was still likely to prove an obstacle in world trade negotiations. While these decisions might curtail the CAP, their effect would only be short-term unless the EU tackled the source of the problem – which would entail a radical overhaul of agricultural policy and a changed political climate. This was especially necessary at the end of the 1990s, as the planned eastward expansion of the EU would incorporate states with large agricultural sectors, by Western European standards, which were generally inefficient.

The **Agenda 2000** programme aimed to reshape the CAP and prepare the rural sectors of the EU for future **enlargement** and integration. Greater emphasis was to be placed on the integration of agricultural policy within the broader socio-economic context of rural areas, and the development of a coherent rural policy. At present there are no links between agricultural, structural and environmental policies. This is considered to be detrimental to the establishment of a consistent rural policy within the EU.

In 2003, according to the then Agriculture Commissioner, Franz Fischler, the current criticisms of the CAP were a sign of the widening gap between the positions of farmers and of civil society. Urgent action was needed to restore mutual understanding between both parties. Civil society is justified in supporting a CAP that provides incentives for producing what people want and not what attracts the highest subsidies. In addition, time and time again, opinion polls have confirmed that what people want is healthy, good-quality food, together with a healthy environment and a viably managed landscape.

In 2002 the European Commission tabled a mid-term review of the CAP, which expressed the opinion that public expenditure for the farming sector must be better justified. Besides supporting farming incomes, the CAP must yield more in return with respect to food quality, the preservation of the environment, **animal welfare**, landscapes, cultural heritage, and the furthering of social enhancement and equity. The review aimed to free farmers from red tape, encouraging them to produce at high standards for the highest market return rather than for the sake of the maximum possible subsidy. According to the Commission, the review would ensure better value for money for European consumers and tax-payers.

To achieve these goals the Commission proposed: to cut the link between production and direct payments; to make those payments conditional on the appliance and maintenance of environmental, food safety, animal welfare and occupational safety standards; to increase EU support for rural development; to introduce a new farming audit system; and to adopt new rural development measures to boost quality production, food safety and animal welfare and to cover the cost of the farming audit.

As for the market policy that remained an essential pillar of the CAP, the Commission proposed to bring to a close the process of cereal reforms, notably with a 5% reduction in the intervention price and a new border protection system. Like all previous reforms of the CAP (e.g. the **Mansholt Plan** in 1968 and the MacSharry Plan in 1991 – see **Ray MacSharry**), these radical proposals had to be approved by the Member States. While **Germany**, the **United Kingdom** and the **Netherlands** wanted reform, **France** appeared less enthusiastic and found support from **Italy**, **Ireland**, **Portugal** and **Austria** in resisting major changes. At a meeting of EU ministers of agriculture in **Luxembourg** in June 2003, agreement was reached on what amounts to a fundamental reform of the CAP, and spending levels were determined for 2007 to 2013.

The reform, according to the Commission, envisages a new way for the EU to support its farm sector and will focus more on the needs of consumers and tax-payers, while giving EU farmers the freedom to produce what the market wants. Significantly, in future the majority of subsidies will be paid independently of the volume of production, through a hectare-based 'single farm payment'. These single payments will be linked to the respect of environmental, food safety and animal welfare standards. This decoupling of income and production represents a major political breakthrough. It is hoped that by cutting the link between subsidies and production EU farmers will become more competitive and market-orientated, while the single farm payment will provide the necessary income stability. There are, of course, familiar shortcomings. In order to secure the reform, it was necessary for the Member States to reach agreement, and to do this many of the original proposals had to be diluted. Indeed, Member States now have an **opt-out**, whereby they can extend the existing direct support for a further two years, to 2007 at the latest, rather than the proposed 2005. In other words, in certain key areas there is only partial decoupling: 75% of all direct support will be decoupled in the cereal sector and 50% in the livestock sector. This will add more administration and bureaucracy to the CAP. A much greater emphasis has been placed on reforms of food quality and safety and animal welfare, because for the first time farmers will be encouraged and supported if they comply with food safety and quality and animal welfare issues (cross-compliance), as often demanded by consumer groups. This cross-compliance will ensure better food quality and helps farmers to actually meet the standards required. Also agreed was a 'modulation' mechanism, whereby the direct payments paid to bigger farms are capped. It is envisaged that modulation will save €1,200m. a year, and funds saved will be channelled to rural areas in order to strengthen rural development within the Member States.

Despite its shortcomings, the Luxembourg agreement does appear to represent a historic shift in the structure of the CAP, because it sets the CAP on an irreversible path towards decoupling production from support, an essential and long-awaited economic reform. However, it remains to be seen whether it can stimulate an adequate response at the **World Trade Organization** discussions in Geneva. It is also worth noting that the French government's decision to reach agreement marks a major turning-point in France's position towards the CAP. France, historically the biggest recipient of agricultural receipts, appears now to have acknowledged that the pre-reform CAP is no longer an option for the EU, in particular in view of enlargement. However, it is likely to resist or delay any reform packages. Those Member States likely to make gains from reform are the traditional advocates of CAP reform, including the United Kingdom, where farmers have traditionally been more market-orientated than their French and Irish counterparts. However, the agreement will also make farmers more cautious about investing, owing to the uncertainty caused by the removal of subsidies. The issue of EU agricultural reform is almost certain to feature as a major aspect of EU activity for the next decade and is being tied in very closely to debates on how the EU is funded and its spending priorities. The UK agreed to give up part of its rebate as part of an overall funding arrangement to cover the EU from 2007 to 2013, but on condition that the CAP was reviewed in a serious fashion. The European Commission is expected to hold a full and wide-ranging review of all EU spending, including the Common Agricultural Policy and the British rebate, and to draw up a report in 2008/09. It should be noted however that all EU Member State governments will be able to take decisions on all subjects covered by the review, but will be able to wield their veto. For now Member State governments have been able to agree a budget for the next financial perspective and have simply postponed the thorny issue of agriculture for the time being. Under the terms of the deal agreed on the budget in December 2005, some €292 billion have been earmarked for agriculture and rural development aid. The importance of agriculture was also in evidence in early February 2005, when the European Commission relaunched the Lisbon Strategy (see **Lisbon Agenda**) for the European Union (EU). The strategy involves agriculture and maintains that any strong economic performance in the future should go hand-in-hand with the sustainable use of natural resources.

COMMON CARRIER LEGISLATION refers to European Communities **legislation** that requires transmission systems to carry energy between any third-party supplier and the consumer at a reasonable tariff.

The **COMMON COMMERCIAL POLICY** (CCP) is at the core of European Union (EU) external relations and has been in place since the **customs union** of the European Communities (EC) was established in the late 1960s. The CCP results from EC competence to regulate non-Member State access to the EC market. The CCP therefore confers on the EC, via Article 133 of the **Treaty of Rome**, so-called 'treaty-making powers'. This means that tariff and trade agreements are no longer concluded by the Member States, but by the

EC. Such agreements are negotiated by the **European Commission** under the supervision of the **Article 133 Committee** and formally adopted by the Council of Ministers (see **Council of the European Union**), normally by a qualified majority. Indeed, it is the European Commission that represents the EC and its Member States in both bilateral and multilateral trade negotiations, such as those conducted within the framework of the former **General Agreement on Tariffs and Trade** (GATT) and the **World Trade Organization**. Most agreements involve granting non–Member States preferential access to the customs union and **internal market** through an increase in or abolition of quotas, or a lowering of the **common external tariff**. However, GATT rules dictated that most agreements must involve the creation of a free-trade area or a customs union within a reasonable period of time and cover substantially all goods. This is true of various **free-trade agreements** concluded on the basis of Article 133 and trade arrangements contained in **association agreements**. Traditionally, the CCP has covered mainly trade in goods, although the EU has tended to be highly protective of its own agricultural markets and therefore access here has been less liberal. With the **Treaty of Nice**, the coverage of the CCP was extended to include trade in services.

COMMON CUSTOMS TARIFF: See **Common External Tariff**

COMMON DEFENCE, perhaps in the form of a common European army, is a long-term aspiration of the European Union and is asserted in the **Treaty on European Union** as the extension of a **common defence policy**.

A **COMMON DEFENCE POLICY** (CDP) has been the goal of the European Union (EU) since the **Treaty on European Union** was signed in 1992. Originally, it was to be pursued as an extension of the **common foreign and security policy** and in co-operation with **Western European Union**, although the gradual transfer of this organization's functions to the EU since the late 1990s has meant that the CDP is being developed very much within the framework of the EU, notably as part of the **European security and defence policy**.

The **COMMON EXTERNAL TARIFF** (CET), also known as the common customs tariff, is a term that refers to an essential element of any **customs union**, and an integral part of the **Treaty of Rome**. A common external tariff, imposed on goods entering any Member State from outside the European Communities (EC), was first introduced in the early 1960s, based on an average of the customs levies previously exacted by the Member States, though with some downward adjustment. Since then the CET has been further lowered from around 10% to less than 5%, in accordance with the EC's acceptance of decisions on tariff barriers and international trade in the **General Agreement on Tariffs and Trade**. Certain exceptions are permitted. The **Council of the European Union** may reduce or waive the CET for a Member State where domestic production of the goods being imported cannot meet demand. The **European Commission** may do the same where there is a general shortage of that product within the EC.

The **COMMON FISHERIES POLICY** (CFP) was provided for by the **Treaty of Rome**. The first proposals for a CFP were not, however, made until 1966, and it was not until 1970 that the **Six** committed themselves to such a policy. The Council of Ministers (see **Council of the European Union**) adopted a limited scheme according to the principle of free access for all European Communities (EC) fishermen within EC waters. The scheme, modelled on the principles of the **Common Agricultural Policy** (CAP), envisaged price support mechanisms and protection for the EC market, with measures to ensure equal competition within the market, modernization of the industry, and **harmonization**, if necessary by intervention, of national policies.

These proposals were adopted by the Six at the same time that they were negotiating terms of entry to the EC with **Denmark**, **Ireland**, **Norway** and the **United Kingdom**. All the applicant states had important fishing interests, and the EC plan was, to some extent, perceived and resented by those states as a stratagem to rush through a common policy that, while it might benefit the Six, did not necessarily take into account their own interests. The fisheries issue is widely believed to have been a factor in the Norwegian rejection of membership, at the referendum of 1972. The EC eventually negotiated a compromise agreement with the other three applicant states, whereby each Member State could, as an interim measure until 1982, restrict entry within a zone of six nautical miles (11.1 kilometres) around its shores, or 12 miles in certain areas, to fishing vessels which had traditionally operated within those limits.

The scheme never worked satisfactorily, either in terms of national interests or in encouraging the preservation of fishing stocks. A major disruptive factor was the extension in the 1970s by many countries bordering the Atlantic Ocean, but particularly by **Iceland**, of an exclusive fishing zone to 200 nautical miles, an action that was subsequently endorsed by the **United Nations** Convention on the Law of the Sea. Deep-sea vessels from the EC were excluded from many of their traditional fishing grounds. They were obliged, if they were not to be forced out of business, to concentrate in EC waters. While the EC also adopted a 200-mile limit in 1977, this did little to obviate the fierce competition within the zone between national fleets, and the inevitable over-fishing that followed.

After much disagreement, a Common Fisheries Policy was adopted in 1983. Its two central elements related to access to stocks and their preservation. As far as access was concerned, it endorsed the principle of all waters being open to all EC fishermen within a 200-mile limit of EC shores (which is inevitably less in the Baltic and Mediterranean Seas). However, individual Member States were permitted to retain an exclusion zone of up to 12 miles, within which fishing rights are restricted to their own fleets, and to vessels from other Member States that hitherto had possessed traditional rights of access.

The central concept of conservation was the **total allowable catch** (TAC). Each year the Council of the European Union agrees on TACs for different species. The TAC is the total amount of that species permitted to be caught in European Union (EU) waters, and each Member State is allotted a quota within each TAC, often only after long and acrimonious bargaining. The operation of the TAC system through the surveillance and inspection policies and practices of the Member States is monitored by a body of inspectors answerable to the **European Commission**. However, problems of verification and enforcement have persisted. Other conservation measures not only relate to the extent of fishing in certain areas, governed by the system of EC licences, but also regulate the size of fish that may be caught, and the type and size of mesh that may be used. Any Member State may introduce further conservation measures within its own zone, as long as these do not discriminate against other vessels from the EU.

Other CFP provisions are modelled on the CAP. Guide prices for all categories of fish are set annually by the Council of the European Union. The EC provides compensation for catches that have to be withdrawn from the market, setting a withdrawal price of between 70% and 90% of the guide price. If both guide and withdrawal prices are higher than world prices, a system of refunds to exporters applies, along the lines of CAP **restitutions**, to maintain the income of the fishing industry. By contrast, when catches in the EU are insufficient to meet market demands, customs duties on imports can be suspended. By the early 1990s quota controls and limited stocks had fallen to below demand, with the shortfall being made up by imports. The volume of cheaper imports deflated price levels, obliging the EU to introduce a system of minimum prices in 1993.

The European Commission has also set common marketing standards and principles on, for example, the size, weight, quality and packaging of fish. The implementation of these standards is the responsibility of the Member States, but they are monitored regularly by the Commission. The CFP was also charged with providing some limited financial assistance to the industry to help with the modernization and restructuring of fishing fleets, but the funds available to it have been very modest, rather less than 1% of the EC **budget**. The basic problem faced by the CFP is that the objective of reducing over-fishing and preserving fish stocks has tended to increase the relative capacity of the fishing fleet, and reductions in capacity have been strenuously resisted by Member

States. In 1991 the Council of Ministers (see **Council of the European Union**) introduced the first of a series of measures intended to address this problem, and in late 1992 it agreed to establish a **Financial Instrument for Fisheries Guidance** (FIFG) as part of the **structural funds**. In 1996, following some controversy over the Commission's proposals to reduce the number of fishing vessels, and the UK government's objection to 'quota-hopping' (in which boats registered in one Member State are bought by operators in other EU countries, which are thus able to gain part of the former Member State's fishing quotas), quotas were set for 1997. These fixed catch reductions at 30% for species most at risk, and at 20% for other over-fished species. Moreover, the Council in 1998 agreed a ban on fishing using drift nets, which would come into effect in January 2002. However, the issues of equal access, capacity and over-fishing persist and remain as politically sensitive as ever.

It was not until 1994 that agreement was reached between the EU fisheries ministers on a revision of the CFP, allowing **Spain** and **Portugal** to be integrated into the CFP by 1 January 1996. A compromise accord was reached on Spanish access to waters around Ireland and South-West Great Britain (the 'Irish Box'); this was strongly opposed by Irish and British fishermen.

In 1999 the Council adopted a new regulation on fisheries that outlined its objectives for the period from 2000 until 2006. It aimed to encourage fishermen to catch only what can be sold; to strengthen the industry organizations and make them more competitive; to protect employment; and to provide greater information for consumers on what they are buying. According to the Commission's 2001 **Green Paper,** much more needed to be done to relieve the depressed state of fisheries in the EU, and the Commission recommended urgent change to the CFP (which had to be revised by 2003). Some degree of reform is vital to tackle the problem of over-fishing, the difficulties of policing 'blue Europe' and the impact of eastern **enlargement** and in particular the future absorption of the Polish fishing fleet into EU waters.

In December 2002 the EU fisheries ministers met in **Brussels** to decide on the much-needed reform of the CFP. Agreement was reached at the end of a five-day consideration of the Commission's proposals on CFP reform. Ministers agreed on three major issues: the need to reform the CFP; the adoption of urgent recovery measures for some cod stocks which were in imminent danger of collapse; and the establishment of TACs and quotas for 2003, including substantial reductions for a number of threatened stocks. In general, the objectives of the CFP have been reviewed to focus more on the sustainable exploitation of living aquatic resources based on sound scientific advice and on the precautionary approach to fisheries management on the one hand, and on sustainable aquaculture on the other.

According to the Commission, the decisions taken in December 2002 would make fisheries management more effective and better able to ensure the long-term viability of the fisheries sector through sustainable exploitation of resources. The Council has accepted the necessity of a more long-term approach to fisheries management, involving the setting of multi-annual recovery plans for stocks outside safe biological limits and of multi-annual management plans for other stocks. It has also endorsed a simpler system for limiting the fishing capacity of the EU fleet in order to reach a better match with available resources. To this end, it will replace the former system of Multi-annual Guidance Programmes (MAGPs), generally regarded as ineffective, with a new system which is designed to give more responsibility to the Member States to achieve a better balance between the fishing capacity of their fleets and the available resources.

The plans were not welcomed by many EU fishermen, for example in areas of the United Kingdom such as Scotland and Northern Ireland where widespread disenchantment was expressed about the future for the fishing communities in these areas. To compensate for the continuing decline of the EU fishing fleet, the EU has instigated a series of socio-economic measures. These include the provision of aid from Member States to fishermen and vessel owners who have temporarily to stop their fishing activity. Aid is also being increased to support the retraining of fishermen to help them convert to professional activities outside the fisheries sector, while allowing them to continue fishing on a part-time basis.

The new measures entered into force on 1 January 2003. They replaced the basic rules governing the CFP since 1993 and substantially amended the Regulation on structural assistance in the fisheries sector through the FIFG. A new Regulation establishing an emergency fund to encourage the decommissioning of vessels (the so-called 'Scrapping Fund') was also adopted.

The problem of over-fishing endured throughout 2003. In view of the high risk of collapse of a number of cod stocks and the difficulty of controlling compliance with low catch limits, scientists from the International Council for the Exploration for the Sea (ICES) and the Scientific, Technical, Economic Committee on Fisheries (STECF) recommended in 2003 a moratorium on the fisheries concerned. Aware of the potential economic and social impact of such measures on fishing communities, the Commission proposed, rather than a moratorium, substantially reduced fishing possibilities for a number of stocks (primarily cod) as well as improved measures to ensure their proper implementation. Accordingly, the TAC reductions were less severe than had been initially proposed. For example, the TACs for Celtic Sea cod stocks and stocks associated with recovery stocks in this area were reduced by 15% (instead of by 47% as initially proposed) for cod in the Celtic Sea, west of Ireland and the English Channel, by 15% (instead of 55.5%) for whiting and by 15% (instead of 33%) for sole. The Council's request that Commission proposals be presented to incorporate within existing recovery plans stocks newly identified as being below safe biological limits also permitted less stringent measures in 2004. For example, the TAC for plaice in the North Sea was reduced by 17% instead of by 41% as initially proposed.

The Council also decided in December 2003 to retain and extend the scope of the interim measures restricting fishing effort adopted by the Council in December 2002 to protect certain cod stocks. These measures, which have been applied in the Skagerrak, Kattegat, the North Sea and west of Scotland since 1 February 2003, will now also include the eastern Channel and the Irish Sea. The aim is to limit the number of days that vessels spend in the areas concerned fishing for endangered stocks, in order to prevent overshooting of quotas. Reinforced inspection and control measures have also been adopted in this context. These measures became applicable from 1 February 2004 and were to remain in force until the Council agreed alternative measures to replace them.

As a corollary to the CFP, the EC signed reciprocal agreements with other European and Atlantic states that permit some limited access to each other's zones and markets. Nevertheless, in early 1995 Spanish vessels fishing in the North Atlantic were the subject of an acrimonious dispute between Canada and Spain, and the EC played a significant role in subsequent negotiations. In 1996, following the publication of a report warning that herring stocks were in danger of being completely eradicated, the EU and Norway agreed an emergency measure to reduce by 50% catches in the North Sea and the waters around Denmark. Further afield, agreements have been signed with some African and Indian Ocean countries that allow EU vessels access to their waters in return for the provision of technical and financial aid.

In late December 2005 the Fisheries Council agreed its latest annual fishing TACs. With regard to cod, fishing possibilities were reduced by 15%, as proposed by the Commission. Conservation is very much at the heart of the Commission's thinking. The effects of these more modest reductions agreed by the Council will be complemented by a further reduction in the number of days that fishermen can stay at sea, and this will also apply to the fleets for which cod is a by-catch but which are responsible for 60% of cod catches. It is hoped that these measures should enable a recovery of cod stocks.

The December 2005 deal also saw reductions in the fishing possibilities on other species. This reduction was as usual smaller than the Commission's proposals, but the general trend of recent times was again reinforced as the overall TACs were lower in 2006 than in 2005. Ministers agreed to further reductions in catches for herring and whiting and a 13% cut in haddock fishing. More positively, ministers were able to agree to a 30% increase in North Sea prawn quotas, a 5% rise in Irish Sea monkfish and a 3% increase in the catch level for hake in most fishing grounds.

These cuts are rarely warmly received by the UK's fishing communities who are always ready to dispute the accuracy of the scientific findings on fish stocks.

They also vent their frustrations about whether other Member States actually enforce the Council's decisions. This is a very significant challenge for the Member State governments and their fishing industries, as failure to enforce fisheries measures works against the interests of fishermen as it leads to over-fishing, depleted fish stocks, smaller catches and shrinking incomes

Interestingly, the European Commission has started to publish its Fisheries Scoreboard (its third appeared in 2005) which now also includes data from the 10 newest Member States. There still seems to be a reporting problem, as facts are not always communicated to the Commission as quickly as the DG Fisheries would like, and this is an area that needs improvement. France, Ireland and Portugal are the worst offenders when it comes to transmitting data about their fleets' fishing effort.

Not surprisingly, more than two-thirds of the infringement procedures cur-rently pending against Member States relate to cases of overfishing. Indeed, the Court of Justice has recently ruled against Belgium, Denmark, Spain, Ireland, Portugal, Finland and Sweden for overshooting their quotas. Moreover, on 12 July 2005, in a landmark case involving France, it also imposed a penalty of €20m. as well as an additional €57m. for each period of six months of non-compliance with a court ruling dating back to 1991. The latest Scoreboard illustrates how only three Member States, Denmark, Sweden and the United Kingdom, fully met their obligations in this area.

Poland is the main fishing nation among the 10 newest EU Member States. The Polish fishing fleet comprises approximately 1,280 vessels and their average age is some 26 years. This particular fishing fleet is involved with three main types of fishing: coastal fleet, cutter fleet and high-seas fleet. The small fishing vessels operate in the territorial waters and in the Vistula and Szczecin lagoons and are after cod, herring and flatfish. The cutter fleet operates in the Baltic Sea and to a lesser extent in the Northeast Atlantic, and is fishing mainly for cod, herring and salmon. The Polish high-seas fleet traverses the North Atlantic in search of shrimp, Antarctic krill and poutassou.

The **COMMON FOREIGN AND SECURITY POLICY** (CFSP) is one of the three **pillars** that form the European Union (EU) created by the **Treaty on European Union** (TEU). The **intergovernmental conference** of 1990 that prepared drafts on political union for the **Maastricht Summit** had as one of its briefs the task of considering collective action by the Member States in the post-**Cold War** era. In part, this came from a desire that the European Communities (EC) should develop an international role more commensurate with their economic standing. It was felt that **European political co-operation** (EPC) was no longer adequate, a view underlined by the different national positions in relation to the Gulf War in 1991. The CFSP became the successor to EPC. Not being part of the EC, which in themselves form a separate pillar of the EU, the CFSP is not subject to normal EC decision-making procedures: direction is given by the **European Council**, not the **European Commission**. The Secretary-General of the Council acts also as the **High Representative** for the CFSP, and in this capacity assists the presidency of the EU, and is responsible for policy planning and monitoring international developments. The actions of the CFSP are also not subject to scrutiny by the **Court of Justice**. It is therefore essentially intergovernmental in character.

The objectives of the CFSP are to safeguard the common values, interests and security of the EU, to preserve peace and strengthen international security, and to promote international co-operation, democracy, the rule of law and respect for **human rights**. While the European Council is free to define how the CFSP is to be implemented, the TEU defines the Member States' duty, firstly to pursue a practice of 'systematic co-operation' through information, consultation and policy co-ordination, and secondly to adopt 'common positions' and 'joint action' when dealing with CFSP matters. The CFSP also includes 'the eventual framing of a common defence policy, which might in time lead to a common defence'. Originally, it was accepted that, until such a position could be reached, the **Western European Union** (WEU) would act for the EU where defence implications arose, and those EU states not members of the WEU were invited to join the organization, at least as observers. Since then, the EU itself has taken a more prominent role in military matters, as seen in the development of a **European security and defence policy** (ESDP) and the creation of a **European rapid reaction force**. This has not been without its problems, given concerns over the impact that such developments might have on the role of the **North Atlantic Treaty Organization** (NATO) and consequently on the effectiveness of that body. Moreover, conflicts in the former **Yugoslavia** illustrated the extreme difficulty of achieving a co-ordinated policy among the Member States, even when there was a predisposition to work together.

That there were difficulties in implementing a CFSP was recognized in the **Treaty of Amsterdam**, which encouraged the adoption of **common strategies**, facilitated decision-making through the introduction of **constructive abstention** and encouraged closer co-operation with the WEU. Thereafter, the **Treaty of Nice** downplayed relations with the WEU and removed the requirement for all the Member States to co-operate on CFSP matters through the introduction of a modified definition of enhanced co-operation. This was followed in 2003 by the adoption of a **European Security Strategy**. Since then, various reforms have been agreed as part of the **Treaty establishing a Constitution for Europe**. These include the creation of a **Union Minister for Foreign Affairs** and a **European Council President**, the establishment of a **European External Action Service**, greater use of **qualified majority voting** and **permanent structured co-operation** in defence matters. Given the doubts surrounding **ratification** of the Treaty establishing a Constitution for Europe, however, these may not come into force, although moves towards the creation of a European External Action Service did begin in 2005.

This, alongside the development of the ESDP, highlights the commitment that exists among the Member States to ensure that the CFSP continues to develop. Despite differences over, for example, Iraq in 2003-06, and concerns that **enlargement** in 2004 would lead to a more Atlanticist outlook within the EU and a greater preference for developing security through NATO, the CFSP enjoys widespread support. It has also enjoyed a number of relative successes in recent years, notably in promoting stability in the **Western Balkans**. This is not to say that its future is without organizational and procedural challenges. Indeed non-ratification of the Treaty establishing a Constitution for Europe will deny it a range of institutional reforms and innovations, thus potentially hampering the EU's capacity to deliver in this important policy area.

COMMON MARKET is a popular alternative name for the **European Economic Community** and, later, for the European Communities (EC). It summarizes the primary economic objectives of the **Treaty of Rome**, a goal that originally was to be achieved by 1970. While in the 1960s it was a relatively neutral term, it later acquired some political connotations, often being used in preference to the term European Communities by those who reject any notion of political integration, insisting that the common market should be the only ambition of the EC.

COMMON STRATEGIES are an instrument for implementing the **common foreign and security policy** (CFSP), which were introduced by the 1997 **Treaty of Amsterdam**. Article 13 of the **Treaty on European Union** sets down the principles and general guidelines for the CFSP. These are decided by the **European Council**. The same body also determines whether to intro-duce common strategies in areas where the Member States share important interests in common. A common strategy defines aims, objectives and timetables involved and, more importantly, outlines the means to be made available by the European Union and the Member States in order to realize them. Common strategies are then implemented by the Council, through the adoption of joint actions and common positions, and the recommendation of common strategies to the European Council.

The **COMMONWEALTH OF INDEPENDENT STATES** (CIS) is the loose association of most of the former constituent republics of the **USSR**, which was established in December 1991 and which in September 1993 agreed on a framework that would serve as the basis of an economic union, and was the focus of much attention by the European Union in terms of political co-operation and economic aid and agreements.

COMMUNICATIONS POLICY: See **European Communications Policy**

COMMUNISTS AND ALLIES is the title of one of the original transnational **party groups** in the **European Parliament** (EP). It consisted of members of national Communist parties and independents elected on a Communist list, and was formed in 1973. It was always dominated by the French and Italian parties but, because these two major national components were invariably deeply divided over both domestic political strategies and those at a European level, the group was one of the least cohesive in the EP. After the 1989 **direct elections** the group formally divided into two separate factions, the Group for the European Unitarian Left and **Left Unity** (LU). While the former still exists as the **Confederal Group of the European United Left/Nordic Green Left**, having 41 MEPs after the 2004 EP elections, LU has disbanded.

COMMUNITARIZATION is a term used to describe the transfer of com-petences to the European Communities **pillar** of the European Union.

COMMUNITY ASSISTANCE FOR RECONSTRUCTION, DEVEL-OPMENT AND STABILIZATION: See **CARDS**

COMMUNITY METHOD is a term often used to describe policy-making procedures undertaken through the institutions of the European Communities, as opposed to those carried out through intergovernmental structures and mechanisms.

The **COMMUNITY PATENT CONVENTION** (CPC) is an initiative aimed at overcoming some of the problems experienced by European companies in registering **patents** and **trademarks**. A general European Patent Convention was signed in 1973. It was designed to eliminate, for companies, the costly procedure of applying for patent protection separately in each country, through the introduction of a single application for European patent protection. A European Patent Office was set up in Munich, **Germany**. The original Con-vention was not a European Communities (EC) instrument, since the Member States could not agree on a common policy, and some did not join the scheme. The major problem was that, while it introduced a common registration procedure, where patent infringements occurred, the plaintiff had to pursue separate litigation in each country where the infringements were alleged to have taken place. The **European Commission**'s proposal for a new Convention remedied this problem by formulating a single EC patent and grievances procedure that complied with the requirements of the **internal market**. The Convention became operative in 1992.

The **COMMUNITY PLANT VARIETY OFFICE**, established in 1995 and located in Angers, **France**, is a decentralized European Communities (EC) agency which implements and applies an EC scheme to allow intellectual property rights to be granted for plant varieties. These rights are valid throughout the European Union.

COMMUNITY PREFERENCE is a term that refers to the situation within the **Common Agricultural Policy** when the price of domestic agricultural products falls below that of imported products.

COMMUNITY PROGRAMME FOR EDUCATION AND TRAINING IN TECHNOLOGY (COMETT) was an initiative established in 1986 as a corollary to, and continuation of, the various initiatives in **research and technological development policy** and **information technology**. The purpose of COMETT was to ensure that the European Communities would have a sufficient reserve of skilled engineers and technicians capable of operating and utilizing the new technologies. To achieve this, COMETT was to promote transnational co-operation between industrial companies and universities in the training of students in new technologies. The key component was that students should receive work experience during their studies by being given a job placement in a company in another Member State. By 1990, more than 1,300 projects had been initiated, and a second programme, COMETT II, was introduced to continue the work until 1994. In April 1990 participation in COMETT was extended to members of the **European Free Trade Association**. COMETT continued as part of the **Leonardo** programme, which began in 1995.

COMMUNITY SUPPORT FRAMEWORKS: See **Structural Funds**

The **COMPANY LAW STATUTE** has long been a contentious issue among European Union (EU) Member States. The original **European Commission** proposal dates back to 1975 and was an attempt to facilitate the establishment of new multinational companies across the European Communities (EC). The proposal encountered immediate opposition, largely as a result of its focus on workers' rights, and was promptly dropped. A second proposal in 1989, which suggested that companies might choose to adopt a company statute in return for certain tax incentives, proved equally contentious. All issues relating to the rights and interests of the labour force can only be decided upon by unanimity in the **Council of the European Union**. These proposals were particularly unacceptable to the German government, which insisted that a European company law statute must contain a requirement for workers' representatives to sit on supervisory boards and to be consulted on all aspects of workforce-related decision-making, in keeping with the German national model.

However, pressure for a European company law statute intensified following the European Council's Nice declaration in favour of harmonizing company law across the EU. Nevertheless, the Council still needed to address concerns among the Member States and some doubts expressed by the **European Parliament**. The latter was anxious to ensure that **legislation** in the area of workers' rights should be subject to the **co-decision procedure** and is continuing to press the case for greater protection of workers' rights within any European company statute.

Finally, however, after some 30 years of debate, on 8 October 2001 the Council Regulation (EC) No. 2157/2001 on the Statute for a European Company (or Societas Europaea, SE) was adopted. Member States had to adopt the laws, **regulations** and administrative provisions necessary to comply with the Directive by 8 October 2004 (the date on which the European Company Statute, or ECS, Regulation, which is directly applicable in the Member States, came into force), or ensure by then that management and labour introduce the required provisions by agreement.

The ECS Regulation gives companies the option of forming a European Company (SE), which can operate on a Europe-wide basis and be governed by Community law directly applicable in all Member States (rather than national law). The Directive lays down the employee involvement provisions to apply to SEs, providing for negotiations between management and employees' representatives in each SE on the arrangements to apply, with a set of back-up statutory 'standard rules' where no agreement is reached. Involvement constitutes the information and consultation of employees and, in some cases, board-level participation. The adoption of the ECS was without doubt a highly significant development in both EU company law and social policy.

COMPETENCE is a term that describes the authority of the European Communities to undertake specific activities. The authority is usually based upon an **Article** of one of the **Founding Treaties**.

COMPETITION POLICY is crucial to the creation of a successful **internal market**. It would be counter-productive to dismantle trade barriers between the Member States if private industry were to remain free to engage in cartel-like restrictions on competition and undermine the advantages of opening up the markets in the first place. Moreover, from an economic viewpoint, the force of competition is to be welcomed as it unleashes dynamic effects that can be transformed into greater efficiencies, innovation and, ultimately, lower prices for the consumer. In short, competition policy describes the objective of striking a balance between the imposition, by **legislation**, of necessary restrictions upon unbridled economic competition, and the elimination of harmful restrictive practices that prevent a coherent integration of markets. As such, it formed an essential part of both the **Treaty of Paris** and the **Treaty of Rome**. Under the terms of the latter, the European Communities (EC) rules: target the existence of cartels and restrictive practices (such as price-fixing and **market-sharing agreements**) designed to undermine the market; seek to ensure that firms do not abuse a dominant position in the market place (under Article 82); aim to inject greater competition into former public utilities such as telecommunications and power (under Article 86); and also seek to impose limitations on governments, prohibiting state **subsidies** that adversely affect competition (under Articles 88–90). In 1990 **merger policy** (which had been present in the Treaty of Paris, but omitted in the Treaty of Rome) was finally added, after much demand from the business community. The merger control regulation (4064/89) quickly established itself as a highly potent weapon in the armoury of the EC competition authorities.

The **European Commission** (and particularly the **Directorate-General** – DG – for competition) is the body entrusted with the task of ensuring that the Member States and companies conform to the provisions of the Treaty. In this policy field the Commission operates as an autonomous and quasi-judicial policy-making institution, largely free from interference from either the **European Council** or the **European Parliament**. The Commission's decisions on competition policy are only subject to review by the European courts. While the Commission's powers were first established in 1962 (under Regulation 17), before the mid-1980s competition policy was a rather low priority. Since then, as a result of a shift in economic philosophy (towards neo-liberalism), the accumulation of case-law and the involvement of a succession of dynamic and forceful personalities (including Peter Sutherland, **Leon Brittan**, Karel van Miert and, more recently, **Mario Monti**), there has been enormous growth in the role and prominence of competition policy. The Commission has the authority to act, either on its own initiative, or upon receipt of complaints from Member States, companies or individuals, without reference to the **Council of the European Union**, concerning possible infringements of EC rules. Its powers to investigate alleged breaches of competition policy are very wide. In the first stage of investigation, its inspectors are entitled to visit companies without prior warning, to see any documents they wish, and to retain photographic evidence. The second stage of the process is a series of hearings with the company concerned. On the basis of the evidence and depositions, the Commission then issues its verdict. If it finds against the company, it has the right to demand a change of policy, impose a fine or combine both courses of action. The level of fines can be substantial, but with an upper limit of €1,000m. or 10% of the world annual turnover, during the previous business year, of the company concerned. In the last 10 years there has been a noticeable trend to impose substantial fines. For example, in November 2001 a group of vitamins producers, including European firms Roche and BAST, were fined a record €855m. for operating an illegal price cartel between 1990 and 1998. Companies that have been found guilty by the Commission have the right of appeal to the **Court of Justice**, the decision of which is final, against either the verdict or the size of the financial penalty. The Commission usually investigates several hundred cases of alleged infringements each year. Through the multitude of appeals against Commission decisions which have come before it, the Court of Justice has built up a substantial body of case-law, which has emphasized that EC competition policy takes precedence over national law, and must be directly applied by national governments.

The application of competition policy has resulted in the outlawing of several kinds of trading agreements based on market-sharing, price-fixing, and **exclusive agreements** on purchasing or distribution. **Patents, trademarks** and works of art are not automatically exempt from the provisions of the policy. The European Commission has also developed a stringent and well-received **merger policy** through a series of legislative acts, the most important being the 1989 Merger Regulation.

Competition policy rules apply to both private and publicly owned companies, and to nationalized industries. Companies that are negotiating or contemplating an agreement that may not satisfy the treaty provisions are obliged to inform the European Commission of their intentions. In addition, companies have the right to apply to the Commission for either a 'negative clearance', which recognizes that there is no threat to competition policy, or an 'exemption', which may be granted if the company or companies can demonstrate that, competition rules notwithstanding, a restrictive agreement should nevertheless be permitted on the grounds that it will provide substantial public benefits. With the **internal market** programme, which did not specifically deal with competition policy, the Commission also devoted considerably more attention to public procurement, and between 1990 and 1992 a series of **directives** on public utilities demanded that public contracts be put out to open tendering.

The European Commission may use its discretion to grant exemptions on the grounds mentioned above, or where the effect on free competition would be minimal. In particular, it has sought to balance a strict application of competition policy with its concern for the viability of small companies. Because it has wished to encourage co-operation between small companies, the Commission has outlined several categories of agreement which it may be prepared to exempt from a general ban: small-scale agreements in cases where turnover is less than €200m. and the market share less than 5%; agreements in various areas such as research and development and the exchange of information; and those which are essentially franchising or sub-contractual. The Commission is also prepared to be flexible where companies are confronted with adverse economic conditions and a sustained decline in demand. In such circumstances, companies may be permitted to collaborate in co-ordinating an orderly reduction in the resulting over-capacity.

The European Commission also monitors government activity on a regular basis. This has been a more difficult task, because of the tendency of governments to shield their own companies from competition through a variety of techniques and mechanisms, which may or may not amount to state aid (see **subsidies**). The Commission is, however, willing to accept exceptions to the general ban on state subsidies that might distort competition. Member States wishing to provide aid to companies are expected to inform the Commission of their intentions. If the Commission rejects the plan, and if the latter goes ahead, it has the authority to demand the repayment of unauthorized subsidies, and even to impose fines on recalcitrant Member States. Categories of state aid that have been exempted from the general rules include grants to areas afflicted by a natural disaster and aid to economically depressed regions that is designed to assist the development of new forms of economic activity. The Commission has also issued guidelines governing state aid to industries severely affected by recession, but has insisted that such aid must have a specific purpose and fixed duration, and be regarded as totally exceptional. In the past, shipbuilding, steel, synthetic fibres and textiles have benefited from these guidelines. Disputes between the EC and the Member States about state aid may, in the last resort, be resolved by the Court of Justice. Competition policy does not necessarily apply to goods imported into the European Union, where several bilateral or international agreements exist, and where some products have been affected by voluntary export restraints.

The workload of the DG for competition has been immense. Concerns have been expressed about inadequate staffing, lengthy time delays in investigating cases under Articles 81 and 82, opaque and unpredictable decision-making and a tendency for some cases to be politicized (especially with regard to merger control). In response, the DG for competition has initiated a series of internal measures to address these problems during the last five years, including a proposal to modify Regulation 17; essentially, this proposal advocated closer co-operation between the Commission and the national authorities that would enable national courts to apply Articles 81 and 82; tougher powers of enquiry for DG COMP and the abolition of the notification system. The Commission hopes that these reforms will enable it to concentrate its limited resources on the more problematic cases. Some concerns have been expressed, principally among lawyers, as to whether or not this process of decentralization would operate efficiently, but the Council approved the proposal (Council Regulation No. 1/ 2003) and it entered into force in May 2004. This new regulation may indeed prove a stroke of genius on behalf of the Commission, as it will actually enhance its role and allow it to determine which cases it intends to investigate and which to pass to the Member State competition authorities. 1 May 2004 is a momentous date in the history of EC competition policy as it also marks the entering into force of a revised merger control regulation (Regulation 139/2004) and the arrival of the 10 candidate countries. All the candidate countries were required to have adopted national competition laws that reflected the principles of the *acquis communautaire* before accession negotiations could be concluded successfully. The EC merger policy was revamped to provide both greater transparency and efficiency and also to respond to growing criticism of administrative procedures and case analysis, and was introduced with a number of other simultaneous internal Commission reforms. Together both regulations actually enhance the 'federal' characteristics of competition governance. The process of reform continues and the Commission is now proposing to reform Article 82; it is also expected to step up its campaign against monopolistic utilities and the politicians who defend such activities. Its principal target will be those companies that control both the supply and distribution of energy. DG Competition also suggested in late 2005 that firms and individuals who have been the victims of deliberate anti-competitive practices should be able to seek financial damages through the courts. This is a bold initiative, which might act as an additional deterrent and from the Commission's own perspective will not involve any additional costs.

In recent years the European Commission has devoted considerable effort to creating an International Competition Network (ICN). This network was established in October 2001 as, essentially, an informal forum in which competition authorities from around the world exchange views and discuss the issue and function of competition policy and its enforcement. It is an almost purely virtual network, but it is emerging as a credible forum that is seeking to encourage and spread best practices.

COMPETITIVENESS was the focus of the **European Commission's White Paper** on Growth, Competitiveness and Employment. This paper, dating from 1994, presented guidelines for pursuing a policy of global competitiveness. The policy comprised four objectives: provision for assistance to those European firms seeking to adapt to the new globalized economy; the ability for firms to exploit the competitive advantages associated with the rapid move to a knowledge-based economy; the ability to foster and promote sustainable industrial development; and the need to reduce the time differential between the pace of change in supply and the corresponding adjustments in demand. The White Paper's recommendations informed negotiations on the new title on employment introduced by the 1997 **Treaty of Amsterdam**. Competitiveness has emerged as a highly salient theme in both the Commission and the **Council**. Its significance is illustrated in the **Lisbon Agenda** and in a new heading of priorities in the annual **budget**.

COMPULSORY EXPENDITURE refers to that element of the **budget** of the European Communities (some three-quarters of the total) that must be spent on policies arising directly out of the **founding treaties** and their amendments. The major item of cost is the **Common Agricultural Policy** (CAP). In reviewing the annual draft budget submitted to it by the **Council of the European Union**, the **European Parliament** is allowed to modify only the proposals on compulsory expenditure.

The **CONCILIATION COMMITTEE** is composed of the members of the **Council of the European Union**, or their representatives, and an equal number of representatives of the **European Parliament** (EP). It meets as part of the **co-decision procedure** when the EP fails to adopt the common position of the Council. The **European Commission** participates in the Committee's proceedings, initiating proposals to overcome any impasse between the Council and the EP's representatives. The aim of the Conciliation Committee is to approve a joint text that is acceptable to all sides and may subsequently be adopted by the Council and by a plenary session of the EP.

CONDITIONALITY is widely used in the context of European Union (EU) external relations and **enlargement**, with the EU making closer ties conditional on non-Member States meeting certain political if not economic conditions. The conditionality underpinning enlargement is based on **applicant countries** meeting the so-called **Copenhagen criteria** adopted in 1993. Once a country is a member of the EU, conditionality is still relevant. Since the **Treaty of Amsterdam**, Member States that do not respect principles of liberty, democracy, respect for **human rights** and fundamental freedoms and the rule of law may have certain of their rights under the **European treaties** suspended.

CONECCS: See **Interest Groups**; **Lobbying**

The **CONFEDERAL GROUP OF THE EUROPEAN UNITED LEFT/ NORDIC GREEN LEFT** (GUE/NGL) is one of the transnational **party groups** in the **European Parliament** (EP). Prior to the 1994 elections it was known as the Group for the European Unitarian Left (GUE) and was one of the two Communist groups that emerged in 1989 following a division of the original **Communists and Allies** group. Dominated by the Italian Communists, GUE had a more Eurocommunist profile than the former French-dominated **Left Unity** group. The group changed its name again in early 1995 when it was joined by **Members of the European Parliament** (MEPs) from **Denmark**, **Finland** and **Sweden**. The fortunes of this party, which remains very much against neo-liberalism, have remained rather stagnant in recent years. After the 2004 EP elections the GUE/NGL group has 41 members (as opposed to 44 in 2002). The GUE/NGL comprises 17 member parties drawn from the 25 Member States. This group also includes five MEPs as individual associate members who are included in the above figures.

CONFERENCE ON SECURITY AND CO-OPERATION IN EUROPE (CSCE): See **Organization for Security and Co-operation in Europe**

CONFERENCES OF THE PARLIAMENTS: See **Assizes**

CONGRESS OF EUROPE was the name of the first post-war European gathering, held in The Hague in May 1948. It was organized by the **International Committee of the Movements for European Unity** and was attended by several hundred delegates from 16 countries, as well as by observers from the **USA** and Canada. Most political groupings except those at the extremes were represented, and many leading political figures attended. The major absentee was a strong delegation from the British Labour Party, in power at the time in the United Kingdom, which had dismissed the Congress as a body of 'unrepresentative interests'. The Congress called for a European assembly, a charter of **human rights** and a European court. It demanded that the European states 'transfer and merge some portion of their sovereign rights so as to secure common political and economic action for the integration and proper development of their common resources'. Few practical measures were adopted, but it did agree to the formation of a **European Movement**. The latter, responding to a request from **Paul-Henri Spaak**, the Prime Minister of **Belgium**, produced a memorandum that contained the first draft for what would become the **Council of Europe**.

CONSTITUTION: The European Union (EU) has no formal constitution although the **European treaties** are regarded as providing the constitutional framework of the EU, and the **Court of Justice** has referred to the **Treaty of Rome** as being the 'Constitutional Charter' of the European Communities. However, the issue of whether the EU should have a constitution was placed on the agenda of the **European Convention** launched in February 2002. This produced a **draft Treaty establishing a Constitution for Europe** which subsequently formed the focus of negotiations in an **intergovernmental conference** convened in October 2003. This produced the **Treaty establishing a Constitution for Europe**.

CONSTITUTIONAL TREATY is the term often used to describe the outcome of the **intergovernmental conference** launched in October 2003. See: **Treaty establishing a Constitution for Europe**.

CONSTITUTIVE TREATIES: See **Founding Treaties**

CONSTRUCTIVE ABSTENTION is employed during consideration of matters of **common foreign and security policy** and allows decisions requiring unanimity within the **Council of the European Union** to be taken without the express support of all Member States. Abstentions do not count as votes in opposition to a proposal.

The **CONSULTATION PROCEDURE** is the oldest and simplest of all decision-making procedures in the European Communities: the **Council of the European Union** has only to consult the **European Parliament** when adopting **legislation** proposed by the **European Commission**. Although the consultation procedure is still used for legislation adopted as part of the **Common Agricultural Policy**, for example, most decisions within the European Union are now adopted under the **co-decision procedure**. (See also **Co-operation Procedure**; **Assent Procedure**.)

The **CONSULTATIVE COMMITTEE OF THE EUROPEAN COAL AND STEEL COMMUNITY** was established in 1951 as a part of the now defunct **European Coal and Steel Community** (ECSC). It was charged with advising the High Authority, the executive of the ECSC, on all aspects of the operation of the ECSC and of the national **coal** and **steel** industries. The Committee assumed a similar role in relation to the **European Commission** following the merger of the executives of the European Communities in 1967. Composed of representatives of producers, employees and consumers, it had a purely advisory and consultative role, with no decision-making authority.

The **CONSULTATIVE COUNCIL OF SOCIAL AND REGIONAL AUTHORITIES** was an advisory body attached to the **European Commission**, and was consulted on issues of regional development. Its role was taken over by the **Committee of the Regions**.

The **CONSUMER COMMITTEE** was established in 1995 as a successor to the Consumers' Consultative Council (CCC), a body that had been established as the Consumer Consultative Committee in 1973. The CCC was active in forwarding opinions and proposals for action to the Commission. However, by 1995 it had 48 members, which meant that it found it difficult to co-ordinate the views of its disparate membership. It was therefore replaced by a Consumer Committee, appointed by the **European Commission**, and consisting of 20 members. The membership is made up as follows: one member from each of the European Consumers' Organization (BEUC), the Confederation of Family Organizations in the European Community (COFACE), the European Community Consumer Co-operatives (EURO-COOP), the European Trade Union Confederation (ETUC) and the Institut européen interrégional de la consommation (IEIC – a grouping of regional bodies concerned with consumer affairs); and 15 representatives from Member States. Meetings are chaired by a senior official from the **Directorate-General** (DG) in charge of consumer policy. The Committee, while only an advisory body, is consulted by the Commission on proposed initiatives that may have a bearing on consumer interests.

CONSUMER CONSULTATIVE COUNCIL: See **Consumer Committee**

CONSUMER POLICY was not mentioned in the **Treaty of Rome**. Although consumer interests and the **European Parliament** pressed for a consumer policy for several years, action was not taken until the Paris summit of the heads of government in 1972. Agreement was reached on the establishment within the **European Commission** of a section, later upgraded to a **Directorate-General** (DG), DG-XI, for consumer and environmental protection, a Consumer Consultative Committee (later the Consumer Consultative Council, or CCC, now known as the **Consumer Committee**) and a Consumer Policy Service (which later became DG-XXIV, for consumer policy and health protection). In April 1975 the Council of Ministers (see **Council of the European Union**) launched a consumer information and protection programme which established five fundamental consumer rights: safeguards against risks to **health and safety**; economic justice; redress for damages; consultation; and information and education. These rights were to be the basis of specific measures of consumer protection. Although consumer policy was strengthened in 1983, when the national ministers responsible for consumer affairs began to meet regularly within the Council of Ministers, the bulk of consumer protection **legislation** was not adopted until after the launch of the Third Consumer Programme of 1986. The action was part of the effort to prepare for the **internal market**, and the **Single European Act** incorporated consumer policy within the treaty framework. A firm legal basis for consumer policy was created via the **Treaty on European Union**.

A large number of measures apply to **foodstuffs**: there are **directives** governing purity standards, additives, the listing of ingredients and 'sell-by' dates (markings indicating the latest date at which a product may be sold). Maximum levels have been set for pesticide residues in fruit and vegetables. Several directives apply to **pharmaceuticals**, referring to everything from the testing to the marketing of a range of products. A further set of directives deal with **dangerous substances**, imposing standards on several industries and strict requirements relating to toxic substances. The European Commission has also worked for the standardization of manufactured products, with directives on tools and component parts, and since 1985 there has been a greater emphasis on safety specifications for manufactured products.

Directives on the protection of consumers' economic interests have been fewer and rather less successful, in part because it has proved much more difficult for Member States to arrive at a consensus. In 1988, however, a directive on product liability came into force. Other directives have given consumers the right to use the courts to complain about misleading advertising, have required that consumer credit agreements should be clearly written and easily understandable, with the real rate of interest being clearly indicated, and have imposed rules relating to door-to-door sales. The least progress has been in the area of consumer information and education, although many of the directives on dangerous substances, foodstuffs and pharmaceuticals have an important information component. The European Commission has insisted on information, such as weight-to-price ratios and the energy consumption of electrical goods, being printed on a wide range of products. As part of its education programme, the Commission has provided some funding for national consumer groups, and sponsored meetings on consumer issues.

CONTINENTAL CAN is the name of a large US multinational company manufacturing metal containers, which had achieved a dominant position (see **dominant firm abuse**) in the West German market through its acquisition of a domestic competitor. When this was followed by the further acquisition of a major Dutch manufacturer, the **European Commission** took the company to the **Court of Justice** under the **competition policy** rules relating to abuse of dominant position. Although the Court ruled against the Commission's argument that Continental Can had created and abused a dominant position, the verdict was significant because it recognized that the Commission has the ability to examine mergers of companies from different Member States.

CONVENTION ON THE FUTURE OF EUROPE: See **European Convention**

CONVERGENCE is a term used to describe the objective of encouraging the economies of the Member States to develop in the same way, especially with regard to inflation, deficits and interest rates. It emerged during the arguments in the 1980s for an **internal market**, and later was applied to the declared objective of **economic and monetary union** by 1999.

CONVERGENCE CRITERIA for progression to stage three of **economic and monetary union** (EMU) were established by the **Treaty on European Union**. The four criteria were: an avoidance of excessive government deficits (i.e. an annual deficit of no more than 3% of gross domestic product – GDP, and no more than 60% of GDP for stock of government debt); a rate of inflation no more than 1.5 percentage points above the average of that of the three best performing Member States; exchange rate stability within the **European Monetary System** over the two previous years, without devaluation; and long-term interest rates to be within two percentage points of the average in the three Member States with the lowest inflation rates in the European Union. However, economic difficulties were such that few states met the convergence criteria. Consequently, a less strict interpretation of the criteria was applied, and in 1998 it was declared that, of those Member States wishing to participate in EMU, only **Greece** had failed to meet the convergence criteria.

CO-OPERATION refers more specifically to intergovernmental co-operation, a process of collaboration by the Member States, with the intention of securing agreement on objectives and strategies without the involvement of supranational institutions. It is the opposite of the **community method**.

CO-OPERATION AGREEMENTS are similar to **Association Agreements** (but less comprehensive), which aim to promote intensive economic co-operation. Co-operation Agreements have been concluded since the mid-1970s by the European Communities with many countries outside Europe, as well as being, before 1991, the favoured form of relationship with Eastern European countries. After 1989 many Central and Eastern European countries preferred to seek **Europe Agreements**, the new form of association agreement being offered to them. Successor states to the **USSR** were offered **Partnership and Co-operation Agreements**.

The **CO-OPERATION PROCEDURE** was introduced by the **Single European Act** in 1987 as a means of enhancing the role of the **European Parliament** in EC decision-making. Although still used for certain decisions in the area of **economic and monetary union**, the procedure has been replaced elsewhere by the **co-decision procedure**.

The **CO-ORDINATION COMMITTEE FOR MULTILATERAL EXPORT CONTROLS** (COCOM) was an association of Western democracies formed in 1949 under the aegis of the **North Atlantic Treaty Organization** (NATO) to regulate the flow of equipment and technology of potential military significance to the **USSR** and its allies. After the ending of the **Cold War**, its members agreed in 1990 to create a more selective core list of embargoed items. In 1993 it began to consider offering membership to the Russian Federation and the Eastern European countries as a way of strengthening their links with the West and helping to prevent military technology reaching what were regarded as potentially aggressive states in other parts of the world. However, the organization was formally dissolved in March 1994.

COPA: See **Committee of Agricultural Organizations in the European Union**

The **COPENHAGEN CRITERIA**, sometimes referred to as the **accession criteria**, are the conditions that countries of **Central and Eastern Europe** must meet if they are to be admitted to the European Union (EU). They were adopted at the **Copenhagen Summit** of the **European Council** in June 1993 and require those countries seeking to join the EU to possess stable institutions which guarantee democracy; to respect the rule of law and human and minority rights; to possess a functioning market economy able to cope with competitive pressure and market forces; and to be capable of meeting the obligations of membership (i.e. adherence to the *acquis communautaire* as well as the *finalité politique* of the EU).

Two **COPENHAGEN SUMMITS** of the **European Council** met specifically to discuss the eastward **enlargement** of the European Union (EU). The first met in 1993 and established the **Copenhagen criteria** for EU membership, while the second, convened in December 2002, formally approved the accession of the first 10 **candidate countries** to the EU. The states were: **Cyprus,** the **Czech Republic, Estonia, Hungary, Latvia, Lithuania, Malta, Poland, Slovakia** and **Slovenia**. Following the successful outcome of the second Copenhagen summit, the **Accession Treaty** was signed and the 10 states joined the EU on 1 May 2004.

CoR: See **Committee of the Regions**

CORDIS stands for Community Research and Development Information Service. It provides a database and summary information on all current research projects within the European Union.

CORE EUROPE refers to the notion that a group of states within the European Union (EU) would opt to forge closer economic, political and military links between themselves, if some of the other states showed a degree of reluctance to pursue the policy agenda of a core group. The concept of core Europe is usually understood to mean **France, Germany** and the **Benelux** states, that is, all the original members of the **European Coal and Steel Community** except **Italy**.

COREPER: See **Committee of Permanent Representatives**

CO-RESPONSIBILITY LEVIES were introduced in 1986 and, along with the later **stabilizers**, were seen as a means of attempting to halt the open-ended subsidies on production and the huge surpluses that the guaranteed price support system had imposed upon the **Common Agricultural Policy**. The levies were set to come into operation whenever predetermined production quantities for a product were exceeded, making them, in effect, a tax on excess output. Many people argued that the levies had been set at too low a level to be properly effective.

COREU is a secure communications system that connects all the foreign ministries of the European Union (EU) Member States. The objective of this link is to improve and foster co-operation in the development of the EU's **common foreign and security policy**.

CORPORATION TAX is a tax levied on company profits. To generalize, the Member States each operate one of three different systems of calculation and application. The question of the **harmonization** of corporation tax has been discussed by the European Communities since 1963, but agreement has been difficult to achieve.

COSAC is the acronym for *Conférence des Organes Spécialisés dans les Affaires Communautaires*, the gathering, every six months, of **Members of the European Parliament** and members of the European Union affairs committees of **national parliaments**.

COST, the acronym used to refer to European Co-operation in the Field of Scientific and Technical Research, is a concept rather than an institution or programme. It is a framework for the preparation and implementation of European projects relating to applied scientific research. It was established in 1970 with a membership of 19 countries, which increased to 25 countries in 1994, including all the Member States of the European Union. In 1997 three new countries joined COST. The COST Secretariat is attached to the **Council of the European Union** and the technical management of projects has been handled by the **European Commission**. Each project, however, has been individually negotiated by those states that wish to participate in it. Several collaborative projects have been pursued in 10 areas: information technology, telecommunications, transport, oceanography, metallurgy and materials science, meteorology, agriculture, food technology, environmental protection and medical research and health. (See also **EUREKA**.)

COSTA v ENEL is the name of an important case in which the **Court of Justice**, in 1964, established the primacy of European Community law and confirmed that it cannot be overruled.

The **COTONOU AGREEMENT** was signed in June 2000 by the European Union (EU) and 77 **ACP** (African, Caribbean and Pacific) **States** and superseded the fourth **Lomé Convention** (1990–2000). It provides longer-term (20-year) support for the EU-ACP relationship, which is to be developed on the basis of five interdependent pillars: comprehensive political dialogue; the enhanced participation of civil society in partnership affairs; a strengthened focus on poverty reduction; a new framework for economic and trade co-operation; and a reform of financial co-operation. The new Agreement therefore places greater emphasis on establishing and maintaining good governance in the **ACP States**. It also envisages the establishment of an EU-ACP free-trade area by 2020, and committed €13,500m. in aid for the first five years of the Agreement. These funds were directed at poverty reduction and at encouraging non-state sectors to participate in the development process. The new Agreement is also notable for its insistence that respect for **human rights**, democratic principles and the rule of law should form the core criteria for aid policy decisions. From a practical perspective, the Agreement can be revisited every five years, as can the aid protocols, which are bound to a similar timetable. Progress is reviewed on an annual basis.

The **COUNCIL FOR MUTUAL ECONOMIC ASSISTANCE** (CMEA), also known as COMECON, was established in 1949 by the **USSR** and subsequently developed into an organ for economic co-operation and co-ordination in the Communist bloc. At first, the European Communities (EC) expressed little interest in an arrangement with the CMEA. Any agreement would have been difficult because of the non-convertibility of CMEA currencies and its operation of a centralized planning and production system, whereby trade was based on an exchange or barter system rather than money transfers. These problems were compounded by Soviet hostility towards the EC. Talks between the EC and the CMEA began only in 1976. They had not produced any results by 1980, when discussions were broken off as a result of the Soviet invasion of Afghanistan. They were not resumed until 1986, after Mikhail Gorbachev's accession to power in the USSR, and a mutual recognition agreement was signed in June 1988. Among other things, it permitted the establishment of diplomatic relations between the EC and individual Eastern European countries: several, including the USSR, established diplomatic posts in **Brussels** with accreditation to the EC. Prior to the 1988 agreement, the EC had signed only limited sectoral agreements with Eastern European countries. The German Democratic Republic (GDR – East Germany) had been in a different position since the 1972 **Ostpolitik** agreement with the Federal Republic of **Germany** (FRG – West Germany), which had given its products access to the EC.

The relationship with the CMEA was confused and disrupted by the events of 1989, which removed the Communist parties from power or forced them to share it. In October 1990 the former GDR automatically became part of the EC when it was subsumed into the FRG by German reunification. At a CMEA meeting in 1990 the new governments of the other Eastern European states expressed strong dissatisfaction with the past performance of the CMEA and its current condition: several declared an interest in EC membership in the medium term. In 1991 it was agreed to replace the CMEA by a two-year interim organization based upon market economy principles, to be called the Organization for International Economic Co-operation. However, with the disintegration of the USSR at the end of 1991, all semblance of continuing collaboration ceased, and the CMEA effectively disappeared.

The **COUNCIL OF THE BARS AND LAW SOCIETIES OF THE EUROPEAN COMMUNITY** (CCBE) is the officially recognized representative organization for the legal profession in the European Union (EU) and the **European Economic Area**.

The **COUNCIL OF EUROPE**, which should not be confused with either the **Council of the European Union** or the **European Council**, was formed in 1949 as Western Europe's first post-war political organization. Its Statute was signed as the Treaty of Westminster by 10 states, and permanent offices were provided for the organization in **Strasbourg**. Its declared objective was to achieve 'a greater unity between its members for the purpose of safeguarding and realizing the ideals and principles which are their common heritage and facilitating their economic and social progress'. These objectives were to be secured through 'discussions of questions of common concern and by agreements and common action in economic, social, scientific, legal and administrative matters and in the maintenance and further realization of **human rights** and fundamental freedoms'. Its membership grew until, by the 1980s, it incorporated all the non-Communist states of Europe.

The Council consists of two bodies: a Committee of Ministers and an Assembly. With each state having one vote and a veto, the Committee of Ministers is essentially an **intergovernmental conference** of foreign ministers meeting twice yearly. Since 1952, the practice of deputies (usually diplomats) representing the ministers has been normal for all but the most symbolic meetings. In relaying **decisions** to the Member States, the Committee is allowed only to make recommendations. States are not obliged to accept decisions of the Council of Europe. Similarly, the Assembly, renamed the Parliamentary Assembly in 1974, is essentially a discussion chamber, with hardly any substantive powers. Ever since its first session in 1949, the majority of the delegates, who are appointed by their **national parliaments**, have been strong supporters of European integration. The fact that it has shared a common home in Strasbourg with the **European Parliament** has helped this commitment. However, the Assembly can only forward recommendations to the Committee of Ministers, which can, and often does, ignore or reject them at will.

The Council of Europe has produced more than 120 conventions and agreements, most of which have been accepted by almost all the Member States. Its greatest achievement, perhaps, was to secure agreement on a **European Convention on Human Rights** in 1950, with a concomitant **European Commission of Human Rights** and a **European Court of Human Rights**, both of which operate under the aegis of the Council. Much of the Council of Europe's success has been in the less politically contentious cultural field. It sponsored, for example, the European Cultural Convention in 1954 and a European Social

Charter in 1961. In 1960 it was handed the social and cultural responsibilities that the **Western European Union** had been granted by the **Treaty of Brussels**.

In the 1950s it also sought to achieve some form of policy co-ordination in agriculture, civil aviation and transport. However, by itself the Council could not advance European integration much beyond such symbolic actions as seating the Assembly delegates in alphabetical order rather than by nationality. The **United Kingdom** and the Scandinavian states were firmly opposed to it becoming anything more than an intergovernmental deliberative body. After the early 1950s it was overtaken by the developments that led to the establishment of the European Communities (EC). While its major historical significance was that it was the first European organization of a political nature, its later importance was twofold. It was the European organization with the broadest membership, albeit limited to democracies, a claim that was later challenged by the formation of the **Conference on Security and Co-operation in Europe**. Also, because of its broad membership, it remained important as a forum where a wide range of ideas and views could be expressed, and as a central clearing-house for co-operation and co-ordination, receiving and discussing annual reports from a wide range of European and other international organizations and agencies, including the EC. The ending of the **Cold War** offered the Council an opportunity of expanding its membership, and in the early 1990s most of the Central and Eastern European countries and the western republics of the former **USSR** (for example Russia) either joined the Council, or at least applied for membership.

COUNCIL OF MINISTERS: See **Council of the European Union**

The **COUNCIL OF THE EUROPEAN UNION** is frequently referred to as the Council of Ministers, and prior to 1993 its full official title was the Council of Ministers of the European Communities. It is not to be confused with either the **Council of Europe** or the **European Council**, although it is closely related to the latter. The Council of the European Union shares executive responsibility in the European Communities (EC) with the **European Commission**. Whereas the Commission represents and defends general European and EC interests, the Council essentially represents the interests of the individual Member States. It evolved into the most powerful of the EC institutions, a position that was only slightly modified by the **Single European Act** (SEA) and the **Treaty on European Union** (TEU). The membership of the Council consists of ministerial representatives of the Member States. Its meetings are serviced by officials from its own secretariat, whose existence was formally acknowledged only in the TEU, and they may also be attended by one or more

Commissioners, depending on the topics listed on its agenda for the day. The Council's headquarters are in the Charlemagne building in **Brussels**, but on three occasions each year (in April, June and October) the Council meets in **Luxembourg**. This is a legacy of the merger of the executives of the EC in 1967: the executive High Authority of the **European Coal and Steel Community** had been based in Luxembourg. Council meetings are normally held in private, although there have been some sessions where elements of the proceedings have been televised. Moreover, spokespersons for each of the member governments hold extensive and detailed press briefings after each Council session.

The Council of the European Union has no fixed membership other than permitting one representative from each Member State. This is because of the wide responsibility the Council has for a broad range of policy sectors and questions. There are, in effect, a range of Councils (currently nine), some of which can even meet simultaneously in parallel sessions. The composition of each Council is determined by a particular policy agenda: if, for example, the topic to be discussed is agriculture, the Council consists of the national agricultural ministers; if the agenda is to deal with **consumer policy** it will be the national ministers responsible for consumer affairs who are in attendance, and so on. When the EC **budget** is to be discussed, the national finance ministers form the Council. At the core of the Council, holding the whole institution together, are the meetings of the national foreign ministers. Collectively they form the **General Affairs and External Relations Council**, and normally meet at least once a month. In addition to discussing European Union (EU) external policy, primarily matters arising as part of the **common foreign and security policy** (CFSP), they have the responsibility for monitoring and co-ordinating the activities of the various manifestations of the Council. This is no easy task as, in a European version of interdepartmental bureaucratic rivalry, it is possible for different Councils to be encouraging development in several different directions at once. In addition, the foreign ministers are expected to tackle more sensitive issues, and broader questions that go beyond the remit of a single specialized ministry. Finally, they are also responsible for preparing the agenda for meetings of the European Council, which, when acting in a decision-making capacity and without the Commission representatives, becomes another version of the Council of the European Union. The various versions of the Council – streamlined in 1999 and again in 2002 – meet on some 100 occasions each year. Most meetings last for only one day, but several can be of longer duration. The meetings of the **Economic and Financial Affairs Council of Ministers** (ECOFIN) have gained in importance with the advent of **economic and monetary union** (EMU) and a new group, known as the **Eurogroup** (EURO-12), was established in 1998, composed of the finance ministers of those Member States participating in EMU.

The Council of the European Union is the essential legislative element of the EC and the only institution with decision-making powers in relation to the other two **pillars** of the EU. While the **right of initiative** for most **legislation** lies with the European Commission, it is only the Council that, after some involvement of the **European Parliament** (EP) and consultation with one or more **advisory committees** and agencies, is empowered to adopt proposals and so legislate for the EC. Other responsibilities include the obligation, in conjunction with the EP, to adopt the EC budget, and the power of appointment to other EC institutions, including the Commission.

To aid it in its tasks, the Council has its own secretariat in Brussels. Central to this are the delegations or **Permanent Representations** that each Member State maintains in Brussels. The **Committee of Permanent Representatives** (COREPER) has the task of ensuring that issues awaiting a decision by the Council have been thoroughly discussed and analysed by Council staff. Where COREPER reaches agreement on proposals, these are normally adopted by the Council without discussion. On all other issues the Council reaches its decision by voting. The way in which the Council votes on issues is defined by the **Treaty of Rome** and its amendments. Depending upon the issue under discussion, a proposal may be adopted by **majority voting**, **qualified majority voting**, or unanimously. The incidence and importance of decision-making by simple majority is negligible, and it is used only for a few minor questions, usually of a procedural nature.

The Treaty of Rome anticipated that, after an initial transitional period, qualified majority voting would become more usual, with unanimity restricted to a few issues of major importance. This plan was disrupted by the **empty chair crisis** of 1965 and the **Luxembourg Compromise** of 1966. The use of qualified majorities remained limited, with the Council preferring not to jeopardize unanimity by pushing issues to a vote. This made for slow progress. Almost all the reviews of EC practices conducted after the mid-1970s commented adversely on the slowness of decision-making, and recommended a greater use of majority voting; this was finally introduced by the SEA. The creation of the EU and its potentially extensive **enlargement** in the early years of the 21st century will probably force further re-examination of the decision-making process. In fact the TEU, the **Treaty of Amsterdam** and the **Treaty of Nice** all extended the use of qualified majority voting to new areas of policy.

The task of directing the Council in its various functions falls to its President. Member States hold the **Council presidency** in rotation, the position shifting from state to state every six months. The foreign minister of the state currently holding the presidency, which coincides with that of the European Council, becomes President of the Council, and is responsible during those six months for organizing the business of the Council, in conjunction with the secretariat. While each foreign minister will, as President, hope to advance those causes which his or her national government deems important, by convention the President is expected to be a neutral arbiter, securing, by compromise and bargaining, Council agreement on as many issues as possible. During each country's presidency, it will host at least one meeting of the European Council. These **summit meetings** are often concurrent with the meetings of various groups of national ministers. These take up long-term issues that may concern the Council of the European Union, but without feeling the need to reach decisions, or being exposed to the pressure of time that characterizes formal Council meetings.

As a result of measures introduced by the Treaty of Amsterdam, the Council must now play a more active role in employment affairs by encouraging Member States to exchange information and best practice in this field. It must also evaluate employment schemes and pilot projects. Its role in protecting **citizens' rights** has also expanded, with a new **Article** permitting the Council to take action, by unanimity, in cases of discrimination. However, the Treaty of Amsterdam also increased the powers of the EP at the expense of the Council, by strengthening the **co-decision procedure**, granting the EP full co-legislative powers in a number of policy areas. The areas in which the Council can take decisions using qualified majority voting have been extended by the Treaty of Amsterdam and Treaty of Nice, although unanimity is still required in core areas such as taxation and in constitutional matters. Attempts to speed up the EU's reaction in times of international crisis have also been introduced as part of reforms to the CFSP. In situations where Member States have common foreign policy interests, the Council of the European Union is to decide by consensus the principles and strategies to be employed in joint actions. If agreement cannot be reached by the Council, the final decision on EU foreign policy actions is to be taken by the European Council. For Member States not opposed to proposed actions but not prepared to participate directly, there is the 'constructive abstention' option. The Secretary-General of the Council of the European Union has been given the title of **High Representative** of the CFSP, supported by a policy planning and early warning unit. Reflecting developments within the CFSP, a **Military Committee of the European Union** has also been established within the Council.

The **COUNCIL PRESIDENCY** rotates in a predetermined sequence (until 1995 it was arranged alphabetically) among the members of the European Union (EU). Each Member State currently holds the presidency for a period of six months and can influence the focus of its presidency and attempt to steer policy agendas accordingly. However, it is extremely difficult to carry through specific **legislation** in this short period. Moreover, there are concerns that this mode of organization will not be productive in an enlarged EU. Hence, the

Treaty establishing a Constitution for Europe envisaged three changes: team presidencies comprising three Member States and lasting 18 months; a **European Council President** in office for two-and-a-half years; and a **Union Minister for Foreign Affairs** chairing Council meetings dealing with foreign affairs. Until then, the Council presidency will rotate as follows: **Austria** in the first half of 2006, followed by **Finland**. In 2007 Germany and Portugal are scheduled for the presidency. Slovenia will take over in the first half of 2008, as the first of the new Member States which joined the EU on 1 May 2004.

The **COUNCIL SECRETARIAT** is a professional civil service that forms part of the **Eurocracy** residing in Brussels. The Council secretariat is considerably smaller than the **European Commission** and in 2000 comprised approximately 2,500 people (of whom around 316 were 'A'-grade officials). The purpose of the Council Secretariat is essentially to draft the six-month legislative programme for each **Council presidency**, providing legal service, briefing government ministers on salient EU issues and preparing the agenda for Council meetings and drafting Council meetings minutes. In terms of structure, the Council Secretariat mirrors the Commission in so far as it is divided into directorates-general, although along very different lines. There is a legal service to represent the Council before the courts. The **Treaty of Amsterdam** provided for the Council secretary-general becoming CFSP **High Representative** and a deputy secretary-general assuming responsibility for the Secretariat. This development meant that the role of the secretary-general changed from civil servant to high-ranking politician. The post is currently occupied by **Javier Solana**. As a result of this change in emphasis it is expected that the Council Secretariat will for the first time become an active participant in the design of policy formulation.

The **COURT OF AUDITORS** (ECA) is a body established in 1977, under the 1975 Treaty of Brussels, replacing an earlier and more limited Audit Board, which was responsible for examining the accounts of **revenue** and **expenditure** for the European Communities (EC). Its powers were limited, and in 1977 it was replaced by a more authoritative Court of Auditors that scrutinizes the accounts of European Communities (EC) institutions and agencies in order to verify that they possess satisfactory financial management, with all revenue having been legally received and all expenditure properly accounted for. The Court publishes an annual report detailing its findings. It may, either on its own initiative or at the request of another EC institution, prepare other, more specific reports. The Court has in the past drawn attention to the existence of wasteful expenditure in several policy areas, and on a few occasions has found evidence of financial mismanagement. While its role has been important in forcing the EC to improve their procedures and introduce a more effective financial regimen, there is widespread agreement that much more needs to be done. The **Treaty on European Union** elevated the Court to the status of an EU institution, with the consequent implications of legality and decision-making authority. Its status was further enhanced by the **Treaty of Amsterdam**, which aimed to ensure better financial management of EC money by introducing measures to curtail fraud by extending the ECA's auditing powers to the second and third **pillars,** and by giving it an additional right to refer cases to the **Court of Justice**. The ECA provides and audits all of the Community's revenue and expenditure. It examines accounts and produces a sound annual financial management plan. It also provides the **European Parliament** and the **Council of the European Union** with a statement of assurance.

The membership of the Court consists of one individual from each Member State, and the ECA has a total staff of around 750. Around 140 are involved in translation and 150 in administration, with the remainder on the Court's audit tasks. Prior to the **European Council** summit in Nice in December 2000 the Commission put forward the suggestion of capping the membership of the Court rather than allowing it to expand with each new accession. This view did not prevail at Nice where agreement was reached by the Member States to maintain the current practice of requiring the Court of Auditors to consist of one member from each Member State. It was generally assumed that having a national member would facilitate co-operation with the national audit offices. Appointments to the Court are made by the **Council of the European Union** for renewable six-year terms and, since Nice, by **qualified majority voting** on the basis of a list drawn up in accordance with proposals made by each Member State. In practice, however, the Council will simply endorse the candidates put forward by the Member States. In making the appointments, the Council must normally select individuals who belong to, or have had experience of, the external audit departments of their own national administration. Exceptionally, individuals with other special qualifications may also be eligible for appointment. The Court elects its President from among its own members, for a renewable term of three years. The Court is based in **Luxembourg**.

The **COURT OF FIRST INSTANCE** (CFI) is an innovation of the late 1980s. Under the **Treaty of Rome** the **Court of Justice** was made responsible for cases brought against the European Communities (EC) by its employees. These cases involved such issues as recruitment, promotion, salaries and disciplinary measures. They were, to a large degree, responsible for the increasing volume of work with which the Court had to cope, accounting for almost one-half of the cases heard. In order to reduce the Court's burden, by removing from its competence minor cases, including those involving EC staff that could easily be handled by a lower court, the **Single European Act** created the Court of First Instance. Composed of one judge from each Member State, but chosen by common accord, the new Court began to operate in September 1989. Its role and status were further enhanced by the **Treaty on European Union** in 1991, but only after the **Treaty of Nice** was it instituted as a genuine court of first instance. Prior to this, it was competent primarily for cases relating to **competition policy** and the **European Coal and Steel Community**. Many other cases went directly to the Court of Justice, bypassing the CFI. Currently it deals with a range of cases covering *inter alia* actions for annulment of EC legislation and actions for a failure to act by an EU institution. In all cases, appeals against its decisions could be directed to the Court of Justice on grounds of its lack of jurisdiction over a case or its misinterpretation of precedents. In 2005, the CFI completed 493 cases, a figure considerably higher than that of 2004 (361 cases). This was mainly due to the transfer of 117 staff cases to the newly created Civil Service Tribunal, established in 2004, and to the increase in the number of judges following **enlargement**. At the end of 2005, however, there were still 1,033 cases pending before the CFI.

The **COURT OF JUSTICE**, based in **Luxembourg**, was, until the establishment of the **Court of First Instance**, the only court of the European Communities (EC). It is concerned primarily with EC law, although its jurisdiction over the other **pillars** of the European Union (EU) is increasing. Overall, it is charged with ensuring that the operation of the EC concurs with the provisions of the **founding treaties** and their amendments. It has no hierarchical links with the courts of the different legal systems of the Member States, and has no jurisdiction over the application and interpretation of purely national laws by the national courts, except in so far as those laws conflict with EC law, which takes precedence over them. Within its area of competence the Court is supreme: there is no appeal against its rulings.

The Court is composed of one judge from each Member State, so that all of the EU's national legal systems are represented. Even after the EU's **enlargement** to 25 Member States in May 2004, there was still to be one judge per Member State. For the sake of efficiency, however, the Court may sit as a 'Grand Chamber' of just 11 judges instead of always having to meet in a plenary session attended by all the judges. (Previously, when there were 13 judges, the 13th, who was necessary to ensure a majority if the Court was divided, was drawn from one of the larger Member States rotating in alphabetical order.) There are also nine **Advocates General**. These have similar privileges to judges, but act more as consultants and advisers than as referees. Under Article 167 of the **Treaty of Rome** (since the **Treaty of Amsterdam** this **Article** is known as Article 223) members of the Court have to be individuals 'whose independence is beyond doubt and who possess the qualifications required for appointment to the highest judicial offices in their respective countries or who are jurisconsults of recognized competence'. While it is the member governments who formally submit nominations to the Court, appointment is made by the Council of Ministers (see **Council of the European Union**). Judges and Advocates General are appointed for renewable six-year terms of office, with one-half of the Court being renewed every three years. The President of the Court is elected by the judges from among their own members for a renewable three-year term.

The Court meets in both plenary sessions and in smaller subdivisions called Chambers. The latter enable the Court to carry a larger case-load at any one time. Important cases, including virtually all those brought by an EC institution or by a Member State, are heard in plenary session, where eight judges constitute a quorum. Other cases are referred to a Chamber, of which there are six. Any Chamber is free to request that a case currently before it should be transferred to the full Court when it considers that the case merits the fullest possible hearing.

In its various guises, the Court hears three different types of case: opinions, referrals and disputes. The least contentious are opinions, which refer to opinions given by the Court on international agreements to which the EC is party. Referrals describe preliminary rulings by the Court on cases brought before it from national court systems. When a point of EC law is raised in a case before a national court, the point at issue is referred to the Court of Justice for a preliminary ruling, because EC law takes precedence over national law. The national court must take this into account in hearing the case before it. Referrals have been an important way in which the Court has been able to ensure that EC law is applied uniformly across all the Member States. Most cases involve disputes. There are four main types of dispute: those between the EC and Member States; between Member States; between EC institutions; and between individuals or corporate bodies (including EC employees) and the EC. Any of these categories can initiate Court proceedings. In the case of an individual, he or she must be able to demonstrate a direct personal interest in the case and its outcome. Under the terms of the **Treaty on European Union** (TEU), disputes between individuals and the EC were made the responsibility of the Court of First Instance, which now has jurisdiction in this fourth area of disputes.

When the Court first receives a written complaint, it has to establish whether the charge falls within its remit and within the time limits stipulated by the treaties. If it decides in the affirmative, the written charge is sent to the defendant, who has one month in which to make a rebuttal. The plaintiff is then granted an additional month in which a response may be made to the defendant's statement. Finally, the defendant has a further month in which to prepare an additional response. Once this process is completed, the case, if not settled out of court, moves to the stage of a formal hearing. The responsibility for a case belongs to a judge rapporteur, who is appointed by the President of the Court. The judge rapporteur, after studying all the documents, sends a preliminary report to the Court, which must then decide whether to hold a preliminary inquiry, which could involve a request for further documentation and/or the need for the two sides in the case to give oral testimony before the Court. It is at this point that the Court decides whether to hear the case in plenary session or to refer it to one of the Chambers. A date for the public hearing is set by the President of the Court. The conduct of the public hearing follows normal legal convention: plaintiff and defendant present their arguments and call witnesses; cross-questioning is done by the judges and the Advocate-General appointed to the case. The Advocate-General acts as a public prosecutor of the kind found in many European legal systems. The Court does not give its verdict immediately upon the conclusion of the public hearing. A further hearing is held some weeks later at which the Advocate-General reviews the oral and written evidence and proposes a verdict. The opinion of the Advocate-General is not final, but in the majority of cases it is a good indication of the likely decision of the Court. If, during their consideration of the evidence, the judges feel they need more information or explanation, they may extend the hearing. Finally, the Court delivers its verdict at a public hearing. Unanimity is not required, and judgments are reached by majority vote. Normally, the case will be heard by an uneven number of judges: where this is not the case and there is no majority, a decision is reached by eliminating the vote of the most junior judge. Judgments are nevertheless collective, to emphasize the independence of the Court from both other EC institutions and national governments. Voting is secret, and the voting record of any individual judge is not known.

The average length of time between the lodging of a complaint and final judgment has been around 23 months. This tardiness has led to considerable complaints about the Court, but the delays are due not only to the lengthy procedure that must be followed, but also to the increasing volume of cases that the Court has had to hear. Even though about one-third of the submissions do not result in a judgment, they have contributed to the Court's burden. While a large number of cases involving EC employees, as well as certain other categories of cases, were transferred in 1989 to a new Court of First Instance, this has had only a marginal effect upon reducing the time taken to reach a judgment. It is hoped that reforms introduced by the **Treaty of Nice**, which include the creation of **Grand Chambers** and **Judicial Panels**, will help reduce the backlog of cases. At the end of 2005, the Court had a total of 740 cases pending. In all, 474 new cases were lodged in 2005, and 574 were successfully dealt with. For the second year in succession, the Court completed more cases than it received.

Apart from EC employees, the largest number of cases have related to agriculture and the **Common Agricultural Policy**, followed by those concerning the **customs union**, **freedom of movement**, **competition policy** and **workers' rights**. The majority of actions has been brought by individuals and companies, mostly protesting against EC **regulations**, although a significant number have been directed against Member States. The **European Commission** has been the most vigorous plaintiff, as well as being the most common defendant. Cases brought by one EC institution against another have been comparatively rare, but the Council of Ministers and the **European Parliament** (EP) have, on occasions, brought each other before the Court. The TEU increased the ability of the EP to bring cases before the Court. Member States have initiated actions less frequently. They have often, however, been the subject of actions brought by the Commission, when the latter alleged failure to carry out their obligations. The most litigious country has been **Italy**, most notably as a defendant, owing mainly to its tardiness in implementing EC **legislation**, but also as the state that has initiated the most actions. The TEU remedied a previous deficiency by giving the Court powers of enforcement (usually fines) against Member States that do not conform to its judgments.

In many ways, the Court has become the most important EC institution, playing a vital role in consolidating and harmonizing the EU. In the cases brought before it both by the Commission and by individuals, it has made a significant contribution towards ensuring that Member States and their governments acknowledge the superiority of EC law and honour their EU obligations. The place of the Court was, however, altered somewhat by the TEU. On the one hand, the increased role of the Court of First Instance suggested that the long-term future of the Court of Justice might well be that of a court of appeal. On the other hand, the Court has traditionally been excluded from the two intergovernmental **pillars**, although this is changing slowly.

PAT COX was President of the **European Parliament** (EP) from January 2002 until June 2004. Pat Cox was a Member of the European Parliament from 1989 to 2004, representing the constituency of Munster in the Republic of **Ireland**. Prior to entering the EP he worked both as an economics lecturer at the Dublin-based Institute of Public Administration and as a journalist. Cox was re-elected to the EP in 1994 and was first elected President of the European Liberal Democrat Group in 1998. Thereafter, he was unanimously re-elected as Group President in June 1999 following the fourth elections to the EP.

CPC: See **Community Patent Convention**

CREEPING COMPETENCE is a phrase that has been used, mainly by critics of further integration, to refer to the extension of the role and powers of the supranational institutions at the expense of the Member States, usually through a more expansive interpretation of the treaties and their amendments.

CREST: See **Scientific and Technical Research Committee**

CROATIA, a country of 4.4m. people, emerged as an independent European state following its secession from the **Yugoslav** federation in 1991. This successful move to independence was due in large amount to **Germany**'s unilateral decision to recognize the new state, even though Croatia's action aroused Belgrade's animosity and led to a short and bitter war with the Serbian minority in Croatia from 1991 to 1994, which included the bombing of the historic city of Dubrovnik. Initially, Croatia was beset by severe problems, which were epitomized by economic stagnation and a high rate of unemployment (which had soared to 20% by 2000) and by the stubbornness and style of authoritarian nationalism created under the President, Franjo Tudjman, who died in 1999. In 2000 the new government was determined to bring Croatia into the European mainstream, and signalled its intention to reform the economy and to apply for membership of the EU. By early 2003 it had made sufficient economic and political progress to apply formally for EU membership, becoming the second former Yugoslav republic after **Slovenia** to do so. In June 2004, following a positive *avis* from the **European Commission**, the **European Council** conferred candidate country status on Croatia and announced that **accession negotiations** would be opened in 2005. Croatia's failure to cooperate fully with the International Criminal Tribunal for the Former Yugoslavia (ICTY) or to hand over General Ante Gotovina, who has been accused of ordering the killing of more than 100 ethnic Serbs and expelling 150,000 in 1995, meant that the planned opening of negotiations in spring 2005 was postponed. Only following confirmation from the ICTY chief prosecutor, Carla del Ponte, that Croatia was now fully co-operating with the ICTY did the EU's Member States agree to open negotiations in early October 2005. The decision was somewhat controversial and was widely seen as part of a deal that allowed **Austria** to drop its opposition to the opening of accession negotiations with **Turkey**. With Gotovina finally captured and handed over to the ICTY in December 2005, the EU signalled its intention to open substantive negotiations on two of the 35 negotiating chapters in 2006. The Croatian government is seeking membership in time to participate in the next **European Parliament** elections in 2009.

CROCODILE GROUP is the name of an action group founded in July 1980 by **Altiero Spinelli** and other **Members of the European Parliament** (MEPs) who wished to persuade the new directly elected **European Parliament** (EP) to develop a plan for a radical reform of the European Communities and a grand strategy for an all-embracing European union. The name derived from the restaurant in **Strasbourg** where the Group first met. The Group met at frequent intervals to plan strategy and formulate proposals, and circulated newsletters (*Crocodile letters*) to all MEPs. Its key argument was that the EP had a duty to consider constitutional reforms and to compile a draft that would be transmitted to the proper constitutional authorities in the Member States for **ratification**. By 1981, it had won the support of a substantial number of MEPs, and the EP voted to establish an Institutional Committee to deliberate on the topic. This process resulted in the **Draft Treaty establishing the European Union**.

CRONOS: See **NEW CRONOS**

CSCE: See **Organization for Security and Co-operation in Europe**

CSF (Community Support Frameworks): See **Structural Funds**

CULTURAL POLICY has been a relatively undeveloped European Communities (EC) policy sector. The EC have supported the initiatives of the **Council of Europe**, which has always been active in seeking to protect and develop the European cultural heritage. It was the rapid advance of technological developments in the 1980s that pushed the EC into greater activity, and the **European Commission** began to define the outlines of a cultural policy. Most of its efforts have been concentrated upon film and television (see **Media Policy**). It has also focused upon free trade in cultural goods, improving the working conditions and prospects of artists, encouraging a wider audience for cultural activities, and preserving the architectural heritage of the European Union (EU). It has emphasized the **freedom of movement** of both artists and their products throughout the EU, although it is agreed that 'national art treasures' should be excluded from these general provisions. Such treasures, however, have to be strictly defined. The EC have attempted to seek greater **harmonization** in various areas, including national copyright laws, public subsidies, resale rights and royalties. Several activities have been sponsored: the EU Youth and Baroque Orchestras; the translation of contemporary literature, especially from the minority languages of the EU; a European Film Festival (held in a different city each year); and the European Theatre in Milan and Paris. The most widely known initiative, perhaps, is the designation each year, beginning with Athens in 1985, of a different city as European City of Culture, where the EC sponsors several events. The most contentious policy has been that contained in the 1991 *TV Without Frontiers* directive, which attempts to protect EU television producers against non-European programmes. Since 1982 grants, as well as loans from the **European Investment Bank**, have been advanced for architectural preservation and restoration, and have benefited some 30 sites which are deemed to be of significance for the EU as a whole or which are located in poorer and undeveloped regions of the EU. A more concerted effort linking these activities was launched in a four-year Action Programme in 1988, and in 1991 the **Treaty on European Union** made specific references to cultural policy. A **Culture 2000** framework programme was proposed in 1998 to cover the period 2000–04. This was to operate in three main areas: legislation favourable to culture, the cultural dimension of existing policies, and culture and external relations. It superseded the **Kaleidoscope, Ariane** and **Raphael** programmes. Further initiatives, however, will depend upon finance, and will probably continue to be opposed by many who fear that an emphasis upon a 'common cultural heritage' will lead to transnational cultural conformity, and damage national and regional cultural diversity. In January 2005 the Commission adopted Decision 2005/56/EC setting up a new Education, Audiovisual and Culture Executive Agency (EACEA). This Agency will be responsible for the management of certain parts of the EU's programmes in the education, culture and audiovisual fields.

The **CULTURE 2000** framework programme was proposed in 1998 to cover the period 2000–04. The programme operates in three main areas: legislation favourable to culture, the cultural dimension of existing policies, and culture and external relations; it was given a budget of €167m. Its main aim is to promote a 'common cultural area' inclusive of cultural diversity and common cultural heritage. Cultural Contact Points promote the programme in Member States and in participating **candidate countries** of **Central and Eastern Europe**. The programme superseded the **Kaleidoscope, Ariane** and **Raphael** programmes. In July 2005 the European Commission adopted an ambitious proposal to establish a new Culture 2007 programme, which would run from 2007 to 2013, taking over from Culture 2000 and extending it, with a proposed budget of €408m.

CUSTOMS 2007 is aimed at helping the customs administrations of the Member States and the **candidate countries** to work more closely together against customs fraud. It has a budget of €166m. for the period 2003–07.

CUSTOMS DUTIES are those taxes levied by states at their border upon imports into their territory. The **Treaty of Rome** committed the Member States to 'the elimination, as between Member States, of customs duties and of quantitative restrictions on the import and export of goods, and of all other measures having equivalent effect'. The removal of internal duties and restrictions, and the imposition of a **common external tariff** (CET), constitute a **customs union**. Customs duties on goods imported from outside the EU are collected by the Member States in accordance with the CET, but they are regarded as part of EC **own resources** and are a source of **revenue** for the EC **budget**.

CUSTOMS UNION is the name of an economic structure whereby a group of states agree to belong to a single tariff area, where there are no **customs duties** on goods circulating within the union, but where there is a **common external tariff** (CET) levied on all imports into the union. The **Treaty of Rome** created a precise timetable for the establishment of a customs union, which was largely completed by July 1968. New members of the European Communities (EC) have been granted a short transitional period of adjustment in which to comply with the full requirements of a customs union. The CET was introduced in the 1960s, but its level was determined by the terms of the several accords with the now superseded GATT (**General Agreement on Tariffs and Trade**), to which the European Union states individually and collectively were party. It was generally accepted that a customs union would not be sufficient to bring about the EC goal of a **common market**, but it was not until the late 1980s that the EC began to consider seriously the problem of non-customs obstacles to the establishment of a common **internal market**. Certain non-Member States – for example, **Turkey** – have signed agreements with the EC whereby they have been incorporated into the customs union.

CYPRUS became a member of the European Union (EU) on 1 May 2004. Prior to this, it concluded an **association agreement** with the European Community (EC) in 1972. The intention was that the agreement would prepare the way for a full customs union between Cyprus and the EC. Developments proved to be much slower than originally anticipated, and were complicated by the *de facto* partition of the island after the invasion of northern Cyprus by **Turkey** in 1974. The EC refused to deal with the administration of the Turkish-controlled sector of the island. In 1987 Cyprus concluded a customs union agreement with the EC, which included arrangements concerning agriculture. The customs union was to come into force in stages over a 10-year period. In 1990, however, Cyprus applied for full membership of the EC. Given the wish of Turkey also to become a member, this created a dilemma for the EC. The **European Commission** published its *avis* in 1993, and indicated that, if partition was not ended, the EC would consider negotiating only with the Greek Cypriot government. Following this *avis*, in 1995 the **European Council**

decided that negotiations with Cyprus would begin six months after the end of the **intergovernmental conference** which was held in 1996–97. Formal negotiations began in March 1998 and were concluded in December 2002. Although some Member States still had reservations about admitting a divided island into the EU, the signing of the **Accession Treaty** in April 2003 committed the EU to admitting Cyprus irrespective of the political situation on the island. Nevertheless, the prospect of membership did lead to improved relations between the two parts of the island, notably in 2003 when travel restrictions were substantially eased. Subsequently, and despite the breakdown of earlier UN-brokered talks, frantic efforts were made during the months leading up to membership on 1 May 2004 to secure agreement on the reunification of the island so that it could join the EU as a single political entity. Although an agreement was reached, it failed to gain the approval of Greek Cypriots in a referendum in April 2004. As a result, only the southern half of the island became part of the EU the following month.

The **CZECH REPUBLIC** signed a **Europe Agreement** with the European Community (EC) in 1993, whereby the EC accepted in principle the possibility of membership. This accord superseded the earlier Europe Agreement signed between the EC and the former Czech and Slovak Federative Republic (Czechoslovakia) in 1991. The first agreement had become obsolete in January 1993 with the creation of two separate states, the Czech Republic and **Slovakia**. There existed a strong body of opinion that the Czech Republic's application could not be considered until the European Union (EU) had been consolidated, and the **European Free Trade Association** states admitted. In 1997 the Czech Republic's 1996 application to join the EU was considered favourably, and **accession negotiations** began in March 1998. The country was deemed to have completed the necessary economic and institutional reforms. The application was considered by the **European Commission** to be integral to its **Agenda 2000** 'for a stronger and wider Europe' initiative, although it noted that investment would be needed to transpose EC rules on agriculture, the environment and energy, and that administrative reforms would be required to 'provide the country with the structures it needs for effective application and enforcement of the full body of Community law.' Although the Czech Republic had long been considered among the best placed of the **candidate countries** to join the EU, this did not prevent the Commission from criticizing its preparations for membership. However, the Czech Republic completed accession negotiations with the EU in December 2002. Following its signing in April 2003, the **Accession Treaty** was approved in a national referendum held in mid-June 2003. On a voter turn-out of 55.2%, 77.33% of those who participated voted in favour of membership. The Czech Republic joined the EU on 1

May 2004. Domestic political infighting contrived to mar the build-up to the occasion, with the prospective Czech member of the European Commission resigning within a week of being nominated. The government had planned to hold a referendum on the **Treaty establishing a Constitution for Europe** in the spring of 2006, but this was 'postponed' following the rejection of the treaty in both **France** and the **Netherlands** in May/June 2005

CZECHOSLOVAKIA: See **Czech Republic; Slovakia**

D

DANGEROUS SUBSTANCES are the subject of several European Communities (EC) **directives** regulating the classification, use, labelling and marketing of many products deemed to be potentially dangerous. These directives cover, *inter alia*, asbestos, glues, paints, pesticides and solvents. The production and distribution of **pharmaceuticals** are also controlled by EC directives. Nuclear-related matters have been handled by the **European Atomic Energy Community** (EAEC) and the **Joint Research Centre**. In 1981 the EC adopted a scheme for the rapid exchange of information between the appropriate national authorities about accidents and risks to **health and safety** that arise from the use of potentially dangerous products, and a system of monitoring accidents caused by consumer goods was subsequently introduced. (See also **Consumer Policy.**)

DAPHNE was a programme, originally launched in 1997, but extended to cover the years 2000–04, which supported projects by non-governmental organizations to combat violence against women, young people and children, especially in the areas of trafficking in women and the sexual exploitation of children. Its successor, Daphne II, runs from 2004 until 2008, with a budget of €50m.

DAVIGNON REPORT is the name usually given to a document which was a product of the **Hague Summit** of December 1969, when the heads of government agreed to return to the theme of political integration. The summit charged the foreign ministers with the responsibility of studying 'the best way of achieving progress in the matter of political unification, within the context of **enlargement**'. Mindful perhaps of the arguments that this had caused in the past, the leaders did not try to be specific as to which route such political progress might follow. The foreign ministers opted for a compromise solution in order to achieve agreement. The conclusions were presented in a report compiled by Etienne Davignon (1932–), political director in the Ministry of Foreign Affairs of **Belgium**. The Davignon Report of 1970 accepted that political integration should ideally begin in a policy sphere where the Member

States, both current and projected, already possessed an identifiable common interest, and recommended that it should be in the co-ordination of foreign policy 'that the first concrete efforts should be made to show the world that Europe has a political vocation'. The Report included several specific recommendations: a regular consultation process of meetings of the foreign ministers, backed by a support group, a Political Committee, formed by the political directors of the national foreign ministries; ongoing liaison between European Communities (EC) ambassadors in foreign capitals; and the issuing, by the EC states, of common instructions on certain matters to their ambassadors abroad. The Report was widely welcomed, and its main recommendations were put into effect more or less immediately. The first ministerial meeting under the new regime was held in Munich, **Germany**, in November 1970, and the EC made their first joint policy declaration, on the Middle East, the following May. The process was judged a success, and a second Davignon Report in 1973 recommended its continuation. This second report stressed the non-binding aspects of political co-operation: its aims were 'to ensure a better mutual understanding of the major problems of international politics through regular information and consultation; to promote the **harmonization** of views and the co-ordination of positions; to attempt to achieve a common approach to specific cases'. The Davignon Reports were the basis of what came to be known as **European political co-operation**.

DE: See **Group of the European People's Party (Christian Democrats) and European Democrats**

ALCIDE DE GASPERI (1881–1954) was the first and longest serving Prime Minister (1946–53) of Italy after 1945. A member of the dominant Christian Democrat Party (DC), he had been a member of the imperial Habsburg Parliament in Vienna before 1914. His opposition to Benito Mussolini led to a four-year prison term, followed by his effective exile in the Vatican. A skilled politician, he maintained successful control of his unwieldy party, and pursued an active pro-Western foreign policy. He was a committed supporter of all initiatives for European integration and was a close confidant of **Konrad Adenauer** and **Robert Schuman**. He believed not only that integration was intrinsically valuable, but also that it would benefit Italy in aiding the country's economic development as well as strengthening its democratic system against potential challenges from the strong political extremes. His efforts on behalf of the European integration project led to his election as President of the Common Assembly of the **European Coal and Steel Community** in 1954, just months before his death. In general terms, he set the tone of Italy's attitude towards

European integration: until 1954 he was perhaps the most consistent supporter of the concept in the European Communities.

CHARLES DE GAULLE (1890–1970) became the first President of the French Fifth Republic in 1958, serving until 1969. His foreign policy was directed towards the restoration of French influence in international affairs, the reassertion of national sovereignty, *rapprochement* with the Federal Republic of **Germany**, less reliance on and 'subservience' to the **USA**, and French leadership of the European Communities (EC). De Gaulle was not averse to economic integration, as long as it served French interests and did not limit French independence of action. For the same reasons, he was hostile to the political implications of the **Treaty of Rome**, preferring a looser intergovernmental structure of independent states. His political plans for the EC were the basis of the 1961 **Fouchet Plan**, which was rejected by the other Member States. The 1963 **Treaty of Friendship** (Elysée Treaty) was a truncated version of the Plan, but provided the basis of the Franco-German axis that came to dominate much of future EC activity. Two further actions stand out in terms of their impact upon the EC. In 1963 and again in 1967, against the wishes of the other Member States, he vetoed the application of the **United Kingdom** to join the EC, fearing that it would lead to undue British and US influence in Europe, and thus the dilution of French influence. The other episode was the **empty chair crisis** of 1965, which resulted in a reassertion of French national power within the EC that reflected de Gaulle's hostility towards **supranationalism** and was personalized in his clashes with the first **European Commission** President, **Walter Hallstein**. While de Gaulle effectively won both disputes, the United Kingdom did eventually join the EC in 1973, and the drive towards integration was renewed in the 1980s. His vision of what the EC should be like politically was partially reflected in the emergence of the **European Council** under one of his successors, **Valéry Giscard d'Estaing**. De Gaulle retired in 1969 and died the following year.

DECISION-MAKING in the European Union is often considered complex, malleable and incomprehensible. There are an estimated 20 to 30 different ways in which **decisions** can be taken, and even then it is necessary to differentiate between policy and administrative procedures. In a 1995 report the **European Commission** itself identified 29 different decision-making procedures. The key to understanding the decision-making processes lies within the **founding treaties** and subsequent **regulations**. The decisions can be classified loosely into different category headings: constitutional decisions (concern the **European Council**); legislative decisions (concern the Commission, the **Council of the European Union** and the **European Parliament** (EP) and are subject to either **consultation, co-operation, co-decision** or **assent procedures**); **trade** policy decisions (Council and Commission); **competition policy** decisions (Commission and courts); **common foreign and security policy** (concerns primarily the Member States, as do **justice and home affairs** issues falling under pillar III); and finally, decisions relating to the **budget** (which fall to the EP and the Council).

DECISIONS are one of three different types of **legal instrument** that the **European Commission** and the **Council of the European Union** are empowered to issue. Decisions by either the Commission or the Council are binding upon the Member States; they may be addressed to named individuals or enterprises. Decisions can be made by either of the European Communities (EC) executives on the basis of the direct authority they possess under the terms of the **Treaty of Rome** and its amendments, or on the basis of earlier **regulations** or **directives**. Decisions made under the **Treaty of Paris** are slightly different: they are binding in their entirety and are thus closer to EC regulations. (See also **Law**; **Opinions**; **Recommendations**; **Resolutions**.)

A **DECLARATION**, as far as the **European treaties** are concerned, is a political statement issued by one or more Member States or the **intergovernmental conference** clarifying provisions of a treaty or outcomes of the negotiations. Of lesser status than a **protocol**, it has limited judicial force; its main purpose is to express the intention of the signatories. Declarations are also often issued following meetings of the **European Council**. The deliberations are usually produced in the form of 'conclusions of the presidency' and supplemented by declarations containing more detailed information on certain points of substance.

DECT: See **Digital European Cordless Telecommunications**

DEEPENING refers to the process of European integration. From its early incarnation as a **customs union** and through its steady evolution to a **common market** and now the **eurozone**, the European Union (EU) has aspired to 'ever closer union' among the peoples of Europe. Since the **Treaty of Paris** the EU's competence, policy remit and powers have steadily increased. The debate on deepening usually occurs alongside that of widening (**enlargement**) and there is a generally held view that the 2004 enlargement to 25 Member States, coupled with the prospect of further enlargement, must be accompanied by further deepening, or the EU will become a weaker entity, as it will be increasingly difficult to reach agreement on key **decisions**. Such thinking was part of the rationale behind the **Laeken Declaration** on the Future of the European

Union, the establishment of the **European Convention** and the convening of a further **intergovernmental conference** in 2003, which led to the adoption of the **Treaty establishing a Constitution for Europe** in June 2004.

DEFENCE: See **Common Defence Policy**; **European Security and Defence Policy**

DEFICIENCY PAYMENTS are a means of ensuring producers a fair price for their products and labour when the costs of the latter are higher than the prices for produce obtainable on the free market. When market prices are too low to cover the costs of production, compensation is given to the producer in the form of subsidies. Deficiency payments have been employed in the **Common Agricultural Policy** as an integral part of the price guarantee system.

JACQUES DELORS (1925–), a former financier and French government minister, was appointed President of the **European Commission** in 1985 and remained in office, serving a record three terms, until early 1995. He insisted that the schedule set down for the implementation of the single **internal market** by 1992 be maintained. He was equally insistent that the European Communities (EC) and the Member States should think beyond economic integration and 1992, towards working for closer political integration. His commitment and efforts made him the most active President since **Walter Hallstein**, and probably the most powerful in the EC's history. In pursuit of his goals, he was prominent in the drafting of the **Charter of Fundamental Social Rights of Workers** (the Social Charter), which he argued had to be adopted as an essential contribution to the internal market. He was also the main author of the Commission proposals (**Delors I**) of 1987 on budgetary reform, which were designed to place the EC **budget** on a sound basis until at least 1992. He chaired the committee, composed mainly of the central bankers of the Member States, mandated by the **European Council** in 1988 to consider how the EC might achieve **economic and monetary union** (EMU): the result was the **Delors Plan**. All three initiatives were, for Delors, to be an integral part of a radical restructuring of the EC by the 1991 **Maastricht Summit**. It was a restructuring in which, he argued, the Commission must be given greater decision-making powers to become a 'real executive', answerable to, and coun-terbalanced by, 'the democratic institutions of the future Federation' (primarily an enhanced **European Parliament**). The Maastricht Summit and the sub-sequent **Treaty on European Union** did not quite live up to Delors' expec-tations in terms of the social dimension, institutional reform or the **opt-outs**

conceded to **Denmark** and the **United Kingdom**. The turmoil in the money markets during 1992 and 1993 further adversely affected his hopes for EMU. Nevertheless, the policies followed by the EC in the 1990s were due in large measure to Delors' efforts.

DELORS I is a name which was given to a set of ambitious budgetary measures put forward in February 1987 by the **European Commission**, as a response to the continued difficulties in funding European Communities (EC) operations (see **budget**). The collection of reforms was intended to enable the EC to realize the aim of implementing an **internal market** by the end of 1992. It outlined four objectives: an increase in EC **revenue**; firmer budgetary discipline; reforms and stricter control of the **Common Agricultural Policy** in order to release more funds for other initiatives, especially in the field of **research and technological development policy**; and increased resources for the **structural funds** and the policy of **cohesion**. The proposed measures proved controversial among the 12 Member States. Three meetings of the **European Council** were necessary before agreement on the reforms could be reached at a special European Council meeting in Brussels in February 1988 under the German presidency. Several states were unhappy about the agricultural component, while the **United Kingdom** insisted that its budgetary rebate, agreed upon in 1984, should continue to be guaranteed. As a result of acceptance of the measures, the EC obtained a more secure budgetary structure for the medium term, and a greater degree of fairness was introduced into the budgetary system. The 1988 deal established the first of the multi-annual **financial perspectives**, which ran from 1988 to 1992, and saw an effective doubling of the money devoted to the structural funds for **Greece**, **Ireland**, **Portugal** and **Spain**. With the agreement secure, the Commission felt able to turn its attention to the issue of **economic and monetary union**.

DELORS II is the popular name of a set of budgetary measures proposed by the **European Commission** in February 1992. It sought a one-third increase in European Communities (EC) **revenue** in order to cover the additional costs imposed by the **Treaty on European Union**, in particular those incurred by the objectives of **cohesion**, improving the competitiveness of EC industry, and greater foreign policy obligations, while still maintaining budgetary discipline and reflecting the ability and willingness of Member States to pay. The proposals' progress was hindered by the difficulties surrounding **ratification** of the Treaty, and final agreement upon a revised version was not reached until late 1992 at the meeting of the **European Council** in Edinburgh in December.

The **DELORS PLAN** is the popular name of a report on **economic and monetary union** (EMU) published in April 1989. The official title is the Report of the Committee for the Study of Economic and Monetary Union. The report was the work of a committee appointed by the **European Council**. Mainly composed of the central bank governors, it was chaired by **Jacques Delors** and outlined a sequence of three stages, with full EMU to be achieved by the end of the 20th century. The first stage would involve consolidating the achievement of free movement of capital, and closer monetary and macro-economic co-operation between the Member States and their central banks. The second stage would consist of a new system of European central banks, before the implementation of full EMU. The European Council, despite British objections, agreed in December 1989 that an **intergovernmental conference** would consider what treaty changes would be necessary for implementation of the Plan. The conclusions were presented at the **Maastricht Summit**, and the relevant provisions in the **Treaty on European Union** on EMU largely followed the structure of the Delors Plan.

DEMANDEUR is the French term often used to refer to those states requesting something (e.g. increased **structural fund** receipts) from the European Union.

DEMOCRATIC DEFICIT is a term that has frequently been applied to procedures and structures relating to the European Union (EU) over the past two decades. It refers to the belief that there is a lack of proper democratic and parliamentary supervision and **accountability** in European Community (EC) decision-making procedures. The lack has occurred because of the diminution of national **sovereignty** and the relative inability of national legislatures, because of legal restraints and pressure of time, to monitor both the **European Commission** and the **Council of the European Union**, and because the **European Parliament** (EP) had insufficient authority to fill the gap.

As European integration has progressed, the question of democratic legitimacy has become increasingly sensitive. The more recent treaties (Maastricht, Amsterdam and Nice) have triggered the inclusion of the principle of democratic legitimacy within the institutional system by reinforcing the powers of Parliament with regard to the appointment and control of the Commission and successively extending the scope of the **co-decision procedure**.

The **Treaty of Amsterdam**, for example, sought to address this problem by expanding the areas in which the EP participates under the co-decision procedure. Members of Member State **national parliaments** may also be able to play a greater role in EC decision-making, since the Treaty includes a **protocol** stipulating that, in the area of **justice and home affairs**, there must be a six-week interval between the tabling of a legislative proposal and its appearance on the Council's agenda. This should permit national members of parliament to participate more directly in EC **decisions**. The Conference of European Affairs Committees of national parliaments of the Member States is also encouraged to provide its views on **subsidiarity**, justice and security, and fundamental rights and freedoms. The EC institutions have also been opened to public scrutiny with easier access to the documents of the European Commission, and to the voting results of the Council of the European Union, where decisions have legal effect. Institutional design and inter-institutional relationships formed a core rationale behind the **Treaty of Nice**, which was agreed in December 2000 and came into force on 1 February 2003. It re-examined such issues as the use of **qualified majority voting** in the Council, allocation of seats in the EP and the extension of the co-decision procedure in an effort to inject greater **accountability** and **transparency** in the **decision-making** processes. More radical measures for reducing the democratic deficit are still under consideration and include stronger powers for the EP through the complete extension of co-decision to all policy areas, a stronger role for national parliaments in scrutinizing EU **legislation**, the desirability of holding regular European referenda and the possibility of electing the Commission president.

DENMARK has had a particularly difficult relationship with the European Communities (EC) over the past decade, as its citizens have twice (in 1992 and 2000) voted against participation in further stages of European integration, namely **ratification** of the **Treaty on European Union** (TEU) and adoption of the single European currency (**euro**) respectively. This reflects a tradition of rather marked 'Euroscepticism' encouraged by a history of notable maritime achievement and long-standing trading links with the **USA**. Originally Denmark declined in the 1940s and 1950s to participate in any integrative venture that went beyond intergovernmental co-operation. In 1960 it became a founder member of the **European Free Trade Association**. However, it reversed its position as a consequence of the UK decision to apply for EC membership, and submitted its own application in 1961, and a re-application in 1967. Denmark was not willing, primarily on economic grounds, to join the EC without the **United Kingdom**, although it was informed that it was not affected by the veto on UK membership. Discussions on accession were resumed in 1970, and the Enabling Act ratifying the **Accession Treaty** was passed by the Danish Folketing (parliament) in September 1972. Because the parliamentary majority was slightly less than the five-sixths' majority constitutionally required to approve any delegation of national sovereignty, a referendum had to be held. In October 1972 the referendum resulted in a vote of 63.3% in favour of EC entry. Denmark formally acceded to the EC on 1 January 1973.

One of the wealthiest Member States, Denmark has been a net beneficiary of the **Common Agricultural Policy** and has benefited from the **internal market**. It has strongly supported a more comprehensive and rigorous **environmental policy** and **workers' rights**, but has had doubts about full monetary union and, to an even greater extent, about a **common defence policy**. Along with the United Kingdom, Denmark has been the least enthusiastic member on the issue of closer political integration. Its policy within and towards the EC has been generally based upon a strict constructionist interpretation of the **founding treaties** and their amendments. Because the country has been governed by relatively weak minority coalition governments since the 1970s, the Danish Folketing has acquired a decisive voice in European affairs. The Folketing rejected the **Single European Act** (SEA), and the Prime Minister had to attempt to bypass the opposition by calling a referendum, before which he made it clear that Denmark's continuing membership of the EC was at stake. Even so, in the referendum he managed to gain only a small majority (56.2%) in favour of ratifying the SEA. Denmark's doubts returned in the aftermath of the **Maastricht Summit**. While the government endorsed the TEU, **ratification** was rejected by a small majority in a referendum held in 1992, a result which threw the EC into disarray. The result was significant because it was the first of several popular expressions of discontent within the EC over the pace of integration, indicating that there were limits to how far governments could proceed without paying attention to their electorates. More specifically, crisis meetings had to be held to maintain the momentum of integration and resolve the Danish problem. At the **Edinburgh Summit** of 1992, the **European Council** dealt with virtually all of the Danish concerns. Denmark was granted a number of exemptions, or **opt-outs**, from provisions of the TEU. The new conditions were subsequently approved by a small majority in a further referendum in 1993. In 1998 a referendum narrowly endorsed the **Treaty of Amsterdam**, which contains **protocols** relating to Denmark and its decision to opt out of certain provisions of the Treaty. Denmark has also opted to remain outside moves towards a single currency and **economic and monetary union**, and again against participating in the first wave of euro membership in September 2000. However, public opinion is believed to have changed, and there has been some speculation that a reorganized referendum would now attract approval for euro adoption. Denmark was also scheduled to hold a referendum on the **Treaty establishing a Constitution for Europe** in the summer of 2005, but postponed the poll in June of that year following the rejection of the treaty in both **France** and the **Netherlands**.

DEP is the acronym for a European Depository Library, where holdings of European Communities documents are less complete than those in a **European**

Documentation Centre (EDC). A DEP is intended primarily for use by the general public.

DEREGULATION has a specific meaning within the European Union. It refers not just to the ending of unnecessary rules inhibiting the working of the economy or to the reduction of government interference, but also more directly to all those measures intended to remove restrictions to **trade** as part of the implementation of the **internal market**.

DEROGATION is a term that refers to a decision by the European Communities (EC) to exempt one or more Member States from the provisions of a **directive**; it may apply to the whole or part of a directive or **regulation**. Member States that feel that their situation constitutes special circumstances may apply to the **European Commission** for a derogation, subject to agreement by the **European Council**. In principle, derogations are meant to be temporary, to permit a Member State time in which to adapt itself to EC requirements more gradually. For example, **Greece**, **Ireland**, **Luxembourg**, **Spain** and **Portugal** all received five-year derogations from the planned start of a single market in **telecommunications** (the liberalization of voice telephony and network operation that began in 1998). In practice, derogations sometimes continue indefinitely. Derogations are most widely granted to new Member States for periods of five or 10 years under the terms of the relevant **accession treaty**.

DÉTENTE is a term first used in the mid-1950s to describe a lessening of the tensions between East and West during the **Cold War**. The term is a highly subjective one: while the hostility of the late 1940s and early 1950s may not have been repeated, the two sides never ceased entirely their competition and rivalry. The importance of *détente* for European integration lies less in its questionable reality, but in the perception by Europe of a lessening of international tension. This perception allowed Western Europe to rely less heavily upon the **USA** and perhaps permitted the Member States of the European Communities (EC) to concentrate more upon their own plans and development. The changes in **Central and Eastern Europe** after 1989 may have, in a way, created a new sense of *détente*, but they also persuaded many that the EC should develop its own **common foreign and security policy**.

DEVELOPMENT AID comes from the **budget** of the European Communities (EC), the **European Development Fund** (EDF), and the **European Investment Bank** (EIB) and falls into several different categories. Firstly, there is the aid provided to the **African, Caribbean and Pacific** (ACP) **States**

(some 77 countries) under the terms of the **Cotonou Agreement** and previously the **Lomé Conventions**. The EC have also concluded agreements with a number of countries in **Asia** and **South and Central America**, which incorporate provisions for development aid. Similar help has been given to the **Maghreb States** and to the **Mashreq States**, as well as to Israel, under **protocols** in the agreements signed between these countries and the EC. A further element of aid is food and emergency provision forwarded to countries requesting EC assistance in coping with severe food shortages or the aftermath of natural disasters. This form of assistance has mainly been given to African and Asian countries, but in July 1989 the EC agriculture ministers agreed to provide food aid to **Poland** as part of what became known as operation **PHARE**. The amount of development aid provided by the EC has been substantial as a proportion of gross national product (GNP). The European Union (EU) is currently the world's largest donor of humanitarian aid and in 1992 the **European Commission** created the **European Community Humanitarian Office** to help provide emergency relief to the former **Yugoslavia**. Collectively, however, the **ACP States** have consumed the largest amount of aid, although, because of their number, the funds have been distributed rather thinly among them. The largest element of aid to ACP States consists of grants from the EDF and low-interest loans from the EIB, together comprising just over two-thirds of EC assistance in this area. EC development aid policy has not been entirely disinterested. Food aid has been a means of reducing EC surpluses, while the aid programmes have benefited EU companies and enterprises, which have won most of the contracts awarded under the programmes. In 2006 some €3.5 billion was available for EDF-backed projects that sought to reform education, modernize health and transport systems, support debt relief and balance of payments difficulties and further institutional development.

DEVELOPMENT POLICY in the European Union (EU) seeks to reduce and ultimately to eradicate poverty in the developing countries and to promote sustainable development, peace and security as well as a stable and democratic political environment in the EU's partner countries.

The central EU institution in this policy area remains the **European Commission**, and specifically **Directorate-General** (DG) Development. It is charged with the role of initiating and formulating the EU's development co-operation policy for all developing countries as defined in Title XX of the **Treaty establishing the European Community**, and to co-ordinate the relations with the sub-Saharan **African, Caribbean and Pacific** (ACP) **States** and the **Overseas Countries and Territories** (OCTs). The **Cotonou Agreement** provides the framework for a 20-year partnership for **development aid** to the 77 ACP countries, funded mainly by the **European Development Fund**. DG

Development is also assisted by specified budget lines in terms of the EU **budget**, prepares strategies for co-operation with ACP countries and OCTs, and also monitors their implementation.

In fulfilling its role, DG Development works in close collaboration and interaction with other services of the European Commission, in particular the EuropeAid Co-operation Office, the **European Community Humanitarian Office** (ECHO), and the Directorates-General for External Relations, Trade, Economic and Financial Affairs, Fisheries, Agriculture, Environment, Transport, Energy and Justice and Home Affairs. It is committed to strong co-ordination and complementarity between the Commission, the EU Member States and organizations such as the World Bank, regional development banks, the OECD and the **United Nations** system. DG Development works in partnership with government, civil society, and the economic and social spheres, including the private sector in ACP countries and other developing countries.

DG: See **Directorates-General**

The **DIALOGUE WITH BUSINESS** website was launched in January 1999. The site is free, accessible in the working languages of the European Union (EU) and acts as a gateway to data, information and advice from a variety of sources at European, national, regional and local level. It also makes available practical tools such as on-line access to business newspapers and directories. The Dialogue with Business website is intended to provide direct access to the **Euro Info Centre** (EIC) network and to Business Contact Points which have been set up at the level of national administrations to deal with country-specific problems related to the implementation of **internal market** rules. In particular, it gives small and medium-sized enterprises access to information and advice about Internal Market opportunities and potential problem-solving mechanisms.

According to Commission statistics, companies are making more than 11,000 requests for information and advice every day to the Dialogue with Business website. This practical and free tool is already helping firms to win new business in the Single Market and to overcome potential obstacles. Technical standards, EU funding opportunities, intellectual property rights and public procurement are proving to be areas of particular interest.

The pursuit of greater interaction between the **European Commission** and the business community was further developed by means of a new initiative on 17 April 2000, the 'Business Feedback Mechanism'. This was created to ensure that future policy-making could take better account of the practical experience of European businesses operating in the Internal Market. Under this initiative, queries from business to 41 Euro Info Centres will be analysed in order to pinpoint which issues give rise to most problems for business. The Commission is expected to consider these views, which will be available on-line, in its future policy-making. The 41 EICs participating in the scheme, covering all Member States, have been selected as the most representative of the 300 such Centres, which provide information, advice and assistance to business on EU-related issues. The 'Business Feedback Mechanism' initiative will help the Commission to fulfil the Lisbon **European Council**'s request to 'pay particular attention to the impact and compliance costs of new proposals' and to 'pursue their Dialogue with Business and Citizens with this in mind'.

The Dialogue with Business website has received more than 2.5 million requests for information and advice since its launch in January 1999. The Business Feedback Mechanism aims to process at least 20,000 requests a year, covering a broad range of sectors such as public procurement, technical **harmonization**, e-commerce, intellectual property rights and environmental regulation. The results will be systematically included in the review of the Internal Market Strategy, which sets legislative and non-legislative priorities for the development of the internal market.

DIANE: See **Direct Information Access Network for Europe**

DIFFERENTIATED INTEGRATION: See *À La Carte* **Europe**

DIGITAL EUROPEAN CORDLESS TELECOMMUNICATIONS (DECT) was an initiative launched in 1991 to develop a system for providing a variety of applications for cordless telephones and communications systems. It has since become a standard developed by the European Telecommunication Standard Institute from 1988, governing pan-European digital mobile telephony.

DIPLOMATIC REPRESENTATION abroad is not yet formally maintained by the European Communities (EC), although the **European Commission** has an External Delegation in most countries and to international organizations. Collaboration between ambassadors of the EC states was developed as part of **European political co-operation**, and in recent years some Member States have agreed to share embassies and missions. The EC also have their own non-diplomatic representation in several international economic forums, such as the **World Trade Organization** (formerly the **General Agreement on Tariffs and Trade**). On the other hand, many states have diplomatic representatives accredited to the European Union, giving the latter a partial diplomatic status. These are often the countries' ambassadors to **Belgium**. (See also **Permanent Mission**; **Permanent Representation**.)

DIRECT EFFECT, together with primacy, is one of the fundamental legal principles underpinning European Communities (EC) **law**. Essentially, by interpreting the **Treaty of Rome** as having established individual rights that had to be protected at Member State level, the **Court of Justice** established the doctrine of direct effect. As a result a mechanism was created for individuals and institutions to challenge the compatibility of national law with EC law. Thenceforth the Court of Justice could be invoked in national policy debates and, more importantly, any national laws that were deemed to run contrary to EC law had to be set aside.

DIRECT ELECTIONS to the **European Parliament** (EP) were provided for by the **Treaty of Rome**. The Council of Ministers (see **Council of the European Union**) declined for some time to initiate the legislation for direct elections, despite considerable agitation by the EP, which even threatened to take the Council to the **Court of Justice** for failing to honour its treaty obligations. The first direct elections were eventually held in June 1979, and since then have been held regularly at five-year intervals. Despite a widespread belief that there should be electoral **harmonization** across the Member States, it has proved impossible to reach an agreement on either a single day for the election, or a common electoral system, although all now use varying systems of proportional representation. The elections are spread over several days because states insist on holding them on the day traditionally used for national elections (Sunday in most countries, Thursday in the others). Counting of votes does not begin until polls have closed in all Member States. Each Member State has also been free to decide upon its own electoral system: this is usually the same as, or is based upon, that used for the election of the national legislature. The **United Kingdom** retained its traditional single member, simple majority constituency system, also known as the first-past-the-post system, except in Northern Ireland, where since 1979 three seats have always been determined by the single transferable vote (STV) method of proportional representation. (Constituencies in the United Kingdom, essentially amalgamations of those for national elections, are determined by the national Boundary Commission.) The UK government, however, introduced a method of proportional representation, using a regional party list system, for the first time in the European elections held in June 1999. All the other Member States employ proportional representation and, with the exception of **Ireland**, which uses the STV method, they all employ a party list system. The lists of candidates submitted by the competing political parties are national lists in most countries, including **Austria**, where direct elections to the EP were held for the first time in late 1996. However, in **Belgium**, **Germany**, **Italy** and **Spain** – as well as **Finland**, where the first elections were held in 1996 – regional party lists are employed, so the region becomes, in effect, a kind of constituency. (See also **Party Groups**.) The latest elections took place in June 2004 and were the first to involve the new Member States from **Central and Eastern Europe** and the Mediterranean. Overall turnout across the EU was 45%.

DIRECT INFORMATION ACCESS NETWORK FOR EUROPE (DIANE), also known as Euronet DIANE, was one of the first European information networks of its kind. It was a **European Commission** initiative to encourage developments in **telecommunications**. Based upon electronic packet switching, it was established in 1980 as a collaborative effort between the European Communities (EC) and the postal and telephone authorities of the Member States. It enabled users to utilize the resources of some 750 databanks and databases in the EC by means of a computer and telephone. The control and management centre for the network is in London, with further regional nodes in other parts of the European Union. (See also **I*M GUIDE**.)

DIRECTIVES are one of three different types of **legal instrument** that the **European Commission** and the **Council of the European Union** are empowered to issue for the adoption of **legislation**. A directive is the most common form of European Union legislation. Directives are binding upon all Member States, but take the form of general instructions on the goal to be achieved, while leaving the way in which it will be attained to the discretion of each Member State. The conditions of a directive are normally met by the Member States introducing national legislation in conformity with European Communities stipulations. (See also **Decisions**; **Law**; **Opinions**; **Recommendations**; **Regulations**; **Resolutions**.)

DIRECTORATES-GENERAL (DGs) are the principal bureaucratic 'ministries' of the **European Commission**, to which they are responsible. The General Secretariat of the **Council of the European Union** and the Secretariat-General of the **European Parliament** also have DGs, but these are fewer in number, have fewer powers and are generally less well known. The duty of the DGs of the European Commission is to carry out, or to ensure that the Member States carry out, European Communities (EC) policy, and to administer allocations from the **budget** to different policy areas and the **structural funds**. They are, in turn, divided into Directorates and Units. Each DG is expected to serve and advise the Commission through the Commissioner or Commissioners who hold the portfolios for its areas of responsibility. Appointment of staff to the DGs is by competition and merit, although the allocation of posts has to ensure a fair distribution between nationals of the Member States. In addition, as far as possible, it is usual for the Director-General in charge of a given DG and any relevant Commissioners not to be of the same nationality.

The European Commission is currently divided into some 24 DGs and 13 Service departments. Until the late 1990s, they were usually identified by number (e.g. DG IV), but, since reorganization in 2000, are now identified by their policy area (e.g. DG for Competition). The policy activities of the DGs are: Administrative Affairs, Audit and Anti-Fraud; Agriculture and Rural Development; Competition; Economic and Monetary Affairs; Education, Training and Culture; Employment, Social Affairs and Equal Opportunities; Energy; Enterprise; Environment; Financial Programming and the Budget; Fisheries and Maritime Affairs; Health and Consumer Protection; Information Society and Media; Internal Market and Services; Justice, Freedom and Security; Regional Policy; Science and Research; Taxation and Customs Union; Transport; Development and Humanitarian Aid; Enlargement; External Relations and European Neighbourhood Policy and Trade. Given the uneven degree of EC development in different policy areas, they have been far from equal in size. Groups of Directors-General meet at intervals to discuss the linkages and overlaps between their areas of responsibility, of which there are many. These have led to 'turf wars' within the College of Commissioners. In particular, the DG responsible for the **budget** attempts to keep an overview of EC **expenditure** – and hence that of all the other DGs – though with less success and authority than national finance ministries.

The DGs are complemented by several other European Commission agencies that carry out specialized functions. These include the **Secretariat-General**, the **Legal Service**, the European **Anti-Fraud Office**, the **Joint Interpreting and Conference Service**, **Eurostat**, the **European Atomic Energy Community** (Euratom) Supply Agency, the Security Office and the **Office for Official Publications of the European Communities**. A few other agencies of the Commission are based in centres throughout the European Union.

DISCRIMINATION can refer to the application of restrictive **trade** practices by one Member State at the expense of goods and companies from other Member States. Equally, it has long been used within the European Communities (EC) to refer to inequitable treatment between individuals based on nationality and, with regard to pay, sex. More recently, the **Treaty of Amsterdam** called on the EC to take measures to combat discrimination on the basis of racial or ethnic origin, religion or belief, disability, age or sexual orientation.

The **DOHA ROUND** is the latest round in a series of ongoing trade negotiations that commenced in the late 1940s. These rounds were designed to work towards a system of more liberalized trade rules and, in more recent times, ones that were fairer to developing countries. This latest trade round was agreed after arduous negotiations during 9–13 November 2001 in Qatar. It resulted in some far-reaching decisions on the future development of the **World Trade Organization** (WTO); these included the launch of a new round of trade negotiations – the Doha Development Agenda (DDA) – comprising both further trade liberalization and new rule-making, underpinned by commitments to substantially strengthen assistance to developing countries. It also sought to assist developing countries to implement the existing WTO agreements. In addition, the meeting approved the long-awaited waiver from WTO rules of the **Cotonou Agreement** between the European Union and **African, Caribbean and Pacific States**.

Each trade round is not a new set of rules, principles or procedures for global trade, but rather a catch-all term for the painstaking discussions that aim to result in such rules. The last successful attempt, the Uruguay Round, ran from 1986 to 1993, before the WTO itself was formed in 1995. Attempts to set up a Seattle Round floundered under the weight of international protests and economic tension in 1999. The initial deal in Doha merely helps to set the agenda for a new set of trade talks, which commenced in 2002. The fact that 142 countries were able to clinch a trade deal in Doha has been greeted as a triumph by governments and commentators around the world. The result was a clear success, given that the gulfs separating various trade blocs were alarmingly wide. But the triumphalism should not disguise the fact that Doha is a preliminary to a deal, rather than a deal in itself. Even if everything goes according to plan – and that is a big 'if' – many years of gruelling negotiations lie ahead before a genuine achievement can be claimed. The key issues dealt with at Doha included the liberalization of agricultural trade; the opening up of the financial services market; the general reduction of tariff barriers; rules on subsidies for steel and textiles; a boost to the dispute settlement system; new 'greener' rules for trade; the labelling of and copyright protection for drinks; and the relaxation on control of drug manufacturing. It quickly became evident that the possibility of reaching a deal was going to be extremely difficult.

In September 2003, in Cancún, Mexico, a summit was held to hammer out agreement on the Doha round, and concentrated on four main areas: agriculture, industrial goods, trade in services, and a new customs code. However, those talks failed because rich and poor countries could not reach agreement, particularly on agriculture. A new alliance of developing nations emerged that refused to sign a proposed agreement which they felt favoured the richer WTO members. A deal was finally reached, however, in Geneva in August 2004. This deal opened the way for full negotiations to start. Analysts say that it is vital that any new deal be agreed before 2007, when what is known as 'fast-track legislation' expires in the US. Without fast-track, which limits the power of the US

Congress to alter trade deals negotiated by Washington, there is little prospect that the US would adopt a new pact.

Following the Geneva meeting, Pascal Lamy, EU Commissioner for Trade from 1999 to 2004, said that he believed the Doha round could be completed by the end of 2005. Potentially the rewards were significant. According to the World Bank, a successful final deal could add $520bn (£280bn; €420bn) to the world economy by 2015, if rich and developing countries cut their tariffs. Most of the benefit would, the World Bank believes, go to poorer countries. Lamy's assertion proved to be too optimistic, however, and the next WTO ministerial meeting in Hong Kong in December 2005 broke up without any agreements being reached. The group of seven WTO members – the EU Member States, the US, India, Brazil, China, Japan and Australia – met again in London in March 2006 to see if they could further advance the talks. The most problematic point of the discussions centred on the support that the richer nations give to their farmers.

DOMINANT FIRM ABUSE is dealt with under Article 82 of the **Treaty of Rome**'s provisions on **competition policy** and refers to companies that enjoy a hegemonic market position for particular products. Monopolies are not problematic in themselves and not the focus of attention but rather only those holding a monopoly, who seek to undermine competition by attempting to eject competitors from the market through the imposition of unfair pricing regimes or by deliberately imposing restrictions on the distributors of their own goods. Article 82 has been more severely limited in operation than the more widely used Article 81, which targets **cartels**, but the **European Commission** has upheld the tenets of the Treaty, and its charges, and when cases have proceeded to such an advanced stage, have usually been supported by the **Court of Justice** (but see **Continental Can**) and the **Court of First Instance**. Perhaps the most famous case of alleged abuse was the Commission's charge against the US-owned International Business Machines Corporation (IBM), alleging that it had infringed the Treaty, firstly by withholding information on new products, and secondly by packaging several of its products together, which obliged a customer to purchase a whole package even when only one item was required. The argument lasted for four years until IBM eventually agreed, in 1984, to modify its practices voluntarily. Firms that are found to have infringed Article 82 are subject to financial levies. Recent activity under Article 82 has seen condemnation heaped on Unilever (for tying its customers to selling certain brands of ice cream in **Ireland**); on British Airways (for granting extra commission to those travel agents who sold BA tickets in preference to Virgin tickets); and on the organizers of the 1998 football World Cup in **France**, where French citizens were given preferential treatment with regard to the sale of tickets for the final stages of the competition. More recently, in June 2005, the Commission imposed a fine of €60m. on the pharmaceutical giant AstraZeneca on the grounds that the company had attempted to prevent low-cost drugmakers from launching a cheaper version of a particular (stomach ulcer) medicine. AstraZeneca immediately denied such allegations and plans to challenge the Commission's decision through the European Courts. Meanwhile in 2004 the Commission ruled that US software company Microsoft Corporation had violated EU competition rules by abusing its near monopoly in the PC operating system. The case against Microsoft has not only been one of the most high-profile examples of Article 82 in operation, but also one of the most contentious, as Microsoft has been highly critical of DG Competition's analysis.

DOOGE COMMITTEE, also known as the Committee on Institutions, is the name of an *ad hoc* group of 'personal representatives' of the heads of government, which the **European Council** agreed to establish at its **Fontainebleau Summit** in June 1984. The task of the group was to examine the possibility of institutional reform of the European Communities (EC) in the light of the **draft Treaty establishing the European Union** issued by the **European Parliament** (EP). Chaired by James Dooge of **Ireland**, the Committee was intended to conduct a preliminary exploration of the positions of the heads of government in order to determine the extent to which there existed common ground for further integration. The Dooge report drew closely on the **Genscher–Colombo Plan** and the EP's Draft Treaty. It issued a preliminary report in December 1984, and its final report was presented for discussion at the **Milan Summit** of the Council in June 1985. The Committee stated that its overall aim was to turn the EC into a 'true political entity with the power to take decisions in the name of all citizens by a democratic process'. It outlined four themes of institutional reform: strengthening both the **European Commission** and the EP – the former to be made more independent and streamlined, with only one Commissioner per country, the latter to be given joint decision-making authority with the Council of Ministers (see **Council of the European Union**); simplifying decision-making in the Council of Ministers by restricting the requirement of unanimity to proposals for new areas of EC action and to applications for EC membership; and allotting a strategic role to the European Council, which, meeting twice instead of three times a year, should concern itself with diplomatic and external affairs, and not the daily routine of the EC.

There were several disagreements over the report at the Milan Summit, with the non-founding Member States all expressing reservations about some sections of the report. In general, however, its major recommendations were not rejected outright. The Committee had also suggested that a special **intergovernmental conference** be established to consider its ideas and construct a reform package from all the reports and initiatives delivered over the previous few years. This proposal was also accepted at the Milan Summit, although **Denmark**, **Greece** and the **United Kingdom** voted against it. The intergovernmental conference prepared the way for the **Single European Act**.

DRAFT EUROPEAN ACT: See **Genscher–Colombo Plan**

The **DRAFT TREATY ESTABLISHING A CONSTITUTION FOR EUROPE** was drawn up by the **European Convention** under the chairmanship of **Valéry Giscard d'Estaing**. It brings together the existing **Treaty on European Union** and the **Treaty of Rome** to create a 'constitution' for the European Union (EU). In addition, the draft contains a variety of policy and institutional innovations and reforms. All this is brought together via four parts. The first, *inter alia*, sets out the objectives of the EU, establishes EU **citizens' rights**, defines the EU's **competences**, presents the EU's **institutions**, determines how the EU shall exercise its competences, establishes mechanisms for **enhanced co-operation**, outlines the EU's **budget**, and determines the mechanisms for accession. The second part incorporates the **Charter of Fundamental Rights**. The third part then outlines in much greater detail the policies (e.g. **economic and monetary union, social policy**) and functioning (e.g. **decision-making**) of the EU. The fourth part contains 'general and final provisions' and is followed by a number of **protocols** and **declarations**.

Following its adoption on the basis of 'consensus' by the European Convention in June and July 2003, the draft Treaty establishing a Constitution for Europe was submitted to the **European Council,** which welcomed it as 'a good basis' for starting negotiations on a '**Constitutional Treaty**'. These negotiations began with the launch of an **intergovernmental conference** (IGC) in October 2003, which was scheduled to complete its work prior to the **enlargement** of the EU on 1 May 2004. Although broad agreement existed on adopting the structure of the European Convention's draft Treaty as the basis for the 'Constitutional Treaty', some of its provisions proved unacceptable to certain Member States, as evident at the Brussels European Council in 2003 when **Spain** and **Poland** rejected replacement of the existing system of qualified majority voting in the Council with a system based on dual majority of Member States and population. This meant that the timetable for the IGC was somewhat disrupted, with negotiations continuing until June 2004 when agreement on the Treaty establishing a Constitution for Europe was finally reached. (See also **Treaty establishing a Constitution for Europe.**)

DRAFT TREATY ESTABLISHING THE EUROPEAN UNION is the name of a document prepared by the **European Parliament** (EP) under the direction of **Altiero Spinelli**. An EP Institutional Committee began drafting the document in 1981. The Draft Treaty originated in the work of the **Crocodile Group** (a group of **Members of the European Parliament** – MEPs – who first met in the *Crocodile* restaurant in Strasbourg) and sought to revive the European project. Spinelli believed that following the first **direct elections** to the EP in 1979 the MEPs were now in a position (in terms of legitimacy) to re-examine the original three treaties establishing the European Communities (EC) in the 1950s. Moreover, it was generally felt that a new treaty was needed to reorder the European institutions and to expand the policy remit. This document proposed greater powers for the **European Commission** and EP, and a severe reduction of the Member States' right of veto on proposed policies. The Commission, which would supervise the implementation of the new treaty establishing a European union, would become the sole EC executive, accountable to the EP and a weakened Council of Ministers (see **Council of the European Union**). The EP would have an independent revenue-raising responsibility and share budgetary powers with the downgraded Council, which was to be only a legislative body, renamed the Council of the Union. The EP approved the Draft Treaty in February 1984, but no action was taken on it directly by either the Council of Ministers or the **European Council**, owing to the sensitivity of many of its suggestions. However, several of its ideas were taken up by the **Dooge Committee** on institutional reform, and subsequently influenced the new integration initiatives of the late 1980s and 1990s.

DRIVING LICENCES were the subject of a **directive** adopted by the Council of Ministers (see **Council of the European Union**) in 1980. The directive required the introduction of a European Communities (EC) driving licence. The first stage of the process began in 1983 with reciprocal recognition by the Member States of each other's licences. Since 1983 licences have been issued with common requirements and common specifications, and from January 1986 driving licences in all EC states had to conform to a common model. The format adopted also satisfies the requirements of the 1968 Vienna International Road Traffic Convention, making it valid in other countries that signed the Convention.

DUAL MANDATE refers to those politicians who are members both of the **European Parliament** (EP) and of a **national parliament**. Before **direct elections** to the EP were introduced in 1979 the double mandate was the norm, as MEPs were selected from within the ranks of their own national parliament. Since 1979, however, double mandates have become less common, as parties tend to discourage, and in some cases refuse to allow, their members to sit in both the EP and their national parliament simultaneously. However, many still exist. Indeed, it is also possible to speak of a triple mandate as some individuals sit in the EP, their national parliament and a regional assembly. The major concern surrounding double (and indeed triple) mandates centres on the degree to which such members can adequately master their individual briefs and represent the electorate at both (or all three) levels. This situation caused general dissatisfaction. A proposal by European Union (EU) Member State governments to abolish dual membership of the EP and **national parliaments** was approved by **MEPs** in 2003 (399 votes in favour of this motion, 111 against with 25 abstentions). The proposal forms part of a number of changes to the 1976 Act on the election of members of the EP. The abolition of the dual mandate took effect at the 2004 elections to the EP, although the **United Kingdom** has negotiated an exemption until the 2009 elections.

The **DUBLIN CONVENTION ON ASYLUM** is a document outlining common formal arrangements relating to asylum throughout the European Union. It was a response to worries that the **internal market** and the **freedom of movement** it entailed would attract large numbers of economic asylum-seekers, especially from Eastern Europe. The Convention was signed by Member States in June 1990 (with the exception of **Denmark**, which signed a year later), but the slowness of the ratification process in many Member States delayed its introduction. It stipulates that when an individual has been refused asylum in one Member State, he or she may not seek asylum in any other signatory state. Even this, however, was deemed to be insufficient after the disintegration of the Socialist Federal Republic of **Yugoslavia**, and in June 1991 the states agreed to establish a Quick Reaction Consultation Centre.

DUBLIN FOUNDATION: See **European Foundation for the Improvement of Living and Working Conditions**

DUMPING is the selling of produce at greatly reduced, below-cost prices, and such practices by any Member State within the European Union (EU) are banned. The **European Commission** has the authority to permit the affected Member States to take appropriate protective measures if the offending country does not heed its recommendations and warnings. One difficulty is that national perceptions of what constitutes dumping can vary, because of different rates and costs of production, and on occasion this has led to disputes between Member States. The Commission can also act by imposing anti-dumping duties where it believes that other countries are engaged in dumping within the EU. By contrast, the policy of disposing of surplus agricultural produce (accumulated under the intervention element of the **Common Agricultural Policy**) at greatly reduced prices abroad has often been claimed by other countries with a major agricultural export industry to constitute a dumping practice.

DUNKIRK TREATY: See **Treaty of Dunkirk**

E

E-EUROPE: See **Information Society**

E NUMBERS are pan-European code numbers identifying a range of food additives. Their use is demanded by various **directives**.

E111 was a form available to European Union citizens entitling them to free or reduced-cost emergency medical treatment in other Member States. The E111 form is no longer valid. EU citizens now need a European Health Insurance Card (**EHIC**) to receive necessary healthcare during a visit to a European Economic Area (EEA) country or Switzerland.

EACEA (Education, Audiovisual and Culture Executive Agency): See **Media Plus**

EAEC: See **European Atomic Energy Community**

EAGGF: See **European Agricultural Guidance and Guarantee Fund**

EAP: See **Environmental Action Programme**

EASA (EUROPEAN AVIATION SAFETY AGENCY): See **Air Transport Policy**

EAST GERMANY: See **Germany**

EBN: See **European Business and Innovation Centre Network**

EBRD: See **European Bank for Reconstruction and Development**

EBU: See **European Broadcasting Union**

EC: See **European Communities; European Community**

ECA: See **Court of Auditors**

ECB: See **European Central Bank**

ECCP: See **European Climate Change Programme**

ECDIN: See **Environmental Chemicals Data Information Network**

ECE: See **Economic Commission for Europe**

ECHO: See **European Community Humanitarian Office**

ECISS: See **European Committee for Iron and Steel Standards**

ECLAS is the **European Commission**'s automated library system. It is accessible online.

ECO-LABEL has been designed as a means of promoting products with a reduced environmental impact and of providing consumers with accurate information about the product. Regulation No. 1980/2000 replaces the earlier 1992 regulation on a European Communities eco-label award scheme. Certain categories are excluded from the new Regulation's scope and include foodstuffs, beverages and pharmaceutical products.

The **ECO-MANAGEMENT AND AUDIT SCHEME** (EMAS) of the European Communities (EC) is a 1993 initiative to promote responsible environmental management in industry. (An existing regulation [No. 1836/93] was replaced by Regulation No. 761/2001.) Participation in the scheme is voluntary. The objective of the new EMAS is to promote continuous improvement in the environmental achievements of all European organizations, while providing the public and interested parties with any relevant information.

ECOFIN: See **Economic and Financial Affairs Council of Ministers**

ECOIN is the acronym of the European Core Inventory of Chemicals.

The **ECONOMIC AND FINANCIAL AFFAIRS COUNCIL OF MIN-ISTERS** (ECOFIN) is one of the three most important formats of the **Council of the European Union** (alongside the **General Affairs and External Relations Council** and the Special Council for Agriculture) through which specific policy areas are addressed. ECOFIN is the name given to the regular meetings of the economic and finance ministers of the Member States, which are held, on average, once a month. The ministers, who also meet in the **Economic and Financial Committee**, discuss both broad and more detailed issues of economic management. Issues pertaining to **economic and monetary union** are discussed by the informal **Eurogroup** (EURO-12) group of finance ministers of the participating Member States.

ECONOMIC AND FINANCIAL COMMITTEE is the name of an institution created by the **Treaty on European Union** as part of the development of **economic and monetary union** (EMU). It was first instituted at the start of the third and final stage of EMU on 1 January 1999, as a replacement for the **Monetary Committee**, although it was not charged with reviewing the monetary situation in the European Communities (EC). The committee comprises senior individuals from Member State finance ministries and representatives from the **European Central Bank**. The Treaty charged it with monitoring the economic situation in the European Union and reporting to and advising the **European Commission** and the **Council of the European Union**. Despite its largely advisory function, the Committee is highly influential, given its policy remit over EMU.

ECONOMIC AND FINANCIAL POLICY is mentioned in the **Treaty of Rome**, which obligates the Member States to co-operate with each other in planning their economic policies. Since the establishment of the European Communities (EC), the Member States have broadly followed similar economic policies, but this has been due less to co-ordination of effort and more to common reactions to worldwide problems and trends in the international economy. The **European Commission** has issued annual economic reports, which have included recommendations, but its advice and suggestions have not been binding upon the Member States. Broad questions of economic policy have been discussed by the **European Council** and have been a concern of what is now the **Economic and Financial Affairs Council of Ministers**.

Further co-operation was achieved through the regular meetings of the consultative **Committee of the Governors of the Central Banks**. These consultation exercises together constituted a reasonable level of co-operation, but they fell short of the level of co-ordination anticipated by the Treaty of Rome. Only in two areas have the EC been able to wield a significant influence upon economic policy. The first is the raising of loans on behalf of Member States through a variety of instruments: the **European Investment Bank**, the **European Coal and Steel Community**, the **European Atomic Energy Community** and the New Community Instrument. The other, prior to **economic and monetary union** (EMU), was the ability to limit exchange-rate fluctuations through the **exchange-rate mechanism** of the **European Monetary System**. More generally, however, EC authority and its **budget** have been too limited to have any kind of decisive impact upon macroeconomic policy analogous to that wielded by national governments. These deficiencies explain the interest in EMU. The details and timetable for EMU set down by the **Treaty on European Union** were intended to provide the EC with a common economic and financial policy by 1999. Eleven Member States were ready to participate as planned by this date, but the reality of four Member States (**Greece**, **Denmark**, **Sweden** and the **United Kingdom**) not taking part in EMU imposed some limitations on that objective. Greece entered EMU in 2001, but the decision for the other three states was to be determined by referenda. Two have already taken place: in Denmark and Sweden. In both instances the respective electorates voted against participation, leaving only the **United Kingdom** still to hold a referendum.

ECONOMIC AND MONETARY UNION (EMU) has been on the European Communities (EC) agenda since 1969, when the **Six** agreed to the principle at the **Hague Summit** and set 1980 as the completion date for full EMU. The **Werner Report** of 1970 established a timetable for the programme. The plans for EMU were effectively destroyed by the severe decline and general turmoil in the international economic climate of the 1970s. The Member States became more introspective in their economic policies, and the idea of EMU by the end of the decade was abandoned. All that survived was the **European Monetary Co-operation Fund**. The **European Monetary System**, launched in 1979, was not a replacement for EMU, though it did constitute a step in that direction. The next step towards EMU was precipitated by the plans for a single market that comprised the substance of the **Single European Act**. Although this treaty did not describe EMU as an immediate objective it did refer to the idea in the preamble to the treaty, which **Jacques Delors** pushed forward and presented to the Hanover meeting of the **European Council** in June 1988. Despite the objections of the **United Kingdom**, the European Council agreed to establish a committee to examine the idea and benefits of realizing EMU; Delors was asked to chair this committee.

EMU was revived formally in June 1989, when the European Council accepted the proposals of the **Delors Plan**, which envisaged a three-stage movement towards the goal, with the first stage, the involvement of all Member States in the **exchange-rate mechanism** (ERM), to begin in July 1990. In Rome in October 1990, the Council endorsed January 1994 as the beginning of the second stage of a more intensive economic and monetary co-ordination in anticipation of the creation of a **European Central Bank** (ECB) and single currency. An **intergovernmental conference** of EC finance ministers began in December 1990. Its deliberations were synchronous with those on closer political integration, and EMU became therefore a major theme of the **Maastricht Summit** and the consequent **Treaty on European Union**. The Treaty provisions relating to EMU broadly followed the outline of the Delors Plan, confirming January 1994 as the date for commencement of closer co-ordination, and preparing for the establishment of a **European Monetary Institute**, which would assume some responsibility from the **Council of the European Union** for monitoring how national policies and budget deficits were conforming to guidelines. The final stage of EMU was set for January 1999. It would entail a **European System of Central Banks** along with the ECB, with the **European Currency Unit** (ECU) becoming the single currency of the European Union (EU) (however, it was decided in 1995 that the new single currency would be the **euro**, which would replace the ECU on a one for one basis).

Participation in the third stage would depend upon individual Member States meeting the following **convergence criteria**: a high degree of price stability measured by an inflation rate no higher than 1.5% above the average of that of the three best performing Member States; a budget deficit no greater than 3% of gross domestic product (GDP) and a governmental debt no greater than 60% of GDP; staying within the permissible fluctuation limits of the ERM for at least two years without any realignment or devaluation; and interest rates no more than 2% higher than the three best performing Member States in terms of price stability. However, it was agreed that EMU would begin in 1999 regardless of how many states had met the criteria. The schedule and deadlines were immediately questioned, not least because **Denmark** and the United Kingdom were later given exemptions, or **opt-outs**, from the final stage. There was also considerable popular opposition in **Germany** to a single currency. Economic and monetary conditions in the 1990s threatened the achievement of EMU. Turmoil and speculation on the money markets in 1992 and 1993 put the ERM under extreme pressure, revealing that the EMU plans and the ERM took little account of the real strength of national currencies.

The United Kingdom and **Italy** were forced to leave the ERM, and many other currencies were devalued. The ERM survived only by extending the permissible fluctuation limits to such an extent that what resulted was almost a system of floating currencies. Equally important was the recession in Western Europe. The economic difficulties were such that by 1994 very few states met the convergence criteria. However, a much less strict interpretation of the criteria was eventually applied, and in 1998 it was declared that, of those Member States that wished to be part of EMU, only **Greece** had failed to meet the criteria. Denmark, **Sweden** and the United Kingdom had already decided not to join in the venture, which was launched in January 1999, after the inauguration of the ECB and the launch of the euro. Greece joined the initial 11 Member States in 2001, leaving only Denmark, Sweden and the United Kingdom outside the so-called **Euroland**; their entry would depend on the outcome of a referendum that would be held in each state when their governments decided they were ready to join. The Danish people rejected membership of the euro in a referendum in September 2000. Full EMU for participating states occurred in 2002, when national notes and coins were replaced by the euro. **Ireland** was the first EU Member State that successfully replaced its former national currency, in early February 2002. In a referendum in Sweden in September 2003 a majority of the voters opted to reject membership of the **eurozone** for the time being at least, while in the United Kingdom a referendum will almost certainly not take place during the term of the 2002–2007 parliament. As regards the States that joined the EU on 1 May 2004, it was considered unlikely that any would adopt the euro until at least two years after accession; in March 2006 Lithuania, for example, applied to join the **eurozone**, seeking membership from 1 January 2007, and Slovenia announced its desire to do the same.

ECONOMIC AND SOCIAL COMMITTEE: See **European Economic and Social Committee**

The **ECONOMIC COMMISSION FOR EUROPE** (ECE) is a regional agency of the **United Nations** established in 1947. Until the formation of the **Conference on Security and Co-operation in Europe**, it was the only European body that allowed the states of both Eastern and Western Europe an opportunity to meet on a regular basis. It concerned itself primarily with the exchange of information and development of ideas in non-contentious areas, especially relating to environmental problems.

ECONOMIC POLICY COMMITTEE is the name of an adjunct to the **Council of the European Union**. It is one of several meeting places for representatives of the economic and finance ministers of the Member States.

ECOSOC: See **European Economic and Social Committee**

ECSAs: See **European Community Studies Associations**

ECSC: See **European Coal and Steel Community**

ECTS stands for the European Communities Course Credit Transfer System, established as part of the European Community Action Scheme for the Mobility of University Students (**ERASMUS**).

ECU is the acronym commonly used to refer to the European Currency Unit. The ECU was introduced in 1979 as a central element of the **European Monetary System** (EMS), namely a common artificial currency unit supporting the **exchange-rate mechanism** (ERM) of the EMS. It replaced the **European Unit of Account** (EUA). While not all the Member States have participated in the ERM, all subscribe to the ECU. Its value was based upon a weighted **basket of currencies**. Each currency received a different 'weight' in the basket, with the allocation of weights being subject to regular review. The weights (in percentages) for each national currency were frozen as follows in November 1993 under the terms of the **Treaty on European Union** (TEU): **Germany** 32.0; **France** 20.4; the **United Kingdom** 11.2; the **Netherlands** 10.0; **Italy** 8.5; **Belgium** 8.2; **Spain** 4.5; **Denmark** 2.7; **Ireland** 1.1; **Portugal** 0.7; **Greece** 0.5; **Luxembourg** 0.3. (The currencies of **Austria**, **Finland** and **Sweden** were not represented in the ECU basket.) The US dollar was used as a reference point. The specified amounts of the national currencies were converted into dollars, and added together to give the value of the ECU, which could then be translated back into national currencies and used for transactions. The central rate of the ECU was used to calculate bilateral central rates for each pair of European Union (EU) currencies. The ECU was supported by the **European Monetary Co-operation Fund** (EMCF), a reserve fund into which the countries participating in the basket had to place 20% of both their gold and dollar reserves. It established itself as an accepted currency in international money markets, widely used in international Eurobond issues, as well as in commercial transactions, loans, bank deposits and cheques. Internally, it became a book-keeping device, fully replacing the EUA for all European Communities transactions and calculations in 1981. It was also originally conceived to evolve into the single currency of the EU once full **economic and monetary union** (EMU) was established. This was confirmed by the TEU, which set completion of the third and final stage of EMU for 1997–99, at which point the ECU would replace the national currencies throughout the participating Member

States. However, at the **European Council** meeting in Dublin, in 1995, it was decided that the ECU would be replaced by the **euro** on 1 January 1999, on a one for one basis. The euro became the new currency unit within the newly established **eurozone**, and replaced the national currencies of those 12 Member States participating in EMU.

ED: See **European Democratic Group**

EDA: See **European Defence Agency**

EDC: See **European Defence Community**

EDCs: See **European Documentation Centres**

EDD: See **Group for a Europe of Democracies and Diversities**

EDF: See **European Development Fund**

The **EDINBURGH SUMMIT** of the **European Council** in 1992 took place in the aftermath of the Danish electorate's rejection of the **Treaty on European Union** and saw the European Council agree on a number of exemptions, or **opt-outs**, for **Denmark** as well as issuing a statement which sought to clarify the principle of **subsidiarity** and highlight the European Union's commitment to **transparency** and greater **openness**.

EDUCATION INFORMATION NETWORK IN THE EUROPEAN COMMUNITY: See **EURYDICE**

EDUCATION, VOCATIONAL TRAINING AND YOUTH POLICY was originally largely excluded from the **Treaty of Rome**, other than as a reference to the reciprocal recognition by the Member States of diplomas, professional qualifications and vocational training. The European Communities have long accepted that national traditions and practices in education are both important and too complex or sensitive to be easily standardized. Initiatives to foster Member State co-operation on educational matters only began to materialize in the 1970s in a series of non-binding **resolutions**. The **Single European Act** emphasized the need for a European dimension in this area.

This manifested itself in a 1988 resolution calling for all Member States to integrate the European dimension into the school curriculum. Education was first recognized as a policy competence when Articles 149 and 150 were inserted into the Treaty of Rome by the **Treaty on European Union**. These spoke of 'the development of quality education by encouraging co-operation ... with a view to developing the European dimension in education' and envisaged, for example, the teaching of Member State **languages** in other European Union (EU) states, plans to encourage greater mobility of students and teachers, and efforts to develop educational exchanges and establish distance learning programmes. The **Treaty of Amsterdam** altered nothing substantial, but did determine that measures relating to education and vocational training were to be adopted under **co-decision procedures**. Progress in these areas has been limited. Even a 1989 **directive** requiring all Member States to recognize diplomas and degrees of three years' study has proved problematic. Education policy continues to confine itself to stressing the need for closer collaboration and mutual understanding, and continues to take the form of **recommendations** to Member States, rather than binding **legislation**. States have been urged to improve training opportunities for, and the cultural integration of, migrant workers; to co-operate in higher education; and to improve the quality and extent of the teaching of EU languages. The few **directives** that have been issued relate to **freedom of movement** in jobs and professions. Since 1995 there have been three main education and vocational training programmes: **Socrates**, to encourage student mobility; **Leonardo** (da Vinci), to promote access to vocational training and life-long learning, training exchanges and cross-border projects, and to foster innovation and entrepreneurship, improve the quality of training and make it easier to obtain and use vocational training and skills in other European countries; and **Youth for Europe**, which aims to facilitate the mobility of young people from disadvantaged backgrounds. In addition, the **Tempus** programme encourages exchanges in higher education between the EU and the states of **Central and Eastern Europe**. These programmes are open to people of all ages because lifelong learning and building a Europe of knowledge know no age barriers.

The two principal EU-run programmes remain the Leonardo programme and the Socrates programme. Together well over €400m. is spent on both annually. The Leonardo programme is complemented by the work of the European Centre for the Development of Vocational Training in the Greek city of Thessaloniki. This agency helps policy-makers in EU institutions, Member States and social partner organizations make informed choices about vocational training policy.

The oldest and probably the best known sub-programme under the Socrates umbrella is **Erasmus**. It devotes more than €100m. annually to grants for students and teachers to spend time at universities in other European countries.

Two thousand universities participate. By 2007, two million students will have studied in another country, thanks to Erasmus. From 2004, a new programme, Erasmus Mundus, aimed to spend more than €40m. annually on promoting Masters courses offered by a consortium of at least three universities in at least three different European countries. Scholarships to take these courses are available to students from any country.

Other Socrates programmes include **Grundtvig** for adult learners and their teachers to develop European teaching materials and networks, and **Comenius** for schools and their teachers. More than 10,000 schools benefit each year from **Lingua** to promote the learning of languages, particularly lesser-used languages, and **Minerva** to apply new technologies in education. (See also **ERASMUS**; **European Centre for the Development of Vocational Training**; **European Schools**; **European University Institute**.)

EEA: See **European Economic Area**

EEA: See **European Environment Agency**

EEC: See **European Economic Community**

EEIG: See **European Economic Interest Grouping**

EESC: See **European Economic and Social Committee**

EFA: See **European Free Alliance**

EFDA: See **European Fusion Development Agreement**

EFDO: See **European Film Distribution Office**

EFTA: See **European Free Trade Association**

The **EHIC** or European Health Insurance Card replaced the E111 form from January 2006 and entitles its holders to reduced-cost, or sometimes free, medical treatment that becomes necessary when people are staying in another EU Member State, a member of the European Economic Area (EEA – i.e. **Iceland, Liechtenstein** and **Norway**) or **Switzerland**.

The EHIC will normally be valid for three to five years and covers any medical treatment that becomes necessary during a holiday or business trip, because of either illness or an accident. The card provides access to state-provided medical treatment only and specifically does not cover people who are intent on travelling to one of the states above just for the purpose of receiving medical treatment.

EIB: See **European Investment Bank**

EIC: See **Euro Info Centres**

EIF: See **European Investment Fund**

EINECS: See **European Inventory of Existing Chemical Substances**

EIS: See **Schengen Information System**

EJN: See **European Judicial Network in Criminal Matters**

ELDR: See **Group of the European Liberal Democrats**

ELECTIONS: See **Direct Elections**

ELECTRICITY has been considered by the European Communities (EC) in the context of its overall **energy policy**. The first programme concerning electricity was drawn up by the Council of Ministers (see **Council of the European Union**) in 1974, and updated in 1980 and 1986. The 1986 review defined objectives for the period up to 1995. It urged continuation of the policy of reducing the reliance of electricity generation on petroleum, which was to constitute less than 15% of total electricity generation by 1995. It further suggested that by 1995 40% of electricity generation should be nuclear-based, rising to 50% by 2000. Owing to subsequent concerns about the safety and costs of nuclear energy, these projections have become less realistic.

Electricity policy forms a core element of the EC's pursuit of an **internal market** for energy. In the case of electricity, its objective is to ensure the free movement of electricity while improving security of supply and the competitiveness of this particular sector. In 1997 a **directive** (96/92/EC) concerning common rules for the internal market in electricity came into force. The

European Commission has subsequently monitored this sector, and in its second report on the state of liberalization in the energy markets, published in May 1999, accepted that substantial progress was being made in relation to the restructuring of this sector across all Member States. It reported that progress had exceeded the original minimum market opening prescribed in the original directive, and that 60% of the electricity market had been liberalized. The Lisbon **European Council** meeting in March 2000 called for a speedier opening up of the European Union (EU) energy market. In March 2001 the Commission adopted a set of measures to liberalize the electricity market fully by 2005. These included a communication on the completion of the internal market, a draft directive amending existing **directives** and introducing common rules for the electricity market, and a draft regulation on conditions or access to cross-border trade in electricity. These initiatives reflect the Commission's zeal to create a genuine internal market that is subject to fair competition and guarantees the rights of the consumer. These moves were complemented by a series of measures to strengthen economic and social cohesion, which includes, for example, the establishment of trans-European energy networks across the continent. These have been in existence for the last decade and have helped to connect both halves of Europe. Indeed, the CENTREL electricity grid (which covers **Poland**, the **Czech Republic**, **Slovakia** and **Hungary**) has been connected to the main European grid since 1995. The EU is currently developing a much broader policy and establishing other close energy links with countries such as Russia, the People's Republic of China and the Balkan states.

ÉLYSÉE TREATY: See **Treaty of Friendship**

EMAS: See **Eco-Management and Audit Scheme**

EMCDDA: See **European Monitoring Centre for Drugs and Drug Addiction**

EMCF: See **European Monetary Co-operation Fund**

EMEA: See **European Agency for the Evaluation of Medicinal Products**

EMEA: See **Euro-Mediterranean Economic Area**

EMEP is the acronym of a co-operative programme set up in 1986 to monitor and evaluate the transmission of air pollutants over long distances.

EMI: See **European Monetary Institute**

EMP: See **Euro-Mediterranean Partnership**

EMPLOYMENT is the focus of a relatively new **title** on employment inserted into the **Treaty of Rome** (Articles 125–130) by the **Treaty of Amsterdam**. The promotion of employment now ranks as one of the European Union's objectives and as a matter of common concern. Member States are encouraged to co-ordinate their employment strategies in moves to combat high unemployment, although there are no plans for a common employment policy. However, under the terms of the Treaty, the **European Council** is to conduct an annual review of the state of employment, and the **Council of the European Union** must play a more active role in employment affairs by encouraging the exchange of information in this field between Member States. This objective was reinforced at the **Luxembourg** jobs summit, an extraordinary European Council meeting convened in November 1997, where it was decided to develop a **European Employment Strategy** built on thematic priorities and described in employment guidelines adopted by the **Essen Summit** meeting of the European Council. Every year these guidelines have to be translated into national action plans for employment by Member States, which are later assessed by the Council of the European Union and the **European Commission** prior to the publication of a joint employment report. An **Employment Committee** was established to oversee the co-ordination of the employment strategies of the Member States.

The **EMPLOYMENT COMMITTEE**, established under the **Treaty of Amsterdam**, replaced the Employment and Labour Market Committee set up in 1996. It comprises two representatives from each European Union Member State and two representatives from the **European Commission**. The Committee is charged with monitoring Member State employment and labour market policies, and promotes their co-ordination and delivers opinions on them. (See also **Standing Committee on Employment**.)

EMPTY CHAIR CRISIS refers to the period of seven months after June 1965, when **France** boycotted meetings of the Council of Ministers (see **Council of the European Union**) and the **Committee of Permanent Representatives** (COREPER), although it continued to send junior representatives to some sessions in order for minor routine business to be carried out. This French ploy effectively paralysed the European Communities (EC). The French protest was over the EC timetable for the increased use of **qualified**

majority voting in the Council of Ministers after January 1966, and over a collection of proposals from the **European Commission**. These included the finalization of the financial regulations for the **Common Agricultural Policy** (of which France was in favour), as well as more powers for the **European Parliament** – especially in relation to the **budget** – and an independent source of **revenue** for the Commission (both of which proposals France opposed). The crisis was resolved by a compromise, which was largely to France's advantage and **Charles de Gaulle**'s satisfaction. The most important element of the resolution was the **Luxembourg Compromise**, which, although maintaining the principle of majority voting, extended to Member States the right to use a veto in the Council of Ministers if they believed that their national interests were being compromised. This agreement among the **Six** undermined the prestige of the Commission and impaired the EC's political development for nearly 20 years, until the **Single European Act**. (See also **Walter Hallstein**.)

EMS: See **European Monetary System**

EMSA: See **European Maritime Safety Agency**

EMU: See **Economic and Monetary Union**

ENERGY POLICY has been a rather problematic area for the European Communities (EC), as it touches on sensitive national concerns. The difficulties were revealed by the different national responses to the petroleum crisis of 1973. In 1974 a **European Commission** energy programme was accepted by the Council of Ministers (see **Council of the European Union**) and has since served as the basis for discussions on energy policy. It was revised in 1980, and again in 1986. The original priority was to reduce EC dependence on petroleum, especially on supplies from politically volatile regions. Within 10 years, petroleum imports had been reduced by one-half thanks to savings achieved through increased efficiency, the successful exploitation of North Sea petroleum, and a diversification of energy sources.

The 1986 revision of energy policy set priority targets until 1995. As far as the supply and use of energy were concerned, it urged that petroleum imports be held at a level below one-third of total EC energy consumption, with greater reliance upon **coal** and nuclear energy, the latter to supply 40% of EC needs by 1995. All developments were to take place within the context of greater efficiency, and a further improvement in energy saving of at least 20% was to be secured by 1995. More financial assistance was to be made available for the exploration of alternative energy sources such as solar, wave and wind energy, in the hope that these would provide up to 5% of EC needs by 2000. The programme also set several further objectives. It recommended more internal trade in natural gas and **electricity** (accepting that little more could be done for trade in petroleum and coal), and called for a common pricing system across all energy sectors. It confirmed the importance of maintaining a contingency supply of fuel reserves equal to 30 days' consumption at power stations (and 90 days' consumption in the case of petroleum stocks), and of more flexibility and co-operation between the Member States. It suggested that the EC should seek to use more effectively its position as a major energy consumer to negotiate agreements with energy suppliers. Finally, it emphasized the need for a major and coherent research and development programme, and for energy policy to be consistent with environmental protection.

The programme was an ambitious one, and doubts were soon raised as to whether all of its objectives could be met. There were potential conflicts between energy needs and environmental protection, and a growing objection to nuclear power. In the 1990s there were three major aspects to energy policy. First, as a consequence of the **internal market**, there was a new stress upon a single energy market. This would entail a liberalization of gas and electricity markets by removing the dominance of state monopolies by 2000. The European Commission issued several **directives**: on price transparency, the transit of energy, and the development of energy infrastructures. The EC also took the lead in the establishment in 1991 of a **European Energy Charter** linking Western with Eastern Europe. Later, in 1996, it would establish as part of its **Mediterranean policy**, a Euro-Mediterranean Energy Forum to assist in the development of co-operation projects. Finally, the Commission linked the development of energy more closely with **environment policy**. The major symbol of this commitment was the proposal for a **carbon tax**.

Much of the proposed energy programme was contentious, since the energy requirements of the European Union (EU) were likely to continue to grow. Given its potential importance, it is surprising that only limited reference was made to energy in the **Treaty on European Union** (TEU): it referred only to the existence of EC powers in the area of energy and the need for the development of European energy infrastructures. Moreover, although it was agreed that the possibility of incorporating energy into the treaty basis of the EU would be reviewed by an **intergovernmental conference** at the end of 1996 considering possible revisions of the Treaty, the **Treaty of Amsterdam** went no further than the TEU. In 1995 the European Commission published a **White Paper** on energy policy, prioritizing security of supply; improving the competitiveness of European businesses; and emphasizing environmental constraints. Following this, in 1997 the Commission proposed a framework programme for the energy sector, which, following approval by the Council of the European Union in December 1998, covered the period 1998–2002. The objective of this programme was to guarantee the coherence and efficiency of EC energy by bringing together all ongoing energy actions and programmes across all EC policies. EC energy policy does not seek to replace Member States' initiatives, nor other EC initiatives, but aims to reinforce cohesion between these different actions. Objectives for this five-year period included: the strengthening of international co-operation; the promotion of renewable energy sources; the encouragement of an efficient use of energy sources; an improvement of safety in the use of nuclear energy; and increased industrial co-operation with **Russia**. The Commission is charged with reviewing the implementation of this framework on an annual basis. In November 2000 the Commission launched a **Green Paper** on the security of energy supply. This aimed to ensure a supply of energy to consumers at reasonable prices while maintaining the competitiveness of the sector and respecting both the environment and sustainable development. It resulted in the **Intelligent Energy – Europe** initiative.

Technology is expected to play a key role in using energy more rationally. There is money for energy research in the EU's Sixth Framework Programme for Research and Technological Development. In addition, the EU planned to spend €200m. from its *Intelligent Energy for Europe* programme between 2003 and 2006 to support research into energy saving, energy efficiency, renewable energies and the energy-related aspects of transport. The focus will be on research programmes that help strengthen security of supply, fight climate change and make industry more competitive. Much has changed in the energy sector in the course of the last two decades. The Lisbon Summit meeting of the **European Council** in March 2000 called for the creation of a genuine single market for energy, and in March 2001 the Commission responded by adopting a series of measures to open up the gas and **electricity** markets completely by the end of 2005. A competitive energy market helps efficient energy use. In the past, national gas and electricity markets were separate 'islands' within the EU, where supply and distribution were in the hands of monopolies. Now, those markets have been opened up to competition. According to the Commission, consumers not only have the right to choose their supplier, but they also have a right to gas and electricity supply at reasonable prices. The Member States have already made progress in implementing two earlier directives (from 1996 and 1998) on liberalizing the electricity and gas markets. Some states have gone further than others, and there has been a notable reduction in prices in the **United Kingdom** and **Sweden** in particular. Problems still persist as a result of limited progress in cross-border trade and differing stages of implementation across Member States. Further progress needs to be made, particularly with regard to the pricing of cross-border trade and the rules for the allocation and management of scarce resources. To facilitate further developments the Commission has established two new consultative bodies: the Electricity Regulatory Forum of Florence and the Gas Regulatory Forum of Madrid. In September

2002 the Commission, increasingly aware of the EU's heavy reliance and dependence on external supplies of petroleum and gas, adopted two directive proposals that were designed to maintain the security of EU energy sources at affordable prices. In March 2003 the Commission raised the issue of energy sources again in a communication to the Council and the **European Parliament** on the consequences of the war in Iraq. Concern was particularly expressed over the impact of the war on the price of petroleum, which had been steadily rising in the months leading up to the outbreak of war. The EU currently obtains 22.9% of its petroleum requirements from **Norway** and 22.5% from Russia, and although OPEC has stated that it will compensate for any shortfalls in Iraqi exports to the EU, the price of petroleum is likely to rise further if the unrest in Iraq lasts for any lengthy period and particularly if it spreads further afield.

By mid-2004 all businesses were free to choose their own supplier of gas and electricity, and consumers were to have followed suit by mid-2007. For their part, all suppliers have guarantees under single-energy market rules that they can have access to the distribution grid and pipeline networks of other EU countries and that they will pay a fair price for access. Safeguards are being built into this free market to protect consumers against blackouts. The lights should not go out because of congestion problems as electricity flows across borders.

Consideration of energy policy has always stoked controversy at the EU level. Nevertheless, the dependence of many EU states on foreign-owned energy sources is unmistakeable. The dangers of such dependency were apparent when Russia threatened to cut off all gas supplies to Ukraine in January 2006 and thereby disrupt gas supplies to Western Europe as they came via Ukraine.

The European Commission published its Green Paper on a Secure, Competitive and Sustainable Energy Policy for Europe in March 2006. The paper seeks to secure sufficient energy supplies and to lay the base for a number of issues, including: a policy on gas storage; a single European electricity grid; the need for a new infrastructure; the construction of new gas terminals from the Caspian Sea and North Africa; a broad debate on the future of nuclear power; and more open energy markets. The Commission's initiatives to liberalize the electricity and gas markets since the early 1990s have met with mixed results, and certain Member State governments have sought to resist proposed mergers in the energy sector. Cases of blatant economic protectionism found illustration in the spring of 2006 when Gaz de France attempted to merge with fellow French supplier Suez, in spite of an Italian offer from Enel to acquire the same company. The French government strongly favoured a merger between purely French companies in an area that it deems to be vital to national security. Spain has also expressed its unease and opposition regarding cross-border mergers in any energy sector. Barroso and his Commission are strong advocates for the creation of large cross-border energy companies that can compete in the single market.

The scene is set for battle between these conflicting positions, but logic suggests that some form of common energy policy is required to tackle Europe's deficiencies and to encourage investment in new forms of energy. The most radical part of the Commission's Green Paper, which hopes to resolve the continent's energy difficulties, centres on a plan for a deal with Russia, which supplies one quarter of Europe's gas.

ENERGY TAX: See **Carbon Tax**

ENGRENAGE is a term that comes from a French expression meaning 'getting caught up in the gears'. It relates closely to the '**Monnet method**' of integration, whereby individuals, governments, interest groups and European Communities institutions, having embarked on a particular course of action, find themselves compelled to take additional measures that deepen European integration.

ENHANCED CO-OPERATION was substantially overhauled at the **intergovernmental conference** convened in Nice in December 2000, specifically by listing in a single provision the 10 conditions necessary to establish enhanced co-operation. Although the essential characteristics of this instrument (whereby enhanced co-operation should only be taken as a measure of last resort) were not changed significantly, there were some notable alterations. For example, the minimum number of Member States required to establish enhanced co-operation was designated as eight, rather than a majority, thus facilitating use of enhanced co-operation on the **enlargement** of the European Union.

In pillar I (the European Communities) and in pillar III (**police and judicial co-operation in criminal matters**) the possibility of opposing enhanced co-operation (by employing a veto) has been removed. With regard to pillar II on the **common foreign and security policy** (CFSP), the deliberations in Nice made it possible to establish enhanced co-operation for the implementation of joint action or a common position; this does not apply to matters of defence. Authorization for enhanced co-operation rests with the **Council of the European Union**, and the Council will decide by **qualified majority voting** (QMV). Member States are still entitled to ask the Council to adopt a decision by unanimity if they are convinced that an issue is of particular importance. When enhanced co-operation concerns an area determined by the **co-decision procedure**, the assent of the **European Parliament** is required. Assuming that the **Treaty establishing a Constitution for Europe** is ratified, a number of significant changes concerning enhanced co-operation will be introduced. First, the minimum number of states needed for enhanced co-operation will change from eight to one-third of the total membership. Second, the launching of enhanced co-operation will no longer require unanimity but QMV. The exception will be the CFSP, where unanimity will still be necessary. And third, in those policy areas where the Council acts by unanimity, member states participating in enhanced co-operation will be able to use QMV and introduce co-decision when adopting measures except those that have either military of defence implications. Finally, the Treaty establishing a Constitution for Europe envisaged a further form of enhanced co-operation – **permanent structured co-operation** – under the European security and defence policy.

ENLARGEMENT is a general term used to describe the process of admission of new states into the European Union (EU). The procedures for enlargement are contained in Article 49 of the **Treaty on European Union**. All applicants for membership must possess a democratic form of government, respect the principles on which the EU is based (i.e. liberty, democracy, respect for **human rights** and fundamental freedoms, and the rule of law), and be prepared to accept not only the provisions of the **European treaties**, but also the *acquis communautaire*, the accumulated **legislation** of the European Communities (EC). Because of the last-mentioned requirement and the desire of both Member States and applicants to protect their own interests as much as possible, negotiations tend to be complex and protracted. The **European Commission** undertakes an analysis of each country's application focusing on both the economic situation and political stability of each state. Thereafter the Commission presents its *avis* to the **Council of the European Union,** where a decision on the applicant will be made. If negotiations are successful and an **Accession Treaty** is signed, this must be ratified by the **national parliaments** of the acceding states, all the Member States and, since the **Single European Act**, also by the **European Parliament** (EP).

The first round of enlargement involved applications in 1961–62, and again in 1967, from **Denmark, Ireland, Norway** and the **United Kingdom**. On each occasion, the UK application was vetoed by **France**, and the other three applicants chose not to pursue the matter further without the United Kingdom. The applications were renewed in 1970, leading to the signing of Treaties of Accession in 1972. As a result of a national referendum, Norway declined to join. The other three states became full members of the EC on 1 January 1973. The second and third rounds involved **Greece, Portugal** and **Spain**, all of which applied for membership after establishing a democratic form of government in the mid-1970s. Greece formally became a member on 1 January 1981, followed by Portugal and Spain on 1 January 1986.

The EC decision to create an **internal market** was a matter of concern to the **European Free Trade Association** (EFTA) states, most of which between

1989 and 1992 eventually submitted formal applications for membership. Negotiations with **Austria, Finland**, Norway and **Sweden** were concluded in 1994, with membership offered subject to **ratification**. Following another national referendum, Norway again declined membership, but the other three states joined the EU on 1 January 1995.

After the collapse of Communism in Eastern Europe in 1989, most of the newly democratized states indicated an interest in seeking membership in the medium term. The EC's response was that this would be limited in the first instance to members of the **Visegrad Group**, namely **Hungary, Poland** and the former Czechoslovakia (see the **Czech Republic** and **Slovakia**). Other applicant states have been **Turkey** in 1987, and **Cyprus** and **Malta** in 1990. These applications initially met with considerable resistance within the EU even though the countries had all signed **Association Agreements**. However, in 1996 the **European Council** decided that **accession negotiations** with Cyprus would begin six months after the conclusion of the 1996 **intergovernmental conference.**

By this time the EU had also received applications for membership from the 10 Central and Eastern European countries with which **Europe Agreements** had already been signed: Hungary, Poland, **Romania**, Slovakia, **Latvia, Estonia, Lithuania, Bulgaria**, the Czech Republic and **Slovenia**. This block of applications constituted the largest enlargement of the EU to date and also the most difficult, given the economic challenges facing the countries of **Central and Eastern Europe**. As a result, the EU progressed with the applications cautiously. In 1997, as part of **Agenda 2000**, the European Commission, using the **accession criteria** established in 1993 at the **Copenhagen Summit**, assessed each country's ability to fulfil membership obligations, and recommended that accession negotiations begin with Hungary, Poland, Estonia, the Czech Republic and Slovenia. Negotiations with these five countries (plus Cyprus) began in March 1998. Meanwhile, the other applicants were included in an 'inclusive and evolutive' accession process, and would have to wait until late 1999 before they, along with Malta – which had renewed its application for membership in 1998 – were recommended for negotiations. Following the recommendation, the European Council, meeting in Helsinki in December 1999, decided to open negotiations in 2000. Moreover, it conferred on all the applicant states, including Turkey, the status of **candidate country.**

The completion of accession negotiations currently requires the closure of 35 chapters, most of which deal with particular areas of the *acquis communautaire* (e.g. **competition policy**, the **Common Agricultural Policy**, telecommunications policy, and **energy policy**). In the case of 10 **candidate countries** – Cyprus, the Czech Republic, Estonia, Hungary, Latvia, Lithuania, Malta, Poland, Slovakia and Slovenia – the then 31 chapters were finally closed in December 2002. This paved the way for the EU to enlarge to 25 Member

States on 1 May 2004. As a consequence, the EU underwent its greatest enlargement to become a union covering another third of the European continent and comprising nearly 500m. people.

Prior to the 2004 enlargement, each of the candidate countries, as well as the Member States, had to ratify the **Accession Treaty** signed on 16 April 2003. Nine candidate countries – the exception being Cyprus – successfully held referenda on EU membership between March and September 2003. At the same time, negotiations with Bulgaria and Romania continued, with the EU committing itself to realizing the two countries' goal of membership in 2007. Turkey, meanwhile, continues to present a more problematic case, and the Commission is working with the Turkish authorities to ensure that the country is able to meet the **Copenhagen criteria**. To this end, the EU provided Turkey with increased financial assistance and agreed to open negotiations in December 2004. The prospects for Turkish accession look decidedly gloomy, especially after President **Jacques Chirac** of France decreed in early 2005 that the French people would be able, through a referendum, to permit or prevent Turkish membership. The issue of Turkey featured as a strong element in the debate leading up to the French referendum on the **Treaty establishing a Constitution for Europe** in May 2005.

Enlargement is not a straightforward process, since it has budgetary implications and threatens to result in institutional paralysis unless there is institutional reform. This is why since the mid-1990s the EU has been seeking to reform its most significant areas of expenditure – the **Common Agricultural Policy** (CAP) and the **structural funds** – as well as its institutions. Progress on the former was made at the Berlin Summit meeting of the European Council in March 1999 when a new **financial perspective** for 2000–06, and reforms to the CAP and structural funds, were agreed. Prior to the 2004 enlargement the EU provided pre-accession assistance to the candidate countries. This included €1,500m. annually under the **PHARE** programme; €1,000m. annually under the **Instrument for Structural Policies for Pre-Accession**; and €540m. annually under the Special Accession Programme for Agriculture and Regional Development (**SAPARD**). Less progress was initially made on institutional reform. Measures introduced by the **Treaty of Amsterdam** prepared the EU only marginally for future enlargement, by avoiding any significant changes to the institutions so as to enable them to cope with the extra demands that would be placed on them. However, the following reforms were introduced as a result: a limit was placed on the size of the EP; the European Commission was to undergo a review process; the **co-decision procedure** was simplified; and agreement was reached on greater use of **qualified majority voting** in the Council of the European Union, to ensure that decision-making was not slowed down unduly. In **protocol**s attached to the **Treaty of Amsterdam** references were made to the fact that each Member State would have only one Commissioner after enlargement: the larger Member States have two Commissioners each at present. The Treaty also promised that a further review of the institutions was to take place if the EU grew to more than 20 Member States. In other words, the key decisions on institutional reform were postponed.

The whole array of institutional issues relating to enlargement was tackled more fully by the **Treaty of Nice**, agreed by the governments of the 15 existing Member States in December 2000. This reformed the Commission, the **Court of Justice** and the **Court of First Instance**; extended qualified majority voting; re-allocated votes in the Council of the European Union; and agreed the distribution of votes and seats in an enlarged EU of 27 members. Yet concerns that the reforms were insufficient to ensure that a substantially enlarged EU could function smoothly persisted. The result was the **European Convention's** reform proposals contained in the **draft Treaty establishing a Constitution for Europe**. Many of these survived the **intergovernmental conference** launched in October 2003 and appear in the Treaty establishing a Constitution for Europe.

The enlargement process is unlikely to end with the admission of all the current applicants, and it is not improbable that in time other European states such as **Albania** and other states of the former **USSR** and of the former **Yugoslavia** will seek EU membership. In fact, **Croatia** submitted its application to join in February 2003 and this was followed in 2004 by **Macedonia**. In June 2004, the European Council announced that accession negotiations with Croatia would begin in 2005, which eventually happened in October of that year. Moreover, membership bids from other countries in Western Europe cannot be ruled out. Norway may apply again and **Switzerland** may reactivate its 1992 application. **Ukraine**, following the 'orange revolution' and the election of the pro-Western Victor Yushchenko, has also expressed great interest in future EU membership.

However, there are increasing concerns being voiced that the EU does not have sufficient 'absorption capacity' to admit more states beyond Bulgaria and Romania in 2007-2008. Such concerns have become particularly prominent following the rejection of the Treaty establishing a Constitution for Europe in the referenda in both France and the **Netherlands**. A widespread assumption is that the EU will have to undergo further institutional reform before it moves beyond a membership of 27. In addition, it is recognized that much needs to be done to convince public opinion in the existing Member States of the value of enlargement. Currently popular support for further enlargement, and in parti- cular the admission of Turkey, is far from universal.

ENTERPRISE POLICY aims to ensure that the European Union (EU) helps to stimulate a climate in which enterprise, industry and innovation flourish.

Enterprise is crucial to the EU's economic growth and the EU hopes to foster and encourage innovative business practices that will create jobs and promote growth. Enterprise policy has been designed at EC level to meet the requirements of the entire business community (whether large or small businesses) and its environment. Article 157 in Title XVI of the **Treaty of Rome** provides the legal basis for enterprise policy. Historically, work on enterprise policy has consisted of three key areas: **small and medium-sized enterprises** (SMEs), innovation and competitiveness, and making the most of opportunities and benefits arising from the single market. The level of European Communities (EC) interest in all three aspects is evident from the number of action programmes and **Green** and **White Papers** dedicated to these matters over the last two decades.

Support for SMEs dates back to 1983 and the adoption of the first EC action programme to assist their development. The business community currently places considerable emphasis on the notion of promoting innovation; in 1995 the **European Commission** produced a Green Paper on this subject, and this led in 1996 to the first action programme for innovation in Europe. This identified several objectives, including the need to promote an innovation culture; to create a good business environment; and to foster more effective links between research, innovation and business.

Enterprise policy has also been facilitated by the Commission's promotion of competitiveness, an initiative that was most apparent in its 1993 'White Paper on Growth, Competitiveness and Employment'. In January 2000 a new **Directorate-General** (DG) for Enterprise policy was created, with a range of responsibilities combining some of those previously held by the DG for Industry with the innovation activities that had previously been dealt with by the information society DG. In March 2000, at a meeting of the **European Council** in Lisbon, the 15 Member States confirmed the promotion of enterprise policy to be a new strategic objective for the EU, a measure which it is hoped will transform the EU into one of the most competitive and dynamic knowledge-based economies in the world, capable of sustained economic growth and higher levels of employment.

In April 2000 the Commission produced a communication on the challenges ahead for enterprise policy, which envisaged an 'Enterprise Europe' by 2005. This was accompanied by a proposal for a multi-annual programme to consider how enterprise policy can meet the challenges of globalization and the new knowledge-driven world economy. In December 2000 a new multi-annual programme on enterprise and entrepreneurship was adopted, focusing specifically on the role of SMEs (which provide the largest number of jobs across the EU) and built on the earlier EC action programmes. The current aims of the Commission's enterprise policy are: to develop an entrepreneurial spirit; to promote an innovative business environment which makes good use of research and technology and fosters competition; to get more from the **internal market** by tackling some of the remaining barriers to trade and to facilitate trade in transport; to provide for greater co-ordination and sharing of experiences among the EU Member States (to include benchmarking and sharing best practice); and lastly, to stimulate new business models in the 'e-economy' through the promotion of new information and communication technologies.

The collection and dissemination of examples of innovative practice are crucial for the success of 'Enterprise Europe'. To facilitate information exchanges and examples of best practice, the Commission aims, through its new Business Environment Simplification Task Force (BEST) procedure, to highlight the results and experiences of businesses engaged in innovation through seminars, conferences, peer reviews and studies. Enterprise policy is financed by various sources. Although the principal source is the multi-annual programme on enterprise and entrepreneurship, grants for training programmes, protecting the environment and fostering co-operation, for example, can be obtained from the **European Investment Bank** and the **structural funds**.

The first **ENVIRONMENTAL ACTION PROGRAMME** (EAP) of the European Communities (EC) was introduced in 1973. The current, and sixth, EAP was proposed by the **European Commission** in January 2001, and is entitled *Environment 2010: Our future, our choice*. It covers the period 2001–2010 and is an integral element of EC **environmental policy.**

The **ENVIRONMENTAL CHEMICALS DATA INFORMATION NETWORK** (ECDIN) is a database that also contains the **European Inventory of Existing Commercial Chemical Substances** (EINECS).

ENVIRONMENTAL POLICY was not specifically mentioned or provided for in the **Treaty of Rome**. The **Single European Act** gave the European Communities (EC) competence, and this was extended into a policy remit by the **Treaty on European Union** (TEU). The objectives are those that the EC has pursued for some time. The aim of EC environmental policy is to preserve, protect and improve the quality of the environment and to protect people's health. The TEU added another dimension: the promotion of measures for dealing with global environmental problems. The concept of sustainable development was enshrined in the **Treaty of Amsterdam** as one of the EC's objectives. Moreover, environmental protection requirements were given greater emphasis in other EC policies, and especially in relation to the single market. Significantly, the Treaty also simplified decision-making by allowing **co–decision**

procedure to replace **co-operation procedure** where the latter had applied to certain parts of environmental policy-making.

Together these objectives simply reflect EC activity since an environment policy was adopted in 1972, after which specific environmental problems were incorporated into a series of five-year programmes for dealing with generalized issues of environmental enhancement and protection. The main policy principles were defined in the first **Environmental Action Programme** (EAP): the polluter must pay the costs of repair to the environment; prevention of environmental damage is preferable to remedial measures; and all EC initiatives in all policy areas must take their likely effect upon the environment into account. The TEU further stressed the precautionary principle and the need for environment policy to take into account the regional economic diversity of the European Union (EU).

Environmental policy has become increasingly significant for the EU. More than 300 **directives** or **regulations** on the environment had been adopted by the mid-1990s. Since then there has been a noticeable decline in the number of regulations and directives, reflecting the sensitivity and controversy surrounding environmental policy or, more accurately, the costs of implementing tougher environmental regimes that impact either on central and local government or on the business community. Nevertheless, activity has concentrated on six broad problem areas: water; **atmospheric pollution**; noise; chemical products; waste disposal; and the preservation and restoration of natural habitats and the conservation of wildlife. Several directives deal with the pollution of all forms of water and with relevant quality standards, and the EC have participated in international conventions dealing with the reduction of pollution in international waterways and rivers. Other directives cover the discharge of pollutants into the atmosphere from industrial plants, and exhaust emissions from motor vehicles. Maximum noise levels have been established for a range of machinery and household equipment. Chemical products have been subject to regulation since 1967. Control of chemicals became more urgent after the Seveso incident in Italy in 1976, leading to a range of further directives on their manufacture and usage, and on safety precautions. A **European Inventory of Existing Chemical Substances** (EINECS) was established in 1986. The EC committed themselves to reducing chlorofluorocarbons (CFCs) by 85% by 2000, and in 1993 the **European Commission** proposed the elimination of hydrochlorofluorocarbons by 2014. To protect natural habitats and conserve wildlife, a number of directives relate to the preservation of species and to scientific experiments on animals. Funds have been provided for the preservation of natural habitats, and the EC have signed several international conventions on the conservation of wildlife. EC **legislation** also covers the dangers posed by radiation. Following the accident at the Chernobyl nuclear power station in the former **USSR** in 1986, maximum levels of radiation contamination in foodstuffs were set.

As part of the EC's efforts to promote awareness of environmental issues and encourage companies to do likewise, an **Eco-Management and Audit Scheme** (EMAS) was set up in 1995. Participation is voluntary and involves industrial companies undergoing an independent audit of their environmental performance. In the area of transport, harmful emissions from road vehicles were to be reduced by 60%–70% by 2010, and measures were agreed to lower the allowable limits for certain chemical substances in petrol and diesel fuel by 2000. Leaded petrol was to be phased out, for most vehicles, by 2000. There has also been legislation concerning the protection of groundwater resources, waste disposal in landfill sites, genetically engineered foods, and trade in endangered species. In 1997 the European Commission agreed to provide funding for 188 environmental projects.

The fourth EAP (1987–92) increased EC activity, conferring stronger powers on the European Commission, including the right to take Member States to the **Court of Justice** for non-compliance with environmental legislation. As part of the task of raising public awareness, 1987 was designated as the European Year of the Environment (EYE), and the Network for Environmental Technology Transfer (NETT) was established to aid the realization of its activities. The pursuance of these objectives was potentially strengthened by the 1990 decision to set up a **European Environment Agency** (EEA) and a special environment fund, **LIFE**. The EC also agreed, in principle, to introduce a **carbon tax**. The importance of these measures and programmes was reiterated in the fifth EAP (1993–2000), which also stressed that EC activity must be more anticipatory, less devoted to problem-solving, focusing more on the causes of environmental problems as part of a commitment to 'sustainable development'. The programme lists several initiatives that should be pursued, including better resource management by industry, the curbing of consumer demand for products that generate pollution, the development of more environmentally friendly agriculture and a more effective management of mass tourism. The sixth EAP (2002–2012), entitled *Environment 2010: Our future, our choice*, was guided by the fifth programme and defines the priorities and aims of EC environmental policy to 2012. Four areas are given particular emphasis: climate change, nature and bio-diversity, environment and health, management of natural resources and waste. It also identifies explicitly the measures needed to implement successfully the EU's sustainable development strategy, which has been given much wider prominence following the adoption of the EU Sustainable Development Strategy in 2001.

In December 2003 the European Commission adopted its first ever Environmental Policy Review. This review should be placed within the context of the 2000 Lisbon Strategy which was supplemented by a third economic **pillar** after the adoption of the EU Sustainable Development Strategy at the Gothenburg **European Council** summit in 2001. The primary objective of this review was to examine the most pressing threats to the environment and to report on developments since 2001 in both EU and national environmental policies. Essentially, this report maintained that more needed to be done to improve the state of the environment and it recommended, in order to ensure a credible policy of sustainable development, that the following three steps must be taken: the integration of environmental concerns into other policy areas; the implementation of existing environmental legislation; and the provision of more information on environmental themes. The challenge confronting the EU and its Member States is to ensure, on the one hand, the development of balanced policies that are designed to stimulate growth and investment, and, on the other hand, the protection of the environment and human health for future generations.

The environment remains an increasingly fundamental aspect of EU activities. An initiative launched in January 2004, deriving from the priorities of the sixth EAP, envisaged a 'Thematic Strategy on the Urban Environment'. This communication from the Commission seeks to identify the problems and challenges facing urban areas. Environmental problems are a global concern and in the last decade there have been high-profile conferences at the international level (Rio de Janeiro, 1992; Kyoto, 1997; and The Hague, 2000) to address the issues of ozone depletion and global warming. However, these have made only modest progress towards tackling the necessary reduction of dangerous emissions. Nevertheless, this international dimension has enabled the EU to establish a global presence in the field of environmental policy, a position that has led it into dispute with the **USA**. The sixth EAP specifically refers to an international context and also to the next phase of EU **enlargement**. As regards the latter, it encourages an extended dialogue with the administrations of all the **applicant countries** over issues such as sustainable development. It also seeks to encourage greater public participation in environmental debates.

EP: See **European Parliament**

EPC: See **European Political Co-operation**

EPU: See **European Payments Union**

EQUAL is a European Communities (EC) initiative funded by the **European Social Fund** which seeks to address discrimination and inequality experienced by those in work and those looking for **employment**. A total of €3,000m. was allocated to the initiative for the period 2000–06. The initiative builds on the work undertaken as part of the New Opportunities for Women (NOW) programme, which ran from 1990 to 1999 and provided support for actions and programmes that would have a significant and beneficial effect on the provision of employment and training opportunities for women. The second round of EQUAL runs from 2004 to 2008.

EQUAL OPPORTUNITIES are the responsibility of a unit within the **Directorate-General** (DG) for Employment and Social Affairs of the **European Commission**. Sometimes also known as Action on Employment and Equality for Women, the unit is charged with developing and implementing European Communities policy on **women's rights**, and also has a duty to ensure that gender equality is taken into account in other policy areas. The fourth Community Action Programme on the Promotion of Equal Opportunities for Women ran from 1996 to 2000. The **Treaty of Amsterdam** contained a new **article** (Article 13) that reinforced the principle of non-discrimination, and authorized the **Council of the European Union** to take appropriate action to combat discrimination based on sex, racial or ethnic origin, religion or belief. (See also **Charter of Fundamental Rights**; **Charter of Fundamental Social Rights of Workers**; **Citizens' Rights**; **Equal Pay**.)

EQUAL PAY policy was laid down in Article 141 of the **Treaty of Rome**. While it refers specifically to gender discrimination, obliging the Member States to 'ensure and subsequently maintain the application of the principle that men and women should receive equal pay for equal work', the Article has been taken to refer to equality in general. A series of **directives** between 1975 and 1986 extended the meaning of equal pay for equal work, as well as enabling those who consider themselves to be discriminated against to take their case, without fear of dismissal or reprisal, to a national tribunal. Where there is a difference of opinion over the meaning of European Communities **law**, the question may be referred to the **Court of Justice**, whose rulings are binding on all national bodies.

ERASMUS stands for European Community Action Scheme for the Mobility of University Students, a programme established in 1987 with the purpose of encouraging students to spend an integral part of their studies at a university in another country of the European Communities (EC). This programme of student mobility was widened to include **European Free Trade Association** (EFTA) countries in 1991 and countries from **Central and Eastern Europe** as well as **Cyprus** in 1998. The periods of study abroad are recognized by the students' home universities by means of a course credit transfer scheme. The original goal was that some 10% of the EC student population would be participants in the scheme by 1992. Despite the problems created by linguistic diversity and different national systems of higher education, ERASMUS proved a huge success. Its popularity increased the costs of the programme at a time when EC expenditure came under closer scrutiny, leading to pressure for the target figure to be reduced to 5% of the student population. ERASMUS encompassed more than just student mobility, and contained chapters on: teacher exchanges; joint preparation of courses, where at least three establishments from different countries pool their resources to create a programme of study, a module, a curriculum or a Master's programme; intensive programmes (such as summer schools); and thematic networks on a subject area or a specific platform for analysis and discussion of a European theme. The Thematic Network in Public Administration (based at Leiden University), for example, is an initiative whereby academics meet on an annual basis to discuss the Europeanization of public administration and to seek co-operation and teaching links across Europe. ERASMUS became part of the **Socrates** programme in 1995.

ERASMUS MUNDUS has been designed as a co-operation and mobility programme in the field of higher education. It aims to promote the European Union as a centre of excellence in learning around the world. It supports European top-quality Masters Courses and enhances the visibility and attractiveness of European higher education in third countries. It also provides EU-funded scholarships for third country nationals participating in these Masters Courses, as well as scholarships for EU nationals studying in third countries.

ERDF: See **European Regional Development Fund**

ERM: See **Exchange-Rate Mechanism**

ERTA **JUDGMENT**: See *AETR* **Judgment**.

ESA: See **European Space Agency**

ESA: See **European System of Integrated Economic Accounts**

ESC: See **European Economic and Social Committee**

ESCB: See **European System of Central Banks**

ESDP: See **European Security and Defence Policy**

ESF: See **European Social Fund**

ESPRIT: See **European Strategic Programme for Research and Development in Information Technology**

ESRO: See **European Space Research Organization**

The **ESSEN SUMMIT** took place in the German city of that name on 9–10 December 1994. It was held mainly to discuss the potential **enlargement** of the European Union (EU) to include countries of **Central and Eastern Europe**, and the policy changes that would be necessary if those countries were to be admitted. The summit brought together the heads of government of the existing Member States, of **Austria**, **Finland** and **Sweden**, which joined the EU in January 1995, and of all those Central and Eastern European states that had signed **Europe Agreements**.

ESTI is the European Solar Test Installation at Ispra, the **Joint Research Centre** (JRC) establishment in Italy.

ESTONIA joined the European Union (EU) on 1 May 2004. It is one of the smallest Member States, with a population of some 1.4m. Following the collapse of the **USSR** in the early 1990s, the Baltic states of Estonia, **Latvia** and **Lithuania** immediately began to develop closer links with Western Europe and particularly the EU. The EU responded by providing technical (see **PHARE**) and financial assistance to Estonia. Relations with Estonia progressed swiftly from a free-trade agreement to a **Europe Agreement**, and then to preparations for eventual EU membership. Estonia applied for membership in November 1995 and participated in the first wave of **accession negotiations**, which began in March 1998. Negotiations were completed in December 2002, the outcome being approved by popular referendum nine months later. In a turn-out of just over 64%, two-thirds (66.8%) of voters voted in favour of accession. Estonia had opted to approve the **Treaty establishing a Constitution for Europe** through the normal parliamentary process rather than holding a referendum, and the government remains determined to press on with **ratification**, even after events in **France** and the **Netherlands**.

ETF: See **European Training Foundation**

ETSI is the European Telecommunications Standards Institute, set up in 1987 to harmonize European technological specifications and standards in the field of

telecommunications. ETSI aims to harmonize standards in the European Union through the development of mandatory norms known as 'common technical regulations'. The Institute is based near Nice, **France**.

ETUC: See **European Trade Union Confederation**

EU: See **European Union**

EUA: See **European Unit of Account**

EUDOR superseded ABEL, which was a database comprising the contents of the 'L' series of the *Official Journal of the European Communities* (OJ), which enabled users to order legal texts, documents and publications directly from the **Office for Official Publications of the European Communities** (EUR-OP). EUDOR is an electronic archive system accessible via the Internet, updated daily, allowing greater **transparency** of, and accessibility to, European law.

EUI: See **European University Institute**

EUMC: See **European Monitoring Centre on Racism and Xenophobia**

EUMETSAT is the acronym of the European Organization for the Exploitation of Meteorological Satellites, a body that was established in 1986. Most of the European Union (EU) Member States belong to EUMETSAT, which does not have formal links with the EU. EUMETSAT formalized the co-operation between the national meteorological institutions, which began with the launch of the first European meteorological satellite in 1977, and took over the operational programme agreed upon in 1981. Funded by the national authorities, EUMETSAT works in conjunction with the **European Space Agency** (ESA).

EURAM: See **BRITE-EURAM**

EURATEX is the European Apparel and Textile Organisation and represents the European textile and clothing industry on matters of common interest. Its main objective is to promote the interests of its members while taking into account the European Union's institutional framework and its international obligations. It resulted from the merger of various textile and clothing organizations, including the Co-ordinating Committee for the Textile Industries in the EEC (COMITEXTIL) in 1994.

EURATOM: See **European Atomic Energy Community**

EUREKA is the acronym of the European Research Co-ordination Agency, a body established in 1985 in Brussels. It originated from an initiative by President **François Mitterrand** of **France** to establish a programme of non-military **research and technological development** that would keep the European Communities (EC) at the forefront in these fields. EUREKA was intended to be responsible for a European Programme for High Technology Research and Development agreed to by several European countries, including non-EC states. EUREKA is more a sponsor of projects than a programme, and in that sense it overlaps with the activities of the European Co-operation in the field of Scientific and Technical Research (**COST**) programme. It has launched well over 100 separate transnational collaborative projects in a diverse number of fields, including factory automation, ceramic turbines, computers, lasers and robotics. It raises most of its funding from private sources or on the capital markets, since the EC and the Member States of the European Union make only relatively small contributions to its budget.

EURES was established in 1994 as the successor to **SEDOC**. SEDOC was the acronym of the European System for the International Clearing of Vacancies and Applications for Employment, an agency established by the **European Commission** to operate a scheme that would permit Member States to exchange information on job opportunities for migrant workers. In 1980 the Council of Ministers (see **Council of the European Union**) adopted a **resolution** on the co-ordination of national employment policies. SEDOC's activities were extended to become a kind of job placement service for the European Communities (EC) as part of the objective of balancing the supply and demand for labour throughout the EC. It was complemented by the Electronic Loan Insurance Scheme for Employment (ELISE), to which it was linked. EURES operates as a network to liaise between the public employment services of the Member States along with those of two other countries and the European Commission in order to exchange data relating to employment. The network also lists 50,000–100,000 employment vacancies daily, and is available online.

EURISTOTE is an online directory of university theses and studies on the theme of European integration.

EUR-LEX is a European Communities database containing the contents of the *Official Journal of the European Communities* (OJ) 'L' and 'C' series. It was to be extended to include all **legislation** in force, along with the treaties, proposals for legislation, and recent judgments of the **Court of Justice**. EUR-LEX is available online, and is updated daily.

The **EURO** (€) was adopted in 1995 as the name of the common currency of the European Union (EU), and was to replace the **European Currency Unit** on a one for one basis at the start of **economic and monetary union** (EMU). By 1998, however, only 11 Member States (the Euro-11) had agreed to proceed with EMU and adopt the euro on 1 January 1999. (**Greece** did not meet the **convergence criteria** at that time – but joined in 2001 – and **Denmark**, **Sweden** and the **United Kingdom**, as seen below, decided not to join.) On 1 January 1999 the conversion rates of the participating Member States between themselves and against the euro were fixed, and a single monetary policy implemented by the new **European Central Bank** (ECB) and the **European System of Central Banks** (ESCB).

The movement towards EMU and a single currency in the EU was slow. However, pressure from business and financial sectors within the EU forced governments to co-operate and to harmonize their approach to introducing a common currency. **Belgium** was the first Member State to announce that its government departments would change over to the euro. In all participant Member States there was to be a transition period between 1999 and 2002 (by which time euro banknotes and coins were to have been introduced), during which national budgets would be drawn up in national currencies, but payments by government departments would be in euros. From 1999 businesses were to be able to make social security contributions and pay taxes in euros. They would also be able to establish capital in euros. Moreover, in participating Member States, with the exception of **Germany**, tax returns would be accepted in euros, and in most participating states people would be able to pay their taxes, including income tax, in euros. Financial markets were also to use the euro.

The three Member States remaining outside the euro area were to continue to work towards EMU. In 1998 Denmark retained the position it held during the **Treaty on European Union** (TEU) debate in 1992, remaining firmly opposed to the idea and the practice of the single currency. Despite broad support from government and business circles, the people of Denmark voted against Danish adoption of the euro by a narrow margin in 2000. Sweden held a referendum in September 2003, as a result of which it too elected not to join the euro area. The UK government, although realizing that British business will participate in the euro area to an extent, remains cautious about full participation and, faced with considerable public opposition to the euro, continues to postpone any plans for a referendum on the issue.

EURO INFO CENTRES are maintained by the European Communities (EC) in major cities of Member States. They mainly provide services for the business community. Pamphlets and documents published by the EC are available from them, often free of charge.

EURO-12 COUNCIL: See **Eurogroup**

EURO-AIM is the European Organization for an Audio-visual Independent Market. It is part of the MEDIA programme (see **Media Policy**), and its purpose is to offer independent producers in Europe a support and advice service for the marketing and sale of their products. EURO-AIM is based in Brussels.

The **EURO-ATLANTIC PARTNERSHIP COUNCIL** (EAPC) is the forum in which members of the **North Atlantic Treaty Organization** (NATO) meet on a regular basis with representatives of its 27 partner countries to discuss political and security-related issues and develop co-operation in a wide range of areas. It replaced the **North Atlantic Co-operation Council** in 1997.

EUROBAROMETER is the name of a series of public opinion polls carried out and published on a biannual basis throughout all the Member States of the European Union (EU) since 1973. The operation is the responsibility of **Eurostat**. All kinds of topics are covered by the questionnaires used for polling purposes. These include questions on knowledge of the EU institutions, questions on the availability of information on the EU and questions on a range of EU policies. As well as providing profiles of the European population, the Eurobarometers are used by the **European Commission** and its agencies for planning purposes.

EUROCODES are common codes for the European construction industry, which are intended to standardize and replace the different national specifications for materials, skills and personnel.

EURO-COOP: See **Consumer Committee**

EUROCORPS is the name given to an integrated transnational military unit formally inaugurated in November 1992, following agreement at the 59th

Franco–German summit in La Rochelle in May 1992. Its origins lay in a joint Franco-German brigade formed in 1991. Its supporters have argued that it could become the nucleus of a European army at the centre of a reconstructed **Western European Union** (WEU), and therefore a central element of security in the European Union (EU). In July 1993 **Belgium** indicated that it would join the Eurocorps. **Spain** agreed to contribute troops to the force in December 1993 and **Luxembourg** joined in May 1996. Based in **Strasbourg**, the Eurocorps became operational in November 1995. From May 1995 it was complemented by two new WEU bodies: Euroforce (based in Florence, **Italy**) and Euromarforce (a maritime force serving the Mediterranean), constituted by **France**, **Italy**, **Portugal** and Spain. Since Eurocorps' establishment, the EU has gradually taken over many of the roles of the WEU as part of the development of a **European security and defence policy** (ESDP). Hence, in June 1999, at the Cologne meeting of the **European Council**, it was announced that Eurocorps would be put at the disposal of the EU for crisis response operations. It was subsequently decided that Eurocorps would become part of the **European Rapid Reaction Force**, a process that began in June 2001.

EUROCRAT is a colloquial term used to describe a bureaucrat or administrator employed by the European Communities.

EURODICAUTOM is a Commission database containing multilingual terms for use by translators.

EUROFER: See **European Confederation of Iron and Steel Industries**

The **EUROGROUP** is the informal council of economic and finance ministers of the 12 Member States participating in **economic and monetary union**. It held its first meeting in **Luxembourg** in June 1998. The group, sometimes also referred to as euro-X or Euro-12 group, was to be a forum for policy co-ordination rather than decision-making, which would still exist under the aegis of what is now the **Economic and Financial Affairs Council of Ministers**, the monthly meetings of the finance ministers of the 25 full Member States of the European Union.

EUROIZATION refers to the process whereby non-participants in **economic and monetary union** link their national currency to the **euro** (€). Examples include Montenegro and **Bosnia-Herzegovina**.

EUROJUST is a European Union body charged with promoting co-operation among Member States authorities dealing with the investigation and prosecution of serious cross-border and organized crimes. Established in 2002, it comprises a representative from each of the Member States. See also **police and judicial co-operation in criminal matters**.

EUROKOM was set up as a teleconference and electronic mail facility that would contain details of organizations and enterprises seeking partners in other Member States for participation in projects of the **European Strategic Programme for Research and Development in Information Technology** (ESPRIT) and the European Research Co-ordination Agency (**EUREKA**).

EUROLAND, sometimes also referred to as the 'eurozone', is an informal way of referring to those 12 European Union Member States (i.e. all apart from **Denmark, Sweden, the United Kingdom** and the 10 Member States which joined the EU in May 2004) participating in full **economic and monetary union**, having replaced their national currencies with the **euro.**

The **EURO-MEDITERRANEAN ECONOMIC AREA** (EMEA) is the medium-term goal of the **Euro-Mediterranean Partnership** and involves the creation of a Mediterranean free-trade area by 2010. Based on the idea of the **European Economic Area**, this is a key element of the European Union's **Mediterranean policy.**

The **EURO-MEDITERRANEAN PARTNERSHIP** (EMP) lies at the heart of the **Mediterranean policy** of the European Union (EU). Often referred to as the **Barcelona Process**, the EMP was launched in 1995 and involves the Member States of the EU and 10 non-Member States in the Mediterranean region: Algeria, Egypt, Israel, Jordan, Lebanon, Morocco, the Palestinian Authority (now Palestinian Autonomous Areas), Syria, Tunisia and **Turkey**. The three main components of the partnership are: political and security partnership; economic and financial partnership; and partnership in social, cultural and human affairs. Agreements have been concluded in a range of specific policy areas such as energy, the environment, media and migration. They are supported through finance from the **MEDA** programme.

EURONET DIANE: See **Direct Information Access Network for Europe**

EURONORMS, or Ens, were originally standards produced by the **European Coal and Steel Community** covering the quality, dimensions, tolerances and methods of testing of steel, as well as providing a glossary of terms. The term was later also used for more general European standards set by **CEN** and **CENELEC**.

EUR-OP: See **Office for Official Publications of the European Communities**

EUROPA is the name of the main **European Commission** Internet information site (europa.eu.int), which provides information on the institutions and activities of the European Communities.

EUROPE AGREEMENTS are types of **Association Agreement** and were concluded by the European Communities with countries in **Central and Eastern Europe** (CEE) subsequent to the latter's democratization after 1989. The first such Agreements were signed in December 1991, and by mid-1995 existed with nine countries (**Bulgaria**, **Czech Republic**, **Estonia**, **Hungary**, **Latvia**, **Lithuania**, **Poland**, **Romania** and **Slovakia**). A further agreement was signed with **Slovenia** in June 1996, which came into effect in early 1999. Each agreement provided for free trade in industrial goods, political dialogue, wide-ranging co-operation and legislative **harmonization**. Bilateral institutions were also established to manage the association created. After concluding Europe Agreements, each of the CEE countries went on to apply for membership of the European Union (EU). All except Bulgaria and Romania joined the EU on 1 May 2004. When devising **stabilization and association agreements** for the countries of the **Western Balkans**, the **European Commission** drew heavily on the structure and content of the Europe Agreements.

EUROPE BY SATELLITE (EbS) is the TV news agency of the European Union. It provides EU-related information for professionals working in television and radio and for other European institutions. EbS transmits via satellite a 'free to air' signal. It can be received in the European Union, as well as the Mediterranean region and central and eastern Europe. For the rest of the world (**Asia**, Africa, Latin America, southern region of the **USA** and north Australia), EbS provides an hour-long selection from its daily transmissions in collaboration with Canal France International (CFI). EbS is also available via the Internet. The Commission wants to make much more of this resource, and sees it as a valuable tool in its communications strategy.

EUROPE DAY refers to 9 May 1950, the day when **Robert Schuman**, the French Foreign Minister, presented **Jean Monnet**'s proposal for the creation of a new European institution that became the **European Coal and Steel Community**. This date marks the birth of what is now known as the European Union (EU), and 9 May is now celebrated across the EU as Europe Day. The day is marked by activities and festivities that aim to enhance the relationship between the EU and its citizens.

The **EUROPE DIRECT INFORMATION NETWORK** was announced as a new initiative in May 2005 and is supposed to provide a new means for the EU to communicate (in theory) with ordinary citizens. The new information centres will provide, among other things, brochures on how the EU works and takes **decisions** and also about EC laws, institutions and policies. It is even intended to host live television broadcasts. The network is open to all Member States and it will have a presence (of some 400+ offices) in every country in the EU except the **United Kingdom**. The UK government's reluctance owes much to its fears that such activities will be deemed as propaganda tools and give rise to greater charges by Eurosceptics of interference by Brussels. However, the network's supporters argue that this is an attempt to encourage debate among the public, especially in the UK, where knowledge of the EU, according to **Eurobarometer** statistics, is particularly weak.

EUROPE OF DEMOCRACIES AND DIVERSITIES was a group comprising a number of anti-European Union parties in the **European Parliament**. Formally known as the Europe of Nations group after the 1994 elections, they regrouped and renamed themselves the Europe of Democracies and Diversities Group after the 1999 elections. Some 16 **Members of the European Parliament** belong to the group. In 2004 this group remodelled itself once again and formed the **Independence and Democracy Group (IND)**.

EUROPE OF THE REGIONS is a phrase that came into common usage in the late 1980s. It was used by those who wished local and regional authorities, many of which already maintained liaison offices in Brussels, to have a greater input into the European Communities. Its importance was recognized by the establishment of the **Committee of the Regions** under the **Treaty on European Union**.

The **EUROPEAN AGENCY FOR THE EVALUATION OF MEDICINAL PRODUCTS** (EMEA) is a decentralized agency of the European Communities established by the **Council of the European Union**. Located in London, it began operations in early 1995. It is responsible for the licensing of all human and veterinary medicinal products in the European Union (EU), and for monitoring their efficacy. Once a **pharmaceuticals** company has obtained a licence, it may sell its products anywhere in the EU, bringing to an end Member States' former protective practices in the interests of their own companies. However, national regulatory bodies continue to operate and provide an alternative means for approving new drugs in the EU.

The **EUROPEAN AGENCY FOR RECONSTRUCTION** (EAR) was established in February 2000 and is based in Thessaloniki, **Greece**. It is responsible for management of the main European Union (EU) assistance programmes in **Serbia and Montenegro** (the former Federal Republic of Yugoslavia) and the former Yugoslav Republic of **Macedonia** (FYROM). It is an independent EU agency, which is accountable to the **European Council** and the **European Parliament**, and is overseen by a governing board (comprising the **European Commission** and representatives from the Member States). The EAR evolved from a previous commitment made by the European Council to assume an active role in helping the reconstruction and recovery of the Kosovo region, but this was extended in late 2000 to cover the whole of the Federal Republic of Yugoslavia. In December 2001 the agency also acquired management responsibility for the FYROM. Since its creation, the agency has overseen the dispersal of over €2bn in assistance. The agency has three main objectives: to conduct immediate physical and economic reconstruction (repair of infrastructure and public utilities); to lay the foundations for the development of a market-orientated economy; and to support the establishment of democracy, respect for **human rights** and the rule of law (e.g. freedom of press and judiciary).

The **EUROPEAN AGENCY FOR SAFETY AND HEALTH AT WORK** is a decentralized European Communities agency, established in 1995 to promote the exchange of information and co-operation on measures dealing with health and safety at work. It is located in Bilbao, **Spain**.

The **EUROPEAN AGRICULTURAL GUIDANCE AND GUARANTEE FUND** (EAGGF), also widely known by its French acronym, FEOGA, was established in 1962 to finance the **Common Agricultural Policy** (CAP). The EAGGF comprises two sections. The Guidance Section of the Fund provides support for agricultural restructuring and modernization, and is, therefore, one of the **structural funds** of the European Community. Its activities have not been controversial, as it takes up only some 5% of the CAP budget. Even so, the amount of its funding has been substantial. The EAGGF is dominated by its

Guarantee Section, which operates the common price structure of the CAP with the objective of maintaining agricultural incomes. It is the Guarantee Section which has been the source of the controversies surrounding the CAP and which has contributed to its soaring costs. In 1988 it was agreed that future increases in EAGGF funding for guarantees would be limited to the rate of growth of the total gross national product (GNP) of European Communities (EC) states. Several further measures were introduced to reduce agricultural production and, in the long-term **budget** proposed by the **European Commission** in 1993, the EAGGF share of EC funds was set to fall further, though still remaining substantial.

The **EUROPEAN ANTHEM** adopted by both the European Union in 1986 and the **Council of Europe** in 1972 for use on ceremonial occasions, consists of the words of Schiller's *Ode to Joy* as set to music in the final movement of Beethoven's Ninth Symphony.

EUROPEAN ARMAMENTS, RESEARCH AND MILITARY CAPABILITIES AGENCY: See **European Defence Agency**

The **EUROPEAN ARREST WARRANT (EAW)** allows a person to be transferred from one Member State to another without the judiciary having to go through a formal extradition procedure, where a person is wanted for criminal prosecution or for a custodial sentence. The Council Framework decision on a European Arrest Warrant was agreed on 13 June 2002 and came into force in January 2004. The following eight Member States applied the regime from that date: **Belgium**, **Denmark**, **Ireland, Finland**, **Portugal**, **Spain**, **Sweden** and the **United Kingdom**. The remaining Member States failed to meet the implementation deadline of 31 December 2003 laid down in Article 34(1) of the Framework Decision on the EAW.

The **EUROPEAN ATOMIC ENERGY COMMUNITY** (EAEC) is also known by its acronym Euratom. One of several sectoral organizations conceived by **Jean Monnet**, the EAEC was established in 1957 at the same time as the **European Economic Community**. At the time, it was regarded by many supporters of integration as potentially the more significant initiative. The aims of the EAEC are defined as promoting research and disseminating technical information; establishing uniform safety standards; facilitating investment and the establishment of the necessary basic installations for the development of nuclear energy; ensuring a regular and equitable supply of ores and nuclear fuels; preventing the improper use of fissile materials; exercising the right of ownership over fissile materials (mainly uranium and plutonium); developing wide commercial outlets; and working for progress in the peaceful uses of nuclear energy. The EAEC has experienced many problems, being from the outset somewhat overshadowed by other developments in the European Communities (EC). Technical problems, costs and worries about nuclear safety have hindered its work, and the EAEC has found it difficult to control and direct national developments.

However, EC **energy policy** has placed considerable emphasis on nuclear energy. In seeking to facilitate nuclear research, the **European Commission** has the right to insist that national programmes are co-ordinated in order to avoid unnecessary duplication of effort. It also undertakes regular reviews of nuclear research and indicates areas of possible future research. It was under the aegis of the EAEC that the **Joint Research Centres** and the **Joint European Torus** were established. Beyond research, the EAEC may also help states to acquire nuclear ores and materials: supply policy is administered through the EAEC Supply Agency. While bound by the obligations of professional secrecy, the Commission is entitled to receive details of all relevant patents sought or obtained in the Member States. In certain circumstances, it may seek licences to use them through a compulsory purchase order, although this would probably be impossible to implement without the consent of the Member State concerned. There have also been several initiatives on **health and safety** standards for workers in the industry. The Commission may also demand the imposition of extra precautions where particularly dangerous experiments are being conducted, especially if these may affect other Member States. The task of the routine monitoring of nuclear installations is, however, the responsibility of the Member States.

From its inception the EAEC was considered the least significant of the three founding communities, and its identity and sense of autonomy essentially disappeared following its merger with the EC executives in 1967 (see **Merger Treaty**). Recent concerns about the safety of nuclear installations and doubts about their economic viability may well further reduce the significance of nuclear energy and the role of the EAEC.

EUROPEAN AVIATION SAFETY AGENCY (EASA): See **Air Transport Policy**

The **EUROPEAN BANK FOR RECONSTRUCTION AND DEVELOPMENT** (EBRD) is a body whose purpose is to provide aid for countries in **Central and Eastern Europe** that have adopted a democratic form of government and have managed the transition towards stable market economies. A proposal from the French President, **François Mitterrand**, for the creation of such a body to assist these regions was accepted in December 1989 by the **European Council** in Strasbourg, which also agreed to the participation of other Western countries (something that had not been part of the original French proposal). The EBRD was sited in London and its first president was Jacques Attali, a close associate of Mitterrand. The bank began operations in March 1991, with a membership of European and other countries belonging to the International Monetary Fund (IMF), as well as the European Communities (EC) and the **European Investment Bank**. The EC took a 51% stake in the enterprise, which set out to help eligible countries with market transition, privatization programmes, direct investment and environmental rehabilitation. In 1992 participation was extended to the successor states of the **USSR**. It was affected by scandal in 1993 when it was disclosed that it had spent more on furnishing its headquarters in London and on expense accounts than it had advanced in loans. In addition, there was a strong view that its establishment had been primarily a political gesture, since it could not provide anything not already available from the IMF and the International Bank for Reconstruction and Development (IBRD – World Bank). The scandal toppled Attali, who was replaced by Jacques de Larosière, and it was under the latter's tenure that the EBRD secured international credibility and began to see returns from its investments in Central and Eastern Europe. With a subscribed capital totalling some €20 billion, the EBRD has a solid capital base. The strength of the Bank's capital and its prudent operational and financial policies are reflected in the EBRD's triple A credit rating. The EBRD has played a significant role in the redevelopment of 27 countries, mostly the former Soviet states and countries of Central and Eastern Europe. As well as boosting economic transformation, the EBRD has promoted political change, with loans conditional on guarantees that countries apply the principles of multi-party democracy and are openly pluralist. By 2006 there were some 60 members who had placed capital subscriptions with the EBRD. Jean Lemierre took office as the fourth president of the European Bank for Reconstruction and Development on 3 July 2000, and was reappointed for a second four-year term of office in 2004.

The **EUROPEAN BROADCASTING UNION** (EBU) is an international federation of broadcasting organizations formed in 1950 and based in Geneva, **Switzerland**. Its membership includes all the Member States of the European Union. The EBU has encouraged collaboration and development within European broadcasting, especially in terms of increasing the European content of programming, but it has no authority over national broadcasting networks. It has collaborated with the **European Commission** on several initiatives. Its most recognizable broadcast in the United Kingdom, outside the sporting arena, remains the annual Eurovision Song Contest.

EUROPEAN BUSINESS AND INNOVATION CENTRE NETWORK (EBN) is a **European Commission** initiative to encourage **small and medium-sized enterprises** (SMEs), and to ensure that they are able to benefit from European Communities **competition policy** and the **internal market**. It is essentially an advisory body that disseminates information on innovations and ideas to companies. (See also **European Venture Capital Association**; **SME Task Force**; and **Business and Innovation Centres**.)

The **EUROPEAN CAPITAL OF CULTURE**, which was known as the European City of Culture until 1999, is one of the best-known examples of the fledgling cultural policy of the European Communities (EC). The programme dates from 1985 and was temporarily included under the EC's **Kaleidoscope** programme for general cultural events; it is now funded as part of the EC **cultural policy**. It has subsequently become one of most keenly sought-after titles among cities across Europe. Cities are chosen by Member States and are given a subsidy by the **European Commission**. Recent Capitals of Culture include Weimar, Avignon, Bergen, Bologna, Brussels, Helsinki, Kraków, Rey-kjavik, Prague and Santiago de Compostela (2000), Porto and Rotterdam (2001), Bruges and Salamanca (2002), Graz (2003), Genoa and Lille (2004), Cork (2005) and Patras (2006). Future cultural capital cities will include Lux-embourg (2007) and Liverpool (2008).

A **EUROPEAN CENTRAL BANK** (ECB) has long been held to be essential to **economic and monetary union** (EMU) as a body with powers to issue the European single currency (the **euro**) and control monetary policy. The **Treaty on European Union** confirmed that the ECB would come into operation at the beginning of the third stage of EMU, between 1997 and 1999. Its leadership is provided by an Executive Board of six individuals, appointed for a non-renewable period of eight years. They formulate policy in conjunction with the governors of the national central banks of the participating Member States, making up a 17-member Governing Council. A General Council is made up of the President and Vice-President of the ECB along with the governors of the national central banks of the 25 Member States.

During stage two of EMU, the ECB was preceded by a **European Monetary Institute** (EMI). In 1993 it was agreed that the ECB would be located in Frankfurt am Main, **Germany**, and it was formally established in June 1998. The first president, appointed for a period of eight years, was Wim Dui-senberg. He was replaced in July 2003 by **Jean-Claude Trichet**, formerly Governor of the Banque de France.

Prior to the launching of stage three of EMU in January 1999, the ECB's capital was just under €4,000m. The national central banks of the Member

States are the only subscribers to and holders of the ECB's capital. The percentage shares of the national central banks of the Member States in the ECB's capital were initially set by the ECB Governing Council in June 1998 (based on the Member States' respective shares in the gross domestic product and population of the European Communities). They were subsequently revised, with effect from 1 January 2004, and are now as follows: **Austria** 2.3019; **Belgium** 2.8297; **Denmark** 1.7216; **Finland** 1.4298; **France** 16.5175; Germany 23.4040; **Greece** 2.1614; **Ireland** 1.0254; **Italy** 14.5726; **Luxembourg** 0.1708; **Netherlands** 4.4323; **Portugal** 2.0129; **Spain** 8.7801; **Sweden** 2.6636; and the **United Kingdom** 15.9764. They were due to be revised again owing to the 2004 **enlargement** of the European Union.

EUROPEAN CENTRE FOR THE DEVELOPMENT OF VOCATIONAL TRAINING (CEDEFOP) is a service agency of the **European Commission**, established in 1975. Originally located in Berlin, CEDEFOP relocated to Thessaloniki, **Greece**, in 1995. It is charged with the task of encouraging the development of vocational and in-service training for adults, and of standardizing national qualifications. It assists the Commission in the preparation of European Union training programmes. Much of its recent work has focused upon the employment problems of women, especially those who wish to return to work after a long absence. Its work is directed by a council consisting of representatives from the national governments, employers, trade unions and the Commission. CEDEFOP is closely involved with the **European Training Foundation**, with **Eurostat** and with the **Leonardo** programme.

EUROPEAN CITY OF CULTURE: See **European Capital of Culture**

The **EUROPEAN CLIMATE CHANGE PROGRAMME** (ECCP) is a European Communities initiative launched in June 2000. Its main purpose is to identify and develop all the necessary elements of a European Union strategy to implement the Kyoto Protocol to the **United Nations** Framework Convention on Climate Change, the purpose of which was to reduce 'greenhouse' gas emissions to 8% below 1990 levels by 2008–12.

The **EUROPEAN COAL AND STEEL COMMUNITY** (ECSC) was the body that emerged from the **Schuman Plan**. It was established by the **Treaty of Paris** of 18 April 1951, which was effective from 23 July 1952 until 23 July 2002 when the ECSC was disbanded. Formed by the **Six** European states (**Belgium**, **France**, the Federal Republic of **Germany**, **Italy**, **Luxembourg** and the **Netherlands**) which later went on to create the **European Economic**

Community (EEC) and the **European Atomic Energy Community** (EAEC or Euratom), the ECSC had as its general objective the fostering of 'economic expansion, growth of employment and a rising standard of living' in the Member States through the development of a common market in **coal** and **steel**. The common market would commence after a transitional period of five years.

The ECSC's historic importance lies in the fact that it was the first European organization to embrace supranationalism. This was represented by the executive High Authority, which was complemented as an executive by a Council of Ministers. Its indirectly elected Assembly, though possessing only advisory powers, was the first European assembly with a legally guaranteed basis. The other institutions of the ECSC were a **Court of Justice** as a final arbiter of the Treaty of Paris, and a Consultative Committee of representatives of national interest groups. This institutional framework was the model used later for the EEC.

The ECSC enjoyed some success in the 1950s, presiding over a large expansion in output, although this was due as much to world economic conditions as to the ECSC. However, it failed to cope satisfactorily with a major crisis in the coal industry in 1959 and to overcome the many barriers to the establishment of a common market. Moreover, it did not by itself make much progress towards political integration. One of its major problems was that it was difficult to achieve co-ordination and integration in only one economic sector; it was difficult, if not impossible, to isolate coal and steel from the national economies in general. This was a major reason for the switch by the Six from **sectoral integration** to the broader EEC.

With the establishment of the EEC and Euratom, the ECSC lost all its independent institutions except for its two executive bodies. In 1967 these were merged with those of the other two European Communities (EC). The ECSC continued, however, to have a semi-independent existence, with its own source of **revenue**, derived from a direct levy upon coal and steel producers, and its own budget out of which it financed development and restructuring plans for the industries. It also set prices and supervised production levels in the coal and steel industries. Much of its activity had to be devoted to helping remedy the severe social and economic consequences of the reduction in the workforces of both industries through early retirement schemes, retraining and redeployment, especially in those regions where these industries had traditionally dominated the local economy. The **European Commission** inherited the powers of the old High Authority over the coal and steel industries, powers which were much more substantial than in most policy areas of the EC, and used them to the extent of seeking the declaration of a state of **manifest crisis**, which gave the Commission even greater powers of direction and punishment. A state of manifest crisis was declared in the steel industry between 1980 and 1988.

The **EUROPEAN COMMISSION**, officially known as the Commission of the European Communities, was established as one of the two executive institutions of the European Communities (EC). As opposed to the the Council of Ministers (see **Council of the European Union**), which represents the Member States, the Commission has been regarded as both the European, or supranational, and the administrative arm of the EC executive. The term refers to both the collectivity of the Commissioners (currently 25 in number) and the administrative apparatus that serves them. The obligations of the Commission are laid down in Article 211 of the **Treaty of Rome** as initiation, supervision and implementation. It was to share decision-making powers with Council of Ministers), but since in most instances the Council cannot take any action in the absence of Commission initiatives, the Commission became, in effect, the central formulator of **legislation** in the EC. As to supervision, the Commission was given a general responsibility to ensure that other EC institutions and the Member States fulfilled those tasks and provisions assigned to them under the **founding treaties**. It had a duty to ensure that **decisions** taken by the Council were carried out, or adhered to, by the Member States, making it responsible for the implementation of EC legislation. In addition to these general areas of constitutional obligation, the Commission came to enjoy further and significant autonomous authority in the operation of the **Common Agricultural Policy** (CAP) and EC **competition policy**. A further area of autonomy lay, after the 1967 **Merger Treaty**, in its inheritance of the substantial decision-making powers of the previous High Authority of the **European Coal and Steel Community**, which gave it the right to act without regard to the Council of Ministers.

These constitutional powers do not give a complete picture of the overall role acquired by the European Commission since 1957. The extent of its activities, along with its unelected nature, has made it the most controversial of the EC institutions. While its original activism under the leadership of **Walter Hallstein** was obstructed by President **Charles de Gaulle** of **France** in the **empty chair crisis**, events internal and external to the EC after the early 1980s contributed to a new dynamism on the part of the Commission, especially under the first half of the presidency of **Jacques Delors** (1985–95). The **Treaty on European Union** (TEU) made few constitutional changes to the Commission's role. Some of those changes recognize an extension of its competence, while others perhaps indicate a reduction in its independence (see below). Moreover, the **Treaty of Amsterdam** stipulates that the President of the Commission must be formally approved by the **European Parliament** (EP). However, the Treaty also enhances the authority of the President as the Commission prepares to review its organization and procedures prior to **enlargement**.

With the establishment of the European Union (EU), the European Commission continued to uphold the **founding treaties** and the *acquis communautaire* by monitoring other institutions and the Member States, although its exclusive **right of initiative** was compromised. In extreme circumstances, it can seek to enforce implementation by prosecuting an offending institution or Member State in the **Court of Justice**. The Commission is also required to advise on matters regarding the treaties, and even volunteers advice where it deems necessary. In order to fulfil this function, the Commission has had to develop a vast network of consultative and advisory bodies and contacts. It continues to take decisions in conjunction with the Council and the EP or, as with the CAP and competition policy, in its own right. The TEU gave it additional initiative authority in the areas of **social policy** and **economic and monetary union**. The Treaty further gave the Commission the right to be fully involved in the work of the two intergovernmental **pillars** that would stand alongside the EC: it can seek to initiate action within these pillars and even propose that some areas of responsibility should be transferred to the EC pillar. The Commission must also carry out the duties and responsibilities conferred upon it by the Council of the European Union. To fulfil all these obligations, the Commission has to utilize a considerable number of resources. It controls the adminis-trative apparatus of the EC, currently employing a workforce of some 17,000 people. These are mainly based in **Brussels**, but some are in **Luxembourg**, in EU offices in Member States or in delegations to non–member countries. Others, primarily engaged in scientific projects, are located in centres through-out the EU.

The Commission is also responsible for the financial management of the EC. It prepares the preliminary draft annual budget that must be submitted to both the Council of the European Union and the EP for approval and adoption. It is further responsible for the administration of the **budget** and the allocation of money from the budget to the **structural funds**, other programmes and salaries. The TEU imposed more stringent controls and **accountability** on the Commission. A further responsibility is the representation of the EC abroad. It is the Commission that negotiates international agreements on behalf of the EC, and that maintains and staffs EC offices in other countries. Finally, because of its multifarious roles, the Commission has one further task. It has become widely regarded as the body that deals with the problems and issues that other EC institutions cannot or will not tackle. An activist Commission can seek to utilize this role to maintain the momentum of integration.

The Commissioners meet formally, as the College of Commissioners, once a week to discuss an agenda that has been prepared in advance. Additional and sometimes more informal meetings can be held to discuss general questions of European development, or more specific problems. If a majority of Commis-sioners are present, a meeting is considered to be quorate and decisions are taken by a simple majority. Once the Commission has taken a decision, however, its members are expected to abide by the principle of collective responsibility.

The Commissioners are, in practice, appointed by the national governments, although formally governments submit nominations for approval by the Council of the European Union. Each Member State is entitled to nominate one Commissioner, while the five largest states (France, **Germany**, **Italy**, **Spain** and the **United Kingdom**) were initially each entitled to nominate a second Commissioner. The accession of **Austria**, **Finland** and **Sweden** to the EU in January 1995, and the virtual certainty that additional countries from **Central and Eastern Europe** would join in the first decade of the 2000s, caused concern that the Commission might become too unwieldy. The Treaty of Amsterdam subsequently envisaged limiting each Member State to one Commissioner following further enlargement, as long as the weighting of the votes in the Council of the European Union had been modified in order to compensate those Member States losing the chance to nominate a second Commissioner. The **Treaty of Nice** also limited the expansion of the Commission following EU enlargement (see below).

On assuming office, each Commissioner has to take an oath of loyalty to the EC, swearing that he or she will serve EC interests exclusively, and will not seek or take instructions from any national government or other body. Commissioners are appointed for a five-year term, which is renewable. The fact that about one-half are not reappointed for a further term suggests that Commissioners who act more independently than their governments might wish do not receive a further nomination. Most Commissioners have previously been national politicians, and normally belong to the party, or one of the parties, making up the government that submits their nomination. A few have previously been bureaucrats, industrialists or trade union leaders. Of the two British appointees, despite the fact that nominations were made by the Prime Minister, one had always been drawn from the ranks of the major opposition party. There is no means of dismissal other than by a collective vote of censure in the EP. Since 1995 terms of office for Commissioners have begun after the election of the EP and coincided with the duration of the Parliament. Since 2004 each Member State has been entitled to nominate one Commissioner. In other words, France, Germany, Italy, Spain and the United Kingdom all lose a Commissioner and in total there are 25 Commissioners. The new team of 25 took up office in November 2004, two weeks later than planned after the mini-crisis of the **Buttiglione** affair.

Before the TEU, the President of the European Commission was appointed by the Council of Ministers for a two-year term, but in practice this was automatically extended to four years, with **Walter Hallstein** and **Jacques Delors** serving even longer. The Presidents of the Commission and the year of their appointment are as follows: Walter Hallstein 1958; Jean Rey 1967; Franco Maria Malfatti 1970; Sicco Mansholt (see **Mansholt Plan**) 1972; **François–Xavier Ortoli** 1973; **Roy Jenkins** 1977; **Gaston Thorn** 1981; Jacques Delors 1985; **Jacques Santer** 1995; **Romano Prodi** 1999. **José Manuel Barroso** was nominated by the **European Council** as President in 2004 and was subsequently approved by the European Parliament. The EP endorsement, it should be noted, was far from being universal and the votes came down as 413–251 for him to succeed Romano Prodi. While the President has rather less authority over Commission members than does a national prime minister over ministers in a government, the view of the President as just one of several Commissioners increasingly belied the true role of the office, which was enhanced and clarified by the TEU. The Treaty ensured that the EP must be consulted on nominations for the presidency, which are made by the Council of the European Union, and the Council's choice then requires **ratification** by the EP, along with the other proposed members of the Commission. Under the terms of the TEU the President now has the formal right to be consulted on the selection of other Commissioners. This enhanced presidential authority reflects the established practice of the President attending **European Council** meetings, representing the EC at international meetings and reporting on proposals and progress to the EP. However, under the terms of the TEU the President did not have the power to dismiss other Commissioners from office, and had only a limited influence upon the distribution of portfolios, which was ultimately a collegiate decision. Some portfolios are more important than others, and larger Member States tend to believe they have a prior claim to these. Equally, each newly appointed Commissioner, because of personal interest or because a policy area is important for his or her own country, will have a personal preference. Before the TEU, six of the Commissioners were also appointed as Vice-Presidents: these offices, however, had little political significance, and the Treaty reduced the number of Vice-Presidents to two.

Each Commissioner has a portfolio, which usually consists of several areas of policy responsibility, and which may not correspond exactly to the fields of activity of the **Directorates–General** (DGs) and the special services that together constitute the administrative arm of the EC. While the relevant sections of the bureaucracy report directly to the appropriate Commissioners, the latter have adopted the French practice of employing **Cabinets**, a group of personally appointed advisers and aides answerable solely to their Commissioner, providing him or her with assistance and liaising with other Commissioners and the various parts of the administration.

The Treaty of Amsterdam increased the Commission's role in formulating international agreements on services and intellectual property rights, to be exercised at the discretion of the Council. The Treaty also stipulated that a further review of the Commission had to be undertaken.

The Commission can be dismissed *en bloc* through a vote of censure by the EP. In January 1999 the EP's Socialist group (see **Group of the Party of European Socialists**) presented a censure motion, in order to ensure the Commission's **accountability** in the face of allegations of fraud, financial mismanagement and nepotism. Although a compromise deal ensured that the motion was defeated, concessions won by the EP during the dispute were widely felt to mark a significant reduction in the extent of the Commission's perceived autonomy. This was reinforced two months later, when an independent report into the allegations found considerable evidence of incompetence and corruption and, while detailing charges against several Commissioners, also judged the Commission to be collectively responsible for a 'dysfunctional' political environment, marked by a culture of evasion and an absence of leadership. On 16 March 1999, for the first time in its history, the Commission resigned *en masse*. The Commissioners retained their positions and exercised limited duties until a new Commission was appointed. The EP ratified the appointment of Romano Prodi as President of the Commission, and of the new Commissioners, in late 1999. The EP also exerted its power in the autumn of 2004 when it successfully threatened to block the incoming Barroso Commission unless Commissioner-designate Rocco Buttiglione was replaced.

The Commission under Prodi, whose term ran until the autumn of 2004, launched a programme of wide-ranging reforms and two important White Papers. The first of these, on governance, proposed to modernize the institutional machinery of the Commission, and the second to increase **transparency**, efficiency and interaction with outside interests (the public, **non-governmental organizations** and the private sector). The Barroso commission has launched a more ambitious five-year programme that was first presented to the EP in January 2005. It seeks to unleash Europe's potential and has placed its emphasis on policies that will bring economic growth and secure and create more jobs. The proposals are not unproblematic and Barroso has been swift to pre-empt left-wing critics by arguing that such 'liberal' policies are essential in order to narrow social disparities and protect the environment. Other priorities include: the need for investment in research and development; greater consideration of how to tackle problems such as climate change; and the sustainable management of natural resources as well as initiatives to bring the states of the **Western Balkans** closer to EU membership.

The Treaty of Nice made a further significant alteration to rules pertaining to the **nomination procedure** for the Commission. Under its terms, the nomination of the President is a matter for the European Council acting by **qualified majority**, rather than unanimity. This appointment still has to be approved by the EP. Once a President is selected, he or she then liaises with the Council to adopt a list of other Commissioners who in turn require endorsement from both the Council and the EP. Moreover, the Treaty of Nice increased the Commission President's powers to allow him or her to decide on how the Commission is structured internally; to enable him or her to allocate portfolios, and if necessary to reassign policy portfolios; and to enable him or her to demand the resignation of an individual Commissioner.

Regarding the future, the **Treaty establishing a Constitution for Europe** envisages further reform of the size of the Commission and in the appointment of the Commission President. Regarding the former, from 2014 the size of the Commission will correspond to two-thirds of the number of Member States. In an EU of 27 members, therefore, there will be 18 members of the Commission. These will be selected on the basis of equal rotation among the Member States. Hence, each Member State will have a national of theirs in two out of every three Commissions. Which Member States provide members of the Commission and when will be determined by a unanimous decision of the European Council. The rotation is to reflect 'satisfactorily the demographic and geographical range' of all Member States. Where the post of Commission President is concerned, it is envisaged that the European Council's role will be reduced to proposing a candidate who will then be elected by the European Parliament.

EUROPEAN COMMISSION HOST ORGANIZATION: See **I*M GUIDE**

The **EUROPEAN COMMISSION OF HUMAN RIGHTS** is a body established in 1953 that operates under the aegis of the **Council of Europe** in **Strasbourg**. Although it has no formal connection with the European Communities, the latter accept the principles that govern the operation of the Commission and acknowledge its role in the field of **human rights**, including the right to investigate alleged infringements of the **European Convention on Human Rights** by and within the Member States. These can be brought before the **European Court of Human Rights**.

EUROPEAN COMMITTEE FOR ELECTROTECHNICAL STANDARDIZATION: See **CENELEC**

The **EUROPEAN COMMITTEE FOR IRON AND STEEL STANDARDS** (ECISS) is a body established in 1986 that replaced an Iron and Steel Nomenclature and Co-ordinating Committee. Its purpose was to replace national iron and steel standards with common European standards.

EUROPEAN COMMITTEE FOR STANDARDIZATION: See **CEN**

The **EUROPEAN COMMITTEE TO COMBAT DRUGS** (CELAD) is a group within the **TREVI** framework established in December 1989. It was intended to follow up work carried out since 1971 by the so-called Pompidou Group of the **Council of Europe** on the promotion of collaborative measures within the European Communities (EC) and between the EC and other states and international organizations on drugs-related problems and issues, especially the illegal traffic in drugs, the monitoring of drugs that have a potential for being misused, and the prevention of the laundering of money gained from drugs-trafficking.

A White Paper on a **EUROPEAN COMMUNICATIONS POLICY** was published in early February 2006. This policy is being presented by the **Commission** as a new approach to explaining what the EU does, and is an attempt to try and close the recognized gap in interest between EU citizens and EU policy-makers. The **Barroso** Commission made communication one of its strategic priorities in 2005, and the White Paper sets out 50 practical steps which the Commission can take immediately to improve communication and thereby enhance democracy and legitimacy within the EU. The White Paper comprises five key parts. These are identified under the following headings: Putting Communication at the Service of Citizens; Taking Work Forward; Working with the Media and New Technologies; Understanding European Public Opinion; and Doing the Job Together. In short, the entire document seeks both to inform and consult the public about EU policies. It is to be welcomed and explores ways that these objectives could be realized. It talks of the need to enhance debate and dialogue through the creation of a European Public Space, and hopes to empower citizens through a number of civic education programmes and more public consultations. It aims to make greater use of the media and, for example, intends to open the EU institutions to the public via web TV. The aims are laudable but the Commission recognizes the necessity of working with Member State governments as well as regional and local authorities, political parties and civil society organizations if it is to successfully engage with the wider public. It will be interesting to observe how the **Council** responds to this paper.

EUROPEAN COMMUNITIES (EC) is a term that describes the unified body that resulted from the merger in 1967 of the administrative networks of the **European Economic Community** (EEC), the **European Coal and Steel Community** (ECSC) and the **European Atomic Energy Community** (EAEC or Euratom). The term was also formerly used to describe collectively the signatories of the three Communities' **founding treaties** and their territories. The singular of the term (European Community) has been widely used as an alternative for both meanings.

The main institutions of the EC are the **European Commission**, the **Council of the European Union** (known as the Council of Ministers until November 1993), the **European Parliament** and the **Court of Justice**. Under the **Treaty on European Union** (TEU), signed in 1992, the EC institutions became one of the three **pillars** of the broader European Union (EU). Although European Union was subsequently the preferred term for the collective Member States, it nevertheless remained correct to refer to the relevant institutions as the EC and to the law made by the Court of Justice as EC law.

Following the first **enlargement** beyond the original **Six** Member States, the EC expanded progressively until, by May 2004, the EU had **Twenty-Five** Member States.

EUROPEAN COMMUNITY (EC) is the often-used singular of the term **European Communities**. Following **ratification** of the **Treaty on European Union** (TEU), it also became the official title of the **European Economic Community** (EEC).

EUROPEAN COMMUNITY ACTION SCHEME FOR THE MOBILITY OF UNIVERSITY STUDENTS: See **ERASMUS**

EUROPEAN COMMUNITY CONSUMER CO-OPERATIVES: See **Consumer Committee**

The **EUROPEAN COMMUNITY HUMANITARIAN OFFICE** (ECHO) is a division of the **European Commission**. This office, established in 1992, is based in Brussels and aims to provide emergency humanitarian assistance and food aid to many parts of the world including the countries of the former **Yugoslavia**, the **African, Caribbean and Pacific** (ACP) **States**, the Near and Middle East, the **Commonwealth of Independent States** and the Far East. ECHO aims to meet the immediate needs of victims of mostly man-made disasters world-wide, in such areas as assisting displaced persons, and health, sanitary and mine-clearance programmes. In 2005 ECHO granted €652,499m. in humanitarian aid, which funded aid and projects in more than 80 countries and zones of conflict world-wide.

EUROPEAN COMMUNITY LAW: See **Law**; **Court of Justice**; and **Court of First Instance**

EUROPEAN COMMUNITY STUDIES ASSOCIATIONS (ECSAs) are nationally-based academic organizations that support research on all aspects of the European integration process. The activities of the European associations are co-ordinated through ECSA-Europe, an umbrella organization largely funded by the **European Commission**. ECSA-US in the **USA** is the largest national group. The representative organization in the **United Kingdom** is the University Association for Contemporary European Studies (UACES).

EUROPEAN COMMUNITY TRADE MARKS OFFICE: See **Office for Harmonization in the Internal Market**

EUROPEAN COMPANY STATUTE: See **Company Law Statute**

The **EUROPEAN CONFEDERATION OF IRON AND STEEL INDUSTRIES** (EUROFER) is a voluntary cartel formed by most of the **steel** producers of the European Communities in 1976. The initiative was taken by the **European Commission**, which hoped that such a body would be able to deal more decisively with a continuing crisis caused by decreasing demand for steel, poor productivity, an under-utilization of capacity, and the reluctance of national governments to accept mass redundancies. EUROFER was meant to work for a rationalization of the industry, assisted by the Commission, through reductions in output, to bring productivity and capacity more in line with demand. It had some limited success, but its voluntary nature could not persuade national governments always to follow its guidelines, nor could it prevent individual companies from taking unilateral action to protect themselves. Today, EUROFER continues to promote co-operation amongst national federations and companies in matters concerning the development of the European steel industry. It also represents the common interests of its members vis-à-vis third parties, notably the EU institutions and other international organizations.

The **EUROPEAN CONFERENCE** was established to provide a framework for dialogue between the European Union and applicant states. It was launched, following a French initiative, at the Luxembourg summit of the **European Council** in December 1997, primarily to provide a forum in which **Turkey**, excluded from the accession process launched in 1998, could participate. It meets once a year at the level of heads of state or government and once a year at foreign minister level. It first convened in London in March 1998. The European Conference brings together the existing **Fifteen** Member States and the **applicant countries**. It creates a multilateral forum for the discussion of questions of interest to both parties, and especially those related to economic affairs, regional co-operation and issues under the **common foreign and security policy** (CFSP) and **justice and home affairs** (JHA) **pillars** of the EU.

The **EUROPEAN CONFIDENCE PACT FOR EMPLOYMENT** was put forward by **European Commission** President, **Jacques Santer**, in January 1996 as part of the proposals to the **European Council** on Action for Employment in Europe (see **employment**). Its main aim was to increase employment in the European Union (EU), and its activities centred on macro–economic policy: improving the **internal market**, adopting employment systems, curbing state aids (see **subsidies**), promoting education and training as well as focusing on the EU's structural policies. Santer travelled to all EU Member States and held numerous meetings with employers and trade unions in order to gain support for his plan. Around 60 trial pacts were established in order to focus attention at the local level on initiatives to combat unemployment. However, in general, Member State governments remained rather unenthusiastic about the proposals, while employers signalled degrees of scepticism about its value. Santer's inability to gain widespread support for the plan represented a significant setback for the Commission. Employment issues were tackled more directly by the Member States in the **Treaty of Amsterdam**.

EUROPEAN CONSTITUTION: See **Treaty establishing a Constitution for Europe**

EUROPEAN CONSUMERS' ORGANIZATION (BEUC): See **Consumer Committee**

The **EUROPEAN CONVENTION**, formally the **Convention on the Future of Europe**, and not to be confused with the **European Convention on Human Rights**, was launched on 28 February 2002 under the chairmanship of the former French President, **Valéry Giscard d'Estaing**. It brought together representatives of the heads of governments and of the parliaments of the Member States and the **candidate countries**, representatives from the **European Commission** and the **European Parliament**, as well as a number of observers. In total there were 207 participants (including alternates) whose task was to debate the issues raised by the **Laeken Declaration** and formulate an agenda for the **intergovernmental conference** (IGC) that began work in October 2003.

The Convention was modelled on that which successfully drafted the **Charter of Fundamental Rights** in 2000, and was a response to growing concerns about popular perceptions of the remoteness of IGCs. Supporters of the Convention believed that it was more likely than an IGC to reach decisions on the future of the European Union (EU) that would accurately reflect the concerns and wishes of EU citizens. While this may have been a key assumption behind the launching of the Convention, the deliberations of the 207 participants failed to generate much popular interest. The same was generally true of the Convention's output, the **draft Treaty establishing a Constitution for Europe,** which was adopted 'by consensus' in June and July 2003 and forwarded to the **European Council**.

The **EUROPEAN CONVENTION ON HUMAN RIGHTS**, the full title of which is the European Convention for the Protection of Human Rights and Fundamental Freedoms, is a document sponsored in 1950 by the **Council of Europe**. It represents an unprecedented system of international protection for **human rights** and enables individuals to apply to the courts for the enforcement of their rights. It came into operation in 1953. All the Member States of the European Union (EU) are signatories of the Convention and, in accepting it, the EU has also accepted the role and predominance in this area of both the associated **European Commission of Human Rights** and the **European Court of Human Rights**. The EU is not a signatory to the Convention although concerns about its democratic credentials and the meaning of citizens' rights have led to some pressure to accede. The EU's response has been to draw up its own **Charter of Fundamental Rights,** which was proclaimed in 2000. Moreover, the **Treaty establishing a Constitution for Europe** contains a provision committing the EU to accede to the Convention.

EUROPEAN CO-OPERATION IN THE FIELD OF SCIENTIFIC AND TECHNICAL RESEARCH: See **COST**

EUROPEAN COUNCIL is the name used to describe meetings of the heads of state or government of European Union (EU) Member States, their foreign ministers, and senior officials of the **European Commission**. It should not be confused with the **Council of Europe**, which is an entirely unrelated body, nor should it be identified too closely with the **Council of the European Union**. The **Treaty of Rome** made no provision for the existence of the European Council, creating some lack of clarity about its constitutional position in, and relationship to, the European Communities (EC). The Treaty had stipulated the Council of Ministers (see Council of the European Union) as the only executive body in the EC representing the national governments. No provision was made for meetings of the heads of state or government, and the latter at first seemingly paid little attention to EC affairs, meeting on only three occasions during the first decade. The problems of the 1960s and the **Luxembourg Compromise** suggested that if the Member States were serious about membership of the EC, then the heads of government, who ultimately controlled the Council of

Ministers, should become more directly involved, particularly in order to give a strategic purpose to the EC on a range of issues where the normal institutional framework could not proceed without the consent of the national governments.

Four *ad hoc* **summit meetings** were held between 1969 and 1974. At the fourth, in Paris, the government leaders accepted 'the need for an overall approach to the internal problems in achieving European unity and the external problems facing Europe'; they agreed to a proposal from President **Valéry Giscard d'Estaing** of **France** that they should meet on a regular basis under the rubric of the European Council. The meetings would take place three times a year (amended in December 1985 to twice yearly) 'to ensure progress and overall consistency in the activities of the Communities and in the work on political co-operation'. The presidency of the Council would rotate between the Member States, changing every six months, with the meetings being held in the capital of the country currently occupying the presidency, and the third meeting each year (until 1985) being held in **Brussels**. Further extraordinary sessions may be arranged, should circumstances demand it. The first meeting was held in Dublin in March 1975.

The principle of rotation emphasizes that all Member States are equal. Despite the heavy workload which the presidency involves, it is particularly important for the smaller states since it offers them the opportunity to become a centre of European, and even world, diplomacy once every few years. All states treat the presidency seriously, and most have attempted to use their presidency to promote numerous potentially important initiatives. **Enlargement** of the EU in 2004 has, however, prompted consideration of moving away from existing practice and establishing a **European Council president** who would hold office for two-and-a-half years.

Before the **ratification** of the **Single European Act** (SEA), the European Council had no legal recognition within the EC. This suited the interests of the Member States, since the more informal atmosphere gave them freedom to discuss broad questions of politics and policy without the pressure of having to come to a decision. The European Council became the only EC institution where such broad-ranging discussions could occur. Each meeting normally lasts for two days. Their informality is indicated by the fact that most meetings are not attended by large numbers of national officials and advisers. Only the foreign ministers accompany their leaders. The only other participants are the President of the European Commission, one of the Vice-Presidents and, since 1983, the Secretary-General. The European Council gatherings also provide an opportunity for informal discussion of more sensitive topics outside the scheduled plenary sessions.

The European Council has become central to the EC. Its emergence confirmed that nothing could be achieved unless the Member States were in agreement, and virtually all the major advances since the mid-1980s have occurred because of European Council agreement on their desirability. However, its presence has sometimes hindered effective decision-making at lower EC levels. Because ultimate authority rests with the government leaders, they have often been expected to resolve relatively minor issues, which other agencies were competent, but either unwilling or unable, to deal with.

The position of the European Council within the EC was acknowledged and regularized by the SEA. It is another version of the Council of the European Union, albeit the most senior. When policy decisions are taken by the European Council that conform to the constitutional requirements of the **founding treaties**, they have the force of EC **legislation**. More generally, European Council agreements are framed as general principles or a broad consensus on future action, which are then passed on to the European Commission and the Council of the European Union for further research, discussion and possible adoption. The **Treaty on European Union** (TEU) strengthened the role of the European Council further. It is directly responsible for the two new **pillars** of the EU: the **common foreign and security policy** (CFSP) and **justice and home affairs** (JHA). It is also the body to which changes in **economic and monetary union** (EMU) will be reported and which will put forward further guidelines for EMU. The European Council's decisions have normally been taken on the basis of unanimity, although on a few occasions a vote has been employed to overcome the resistance of one or two Member States. In 2002, new rules governing the organization and proceedings of the European Council were adopted to ensure its effective functioning in the EU of **Twenty-Five**. These effectively limit the duration of the meetings to two days, enhance the preparatory role of the **General Affairs and External Relations Council**, limit the size of each meeting and, as with formations of the Council of the European Union, strengthen the role of the presidency as chair.

Further change has also been introduced as a consequence of a declaration annexed to the **Treaty of Nice**. This stipulated that, as from 2002, one European Council meeting per presidency would be held in Brussels, and went on to declare that once the EU comprised 18 Member States, all European Councils would be held in Brussels. In practice, formal meetings of the European Council have all been held in Brussels since the Italian presidency in the second half of 2003. The **Treaty establishing a Constitution for Europe** if approved, would have provided for the election by **qualified majority** of a **European Council president** to give greater coherence and direction to EU initiatives. This post was scheduled to last for a period of two and a half years with the possibility of one further term.

A **EUROPEAN COUNCIL PRESIDENT**, to be elected by the other members of the **European Council** for a term of two-and-a-half years, is one of the institutional innovations contained in the **Treaty establishing a Constitution for Europe**. The post holder will have five key tasks: chairing the European Council and driving forward its work; ensuring proper preparation for meetings and continuity in co-operation with the Commission President; facilitating cohesion and consensus within the European Council; reporting to the **European Parliament** after each European Council meeting; and ensuring the external representation of the EU on issues concerning the **common foreign and security policy**.

The **EUROPEAN COURT OF HUMAN RIGHTS**, which is based in **Strasbourg**, operates under the aegis of the **Council of Europe**. It hears cases concerning individuals and practices in those states that are party to the **European Convention on Human Rights**. Cases may be brought by individuals or by the **European Commission of Human Rights**. All the Member States of the European Union (EU) have ratified the Convention, and the EU has accepted the jurisdiction of this court in the sphere of **human rights**.

EUROPEAN COURT OF JUSTICE: See **Court of Justice**

EUROPEAN CURRENCY UNIT: See **ECU**

The **EUROPEAN DEFENCE AGENCY** (EDA) was established in July 2004 to support Member States' efforts to improve European defence capabilities in the field of crisis management and to sustain the **European security and defence policy**. Its key functions relate to defence capabilities development; armaments co-operation; the European defence technological and industrial base and defence equipment market; and research and technology. The EDA is the forerunner of the **European Armaments, Research and Military Capabilities Agency** envisaged in the **Treaty establishing a Constitution for Europe**.

The **EUROPEAN DEFENCE COMMUNITY** (EDC) was an initiative based on the 1950 Pleven Plan (named after former French premier, René Pleven). It was established by a treaty signed in Paris, in May 1952, by representatives of the **Six** states that had formed the **European Coal and Steel Community** (ECSC). Attempts to persuade other European countries, especially the United Kingdom, to join the venture failed. The origins of the EDC lay in the evaluation by the **USA**, as a result of the Korean War, of its global commitments, and in US demands for an increase in European support for the

North Atlantic Treaty Organization (NATO), either by increased expenditure, or through the rearmament of the Federal Republic of **Germany** (FRG – West Germany). However, no state was willing to consider increased expenditure, and none, apart from the FRG, really desired West German rearmament. The EDC was a device to permit rearmament without a separate and independent West German military contingent under national command. It also served a European purpose, being viewed as a further sectoral advance towards integration, with an institutional framework modelled upon that of the ECSC. Unlike the ECSC, however, it was not to be a partnership of equals: more restrictions would be placed upon the FRG.

The proposal provoked a great deal of opposition throughout the Six, but especially in **France**. No French government, fearing defeat, dared for some time to submit the Treaty to a parliamentary vote. The French legislature finally defeated it on a technicality in August 1954, and the EDC project was abandoned. West German rearmament nevertheless occurred on a national basis within NATO, supervised, at least implicitly, by the newly created but virtually non-existent **Western European Union** (WEU). At the same time, the collapse of the EDC was widely regarded as a major setback for European integration. (See also **European Political Community**.)

EUROPEAN DEMOCRATIC ALLIANCE: See **Group of the European Democratic Alliance**

The **EUROPEAN DEMOCRATIC GROUP** (ED) was one of the **party groups** in the **European Parliament** (EP). It was formed in 1973 by the British and Danish Conservative parties, which rejected membership of the European People's Party (PPE), feeling a lack of sympathy with the latter's Christian Democratic tradition and commitment to federalism. Dominated by its British representatives, it enjoyed some considerable influence in the EP in the mid-1970s, but its subsequent decline led it to seek collaboration with the PPE. A proposal by the British representatives to join the PPE after the 1989 **direct elections** was rejected on the grounds of the former's lack of commitment to European ideals. However, agreement on a merger was reached in 1992, and the ED effectively ceased to exist, becoming part of the Group of the European People's Party. See also **Group of the European People's Party (Christian Democrats) and European Democrats**.

The **EUROPEAN DEMOCRATS** (DE) sit with the Group of the European People's Party in the **European Parliament**. See **Group of the European People's Party (Christian Democrats) and European Democrats**

EUROPEAN DEPOSITORY LIBRARIES: See **DEP**

The **EUROPEAN DEVELOPMENT FUND** (EDF) was established under the terms of the First **Yaoundé Convention** of 1963, and was retained in the subsequent **Lomé Convention** between the European Communities (EC) and the **African, Caribbean and Pacific** (ACP) **States**. It was set up to provide grants to the **ACP States** for development programmes, focusing after 1984 on rural and agricultural projects, and on broad integrated development programmes. As the Member States were signatories of the 1963 Convention in their own right, and as they are eager to control spending in this area, the EDF is not included in the development section of the EC **budget**, much to the dissatisfaction of many in the **European Parliament**. Under the **Cotonou Agreement**, the EDF was allocated €13.5bn for the period 2000–05. In 2006 some €3.5 billion was available for EDF-backed projects that sought to reform education, modernize health and transport systems, support debt relief and balance of payments difficulties and further institutional development. **See also Development Aid**.

EUROPEAN DOCUMENTATION CENTRES (EDCs) are information centres that contain European Communities (EC) documentation. Their function is to stimulate the development of European studies in academic institutions and to provide an information service on the EC to the public. They are usually based in university libraries, and can also be found in non-EC countries. See also **Europe Direct Information Network**.

The **EUROPEAN ECONOMIC AND SOCIAL COMMITTEE** (EESC), which was also known by the alternative acronyms of ESC and ECOSOC, is not to be confused with the **United Nations** Economic and Social Council, which uses the same abbreviation. It is one of the main European Communities (EC) bodies set up by the **Treaty of Rome**. It was established as a non-political body that enables those active in economic and social fields to voice opinions on EC policy formulation. It has a purely advisory function, but the **European Commission** and the **Council of the European Union** are mandated to consult it on a wide range of issues before they can arrive at a **decision**. The **Single European Act** and the **Treaty on European Union** extended the areas on which it had to be consulted (to environmental and regional issues). In practice, both the Council and the Commission have consulted the EESC on a number of other non-mandatory topics, though they do not always heed its advice. The EESC issues some 170 advisory documents and opinions each year and the **Treaty of Amsterdam** also allows for the EESC to be consulted by the **European Parliament**.

Its membership, which is drawn from national interest groups throughout the Member States, increased from 222 to 317 with **enlargement** on 1 May 2004. The members are appointed for a four-year period, which is renewable. In the enlarged body, **Germany, France, Italy** and the **United Kingdom** each have 24 members; **Spain** and **Poland** 21 each; **Belgium**, the **Czech Republic, Greece, Hungary**, the **Netherlands, Portugal, Austria** and **Sweden** 12 each; **Denmark, Finland, Ireland, Lithuania** and **Slovakia** 9 each; **Estonia, Latvia** and **Slovenia** 7 each, **Cyprus** and **Luxembourg** 6 each, and **Malta** 5. Each national delegation consists of three separate categories: workers, employers and a miscellany of other groups such as farmers, consumers and the self-employed. Members are nominated by national governments, normally after consultation with the major national interest groups, and appointed by the Council of the European Union. It elects its own chairman for a period of two years, and it is conventional for the chairmanship to rotate between the three categories of membership. Participation in EESC is a part-time commitment, and appointees are expected to be granted time off from their employment to attend meetings. Much of its work is done in specialized working groups, which correspond to the major policy concerns of the EC. The groups provide draft opinions for approval in a plenary session of the Committee. EESC has often been divided between left and right, between workers and employers, on many social and economic questions. How effective it has been in directly influencing proposed EC **legislation** is debatable. Its relevance has often been sidelined by both the Commission and the Council, as the former prefers to deal directly with sectoral organizations.

Also, the Committee's internal divisions have reduced its potential impact, and its major participants have often used other channels to make their opinions known. The Committee produces some 200 consultative documents annually in response to requests from the Commission and the Council, but also publishes reports on its own initiatives. The **Treaty of Nice** did not alter the number and distribution per Member State of the seats of EESC. However, the Treaty does note that the total number of members of the Committee should not exceed 350. The Treaty also modified the description of EESC members, stating that the Committee should consist of 'representatives of the various economic and social components of organized civil society'.

The impact of the EESC has been rather limited. It can be seen as representing an attempt at fostering a type of corporatist interest intermediation that suited the 1950s environment. Almost 50 years later its influence has waned to a large degree, as many of the groups it seeks to represent have established more direct means to influence policy formulation.

The **EUROPEAN ECONOMIC AREA** (EEA) is a trading area agreed upon in 1991 by the European Communities (EC) and members of the **European**

Free Trade Association (EFTA). It was a consequence of fears by the EFTA countries that the development of the **internal market** might negatively affect their own economies. In 1989 they agreed upon a joint approach to the EC, using the phrase European Economic Space to describe the kind of structured partnership they wanted. Negotiations began in June 1990, and were completed by November 1991, largely upon EC terms, with an agreement on participation in the internal market. **Ratification** was delayed because of a query by the **Court of Justice** (ECJ) about the constitutional compatibility with the **founding treaties** of the proposed arbitration procedures. This led to the EFTA states having to create their own EFTA court and greater powers being placed in the hands of the ECJ. A referendum in **Switzerland** in 1992 rejected involvement in the EEA, and it came into existence without Swiss participation in January 1994. Although **Liechtenstein** had voted to join the EEA in a referendum held one week after the Swiss vote, the nature of its **customs union** with Switzerland made participation in the EEA problematic. When a number of necessary modifications had been made to the customs union, Liechtenstein voted again to join the EEA, in a second referendum held in April 1995. By this time, the EEA had lost three of its EFTA members, **Austria**, **Finland** and **Sweden** having joined the **European Union** (EU) on 1 January 1995. Indeed, from a positive perspective the EEA helped pave the way for their accession. However, the departure of these countries from EFTA turned the EEA into a rather more minor economic arrangement than the one originally envisaged. Despite expectations to the contrary, the EEA has survived and continues to expand its scope. It therefore provides an adequate basis for relations between the EU and three of the most economically developed European non-EU states (**Iceland**, Liechtenstein and **Norway**), none of which is actively seeking membership at the present time.

EUROPEAN ECONOMIC COMMUNITY (EEC) was the official title of the organization established by the **Treaty of Rome** in 1958. The administrative network of the EEC was formally merged with that of the **European Coal and Steel Community** (ECSC) and the **European Atomic Energy Community** (EAEC or Euratom) in July 1967, after which the three bodies were collectively known as the European Communities or European Community (EC), although the abbreviation EEC remained in common usage, somewhat erroneously, to describe the Communities collectively. It also often carried a political connotation, being used by people who wished to emphasize that the EC should remain an economic organization without any implications of political union. The **Treaty on European Union** (TEU) confirmed that the EEC would in future be referred to as the European Community, and the founding Treaty of Rome was amended accordingly.

The **EUROPEAN ECONOMIC INTEREST GROUPING** (EEIG) is an arrangement established to enable Member States to collaborate more effectively on possible joint projects and enterprises. It falls under the European Union's single market strategy and is designed to create more competitive consortia. The best illustration of an EEIG is **Airbus**. EEIG provides a legal structure for companies of different Member States to link their activities while at the same time retaining economic and legal independence. By the end of 1997 there were more than 800 EEIGs operating in a variety of areas. The Regie initiative promotes EEIGs.

EUROPEAN ECONOMIC SPACE: See **European Economic Area**

EUROPEAN EMPLOYMENT STRATEGY: Each year, the **European Council** agrees on a series of guidelines setting out common priorities and individual objectives for Member States' employment policies. The overall aims include creating jobs, improving job quality, making it easier for people to balance the demands of work and personal life, promoting active ageing and ensuring that race, gender or disabilities do not limit opportunities for employment in the formal economy.

Each EU government produces its own annual action plan describing how it is putting the guidelines into practice. Progress is measured against some 100 indicators, ranging from basic economic figures (e.g. gross domestic product (GDP) growth and unemployment levels) to the availability of career breaks and childcare.

EUROPEAN ENERGY CHARTER is the name of a document inspired by the European Communities (EC) and signed at The Hague in December 1991 by 38 countries. By 2006 there were 51 signatories (51 states plus the EC) throughout Europe and the former **USSR**, as well as the **USA**, Canada and **Japan**. Its purpose was to make European energy supplies more secure by linking the natural resources of Eastern Europe with the West through a grid of supply lines. In return, Eastern Europe would receive investment from Western countries, and the EC proposed to extend the **Organization for the Promotion of Energy Technology** (OPET) scheme for the international transfer of energy-efficient and environmentally friendly technologies to Eastern Europe and the **Commonwealth of Independent States** (CIS). A further objective was to strengthen the Eastern democracies by easing their balance of payments problems, and to offer the Russian Federation an alternative to membership of the petroleum producers' cartel, the Organization of Petroleum Exporting Countries (OPEC).

The **EUROPEAN ENVIRONMENT AGENCY** (EEA) was established in May 1990 by the European Communities (EC) to collect and disseminate detailed information on environmental questions and problems, including air quality, water quality, state of the soil, land use, waste management, noise emissions and coastal erosion. Membership of this body is open also to non-European Union (EU) states. Its inauguration was blocked by **France** because of its dispute with the EC over the future permanent location of the **European Parliament** and controversy over the siting of other European agencies. In November 1993, however, it was agreed that the EEA would be located in Copenhagen. The Agency has 29 member countries and was the first EU body to have members from the 13 candidate states. After EU **enlargement** in May 2004, members comprise the EU of **Twenty-Five** plus **Bulgaria, Iceland, Liechtenstein, Norway, Romania** and **Turkey**. Membership negotiations are under way with **Switzerland**.

The **EUROPEAN EXTERNAL ACTION SERVICE** was due to be established following signature of the **Treaty establishing a Constitution for Europe** in late 2004. Viewed as an embryonic EU Foreign Ministry, the European External Action Service will assist the **Union Minister for Foreign Affairs**.

The **EUROPEAN FEDERALIST MOVEMENT** has been the main proponent of the federalist ideal for Europe since the 1950s. **Altiero Spinelli**, who largely inspired it, led the movement until 1962. It had little impact upon European developments, although, thanks to Spinelli, some of its ideas can be found in the **draft Treaty establishing the European Union**.

The **EUROPEAN FIGHTER AIRCRAFT** programme was the first major joint European armaments project, although it was not a European Communities project. It consisted of an agreement in 1985 by the arms procurement directors of **Germany, Italy, Spain**, and the **United Kingdom** to work collectively towards the development of a replacement for aircraft that would be obsolete by the mid-1990s. The first aircraft were scheduled to be in service by 1997, but rising costs, technical problems, and the lower priority given to defence after the ending of the **Cold War** created doubts about the programme's viability and necessity. After 1992 the programme was scaled down in size and renamed the Eurofighter 2000 project.

The **EUROPEAN FILM DISTRIBUTION OFFICE** (EFDO) was established under the MEDIA programme (see **Media Policy**) to sponsor and help to market European-produced films. The Office is based in Lisbon.

A **EUROPEAN FLAG** was adopted by the European Communities (EC) in 1986. Its design is a crown of 12 five-pointed stars set against an azure background. It is the same flag as that used by the **Council of Europe** since 1955; hence it was merely coincidental that the number of stars on the flag corresponded to the membership of the EC from 1986 to 1994. The stars were placed in a circle to represent the union of the European states. The flag is flown over the EC headquarters in **Brussels**, and is otherwise used at national and international meetings and ceremonies where the European Union is represented.

The **EUROPEAN FOOD SAFETY AGENCY** was established in 2002 following various food safety scares in the 1990s, notably BSE (see **Bovine Spongiform Encephalopathy**). Its purpose is to provide independent scientific advice on all matters linked to food and feed safety, including animal health and welfare and plant protection. It also provides scientific advice on nutrition in relation to Community **legislation**. (See also **Foodstuffs.**)

EUROPEAN FOUNDATION FOR THE IMPROVEMENT OF LIVING AND WORKING CONDITIONS is the name of a **European Commission** agency established in 1975 and based in Dublin. It holds a broad mandate to research and formulate policy on the improvement of the working and living environment of employees, and has focused on **health and safety** policy. It is staffed by representatives of the Commission, the Member States and employers' and employees' organizations.

The **EUROPEAN FREE ALLIANCE** (EFA/ALE) forms part of the **Group of the Greens/European Free Alliance** in the **European Parliament**. It is made up of representatives of 'stateless nations'.

The **EUROPEAN FREE TRADE ASSOCIATION** (EFTA) was established by the **Stockholm Convention** of 4 January 1960. It consisted of seven states – **Austria**, **Denmark**, **Norway**, **Portugal**, **Sweden**, **Switzerland** and the **United Kingdom** – which were unwilling or, for various reasons, unable to accept the supranational and **common market** principles of the **Treaty of Rome** and the **European Economic Community** (EEC). EFTA's objectives were limited to securing a gradual elimination of **tariffs** on trade in most industrial goods between its members. It did not have an agricultural policy or any kind of **common external tariff** (CET), and its institutional structure was to be limited to a Council of Ministers that would meet only two or three times a year, although a council of heads of national delegations was to meet every two weeks. It brought together a very disparate group of countries that seemed to be agreed on only two things. Firstly, they agreed on a rejection of the sequence of events postulated by the Treaty of Rome, apart from the establishment of a free-trade area. Secondly, they believed that some form of unity would place them in an advantageous position *vis-à-vis* the EEC compared with the position they would be in if each country separately attempted to negotiate some accommodation with it.

Within its limited terms of reference, EFTA worked quite well, establishing its free-trade area fairly quickly. After the late 1960s, it collaborated quite closely with the European Communities (EC). When Denmark and the United Kingdom joined the EC in 1973, they left EFTA. The remaining EFTA states, which now also included **Iceland** and **Liechtenstein**, with **Finland** as an associate, negotiated a series of **Free Trade Agreements** with the EC, which came into force in 1973. With some variations from country to country, these agreements provided for the gradual introduction of free trade in industrial goods (but not in agriculture). The relationship was the province of a joint EC–EFTA executive committee meeting twice yearly. While the EFTA states avoided the obligations of full EC membership, the disadvantage was that they were not party to EC **decisions**, many of which had an important effect upon their own economies. The arrangement, however, worked quite well, and by the 1980s EFTA had moved very close to the EC in its economic practices.

In the late 1980s, the EFTA states felt obliged to review their situation in the light of the **Single European Act** and the EC decision to establish an **internal market**. In 1989 the creation of a broad European Economic Space was proposed which, after protracted negotiations, came into being, albeit without Switzerland's participation, as the **European Economic Area** (EEA) in 1994. However, the EFTA states began to conclude that even EEA membership would leave them at a disadvantage and thus Austria, Finland, Norway and Sweden all applied for membership of the EC. In January 1995 Austria, Sweden and Finland joined the European Union (EU), Norway having withdrawn its application following a referendum result that rejected EU membership. EFTA was left as a rump whose viability was in considerable doubt.

The **EUROPEAN FUSION DEVELOPMENT AGREEMENT** (EFDA) took over the operations of the **Joint European Torus** in 2000. The Agreement aimed to promote collaboration in the field of nuclear fusion research by Member States of the European Union, **Switzerland** and certain **candidate countries** of **Central and Eastern Europe** (the **Czech Republic**, **Hungary** and **Romania**). The former two countries joined the EU in May 2004. EFDA also manages the **ITER** nuclear research project. Two support units are based in Garching, **Germany,** and Culham, **United Kingdom**; these units integrate research carried out in various centres into the European Fusion Programme.

The **EUROPEAN GROUP ON ETHICS IN SCIENCE AND NEW TECHNOLOGIES** (EGE) was established in 1998 to advise the **European Commission** on ethical aspects of science and technology. An independent and multidisciplinary group, the EGE has provided opinions on a range of issues including: human embryo research, doping in sport, human stem cell research, clinical research in developing countries and genetic testing in the workplace.

EUROPEAN INFORMATION SYSTEM: See **Schengen Information System**

The **EUROPEAN INVENTORY OF EXISTING CHEMICAL SUBSTANCES** (EINECS) is a programme set up by the **European Commission** in 1986 as a response to widespread alarm about the hazards to both individuals and the environment of many chemical products. The inventory, which forms part of the **Environmental Chemicals Data Information Network**, is intended to record all commercially available chemical products. The Commission uses it to evaluate and control their application, and in the formulation of **consumer policy**, **environmental policy** and **health and safety** policy.

The **EUROPEAN INVESTMENT BANK** (EIB) was set up by the **Treaty of Rome** as a separate and autonomous institution within the European Communities (EC). Based in **Luxembourg**, the EIB was designed to be a bank for the financing of capital investment that would benefit EC development. The EIB has evolved since 1958 in both importance and stature and today is the world's largest bank of its kind, with loans totalling €45,780m. in 2004. The Member States are the basic members of the Bank, collectively subscribing to its capital. The subscription rates were revised in early 1995, giving the following allocations (in percentages): **France**, **Germany**, **Italy** and the **United Kingdom** 17.8 each; **Spain** 6.5; **Belgium** and the **Netherlands** 4.9 each; **Sweden** 3.3; **Denmark** 2.5; **Austria** 2.4; **Finland** 1.4; **Greece** 1.3; **Portugal** 0.9; **Ireland** 0.6; **Luxembourg** 0.1.

The ultimate decision-making body of the EIB is the Board of Governors, normally consisting of the finance ministers of the Member States. The Board normally meets only once a year. Supervision of the daily operations of the Bank is performed by a part-time Board of Directors, composed of nominees from the Member States and from the **European Commission**. The management of operations is the responsibility of a Management Committee composed of the Bank's President and seven Vice-Presidents, nominated by the Board of Directors and appointed by the Board of Governors for renewable six-year terms.

In addition to its subscription capital, the EIB raises funds on the international capital markets, where it enjoys the highest possible credit rating. Its bonds are regularly rated 'AAA' by the leading rating agencies. As it works on a non-profit basis the EIB can pass on to projects the excellent conditions obtained as an AAA borrower. The EIB has three general aims: to assist less developed regions, to help to modernize the economy of the European Union (EU), and to support projects that are of interest to more than one Member State. It provides fixed-rate loans, usually for periods of between five and 12 years (but up to 20 years for infrastructural projects), and occasionally also guarantees loans and credit.

National governments, regional authorities and companies may all apply for EIB loans or guarantees. The EIB never provides all the funding for a project. It will consider only large-scale projects, and will normally advance up to 50% of the projected costs. The balance has to be met by loans from other sources, the applicant's own resources or state assistance. Some 5% of EIB activity is devoted to external aid programmes, mainly to the **African, Caribbean and Pacific** (ACP) **States** under the terms of the **Lomé Convention**. Under the terms of Lomé's successor, the **Cotonou Agreement**, €3,900m. was to be channelled to projects in **ACP States** between 2002 and 2006. The Bank publishes an annual report of its operations, with details of the projects it has funded. With a level of lending approaching that of the International Bank for Reconstruction and Development (IBRD – World Bank), it arguably constitutes the most successful of the funds available from the EC. After 1994 it administered a **European Investment Fund** (EIF) that was intended to promote economic growth and reduce unemployment through the provision of financial aid for major infrastructural projects, and for capital investments by smaller companies.

The responsibilities of the EIB were extended in June 1998 to include the Amsterdam Special Action programme, which allows the EIB to lend money for health and education projects and to provide risk capital for small and medium-sized companies, particularly in new high-technology areas. In recent years the EIB has tended to move its focus from long-term infrastructure projects towards supporting initiatives that increase employment and facilitate research and development across the EU. In 1999 the Bank established the Balkan Task Force, a group of experts whose task is to examine the infrastructure needs of the **Western Balkans**. (See also the **European Central Bank**.)

EUROPEAN INVESTMENT FUND (EIF) is the name of a body proposed by the **European Council** in 1992, as part of a collection of measures designed to combat the economic depression prevalent in the early 1990s, with the objective of providing additional aid for transnational infrastructural projects. The Fund was established in 1994 by the **European Investment Bank** (EIB), the European Communities (represented by the **European Commission**) and a group of 76 banks and financial institutions from throughout the European Union. The EIB subscribed 40% of the EIF's **ECU** 2,000m. capital. The Fund assists **small and medium-sized enterprises** (SMEs) and provides guarantees for the long-term financing of European infrastructure projects, in particular **Trans-European Networks** (TENs). The EIF became operational in 1995.

The **EUROPEAN JUDICIAL NETWORK IN CIVIL AND COMMER-CIAL MATTERS** was established in 2001 as part of the European Union's activities in the area of **justice and home affairs** following the **Tampere Summit** of the **European Council**. The network consists of representatives of the Member States' judicial and administrative authorities and meets several times each year to exchange information and experience and promote co-operation in the areas of civil and commercial law.

The **EUROPEAN JUDICIAL NETWORK IN CRIMINAL MATTERS** (EJN) was established in 1998 and plays a major role in the European Union's efforts to promote **police and judicial co-operation in criminal matters**. It brings together experts from the Member States dealing with criminal matters and has a Secretariat in The Hague linked to that of **Eurojust**.

The **EUROPEAN MARITIME SAFETY AGENCY** (EMSA) was created in 2002 to promote an improved maritime safety system within the European Union. The Agency was due to move to Lisbon, from Brussels, in 2006. Its main goals are to reduce the risk of maritime accidents, marine pollution from ships and the loss of human lives at sea.

EUROPEAN MONETARY AGREEMENT: See **European Payments Union**

The **EUROPEAN MONETARY CO-OPERATION FUND** (EMCF) was established in 1973. By the end of that decade it was the only survivor of plans made in the early 1970s for **economic and monetary union** (EMU). In 1979 it was incorporated into the **European Monetary System** (EMS), where it was the reserve fund that supported the European Currency Unit (**ECU**). Member States participating in the **basket of currencies** that determined the value of the ECU were required to deposit 20% of both their gold and dollar reserves with the Fund. The EMCF was used to regulate the interventions made on the exchange markets by the central banks of the Member States to support the **exchange-rate mechanism** of the EMS, and it kept account of short-term borrowings used to support currencies. Its most important credit facility was its Very Short-Term Financing Facility (VSTF), which permitted borrowing by the central banks, with the proviso that credit must be settled within 45 days. It was superseded by the **European Monetary Institute** in January 1994, at the beginning of stage two of EMU.

The **EUROPEAN MONETARY INSTITUTE** (EMI) was established under the **Treaty on European Union** (TEU) and superseded the **European Monetary Co-operation Fund**. Its operations began with the commencement of stage two of **economic and monetary union** (EMU) and were completed shortly before stage three was launched on 1 January 1999. The EMI's role was to facilitate closer co-operation between the central banks of the Member States, co-ordinate monetary policies, monitor the **European Monetary System** and eventually advise the **European Council** as to whether the conditions for stage three of EMU had been met. Located in Frankfurt am Main, **Germany**, it was the forerunner of the **European Central Bank** (ECB), which effectively replaced it in 1998.

The **EUROPEAN MONETARY SYSTEM** (EMS) constituted the second attempt by the European Communities (EC) to secure some form of monetary co-operation after the failure of the plans of 1970 for **economic and monetary union** (EMU). The EMS, established in 1979, was a more limited and practical attempt to secure, in the first instance, a zone of monetary stability in Western Europe. The core of the EMS was the **exchange-rate mechanism** (ERM), which linked the currencies of the participating Member States and limited the amount by which each currency was permitted to fluctuate against its counterparts. If a currency went beyond these limits, the central banks, with the help of the **European Monetary Co-operation Fund**, intervened in the exchange markets, selling or buying as the case might be, to maintain the currency within the agreed limits. A central rate was calculated for each currency on the basis of the central rate of the European Currency Unit (**ECU**), a notional EC currency that existed alongside the national currencies. Special arrangements existed to provide help for countries that ran into short-term difficulties. Where a currency persistently had difficulty in staying within its agreed limits, the EMS made provision for its realignment.

The EMS had some considerable success in the 1980s. It was widely credited with contributing to the fall in inflation levels and to a growing economic **convergence** of the Member States. While the EMS was not a replacement for EMU, as it was unable to impose economic policy restraints upon the states, by the late 1980s it was widely felt that conditions were more appropriate for the

EC to move on to full EMU. One weakness was that not all the Member States were members of the ERM. The plans for EMU contained in the **Treaty on European Union** (TEU) were disrupted during the currency crises of 1992–93, with the **United Kingdom** and **Italy** leaving the ERM, which itself greatly extended the permissible limits of currency fluctuation. While these events may have delayed the EMU programme, they did not seriously affect the existence of the EMS, which remained essentially an instrument of co-operation in monetary policy until the formal establishment of EMU.

EUROPEAN MONITORING CENTRE FOR DRUGS AND DRUG ADDICTION (EMCDDA) is the name of an agency agreed upon by the European Communities (EC) in 1991 to collect objective and reliable information that would enable the EC and the Member States to take effective steps to reduce the production, consumption and trafficking of drugs. The Centre, which opened in September 1995, is located in Lisbon.

The **EUROPEAN MONITORING CENTRE ON RACISM AND XENOPHOBIA** (EUMC) was established by the European Union (EU) in 1997 to study and review the extent and development of racism, xenophobia and anti-Semitism in Europe, and to report its findings to the EU. EUMC works with the **Council of Europe**, the **United Nations** and other international organizations. It aimed to establish a European Racism and Xenophobia Information Network (RAXEN), which would collect statistics on racist incidents and pass them to EUMC. The latter was to use the materials gathered to construct a European database for conducting research and disseminating information on racism and how to combat it. EUMC has set up a series of 'Round Table' discussions on racism and has launched some of its own research initiatives.

EUROPEAN MOVEMENT is the name of an influential pressure group working for integration in the late 1940s and early 1950s. It was founded at the **Congress of Europe** of 1948. It was the Movement that drew up the first draft of what was to become the **Council of Europe**. While its influence faded after the early 1950s, it remained active in supporting schemes for further political integration. With a membership that covers most European countries, it has come to act more as an umbrella organization, disseminating information to all groups, associations and institutions with an interest in European affairs, and liaising between them.

EUROPEAN NATO refers superficially to all members of the **North Atlantic Treaty Organization** (NATO) except the **USA** and Canada. It more precisely refers to the original European NATO membership of 1949, including **France**, despite the latter's partial membership of NATO, and with the addition of **Germany**. It is a descriptive expression rather than a specific subgroup within NATO, and has often been used in the context of the need to strengthen the European pillar of NATO. As a general term, it embraces those institutional expressions of a common European defence interest: the former **Eurogroup** and **Independent European Programme Group**, and **Western European Union**.

The **EUROPEAN NEIGHBOURHOOD POLICY (ENP)** is the EU's initiative to place relations with neighbouring regions (i.e. Eastern Europe, the Middle East and the Southern Mediterranean, but not **South–Eastern Europe**) on a new footing following enlargement in 2004. It aims to 'reduce poverty and create an area of shared prosperity and values based on deeper economic integration, intensified political and cultural relations, enhanced cross-border cooperation and shared responsibility for conflict prevention between the EU and its neighbours ... [and to] anchor the EU's offer of concrete benefits and preferential relations within a differentiated framework which responds to progress made by the partner countries in political and economic reform'. To this end a range of ENP Action Plans are envisaged. These contain an agenda of political and economic reforms with short- and medium-term priorities, and Plans have so far been agreed with Israel, Jordan, Moldova, Morocco, the Palestinian Authority, Tunisia and Ukraine. Action Plans with a further five 'neighbours' – Armenia, Azerbaijan, Georgia, Egypt and Lebanon – were started in 2005. The Action Plans envisage increased trade relations, involvement in the EU's internal market, and cooperation on justice and home affairs, energy, transport, information society, environment and research and innovation, and social policy. It has been proposed that financial assistance worth almost €15 billion be provided through a European Neighbourhood and Partnership Instrument for the period 2007–2013. EU membership, however, is not envisaged as part of either the Action Plans or the ENP more generally.

EUROPEAN ORGANIZATION FOR NUCLEAR RESEARCH: See **CERN**

EUROPEAN ORGANIZATION FOR THE EXPLOITATION OF METEOROLOGICAL SATELLITES: See **EUMETSAT**

The **EUROPEAN PARLIAMENT** (EP) originated in the **Strasbourg**-based advisory Assembly of the **European Coal and Steel Community** (ECSC).

With the establishment of the **European Economic Community** (EEC) and the **European Atomic Energy Community** (EAEC or Euratom) in 1958, one Parliamentary Assembly was created to serve all three Communities, with a membership of 142, which had increased to 626 by January 1995 and further to 732 by June 2004. Members were initially appointed by the **national parliaments** from among their own members, although the **Treaty of Rome** had called for the introduction of **direct elections**. The powers of the Assembly were defined as the supervision of both the **European Commission** and the Council of Ministers (see **Council of the European Union**), and participation in the legislative and **budget** processes. Essentially, however, it was allotted a secondary position in the institutional framework, being more of an advisory and consultative body than a genuine decision-making body.

From the outset, the Assembly, which was firmly in favour of rapid moves towards political union, was dissatisfied with its secondary role, campaigning constantly for greater influence and authority. In 1962 it took the symbolic step of calling itself the European Parliament: although this was accepted by the European Commission (but not by the Council of Ministers), the EP was given a legal basis only in the **Single European Act** (SEA) of 1987. The EP also asserted a right to meet whenever it wished, circumventing the Treaty of Rome's provisions for an annual session by simply dividing the latter into several segments of time, spanning the whole calendar year. Some slight increases in powers were granted by the 1970 **Treaty of Luxembourg**, with a further modest increase in budgetary influence in 1975, when the EP was given the right to reject the budget in its entirety with effect from 1977. The SEA, the **Treaty on European Union** (TEU), the **Treaty of Amsterdam** and the **Treaty of Nice** extended the EP's competences further by introducing the **co-operation procedure** and **assent procedure** under the SEA and introducing the **co-decision** procedure under the TEU and extending it under both the Amsterdam and Nice Treaties. Even so, the EP remains the weakest of the EC central institutions.

The EP is not a true legitimating body for the European Union (EU). Although it has to approve **Accession Treaties** and **Association Agreements**, it plays no active role in their negotiations, and has only a minor role in any constitutional revision of the EU treaties. Its representative character has also been criticized. Owing to the refusal for several years by the Council of Ministers to adopt the necessary legislation, the first **direct elections** to the EP were not held until 1979. Since then the EP has been elected at five-yearly intervals. In 2004 the sixth parliament was elected. However, it is not a true representative body because small Member States are considerably over-represented in it at the expense of the larger states. There is no standard electoral system across all the Member States, and electorates tend to use the elections to express a verdict on their national government and domestic problems: there has never been a true

European election. Furthermore, electorates tend to have only a vague perception of the EP, often seeing it as secondary to their own national legislatures. The fact that EP sessions have often been attended by less than one-half of its members has not helped its cause.

The TEU strengthened the EP's right of scrutiny and supervision. The EP was given a formal right to establish committees of inquiry, to appoint an **Ombudsman** from among its members to investigate complaints of maladministration in EC institutions, and to be consulted on the nomination of a new President of the European Commission and to ratify the choice of President and members of the Commission. Furthermore, in accordance with the Treaty of Amsterdam, the EP must formally approve the appointment of the President of the Commission. These powers are in addition to its right to put both oral and written questions to the Commission, a duty it has taken seriously. Members of the Commission and its bureaucracy also attend meetings of the various EP committees. The EP has the right to submit questions to the Council of the European Union, which responds through ministers of the Member State currently holding the Council presidency, who attend EP plenary sessions to deliver the Council's replies. Since 1981 the head of government currently occupying the presidency of the **European Council** attends the EP after each European Council **summit meeting** to report on its proceedings. The EP's most severe power – to censure and thus collectively dismiss the Commission – requires a two-thirds' majority of the votes cast, which must also be a majority of the total EP membership; there is no power to dismiss an individual Commissioner. A censure motion was initiated in January 1999, following allegations of financial and other irregularities against the European Commission, and although a compromise deal ensured that the motion was defeated, the concessions won by the EP during that dispute were felt to represent an important shift in the balance of power from Commission to Parliament.

The role of the EP was further enhanced by the TEU's introduction of a co-decision procedure that builds upon the co-operation procedure introduced by the SEA. While these decision-making procedures make the legislative process highly complex, they broadly follow five phases. The Commission first presents a proposal to both the Council of the European Union and the EP. The EP is entitled to give an opinion that must be considered by the Council. A suitably revised version approved by **qualified majority voting** is returned to the EP and, if the EP rejects the common position proposed by the Council, the issue is referred to a Conciliation Committee which may result in approval, rejection or further amendment. Amendments can lead to a repetition of the evaluation process by the Council and EP. The new procedure gives the EP a decision-making role and a potential power of veto. The procedure applies only to those **Articles** of the Treaty that specifically refer to its use. The co-operation procedure introduced by the SEA applies to other policy areas, mostly in the area of

economic and monetary union: under the co-operation procedure, where the Council rejects an EP opinion, it must give a reasoned common position that will become law unless the EP proposes amendments. The Council can override such amendments only by a unanimous vote.

The Treaty of Amsterdam simplified the decision-making process, while extending the EP's powers. Co-decision between the Council and the EP was extended into a wider range of policy areas, and the EP may be consulted in decisions taken by unanimity in Council. International agreements, treaty decisions and the accession of new Member States all require the assent of the EP. The Treaty also calls for the EP to establish a formal code of conduct by which to regulate its members.

On **ratification**, the Treaty of Nice was to introduce a new distribution of seats in the EP. With the exception of **Germany** and **Luxembourg** the arrangements envisaged a reduction in the number of seats allocated to the **Fifteen** Member States at that time. This was deemed necessary for an enlarged EU with up to 27 members. Following the **enlargement** of the EU (to 25) on 1 May 2004, elections to the EP took place in June 2004, and were contested across all 25 Member States. These elections may have been the largest in the EU's history, but the overall turnout was disappointing. Only some 45% (i.e. the lowest in EP elections) of the total eligible electorate in the EU turned out to cast their vote. There were wide discrepancies at the national level. For example, **Belgium** topped the turnout poll at almost 91% and was followed by **Malta** (82.37%) and **Cyprus** (71.19%). More ominously the turnout in **France** and Germany fell again from 1999 figures to 42.76% and 43% respectively. Surprisingly, turnout was generally very low in the latest members; for example, 28.3% in **Slovenia** and the **Czech Republic**, 26.8% in **Estonia**, just under 21% in **Poland**, and the appallingly low 17% in **Slovakia**. Turnout in the **United Kingdom** bucked the trend and rose considerably from just over 23% in 1999 to almost 39% in 2004, but this vote included a healthy showing for the high-profile campaign of the very **Eurosceptic** United Kingdom Independence Party, which picked up 12 UK seats. Most of these MEPs then opt to belong to seven **party groups** within the parliament or opt to remain unattached to any group.

The EP also has substantial budgetary powers, where it again shares authority with the Council of the European Union. It must approve the budget: if it fails to do so, EU expenditure is frozen at the previous year's level, with only one-twelfth of the budgetary expenditure approved for the previous year being available each month until the issue is resolved. The EP's freedom of action is substantially greater on **non-compulsory expenditure**. However, while it can block a budget, it cannot substitute one of its own.

The EP was provided for further powers under the proposed **Treaty establishing a Constitution for Europe**. Essentially, it would have extended the use of co-decision and, significantly, given the EP greater say over both the final settlement of the **budget** and the **common agricultural policy**. The treaty also capped the size of the EP to 750. The EP normally meets for one week each month (except in August), with further meetings in March and October when agricultural prices and the budget are considered. Most of its work is done in its 17 specialized committees, which correspond to different policy areas and European Commission agencies. Committee memberships are determined by the **party groups** in proportion to the number of seats they occupy in the EP. **Members of the European Parliament** (MEPs) sit not by nationality, but in transnational party groups, which have official recognition and receive administrative expenses. MEPs who choose not to belong to a party group are each entitled to serve on one committee. Each committee appoints a *rapporteur*, who draws up the programme for discussion and prepares drafts for resolution by the committee, which are then presented to the full EP.

The MEPs elect a president who serves for a two-and-a-half year term. The current EP president is **Josep Borrell**. In all its functions the effectiveness of the EP is diminished by two structural conditions. The first is the fact that it conducts its business in 20 **languages**, and all the costs and consequences of translating its oral and written business. The second condition is that its operations are dispersed across three Member States. Plenary sessions continue to be held mainly in Strasbourg. Most committees meet in Brussels in order to be close to the executive centre of the EC; after 1994 some plenary sessions were also held there. By contrast, much of the supporting secretariat is located in Luxembourg, and must move to Brussels or Strasbourg, along with the necessary documentation and paraphernalia, for EP sessions. France and Luxembourg have resisted the EP's efforts to relocate all its operations to Brussels, and in 1992 and 1997 it was confirmed that the present, unsatisfactory arrangements would remain until the Member States could unanimously agree upon a change.

EUROPEAN PARTNERSHIPS were launched in 2003 and are being concluded by the European Union (EU) with the countries of the **Western Balkans**. They are similar to **accession partnerships** in that they identify short- and medium-term priorities which the countries need to address in order to integrate with the EU. It is envisaged that the successful fulfilment of the priorities will equip the countries with the institutional and legislative framework and administrative capacity required for a functioning democracy and market economy. It should also speed up their progress towards EU membership.

A **EUROPEAN PASSPORT** was first proposed in 1974. In 1981 the Member States agreed upon the size and layout of a common format burgundy-coloured passport that would be marked 'European Community'. It was due to be introduced in January 1985. While only three Member States met the deadline, all began to comply over the next few years. European passports were marked 'European Union' from 1995.

EUROPEAN PATENT CONVENTION: See **Community Patent Convention**

The **EUROPEAN PAYMENTS UNION** (EPU) was established in 1950 under the auspices of the **Organisation for European Economic Co-operation** (OEEC). It was intended to tackle the problem of reciprocal credits and facilitate multilateral trade once the **Marshall Plan** had come to an end. The EPU proved to be highly successful, and in 1959 was replaced by a broader European Monetary Agreement, which fulfilled the same purpose. It contributed to the ability of the **Six** to co-operate economically in the 1950s, and it was used by the **European Economic Community** (EEC) during the latter's first year of operation.

EUROPEAN PEOPLE'S PARTY AND EUROPEAN DEMOCRATS: See **Group of the European People's Party (Christian Democrats) and European Democrats**

EUROPEAN POLICE OFFICE: See **EUROPOL**

EUROPEAN POLITICAL COMMUNITY was the name of a concept that arose out of the attempts to establish the **European Defence Community** (EDC) in the early 1950s; it was based on the view that a common defence structure ideally required a correspondingly unified foreign policy. It involved only the **Six** countries that had established the **European Coal and Steel Community** (ECSC) and which had committed themselves to the EDC. The unratified EDC treaty required its proposed Common Assembly to study ways of establishing federal institutions. The ECSC Assembly was transformed into an *ad hoc* EDC Assembly to consider a more wide-ranging political co-operation than could be provided by the ECSC and EDC. The Assembly began its work in September 1952 and reported six months later in favour of a European Political Community that would go beyond **sectoral integration** and form the basis of a comprehensive political federation to which the ECSC and EDC would be subordinated. A draft treaty, with a proposed institutional structure based upon the ECSC model, was drawn up in March 1953. However, the EDC treaty had still not been ratified by any state when the Political Community treaty was published. Despite the significant implications of the proposed European Political Community, it was the subject of very little debate; its fate was totally dependent upon the EDC. The important arguments of the time concerned the EDC treaty, the **ratification** or rejection of which would determine the fate of the European Political Community. The refusal of **France** to ratify the EDC treaty in August 1954 effectively meant the abandonment of the draft Political Community treaty.

EUROPEAN POLITICAL CO-OPERATION (EPC), also known by the acronym POCO, was more of a concept than a structure. It was a term used to describe co-operation in foreign policy and foreign affairs by the Member States of the European Communities (EC). Its origins lay in the **Davignon Report** of 1970, and its objectives were to ensure a better mutual understanding of international problems and issues among the Member States through a regular process of consultation and exchange of information, to work towards a **harmonization** of views and a co-ordination of foreign policy positions, and, where appropriate, to attempt to establish a common EC position. The first ministerial meeting under EPC took place in 1970 and the first joint statement, on the Middle East, was issued in May 1971.

EPC was not based on the **founding treaties**, and its development occurred outside the institutional framework of the EC. It developed as an essentially intergovernmental operation involving close and continuing liaison between the national foreign ministries, with an ongoing consultation process involving ambassadors from the EC states to foreign countries and the **United Nations** (UN), and the issuing of common instructions by the foreign ministries to their diplomatic representatives abroad. Three major types of initiative emerged from EPC. The first was the practice for the EC, wherever possible, to have a single representation and single position in international meetings: the EC position was normally presented by the country occupying the presidency of the Council of Ministers (see **Council of the European Union**). In particular, great efforts were made to ensure that the Member States agreed upon a common position on issues in the UN General Assembly. The second element of EPC involved the adoption of common policy statements and initiatives by the **European Council**, occasionally leading to action towards developing a common policy position. Finally, the most specific outcome of EPC was agreement to impose common economic **sanctions** on named countries.

The **Single European Act** regularized the position of EPC within the EC framework, committing the Member States to 'endeavour jointly to formulate and implement a European foreign policy'. It also provided EPC with a small secretariat in Brussels, and made it responsible for the political and economic aspects of a security policy. Despite its intergovernmental character and the non-binding nature of its agreements, EPC proved to be a successful operation, although one that was far from constituting a European foreign policy. It was the changing nature of world politics after 1989, as much as the desire for further integration, which led the EC to reconsider EPC. With the **Treaty on European Union** (TEU), EPC was replaced by the **common foreign and security policy** (CFSP).

The **EUROPEAN PRIVATE EQUITY AND VENTURE CAPITAL ASSOCIATION** (EVCA) was formed in 1983 and is intended to promote the discussion and study of the management and investment of venture capital. Supported by the **European Commission**, EVCA has as its broader aim to develop a European capital market. It has been particularly concerned with the development of small and medium-sized companies. Projects developed under EVCA have received a maximum of 30% funding from the European Communities (EC), and are required, ideally, to complement other EC policies and programmes. (See also **European Business and Innovation Centre Network**.)

EUROPEAN PROGRAMME FOR HIGH TECHNOLOGY RESEARCH AND DEVELOPMENT: See **EUREKA**

A **EUROPEAN PUBLIC PROSECUTOR'S OFFICE** was envisaged in the **Treaty establishing a Constitution for Europe**. Provided the Member States unanimously had agreed on its establishment, the office would have been responsible for 'investigating, prosecuting and bringing to judgment ... the perpetrators of, and accomplices in, offences against the Union's financial interests'. Its powers could have been further extended, by unanimity, to include 'serious crime having a cross-border dimension'.

The **EUROPEAN RAPID REACTION FORCE** (ERRF) was formed in 1999–2003 to support the European Union's (EU) efforts to move beyond a **common foreign and security policy** and establish a **European security and defence policy**. Technically, the ERRF is not a standing force. Instead, it is based on commitments from the Member States to ensure that the EU has at its disposal an ERRF of 60,000 troops that can be mobilized at 60 days' notice. Currently, there is a resource of 100,000 persons and approximately 400 combat aircraft and 100 vessels on which the EU can draw. The ERRF has been deployed to date in **Macedonia** (Operation Concordia) and the Democratic Republic of Congo (Operation Artemis).

EUROPEAN RECOVERY PROGRAMME: See **Marshall Plan**

The **EUROPEAN REGIONAL DEVELOPMENT FUND** (ERDF) is one of the four **structural funds** and was established in 1975. It is the central element of efforts by the European Communities (EC) to develop an effective **regional policy**. It is run by a Regional Fund Committee, structured along the lines of the **Management Committees** of the **Common Agricultural Policy** (CAP), and a Regional Policy Committee consisting of two representatives from each Member State and the **European Commission**, with a chairperson elected from among the government representatives, and with a secretariat provided by the Commission.

The bulk of ERDF expenditure is devoted to specific projects for regional infrastructural developments proposed by the Member States, including grants to enterprises as well as for public works. While only national governments may bid for support from the Fund, these projects often originate from regional and local authorities, other public bodies, or private companies. Financial assistance from the ERDF is mainly focused on: supporting **small and medium-sized enterprises** (SMEs); promoting productive investment; and improving infrastructure and further local development. One of its prime aims is to create employment by fostering competitive and sustainable development.

The ERDF is also used to support EC programmes proposed by the Commission as being of particular importance, often to two or more regions, and it may also be used to support national programmes deemed to possess a value for the European Union (EU) as a whole. Each Member State must submit a list of the programmes and projects for which it is seeking support. National programmes and some major individual projects are evaluated by the Regional Policy Committee. Decisions on smaller projects may be taken by the Regional Fund Committee. To be considered by the ERDF, national programmes must receive Commission endorsement. They must be located in those regions which the Member State has designated as being eligible for support under its own regional aid schemes; they must be consistent with EC objectives; and they must appear to be economically worthwhile. The ERDF operates under the principle of **additionality**, providing a maximum of 50% of the costs, with the Member State having to fund the remainder.

Originally, ERDF resources did not go exclusively to the poorest regions of the EC. Each Member State was allocated a percentage quota of the Fund, against which it could bid for support. This provided aid for the weakest regions in each country, no matter how healthy they might be in the context of the EC as a whole. The quota system was a constant source of contention among the Member States. A limited non-quota element (totalling only 5%), to be utilized by the European Commission for its own programmes, was added in 1979, and in 1985 quotas were abandoned in favour of a percentile range of the ERDF budget being allocated to each Member State; the range indicates the maximum and minimum levels of support a state can receive, provided that an appropriate number of eligible programmes submitted receive endorsement.

In 1987 the Commission introduced a five-year budgetary package to cover all EC expenditure. As part of this the Commission proposed the reform of, and increased resources for, the structural funds in the period from 1988 to 1992. This so-called proposal, which became known as **Delors I**, was supported at a special **European Council** summit in Brussels in 1988. The issue had proved to be problematic, as the UK Prime Minister, **Margaret Thatcher**, had strong reservations over aspects of regional funding and preferred to let market liberalization erode regional disparities within Member States. However, the German Chancellor, **Helmut Kohl**, sympathized with the four poorest EC states (**Ireland**, **Greece**, **Portugal** and **Spain**) and wished to compensate them financially. Under the agreement reached, EC structural spending rose from 15% to 31% of total spending. **Jacques Delors**, then President of the Commission, described the European Council's decision as a 'second Marshall Plan'. The 1988 reform radically revised structural policy by introducing a number of new principles, Additionality, Partnership, Programming and Concentration, and identified five priority objective areas (development of lagging regions under objective 1; conversion of regions facing industrial decline under objective 2; combating long-term unemployment under objective 3; combating youth unemployment under objective 4; and development of rural areas under objective 5).

In 1992 the Commission proposed an ambitious new five-year budgetary package (**Delors II**) to the European Council. At the Edinburgh summit in December the European Council agreed to double EC assistance to the least prosperous regions. The decision again reflected pressure from the four poorest states and the willingness of **Germany** (albeit now more reluctant post-unification in 1990) largely to finance it. When **Austria**, **Finland** and **Sweden** joined the EU in 1995 a new objective was created to help low–population density regions (objective 6). By 1999 structural and cohesion funds made up more than one-third of the EC **budget**. Spending had risen from **ECU** 18,000m. in 1992 to ECU 31,000m. by 1999.

The current multi-annual programme runs from 2000 to 2006 and was determined at the European Council summit in Berlin in March 1999. This followed the Commission's action plan, **Agenda 2000**, which aimed to provide the EU with a new financial framework in preparation for **enlargement**. Under this framework, the funds available for spending in structural assistance were to decrease. Spending on such assistance was still to account for about one-third of the EC's total budget for this period, some €195,000m. (at 1999 prices). In 2003 spending on the EU's structural operations (including the **Cohesion Fund**) accounted for 34.3% of the EU budget (€33,164m.). Financial assistance has been concentrated, moreover, on the most needy areas and to this end the number of objective areas was reduced from seven to three and redefined. The bulk of the funds available was designated for the new objective 1 areas (i.e.

towards the development and structural adjustment of the least developed regions), the poorest EU areas, which consisted mainly of eastern regions of Germany, Greece, **Italy**, Spain and Portugal. In 2003, for example, €21,577m. was directed to these areas. In contrast, €3,652m. was spent on objective 2 regions (to support the economic and social conversion of areas facing structural difficulties) and €3,719m. on the new objective 3 areas (supporting the adaptation and modernization of policies and systems of education, training and employment). Negotiations for the new multi-annual programme (2007–13) commenced in early 2004. Member States are unlikely to increase the amount of money spent in this area and there are already calls to reduce funding and cut back the money available to the EU **budget** and to end the **United Kingdom budget rebate**. It looks increasingly likely, however, that Cornwall will be the only region in the United Kingdom to fulfil the objective 1 criteria.

EUROPEAN RESEARCH CO-ORDINATION AGENCY: See **EUREKA**

EUROPEAN RIGHT (DR) was the name of one of the cross-national **party groups** in the **European Parliament** (EP) until 1994. It was formed after the 1984 **direct elections** by extreme right-wing and neo-Fascist groups. Because of the political attitudes of its members, the DR was the most isolated group in the EP, with no other group willing to be associated with it: indeed, in 1984 other party groups strove to avoid having to be seated beside it. Its share of the vote has dwindled over the last decade to such an extent that it was neither represented in the 1999–2004 parliament nor in the current one (2004–09).

The **EUROPEAN ROUND TABLE OF INDUSTRIALISTS** (ERT) is an influential **Brussels**-based organization that seeks to promote the interests of business in the strategic thinking of the European Union (EU) and in particular the **European Commission**. It was established in 1983 and is comprised of around 45 chief executives of the largest firms across the EU. These include representatives, for example, from the **United Kingdom** (AstraZeneca, British American Tobacco and BT), from **Germany** (Siemens, Volkswagen and Bayer), from **France** (Suez, Renault and Total) and from **Italy** (Pirelli and Fiat). ERT members strongly endorse the benefits of European economic integration and the role of business within it. First, they believe that a dynamic, wealth-producing industrial sector benefits society as a whole. Membership is personal and not corporate, but it is by invitation only. The ERT is funded by multinational firms and maintains some 10 personnel in Brussels. In terms of sectoral areas, the ERT has taken a particular interest in information technology and life-long learning skills. It was highly influential in the development of plans to complete the **internal market** and to promote **Trans-European Networks**. (See also **interest groups**.) The ERT strongly encourages the promotion of the **Lisbon Agenda**, but also recognizes that European industry cannot flourish unless it is competitive with other businesses around the world. The prevailing economic and social policy framework is, the ERT argues, crucially important and must be flexible enough to adapt to changes in global conditions. ERT constantly demands policies which provide that flexibility and enable European companies to build and improve their competitive strengths.

EUROPEAN SCHOOLS have been established by the **European Commission** in several countries. They are intended primarily for the children of European Communities employees, in particular those working in a Member State other than their own. Subject to the availability of space, they are open to other pupils. The schools try to provide a European education by offering an international syllabus in which tuition is given in several European Union **languages**. The syllabus leads to the European Baccalaureate, a recognized system of academic attainment that allows for entry to universities. The headteachers are appointed by an intergovernmental committee on which the Commission is also represented. Each national government appoints a proportion of the other teaching staff.

EUROPEAN SECURITY AND DEFENCE IDENTITY (ESDI) is often used to describe the goal of increased co-operation within the **North Atlantic Treaty Organization** (NATO) between its European members, particularly after 1994. Such co-operation was designed to complement the development of the **common foreign and security policy** of the European Union. More recently, efforts to develop a **European security and defence policy** have promoted the ESDI.

The **EUROPEAN SECURITY AND DEFENCE POLICY** (ESDP) is a relatively recent development, emerging from the **common foreign and security policy** (CFSP) and European Union (EU) efforts to assume a greater role in military and defence matters since the late 1990s. It thus represents a step towards establishing a **common defence policy** and ultimately a **common defence** for the EU. As part of the ESDP, the EU has assumed greater responsibility for the so-called **Petersberg tasks** – humanitarian and rescue operations, peace-keeping activities and combat-force tasks in crisis management, including peace-making – and established a **European rapid reaction force** of 60,000 persons to carry out the full range of them at short notice. In addition, new institutional structures have been put in place, notably the **Military Committee of the European**

Union and the Military Staff of the European Union. These provide military expertise and support to the ESDP, including the conduct of EU-led military crisis management operations. Closer links have also been developed with the **North Atlantic Treaty Organization,** but the Iraqi war in early 2003 clearly laid bare the differences and disagreements between the members of both the EU and NATO on security issues. In an attempt to give greater strategic direction to the ESDP, the **High Representative** for the CFSP, **Javier Solana**, subsequently devised a **European Security Strategy** for the EU. This was formally adopted by the **European Council** in December 2003. Further initiatives designed to promote the development of the ESDP were agreed as part of the **Treaty establishing a Constitution for Europe**. These include **permanent structured co-operation**, creation of a European Armaments, Research and Military Capabilities Agency (see **European Defence Agency**), and the introduction of a mutual assistance clause in the event of a Member State being the victim of armed aggression on its territory.

A **EUROPEAN SECURITY STRATEGY** entitled 'A Secure Europe in a Better World' and devised by the EU's **High Representative, Javier Solana**, was adopted by the **European Council** in December 2003. The strategy is to guide the **Common Foreign and Security Policy** and the **European Security and Defence Policy**. It consists of three main objectives: addressing threats posed by terrorism, nuclear proliferation and regional conflicts; building security in the EU's neighbourhood; and establishing an international order based on effective multilateralism. It commits the EU to greater activity in realizing these objectives, an enhancement of capabilities, greater coherence, and increased co-operation with other parties (e.g. the **USA** and **Russia**).

EUROPEAN SOCIAL CHARTER: See **Charter of Fundamental Social Rights of Workers**

The **EUROPEAN SOCIAL FUND** (ESF) was established as required by the **Treaty of Rome** in order for the European Communities (EC) to develop 'employment opportunities for workers', to raise their standard of living, and to make 'the employment of workers easier', especially by 'increasing their geographical and occupational mobility within the Community'. From its inception in 1960, therefore, the ESF has been concerned with the specific field of employment and training rather than with broad issues of general social welfare. During the 1960s the Fund's operations were limited, being confined mainly to the retraining of workers made redundant by structural economic change. With the dramatic increase in unemployment after 1973, the role of the Fund was redefined and enhanced in terms of retraining, redeployment and the provision of vocational training for young people. Persisting high levels of unemployment, and budgetary restrictions, obliged the ESF to narrow its priorities, and it refocused its activities on retraining and the development of employment skills among young people, with particular attention being paid to the long-term unemployed and women. In 1988 it was agreed that 75% of ESF resources would be spent on projects for people under 25. These funds included substantial amounts spent on the (now-defunct) Programme for the Vocational Training of Young People and their Preparation for Adult and Working Life (PETRA) and EUROFORM initiatives. In addition, the ESF was obliged to focus more intensively on the most economically disadvantaged regions of the EC.

In 1999 a new **regulation** was adopted by the **Council of the European Union** and the **European Parliament,** laying down general provisions on, and the three new objectives for, the **structural funds**. On the social front, the regulation provides for action in five general areas. These include: the development of active labour market policies to combat unemployment; the promotion of **equal opportunities** for all in terms of access to the market and particularly for those at risk from social exclusion; the promotion of vocational training; the promotion of a skilled, well-trained and flexible workforce; and specific measures to improve access to the labour market, especially for women. These objectives are in line with the EC strategy and guidelines on **employment.**

ESF resources are available for both large- and small-scale projects proposed or accepted by a Member State. It operates under the principle of **additionality**, normally providing only 50% of the projected costs of a scheme, the balance having to be met by the Member State. In poor regions that have been given absolute priority status, the ESF contribution is permitted to rise to 75%. A small proportion (some 5%) of ESF expenditure is reserved for other more general purposes or special operations defined by the **European Commission**, which typically involve contributions from several EC sources combined into an integrated programme. The ESF is managed by a Social Fund Committee, and consumes some 8–10% of the EC **budget.** The European Social Fund spent €60bn between 2000 and 2006. Special attention was paid to funding for areas of the EU with particularly high levels of unemployment or low average incomes. Around €3bn was reserved during this period for the **EQUAL** programme. In 2006 the ESF provided some €11.6m. to promote better jobs and working conditions. The money will be directed towards initiatives that develop human resources, secure better integration in the workplace and ensure equality between the sexes.

The **EUROPEAN SPACE AGENCY** (ESA) was established in 1975. It represents a consortium of countries that produce the **Ariane** rocket used to send commercial satellites into space. Its origins lie with the inadequacies of the first collaborative European organization for space research, the **European Space Research Organization** (ESRO), and led to its re-evaluation by a European Space Conference. Negotiations between 1971 and 1973 produced an agreement to establish ESA as a replacement for ESRO. ESA's 17 Member States are Austria, Belgium, Denmark, Finland, France, Germany, Greece, Ireland, Italy, Luxembourg, the Netherlands, Norway, Portugal, Spain, Sweden, Switzerland and the United Kingdom. Canada, Hungary and the Czech Republic have co-operative status and participate in certain ESA projects. ESA is an independent European agency that employs some 2,000 people and has its headquarters in Paris as well as a number of other centres such as ESTEC. ESTEC, the European Space Research and Technology Centre, is the design hub for most ESA spacecraft and technology development, and is situated in Noordwijk, the Netherlands.

ESA is governed by a Council, which comprises members from each of the ESA member states. ESA does not form part of the European Union (EU). There are, however, close ties between the two organizations and they are linked by a common aim: to strengthen Europe and benefit its citizens.

ESA is funded by its member countries, and its objective is 'to provide and to promote, for exclusively peaceful purposes, co-operation among European states in space research and technology and their space applications, with a view to their being used for scientific purposes and for operational space applications'. ESA has been active in satellite development, and in 1984 adopted the long-term 'Horizon 2000' programme to work towards manned European space flight. The 'Horizon 2000 Plus' extension programme, covering the years 2005–16, was initiated in 1994 for the inclusion of projects using new technologies and for participation in future international space activities. ESA has earned a reputation for competence and by March 2002 had launched 17 scientific satellites and probes. (See also **EUMETSAT**.)

ESA's ties with the EU have developed considerably in recent years because of the increasing role of space in strengthening Europe's political and economic role. The necessity of ensuring Europe's guaranteed access to space is becoming ever more apparent as satellites are used to improve communications and navigation, monitor the environment, strengthen technology and increase scientific knowledge. To this end ESA has also set up a liaison office in Brussels to facilitate relations between the two organizations. Recent joint initiatives include Galileo, a European global navigation satellite system and the Global Monitoring for Environment and Security suite of services, known as GMES. A forthcoming initiative concerns satellite-based measures to overcome the digital divide within Europe.

In January 2003 the then European Research Commissioner, Philippe Busquin, introduced a **Green Paper** on European Space Policy, prepared in co-operation with ESA. The Green Paper examined Europe's strengths and weaknesses in the space sector and sought to launch a debate on Europe's space policy and to increase awareness of the strategic importance of space and space policy for Europe and its citizens. In November 2003 the ESA Council adopted the Framework Agreement, previously endorsed by the EU Council in October 2003. Its origins date from an ESA Ministerial Council meeting in November 2001 that gave clear directions on the Agency's evolution and policy, and called for a Framework Agreement to formalize co-operation between ESA and the EU.

This Agreement marks a milestone in ESA/EU relations. It recognizes that both parties have specific complementary strengths, and commits them to working together. The Agreement has two main aims: firstly, the establishment of a common basis and appropriate practical arrangements for efficient and mutually beneficial co-operation between ESA and the EU; and secondly, the progressive development of a European space policy to link the demand for services and applications in support of EU policies with the supply, through ESA, of the space systems and infrastructure needed to meet that demand.

As a result the EU adopted this action plan for implementing an enlarged European space policy in November 2003. Drafted by the EU and ESA, the White Paper includes proposals for joint ESA–EU space activities and takes the Framework Agreement as its basis for implementation.

The **EUROPEAN SPACE RESEARCH ORGANIZATION** (ESRO) was a multi-purpose organization established in 1961 with the participation of several European countries. It was intended both to carry out scientific research and to design and develop European satellites built on a collaborative basis by its members. During its existence, it was beset with disputes between scientists, and arguments over both projects and costs between the participating countries. It became the core of the **European Space Agency** established in 1975.

EUROPEAN STANDARDS COMMITTEE: See **CEN**

The **EUROPEAN STRATEGIC PROGRAMME FOR RESEARCH AND DEVELOPMENT IN INFORMATION TECHNOLOGY** (ESPRIT) was a European Communities (EC) initiative established in 1984. In order to foster and increase co-operation by the Member States in science and technology **research and technological development**, the EC sponsored a pilot scheme involving 38 separate contracts that entailed co-operation between companies from at least two Member States. On the basis of this experience, ESPRIT was launched as a five-year programme to develop EC resources in information technology to full-systems capability based on semiconductor technology. A series of projects were conducted under the auspices of ESPRIT in a number of technology areas. The overall programme was defined by a specially commissioned Task Force for Information Technology and Telecommunications, which in 1987 was fully absorbed within the **European Commission**. EC funding, which extended to a maximum level of only 50% of the projected research and development costs, was available only for applications that included companies, universities or research institutes from at least two Member States. The programme was deemed to be a success in terms of the number of projects funded, the number of participants involved and the practical applications resulting from them, and it was agreed in 1994 to extend ESPRIT for a further five-year term. The extension was given funds triple those available for the first programme, and the new schedule called for a concentration of effort in applied technologies, information technology processing systems and microelectronics. As part of a new Framework Programme in 1998, ESPRIT was subsumed into the **Information Society Technologies** (IST) programme.

EUROPEAN SYSTEM FOR THE INTERNATIONAL CLEARING OF VACANCIES AND APPLICATIONS FOR EMPLOYMENT: See **EURES**

The **EUROPEAN SYSTEM OF CENTRAL BANKS** (ESCB) came into existence in 1998 once the date for the third and final stage of **economic and monetary union** (EMU) had been set. It coexists with the **European Central Bank** (ECB), having the responsibility of maintaining price stability, defining and implementing a common monetary policy, and supervising the foreign reserves and foreign exchange operations of the Member States. It consists of the national central banks of the 25 European Union Member States, along with the ECB, although those Member States not participating in EMU are unable to take part in decision-making in this area.

The **EUROPEAN SYSTEM OF INTEGRATED ECONOMIC ACCOUNTS** (ESA) was established to assist in the development of a European information system in connection with the **internal market**. This was to be compatible with the System of National Accounts (SNA), which was to be used to monitor the development of **economic and monetary union** (EMU).

EUROPEAN TELECOMMUNICATIONS SATELLITE ORGANIZATION: See **EUTELSAT**

The **EUROPEAN TRADE UNION CONFEDERATION** (ETUC) is the major umbrella organization for Member States' national trade unions, and for union federations outside the European Union. In 2006 ETUC comprised 79 national trade union confederations from 35 countries in Europe, and 11 associations representing European industry, resulting in a total membership of some 60m. people. Other trade union structures such as Eurocadres (the Council of European Professional and Managerial Staff) and EFREP/FERPA (European Federation of Retired and Elderly Persons) operate under the auspices of the ETUC. In addition, ETUC co-ordinates the activities of the 39 Interregional Trade Union Councils (ITUCs), which organize trade union co-operation at cross-border level. ETUC was founded in 1973, and since 1975 it has claimed to speak on behalf of all the major unions in the European Communities (EC). Based in **Brussels**, it is represented on several EU committees and organizations, and is generally recognized as a body with a legitimate interest in EU affairs. ETUC is recognized by the European Union, by the **Council of Europe** and by **EFTA** as the only representative cross-sectoral trade union organization at European level.

ETUC exists to speak with one voice on behalf of workers in Europe. It strives to promote the 'European Social Model' which ETUC believes should embody a society combining sustainable economic growth with ever-improving living and working standards, full employment, social protection, equal opportunities and social inclusion. ETUC campaigns constantly for the EU with a strong social dimension. It has developed close relationship with the **European Parliament**, has membership of a number of advisory bodies, consults other social partners and takes part in discussions on the **Lisbon Agenda**. ETUC has been particularly active in supporting EU initiatives on **workers' rights**, notably the **Charter of Fundamental Social Rights of Workers**, but less active in seeking to promote industrial development. Under the **Treaty on European Union** (TEU, as amended by the **Treaty of Amsterdam**) ETUC is recognized as one of the three 'social partners', alongside industry associations such as the **Union of Industrial and Employers Confederations of Europe** (UNICE), with which the **European Commission** negotiates draft social and economic legislation. In 2004, ETUC was particularly vocal on a number of issues. For example, it strongly condemned calls for a longer working week, urged the Dutch presidency of the **European Council** to push for a greater social agenda and supported the **Treaty establishing a Constitution for Europe** as a starting point for progress towards greater social values in the EU. ETUC has played a key role in helping to formulate key parts of EC/EU legislation, for example the European Works Councils Directive of 1994 and the Information and Consultation Directive of 2002. More recently it has also been active in organizing a number of high-profile demonstrations or Action Days to coincide with **summit meetings** or to protest about the impact of policies that threaten to undermine the 'European Social Model'.

The **EUROPEAN TRAINING FOUNDATION** (ETF) was established by the Council of Ministers (see **Council of the European Union**) in 1990. In November 1993 it was agreed that the Foundation was to be located in Turin, **Italy**. The ETF is open also to states outside the European Union (EU). Its aims are to develop vocational training and retraining, and to channel aid to training projects, particularly those concerning Eastern Europe, and especially the **candidate countries**. It has also been made responsible for co-ordinating EU higher education programmes in the **PHARE** states of **Central and Eastern Europe**. (See also **European Centre for the Development of Vocational Training**; **TEMPUS**.)

EUROPEAN TREATIES is becoming a frequently used term referring to the combination of **founding treaties** (see **Treaty of Paris**; **Treaty of Rome**), **accession treaties** and amending treaties (e.g. the **Single European Act**, **Treaty on European Union**, **Treaty of Amsterdam** and the **Treaty of Nice**), which make up the treaty base of the European Union (EU). Currently, consideration is being given to the consolidation of most of these as part of an EU **Constitution** or **Constitutional Treaty**.

EUROPEAN UNION (EU) is the name of the body established in 1993 by the **Treaty on European Union** (TEU), although its exact status was not fully and clearly defined by the Treaty. It has a notional structure consisting of three **pillars**. At the centre is pillar I which comprises the European Communities (EC). This is complemented by two pillars of intergovernmental co-operation: **common foreign and security policy** (pillar II) and **justice and home affairs** (pillar III). This pillar structure enhances the powers of the **European Council**, whose role encompasses all the components of the EU. The supranational institutions, meanwhile, concern themselves mainly with matters covered by pillar I. Hence, the **European Commission** has only a limited role in pillars II and III. The same is true of the **Court of Justice** and the **European Parliament**. While the EU is a political entity that seeks to improve and deepen the relationships between the Member States, and one which claims to have its own **citizenship**, it nevertheless accepts the principle of **subsidiarity** and recognizes national identity. In addition, it is not described by the TEU as a fixed structure, but a 'new stage in the process of creating an ever closer union'. Further timetables and targets were therefore established, most of which were reviewed by an **intergovernmental conference** (IGC) in 1996. This produced the **Treaty of Amsterdam** which reformed elements of each of the EU's three pillars, notably pillar III, various activities of which were 'communitarized' (i.e. moved to the first supranational pillar) and whose title was consequently changed to **police and judicial co-operation in criminal matters**. Further reforms were introduced via the **Treaty of Nice** in 2003. What shape the EU will have in the future was a key focus of debates within the **European Convention** in 2002–2003 and the subsequent IGC launched in October 2003.

EUROPEAN UNION LAW can be used as a generic term to describe all the law produced by the European Union (EU). To some, however, there is a need to distinguish between, on the one hand, the law of the supranational European Communities (EC) and the *acquis communautaire* – EC law – and, on the other, the law that has been and is created under the EU's two intergovernmental **pillars** covering the **common foreign and security policy** and **police and judicial co-operation in criminal matters.**

EUROPEAN UNION OF FEDERALISTS is the name of an organization established in 1946 to harness and combine, on a transnational basis, the energy and ideas of the several groups and organizations that had emerged in 1945 to advocate a federal European state. While supporting the **Congress of Europe**, it was effectively superseded after 1948 by the **European Movement**. By 1950, both federalism and the Union itself had fallen out of favour. Riven by internal disputes, it disintegrated in 1956.

The **EUROPEAN UNION SATELLITE CENTRE** was established in 2001. Situated in Torrejón in **Spain**, it is an agency of the Council of Ministers (see **Council of the European Union**) responsible for producing satellite imagery to aid decision-making in the field of the **common foreign and security policy**, notably where crisis monitoring and conflict prevention are concerned.

The **EUROPEAN UNIT OF ACCOUNT** (EUA) was the book-keeping device introduced by the European Communities (EC) for recording the relative value of payments into and from EC accounts. In 1981 it was replaced by the **ECU**, which in turn was replaced by the **euro** in 1999.

EUROPEAN UNITARIAN LEFT: See **Confederal Group of the European United Left/Nordic Green Left**

The **EUROPEAN UNIVERSITY INSTITUTE** (EUI) was founded in 1976 as part of the European Communities (EC) policy of encouraging co-operation in higher education. Based in Florence, **Italy**, the EUI is an establishment for research and training in postgraduate education, offering doctoral programmes in economics, history and civilization, law and political and social sciences.

Entry for students is competitive. Those accepted on the programmes are funded by their national governments and are expected to have some competence in more than one **language** of the European Union. Staff appointments, made on the basis of open competition, are funded by the EC and are for fixed terms of between three and seven years. The EUI is the depository for the historical archives of the EC institutions.

The **EUROPEAN VOLUNTARY SERVICE** (EVS) programme enables young people between the ages of 18 and 25 to participate in voluntary work within other Member States of the European Union. The programme, which was piloted in 1996, proved to be so successful that the **European Parliament** and the **European Council** supported a proposal to grant the EVS a budget of **ECU** 47.5m. for 1998–99. The programme subsequently proposed to encourage short-term projects, as well as exchange visits, involving multinational groups and third countries. EVS forms part of the **Youth Programme.**

EUROPEAN YOUTH FORUM is the name of a body established in the mid-1970s as a contribution to the European Communities' educational objective of achieving a better mutual understanding in higher education between the Member States. It was set up to advise and aid the **European Commission** on policy issues that concern young people. Its membership consists of the leaders of the national student and youth organizations. The Forum's impact has been limited, not least because, by its very nature, there is a lack of continuity in its membership. (See also **Youth for Europe**.)

EUROPEANIZATION (or arguably, and more accurately, EUization) is a popular theme of current academic research and is used most often to describe and assess the impact that the European Union (EU) exerts on both Member States and non-member states, notably in terms of domestic legislation, policy priorities and administrative structures. Discussions of Europeanization can be measured by looking at the EU's impact on public policies, politics and the public. It affects much more than just Member State governments, and can be applied to a whole range of non-governmental actors who have likewise adjusted their activities and responses to EU structures and activities. The term remains a very fashionable one in contemporary academic literature, but it is often a disputed concept.

EUROPOL stands for European Police Office, an agency that was established in The Hague under the terms of the **Treaty on European Union**. Its objective is to co-ordinate national police activities in the Member States more effectively, as an integral element of **justice and home affairs**, especially in combating drugs-trafficking, fraud and terrorism. The Convention establishing the agency was not signed until June 1995, entering into force in October 1998, but the **Europol Drugs Unit** was already in operation. EUROPOL became fully operational on 1 July 1999. Starting in January 2002, its mandate was extended to include all serious forms of international crime.

The **EUROPOL DRUGS UNIT** operated from 1995 until 1999 before being replaced by **Europol**.

EUROSCEPTICS is a phrase used to describe those people who opposed the **Treaty on European Union** and attempts by the European Communities (EC) to introduce further integration. Their preference is for intergovernmental and free-trade co-operation only. Although opposition to the activities and aims of the European Union can be traced back to the very early days of EC member-ship in many states, Euroscepticism emerged as a particular feature of **United Kingdom** politics in the late 1980s, especially under the final years of **Margaret Thatcher**'s premiership. Then opposition within conservative ranks to the Maastricht Treaty (see **Treaty on European Union)** bedevilled the **John Major** governments and has continued to cast increasing shadows over the second and third **Tony Blair** administrations. Indeed, at the 2004 **European Parliament** (EP) elections, the avowedly anti-EU United Kingdom Indepen-dence Party captured 12 seats and threatened 'to wreck the parliament'. The rising tide of Euroscepticism is not just confined to the UK: there is evidence of similar tendencies emerging in many of the current EU states. The evidence of this reality was felt by both the Dutch and French governments in the late spring of 2005 when their respective electorates voted against the **Treaty establishing a Constitution for Europe**. Indeed, within the EP these more critical voices are represented largely by the **Independence and Democracy Group**.

EUROSTAT is the abbreviated and popularized form of the Statistical Office of the European Communities. It is one of the special services under the jurisdic-tion of the **European Commission**, and is responsible for the collection and publication of statistics covering the whole range of the economic and social affairs of the European Union. While the information is intended in the first instance for use by the Commission and its administration, its documentation is publicly available, both in book form and in databases such as **New Cronos**.

The **EUROZONE** consists of those Member States that are full participants in **economic and monetary union** and have adopted the **euro**.

EURYDICE is the commonly used name for the Education Information Network in the European Community. It was established in 1980 and was one of the European Communities' first essays into both **information technology** and the development of collaboration in **education policy**. The networked information service was based upon databanks of educational statistics, and was available for use by the **European Commission** and national education officials. The programme continued as part of **Socrates** in 1995.

EUTELSAT is the acronym of the European Telecommunications Satellite Organization, an organization established in 1977 in order to foster collaboration in the development of a European communications satellite system, and in the co-ordination and implementation of requirements relating to satellites being developed by the **European Space Agency**. EUTELSAT has no direct links with the European Union (EU), although all the EU Member States are represented. In 2001 Eutelsat was restructured as a company incorporated under French law and now markets its services through a network of partners who include leading telecommunications operators and service providers.

EVCA: See **European Private Equity and Venture Capital Association**

EVS: See **European Voluntary Service**

The **EXCHANGE-RATE MECHANISM** (ERM), along with the **ECU**, was one of the core components of the **European Monetary System** (EMS) established in 1979. It was the central instrument by which the EMS sought to stabilize and limit currency fluctuations. Under the ERM a currency received a central exchange rate against the ECU, the value of which was derived from a **basket of currencies**. From these central rates, a grid of cross-parities was constructed, within which bilateral central rates were calculated for each pair of currencies participating in the ERM. For each currency there was a permissible range of fluctuation around these central rates, as well as a divergence indicator (a threshold point that indicated that the margins of permissible fluctuation were in danger of being breached.) The permissible range was set at $\pm 2.25\%$, with a broader range of $\pm 6.0\%$ for some currencies. The divergence indicator was 75% of this range. Normally, a currency would have reached the divergence threshold before it hit its bilateral limit, but because each currency had a different weighting in the ECU basket, this was not always the case. When the limit for a currency was breached or its divergence indicator triggered, the central banks of the affected states intervened in the exchange markets to keep the currency within the prescribed limits. The banks were supported by the **European**

Monetary Co-operation Fund (EMCF), which supplied short-term credit facilities, but the national authorities could also have been required to take appropriate domestic measures to correct the situation, such as changing interest rates or adopting an incomes policy. Where it proved persistently difficult to hold a currency within its permissible range, mechanisms were available for realigning its central rate. There were 12 exchange rate realignments between 1979 and 1989.

The ERM was credited with contributing to the much lower levels of currency fluctuation in the 1980s, and to the increasing economic **convergence** of the Member States. Its weakness was that not all the Member States were part of it. **Greece** stayed outside the ERM until 1998; **Spain** joined the wider band in 1989, as did the **United Kingdom** in 1990 and **Portugal** in 1992. The 1989 **Delors Plan** saw the ERM as an integral element of **economic and monetary union** (EMU). It called for all Member States to join the ERM as an essential condition for the first of three stages of progress towards full EMU. Partly because of the incorporation of the ERM into the EMU timetable, and partly because of the interpretation of the ERM's previous success, it became a more rigid mechanism after 1990, the scope for adjustments – at least without causing a crisis in the system – being greatly reduced. A more rigid system, however, tended to discount the substantial variations in national economic performance and currency strengths as perceived by the international money markets. The Danish referendum rejecting the **Treaty on European Union** in 1992 was a catalyst for great anxiety and uncertainties in the exchange markets, compounded by the dominance within the ERM of **Germany** which, faced with the escalating costs of reunification, was pursuing a strong domestic anti-inflation policy. The consequent high German interest rates forced other ERM members to pursue similar policies, leading to severe economic problems in several countries. In September 1992 a wave of speculation was unleashed against ERM currencies. Despite massive central bank intervention, there were several involuntary devaluations, and **Italy** and the United Kingdom withdrew from the ERM. Further speculative pressure in August 1993, especially against the French franc, resulted after much acrimony in an extension of the broad range of permissible fluctuation to such a degree that, with only Germany and the **Netherlands** agreeing to stay within the narrow band, the ERM effectively ceased to be a regulatory mechanism. These episodes cast severe doubts on the viability of the timetable for EMU. **Austria** joined the ERM in January 1995 and a further realignment of exchange rates took place in March 1995, when the Spanish peseta was devalued by 7% and the Portuguese escudo by 3.5% in relation to other currencies. **Finland** joined the ERM in October 1996, and Italy rejoined in November of that year. Greece entered the ERM in March 1998.

The need for the ERM, in its original form, ended when the final stage of EMU started on 1 January 1999 (with 11 of the Member States taking part –

Denmark, Greece, **Sweden** and the United Kingdom did not participate, although Greece subsequently met the **convergence criteria** and took part in EMU from 2001) and when the **euro** was introduced as a single currency. However, the ERM was to continue, as ERM2, from 1 January 1999, to regulate the relationship between the euro and the currencies of Member States remaining outside EMU, although some of the non-participating Member States indicated they would not take part in ERM2.

EXCHANGE RATES: See **Bretton Woods**; **Exchange-Rate Mechanism**; **European Monetary System**; **Snake**

EXCISE DUTIES: See **competition policy**; **harmonization**; **internal market**; **White Paper**

EXCLUSIVE AGREEMENTS between companies have been banned under the European Communities' **competition policy**. The ban covers exclusive purchasing agreements on a wide variety of products, several kinds of exclusive distribution agreements, including **market-sharing and price-fixing agreements**, and the use of **patents** and **trademarks**.

EXPENDITURE from the **budget** of the European Communities (EC) comes from EC **own resources**, and is expected to fund both the policies pursued by the EC, and their own running and administrative costs. The largest element of expenditure is on agriculture, which absorbs about one-half of the budget. The **structural funds** absorb a further 30%. Most other policies and programmes each receive less than 5% of the budget. The **Court of Auditors** is responsible for ensuring that all EC expenditure has occurred in a legal manner.

EXTENSIFICATION is a term which is used to describe a reduction in the level of intensive farming, whereby the decrease in agricultural income that might result from lower output is compensated for by a lesser use of fertilizers and pesticides, and the consequent savings.

The draft **EXTERNAL FRONTIERS CONVENTION** proposed determining controls on the crossing of the European Union's (EU) external borders by nationals of non-member states, thereby facilitating the implementation of common EU policies on **visas** and **immigration**. The draft was eventually abandoned because of **Spain**'s desire for Gibraltar to be excluded from the Convention. (See also **Schengen Agreement**.)

EXTERNAL RELATIONS is a collective term which describes the formal bilateral and multilateral trading agreements made by the European Communities (EC) with third countries, for example: **Association Agreements, Co-operation Agreements, Europe Agreements, Partnership and Co-operation Agreements** and the **Cotonou Agreement**. It also refers to attempts by the Member States to develop, outside the institutional structures of the EC, a common set of foreign policies through **European political co-operation** and the **common foreign and security policy**.

F

The *FACTORTAME JUDGMENT* of 1990 (*R v Secretary of State for Transport, ex parte Factortame Ltd*) was an important verdict by the **Court of Justice**, confirming that national legislation in conflict with European Communities law must be suspended. More specifically, the Court ruled that a Member State cannot be liable unless it can be established that the state has severely and deliberately disregarded EC **law**. In order to determine this the following criteria have to be considered: the clarity and precision of the directive; the level of discretion left to the member state to implement the **directive**; whether damages were intentional and whether the failure to implement EC law can be explained by other extenuating circumstances.

The **FAROE ISLANDS** have internal autonomy under Danish sovereignty (see **Denmark**). The parliament of the Islands opposed entry into the European Communities (EC). After extensive negotiations, mainly over fishing rights, an agreement was reached in January 1972. The Islands were granted special status, with the option of applying for full membership by the end of 1975. The Islands, however, have continued to reject membership, and participate only in free-trade arrangements with the European Union. Thus, common EC policies do not apply to the Faroe Islands.

FAIR stands for Fisheries, Agriculture and agro-Industrial Research programme. Established in 1994, this programme replaced all previous agricultural research programmes: AIR, CAMAR, ÉCLAIR, FAR and FLAIR. The objectives of FAIR were: 'To contribute to the improvement of the competitiveness of European agro-industry and primary production by the development of new technologies compatible with sustainable growth and taking account of consumer needs; to improve the quality of agricultural, forestry and fish products in general and food products in particular; to contribute to the implementation of the Community's agriculture, rural development, fisheries, environment and **internal market** policies; to contribute to a better match between the production and utilization of biological primary materials.' It was subsumed into the **Quality of Life and Management of Living Resources Programme** in 1999.

FEDERAL REPUBLIC OF GERMANY: See **Germany**

The **FEDERAL REPUBLIC OF YUGOSLAVIA** (FRY): See **Serbia and Montenegro**

FEDERALISM is a system of government where different levels of authority (usually national and regional) exercise responsibility for particular areas, and maintain their own institutions, and whose specific powers are constitutionally guaranteed. The term has been used loosely and confusingly in the context of the European Union to describe the result of both centralization and decentralization. **Eurosceptics** have used the term to criticize what they see as an undue concentration of power at the supranational level of the European Communities institutions, while others see federalism as the way of preventing such a concentration. In discussions of the **European Council**, it has been used vaguely to refer both to the acquisition of more authority by the supranational institutions and to decentralization, with respect not only to the Member States, but also beyond them to the regions. However, by themselves, concepts such as the **Europe of the Regions** or **subsidiarity** do not fully represent a proper federal structure.

FEOGA: See **European Agricultural Guidance and Guarantee Fund**

FIFTEEN or Europe of the Fifteen, is a term sometimes used to describe the membership of the European Union after January 1995, when **Austria**, **Finland** and **Sweden** joined the existing **Twelve** Member States.

FIFTH DIRECTIVE is the name of the first of several major **European Commission** initiatives relating to the structure of industrial companies and the protection of **workers' rights**. The Directive was proposed in 1972, and its target was those limited companies in the European Communities with a payroll of more than 500 workers. The Directive established conditions for the structure of such companies which, modelled to some extent on the experience of the Federal Republic of **Germany** (West Germany), would entail obligatory worker representation on supervisory boards. It faced powerful opposition from employers' organizations and some Member States, and failed to gain the necessary unanimous approval in the Council of Ministers (see **Council of the European Union**). The idea of worker representation was eventually incorporated into the **Charter of Fundamental Social Rights of Workers** (the Social Charter) and the Social Chapter.

FINALITÉ POLITIQUE is a term used to describe the possible end goals and structure of the European Union. Beyond the references to an 'ever closer union' in the **Treaty of Rome** and **Treaty on European Union**, there is nothing specific written in the treaties regarding this *finalité politique*, although discussions on a **constitution**, particularly in the context of the **Laeken Declaration**, have led to increased pressure to define it. For many, however, the current situation where the *finalité politique* is left undefined is attractive, since it allows for greater flexibility within the process of European integration.

The **FINANCIAL INSTRUMENT FOR FISHERIES GUIDANCE** (FIFG) was established in 1992, and is the main instrument whereby the European Union (EU) affords aid to the fisheries sector under the **Common Fisheries Policy** (CFP). It aims to support the CFP and, in pursuance of that objective, it seeks to help to achieve lasting balance between fish stocks and fishing; to strengthen the competitiveness of operating structures and to develop economically viable firms in the sector; to improve supplies and enhance the commercial value of fishery and aquaculture products; and to help revitalize areas dependent on fisheries and aquaculture. It advocates a restructuring of the industry and is encouraging a reduction in fishing in European Communities (EC) waters, the decommissioning of vessels, establishing joint ventures with foreign investors, increasing competitiveness and assistance for the aquaculture industry, while also promoting economic and social cohesion. National and regional authorities are obliged to contribute to projects, although increased funding is available for poorer regions of the EC. Decision-making concerning the FIFG can be broken down into two stages. In the first a Member State submits a draft programme to the Commission for structural interventions in the fisheries sector: this sets out the strategy and priorities for assistance, as well as a request for funding, in the form of a coherent package of multi-annual measures. Thereafter the Commission negotiates the programme on the basis of this draft with the Member State, and having reached an agreement with the Member State, approves it. The competitiveness of the EU fishing fleet also remains crucial and the FIFG provides support for building and modernizing vessels. FIFG support is also available to the aquaculture sector and for the creation of protected coastal areas. Port facilities, processing, marketing and promotional operations can also attract funding. In addition, the private sector, through the producers' organizations, can apply for funding for various measures relating to the management of the resource and/or fishing effort. Finally, financial contributions to redundancy payments and pensions for fishermen retiring early may also be made. (See also **PESCA**.) Programmed expenditure under the FIFG for 2000–2006 amounted to €3,746m. Over this specific period the EU contribution was able to amount to 75% of the planned total cost of infrastructure in less-developed regions (Objective 1) and 50% in other regions. Where the aid goes to enterprises, the Community contributions were limited to 35% and 15%, respectively.

FINANCIAL PERSPECTIVES are the multi-annual **budget** programmes of the European Communities. The first, often referred to as the **Delors I** package, covered the period 1988–92 and was adopted in 1987 in an attempt to limit the annual wrangling over the budget between what is now the **Council of the European Union** and the **European Parliament** (EP) and provide a firmer foundation for medium-term policy planning. The second financial perspective, the so-called **Delors II** package, covered the years 1993–99. A further perspective was agreed at the Berlin summit of the **European Council** in March 1999 and was designed to finance **enlargement.** It was to cover the period until 2006. Each financial perspective is accompanied by an **inter-institutional agreement**, and understanding between the **European Commission**, the Council of the European Union and the EP, by which they commit themselves in advance to observing agreed limits on the main budgetary priorities and establish a framework for Community expenditure in the form of the financial perspective over a particular time period. In other words, the financial perspective shows the maximum amount and the composition of foreseeable Community expenditure. The main categories of Community expenditure are divided into headings; each of these headings carries an amount of commitment appropriations for each year. The headings are agriculture; structural operations; internal policies; external action; administration; reserves; and pre-accession aid. Negotiations among the Member State governments for a new financial perspective running from 2007 to 2013 proved contentious, but a deal was finally reached in December 2005.

FINANCIAL POLICY: See **Economic and Financial Policy**

FINEFTA is the name of the former agreement between **Finland** and the **European Free Trade Association** (EFTA). Because of its proximity to the **USSR**, and the particular relationship they had, Finland, which had participated in the discussions that led to the establishment of EFTA, originally felt it could not become a full member of the organization. Under FINEFTA, it was given associate status, with more or less the same rights as a full member. Finland became a full member of EFTA in 1986 and remained so until it joined the European Union in January 1995.

FINLAND was restricted in its relationships with other Western European countries by the Finno-Soviet Pact of Friendship, Co-operation and Mutual

Assistance, which had been signed with the **USSR** in 1948. This in effect forced Finland to pursue a foreign policy based on **neutrality**, making its government wary of participation in any organization that the USSR might interpret as violating the terms of the treaty. Hence for a number of years Finland played a minimal role in Western European developments. In the early 1960s it did not approach the European Communities, as did the other Nordic states, for some form of association. Moreover, it became only an associate member of the **European Free Trade Association** (EFTA – see **FINEFTA**). However, it later joined the EFTA states in seeking some form of closer co-operation with the EC. The signing of a **Free Trade Agreement** was delayed until 1973, again because of arguments over whether it violated Finland's neutrality, and doubts about its acceptability to the USSR. The Agreement came into force in January 1974 with an accelerated rate of tariff reductions, in order to synchronize the date for implementation with that for the other EFTA states. Finland became a full member of EFTA in 1986 and in the more relaxed atmosphere of the late 1980s felt able to join the other EFTA states in negotiations with the EC over a **European Economic Area**. In 1992, after much discussion, it formally submitted an application to join the EC. Negotiations were completed by 1994 and endorsed by a popular referendum, allowing Finland to join the European Union on 1 January 1995. Finland has been the only Nordic EU member to adopt the euro as the national currency.

FISCALIS 2007 is a five-year programme launched in 2003 to improve the operation of taxation systems in the **internal market**. European Union funding amounts to €44m. The programme builds on the Fiscalis programme that operated in 1998–2002 and complements the **Customs 2007** programme.

JOSCHKA FISCHER (1948–) served as Federal Minister of Foreign Affairs and Vice-Chancellor of the Federal Republic of **Germany** from 1998 until 2005 . He became Germany's first 'green' foreign minister following the general election victory of the Social Democratic Party and its decision to enter into a coalition government with *Die Grünen*, the Greens. Fischer was elected as one of the first members of the Green Party in 1983 and has emerged as one of Germany's most popular and trusted politicians. Early in 2001, however, his career faced a crisis over his activities as a militant left-wing activist in the 1970s. He apologized for this and retained his portfolio following the re-election of the Red–Green coalition government in 2002. A committed supporter of the European Union, Fischer was instrumental in promoting discussion of further political integration and a European **constitution**. He was also noted for overseeing the deployment of German forces, albeit under the umbrella of the **North Atlantic Treaty Organization**, during the Kosovo conflict in 1999.

FISHERIES: See **Common Fisheries Policy**; **North Atlantic Fisheries Organization**

FLANKING MEASURES is a term used in the European Union to describe measures or actions intended to support the implementation and objectives of a specific common policy or programme, but which are not integral to it. The term is most often used in the context of the **internal market**. Among the most prominent flanking measures are those concerning **economic and monetary union**, **competition policy**, **social policy** and **environmental policy**.

FLEXIBILITY is a term used to describe the effects of different approaches to **integration**, such as **multi-speed Europe**, *à la carte Europe* and **two-speed Europe**. It is also used to describe the effects of the mechanisms for **enhanced co-operation** introduced by the **Treaty of Amsterdam**.

The **FONTAINEBLEAU SUMMIT** of the **European Council**, held in France in June 1984, was one of the most decisive in the history of **summit meetings**. It dealt conclusively with several major issues, which had hindered the development of the European Communities (EC) for a number of years. Agreement was reached on the **United Kingdom**'s budgetary position, raising the limit of **value-added tax** contributions to the EC **budget** to avoid threatened insolvency, limits were placed upon **Common Agricultural Policy** spending, and the way was opened for the entry into the EC of **Portugal** and **Spain**. By resolving such issues and authorizing the establishment of a **Committee for a People's Europe** and the **Dooge Committee**, the summit contributed to the EC's later progress towards further integration.

FOOD AID: See **Development Aid**

FOODSTUFFS are the subject of several European Communities **directives** intended to protect the **health and safety** of consumers and strengthen **consumer policy**. The directives govern the manufacturing, labelling and marketing of foodstuffs. Their provisions include: the publication of listings of permitted substances and additives along with the requisite purity standards; regulations governing the production of a range of foodstuffs; the fixing of maximum permitted levels for pesticide residues in fruit, vegetable and oil products; and regulations specifying that a list of ingredients and their quantities, as well as a 'best before' date, must be included on the labelling of foodstuffs. In addition, a general ban has been placed upon the use of animal growth promoters containing substances that might generate adverse hormonal or other side effects. The **European Parliament** in 2002 proposed stricter labelling regulations for foodstuffs containing genetically modified ingredients. Following a proposal in the **European Commission**'s 2000 **White Paper** on food safety, a **European Food Safety Agency** was created.

FOREIGN POLICY: See **Common Foreign and Security Policy**; **European Political Co-operation**

FORESTRY has been the subject of several European Communities initiatives designed to combine the economic development of the industry with measures for environmental protection and conservation. The initiatives were brought together in the Forestry Sectoral Research and Technology (FOREST) action programme of 1990. This was later absorbed into AIR in 1991, and then into **FAIR**, which was subsequently subsumed into the **Quality of Life and Management of Living Resources Programme**. In 1999 the **Council of the European Union** adopted a **resolution** on a Forestry Strategy for the European Union (EU). The EU also dedicates approximately €120m. a year to forest conservation and management projects in less-developed countries.

FORMER YUGOSLAV REPUBLIC OF MACEDONIA: See **Macedonia**

FORTRESS EUROPE is a term popularized in the 1980s and early 1990s that summarizes the concerns expressed by politicians and economists in several countries about some of the possible consequences of the **internal market**. It refers to fears that while the European Union would have free trade within its borders, it might adopt a more protectionist attitude towards imports from the rest of the world. These concerns have been expressed most strongly by the **USA**, which believes that in some respects the European Communities have always been unduly protectionist. The term has also been used in the context of the increasing stringency of border controls and **immigration policies** in the Member States, as the prospect of internal **freedom of movement** becomes increasingly real.

FORZA EUROPA GROUP (FE) was a **party group** in the **European Parliament** in 1994–95. It consisted of Italian **members of the European Parliament** from the national centre-right party, Forza Italia; it was the only group formed exclusively from members of a single national party. In mid-1995 FE merged with the **Group of the European Democratic Alliance** (RDE) to form the **Union for Europe of the Nations Group** (UPE/UEN).

FOUCHET PLAN is the name commonly given to the outcome of a proposal by President **Charles de Gaulle** of **France** in 1961 that the **Six** members of the **European Economic Community** (EEC) should explore ways of achieving a 'Union of States'. A committee, headed by Christian Fouchet of France, considered the matter and produced a draft treaty in November 1961. A modified second version was produced the following year. The ingredients of the Plan included a council of heads of government or of foreign ministers where decisions would be taken only by unanimous agreement, a permanent intergovernmental secretariat and four permanent intergovernmental committees to take responsibility for the policy fields of foreign affairs, defence, commerce and cultural affairs. The scheme was opposed by most of the other five states, especially the **Netherlands**. The Plan represented a considerable shift in direction from that envisaged by the **Treaty of Rome**, and in addition the smaller states wished first to settle the question of **enlargement**, particularly the possible entry to the EEC of the **United Kingdom**. With France unable to generate support among its partners, the Plan was abandoned in 1963. A truncated version survived in the form of the 1963 **Treaty of Friendship** between France and the Federal Republic of **Germany** (West Germany).

FOUNDING TREATIES is a phrase, like 'constitutive treaties', that refers to the four documents that established the European Communities and the European Union: the **Treaty of Paris** of 1951 establishing the **European Coal and Steel Community** (ECSC), the two treaties of 1957 (see **Treaty of Rome**) establishing the **European Atomic Energy Community** (EAEC or Euratom) and the **European Economic Community** (EEC), and the **Treaty on European Union** (TEU) of 1992. The founding treaties have all been amended by, among others, the **Single European Act**, the TEU, the **Treaty of Amsterdam** and the **Treaty of Nice**. The founding treaties and the amending treaties are increasingly referred to as the **European treaties**. Assuming that it is ratified, the **Treaty establishing a Constitution for Europe** will replace the Treaty of Rome and the TEU.

FRANCE has been one of the most prominent supporters of European integration since 1948. It provided a location for the **Council of Europe** in 1949. The **European Coal and Steel Community** was initially conceived by **Jean Monnet** and was realized by **Robert Schuman**. France was a founder member of the European Communities (EC), and its involvement in their development has been such that French governments have taken an almost proprietorial interest in the EC. Their actions have had important consequences for the EC, even if not always to their benefit. The policies of President **Charles de Gaulle** (1959–69), for example, profoundly altered the nature of the EC and delayed its **enlargement**. His successor, Georges Pompidou (1969–74), opened the way to enlargement in return for obtaining the kind of **Common Agricultural Policy** (CAP) that France wanted. President **Valéry Giscard d'Estaing** (1974–81) proposed the **European Council** and co-sponsored the **European Monetary System**. The tradition was maintained by **François Mitterrand** (1981–95), who campaigned strongly for further intensive integration, and by **Jacques Chirac** (1995–). In 2000 the French presidency of the European Council was responsible for bringing about the conclusion of the 2000 **inter-governmental conference** and the adoption of the **Treaty of Nice**.

France has benefited economically from the EC, above all from the CAP. Just as the EC provided the Federal Republic of **Germany** (FRG – West Germany) with an outlet for its export-orientated industry, so it gave France a bigger market for its large and variegated agriculture, although by the 1980s some French products faced severe competition from cheaper Mediterranean produce. On the whole, the French attitude towards the EC has been highly utilitarian, and governments have always been prepared to emphasize national interests should this seem advisable for domestic political and economic reasons. Nevertheless, its political influence within the EC has been greater than that of any other Member State. To some extent, this was due to its close relationship with the FRG. The EC served one basic purpose of French foreign policy: to influence, even perhaps control, the FRG. That reason decreased in importance after German reunification. In particular, the currency crises of 1992–93 indicated that the two countries had different economic concerns. In the 1990s there emerged a stronger anti-integration mood, as exemplified by the 1992 referendum on the **Treaty on European Union**. This was held by President Mitterrand to emphasize France's European commitment, but he narrowly escaped a humiliating defeat, because government policy, intended to enable the country to meet the criteria for participation in **economic and monetary union**, contributed to high levels of unemployment. His successor, **Jacques Chirac**, proved less fortunate when in May 2005 the French people (on a 70% turnout) rejected (by 55% to 45%) the **Treaty establishing a Constitution for Europe**. When Chirac had opted to call a referendum support for the treaty was relatively high and it was expected that the treaty would find easy endorsement. However, in retrospect, support for the 'no' campaign rose steadily from January 2005 and the final outcome owes much to a variety of concerns over issues such as the 2004 enlargement, the next wave of enlargement, a UK economic blueprint being imposed on the EU and some dissatisfaction with Chirac's decade-long rule.

FRANCO-GERMAN MIXED BRIGADE: See **Eurocorps**

FRANCO-GERMAN TREATY OF FRIENDSHIP: See **Treaty of Friendship**

The ***FRANCOVICH JUDGMENT*** is the common name of a case (*Francovich et al* v *Italy*) heard by the **Court of Justice** in 1992. The Italian government was accused of not implementing European Communities (EC) rules. Specifically, it had failed to implement Directive 80/987/EEC that seeks to protect employees in cases of insolvency, despite several reminders from the Commission. A worker named Francovich duly opted to initiate legal proceedings against the Italian government for his lost pension rights when his company became insolvent. In finding against Italy, the Court established the principle that individuals could appeal against the non-implementation of EC law by Member States on the grounds that their individual rights had been infringed. It also confirmed that Member States found guilty could be deemed liable and fined.

FRAUD rose to prominence on the political agenda of the European Communities (EC) in the 1990s. In particular there were growing concerns about the amount of the EC **budget** that was being lost through fraud, concerns that were often reinforced by the annual reports of the **Court of Auditors** and criticisms coming from the **European Parliament**. On top of these came the allegations of corruption that led to the downfall of the **European Commission** under President **Jacques Santer** in 1999. Early concerns led to the creation in 1994 of an **Advisory Committee for the Co-ordination of Fraud Prevention**, which was followed in 1999 by the establishment of a European **Anti-Fraud Office** (OLAF) within the Commission. Beyond combating fraud within the institutions and policies of the EC, much attention has also been focused since the early 1990s on the need to counter cross-border fraud. Hence, combating fraud features as one of the activities to be pursued as part of policy on **justice and home affairs**. Concerns about fraud have also been instrumental in moves to create a **European Public Prosecutor's Office**.

FREE TRADE AGREEMENTS are signed by the European Communities (EC) with European countries that, at the time of signing, have traditionally not been applicants for membership. They provide for a phased introduction of industrial free trade. Notable signatories have been members of the **European Free Trade Association** and the Baltic States (see **Estonia, Latvia and Lithuania**).

FREEDOM OF MOVEMENT lies at the heart of the objectives outlined in the **Treaty of Rome**, which required the abolition of barriers to the 'freedom of movement for persons, services and capital'. Frontier formalities and checks, different indirect tax rates, government appointive, contractual and procurement policies, and the national basis of many professional qualifications all effectively hindered the establishment of free movement. While some slight progress was made towards removing the barriers, a significant impetus was not achieved until the decision to establish the **internal market** was made. The principle was reconfirmed and formally applied to goods by the **Treaty on European Union**, but the objective had still not been fully realized by the late 1990s. The **Treaty of Amsterdam** attempted to make improvements in this field by setting a timetable of five years within which an area of freedom, justice and security should be established. Common rules on **immigration, asylum** and **visa policy** were intended to promote greater freedom of movement between the Member States. International crime was to be dealt with through improved co-operation between national police forces and customs authorities. Moreover, the **Schengen Agreement** was incorporated into the Treaties.

FUNCTIONALISM is an early theory of integration on which **neo-functionalism** draws. It holds that the creation of international agencies is the consequence of a shared need among states for technocratic management of policy.

FYROM: See **Macedonia**

G

G-7: See **G-8**

G-8, or the Group of Eight, is an exclusive club comprising the world's seven most industrialized states along with Russia. Originally known as G-7, this was officially the title of meetings between the finance ministers of Canada, **France**, **Germany**, **Italy**, **Japan**, the **United Kingdom** and the **USA**, a practice that was established in Tokyo in May 1986. The term was also used more generally to describe the summit meetings of the heads of government of the same seven countries, which began at Rambouillet, France, in 1975 (although Canada did not become involved in the G-7 process until some months after the initial meeting). Leaders of the **USSR** and, later, **Russia** were invited to attend the summits after 1991. Russia demanded equal representation and became a full member in 2002, thereby making the group G-8. Originally intended to discuss common economic problems, after 1989 the summit agendas became increasingly political. The European Union is represented by the President of the **European Commission** and by the President of the **European Council**.

G-24, or the Group of Twenty-Four industrial countries, is a loose intergovernmental association formed in 1989 by the member states of the **Organisation for Economic Co-operation and Development**. The group includes most of the Member States of the European Union (that is, the **Fifteen** together with the **Czech Republic**, **Hungary**, **Poland** and **Slovakia**) plus Australia, Canada, **Iceland**, **Japan**, **Liechtenstein**, New Zealand, **Norway**, **Switzerland** and the **USA**. Its objective is to facilitate the channelling of economic aid and to provide advice to the emerging political regimes and market economies of **Central and Eastern Europe**. Its aid activities, primarily the **PHARE** programme, are co-ordinated by the **European Commission**, thus enabling the Commission to carve out for itself a major international role.

GATT: See **General Agreement on Tariffs and Trade**

GENERAL AFFAIRS AND EXTERNAL RELATIONS COUNCIL is the name of the body usually regarded as the most senior manifestation of the **Council of the European Union** and its central co-ordinating body. Known prior to 2002 as the General Affairs Council, it is the regular meeting of the national foreign ministers at which broad issues of foreign policy are discussed. Often, the foreign ministers are also called upon to consider a range of other questions. These may concern particularly difficult political problems, those that arise out of a conflict of interests between different departmental or policy area meetings of the Council, or those that cannot easily be assigned to a particular departmental competence. In forming the Council, the foreign ministers are also widely regarded as the personal representatives of the heads of government, keeping the latter briefed on the views of other Member States.

The **GENERAL AGREEMENT ON TARIFFS AND TRADE** (GATT) was a convention signed in 1947 by 23 countries (although the number of contracting parties subsequently increased to several times that number), and maintained as a specialized agency of the **United Nations**. Its intention was to secure a pattern of free trade in the post-war world. GATT's objectives were to work towards an orderly framework for international trade, through the elimination of unilateral actions by states and the gradual reduction of tariff barriers. The organization was based upon the principle of non-discrimination: trade advantages offered by one country to another had to be extended to all. There were, however, many exceptions to the principle of non-discrimination. The **Treaty of Rome** specified that the European Communities (EC) should represent the Member States and their interests in external trade affairs and negotiations. Accordingly, the **European Commission** represented the Member States in all GATT rounds of negotiations after the **Kennedy Round** of the 1960s. While GATT was generally successful, the later negotiations were highly contentious as the agenda extended from manufactured products to cover, for example, agriculture, copyright and services. The **Uruguay Round** of negotiations of 1986–94 was dominated by arguments between the EC and the **USA**, which had been highly critical of what it perceived as EC protectionism in a variety of areas, particularly in relation to the **Common Agricultural Policy** (CAP). French objections to lowering protection for its farmers caused considerable tension and the US government threatened to walk away from the entire Round unless the CAP was tackled. This position found sympathy among some EC Member States, including the United Kingdom. The Blair House Agreement of November 1992 between the EC and the USA greatly limited financial assistance to EC farmers and antagonized Paris. The French government threatened to boycott the discussions until **France** secured concessions at a special EC **summit meeting** in December 1992. Negotiations on a successor to GATT were completed in 1993, and on 1 January 1995 the **World Trade Organization** was established.

GENERALIZED SYSTEM OF PREFERENCES (GSP) is a term that refers to preferential treatment granted by the European Communities (EC) to some exports from countries not otherwise associated with them in a formal agreement. GSPs were first proposed in 1968 by the **United Nations** Conference on Trade and Development (UNCTAD), and the EC introduced their own scheme in 1971. It applies only to some developing countries, but is of limited value as, in practice, these countries are preferred to only a very small number of industrialized states, and the GSP applies to only some of their products.

HANS-DIETRICH GENSCHER (1927–) was a long-serving Minister of Foreign Affairs (1974–92) of the Federal Republic of **Germany** (West Germany) and a strong supporter of European integration. He was the principal architect of the **Genscher–Colombo Plan**, on which he subsequently collaborated with the Italian Minister of Foreign Affairs, Emilio Colombo, arguing that implementation of the Plan was necessary to revive the integrationist objectives of the European Communities. Genscher, alongside the German Chancellor, **Helmut Kohl**, was quick to seize the opportunity presented by the collapse of communist rule in **Central and Eastern Europe** to pave the way for German reunification in 1990.

GENSCHER–COLOMBO PLAN is the name given to an initiative for political union sponsored by **Hans-Dietrich Genscher** and Emilio Colombo. Presented in the form of a Draft European Act and draft declaration on economic integration, it argued for more common policies, especially in foreign affairs; for greater cultural and legal co-operation; that the **European Council** should report annually to the **European Parliament** (EP), with the latter being able to submit proposals on all aspects of European union to the Council; and that the use of **qualified majority voting** in the Council of Ministers (see **Council of the European Union**) should be significantly increased. It further recommended the establishment of a mechanism whereby the Member States could rapidly convene meetings of the European Communities (EC) institutions in response to crises. At the heart of the Plan was a belief that the role of the EC institutions should be made more explicit, especially that of the European Council. Various Member States, including the Federal Republic of **Germany** (FRG – West Germany), objected to several of the proposals. In London in November 1981, the European Council invited the Member States' foreign ministers and the **European Commission** to consider and report on the Plan. When it was eventually discussed by the European Council at Stuttgart, FRG, in June 1983, no action was taken other than the signing of a **Solemn Declaration on European Union**. The major supporter of the Genscher–Colombo Plan was the EP, and many of its ideas found their way into the EP's own Draft **Treaty on European Union**.

GERMANY was occupied after its military defeat in 1945 by the four victors: France, the **USSR**, the United Kingdom and the **USA**. Each of these states administered a part of Germany. The original intention was to demilitarize, de-Nazify and re-educate the German people before returning the reins of power to a German government. The onset of the **Cold War** between the USSR and the USA led to the division of Europe and the division of Germany in 1949. From then until October 1990, two separate countries, the Federal Republic of Germany (FRG – West Germany) and the German Democratic Republic (GDR – East Germany) existed in Germany. The FRG was a founder member of the European Communities (EC), and one of the most European-orientated of the Member States, although there was not necessarily a strong correlation between this commitment and West German influence within the EC. On the whole, German influence in the EC has been monetary and economic rather than political. It was the largest and richest Member State, with the strongest economy and manufacturing system, and after 1979 its currency dominated the **European Monetary System**. Its lesser political influence was, in part, the result of its historical legacy. In the 1950s, West German commitment to European integration was seen by **Konrad Adenauer** not only as a means of access to important markets for its export-orientated economy, but also as a central element of his strategy to link the FRG firmly in a Western alliance, rehabilitating it in the eyes of its neighbours and allaying fears of a possible future resurgence of German militarism. Adenauer also saw European integration as being based upon a Franco-German *rapprochement*, even if this meant that the FRG would, because of post-war realities, be the junior partner. The *rapprochement* was formally acknowledged in the 1963 **Treaty of Friendship**.

It was not until the 1970s that the FRG began to seek to exert a political influence in the EC more commensurate with its economic strength. Its support was more tempered by an evaluation of the consequences of EC policies for West German national interests. Between 1974 and 1982 Chancellor **Helmut Schmidt** was particularly concerned, in a period of general economic downturn, about the cost of EC initiatives. His successor, the longest serving post-war German Chancellor, **Helmut Kohl** (1982–98), was a more unreserved supporter of further integration, and active in the initiatives of the 1980s – the single market (see **internal market**), **economic and monetary union** and moves towards deeper political integration – which culminated in the **Treaty on European Union**.

The GDR had been given access to the EC for its products as a result of the **Ostpolitik** treaties, and upon German reunification automatically became part of the EC. The reunited Germany was subsequently the largest unit in the EC by an even greater margin, and Kohl increased the pressure for political union. His reasoning was much the same as that of Adenauer: the reduction of German sovereignty within a political Europe would also reduce fears abroad of German power and limit the effect of potential German nationalism. Nevertheless, there was resistance in Germany to Kohl's commitment to European union, especially over the replacement of the German Mark by a single European currency. However, the coalition governments under **Gerhard Schröder** (1998–2002; 2002–05) maintained Germany's pro-European Union (EU) stance and saw German entry into EMU in January 1999. Today Germany remains strongly in favour of the EU, but its government is prepared to raise its concerns with the EU more often than it has in the past, as for example, over its contributions to the EC **budget,** which it believes are too high. Both houses of the German parliament convincingly endorsed the **Treaty establishing a Constitution for Europe** in May 2005. In the *Bundestag* (lower house) some 569 votes were cast in favour of the treaty with only 23 against. In the autumn of 2005 **Angela Merkel** was elected the first female German Chancellor and heads a grand coalition government between the Christian Democrats and the Social Democrats. Merkel is largely credited with being responsible for securing agreement on the budgetary settlement for the period 2007-13.

VALÉRY GISCARD D'ESTAING (1926–) has a long and distinguished record in French and European politics. He was elected to the French National Assembly at the age of 29 and rapidly emerged as a leading figure, serving as finance minister and, ultimately, as the President of **France** between 1974 and 1981. He was one of the most influential figures within the European Communities (EC) in the 1970s. He established a close relationship with **Helmut Schmidt** of **Germany**, with whom he sought to utilize and develop the EC as an instrument of pragmatic political co-operation and economic integration in which the **European Commission**, which he disliked, would have a more subordinate role. He was largely responsible for the formalization of what had become the reality of the EC: the involvement of heads of state and of government in the operation and development of the EC as a countermeasure to the setting of goals that were unrealistic and overly ambitious. It was he who in 1974 argued for the institutionalization of **summit meetings** in the form of a **European Council**. While he supported the creation of the **European Monetary System**, he opposed the entry of **Spain** for fear of its challenges to

French agriculture. His more pragmatic approach may have brought short-term gains to the EC, but it could be said to have contributed to the accumulation of more long-term issues with which the European Council had to struggle in the 1980s.

After his defeat by François Mitterrand in the presidential election of 1981, Giscard went on to serve as a **Member of the European Parliament** in the 1980s. His intimate knowledge of the workings of the European Union was clearly an instrumental factor in his appointment as President of the **European Convention** set up in February 2002 following the **Laeken Declaration** in December 2001. A more important factor was the support he had from **Jacques Chirac**, the French President and a former protégé and Prime Minister of France under Giscard in the 1970s. Giscard chaired the 207-member Convention and after more than 16 months of deliberation formally presented a **Draft Treaty establishing a Constitution for Europe** to the Italian presidency of the European Council in July 2003. The text served as the basis for the negotiations of the **intergovernmental conference** that began in October 2003 and resulted in the **Treaty establishing a Constitution for Europe**. Its rejection by the French people in the May 2005 referendum was a clear disappointment to Giscard, who subsequently campaigned in favour of the **Constitutional Treaty**'s rejuvenation. At the same time he spoke passionately against the admission of **Turkey** into the EU.

GLOBAL MEDITERRANEAN POLICY: See **Mediterranean Policy**

GLOBALIZATION is one of the major challenges facing the European Union (EU). The phenomenon refers to a process of economic integration on a global level. The main characteristics and driving force behind globalization are: the liberalization of international trade (through the **World Trade Organization** – WTO) and capital movements; developing technological progress and the advance of the information society; and the process of deregulation. All taken together they stimulate international trade by removing barriers and promoting new forms of technology. Many EU policy areas have a global dimension, such as trade policy, **competition policy**, **environmental policy** and the **common foreign and security policy**. Some regard globalization with alarm and question how democratic, accountable and legitimate are some of these new forums such as the WTO, and who is taking decisions on the public's behalf. Recent years have seen the emergence of a well co-ordinated anti-capitalist protest movement at gatherings of the WTO and, on occasions, the **European Council**.

GOLDEN TRIANGLE is a phrase that has often been used to describe what is commonly perceived to be the economic centre and motivating force of the

European Communities, an area bounded by Paris, the German Ruhr area and Milan (Italy).

FELIPE GONZÁLEZ MÁRQUEZ (1942–) became Prime Minister of **Spain** in 1982. He committed himself fully to membership of the European Communities (EC) as a means of regenerating the weak Spanish economy, and fervently supported moves to intensify European integration, while demanding and ensuring that Spain would continue to be a major beneficiary of EC funding. Conversely, his commitment to **economic and monetary union** imposed severe strains upon Spain. However, he was re-elected in 1993 after winning the Basque and Catalan national votes, and remained Prime Minster until his election defeat in 1996.

The **GOVERNANCE WHITE PAPER** was launched in mid-2001 and sought to open up a debate on the nature and workings of European governance, and essentially contains a set of recommendations on how to enhance and open up democracy in the European Union (EU). The Paper considers how it might be possible to inject the EU institutions with greater legitimacy among the citizens of the EU. Two points should be made about it. Firstly, the timing (late July) was unfortunate and it restricted its impact in the media. Secondly, there was a degree of confusion as to the meaning of the term 'governance' across the Member States (the word does not exist in some languages). Together these ensured lower attention in the media for what amounts to the beginnings of a serious and far-reaching debate. On assuming the presidency of the **European Commission**, **Romano Prodi** had placed considerable emphasis on the concept of governance and identified new forms of European governance as one of his four strategic priorities. Definitions of governance vary widely but the term can best be understood as the rules, processes and practices that affect how powers are exercised at the European level. The White Paper was followed by a public consultation that ended in March 2002 and the Commission pledged to report back with its conclusions by the end of that calendar year. Its findings would be used to provide a firm basis for further inter-institutional co-operation on reforming European governance within the constraints imposed by the existing **founding treaties**.

The Governance White Paper is inevitably interwoven with and forms part of the ongoing 'future of Europe' debate, and it was expected that both would inform and pave the way for further institutional changes at the **Intergovernmental Conference** (IGC) scheduled for 2004. The Commission, bound by the **Laeken Declaration**, is actively involved with the **European Convention** preceding the IGC and is using this White Paper as its reference point.

GRAND CHAMBERS are an innovation of the **Treaty of Nice**. They are composed of the President of the **Court of Justice** and eight other judges.

GREECE was one of the first countries to approach the **European Economic Community** (EEC) for some form of association in the late 1950s. An **Association Agreement** was signed in July 1961, coming into effect in November 1962. A **customs union** was to be introduced gradually over a period of 10 years, but, in order to aid the development of Greek industry, a transitional period of 22 years was to apply to most Greek industrial goods. The EEC also agreed to provide loans to Greece during the first five years of the Agreement. The association was soon, however, 'frozen' following the military coup of April 1967 in Greece, its provisions not being reactivated until the restoration of a civilian democratic regime in July 1974. Six months later, the new Greek government notified the European Communities (EC) that it wished to apply for full membership, with similar transitional arrangements to those that had been part of the first **enlargement** process. The Association Agreement was restored in December 1974, and a formal application to join the EC submitted in June 1975. Negotiations took four years, and the **Accession Treaty** was signed in Athens in May 1979, with **ratification** occurring the following month. Greece became the 10th member of the EC in January 1981.

After its electoral victory in October 1981, a new left-wing government criticized the terms of membership accepted by its conservative predecessor for creating and exacerbating economic problems in Greece, and demanded a special status that, based upon a renegotiation of the terms, would take account of what was claimed to be the very different nature of the Greek economy. In 1983 the **European Council** recognized Greece's 'special problems', and negotiations culminated in several concessions to Greece and the adoption in 1985 of the **Integrated Mediterranean Programmes** (IMPs). Greece had earlier indicated that its acceptance of the entry of **Portugal** and **Spain** was conditional upon a satisfactory resolution of its complaints.

As one of the poorest members of the EC, Greece has been a major beneficiary of EC programmes and has been keen to see their expenditure increased. More or less the whole country has priority status for the **structural funds**, and it is a major recipient of the **cohesion policy**, in the form of the **Cohesion Fund**. Under left-wing governments in particular, Greece's attitude towards the EC, especially in terms of foreign policy, has been more openly influenced by national interest than that of most Member States, and this has occasionally caused some irritation among its partners. This national interest often emerges over relations with **Turkey** and **Cyprus**. Overall, however, any assessment of Greek membership must be a positive one. The tensions of the early years of Greek membership have been replaced by a much more pro-European Union

(EU) stance of a younger and less ideological leadership. The country has adapted well to EU membership. The Greek people have consistently proved to be some of the most integrationist within the EU; the economy has grown and there has been consistent political stability. Greece joined the **exchange-rate mechanism** (ERM) in March 1998. However, Greece's inability to meet the criteria for **economic and monetary union** (EMU) was never in doubt, and in 1998 it was the only Member State wishing to participate in EMU that was excluded from doing so. This did not dilute Greek determination to join and the country, after meeting the criteria for joining, acceded to EMU in 2001. Greece successfully and overwhelmingly ratified the **Treaty establishing a Constitution for Europe** in April 2005. The document was backed by 268 votes in the 300-member parliament. Only 17 lawmakers voted against, while another 15 decided to abstain.

GREEN CURRENCIES were introduced into the **Common Agricultural Policy** at the end of the 1960s, as a way of preserving the common price structure that had been established after 1962 for most agricultural products. The ability to maintain the common price structure depended upon the continuation of fixed exchange rates. By the end of the 1960s the **Bretton Woods** system of fixed exchange rates was becoming more difficult to sustain, and several currencies had been revalued. The European Communities decided to retain the common agricultural prices at their original level: these prices, expressed in the currencies of each of the Member States, were the green currencies. They were artificial price figures that bore no relationship to the actual market prices of agricultural products. In effect, each agricultural product had two prices: its real value and one expressed in green currencies. To adjust the common price structure and the green currencies to the real world, the difference between the two values was covered by **Monetary Compensatory Amounts** (MCAs). The **European Commission** tried for some time to end the system of green currencies, and in 1984 agreement was reached on phasing out MCAs by 1989. In the event, they did not disappear until 1993.

GREEN GROUP: See **Group of the Greens/European Free Alliance**

A **GREEN PAPER** is a Commission document that is intended to stimulate public debate and launch a process of consultation at European level on a particular topic. The Commission produces some 10 Green Papers every year. These consultations may then lead to a **White Paper** (e.g. **Governance White Paper**), which translates the conclusions of the debate into practical proposals for European Communities action.

GREENLAND, a Danish colony since 1721, was incorporated into **Denmark** in 1953. It became part of the European Communities (EC) in 1973, even though in the 1972 Danish referendum some 70% of Greenland's electorate opposed membership. In 1978 Denmark accepted home rule for Greenland, and the enabling legislation included a provision for Greenland to withdraw from the EC if it wished. A narrow majority in favour of withdrawal was recorded in a 1982 referendum on the issue and Denmark, still responsible for Greenland's foreign affairs, requested that the **European Commission** revise the treaties to permit withdrawal and the inclusion of Greenland among the **Overseas Countries and Territories** (OCTs). Agreement on the final terms was reached in February 1985, with OCT status being conceded to the island. Greenland remains the only territory to have left the EC.

The **GROUP FOR A EUROPE OF DEMOCRACIES AND DIVER-SITIES** (EDD) is one of the **party groups** in the **European Parliament** (EP). Its members favour 'a stable and democratic Europe of Nation States' and are not in favour of further European integration and centralization. In 2002 the Group had 18 members in the EP, from four countries (**Denmark**, **France**, the **Netherlands** and the **United Kingdom**). This group represented a varying Eurosceptic voice in the EP and re-formed as the **Independence and Democracy Group** in June 2004. This group increased its representation in the EP to 37 seats following the 2004 elections.

GROUP OF EIGHT: See **G-8**

GROUP OF SEVEN: See **G-8**

The **GROUP OF THE ALLIANCE OF LIBERALS AND DEMO-CRATS FOR EUROPE** (ALDE) was formed on 14th July 2004 following the 2004 **European Parliament** (EP) elections. This new group (which arose essentially from the **Group of the European Liberal Democrats**) has 90 **Members of the European Parliament** (MEPs), who are drawn from 19 of the Member States. It is led by Graham Watson (**United Kingdom** MEP). This group constitutes the third largest grouping in the EP and is certain to play a leading role in parliamentary activities. Its interests for the next parliamentary session have been presented in a 10-point programme that espouses amongst other things: the need for the EU to bridge the gap between its economic and political dimensions and to allow it to speak with one voice on the international stage; to secure greater democratization of the EU; to demand the protection of all minorities; to aspire to a common economic policy; and to aim to make the

EU the world leader in environmental protection and to ensure that globalization works for everyone. Two of its members, Luigi Cocilovo (**Italy**) and Janusz Onyszkiewicz (**Poland**), were elected as vice-presidents of the EP in July 2004.

The **GROUP OF THE EUROPEAN DEMOCRATIC ALLIANCE** (RDE) was one of the **party groups** in the **European Parliament**. It was formed in 1973 (as the Progressive Democratic Group), largely as an arrangement of convenience, by the French Gaullist party (known as the Union des Démocrates (UDR) until 1976, as the Rassemblement pour la République (RPR) from then until 2002, and as the Union pour un Mouvement Populaire (UMP) since then), and the nationalist Irish party, Fianna Fáil, neither of which regarded any of the other available party groups as a natural home. While there were strains within the RDE, a common position was found in several policy areas, including agricultural, regional and social policy. In mid-1995 the RDE merged with **Forza Europa** to form the **Union For Europe of the Nations Group.**

The **GROUP OF THE EUROPEAN LIBERAL DEMOCRATS** (ELDR) was one of the oldest **party groups** in the **European Parliament** (EP). In 2002 it was the third largest group in the EP, containing 53 **Members of the European Parliament** (MEPs), although the Group was considerably smaller than the **Group of the Party of European Socialists** (PSE) and the Group of the European People's Party (PPE). The ELDR historically played a pivotal role between these two larger forces. Generally centrist in orientation, it experienced strains between its left- and right-wing elements, which reduced its cohesion and effectiveness. The arrival of the Nordic centre parties in the ELDR increased group heterogeneity. Throughout its existence the ELDR remained fully committed to deeper European Union integration. Following the 2004 European elections, the ELDR was replaced by the **Group of the Alliance of Liberals and Democrats for Europe** (ALDE). See also **Group of the European People's Party (Christian Democrats) and European Democrats**.

The **GROUP OF THE EUROPEAN PEOPLE'S PARTY (CHRISTIAN DEMOCRATS) AND EUROPEAN DEMOCRATS** (EPP–ED) unites Christian Democrat, Conservative and other mainstream centre and centre-right political forces from across the 25-member European Union. The current group has its origins in the Group of the European People's Party (EPP), which was one of the first transnational **party groups** to emerge in the **European Parliament** (EP). Christian Democrats had dominated the assembly from 1951 through to 1975 and, in anticipation of the introduction of **direct elections**, in

1976 they formed the EPP, self-consciously constituting a party rather than a federation of national groups. The EPP was strongly committed to European integration, desiring more powers to be given to the supranational institutions, and favoured a federalist structure for Europe. While broadly Christian Democrat and moderate centre-right in orientation, it contained both progressive and conservative strands, which were not always exactly consistent with national delegations. Since 1979 it has generally been either one of the two largest party groups in the EP, and in 1992 it also absorbed the **European Democratic Group** (ED). Following the 1999 elections, it became the largest group, with 233 Members of the European Parliament. The results of the 2004 EP elections guaranteed the EPP–ED its relative majority with some 268 seats (out of 732) (although by April 2006 this had fallen to 264). This group remains the largest parliamentary group, and is the only one with deputies from all Member States of the Union. Strength of numbers has ensured that EPP–ED Group Members hold a range of key positions within the Parliament – including the chairmanships of many of the EP's 17 committees, half of its 14 Vice-Presidencies, and four of its five Quaestorships. Within the 17 parliamentary committees, EPP–ED Group Members are best placed to secure the right to express the EP's position on key pieces of draft **legislation** and other major reports; the Group gets more of these rapporteurships on more important subjects than any other group.

GROUP OF THE EUROPEAN UNITARIAN LEFT: See **Confederal Group of the European United Left/Nordic Green Left**

The **GROUP OF THE GREENS/EUROPEAN FREE ALLIANCE** in the **European Parliament** (EP) was formed in July 1999, and is made up of mostly Greens and environmentalists alongside representatives of 'stateless nations'. It first emerged after the 1984 **direct elections** when nine representatives of national Green parties were elected to the EP. Under EP rules, however, this was an insufficient number to be recognized as a separate party group, and consequently the Green representatives joined with a heterogeneous collection of other **Members of the European Parliament** (MEPs) to form the **Rainbow Group**. The Green Group did not become a separate **party group** in 1989 following a significant increase in membership. It has continued to evolve. The Group of the Greens/European Free Alliance in the EP is the product of the political will of two separate and progressive European political families to co-operate in order to strengthen their mutual political interests in the European Parliament. The Group has since established itself as one of the main voices within the parliament. Following the June 2004 elections, it had 42 MEPs from 13 Member States (a marginal decrease from some 45 MEPs following the 1999 elections). The MEPs come from **Austria, Belgium, Denmark, Finland, France, Germany, Italy, Latvia, Luxembourg**, the **Netherlands, Spain, Sweden** and the **United Kingdom**. The group is now the fourth largest force in the EP. The Co-Presidents of this group are Monica Frassoni and Dany Cohn-Bendit.

The **GROUP OF THE PARTY OF EUROPEAN SOCIALISTS** (PSE), formerly known as the Socialist Group, is one of the **party groups** in the **European Parliament** (EP). Between 1973 and the late 1990s it was consistently the largest group in the EP. Despite the common political background of its representatives, the group has often been divided by major ideological and policy issues. While it permits free votes in debates, it makes great efforts to develop a common position on as many issues as possible, by means of pre-committee caucuses and working parties. The party group brings together the social democratic and socialist parties across the European Union. The largest national groups within the PSE come from the Social Democratic Party in **Germany** and the Labour Party in the United Kingdom. The PSE supports deeper integration, particularly in the environmental and social fields. In terms of representation the PSE became the second major party following the 1999 EP elections when it secured 181 Members of the European Parliament. Despite an increase in representation (to 200) within the parliament following the 2004 elections, it remains the second major force.

The Socialist Group is a major force and its input to, and support of, the legislative work of Parliament is becoming indispensable. Under the leadership of the Group President, Martin Schulz, the 200 Members from 23 Member States work to enhance perspectives for European society and to implement changes. The Group's activities are co-ordinated by the Bureau, which comprises the Group President, the seven Vice-Presidents and the Treasurer. The National Delegation members along with the staff and secretariat contribute enormously to the Group's work.

GROUP OF TWENTY-FOUR: See **G-24**

GROUPS IN THE EUROPEAN PARLIAMENT: See **Party Groups**

The **GRUNDTVIG** programme is designed to promote and encourage adult education. The Commission's action in this area is aimed at enhancing the European dimension of lifelong learning. It supports a wide range of activities designed to promote innovation and the improved availability, accessibility and quality of educational provision for adults, by means of European co-operation.

GSP: See **Generalized System of Preferences**

GUARANTEE THRESHOLDS were introduced in 1986 as a means of limiting the open-ended nature of production subsidies in the **Common Agricultural Policy** that had been a consequence of the guaranteed price system. With the imposition of guarantee thresholds on agricultural products, an upper limit has been placed upon automatic financial support, with no subsidies given for production that exceeds the thresholds.

GUE/NGL: See **Confederal Group of the European United Left/Nordic Green Left**

GUIDE PRICES are prices offered to farmers for beef and veal under the **Common Agricultural Policy**. They are the same as **target prices**. Guide prices also apply under the **Common Fisheries Policy**.

The first **GULF WAR** occurred in early 1991 when a **USA**-led coalition of states attacked Iraq. The origins of this international crisis date to August 1990, when Saddam Hussain, the Iraqi President, launched an invasion of Kuwait. At this point in the development of the European Union (EU), plans were being laid in the **intergovernmental conferences** that resulted in the **Treaty on European Union** (TEU). The Gulf War was significant as it focused the attention of Member States on the issue of whether the EU should have some form of political and even a military role. This would have been a major step in EU integration. The **European Defence Community** project of the early 1950s had proved just how controversial this area was, and little had changed some 40 years later. The Gulf War and the conflicts in **Yugoslavia** in the early 1990s could not persuade the governments of the Member States to allow the EU a substantial military role. However, the TEU began the process, albeit tentatively. Throughout the 1990s doubts still lingered, principally in the USA, regarding Iraq's military capabilities and intentions and these were fuelled by Saddam Hussain's efforts to block several UN-backed searches for Weapons of Mass Destruction. Frustrated and angered by Iraq's defiance, the US government under George W. Bush, with the diplomatic and military support of the governments of the **United Kingdom**, **Spain** and **Poland**, finally launched a second Gulf War in March 2003. On this occasion Saddam Hussain's regime was overthrown with relative ease, but to the detriment of the United Kingdom's relations with both **France** and **Germany**, which strongly opposed the war.

GYMNICH MEETINGS is a term that refers to specialist ministerial meetings that are held in conjunction with the **summit meetings** of the **European Council**. They are designed to be informal and private sessions without any detailed agenda, in order to permit ministers to consider longer-term issues and problems without being pressurized to reach a decision. The name derives from Schloss Gymnich in **Germany** where the first such gathering was held.

H

HAGUE CONGRESS: See **Congress of Europe**

The **HAGUE SUMMIT** of December 1969 was only the third summit meeting of the **Six** since the **Treaty of Rome**, and the first since the French vetoes on British membership of the European Communities (EC) and the **empty chair crisis**. The newly elected French President, Georges Pompidou, took the initiative in calling for a summit meeting that would address directly the several problems and issues facing the Six. The summit opened the way to the **enlargement** of the EC; it established guidelines for the consolidation and development of common policies; and it reaffirmed political union as the ultimate objective of the EC. More specifically, it endorsed proposals for the financing of the **Common Agricultural Policy**, for extending the budgetary powers of the **European Parliament**, for full **economic and monetary union** to be reached by 1980, and for the development of closer political co-ordination. It heralded the new style of decision-making focusing on strategic leadership from heads of government and state, later institutionalized through the **European Council**, which would characterize the EC after 1970.

WALTER HALLSTEIN (1901–82) was the first President of the **European Commission**, serving from 1958 to 1967. He had led the West German delegation to the conference that discussed the **Schuman Plan** in 1950, and had attended the meeting in **Messina** in June 1955 that agreed to establish a **common market**. He believed strongly in economic and political integration, enjoyed considerable personal prestige throughout the **Six**, but especially in **France**, and in 1958 began to make the Commission the motivating force of the European Communities (EC). His vigorous leadership contributed to the rapid development of the EC in their first years of operation. Hallstein saw the Commission as the nucleus of a future European government and on one occasion said that he could be regarded as a kind of European Prime Minister. He held a large part of the responsibility for some of the proposals rejected by President **Charles de Gaulle** and which led to the **empty chair crisis** of 1965. Hallstein interpreted the resolution of the crisis through the **Luxembourg**

Compromise as effectively reducing the primary role of the Commission as the initiator of policy and the core of the EC. With his chances of re-election as President doubtful in 1967, he chose instead to resign.

HARD CORE: See **Core Europe**

The **HARD ECU** was conceived by the UK government in 1990 as an alternative to the **Delors Plan**, which proposed a single currency and a **European Central Bank** as the integral elements of **economic and monetary union**. The alternative proposal was for a strong European Currency Unit (**ECU**) – the Hard ECU – that could not be devalued and would exist alongside the national currencies within a framework administered by a European Monetary Fund. It failed to generate support from other governments.

HARMONIZATION is a phrase used to describe the process whereby national policies and standards are brought more closely in line with one another. To many, it is synonymous with **approximation**, although legally speaking it involves a greater degree of integration. The harmonization and approximation of **legislation** is central to the **internal market** programme. Legislative harmonization and approximation with the *acquis communautaire* also feature as an obligation placed on non-Member States in their relations with the European Union.

HEADS OF GOVERNMENT: See **European Council**; **Summit Meetings**

The **HEALTH POLICY** competences of the European Communities (EC) are limited to the promotion of public health. They do not concern the organization of healthcare provision. Hence, the efforts of the EC have been restricted to co-ordinating and enhancing national policies on health awareness and health protection. This has led to campaigns on AIDS, cancer and drug dependence. In January 2003 a six-year action programme for public health with €312m. of funding was launched. It comprises three main objectives: health information, rapid reaction to health threats and health promotion through addressing health determinants. These are to be achieved via co-operation between Member States and dialogue with key players in health promotion such as non-governmental organizations.

HEALTH AND SAFETY, particularly with regard to the provision of satisfactory conditions for workers at their place of employment, have been a long-standing concern of the European Communities (EC), and were reconfirmed in the **Treaty on European Union**. General policy initiation in the area of health and safety is the responsibility of two **European Commission** agencies, the Advisory Committee on Safety, Hygiene and Health Protection at Work and the **European Foundation for the Improvement of Living and Working Conditions**. A more specific occupational remit rests with the Mines Safety and Health Commission. Health and safety also figure prominently in EC **consumer policy** and **environmental policy**. As a result of the **Single European Act**, **directives** and **regulations** on health and safety required only a **qualified majority vote** in the **Council of the European Union**. Hence supporters of several initiatives, notably the **Working Time Directive** and many deriving from the Social Chapter (see **Charter of Fundamental Social Rights of Workers**), attempted to have the Council consider them under the rubric of health and safety, before the **Treaty of Amsterdam** incorporated the **protocol** based on the Social Chapter into the **Treaty of Rome** and extended the use of qualified majority voting to this area.

EDWARD HEATH (1916–2005) was the leader of the United Kingdom's delegation to the negotiations over British entry to the European Communities (EC), held in 1961–63. As Conservative Prime Minister after June 1970, he was responsible for the renewal of discussions on British entry that were made possible by the decision of the 1969 **Hague Summit** on **enlargement**. Heath had always been a committed supporter of European unity, the necessity of which had been the theme of his first speech in the House of Commons. Despite a growing popular rejection of the EC, he successfully ensured the support of the majority of his own party for membership. His major concerns in the negotiations were to secure a satisfactory transitional period of adjustment, and the adoption by the EC of a **regional policy** that would benefit the weaker British economy. His defeat in the 1974 general election led to a Labour Party government that was much more sceptical about, and badly divided over, membership of the EC, which contributed to the United Kingdom's isolated position in the EC, and possibly to a reduction of its potential influence in the organization.

HELSINKI FINAL ACT: See **Organization for Security and Co-operation in Europe**

HELSINKI GROUP: See **Accession Negotiations**

HIGH AUTHORITY: See **European Coal and Steel Community**

The **HIGH REPRESENTATIVE** is a post created under the terms of the **Treaty of Amsterdam** to provide a higher profile for the European Union's (EU) **common foreign and security policy** (CFSP). The **Secretary-General of the Council of the European Union** acts as the High Representative and, drawing on the French acronym for the CFSP, is often referred to as Monsieur/Madame PESC. The High Representative, along with the European Commissioner responsible for external relations and the representative of the **Council presidency**, constitute the EU's **Troika**, which represents the EU internationally. The current High Representative is **Javier Solana**. He is expected to become the first **Union Minister for Foreign Affairs,** assuming that the **Treaty establishing a Constitution for Europe** is ratified.

HUMAN RIGHTS have become an increasingly important issue in debates over the role and future of the European Union (EU) since reference to respect for fundamental rights was included in the **Treaty on European Union** (TEU) in 1993 and later expanded by the **Treaty of Amsterdam**, which declared the EU to be founded on respect for human rights and fundamental freedoms. The rights themselves are not explicitly listed anywhere in the EU's treaty base. Instead, reference is made to the **European Convention on Human Rights** (formally the Convention for the Protection of Human Rights and Fundamental Freedoms) adopted by the **Council of Europe** in 1950, and to the constitutional traditions of the Member States. This did not prevent the drawing up in 2000 of a **Charter of Fundamental Rights** of the EU. Nor has it prevented the EU in its external relations from making respect for human rights a precondition for closer ties and, indeed, membership. The EU has not, however, signed the European Convention on Human Rights, the **European Court of Justice** ruling in 1996 that it did not have the competence to do so.

That human rights enjoy an increasingly higher profile in the EU is underlined by the fact that a Member State's suspected breach of them may be investigated. Ultimately its voting rights, as well as other rights deriving from the TEU and **Treaty of Rome**, may be suspended where a serious and persistent breach is confirmed.

HUMANITARIAN ASSISTANCE is an area in which the European Union is active as part of the common foreign and security policy. To this end it funds a **European Community Humanitarian Office**. Formal recognition of its involvement in humanitarian assistance work is contained in the **Treaty establishing a Constitution for Europe**.

HUNGARY indicated, soon after the fall of the Communist regime in 1989, that it wished for a closer relationship with and eventual membership of the

European Communities (EC) once it had adapted its economy to market conditions. A **Europe Agreement** was signed in 1991, and the EC accepted in principle the possibility of membership, although not for a number of years. Hungary submitted a formal application for membership in March 1994. In **Agenda 2000** it was recognized as one of the best-placed applicants for membership and was invited to open **accession negotiations** in March 1998. These were concluded in December 2002 and in the following April almost 84% of those participating in a referendum opted for accession to the European Union (EU). The Hungarian government welcomed the result and duly signed the **Accession Treaty** on 16 April 2003. The vote was not regarded, however, as an emphatic endorsement of EU membership: only 46% of the electorate actually participated in the referendum. Following its entry into the EU on 1 May 2004, Hungary became the second country to ratify the **Treaty establishing a Constitution for Europe** with a parliamentary vote (304 votes to 9) in December 2004.

I

I*M GUIDE, which stands for Information Market Guide, formerly the **European Commission Host Organization**, is an information service on databases, databanks, host organizations, database producers, etc., in the European Communities (EC). It was part of the INFO 2000 project, itself a component of the EC **information society** policies.

ICELAND played little part in European developments during the first two decades following the Second World War. It joined the **European Free Trade Association** (EFTA) only in March 1970. The following November it began talks with the European Communities (EC) along with the other non-applicant EFTA states, and formal negotiations began the following year. These were hindered by Iceland's unilateral decision in 1972 to expand its territorial fishing limits to 50 nautical miles (93 kilometres). Although a **Free Trade Agreement** was ratified in February 1973, the EC insisted that a satisfactory settlement of the fishing dispute had to be reached before Iceland would be allowed to obtain the full benefits of the Agreement, and an acceptable compromise was not reached until July 1976. After this, there were no significant qualitative changes in the relationship with the EC until the late 1980s, when discussions followed by negotiations on the **European Economic Area** began. This arrangement satisfied Iceland's desire for access to the **internal market**. Hence, unlike most of its EFTA partners, Iceland did not apply for EC membership. Opposition to an application persists at government level. This has not, however, prevented relations with the European Union (EU) from developing further. Iceland, along with Norway, has negotiated participation in the **Schengen Agreement** and regularly associates itself with EU positions adopted as part of the **common foreign and security policy**.

IDEA is an electronic directory of European Union (EU) institutions, the Inter-institutional Directory of the EU, accessible via the Internet and in book form.

IEPG: See **Independent European Programme Group**

IFOP is the acronym of a financial guidance instrument for fisheries that was established in 1994. It was intended to take over the financing of adaptation and modernization of fisheries structures within the ambit of the **structural funds**.

IGC: See **Intergovernmental Conference**

IMMIGRATION POLICY was a low priority for the European Communities (EC) until the 1980s, and Member States were free to pursue their own policies. A more structured approach began to emerge after the creation of **TREVI** (*Terrorisme, Radicalisme, Extrémisme, Violence Internationale*), and an ***Ad Hoc* Group on Immigration** was established in 1986 to work for greater co-operation on improving controls at the external borders of the EC and on the granting of visas. Although the political changes in **Central and Eastern Europe** after 1989 contributed to greater immigration pressure, the Member States were reluctant to relinquish total control of immigration policy to the EC. Under the **Treaty on European Union**, only visas became a **competence** of the EC, immigration being incorporated into the intergovernmental **pillar** of **justice and home affairs**. Closer co-operation in immigration policies was also a feature of the **Treaty of Amsterdam**, which conferred powers on the EC in areas of migration and asylum. The Commission believes that the ideal approach to the issue of immigration is an open procedure for co-ordination that will lead to the identification of common objectives that will, in turn, create pressure for a European response. To this end the Commission undertakes to co-ordinate national policies, to exchange best practices, to monitor the impact of Community policy and to organize regular consultations with third countries. At the 1999 Tampere **European Council**, the Member States set out the four key areas for the development of a common policy on asylum and immigration. These were: a solid partnership with the countries of origin; the establishment of a common European asylum system; fair treatment of third country nationals; and a more efficient management of migration flows. In 2000 and 2001 the **European Commission** proposed several new measures that would facilitate the development of a common policy on asylum and migration. For example, the Commission proposed a directive on family reunification and another on the status of third country nationals who have been long-term residents. In addition, the Council adopted **directives** on the mutual recognition of decisions on the expulsion of third country nationals and on harmonizing financial penalties imposed on carriers transporting into the Community third country nationals lacking the documents necessary for admission. To assist the Member States in their examination of immigration, the **Council of the European Union** established the Centre for Information, Discussion and Exchange on the Crossing of Frontiers and Immigration (CIREFI) in 1992. This collects information on a range of issues including: legal immigration; illegal immigration; the entry of aliens through facilitator networks; and the use of falsified documents. As well as providing advice, it also encourages the exchange of information. CIREFI reports to the Council on an annual basis. Since May 1999 an early warning system for the transmission of information on illegal immigration has been operational. In June 2002 immigration policy was discussed at a **summit meeting** held in Seville, **Spain**. (See also **Schengen Agreement**.) The availability of comparable statistics is of crucial importance for the effective monitoring of the immigration policy. At present, **Eurostat** compiles migration data in its work on demography. However, the data collected do not give reasons for migration or its duration. The Commission has suggested that statistics on legal entry and stay be compiled on a monthly basis. By the start of 2004 the issue of immigration had emerged again as a major theme in the domestic arenas of practically all the Member States. Much of the media interest in the subject was directly linked to the implications of **enlargement** of the EU in May 2004 and was somewhat sensationalist. Given public attitudes and the recent successes of extreme right-wing political movements in parts of Europe, most Member States, with the notable exception of **Ireland** and the **United Kingdom**, have decided to impose restrictions on the free movement of people from **Central and Eastern Europe**.

IMP: See **Integrated Mediterranean Programmes**

IMPLEMENTATION is a crucial aspect of the process of European integration. As the European Communities (EC) have evolved, so the body of laws and commitments aimed at establishing a genuine **internal market** has expanded. These laws have to be adhered to at national level, such as, for example, **environmental policy** and **competition policy**, if the project is to operate effectively and efficiently. However, this is not unproblematic, as Member States may seek to delay or resist implementation for a variety of reasons ranging from a dislike of a particular piece of **legislation** to not possessing sufficient technical expertise to apply EC rules. Implementation centres on the following three broad areas: transposition of EC law into national law; the application of EC law by the relevant national authorities; and the enforcement of EC law including penalties for non-compliance. The **European Commission** has general responsibility for all implementation issues but, given its limited resources, it relies heavily on other specialized agencies (e.g. **European Agency for the Evaluation of Medicinal Products**) or on complaints from the wider public to inform it of cases of non-implementation. In order to both embarrass non-compliant Member States, and accelerate implementation relating to the completion of the single market, the **Directorate–General** responsible for the internal market initiated an internal market scoreboard to reveal the degree of implementation in each of the Member States. This sort of **transparency** seems to work, but continues to reveal the existence of numerous infringements. Many questions remain over the ability of the **candidate countries** to implement the full *acquis communautaire* on joining the European Union. Derogations or transitional periods are likely to be granted. Overall, the Commission does very little in the way of direct implementation and is much more concerned with indirect implementation, i.e. ensuring that the Member States carefully transpose EC laws into national laws. One of its few areas of direct implementation is **competition policy**.

The **INDEPENDENCE AND DEMOCRACY GROUP (ID)** was established following the 2004 **European Parliament** (EP) elections in June 2004. It emerged following the rebranding of the former Group for a Europe of Diversities and Democracies (EDD) within the European Parliament. The new group is numerically considerably stronger than the EDD, and in the current parliament initially had 37 deputies (from nine Member States) as opposed to 17 (from four) in the 1999–2004 parliament. In 2006, however, the delegations from Italy (Lega Nord) and Poland left the group, reducing the number of deputies to 22. The group is co-chaired by Jens-Peter Bonde, a Danish **Member of the European Parliament** (MEP) and Nigel Farage, a UK MEP, and is essentially a marriage of convenience between two factions who have combined to fight and prevent the **ratification** of the **Treaty establishing a Constitution for Europe**. However, they share differing perspectives on the process of European integration itself. One, a more moderate wing, seeks greater **transparency** in terms of EU decision-making and certainly does not advocate leaving the EU, while the second seeks nothing less than withdrawal from the EU. National groups such as the June movement in **Denmark** and the French Mouvement pour la France represent elements of the former position while the United Kingdom Independence Party is the best example and the most numerous force (10 deputies) in the latter group.

The **INDEPENDENT EUROPEAN PROGRAMME GROUP** (IEPG) was created in 1976 as an attempt to stimulate a European defence industry. It was a product of the Eurogroup within the **North Atlantic Treaty Organization** (NATO). Its major objective was to secure co-operation in weapons programmes, and research and development to counterbalance the domination of the **USA** in this field. The hope was that, if the members could combine their procurement plans, the resulting orders would be large enough to sustain an economically viable European defence industry. While the Group achieved some success, there was also resistance, especially among the larger states, to the implication of a division of labour and specialization between the national industries. The scaling down of defence requirements after the end of the **Cold War** placed more doubts on its objectives. Nevertheless, regular meetings of national defence ministers continued to take place under the auspices of the IEPG, along with meetings of the administrative directors of the national military procurement agencies. In January 1994 the Eurogroup, and consequently also the IEPG, ceased to operate.

INDUSTRIAL POLICY has not been developed by the European Communities (EC) in any comprehensive or integrated form, although the **European Commission** launched a discussion paper dealing with a general EC industrial policy in November 1990. This new emphasis represented nothing less than a complete transformation in Commission thinking as it moved away markedly from espousing direct intervention in the economy to one of seeking to boost European industrial competitiveness. The change was later reflected in the restructuring of the Commission in 2000 that saw the former **Directorate-General** (DG) III (Industry) being rebranded as DG Enterprise. Indeed, industrial policy has likewise been rebranded as enterprise policy. The **Treaty on European Union** in 1993 provided industry with its own specific **article**, Article 157, inserted in the **Treaty of Rome**. This requires the Member States to secure the conditions necessary for the competitiveness of EC industry. The EC are empowered to take special measures to boost industry, but only so long as these measures do not interfere with or distort competition. In 1995 the Commission presented an action programme that contained four major priority areas to strengthen industrial competitiveness. These were: solidifying the **internal market**; encouraging **research and technological development**; promoting the **information society**; and promoting industrial co-operation. Collectively, however, EC enterprise policy, research and development policy, **regional policy, social policy, competition policy, workers' rights, energy policy, transport policy** and **environmental policy** can be said to constitute an industrial policy. The basic concern has been to increase the efficiency and competitiveness of any industry within a free-market ethos. Apart from policies aimed at specifically targeted industries such as **coal** and **steel**, further general objectives have been industrial development in the poorer regions of the European Union (EU), a restructuring of traditional, declining industries including retraining for those workers needing to be redeployed, and the encouragement of transnational collaboration in new technology-orientated industries.

While modern and often successful, European business and industry cannot afford to rest on their laurels. It is a constant challenge to remain competitive and keep up with technology. Meeting the challenge successfully is essential for sustainable growth and for greater prosperity and, consequently, EU enterprise policy seeks to play its part by fostering innovation, entrepreneurship and competitiveness in manufacturing and services. Innovation and entrepreneurship have emerged as central tenets of enterprise policy. The **European Commission** is the focal point for ensuring that innovation policy is coherent and cohesive across the EU, for benchmarking performance, for disseminating best practice, and for highlighting lessons to be learned from any failure of the market economy that might justify state intervention.

The EU's 25 million **small and medium-sized enterprises** (SMEs) are already the backbone of EU industry, and are the main focus of pro-active enterprise policies based on applying the principle 'think small first'. To this end specific programmes have been devised to ensure that SMEs participate in EU-funded research and innovation projects. The rules on state aid (see **subsidies**) and other forms of funding are more generous for SMEs than for large firms. Entrepreneurs, and SMEs in particular, can obtain help in finding partners through the Innovation Relay Centre network in more than 30 countries. These are part-funded by the Commission.

Through its Entrepreneurship Action Plan, the Commission is promoting a more entrepreneurial mind-set, encouraging more people to set up businesses, helping those businesses grow and become more competitive, improving the flow of finance and creating a more SME-friendly regulatory and administrative environment. Indeed, the EU granted some €90m. annually from 2001 to 2005 for SME-orientated projects in the EU and the three **candidate countries**, **Bulgaria**, **Romania** and **Turkey**. Money was provided, for example, to facilitate the participation of European SMEs in a knowledge-based, internationalized economy and to give business easier access to networks such as the **Euro Info Centres** in more than 40 countries.

Enterprise policy is co-ordinated closely with other policies, in particular the single market (see **internal market**), research and innovation and information society policy. Conversely, when the EU is formulating policy on trade, education and training, or the environment, the business impacts are taken into account.

The **INFORMATION SOCIETY** has been gradually emerging in Europe as a result of advances in technology and communication (see **information technology**). One of the European Union's (EU) current priorities is to ensure that businesses, governments and citizens play an active role in shaping and participating in the global knowledge- and information-based economy. To achieve this, the **European Commission** actively wishes to stimulate research into the development and deployment of new information and communication technologies. It also wishes to set up and maintain a framework of regulation and standards that is designed to generate competition. In an attempt to encourage and promote a coherent information society within the EU, there have been a number of research and development programmes in fields of information technology and telematics since 1984. Programmes within the different fields are considered essential to the economic growth and competitiveness of the EU, and to the creation of new jobs and markets. In 1994 the European Commission Vice-President, Martin Bangemann, issued a report recommending that an Action Plan would be necessary to ensure that Europe also played its part in the global information society. Maintaining and improving international competitiveness is also an important element of the information society programmes, one of the earliest of which was the **European Strategic Programme for Research and Development in Information Technology** (ESPRIT). By the end of the 1990s the latest technological developments (such as the Internet and the emerging knowledge-based economy) required a fresh impetus, which culminated in the 1999 Commission communication on 'eEurope – An information society for all'. This was accepted by the **Council of the European Union** in 2000, and the Council in turn asked the Commission to elaborate an eEurope Action Plan. This was adopted at the 2000 Feira summit of the **European Council**. The Commission's eEurope 2002 Action Plan identified a series of targets that included securing a cheaper, faster and more secure Internet; greater investment in people and skills; and finding ways to stimulate the use of the Internet.

The importance of the information society cannot be overestimated as it has had a significant effect on certain areas of EU public policy and, for example, has accelerated the liberalization of the **telecommunications** sector. The EU's policy for the information society comprises the following four pillars: telecommunications policy; support to bring about technological development in information and communication technologies; to contribute to creating the necessary conditions to ensure competitiveness exists; and to promote **Trans-European Networks** in transport, telecommunications and energy.

The **INFORMATION SOCIETY TECHNOLOGIES** (IST) programme was set up in 1998 as part of the European Communities **information technology** initiatives, and superseded various separate programmes including the **European Strategic Programme for Research and Development in Information Technology** (ESPRIT) and **ACTS** in order to create a single integrated programme in this area. Four main topic areas were: systems and services for the citizen; new methods of work and electronic commerce; multimedia content and tools; and essential technologies and infrastructures.

INFORMATION TECHNOLOGY became a major European Communities (EC) theme in the 1980s. Concerned that Europe might fall behind its major competitors in the rapidly expanding and changing field of information technology, partly because the high costs involved might deter investment and development by private companies, and partly because the protected national public sector markets in electronics might lead to duplication of effort, the EC have been particularly keen to encourage transnational collaboration. A way forward was suggested by the successive programmes of FAST (Forecasting and Assessment in the Field of Science and Technology), as a result of which several collaborative **research and technological development** projects were developed: SPRINT (the Strategic Programme for Innovation and Technology Transfer); the **European Strategic Programme for Research and Development in Information Technology** (ESPRIT); and **RACE** (Research and Development in Advanced Communications Technologies in Europe). More specific programmes have been established to develop information technology in such diverse areas as banking and financial services (Development of Integrated Monetary Electronics – DIME), road traffic flow and control (Dedicated Road Infrastructure for Vehicle Safety in Europe – DRIVE), teaching using computers (Developing European Learning through Technological Advance – DELTA), and medicine (Advanced Informatics in Medicine – AIM). The EC also established information technology programmes to assist in their own operations, including: Co-operation in Automation of Data and Documentation for Imports/Exports and Agriculture (CADDIA); Customs Handling of Import and Export Freight (CHIEF); and Inter-institutional Integrated Services Information System (INSIS). The EC institutions have several associated information networks, such as the **European Commission Host Organization** (ECHO), which provides access to several EC information networks, and the **I*M Guide**, which allows users to tap into the resources of databanks. There are also databases, such as **New Cronos**, which contain European Union statistics.

INFRINGEMENT PROCEDURES relate specifically to the implementation of European Communities (EC) laws. The **Treaty of Rome** charged the **European Commission** with the responsibility of ensuring that all laws and rules are applied. In its guise as guardian of the treaties, the Commission can initiate infringement proceedings under Article 226 against a Member State for failure to do so. Most of the infringement issues relate to the free movement of goods, free movement of people and free movement of capital as well as to decisions relating to public procurement and financial services. The Commission becomes aware of infringement by various means, as anyone residing in the European Union or outside can lodge a complaint with the Commission against a Member State on any issue that is deemed to be inconsistent with EC law. The Commission then decides whether to take the issue any further. If it does, the Commission in the first instance may wish to bring the infringement to an end after presenting a letter of formal notice to the Member State government concerned. Approximately 1,000 such letters are generated each year. This reasoned opinion alerts the Member State concerned to the details of the infringement and asks the country to comply with EC law. If the state in question declines to end the infringement or ignores the letter, the Commission can then take the case to the **Court of Justice**. The **Treaty on European Union** gave the Courts the authority to levy fines against states infringing EC law. The Commission is also empowered under Regulation 1/2003 (an updated version of Regulation 17/62) to take action against a private company or a series of private companies for infringing the **competition policy** rules. In the last decade this has led to the imposition of ever more substantial fines on the companies concerned.

INLAND WATERWAYS form an essential part of the transport network of much of the European Union, especially for raw materials and industrial products. In 1976 the Member States agreed to recognize, on a reciprocal basis, each other's decisions on the navigability and control of inland waterways. The type and technical specifications of commercial craft permitted to use the waterways have been subject to European Communities **regulations** since 1982, and the **European Commission** has continued to work towards broader international co-operation throughout the whole of Europe.

INNER CORE is an expression used to refer to a group of Member States that may wish to pursue deeper integration at a much quicker pace than would find agreement among all Member States, where unanimity is required. The concept is an old one and can be traced back to discussions on differentiated integration that have surfaced since the founding of the European Communities. (See also **enhanced co-operation**; **flexibility**; **variable geometry**.)

INSTITUTIONS in the context of the European Communities (EC) are the central decision-making bodies of the organization. They possess a special status in EC treaties and practice. The **Treaty of Rome** currently identifies five main European Union institutions. These are the **Council of the European Union**, the **European Commission**, the **European Parliament**, the European **Court of Justice** and the European **Court of Auditors**. Not all EC agencies are institutions in this sense. (See **European Economic and Social Committee**; **European Investment Bank**; **European Council**; **Committee of the Regions**; and **European Central Bank**.)

The **INSTRUMENT FOR STRUCTURAL POLICIES FOR PRE-ACCESSION** (ISPA) is a European Communities initiative to strengthen the infrastructure of the **candidate countries** of **Central and Eastern Europe** in order to prepare them for membership of the European Union. ISPA operates in the area of transport and the environment. It was agreed by the Council in June 1999 and stems directly from the **Commission's Agenda 2000** communication. The programme was scheduled to run from 2000 to 2006 and had an annual budget of €1,040m. for its duration. Financial assistance has been granted to environmental projects that enable the recipients to meet existing EU environmental standards and to initiatives in the transport sector that foster **Trans European Networks**. Between 2000 and the end of 2004 the Commission had allocated some €5.65 billion to ISPA projects. It should be noted that upon accession to the EU a country will automatically lose its entitlement to support under the ISPA. In 2005, therefore, the principal beneficiaries of the programme were **Bulgaria** and **Romania**.

INSURANCE was one of the professional services identified by the **European Commission** in its 1985 **White Paper** on the **internal market** that should be open to **freedom of movement** throughout the European Communities. While considerable liberalization has occurred, several national obstacles still hinder the emergence of a common insurance market.

INTAS is an independent international association that was originally established in 1993 to promote co-operation between scientists in Western Europe and those in the newly independent states of the former **USSR**. In 2006 its membership comprised the 25 Member States of the enlarged European Union, plus **Bulgaria**, **Iceland**, Israel, **Norway**, **Romania**, **Switzerland** and **Turkey**.

The **INTEGRATED MEDITERRANEAN PROGRAMMES** (IMPs) were a collection of European Communities (EC) aid initiatives established in 1985. The programmes were a response to the demand by **Greece** in 1981 for a renegotiation of its terms of entry to the EC, on the grounds that the structure and level of development of its economy differed markedly from those of the other Member States and merited special treatment. The IMPs were intended to improve social and economic conditions in all Mediterranean areas of the EC during a seven-year period. Using the resources of the **structural funds**, the **European Investment Bank** (EIB) and the New Community Instrument, funding was to be made available over a period of seven years for combined programmes designed to develop and modernize the socio-economic structure of those Mediterranean regions of the EC largely dependent on agricultural production. The Member States in receipt of IMPs were also expected to contribute towards the financing of approved projects. The work started by IMPs continued within the **MEDA** programme.

INTEGRATION THEORY refers to explanations, primarily produced by political scientists, to explain the logic and factors behind the European integration process. There now exists a huge and ever-expanding literature on European integration, but there is no single meta-theory that explains the entire process. Instead there is a wide diversity of opinion that essentially divides into two major approaches, namely **intergovernmentalism** and **supranationalism**. The first derives from the study of international relations and regards the Member States as the key figures in determining the shape and pace of integration. In contrast, the second approach prefers to extol the role of the supranational institutions and other interested parties (such as the business community) in pushing and demanding deeper integration. In reality both approaches can help to explain different stages and indeed levels of the decision-making processes. Whereas major 'constitutional changes' are certainly determined by the Member States in the **intergovernmental conferences** and involve a process of stating preferences and a considerable degree of bargaining, the day-to-day decisions in policy areas are left to the European Communities institutions, while much of the policy formulation allows considerable scope for interest groups to express their views and have them incorporated into policy development. Alongside these 'classic' theories, there have emerged in recent years a number of mid-range theories or approaches to EU integration and public policy studies that come under the headings of, for example, policy network analysis, multi-level governance and constructivism.

INTELLIGENT ENERGY – EUROPE is a support programme for non-technological actions in the field of energy (i.e. energy efficiency and renewable energy sources). It is intended to support the European Union's policies on energy as well as sustainable development.

INTEREST GROUPS seek to influence the European Union (EU) public policy process by forging close relations with the principal institutional actors, primarily the **European Commission**, and, increasingly, the **European Parliament** (EP) since the **Treaty on European Union** and the arrival of the **co-decision procedure**, and, to a lesser extent, the **Court of Justice**. The **Council of the European Union** cannot be lobbied directly and thus interest groups focus their attention on their national capitals. However, interest groups form a vital part of policy development, although their significance varies from group to group and from policy area to policy area. Some, such as the

European Round Table of Industrialists, are clearly influential and have easy access to the institutions. Interest groups have been a feature of European Communities (EC) business activity from the very outset. Given the EC's original economic activities, the first groups to establish themselves in Brussels were representatives from the business (**Union of Industrial and Employers' Confederations of Europe** – UNICE) and agricultural (**Committee of Agricultural Organizations in the European Union** – COPA) communities. By the end of the 1970s trade unions and other new movements such as environmentalists had established a presence. Their influence was initially limited until the **Single European Act** and later treaties transformed decision-making by enhancing the power of the EP and sought to establish a genuine **internal market** requiring EC-wide rules. By the late 1980s there was a noticeable expansion in the formation of interest groups. The emphasis on regions (see **Committee of the Regions**; **Europe of the Regions**) in the late 1980s and the 1990s added another dimension and led to the establishment of many offices representing sub-national authorities. By the late 1990s it was estimated that there were some 3,000 interest groups operating in Brussels, employing some 10,000 people. Around 700 Euro-groups exist and most are also based in Brussels. The Commission has set up a database, CONECCS (Consultation, the European Commission and Civil Society), of around 1,000 organizations working at EC level, covering approximately 100 branches of activity. (See also **lobbying**.)

An **INTERGOVERNMENTAL CONFERENCE** (IGC) is the set of negotiations between the governments of the Member States launched with a view to amending the **founding treaties**. The IGC provides a forum through which the European Communities (EC), or more specifically the **European Council**, have chosen to explore in detail new organizational and other infrastructural initiatives. They have become key events in the integration project and are used to seek agreement on **resolutions** approved in principle by the Council, and to plan their details. There have been seven major IGCs in the history of the EC and five of these have occurred since the **Single European Act** was negotiated in the mid-1980s. The most important were the two conferences that began in 1990 to discuss **economic and monetary union** and **political union**, which formed the basis of the **Treaty on European Union**. Two further conferences on the future political integration of the European Union (EU) were held in 1996 and 2000, and the measures suggested at these IGCs were formalized respectively in 1997 in the **Treaty of Amsterdam** and in 2000 in the **Treaty of Nice**. Following the December 2001 Laeken Summit a new means for discussing and debating the future structure and powers of the EU – the **European Convention** – was launched. This allowed the views of a much wider range of interested parties to be brought together in preparation for the IGC that began its work in October 2003. This produced the **Treaty establishing a Constitution for Europe**.

INTERGOVERNMENTALISM relates primarily to one approach of academic discourse on European **integration theory**. It assumes the supremacy of national governments in the integration process and in treaty design, and downplays the role of the supranational institutions, the **European Commission**, the **European Parliament** and the **Court of Justice**, and other actors (e.g. the business community).

INTERIM AGREEMENTS are often concluded by the European Communities to implement the trade provisions of international agreements that contain a mixture of European Union and Member State competences, such as **Partnership and Co-operation Agreements** and **Europe Agreements**, pending the **ratification** of such agreements.

INTER-INSTITUTIONAL AGREEMENTS are agreements made between the **Council of the European Union**, the **European Commission** and the **European Parliament** in order to run the European Union more efficiently. They currently involve a range of legal, organizational and budgetary arrangements, and there are some 30 in existence. The most widely known are the Inter-Institutional Agreements on the **budget** in 1988, 1993 and 1999, which determined levels of expenditure on multi-annual spending programmes.

An **INTERNAL MARKET** achieved by 'progressively approximating the economic policies of Member States' was an immediate general objective of the **Treaty of Rome**. The Treaty set down a specific timetable for the achievement of the **common market**. It was to be reached in a series of stages, and completed within 12 to 15 years. Although the **Six** successfully abolished quota restrictions and **tariffs** on internal trade, the broader objective was not attained within the stipulated time limit. It was not until the 1980s that the European Communities (EC) began to consider with greater urgency the need to tackle the numerous non-tariff barriers (so-called physical, technical and fiscal barriers) that restricted the **freedom of movement** of people, goods, services and capital. There was concern that the EC were not enjoying the economic advantage over their main trading rivals that their large population should provide. **European Commission** initiatives on economic liberalization were accumulating in the Council of Ministers (see **Council of the European Union**), where the effective requirement of unanimous agreement was seen as a major obstacle to any rapid progress. **Jacques Delors**, the incoming President of the Commission, had recognized the potential of pushing for a genuine internal market as a means of not only increasing trade and prosperity among the **Ten**, but also of relaunching the European integration project. In a tour of Member State capital cities in the latter half of 1984 he found a general consensus in favour of the creation of an internal market, which he then presented to the **European Council** in **Brussels** in March 1985.

The Council accepted the principle of establishing a single market within a specified deadline, and instructed the European Commission to draw up a detailed programme, according to which the internal market would be completed by December 1992. The Commission responded with a **White Paper** prepared by Francis Cockfield, which listed some 300 actions (subsequently reduced to 282), with a timetable for each that would need to be taken. Three months after its Brussels meeting, the European Council set in motion the developments that resulted in the **Single European Act**. This made the process of **harmonization** less subject to delay by amending the provisions relating to voting in the Council of Ministers. By 1992, most of the measures included in the White Paper had been adopted (although many still required **implementation** at national level). The effort to complete the internal market helped to revive the EC. It also persuaded the **European Free Trade Association** (EFTA) countries to seek a closer relationship with the EC, and possibly even membership. And it led directly to renewed pressure for both **economic and monetary union** and closer political integration, and so indirectly to the **Treaty on European Union**. The **Treaty of Amsterdam** also introduced measures to improve freedom of movement within the European Union, which could have an impact on the internal market. Other measures that had to be agreed at European level included greater combating of state aids (see **subsidies**), more market liberalization (especially in the energy sector), a more concerted **research and technological development** strategy, greater assistance for small and medium-sized businesses, better **Trans-European Networks**, greater labour mobility and, most controversially of all, fiscal harmonization.

INTERNATIONAL COMMITTEE OF THE MOVEMENTS FOR EUROPEAN UNITY was the name of an umbrella organization founded in December 1947 to co-ordinate and act as a link between the several bodies and groups that argued for political and economic integration in Europe. It organized the 1948 **Congress of Europe**.

The **INTERNATIONAL RUHR AUTHORITY** (IRA) was an agency established in April 1949 to supervise coal and steel production in the Ruhr region of **Germany**. It was intended to ensure that the Ruhr's resources in the new Federal Republic of Germany (FRG – West Germany) would not be used for aggressive purposes. As an alternative to keeping the FRG under military control, **France** had seen the IRA as a means of maintaining influence over German policy. The IRA was abandoned in 1950 as being unworkable. Its failure was one factor that made France look favourably upon the **Schuman Plan** as an alternative means of influencing German **coal** and **steel** production.

INTERNATIONAL SPACE STATION: See **COLUMBUS**

INTERREG is the name of a **structural funds** initiative intended to assist border areas of the European Union (EU) to overcome problems of development caused by their relative isolation either within a national economy or within the EU as a whole. It is financed solely through the **European Regional Development Fund**. INTERREG II was introduced in 1994 to encourage transnational spatial planning. INTERREG III was to cover the period 2000–06, and was given a budget of €4,875m. This latest phase of INTERREG is designed to strengthen economic and social cohesion throughout the EU. It aims to do this through the promotion of balanced development of the Continent through cross-border, transnational and interregional co-operation. It places particular emphasis on integrating remote regions and those that share external borders with **candidate countries** of **Central and Eastern Europe**.

INTERVENTION AGENCY is the name of the body that, under the **Common Agricultural Policy**, intervenes to purchase produce when market prices fall below previously agreed **intervention prices**.

INTERVENTION PRICE is the lynchpin of the **Common Agricultural Policy**. It is a price support mechanism that ensures that if a product cannot be sold at an agreed price for that year then it goes into 'intervention' and is purchased and stored by the European Communities. The cost is borne by the **budget**. In other words, intervention prices are fixed prices for farm commodities and are the minimum prices that producers are guaranteed for their commodities. When market prices fall below this level, produce is purchased by an **Intervention Agency** at the guaranteed price.

INVESTITURE is a term that refers to the process of conferring authority on the **European Commission** to act as a governmental body for the European

Communities. Because the membership of the Commission is now approved by both the **Council of the European Union** and the **European Parliament**, the term 'double investiture' is used. (See **nomination procedure**.)

The **INVESTMENT SECURITIES DIRECTIVE** of 1989, introduced in 1993, is a **directive** designed to permit a company authorized in one **Member State** to offer its services throughout the European Union without the need to acquire further authorization. It also set standards for solvency and the protection of investors.

INWARD INVESTMENT refers to the establishment of operations within the European Union (EU) by non-EU companies. The potential of the large EU market, the **common external tariff** and, more recently, the **internal market** and the **European Economic Area** have encouraged multinational companies to invest within the EU. On the whole, inward investment has been welcomed despite concerns that it might encourage over-capacity or weaken indigenous industries. To ensure that plants owned by external investors do not simply assemble components produced outside the EU, the European Communities have ruled that 60% of the manufactured product of such operations, measured by ex-factory prices, must be locally made.

The **IOANNINA COMPROMISE** takes its name from an informal meeting of foreign ministers in Ioannina, **Greece**, in March 1994. The issue in question centred on **qualified majority voting** rules within the **Council of the European Union** after the 1995 **enlargement** of the European Union (EU). In preparation for an EU of 16 Member States (later modified to 15 when the Norwegian people rejected EU membership in the latter half of 1994) the number of weighted votes in the Council was due to increase from 76 to 87. Prior to the 1995 enlargement the blocking minority was 23 votes, and, after enlargement, it was felt that this should be increased to 26. The **United Kingdom** and **Spain** objected strongly and argued that even with the arrival of new EU members the blocking minority should remain at 23. This was the background to the discussions and compromise reached at Ioannina. The UK position has also to be understood against the backdrop of domestic politics and the strong anti-EU sentiment among Conservative backbenchers. The compromise agreed states that if members of the Council representing a total of between 23 and 25 votes indicate their desire to oppose the adoption of a decision by a qualified majority, the Council will do all in its powers to reach a satisfactory conclusion that can be adopted by at least 65 votes. The compromise was essentially a device for the UK government to preserve its dignity, and the compromise in effect has had no practical impact on EU decision-making. A declaration annexed to the **Treaty of Amsterdam** extended the compromise until enlargement in 2004–05.

The second **IRAQ WAR** that commenced in March 2003 clearly revealed the sensitivities and difficulties within the EU on efforts to create a **Common Foreign and Security Policy**. EU Member States were deeply divided on the US invasion of Iraq and (leaving aside the four neutral countries – **Austria, Finland, Ireland** and **Sweden**) can be grouped into two camps. The first group supported the American attempt to topple President Saddam Hussein and included amongst others **Italy, Poland, Spain**, the **United Kingdom** and a number of the newest Member States in Central and Eastern Europe. In contrast, the governments of both **France** and **Germany** resolutely criticized the US move and led Donald Rumsfeld, the US Secretary of State for Defense, to talk of old and new Europe. Although the Saddam regime was swiftly defeated by superior fire power, all subsequent efforts to restore civil order and bring democracy to Iraq have much been harder to achieve. On the ground, the US-led coalition forces have faced almost daily armed rebellions and guerrilla-style attacks. They have lost over 1,000 personnel in the process. Insurgents continually target civilians, Iraqi security forces and international agencies, and the dangers of the country spilling into full-scale civil war look only too real.

IRELAND did not become involved in most post-war European developments, in part because of its neutral status. It did not participate in the development of multilateral trading agreements, and became associated with the **European Free Trade Association** only in December 1965 through signing a free-trade area agreement with the **United Kingdom**. Its application to join the European Communities (EC) was closely related with that of the United Kingdom, because of the strong economic links between the two countries; both subsequently joined the EC in January 1973. Ireland has generally been a supporter of more economic and political integration and the Irish electorate endorsed the **Single European Act**, the **Treaty on European Union** and the **Treaty of Amsterdam** in referenda. Ireland has also been the greatest single net beneficiary of the **Common Agricultural Policy** and the **structural funds**, which have significantly helped to boost the Irish economy. The economic success of Ireland ensured that the country easily met the economic criteria to join **economic and monetary union**, and also meant that Ireland would lose objective 1 status in relation to structural funds after 2006 (see **European Regional Development Fund**). Interestingly, in the 1990s Ireland had one of the worst records among the Member States on the implementation of EC **directives**. However, **Eurobarometer** frequently reveals that Ireland remains one of the most pro-European Union (EU) Member States, and this is certainly the case, despite the much-publicized rejection of the **Treaty of Nice** in a referendum in June 2001. This result shocked the Irish political system, but the outcome owed more to the low turn-out of voters (some 34%) and to the inability of the major Irish political parties to campaign seriously on the issue, than to any sudden change in opinion of the Irish public towards the EU. Indeed, Eurobarometer continued to show Ireland as one of the most pro-EU Member States. In a second referendum on the Nice Treaty held in October 2002 the majority (some 62.89%) of those who participated supported the Treaty, and thus paved the way for the **enlargement** of the EU. Nevertheless, the turn-out for the referendum was still regarded as problematic since only some 48.45% of the electorate opted to vote.

IRISH REPUBLIC: See **IRELAND**

ISDN stands for Integrated Services Digital Network. In 1989 the European Communities (EC) launched an initiative to raise the international competitiveness of the EC **telecommunications** industries through the provision of a range of compatible and harmonized services.

ISIS is the acronym for the Information Society Initiatives in Standardization programme introduced in 1995 to support the development of standards in information society domains.

The **ISOGLUCOSE CASE** relates to a 1980 ruling by the **Court of Justice**. This case represented one of the Court's landmark decisions in the development of the European Union. The case centred on a complaint brought to the Court by the **European Parliament** (EP) with specific reference to the **consultation procedure**. Although this procedure recognized the Council of Ministers (see **Council of the European Union**) as the sole decision-maker, the **founding treaties** implied that the Council could only make legislative **decisions** once it had received the EP's opinion. In this particular instance, the Council had proceeded without waiting for the EP's response, which in this case went against the Council's decision. In Isoglucose, the Court upheld the EP's right to be consulted, and this marginally strengthened the EP's political position within the European Communities. Although following the case the EP still had few powers, this decision enabled the EP to delay the Council in its decision-making.

ISPA: See **Instrument for Structural Policies for Pre-Accession**

IST: See **Information Society Technologies**

ISTC is the acronym for the International Science and Technology Centre, which was established in 1994 in order to encourage scientists and engineers previously involved with weapons and warfare research in the former **USSR** to co-operate and to collaborate for peaceful purposes with their counterparts in the **USA**, **Japan** and the European Union.

ITALY was one of the founder members of the European Communities (EC) and generally has been a supporter of the principle of economic and political integration. Since 1957 it has favoured **supranationalism**, arguing for reforms that would strengthen the **European Commission** and the **European Parliament**. In 1986 it initially refused to sign the **Single European Act** as a protest against the inadequate nature of its proposed reforms. While the richer, more industrialized northern regions of the country have benefited substantially from EC membership, the poorer south has remained relatively impoverished, despite the infusion of substantial EC funding. On the other hand, Italy has been the subject of the greatest number of complaints against a Member State (some one-third of the total) brought before the **Court of Justice**. The major reason has not been a reluctance to comply with EC **legislation**, but the cumbersome nature of the Italian parliament, which makes approval of any legislation a lengthy process. Most of the charges have related to Italy's failure to apply **directives** within the specified deadlines. Popular antipathy in Italy to the old political élites and parties, which were the subject of numerous national corruption charges after 1990, led to a new style of government that was more critical of the EC, the European Union (EU) and their objectives. In addition, speculative pressure in 1992 forced Italy to leave the **exchange-rate mechanism** (ERM). The country re-entered the ERM in November 1996, and Italy was one of the 11 Member States to embrace **economic and monetary union** in January 1999. Critics questioned the degree to which Italy had actually met the **convergence criteria**, but there can be no doubting that the decision to join was politically motivated, and one that aroused a considerable degree of sensitivity in Rome. The return of **Silvio Berlusconi** as Prime Minister in 2001 added an extra degree of controversy to the EU–Italian relationship as Berlusconi's style of leadership (for example, during the much criticized Italian presidency of the EU in the second half of 2003) and political gaffes angered other heads of government. Yet, there can be little doubt that talks in February 2004 and the emergence of a putative *directoire* comprising **France**, **Germany** and the **United Kingdom** to lead the EU has aroused Italian sensitivities. Whether Berlusconi's dismissal of such meetings as a 'big mess' serves Italy's interest in promoting it as an equal player remains open to question. Italy became the first of the founding states of the European Union to ratify the **Treaty establishing a Constitution for Europe** by parliamentary vote in April 2005.

ITER stands for the International Thermonuclear Experimental Reactor, an international co-operation project comprising the Member States of the **European Atomic Energy Community** (EAEC or Euratom), plus **Japan**, the **USA** and countries of the former **USSR**. (See also **European Fusion Development Agreement**; **Joint European Torus**.)

J

JAPAN has been regarded by the European Union (EU) as a major economic competitor, and perhaps also as an example to the EU, especially in terms of new technological industries. Much of European Communities (EC) **research and technological development policy** has been determined by the perceived need to compensate for the advantage that Japan is believed to hold. More generally, trade relations between the EU and Japan have been fraught with problems. The main reason is the large trade deficit that the EU has incurred with Japan. In the period 1993–2004, Japanese exports to the EU increased by almost 40% from €50,100m. to €73,500m., while EU exports to Japan rose from €28,800m. to €43,100m. In addition, Japanese exports are concentrated in a few important consumer fields, such as cars, electronics and computers. Japan has traditionally been slow to ease the entry of imports to its domestic market by relaxing or removing a range of non-tariff barriers. On the other hand, the **European Commission** has regulated the entry of several Japanese products and has passed several anti-**dumping** measures. In addition, Member States have imposed several restrictions on Japanese imports: the best known, perhaps, have been the so-called voluntary agreements limiting the volume of imports of Japanese cars. However, many Japanese companies have invested in the EU. Although the focus of EU meetings with Japanese ministers and officials has in the past been on the persistence of the trade imbalance, recent years have seen a shift in emphasis to requests for deregulation and structural reforms in Japan. In addition to the long-established bilateral negotiations and contacts on economic issues, a political dialogue between the EU and Japan also exists. This, dating back to a 1991 declaration, has yet to be fully developed. Considerable progress has been made over the course of the last decade and relations are generally good. Indeed, as part of the declaration an annual meeting is held between the European Commission president, the European Council presidency and the Japanese Prime Minister. The 13th such summit took place in Tokyo in June 2004 and was followed by one in Luxembourg in May 2005.

ROY JENKINS (1920–2003), or as he became, Baron Jenkins of Hillhead, was President of the **European Commission** from 1977 to 1981. At the time of his appointment a senior political figure in the Labour Party in the United Kingdom, he had always been strongly in favour of that country joining the European Communities (EC): in 1971 he led a party minority in the House of Commons which voted in favour of the terms of entry to the EC, thus defying the three-line whip (a mandatory voting instruction) imposed by his party leadership. Jenkins' appointment as President raised hopes for a renewed momentum in EC developments after the presidency of **François–Xavier Ortoli**. These expectations were largely unfulfilled. A UK President did not end continuing UK scepticism about the EC and complaints about its budgetary contribution, but Jenkins did develop the concept of the **European Monetary System** and successfully fought for the right of the Commission President to attend the meetings of the Group of Seven (see **G–8**). The first achievement helped to reopen the debate on **economic and monetary union**, while the second increased the prestige and visibility of the Commission.

JET: See **Joint European Torus**

JHA: See **Justice and Home Affairs**

JICS: See **Joint Interpreting and Conference Service**

JOINT ACTIONS are among the measures that can be adopted by the **Council of the European Union** under **common foreign and security policy** (CFSP). They commit the Member States and are normally adopted unanimously. However, joint actions may in certain circumstances be adopted by a **qualified majority vote**. In all cases, the objectives of a joint action, its scope, the means to be made available to the EU, and the conditions governing implementation, must be laid down.

JOINT EUROPEAN TORUS (JET) was one of the principal operations of the nuclear policy of the European Communities. Established in 1978, based at Culham in the United Kingdom, and built and funded by the **European Commission**, JET was the central institute for all West European research into nuclear fusion. Some non–Member States also participated in the project (**Japan**, the **USA** and countries of the former **USSR**). JET was one of only four such centres in the world, and its objective was to develop nuclear fusion as a safer, cleaner, more efficient and economic source of energy than a nuclear fission reactor. It maintained links with similar institutes in other parts of the world. In 2000 the **European Fusion Development Agreement** took over JET's operations. (See also **ITER**.)

JOINT INTERPRETING AND CONFERENCE SERVICE (JICS) is a language service established by the European Communities (EC) as an agency of the **European Commission** in 1985. In addition to providing appropriate support to EC institutions, one of its objectives is to assist in the training of conference interpreters.

The **JOINT RESEARCH CENTRE** (JRC) is an organization established under the **European Atomic Energy Community** (EAEC or Euratom). Directed by the **European Commission**, but relying for much of its funding on individual contracts, it is, in fact, a collection of seven institutes based in Geel (**Belgium**), Karlsruhe (**Germany**), Ispra (**Italy**), Petten (**Netherlands**) and Seville (**Spain**). While nuclear research and development remain major concerns of the institutes, their research efforts have diversified to incorporate safety standards and measurements, systems engineering, safety technology, **information technology**, electronics, environmental protection, food and drug analysis and space applications. An Institute for Health and Consumer Protection was established in 1998 as part of the restructuring of the JRC.

JRC: See **Joint Research Centre**

JUDGES: See **Court of First Instance**; **Court of Justice**

JUDICIAL PANELS may be established by the **Council of the European Union** to exercise judicial competence in specific areas. The **Treaty of Nice** introduced provisions for the panels in an attempt to speed up legal proceedings. Explicit reference was made to establishing a judicial panel for cases brought by European Union personnel.

JUSTICE AND HOME AFFAIRS (JHA) was the title given to the inter-governmental third **pillar** of the European Union (EU) when it was established by the **Treaty on European Union** in 1993. The origins of the pillar can be found in the co-operation on anti-terrorism measures and external border security being undertaken by the Member States under the umbrella of **TREVI** (*Terrorisme, Radicalisme, Extrémisme, Violence Internationale*). Faced with increasing problems in the late 1980s and early 1990s in these and other areas such as asylum, immigration, drugs trafficking and fraud, many of the Member States were persuaded that something more formal and structured than TREVI was desirable. A further factor was the difficulties faced by the countries that had signed the **Schengen Agreement** in their efforts to agree on a **harmonization** of policies. While the provisions for JHA often simply gave a more formal recognition to already well-established co-operative procedures, the socio-economic environment in the mid-1990s and difficulties in the operation of the pillar pushed the Member States towards consideration of a less intergovernmental approach to JHA co-operation. On the other hand, several Member States were not prepared to consider incorporating JHA fully into the European Communities institutional structure, and this resistance inevitably placed limits upon its scope for action. The **Treaty of Amsterdam** transformed JHA by transferring a number of areas under the third pillar to the **Treaty of Rome**, and hence to the first, supranational, pillar of the EU as part of its aim of creating an **area of freedom, security and justice**. At the same time, pillar III was renamed **police and judicial co-operation in criminal matters** to reflect more precisely the areas of activity left for intergovernmental co-operation. (See also **Tampere Summit**.)

JUSTICIABLE means that, under the terms of the **European Treaties**, a matter under dispute can be submitted to the **Court of Justice** or the **Court of First Instance** for resolution.

K

KALEIDOSCOPE is the name of an initiative introduced in 1996 under the European Communities' cultural policy. The programme is intended to promote contemporary artistic creativity, encourage the training and mobility of young artists in all cultural areas, and support innovative cultural events with a European dimension, as well as seeking to encourage greater public awareness of Europe's cultural heritage. Although most of the activities that the programme financed were rather small-scale and amounted individually to a maximum of ECU 50,000, there were a number of larger projects such as the European Community Youth Orchestra and the **European Capital of Culture**. In 2000 the **Culture 2000** framework programme, which ran until 2004, replaced the previous activities of Kaleidoscope and aimed to implement a new approach to cultural action. (See also **Ariane**; **Raphael**.)

KALININGRAD, formerly known as Königsberg, was part of German East Prussia until this territory was annexed by the **USSR** in 1946. The territory offered the USSR direct access to the Baltic Sea and was one of the most militarized places in Europe during the **Cold War**. However, the dissolution of the USSR in the early 1990s has transformed the Kaliningrad region into what is effectively a Russian exclave which is cut off geographically from **Russia** by **Lithuania**, **Latvia** and Belarus, and whose economic situation has been desperate for much of the time since. In 1992 it was declared a 'free economic zone' in the hope of attracting foreign investment. The **enlargement** of the European Union (EU) and the **North Atlantic Treaty Organization** (NATO) to include **Poland** and Lithuania have heightened fears that the exclave could become completely isolated. Hence, the Russian government has been keen to ensure land access to Kaliningrad. Its initial proposal of a closed land corridor was rejected by Lithuania and the EU during **accession negotiations**. Instead, agreement was reached in 2002 on introducing special transit arrangements for Russian citizens from 1 July 2003. Sensitive to the economic situation of the enclave, the EU established Kaliningrad as a priority area in the 2002–03 **Technical Assistance to the Commonwealth of Independent States** programme. This followed earlier financial assistance aimed at tackling severe environmental problems in the region, and was followed by funding worth €50m. for the period 2004-2006. This is aimed at improving *inter alia* border crossings, local economic development, administrative capacity building, and the environment situation in the territory.

KENNEDY ROUND, named after President John F. Kennedy of the **USA**, was the name given to the sixth series of negotiations (1964–67) on tariff reductions held by the **General Agreement on Tariffs and Trade** (GATT). It was the first series of GATT talks where the **European Commission** was the sole representative of the European Communities (EC), according to the terms of the **Treaty of Rome**, which stipulated that the EC were to represent the Member States in issues of external trade. As a result of the discussions, the EC **common external tariff** was reduced, on average, by some 35%.

NEIL KINNOCK (1942–) became one of the UK members of the **European Commission** in 1995 and assumed responsibility for transport. Prior to this appointment he had limited experience within the European Union, and his move to **Brussels** surprised many. He had spent his political career in Westminster, where he served as leader of the Labour Party from 1983 until 1992, when he resigned after Labour's election defeat, and was largely responsible for undertaking the full-scale review of the party that led to the emergence of 'New Labour' in the 1990s, which preceded **Tony Blair**'s election victory in 1997. Kinnock was one of the few members of the **Jacques Santer** Commission (1995–99) to return to Brussels, becoming a senior figure in the **Romano Prodi** Commission. With his accession to the post of Vice-President for Administrative Reform in 1999, he took responsibility for overhauling the structure and internal machinery of the Commission. He stepped down from the Commission when his term of office ended in November 2004.

The **KIRCHBERG DECLARATION** dates from May 1994, when it was issued by the leaders of the **Western European Union** (WEU). Essentially it established categories of WEU membership. The four categories listed are: full members, which are members of both the **North Atlantic Treaty Organization** (NATO) and the European Union (EU), such as the United Kingdom; associate members, which are members only of NATO and not the EU; associate partners, which are members of neither NATO nor the EU; and finally, observers, such as **Ireland**, which are members of the EU but not of NATO.

HELMUT KOHL (1930–) became Chancellor of the Federal Republic of **Germany** (West Germany) in 1982, and was elected Chancellor of the reunified

Germany in 1990, remaining Chancellor until his defeat at the September 1998 federal elections. A long-term advocate of **supranationalism**, he supported the moves towards integration in the 1980s that culminated in the **Single European Act**, while still seeking to defend German interests in the European Communities (EC). His commitment led to Germany's willingness to see the doubling of the **structural funds** in 1988 and the creation of the **Cohesion Fund** in 1993 to facilitate the reduction of economic disparities in the four poorest European Union (EU) Member States (**Greece**, **Ireland**, **Portugal** and **Spain**). Wishing for a stronger **European Commission** and **European Parliament**, he called for European political union on several occasions, establishing a close alliance with President **François Mitterrand** of **France** in April 1990, and with the then Commission President, **Jacques Delors**. Following the collapse of the Communist regime in the German Democratic Republic (East Germany) in 1989 and German reunification in October 1990, Kohl's role in the EC increased. Reunification, in his view, gave a greater urgency to European union, for only through unification could concerns be allayed in other countries about a potentially more powerful Germany. Ultimately, the **Treaty on European Union** (TEU) did not entirely meet all his objectives, and there was opposition in Germany to some of its provisions (and specifically to **economic and monetary union** – EMU). After the TEU, Kohl continued to take a lead in pressing the EU to move swiftly to full EMU. In the mid-1990s he was a committed supporter of **enlargement** and sought greater European co-opera-tion in the fields of **justice and home affairs**. He leaves a substantial legacy and will undoubtedly be identified as one of the most influential figures in the history of EU integration. Following his defeat in 1998 the prospects of Kohl becoming an international elder statesman seemed almost assured until he became embroiled in a political scandal on financial irregularities over party funding which had occurred during his term as party leader of the Christian Democrats. This scandal tarnished his political reputation considerably.

NEELIE KROES took up her position as a member of the **Barroso** Com-mission in November 2004 and is the Commissioner in charge of **competition policy**. She is one of the new Commission's free marketeers and is a member of the Dutch Liberal Party. Since the mid-1980s Kroes has emerged as one of the most powerful and well-known businesswomen in the **Netherlands**. She served several terms as Dutch transport minister in the 1980s and in her new role has focused her attention on continuing **Mario Monti**'s efforts to tackle state aids (see **subsidies**) and, especially, cartels.

L

The **LAEKEN DECLARATION** on the Future of the European Union was adopted by the **European Council** at its summit in Laeken, **Belgium**, on 15 December 2001. The Declaration followed a similar Declaration on the Future of the Union adopted a year earlier at the same time as the **Treaty of Nice** and was significant for the issues it raised for consideration by the **European Convention**, which was launched in late February 2002. The Laeken Declaration begins by identifying the two key challenges facing Europe: the need to bring the European Union (EU) closer to is citizens; and defining the role for the EU in a fast-changing globalized world. It then proceeds to raise more than 50 questions and issues for the Convention to address. These include a better division and definition of the EU's competences; **simplification** of treaties and legislative measures; the need for more democracy, **transparency** and efficiency; and steps towards a **constitution** for the EU.

The **LAMFALUSSY PROCEDURE** refers to a novel approach to the process of European **legislation** and regulation. It originated in February 2001, when a 'Group of Wise Men' headed by Baron Alexandre Lamfalussy presented a Report on the Regulation of European Securities Markets to the **Council of the European Union**. The report provided a clear and coherent argument calling for a change in European legislative and regulatory structures. Essentially, the authors of the report identified the economic benefits of further financial market integration in Europe, highlighted the key factors slowing down that integration process and arrived at the conclusion that the then existing regulatory system was unable to cope with the accelerating pace of market change. To overcome and improve the deficiencies, the Group agreed upon what has become known as the Lamfalussy procedure. It is a four-level approach to law-making, based partially on procedures existing (but not widely used before in the area of financial markets) in the European Union (EU) constitutional framework, partially on experience in Member States, but partially new and innovative. According to the Lamfalussy proposals, financial markets legislation and regulation should usefully involve the following four levels: framework principles to be decided by normal EU legislative procedures, i.e. in co-decision between Council and Parliament (EP – see **European Parliament**) upon a proposal by the Commission (see **European**

Commission); implementation legislation by the Commission upon proposal by the newly established Council of European Securities Regulators (CESR) in consultation with Member States through an EU Securities Committee; intense co-operation and networking between securities regulators in CESR to ensure consistent and equivalent transposition of level I and II legislation; strengthened enforcement, basically through Commission action, but with co-operation from Member States, regulators, and the private sector. In the area of securities markets legislation, the Lamfalussy procedure was applied for the first time for the new Directives on Market Abuse and on Prospectuses. The first impressions are mixed; it may seem that not all of the parties involved have fully understood (or fully appreciate) the mechanics as intended by the 'Wise Men'. Proposals have been made to extend the application of the Lamfalussy process beyond securities markets into other financial areas (notably banking, insurance and investment funds).

LANGUAGES are both an indication of the diversity of the European Union (EU) and a barrier to effective integration. Prior to **enlargement** in 2004, the EU had 11 official languages: Danish, Dutch, English, Finnish, French, German, Greek, Italian, Portuguese, Spanish and Swedish. With 10 countries joining, a further nine languages were to become official languages of the EU: Czech, Estonian, Hungarian, Latvian, Lithuanian, Maltese, Polish, Slovak and Slovenian. Any one official language may be used in EU meetings; all official documents from all EU institutions need to be translated into all languages; and simultaneous interpreting between all languages is provided for most EU meetings (e.g. of the **European Council**, the **Council of the European Union**, the **Court of Justice** and the **European Parliament**). In May 2005 the Irish language was officially recognized as a working language by the EU. Irish is the 21st language to be given such recognition by the EU. Prior to this development Irish had been recognized as a treaty language only.

The cost of translation is considerable, there being more than 400 different translation combinations, but arguably necessary if the EU's citizens are to be able to understand the **decisions** and laws that affect them. Within the **European Commission**, costs are reduced since the administration conducts most of its daily business in English and French. Other institutions have yet to follow suit to the same extent although many committees do conduct their business in either English or French. (See also **LINGUA**.)

LATIN AMERICA: See **South and Central America**

LATVIA regained its independence from the then **USSR** in 1991. Soon thereafter it began negotiations with the European Communities (EC) on a

Free Trade Agreement, which was concluded in 1994. By the time the subsequently negotiated **Europe Agreement** was signed in 1995, attention was focusing, however, on an application for membership of the European Union (EU) which was duly submitted on 27 October 1995. Although the **European Commission's** *avis* in 1997 was supportive of Latvia's desire to join the EU, it did not recommend **accession negotiations**, primarily because of concerns over the insufficient progress made with economic reform. Instead, Latvia had to wait for the Helsinki **summit meeting** of the **European Council** in December 1999 before being invited to negotiate membership. Despite coming late to accession negotiations, Latvia was among the **candidate countries** that concluded negotiations at the **Copenhagen summit** in December 2002. The Latvian electorate subsequently endorsed the terms of accession in a referendum in September 2003. In a turn-out of 72.5%, more than 67% voted in favour of EU membership. Latvia joined the EU in May 2004 and a year later approved (by parliamentary vote) the **Treaty establishing a Constitution for Europe**.

LAW in the context of the European Communities (EC) is ultimately based upon the **Treaty of Rome**, according to which EC law takes precedence over national law. EC law derives from two sources. The first is **legislation** initiated and applied by the **European Commission** and adopted by the **Council of the European Union**. The second is the body of case-law arising from rulings given by the **European Court of Justice** and the **Court of First Instance** in interpreting the provisions of the treaties and EC legislation. Since the establishment of the European Union (EU), some sources also refer to **European Union Law**. This arguably differs from EC law in that it derives from the EU's two intergovernmental **pillars**. (See also **soft laws**.)

LDR: See **Group of the European Liberal Democrats**

LEADER is the acronym of a **structural funds** initiative, launched in 1991, to preserve the diversification of rural socio-economic structures within the European Union through the establishment of networks of rural development groups using new communications technologies, and the promotion of rural tourism. It continued as LEADER II in 1994 before being replaced by LEADER+ in 2000.

LEFT UNITY (LU), also known by the French title *Coalition des Gauches* (CG), was a transnational **party group** in the **European Parliament** between 1989 and 1994. It was formed as a result of the division of the original **Communists**

and Allies group into two factions. LU, dominated by French Communists, was the more ideological and Marxist-Leninist of the two Communist groups.

The **LEGAL INSTRUMENTS** of the European Union include **directives**, **regulations** and **decisions**. The **Treaty establishing a Constitution for Europe** envisages their replacement with a new range of instruments: European Laws and European Framework Laws, European Regulations and European Decisions.

LEGAL PERSONALITY is a concept which means that a body has the right under international law to take autonomous actions rather than relying upon governments to act on its behalf. The **Treaty of Rome** conferred legal personality upon the European Community (EC). This means that the EC can act in law as an independent party, enter into legally binding agreements, and be subject to constitutional legal proceedings. The legal personality of the EC is distinct from that of the Member States. By contrast, the **Treaty on European Union** does not explicitly confer legal personality on the European Union (EU). The fact that agreements can and have been concluded in the name of the EU has strengthened the argument that the EU does in practice have legal personality. Assuming that it enters into force, the **Treaty establishing a Constitution for Europe** will resolve the current situation by conferring legal personality on the EU.

The **LEGAL SERVICE** is a service of the **European Commission**. Its major task is to prepare and evaluate, from a legal perspective, European Communities (EC) **legislation**. It has to ensure that all legislation, before being printed in the *Official Journal of the European Communities,* has the same precise legal meaning in all EC **languages**.

LEGISLATION is enacted by complex procedures in the European Union (EU). The **Council of the European Union** and the **European Parliament** (EP) or the **European Commission** are empowered to issue three different kinds of legislation: **regulations**, **directives** and **decisions**. The **Court of Justice** institutes a fourth source of legislation: rulings given by the Court on the cases that come before it constitute a body of case-law which affects the interpretation and implementation of European Communities (EC) and national law. In addition there is so-called '**soft law**'.

The EC equivalent of national legislation is the combination of regulations and directives. The first stage of both lies with the Commission, which has the **right of initiative**. If adopted by the Council, the Commission's proposal becomes either a regulation or a directive. The distinction between the two is important. Regulations are more rigorous, the highest form of legislation. They are fairly detailed instructions, applicable throughout the EU, and directly binding upon all Member States. Directives are also binding, but take the form of general instructions on the goal to be achieved, while leaving the way in which it will be attained to the discretion of each Member State. The conditions of a directive are normally met by the Member States introducing national legislation in conformity with EC stipulations.

Decisions by either the Commission or the Council are also binding upon the Member States; they may be addressed to named individuals or enterprises. Decisions can be made by either of the EC executives on the basis of the direct authority they possess under the terms of the **Treaty of Rome** and its amendments, or on the basis of earlier regulations or directives. (Decisions made according to the provisions of the **Treaty of Paris** were slightly different: they were binding in their entirety upon Member States and were thus more similar to regulations.)

Under the Treaty of Rome and its amendments, the Commission and the Council can also issue **recommendations**, which, like **opinions**, and in contrast to the pronouncements described above, do not constitute instructions but merely express an EC preference that Member States are free to ignore. (However, recommendations made under the Treaty of Paris were binding as to the final result, but not the means to achieve it, rather like EC directives.)

Whereas originally, decisions to adopt EC legislation involved either the Commission or the Council, the EP now has a significant role to play. In 1987 the **Single European Act** introduced the **co-operation procedure**, which allowed the EP to table amendments to and reject proposed legislation. It also made **ratification** of **Association Agreements** and **accession treaties** conditional on the assent of the EP (see **assent procedure**). This was followed in 1993 by the introduction via the **Treaty on European Union** (TEU) of the **co-decision procedure**, along with a requirement that certain legislative proposals be adopted jointly by the Council and the EP. Since the TEU, the **Treaty of Amsterdam** and the **Treaty of Nice** have extended use of the co-decision and assent procedures, thus enhancing the EP's role in the legislative process.

The **LEGITIMACY** of the European Communities (EC) prior to the early 1990s was hardly challenged thanks to the permissive consensus that surrounded the European integration project. Since then, and in particular since the establishment of the European Union (EU), the legitimacy of the EC and the EU has been increasingly challenged. This has been evident in the criticisms coming not just from politicians, but also from the citizens of the EU, as evidenced by the **ratification crises** surrounding the **Treaty on European Union** and the **Treaty**

of Nice, and the low and falling turn-out of voters in **European Parliament** elections. Major concerns focus on the perceived inability of the EU to deliver benefits to the people and to solve problems; lack of popular identification with and support for the EU; the alleged intrusiveness of the EU as it increasingly touches on areas traditionally viewed as being the preserve of national governments; and concern over the direction in which the integration project is heading. How to remedy the declining legitimacy of the EU, as well as associated problems concerning the EU's **democratic deficit**, informs many of the issues on the agenda of the **European Convention** launched in February 2002.

LEONARDO (full title: Leonardo da Vinci) is the name of a phased action programme on the implementation of a comprehensive European Communities **education, vocational training and youth policy** to absorb and replace all existing initiatives in the area of vocational training. The first phase of the programme started in 1995, superseding EUROTECNET, the **Community Programme for Education and Training in Technology** (COMETT), the Programme for the Vocational Training of Young People and their Preparation for Adult and Working Life and FORCE. In 1998 young people from **Hungary**, the **Czech Republic**, **Romania** and **Cyprus** were able to take part in vocational exchanges to European Union countries under the programme. Currently 31 states are involved in the programme, which aims to strengthen the skills and competences of people, and especially young people, through, *inter alia*, work-linked training and apprenticeships. Leonardo also seeks to improve the quality of, and access to, continuing vocational training and life-long acquisition of skills and competences with a view to developing adaptability, particularly to new technological changes. The emphasis of this programme is on lifelong learning; the use of new information and communication technologies (ICTs); the participation of **small and medium-sized enterprises** and craft industry; and support for the most vulnerable categories of people in the labour market, including the disabled. The second phase of the Leonardo programme runs from January 2000 to 31 December 2006. The central objective of the programme is to consolidate a European co-operation area for education and training. To this end, the programme actively supports the lifelong training policies conducted by the Member States. It supports innovative transnational initiatives for promoting the knowledge, aptitudes and skills necessary for successful integration into working life and the full exercise of citizenship, and affords scope for links with other Community initiatives – particularly the **Socrates** and **Youth** programmes – by supporting joint actions.

LEVIES: See **Budget**; **Common Agricultural Policy**; **Own Resources**

LIBERAL, DEMOCRAT AND REFORM GROUP: See **Group of the European Liberal Democrats**

LIBERAL INTERGOVERNMENTALISM is one of the most prominent approaches to understanding the major decisions in the history of the European Union. In contrast to **neo-functionalism**, it focuses on national preferences, interstate bargaining and institutional delegation. As a consequence it tends to downplay the significance of geostrategic factors, ideology and supranational institutions in decision-making.

LIBERALIZATION refers, in the context of the European Communities, to the process of establishing the **internal market** by eliminating unnecessary obstacles and restraints to trade.

LIECHTENSTEIN developed a customs union and common currency with **Switzerland** in 1923, and therefore enjoyed a close relationship with the **European Free Trade Association** (EFTA) after that organization was formed in 1960, but only became a full member of EFTA in 1991. In December 1992 Liechtenstein voted in favour of the **European Economic Area** (EEA), one week after participation in the latter had been rejected by a Swiss referendum. The vote seemed to indicate that Liechtenstein saw the EEA as a way of preserving its prosperity and of becoming more politically independent of Switzerland. However, full membership of the EEA could not be realized until the 1923 agreement with Switzerland had been modified. When the necessary adjustments to the customs union had been completed, membership of the EEA was endorsed by 55.9% of the vote in a further referendum held on 9 April 1995. Despite close ties with the European Union, Liechtenstein has expressed scant interest in joining, not least because membership would most likely necessitate changes to its position as a tax haven.

LIFE is the name of a financial instrument for environmental matters, agreed upon in 1992. Its objectives are to provide financial aid for environmental activities, to support the implementation of various aspects of **environmental policy**, and to aid the European Communities (EC) in meeting the obligations of international environmental agreements and conventions to which they are a signatory. It also provided aid for certain non-EU states (those that bordered the Mediterranean and the Baltic Sea) that applied to join the EU in the late 1990s. LIFE was also charged with the supervision of various EC environment programmes. It replaced various earlier programmes including MEDSPA, which operated in the Mediterranean region. The third phase of LIFE, as agreed by both the **Council** and the **European Parliament** under the **co-decision** procedure in 2000, began in January 2000 with an initial budget of €640m., and was originally scheduled to end in December 2004. However, this programme was extended until the end of 2006 with the provision of an additional €317m. of funding. LIFE comprises three main themes. These are: LIFE-Nature (and the conservation of natural habitats); LIFE-Environment (to promote new innovative methods and techniques to aid EU environmental policy); and LIFE-Third countries (to enable states to develop the institutional structures to handle the development of environmental policy).The percentage of the budget for each theme is allocated in shares of 47%, 47% and 6% respectively. The new LIFE+ programme, due to start in 2007, will replace the present LIFE III programme.

LINGUA is the name of an action programme on the promotion and development of the teaching of the 21 official **languages** (with the addition of Letzeburgisch) of the European Union, and the exchange of foreign-language teachers between the Member States. It was a continuation of the 1984 commitment to ensure that schoolchildren would acquire a working knowledge of two other European Communities (EC) languages by the time they reached the statutory school leaving age. More generally, it was intended as a contribution to increasing the cultural cohesion of the EC through creating awareness of languages and the notion of 'Europe' among the general public. LINGUA was opposed in the Council of Ministers (see **Council of the European Union**) by the **United Kingdom** in 1989, on the grounds that its objectives were not provided for by the EC treaties. In adopting LINGUA by a **qualified majority**, the Council accepted that the United Kingdom would initially be excluded from the programme. In 1995 LINGUA was incorporated into the **Socrates** and **Leonardo** programmes. Today the Lingua action centres on language learning and teaching and has three main aims. These are: to encourage and support linguistic diversity throughout the EU; to contribute to an improvement in the quality of language teaching and learning; and to foster and facilitate access to lifelong language learning opportunities. To achieve these action and activities have been divided into two parts. *Lingua 1* seeks to raise citizens' awareness of the Union's multilingual wealth, encourage people to learn languages throughout their lifetime, and improve access to foreign language learning resources across Europe. *Lingua 2* seeks to ensure that a sufficiently wide range of language learning tools is available to language learners.

The **LISBON AGENDA** (or **STRATEGY**) was the product of a special **European Council** held in the city of Lisbon in March 2000. It was decided on that occasion to set the EU a ten-year strategic goal of becoming 'the most competitive and dynamic knowledge-based economy in the world, capable of sustaining and encouraging economic growth with more and better jobs (some 20m. more jobs) and greater social cohesion'. To this end, the Council established a series of targets, which included raising the employment rate and increasing the number of women in employment. Various mechanisms have since been developed to enable these goals to be achieved in areas such as **employment**, innovation, enterprise, liberalization and the environment.

Progress has been reviewed on an annual basis each spring and, where necessary, updated. In retrospect, these targets were over-ambitious. They were agreed at a time of growing economic and business confidence. It was the height of the 'dot.com' boom and economic prospects looked rather good. By 2005 it was clear that the European Union was far from being a beacon of economic growth. In fact growth rates in **France**, **Germany** and **Italy** had been disappointing. Instead of things getting better, in many European countries the economic outlook had actually deteriorated. In France and Germany, for example, unemployment is around 10%. Economic growth in the eurozone was forecast at only 1.6% for 2005, compared with 3.6% in the **USA**. Overall, the EU was struggling to compete with the US, and European leaders were increasingly aware of the acute dangers and challenges to EU economic success that was presented by the rapidly growing competition from the Asian economies. The EU leaders realized that something had to be done to secure EU economic competitiveness, but also recognized some of the difficulties in trying to push for liberalization and greater economic reform. One of the clearest illustrations of such difficulties was revealed by the resistance to the EU's drive to open up the services market and particularly, the fate of the **Bolkestein Directive** in 2005. The Commission has argued that the opening up of this important sector would have created 600,000 new jobs and that the ensuing increase in output in the EU economy would be in the region of €33,000m. (£23,000m.; US \$43,500m.). The EU leaders agreed their determination to pursue the Lisbon objectives in early 2005, but scaled back their ambitious targets.

LITHUANIA, like its Baltic neighbours, **Estonia** and **Latvia**, regained its independence from the **USSR** in 1991. It then proceeded to conclude a **Free Trade Agreement** (1994) and a **Europe Agreement** (1995) with the European Union (EU) before applying to join the EU in December 1995. In its *avis* on the application, the **European Commission** expressed concern at the economic preparedness of Lithuania for membership. Consequently, Lithuania was not included among the countries from **Central and Eastern Europe** invited to open **accession negotiations** in early 1998. It did, however, start negotiations two years later, following a positive regular report from the Commission in October 1999 and an invitation to negotiate from the Helsinki

European Council in December 1999. Although a latecomer to negotiations, by mid-2002 Lithuania had completed negotiations on more than two-thirds of the 31 negotiating chapters. As anticipated, the remaining chapters were closed by the time of the **Copenhagen summit** of the **European Council** in December 2002. Lithuania therefore joined nine other **candidate countries** in signing the **Accession Treaty** in April 2003. In the following month, of the 63.4% of the electorate who participated in a referendum, 91.1% voted in favour of joining the EU. Lithuania joined the EU on 1 May 2004 and became the first EU Member State to successfully ratify the **Treaty establishing a Constitution for Europe** in November 2004. In March 2006 Lithuania applied to join the **eurozone**, seeking membership from 1 January 2007.

LOBBYING of major institutions of the European Communities (EC) and the European Union (EU), such as the **European Commission** and the **European Parliament** (EP), has grown dramatically since the mid-1980s, primarily as a consequence of the increase in the amount of **legislation** emanating from the EC and EU. Lobbyists range from individual companies and single-issue pressure groups to trade associations and so-called Eurogroups such as the **European Round Table of Industrialists**. In addition, a range of regional interests are represented in Brussels seeking to gain influence over the decision-making process. The Commission has set up a database, CONECCS (Consultation, the European Commission and Civil Society), of around 1,000 organizations working at EC level and covering approximately 100 branches of activity. (See also **interest groups**.)

The **LOMÉ CONVENTION** is the title of a series of agreements named after the capital of Togo, and until the entry into force of the **Cotonou Agreement**, was the central element of the European Communities' (EC) relations with developing countries. It derives from a commitment in the original **Treaty of Rome** to develop a relationship between the original **Six** members of the **European Economic Community** (EEC) and their former colonies, in order to promote the interests of the latter and 'to lead them to the economic, social and cultural development to which they aspire'. The first agreements towards these ends were the **Yaoundé Convention** agreements of 1963 and 1969. The First Lomé Convention (Lomé I), signed in 1975, was an extension of the Yaoundé Conventions to involve the EC more formally in development activities in more countries. The recipient states, some of which already had agreements with the EC (e.g. the Arusha Agreements with Kenya, Tanzania and Uganda), were known as the **African, Caribbean and Pacific** (ACP) **States**. Three further Lomé Conventions were signed in 1979, 1984 and 1989.

There were two central themes to the Lomé Conventions. The first was the provision for duty-free access to the EC, on a non-reciprocal basis, for most

ACP exports. There has always been discontent on the part of the ACP States over two major exceptions to the principle of free access: those agricultural products that would compete with European Union (EU) produce protected by the **Common Agricultural Policy**; and textiles, which have been governed by the **Multi-Fibre Arrangement**. However, exemptions have been made in the case of sugar, despite sugar beet over-production in the EU, according to which the EU buys an annual quota of ACP sugar at high EU prices. The second theme is **development aid** through grants from the **European Development Fund** (EDF) and low-interest loans from the **European Investment Bank**. Although funding has increased substantially since 1975, it has to be shared among a great number of eligible recipients. Lomé II introduced further assistance for ACP countries whose export earnings are heavily dependent on one or a few staple products, and which are consequently more exposed to market fluctuations, with the establishment of the System of Stabilization of Export Earnings (STABEX). More specialized assistance was subsequently provided through the System for Safeguarding and Developing Mineral Production (SYSMIN). Neither form of assistance survived the transition to the Cotonou Agreement. Under Lomé III, the EDF set agricultural and rural development as a first priority, with an emphasis on food crops as opposed to cash crops, small EC-based projects, and measures designed to combat drought and desertification. Lomé IV continued these broad emphases, but offered more money for shorter-term structural projects and increased the proportion of grants, as opposed to loans, made under STABEX.

The Lomé Conventions created a legal framework for bilateral co-operation, and a series of joint institutions were made responsible for supervising the operation of the Conventions and the implementation of their programmes: these were the ACP-EU Council of Ministers, a Committee of Ambassadors and a Joint Assembly of representatives from the **ACP States** and the **European Parliament**.

LU: See **Left Unity**

JOSEPH LUNS (1911–2002) of the **Netherlands** is perhaps best known as a vigorous and effective Secretary-General of the **North Atlantic Treaty Organization** (1971–84). Earlier, as Dutch foreign minister from 1956 to 1971, he had been the most forthright opponent of the proposals by President **Charles de Gaulle** of **France** for a form of political union in which decisions would be taken by unanimous agreement, and he played a major role in the rejection of the **Fouchet Plan**. He was a firm supporter of **enlargement**, and strongly criticized the French veto in 1963 of the British application for membership.

LUXEMBOURG participates with **Belgium** and the **Netherlands** in the **Benelux** Economic Union and was a founder member of the European Communities (EC). Currently one of the smallest Member States, and one that has always been exposed to external influences, it has perhaps had fewer reservations than most about diminution of national sovereignty and independence. Its governments have been strong supporters of initiatives for further integration, especially those relating to institutional reform, and several of its statesmen have figured prominently in the development of the EC. Several European institutions are based in Luxembourg rather than in Brussels: the **European Court of Justice** and the **Court of Auditors**, the **European Investment Bank** and part of the **European Commission**'s staff, as well as that of the **European Parliament**. Luxembourg was also the headquarters of the **European Coal and Steel Community** before 1967. Luxembourg has been one of the most pro-EU minded Member States and was determined to go ahead as planned with its referendum on the **Treaty establishing a Constitution for Europe** in July 2005, even after the rejections in **France** and the Netherlands. A majority – 56% – of Luxembourg's voters approved the constitution, and Prime Minister Jean-Claude Juncker, who had threatened to resign in the case of a 'no' vote, claimed the treaty had been resurrected by the vote.

The **LUXEMBOURG COMPROMISE** is the name of the agreement reached by the **Six** in January 1966 that resolved the **empty chair crisis** between **France** and the other five Member States. It was essentially acquiescence to French demands regarding **supranationalism**, and it specifically dealt with the operation of the Council of Ministers (see **Council of the European Union**) and the permissible use of **qualified majority voting** (QMV). The essential sentence of the Compromise states: 'Where, in the case of decisions which may be taken by a majority vote on a proposal from the Commission, very important interests of one or more partners are at stake, the Members of the Council will endeavour, within a reasonable time, to reach solutions which can be adopted by all the Members of the Council while respecting their mutual interests and those of the Community'. The Member States also noted that 'there is a divergence of views on what should be done in the event of a failure to reach complete agreement', but that 'this divergence does not prevent the Community's work being resumed in accordance with the normal procedure'. In essence, the Six agreed to accept the right of any Member State to veto proposals before the Council of Ministers whenever it believed its own national interests might be adversely affected.

The Compromise decisively altered the direction of the European Communities and the balance of power within it. It reduced the importance of the **European Commission**, emphasized the centrality of the member governments and delayed the completion of the **common market**. Despite all the rhetoric and initiatives for closer integration, it set the tone for EC developments until the mid-1980s. This is despite the fact that, as a document outside the framework of the treaties, the Compromise possesses no legal force. In practice, the phrase 'very important interests' has had an unrestricted definition. It was not that the Member States chose to exercise a veto under the terms of the Compromise. Rather, the Council of Ministers chose to rely more upon unanimous agreement or consensus, being generally unwilling to proceed with any issue to the point where a veto might be invoked. This was a major factor in the steady accumulation of European Commission initiatives and proposals awaiting consideration by the Council of Ministers. The Luxembourg Compromise, in fact, has rarely been put to use.

The widespread feeling that the Compromise was nevertheless hindering European developments was one of the factors that persuaded the Member States to include institutional reform in the **Single European Act** (SEA) of 1986. By reducing the number and kinds of issues requiring unanimous approval in the Council of Ministers, the SEA succeeded in limiting the potential impact of the Luxembourg Compromise in the future. However, neither the SEA nor the subsequent **Treaty on European Union** disposed of or regularized the Compromise. Nevertheless, due in part to a change in the rules of procedure of the Council, scant use of the Compromise has been made since. Indeed, many authorities contend that it is now obsolete. However, the **Treaty of Amsterdam** introduced what has been referred to as a Luxembourg Compromise Mark II, where **decisions** are taken by QMV as part of the **common foreign and security policy**.

LUXEMBOURG GROUP: See **Accession Negotiations**

M

The **MAASTRICHT SUMMIT**, held in the town of that name in the **Netherlands** in December 1991, was one of the most decisive meetings of the **European Council**. It had been preceded by two **intergovernmental conferences** on political and monetary union. These provided the agenda of the **European Council,** which, after much often-acrimonious discussion, agreed upon a fundamental revision of the **Treaty of Rome** in the form of the **Treaty on European Union**.

MAASTRICHT TREATY: See **Treaty on European Union**

MACEDONIA, more correctly known as the Former Yugoslav Republic of Macedonia (FYROM), was part of **Yugoslavia** from 1919 until its declaration of independence in 1991. The decision on the country's name drew a hostile response from **Greece**, which had a province of the same name, and the Greek government feared that any international recognition of the new 'Macedonian' state might encourage a false claim to future territorial expansion. Greek opposition culminated in thwarting the European Union's (EU) recognition of Macedonia's independence from Yugoslavia until 1995, by which time the new state had become known as the FYROM. Once recognized, the FYROM concluded a **Trade and Co-operation Agreement** with the European Communities in 1997. A **Stabilization and Association Agreement** (SAA) followed in 2000, along with medium-term financial assistance via the **CARDS** programme. While it was keen to join the EU, civil unrest in 2001 put paid to the FYROM's chances of joining the countries of **Central and Eastern Europe** in **accession negotiations**. The FYROM was nevertheless recognized as a **potential candidate state**. Successful **ratification** of its SAA in early 2004 was scheduled to be swiftly followed by the submission of an application for EU membership on 26 February 2004. The death in an air crash of the country's president, Boris Trajkovski, earlier on that day meant that the application was postponed to 22 March 2004. The **European Commission's** response to the application came in November 2005 and was positive. The following month the European Council upgraded the status of FYROM to

candidate country, although no timetable was given for the opening of accession negotiations.

HAROLD MACMILLAN (1894–1986), Conservative Prime Minister of the **United Kingdom** from 1957 to 1963, reversed the United Kingdom's post-war policy of non-involvement in any European venture that went beyond inter-governmental co-operation. In July 1961 he announced that the United Kingdom would seek membership of the European Communities (EC). Several factors influenced this reversal of policy: the unsatisfactory nature of the **European Free Trade Association** in relation to the EC as an outlet for British trade; the diminishing influence of the United Kingdom in world politics; and the persistently poor performance of the British economy. While Macmillan accepted and cited the economic reasons why the United Kingdom should join the EC, he also believed that entry was politically necessary 'to preserve the power and strength of Britain in the world'. The British application was initially and unilaterally vetoed by **France** in January 1963.

RAY MACSHARRY (1938–) of **Ireland** served as Commissioner with responsibility for Agriculture and Rural Development from 1989 to 1992 and was largely responsible for the largest overhaul to that date (since Sicco Mansholt – see **Mansholt Plan**) of the **Common Agricultural Policy** (CAP). MacSharry's efforts at reforming the CAP, which had become a huge drain on the European Communities' (EC) limited budgetary resources, need to be set against the wider global effort under the **Uruguay Round** of the **General Agreement on Tariffs and Trade** (GATT) to liberalize world trade and to reduce the levels of protection for the EC agricultural sector. This Round had seen the inclusion of agriculture for the first time, largely at the insistence of the **USA**. The 1991 MacSharry Plan sought to reconcile the goals of reducing agricultural surpluses and abolishing trade-distorting export subsidies while simultaneously trying to maintain high farm incomes. His plans to reduce farm income support aroused considerable anger in **France** and Ireland but had the backing of a majority of EC states including the **United Kingdom** and the **Netherlands**. The Council of Ministers (see **Council of the European Union**) adopted MacSharry's proposals in 1992. In 2002 MacSharry was appointed the Irish representative to the **European Convention**.

The **MAGHREB STATES** of **Algeria**, **Morocco** and **Tunisia** signed a collective bilateral trade and aid agreement with the European Communities (EC) in 1976, covering financial, industrial and technical affairs. The agreement allowed duty-free access to the European Union for most industrial products from these states and special concessions for some of their agricultural produce. An **Association Agreement** was signed between the EC and Tunisia in 1995, and with Morocco in 1996; negotiations began with the Algerian government in 1997 with the aim of concluding an Association Agreement that would incorporate commitments to working towards **human rights** and democracy. A draft agreement was initialled in 2001. The states also have access to EC **development aid**, and a new financial arrangement was negotiated in 1991. Since then, their relations with the EC have developed within the context of the **Euro–Mediterranean Partnership** and proposals to establish a **Euro–Mediterranean Economic Area** by 2010.

JOHN MAJOR (1943–) was Conservative Prime Minister of the **United Kingdom** from 1990 to 1997, succeeding **Margaret Thatcher**. He declared his intention early on to place Britain 'at the heart of Europe'. While certainly more favourably disposed towards European involvement than his predecessor, he faced determined opposition from some members of his own party. In order to balance the various interests within the party, he was forced to act cautiously during the **Maastricht Summit** and secured **opt-outs** for the United Kingdom from **economic and monetary union** and the new **social policy** developments. These policies served only to reinforce perceptions that seemed to confirm the view of several other Member States that the United Kingdom remained a half-hearted participant in the European Communities. Major's negotiating position was severely weakened when the Conservatives were left with a narrow majority in Parliament after the 1992 elections. As his majority of 16 Members of Parliament (MPs) shrank during the period from 1992 to 1997, the influence of a small group of **Eurosceptic** MPs grew and effectively restricted his movements with regard to the European Union.

MAJORITY VOTING is one of the ways in which **decisions** may be taken in the **Council of the European Union**. Simple majorities apply only to a limited number of minor issues, usually dealing with procedural matters. It is unlikely that the Member States would accept it as the normal mode of decision-making. Member States do, however, accept the use of **Qualified Majority Voting**.

MALTA initially played little part in the European integration process. It gained independence from the **United Kingdom** in 1964, joined the **Council of Europe** in 1965, and in 1970 concluded an **Association Agreement** with the European Communities (EC). The agreement was regarded by the EC as another element of their **Mediterranean policy**, and constituted a progressive move towards a **customs union**. Owing to domestic politics, however, little came out of the relationship. In July 1990, however, Malta formally applied for EC membership, receiving a favourable *avis* in 1993. In 1996 the incoming Labour government decided, however, to freeze its application. A change of government in 1998 led Malta to revive its application, and in February 1999 the **European Commission** recommended that **accession negotiations** should begin, alongside those taking place with certain countries of **Central and Eastern Europe** and with **Cyprus**. Of all the **candidate countries**, Malta was often judged to be the one applicant state that was most likely to reject membership, and the outcome proved a difficult one to predict to the very end, as the country seemed evenly split on the issue. On 8 March 2003 91% of the Maltese electorate participated in a referendum on membership of the European Union (EU). The final result showed that 53.6% of those who participated in the referendum supported accession, while 46.4% voted against. This vote was further endorsed a month later when the pro-EU Nationalist Party defeated the Labour Party in a general election. This paved the way for Malta to join the EU (as the smallest Member State, with some 380,000 citizens) in May 2004. Malta's accession to the EU poses very few policy-related problems.

MANAGEMENT COMMITTEES, set up in 1962, are part of the structure of the **Common Agricultural Policy** (CAP). The remit of the CAP is so broad, with varying economic and climatic conditions affecting different products, that it has been divided according to the product. Each commodity has its own Management Committee, composed of national government officials. The role of the Management Committees is to assist the **European Commission** in formulating regulations for the implementation of **decisions** made by the **Council of the European Union**, in order to achieve a uniform application of decisions that nevertheless takes account of different national circumstances. The Committees are also responsible for fixing levels of export refunds and import levies. Their opinions are not binding on the Commission but, if a Commission proposal is rejected by a Committee, the proposal must be presented to the Council for consideration.

PETER MANDELSON (1953–) was nominated as the **United Kingdom**'s incoming European commissioner in July 2004 and he took up his position in November 2004. He was born in London and graduated from St. Catherine's College, Oxford, in 1976 with a degree in Philosophy, Politics and Economics. Mandelson first came to prominence as the Labour Party's director of communications from 1985 to 1990 and was seen as a leading figure in its attempt to modernize and reform. He became a Member of the UK Parliament at the 1992 general election, representing the constituency of Hartlepool (1992–2004), and was highly instrumental in the campaign that brought the Labour Party back to power in 1997. As a close ally of **Tony Blair**, leader of the Labour Party and Prime Minister, he was appointed first to a junior ministerial post and then to the Cabinet in 1998 as Secretary of State for Trade and Industry (July–December 1998). His rapid rise proved temporary because, after allegations of financial misconduct, he resigned in December 1998. Unusually for a disgraced minister, he received a second opportunity when he was appointed as Secretary of State for Northern Ireland in 2000. Once again he became embroiled in a political scandal (over the granting of UK passports) and was forced to resign in 2001, although he was later cleared of any wrongdoing. His latest 'comeback' and posting to **Brussels** was greeted with surprise by many commentators but it is widely expected that he will emerge as a highly competent member of **Barroso**'s new team. Mandelson has been given a high profile portfolio in the new Commission, where he is the Commissioner with responsibility for trade policy and trade negotiations. He has rapidly emerged as a leading figure within the Barroso team and has strongly pushed the case for economic reform and called for changes to the common agricultural policy. He has long been a committed European and has sought to exert a strong pro-European influence on Tony Blair.

MANIFEST CRISIS is a term that describes what amounts to a state of emergency in either the **coal** or the **steel** industry. It is part of the substantial powers of direction that the **European Commission** inherited from the High Authority of the **European Coal and Steel Community**. A declaration of manifest crisis requires the assent of the **Council of the European Union** and, if granted, gives the Commission wide authoritarian powers, including the ability to impose **production quotas** on individual companies and to exact severe financial penalties if these are exceeded. A state of manifest crisis was invoked in the steel industry in 1980. It placed more than 80% of the steel production of the European Communities (EC) under compulsory EC control, with the companies liable to fines if they transgressed Commission rules. The austerity programme was formally ended in June 1988.

MANSHOLT PLAN is the name of the document that was the origin of the **Common Agricultural Policy** (CAP). Named after the Dutch statesman Sicco Mansholt, in its final version of 1968 equal importance was given to price guarantees and to a restructuring and modernization of agriculture. Prior to this, the vast majority of agricultural expenditure was being directed towards price support rather than modernization schemes. The plan accepted that rationalization would incur heavy short-term costs, and proposed an extensive programme of compensation. In the longer term, it suggested that rationalization would produce a more cost-effective agriculture, so limiting the amount of **expenditure** required for price guarantees. The agricultural sector protested at the plans, and there were large demonstrations in **Brussels**. The CAP outline adopted by the European Communities (EC) in 1972 was a moderated version of the Mansholt Plan. It gave a greatly reduced emphasis to structural reform, an emphasis that disappeared almost completely when the policy began to operate. At the time, farming organizations almost everywhere in the EC rejected the plan, and Mansholt was much reviled by farmers.

A **MARKET ACCESS STRATEGY** was devised by the **European Commission** in 1996 as a means of promoting European Union (EU) exports. It aims to provide information for businesses regarding trade policy questions, to improve access for EU exporters to other markets and to increase the efficiency of EU **trade** policy.

MARKET-SHARING AGREEMENTS are banned by the **European Commission** on the grounds that they run contrary to the rules of European Communities (EC) **competition policy**, and particularly to Article 81 of the **Treaty of Rome**, which targets restrictive agreements and cartels. Cartels remain an endemic feature of European business activity. The Commission, particularly since the early 1990s, has endeavoured to combat these agreements through the levying of fines on companies engaged in such practices.

The **MARSHALL PLAN** or the European Recovery Programme, named after US Secretary of State George Marshall (1880–1959), was an extensive programme of US aid to assist and stimulate economic reconstruction and recovery in Europe after the Second World War. It came into operation in 1948 and brought both economic and military stability and facilitated the reconstruction of Western Europe. The **USA** insisted that the allocation and operation of priorities had to be a European responsibility. The result was the formation of the **Organisation for European Economic Co-operation**. The Marshall Plan played an instrumental role in promoting European integration that indirectly can be said to have inspired the Schuman Declaration (see **Robert Schuman**; **Schuman Plan**). Reconciliation was an integral aspect of US foreign policy towards Western Europe, particularly given the onset of the **Cold War** in the late 1940s. When the Plan ended in 1952, some US $17,000m. had been given to Western Europe, to the latter's considerable financial and psychological benefit, as well as providing Western Europe with experience in intergovernmental co-operation.

MASHREQ STATES is a term used to describe Egypt, Jordan, Lebanon and Syria, with which the European Communities (EC) signed a collective bilateral trade and aid agreement in 1977. In addition to granting **development aid**, the agreement allowed the Mashreq states to export several manufactured products to the EC duty-free. A further collection of financial aid measures was negotiated in 1991. Since then, relations between the EC and the Mashreq states have developed within the context of the **Euro-Mediterranean Partnership** and a proposal to establish a **Euro-Mediterranean Economic Area** by 2010.

MCAs: See **Monetary Compensatory Amounts**

CHARLIE McCREEVY was nominated as the Irish representative to the **Barroso** Commission in 2004 to be the Commissioner with responsibility for the internal market and services. Prior to this he had served under **Bertie Ahern**'s two administrations as the Irish Finance Minister. He has been widely credited with presiding over the EU's best-performing economy and is a staunch free marketeer. He has slowly developed a recognizable profile and in particular has condemned attempts by certain Member States to protect their utility sectors from greater competition.

MEDA is the acronym for a Mediterranean Special programme (launched in Barcelona in 1995) that aimed to introduce financial and technical measures in parallel with economic and social structural reforms in the **Euro-Mediterranean Partnership**. It was modelled on the aid programmes **PHARE** and **Technical Assistance to the Commonwealth of Independent States** (TACIS). The MEDA programme commenced in 1996 and replaced all the bilateral **protocols** between the European Union and the so-called MED-12 non-Member Mediterranean states (**Algeria**, **Cyprus**, Egypt, Israel, Jordan, Lebanon, **Malta**, **Morocco**, the Palestinian Authority (now Palestinian Autonomous Areas), Syria, **Tunisia** and **Turkey**).

MEDIA PLUS was the third phase of the MEDIA Programme (measures to encourage the development of the audiovisual industry – see **Media Policy**). It ran from 2001, originally scheduled to last until 2005, but this was later extended to the end of 2006. MEDIA aims to stimulate the distribution and development of European audiovisual works and to boost production companies. The genres concerned are fiction (cinema and television), creative documentaries, animated films and multimedia. To this end the scheme provides financial assistance and support for continuing (and initial) vocational training programmes to instruct audiovisual-industry professionals in business management, scriptwriting techniques and new technologies. A proposal for a new programme to support the European audiovisual sector (MEDIA 2007) was adopted by the Commission in July 2004. In January 2005 the Commission adopted Decision 2005/56/EC setting up a new Education, Audiovisual and Culture Executive Agency (EACEA). This Agency will be responsible for the management of certain parts of the EU's programmes in the education, culture and audiovisual fields, and it officially took over the operational management of the MEDIA programme as of 1 January 2006.

MEDIA POLICY, or at least that element which relates to film and television, represents the one area of **cultural policy** where the European Communities (EC) have been noticeably active. While the **European Commission** aims to encourage co-operation within the European Union, it has also been restrictive in seeking to control the effect on Europe of direct broadcasting by satellite and cable networks. The first draft **directive** in 1985 established a plan for the adoption by the Member States of the television standards sponsored by the **European Broadcasting Union**, their immediate use in direct satellite broadcasting, and their gradual introduction into both cable and ground transmitter systems. This plan later encountered difficulties. A second and highly controversial directive, entitled *Television Without Frontiers,* came into force in 1991. It is designed to ensure increasing co-ordination in broadcasting, and requires the Member States to ensure that a specified and substantial proportion of their national production and broadcast programmes are of European origin. Through the MEDIA (Measures for Encouraging the Development of the Audio-visual Production Industry) and SCRIPT (Support for Creative Independent Production Talent) programmes, the EC have also contributed to the financing, production and distribution of co-operative multilingual European broadcasting, and to the annual Geneva-Europe Prize for the best television scripts for fiction series. Funding is also provided for a media business school, a **European Film Distribution Office** and a European Group of Cinema and Audio-visual Financiers.

MEDICI stands for Multimedia for Education and Employment through Integrated Cultural Initiative, a programme established by **Directorates–General** X and XIII to encourage innovative use of multimedia technology for the promotion of Europe's cultural heritage, through partnerships between museums, cultural institutions and industry. Its secretariat is based in Milan, **Italy**.

MEDITERRANEAN POLICY, sometimes known as the Global Mediterranean Policy, is a term which is normally used to describe, not a policy in the sense of a coherent integrated programme, but the varied collection of trade agreements that the European Communities (EC) have signed with almost all the states that border the Mediterranean Sea, as well as various educational, economic and scientific initiatives that have the Mediterranean as their focus. A **European Commission** initiative of 1994 envisaged the creation of a **Euro-Mediterranean Economic Area** by 2010, which would include the **Maghreb** and **Mashreq** countries, Israel, the Palestinian Authority (now Palestinian Autonomous Areas) and **Turkey**. Despite the initial enthusiasm that accompanied the 1995 **Barcelona Declaration** that launched the process, there remains a great degree of scepticism as to how effective the European Union's (EU) policy towards these Mediterranean countries will be. There are several possible reasons for this. Firstly, a great deal of distrust and suspicion still prevails among these states and greater efforts will be needed to ensure increased co-operation from them. Secondly, some of the existing MED-12 states (**Algeria**, Egypt, Israel, Jordan, Lebanon, **Morocco**, Palestinian Autonomous Areas, Syria, **Tunisia** and **Turkey**) are likely to become EU Member States, while two, **Cyprus** and **Malta**, already have. This raises questions over existing trade relationships. **Accession negotiations** were successfully concluded with Cyprus and Malta, and both states joined the EU in 2004. Meanwhile Turkey has applied to join, although the latter's current economic difficulties and the political sensitivities Turkish accession would raise ensure that for the time being the country must settle for the existing customs union rather than for full EU membership.

MEMBER STATES is a term that is used to refer to the current 25 countries that comprise the European Union. These are **Austria**, **Belgium**, the **Czech Republic**, **Cyprus**, **Denmark**, **Estonia**, **Finland**, **France**, **Germany**, **Greece**, **Hungary**, **Ireland**, **Italy**, **Latvia**, **Lithuania**, **Luxembourg**, **Malta**, the **Netherlands**, **Poland**, **Portugal**, **Slovakia**, **Slovenia**, **Spain**, **Sweden** and the **United Kingdom**.

MEMBERS OF THE EUROPEAN PARLIAMENT (MEPs) are elected for fixed five-year terms. In the **European Parliament** (EP), MEPs sit in transnational **party groups**, not by national party affiliations or in delegations, although a minority of MEPs prefers to sit as non-aligned independents. MEPs are paid the same salary as the national parliamentary representatives in their own country: there is therefore a substantial range in salary levels. All MEPs, however, receive the same level of European Communities resources, including allowances for research, secretarial assistance and travel. Many still hold a **dual mandate** but can only draw on either their salary and expenses as an MEP or as a member of their national parliament, but not both. In the 1999–2004 parliament there were 626 MEPs. The number was to increase with the accession of the former 10 **candidate countries**. Initially, the increase was to be to 788, but following the introduction of changes contained in the **Accession Treaty**, the number following the EP elections in June 2004 was revised to 732.

MEPs: See **Members of the European Parliament**

MERCATOR is the European Network for Regional or Minority Languages and Education, a network for the exchange of information and documentation on minority languages within the European Union.

MERGER POLICY is a leading aspect of current European Communities (EC) **competition policy**. It is, however, a belated weapon in the armoury of the **European Commission** as it was omitted completely from the **Treaty of Rome**. The concept of a European merger control regime was first proposed by the Commission as a draft **regulation** in 1973. Its aim was to give the Commission the ability to approve in advance any proposed transnational mergers, leaving the Member States with the responsibility of policing mergers within their own territory. The Commission initiative and three subsequent efforts all failed to find any substantial favour within the Council of Ministers (see **Council of the European Union**). Finally, however, a renewed proposal in 1987 was submitted, approved in 1989 and came into force in September 1990. The regulation owed much to the growing demands from the business community for an integrated policy with regard to merger rules at the European level, thus avoiding the existing confusions and discrepancies in approach to mergers across the EC. Their calls were also vindicated by the business restructuring that was occurring prior to 1992 and the **internal market** initiative. The regulation required that all proposed mergers of companies with an aggregate world turnover of €5,000m., and where at least two of the companies involved have a turnover within the European Union (EU) of more than €250m. (unless they each realize more than two-thirds of their European turnover in one Member State), and that are likely to affect EC **competition policy**, be submitted to the Commission for assessment and approval. As such, the regulation was designed to cover only the largest mergers, some 50 to 60 a year in the early years. Proposed mergers that fall below these levels, which constitute the majority of cases, remain the responsibility of the national authorities. The number of proposed mergers notified to the Commission increased during the 1990s so that by the end of that decade almost as many as five times the number were being processed than at its beginning. In 2001, for example, some 335 mergers were notified to the Commission. The reactions of Member States to enforcing the regulation against their own industries have been mixed, but the merger regulation has been hailed as a substantial success for the speed in which cases are processed, although some critics point to potential weaknesses in terms of economic analysis. Most cases are dealt with within one month and the remainder within a further four months. By December 2002 the Commission had formally closed some 2,000 cases. Only about 100 of these had become subject to more detailed Phase Two four-month investigations. Outright prohibitions are very rare and currently represent less than 1% (18 at the end of 2002) of all notified transactions. A 2001 Green Paper heralded a revised examination of merger thresholds that led the Commission to adopt a far-reaching reform of merger policy in December 2002 and which, in turn, formed the precursor to a new merger regulation that was agreed by the Council (for Economic and Monetary Affairs) in January 2004. The new merger regulation came into force on 1 May 2004. Essentially, the new regulation forms part of a package of comprehensive reforms for improving what has already been hailed as a major success story. The new package of reforms builds on 13 years of experience and includes guidelines on the assessment of mergers between competing firms and the Commission. The Commission itself has already introduced a set of best practices on the conduct of merger investigations, including the appointment of a chief economist in merger cases, that are designed to streamline decision-making and to make it more transparent. These initiatives were designed to restore Commission credibility in merger cases, particularly after the Court of First Instance overturned for the first time in the history of EU merger policy three Commission prohibition orders in 2002, severely reprimanded the Commission for its methods and procedures and stressed the need for greater economic analysis that stands up to scrutiny.

MERGER TREATY is the name often given to the treaty that formally integrated the executives of the **European Atomic Energy Community**, the **European Coal and Steel Community** and the **European Economic Community** (EEC). While technically there were still three **European Communities**, it became commonplace thereafter to refer to them collectively as the **European Community**. The Treaty created a single **European Commission** and a single Council of Ministers (see **Council of the European Union**), and was signed on 8 April 1965, coming into effect on 1 July 1967. The degree of personal animosity between **Charles de Gaulle** and **Walter Hallstein** ensured that the latter, who by this stage was the outgoing president of the EEC Commission, was not nominated for the position of President of a single Commission.

ANGELA MERKEL (1954-) made history on 22 November 2005 when she was elected by the *Bundestag* (parliament) as Germany's first ever female Chancellor. It should be noted that she is also the first former citizen of East Germany to lead the re-unified Germany and this may help to heal continuing divisions between the two halves of Germany. As chairwoman of the **Christian Demo-cratic Union** (CDU) she leads a 'grand coalition' with its sister party, the **Christian Social Union** (CSU) of Bavaria, and with the **Social Democratic Party of Germany** (SPD). This grand coalition comprises the two largest parties in Germany and came about following the indecisive outcome of the federal elections that took place in September 2005.

Merkel's CDU/CSU polled 35.2% (CDU 27.8%/CSU 7.4%) of the vote to the SPD's 34.2%. Neither the former SPD–Green coalition nor the CDU/CSU and its preferred coalition partners, the **Free Democratic Party**, held enough seats to form a majority in the Bundestag. Not surprisingly both **Gerhard Schröder** and Merkel claimed victory. A grand coalition may not have been a desirable outcome, but it was the only logical step given the distribution of seats in the new parliament. A deal between the two parties was reached after intense discussions that supplied Merkel with the Chancellorship and the SPD with 8 out of 16 seats in the cabinet.

The grand coalition will pursue a mix of policies and intends to cut public spending whilst increasing **VAT, social insurance** contributions and the top rate of **income tax**. Its agenda is going to prove contentious, especially any moves to remove employment protection for employees during their first two years in a job, along with its aims to freeze pensions and withdraw subsidies for first-time home buyers. On foreign policy, Germany will maintain its strong ties with **France** and Eastern European states, particularly **Russia,** and seek to build bridges post-Schröder with the United States. Significantly, Angela Merkel's first foreign trip took place the day after she was sworn in as Chancellor when she went to Paris for a meeting with the French president, **Jacques Chirac.** This move signalled the intention of keeping alive the special Franco-German part-nership. Merkel made her first major foray into EU politics when she attended the **European Council** summit in mid-December 2005, and she was credited with the instrumental force in helping to secure agreement on the **budget** and EU financing for the period 2007-13.

The **MESSINA CONFERENCE** was the meeting of the foreign ministers of the **Six**, held in the Italian city of that name in June 1955. Its aim was to consider new initiatives in integration after the failure of the proposals for a **European Defence Community** and **European Political Community**. An invitation to participate officially was extended to the United Kingdom, but was not accepted. The ministers agreed to begin 'a fresh advance towards the building of Europe' and to create a market that was 'free from all customs duties and all quantitative restrictions'. They also proposed a pooling of information and work on the uses of nuclear energy. The meeting established an intergovernmental committee, headed by **Paul-Henri Spaak** of **Belgium**, which was to consider and elaborate upon the proposals before submitting its report. The conference was the first stage of the process that culminated in the two **Treaties of Rome,** which established the **European Economic Community** and the **European Atomic Energy Community**.

MFA: See **Multi-Fibre Arrangement**

The **MIDDLE EAST** has, since the early 1970s, been a region that has attracted the attention of the European Communities. It was, for example, the focus of early attempts to forge closer foreign policy co-ordination among Member States through **European Political Co-operation**. Trade agreements have also been signed with countries in the region, many of which have since been replaced by new arrangements agreed as part of the European Union's efforts to promote a **Euro-Mediterranean Partnership** that includes the Middle East.

The **MILAN SUMMIT** held in **Italy** in June 1985 was one of the more decisive sessions of the **European Council**. The Council was to consider the report from the **Dooge Committee** on institutional reform of the European Communities (EC) and the report from the **Committee for a People's Europe**, both of which had been commissioned at the 1984 **Fontainebleau Summit**, as well as the decision at the Council's previous session in Brussels to establish a detailed timetable for the completion of an **internal market**. It was perhaps the first summit to be dominated by discussions on a comprehensive overhaul of the EC as established primarily by the **Treaty of Rome** almost 30 years earlier. In a way that was quite unprecedented for the European Council, which hitherto had always proceeded according to the principle of **unanimity**, a vote was called for on the establishment of an **intergovernmental conference** to discuss institutional reform; only a simple majority was needed. **Denmark**, **Greece** and the **United Kingdom** opposed the proposal, but were outvoted by the other seven Member States and subsequently agreed to participate in the conference, which led, some six months later, to the **Single European Act**. At the time, the Milan Summit seemed more of a failure than a success as it had clearly revealed a degree of opposition from Denmark, Greece and the United Kingdom towards any deeper integration. In retrospect, it is now recognized as a watershed in the history of European integration and one that relaunched the European integration project.

The **MILITARY COMMITTEE OF THE EUROPEAN UNION** was created in 2000 as part of the development of the European Union's **European security and defence policy**.

MINERVA is an action of the **SOCRATES** programme. MINERVA aims to promote and assess the use of information and communication technologies (ICT) in education and in open and distance learning (ODL) in education. MINERVA Action has three main objectives: firstly, to promote understanding among teachers, learners, decision-makers and the public at large of the implications of the use of ICT in education, as well as the critical and responsible use of ICT for educational purposes; secondly, to ensure that pedagogical considerations are given proper weight in the development of ICT and multimedia-based educational products and services; and thirdly, to promote access to improved methods and educational resources as well as to results and best practices in this field. To these ends it aims to create a dialogue at the European level in order to exchange ideas and approaches for the use of ICT. Through MINERVA, the **European Commission** supports four major types of activity which generally run for two years: firstly, projects to better understand and foster innovation; secondly, activities to design new teaching methods and resources; thirdly, activities intended to communicate and provide access to the results of projects in order to increase the publication of their findings; and lastly, projects intended to network and encourage the exchange of ideas.

MINORITY RIGHTS, unlike **human rights**, are not among the various rights that the Member States of the European Union (EU) are expressly obliged to uphold under the **Treaty on European Union**. The EU does, however, insist in the **Copenhagen Criteria** for accession to the EU that respect for the rights of minorities is a prerequisite for membership.

FRANÇOIS MITTERRAND (1916–96) was President of **France** from 1981 until 1995. His policy towards the European Communities (EC) tended to emphasize closer political and economic integration to a greater extent than that of his predecessors, while still seeking to preserve and strengthen French interests and influence within the organization. His first major initiatives were taken during the French presidency of the **European Council** in 1984. In a major speech to the **European Parliament**, he called for a renewal of the EC on the basis of the **Solemn Declaration on European Union** signed by the European Council the previous year, for a revision of the **Treaty of Rome** that would give the EC greater powers in more areas, and for the adoption of many more common policies. These were all themes that he reiterated later in the 1980s, after he had played an instrumental role at the 1984 **Fontainebleau Summit**, which resolved several important issues, such as the complaints of the **United Kingdom** with regard to the EC **budget**, which had been impeding EC progress. It was President Mitterrand who encouraged the development of the European Research Co-ordination Agency (**EUREKA**), and was instrumental in the reactivation of **Western European Union**. A strong supporter of EC institutional reform, economic **harmonization** and further political integration, he established a close relationship with the German Chancellor, **Helmut Kohl**, and the Commission President, **Jacques Delors**. Their common interests provided much of the impetus for change that culminated in the **Treaty on European Union**. Mitterrand's place and reputation as one of post-war Europe's most prominent statesmen is assured. Through his strong commitment to a successful Franco-German partnership he helped further to stabilize relations between the two states and was able to develop the European Union into a more dynamic system. While EC developments owed much to Mitterrand's efforts, the effect of the latter was not always positive. He continued to seek limitations on free trade in industry and agriculture to protect French interests, and his insistence on a strong French currency created high interest rates and unemployment problems in France.

MOLDOVA gained its independence from the **USSR** in 1991 and has since struggled with the political and economic challenges of the transition from Communist rule to democracy and a market economy. It also endured a civil war that left the country divided between Moldova proper and the separatist and pro-Russia Transnistria. Relations with the European Union (EU) have nevertheless developed, primarily on the basis of a **Partnership and Co-operation Agreement** signed in 1995 and financial assistance under the **Technical Assistance to the Commonwealth of Independent States** (TACIS) programme. Since then, Moldova has expressed interest in some form of **association agreement** with the EU and joined the Stability Pact for South-Eastern Europe in 2001. The EU's response has been to include Moldova in its **European Neighbourhood Policy**. This resulted in an Action Plan designed to promote closer ties between the EU and Moldova. Evidence of the EU's increasing engagement with Moldova – soon to be a country on the EU's border once **Romania** joins – came with the appointment of a an EU Special Representative on Moldova whose role is to strengthen the EU's contribution to the resolution of the Transnistria issue.

MONETARY COMMITTEE was the name of a body of senior officials from the national finance ministries and the national central banks of Member States that was established in 1958. It met monthly in Brussels, a chair being elected from its own membership for a period of two years. The Committee's objective was to advise the **European Commission** on monetary policy, performing, to some extent, some of the functions of COREPER (see **Committee of Permanent Representatives**) in the area of monetary affairs. Under the **Treaty on European Union**, it was given the task of co-ordinating the monetary policies of the Member States during the first stage of **economic and monetary union** (EMU). It was dissolved during the third stage of EMU and replaced by an **Economic and Financial Committee**.

MONETARY COMPENSATORY AMOUNTS (MCAs) were introduced into the **Common Agricultural Policy** (CAP) as a temporary measure to ease the problems created by the decision, following the collapse of the **Bretton Woods** system of fixed exchange rates, to retain the common agricultural prices at their original level of exchange. These prices would form the **green currencies**. In order to compensate farmers for loss of income caused by currency fluctuations, MCAs would constitute the difference between the common price structure and prices determined by existing exchange rates in both the internal and external trade of the European Communities (EC). Originally, it was agreed that national governments would finance MCAs, but the EC took control of MCA financing for external trade in 1972 and for internal trade in the following year. MCAs were intended to last only until the EC established a definitive financial system for the CAP and introduced a coherent monetary policy. The failure of both of these objectives effectively meant that MCAs became permanent. While providing some form of short-term price stability in the context of floating currencies, MCAs introduced a high degree of complexity into the CAP, varying both between different products and, because of currency fluctuations, over time. At their nadir in 1973, some MCAs were liable to change almost from week to week, and they steadily grew as a proportion of agricultural expenditure. Greater currency stability in the 1980s persuaded the **European Commission** that MCAs hindered rather than helped the **common market**. In 1984 the Commission persuaded the Member States to phase out MCAs by 1989, although it was eventually agreed that they would only be fully dismantled by the end of 1992.

MONETARY POLICY is fundamental to **economic and monetary union** (EMU). Decision-making in this area varies with regard to the topic in question: for the issue of coins by the Member States the **co-operation procedure** applies, after consultation with the **European Central Bank** (ECB); for the formulation of exchange-rate policy guidelines, the **Council of the European Union** decides by **qualified majority voting** (QMV) following a recommendation from the ECB; for technical adjustments to the Statute of the **European System of Central Banks**, the Council decides by QMV on a recommendation from the ECB after consulting the **European Commission** and obtaining the assessment of the **European Parliament** (EP); for the exchange rate of the **euro** against non-EMU currencies, the Council decides by **unanimity**, following a recommendation from the ECB or the Commission and after consulting the EP.

The **MONETARY POLICY COMMITTEE** is the name of an adjunct to the **Council of the European Union**. Along with the **Economic and Financial Affairs Council of Ministers** and the **Economic Policy Committee**, it is one of the bodies that provide a regular meeting place for representatives of the economic and finance ministers of the Member States.

JEAN MONNET (1888–1979) probably contributed more than any other single individual to the post-war developments that culminated in the European Communities (EC). Although he was pragmatic in his approach to integration, his contribution was in the form of ideas rather than as a practising politician. Monnet already had a distinguished diplomatic and business career when, in 1940, he contributed to the formulation of the plan for an Anglo-French Union subsequently advocated by **Winston Churchill**. After the Second World War, Monnet was appointed head of the French Planning Commission in charge of the Modernization Plan. His experiences there persuaded him that no European country could, by itself and using its own resources, plan an effective programme of economic growth, development and prosperity. While Monnet's ultimate objective was a European political union, he tended to be suspicious of ostentatious political gestures. He believed that a programme of integration had to be practical and long-term: effective political integration could only be built on an accretion of proven and accepted experiences of co-operation. For Monnet, the means of achieving progress was a gradual integration of discrete economic sectors that would, through a process of **spillover**, lead in time to full economic and political union.

Monnet was the original conceiver of the **Schuman Plan**, and was appointed as the first President of the High Authority of the **European Coal and Steel Community**. He was the originator of the Pleven Plan that produced the ill-fated **European Defence Community** (EDC). When the EDC collapsed, Monnet resigned from the High Authority to found the **Action Committee for a United States of Europe**. He successfully sponsored the creation of the **European Atomic Energy Community,** which, after the collapse of EDC, he thought had more chance of success than the proposal for a **common market**.

Monnet's vision of a united Europe was not exclusive. While believing that reconciliation between **France** and **Germany** was essential, it was a matter of regret to him that only six countries were willing to participate in experiments in integration. He continually urged the **Six** to encourage other states to join them; in particular, he believed that European integration would be incomplete without the involvement of the United Kingdom. Monnet's labours are commemorated in several ways by the EC, mainly through the funding of Monnet fellowships and other positions in the field of education.

MONNET METHOD is the term used to describe a strategy of integration based on **spillover** from one area of activity to another. It proved successful in the early years of European integration and again under Jacques Delors in the late 1980s and early 1990s. Since then, it has proved more difficult to implement.

MARIO MONTI (1943–) was appointed one of the two members of the **European Commission** from **Italy** in 1995. His term was renewed in 1999. In his first term as Commissioner, Monti was responsible for the **internal market**, financial services and financial integration, customs and taxation; from 1999 he had responsibility for **competition policy**. An academic in the field of economics by profession, he is regarded as a highly capable individual who masters his brief with ease. His record as competition commissioner was highly impressive and there he became famous for starting a long and drawn-out anti-monopoly lawsuit against Microsoft. He had developed into one of the **Prodi** Commission's heavyweights, but his hopes of continuing within the new **Barroso** Commission were dashed when he failed to secure reappointment. His preferred successor was **Rocco Buttiglione**.

MOROCCO, one of the **Maghreb States**, entered into a bilateral trade and aid agreement with the European Communities (EC) in 1976. A decade later, in 1987, it submitted a formal application for membership, but was informed by the EC that because Morocco is not a European state it was not eligible for membership. An **association agreement** was signed with the European Union in 1996, and the country is now part of the **Euro–Mediterranean Partnership.**

MULTI-FIBRE ARRANGEMENT (MFA), the full title of which is the Arrangement Regarding International Trade in Textiles, was first negotiated within the **General Agreement on Tariffs and Trade** (GATT) in 1973. It was an agreement between Western industrial states and suppliers of low-cost textile goods from developing countries. The textile industries of the developed world had already been severely damaged by low-cost imports, and the MFA was established as a means of controlling imports in such a way that Western markets would be gradually opened to developing countries as an orderly contraction and restructuring of the Western textile industries was taking place. In practice, the MFA operated as a protectionist mechanism restricting the level of low-cost imports. In the renegotiations of the MFA in 1977, 1981 and 1986, Western governments successfully imposed stricter quotas on the developing countries. Textiles were hence generally excluded from GATT and the European Communities' commitment to free trade. However, as a result of the **Uruguay**

Round of GATT trade negotiations, the MFA was to be progressively eliminated, over a 10-year period.

MULTI-SPEED EUROPE is a term that is used to describe the notion of differentiated integration, whereby common objectives are pursued by a group of Member States that are both willing and able to advance them. The term assumes that the other Member States, which may be temporarily unable or not willing to advance a given objective at that moment in time, will join the participating Member States at a later date.

MUTUAL RECOGNITION, as a principle, is essential for the proper functioning of the **internal market**. It means that when a product is legally manufactured and marketed in one Member State, it may be freely offered for sale in other Member States, irrespective of whether it complies with the relevant national legislation in that country. The principle was established by the **Court of Justice** in 1979 in the ***Cassis de Dijon*** case.

N

NACC: See **NORTH ATLANTIC CO-OPERATION COUNCIL**

NAFO: See **NORTH ATLANTIC FISHERIES ORGANIZATION**

The **NATIONAL ASSEMBLY FOR WALES EU OFFICE** was established in 2000 and acts as a link for this region of the **United Kingdom** with the European Union (EU) and its institutions. The Office is staffed by Assembly officials and is directly accountable to the National Assembly of Wales. It is also part of the United Kingdom Permanent Representation (UKREP) family and works closely with officials from UKREP and alongside the Office of the Northern Ireland Executive in Brussels (ONIEB) and **Scotland Europa**. The office was set up as a consequence of devolving powers to Wales in 1999. The Assembly seeks to engage directly with the EU across a broad front and the Brussels Office has several functions. These include: providing intelligence and information for ministers and committees from the Welsh Assembly; taking a policy lead on EU horizontal issues and constitutional developments; providing specialist support and acting as a focal point for Assembly visitors and staff based in Brussels; acting as the public face of the Assembly in Brussels; and representing the Assembly on a range of Brussels-based working groups.

NATIONAL PARLIAMENTS have always played a role in the development of the European Communities (EC) and European Union (EU), not least in adopting the necessary implementing legislation for **directives**, undertaking the **ratification** of treaties and agreements, and scrutinizing the activities of the EU and national governments. To these ends, national parliaments have created specialized committees dealing with EU matters. These committees meet with a group of **Members of the European Parliament** every six months under the umbrella of **COSAC** (*Conférence des Organes Spécialisés dans les Affaires Communautaires*). Meetings of the Conference of Presidents and Speakers of Parliaments in the EU are also held every six months. Less regular are the so-called **assizes** (or Conferences of the Parliaments) that are supposed to meet to discuss major developments in the EU.

Despite such involvement in EU affairs, concerns have long been voiced that closer integration at the EU level is leading to a reduction in the powers and roles of national parliaments. Moreover, there have been persistent concerns about the **democratic deficit** within the EU. Various, often half-hearted, attempts have been made to remedy the situation. Hence, the **Treaty of Amsterdam** sought to improve the flow of information on EC/EU matters to national parliaments, particularly on matters concerning **Police and Judicial Co-operation in Criminal Matters**, and to encourage a greater input from COSAC on the legislative activities of the EC/EU. These did little, however, to assuage concerns. Consequently, one of the main issues highlighted in the *Declaration on the Future of the Union*, adopted at the Nice **European Council** meeting in December 2000, was the 'role of national parliaments in the European architecture'. This was developed in the **Laeken Declaration**, which called on the **European Convention** to look at what role national parliaments should play in the future, possibly as part of a new institution in which they would be represented alongside the **European Parliament** and the **Council of the European Union**. The hope was that an increased involvement of national parliaments might help improve the **legitimacy** of the EU and reduce the **democratic deficit**.

NATO: See **North Atlantic Treaty Organization**

NEGATIVE ASSENT is a phrase that has been used in the **United Kingdom** to describe the power of veto over **legislation** and the generally enhanced authority given to the **European Parliament** under the **Treaty on European Union** by the latter's implementation of the **co-decision procedure**, which created a joint decision-making mechanism.

NEO-FUNCTIONALISM is a term that has often been used to describe the actual process of integration pursued by the European Communities. It refers to the placing of emphasis on a process of economic and political co-operation in limited and specified areas, rather than a commitment to a grand design such as **federalism**. Central to neo-functionalism is the idea of **spillover**, whereby co-operation in one area creates demands for and leads to co-operation in another. The appropriateness of neo-functionalism in explaining the process of integration has been challenged by, *inter alia,* **liberal intergovernmentalism**.

NETD@YS EUROPE is an annual operation designed to illustrate how the new forms of electronic media and the expanding information society can help facilitate learning and research. The one-week operation commenced in 1997 and was initially focused on schools, but in recent years it has been extended to cover youth clubs, libraries, cinemas, museums and vocational training centres. This operation facilitates projects that are financed from a **European Commission** grant and involve partnerships between at least two European states.

The **NETHERLANDS** has been deeply involved in European integration ever since 1945. Its government-in-exile during the Second World War agreed on the establishment of the **Benelux** Economic Union and the Netherlands was also a founder member of the three European Communities (EC). Several of its statesmen have made major contributions to European co-operative efforts. In the 1960s the Netherlands was a strong supporter of **enlargement**: it opposed the **Fouchet Plan**, wanting the question of enlargement to be settled first, and supported closer links between the EC and the **European Free Trade Association**. It also, albeit unsuccessfully, urged a reactivation of **Western European Union**. With its efficient agriculture, the Netherlands was a strong advocate of the **Common Agricultural Policy**, of which it has been a major beneficiary. It later stressed the need for a stronger **environmental policy**, and after 1989 emphasized the importance of developing closer political links with **Central and Eastern Europe**. It has persistently supported closer economic and political collaboration, favouring institutional reform and a substantially greater role for the **European Parliament**. As the host of the **Maastricht Summit**, which was to consider a constitutional reform of the EC, it was responsible for constructing the summit agenda. The Netherlands produced a draft that went beyond what most Member States were prepared to accept, and it had to moderate its position, making the **Treaty on European Union** less comprehensive than it desired. It proved more successful in handling the end stages of the 1996 **Intergovernmental Conference**, which led to the **Treaty of Amsterdam**. The Dutch government took a bold decision when it opted to hold a referendum on the **Treaty establishing a Constitution for Europe**. Referenda are practically alien to Dutch political culture and it was assumed that the generally pro-EU Dutch population would simply endorse the government's position on the constitutional treaty. However, on 1 June 2005, three days after the French 'no' vote, some 62% voted against the treaty in the Netherlands, and so plunged the EU into a state of crisis.

NEUTRALITY, in some form, characterizes the foreign policies of six of the Member States comprising the European Union: **Austria**, **Cyprus**, **Finland**, **Ireland**, **Malta**, and **Sweden**. It means that in times of war the neutral states refrain from becoming engaged in the conflict and treat the belligerents equally. For most of the **Cold War**, this meant that Austria, Finland and Sweden felt unable to join the European Communities. Once they did apply for membership in 1989–92, concerns were raised about the impact that their membership and continued adherence to neutrality would have on plans for **common foreign and security policy** (CFSP). In practice, the neutral countries have not raised significant or insurmountable objections to the development of CFSP.

NEW CRONOS is the name of the main statistical database of the European Communities, previously known as CRONOS and covering every economic and social sector. It is compiled by **Eurostat**, the Statistical Office, and is divided into nine themes: general statistics; economy and finance; energy and industry; population and social conditions; agriculture, forestry and fisheries; external trade; distributive trades, services and transport; the environment; and research and development. These themes are themselves subdivided into various domains of information. New Cronos comprises more than 100m. items of social and economic statistical data covering the European Union (EU) Member States, and, in some cases, the **USA**, **Japan** and other main economic partners, including countries, especially those of **Central and Eastern Europe**, that have applied for membership of the EU.

NEW NEIGHBOURHOOD: See **Wider Europe – New Neighbourhood**

The **NEW TRANSATLANTIC AGENDA** (NTA) of 1995 represents an extension of the 1990 **Transatlantic Declaration** and provides a framework for European Union (EU)–US partnership and co-operation across a wide range of activities. The NTA contained four main priorities: to promote peace and stability, democracy and development throughout the world (e.g. joint co-operation over the former **Yugoslavia** and the **Middle East**); to respond effectively to global challenges (e.g. co-operation in fields such as public health); to contribute to the growth of world trade; and to build closer links between Europe and the **USA**. The last two points have led to a number of transatlantic dialogues being established in areas such as the environment, consumer protection and business issues. The NTA was accompanied by an EU–US Joint Action Plan that contained 150 specific areas of action. The aims were diverse and ranged from promoting economic reform in **Ukraine** and combating AIDS, to developing closer links between universities and colleges on both sides of the Atlantic. Since 1995 the EU and the USA have made considerable progress in many of these areas, from combating illicit drugs to educational training. In May 1997 both parties reached agreement on Customs Co-operation and Mutual Assistance in Customs Matters and in 1998 signed a Mutual Recognition Agreement, which covers particular goods such as pharmaceuticals and medical devices and telecommunications equipment. In 1998 a further development included the launch of the Transatlantic Economic Partnership, which sought to develop a regular dialogue on multilateral trade issues.

The NTA launched an era of unprecedented co-operation on a wide range of political, economic and civil society issues between the EU and the USA, although this has not by any means resolved all differences between the two economic powers over issues such as the environment, the structure of labour markets and economic protection of the US steel industry. The EU–US partnership is a highly strategic relationship. It represents an ongoing means for dialogue on a range of issues that have evolved into formal biannual EU–US summits between the Presidents of the **European Council** and the **European Commission** and the President of the USA.

In May 2002 leaders from both the EU and the USA met in Washington, DC, and agreed to establish a Positive Economic Agenda, which foresaw a highly developed scheme of bilateral co-operation in specific sectors, including financial markets, the insurance sector, organic farming, electronic tendering and electronic customs.

NGO: See **Non-Governmental Organizations**

NICE TREATY: See **Treaty of Nice**

NINE is a popular term referring to the membership of the European Communities after the first **enlargement** of 1973. It is used to describe the collectivity of the nine Member States between 1973 and 1981: the **Six** founder members, plus **Denmark**, **Ireland** and the **United Kingdom**.

ÉMILE NOEL (1922–96) was the first Secretary-General of the **European Commission**. Appointed to the position of Executive Secretary of the Commission of the **European Economic Community** (EEC) in 1958, from 1967 to 1987 he served as head of the **Secretariat-General** of the European Commission, the most senior administrator, and assistant to the Commissioners. He played a major role in the development of the European Communities (EC) over three decades and, by leadership and example, contributed much to the ethos and consolidation of the EC administration.

NOISE is the subject of several European Community (EC) **directives** agreed as part of the EC's **environmental policy**. Maximum noise limits have been set for a wide range of commercial and domestic equipment. Manufacturers of many household appliances are required, moreover, to indicate the noise level on the packaging. Limits have also been set for decibel levels in the workplace.

NOMENCLATURE OF TERRITORIAL UNITS FOR STATISTICS (NUTS) describes a classification of regions in the European Union (EU) by the Statistical Office of the European Communities (**Eurostat**). The NUTS system has three levels: each level 1 unit is normally sub-divided into a certain number of level 2 units, and level 2 units are composed of smaller level 3 units. NUTS units often correspond to national administrative divisions, but are sometimes *ad hoc* groupings of smaller national units for the purposes of EU regional statistics. Not all Member States are sub-divided at all three levels.

The **NOMINATION PROCEDURE** is used to nominate the **European Commission** and its President. Originally, nomination involved only the 'common accord' of the governments of the Member States. Following the adoption of the **Treaty on European Union**, the **European Parliament** (EP) was involved more, and the procedure split into four stages: nomination of the Commission President; nomination of the remainder of the Commission; approval by the EP; and appointment by 'common accord' of the Member States. The **Treaty of Amsterdam** further involved the EP, requiring its approval of the Commission President before the rest of the Commission was nominated. Under the terms of the **Treaty of Nice**, the **Council of the European Union** would take over the responsibilities of the Member States and make **decisions** in this procedure by **qualified majority voting**.

NON-COMPULSORY EXPENDITURE refers to that part of the European Communities (EC) **budget** (about 40%), which relates to policies that are not directly provided for by the **Treaty of Rome** and its subsequent amendments. In practice, it includes most EC **expenditure** except that on agriculture. After 1988 greater emphasis was placed upon 'privileged' non–compulsory expenditure, a phrase that refers to spending on long-term programmes. This development has been criticized by the **European Parliament** (EP) for reducing its ability to influence the budget. The EP has greater influence over the non-compulsory part of the budget, and has continually sought a redefinition and expansion of what that term covers. However, EP amendments to non-compulsory expenditure are not allowed to exceed an overall maximum figure previously set each year by the **Council of the European Union**. The criteria that determine the maximum level are the trend in gross national product (GNP), the average variation in the budgets of the Member States, and the trend during the previous year in the cost of living.

NON-GOVERNMENTAL ORGANIZATIONS (NGOs) is a term which, when used in the context of the European Union (EU), refers to those **interest groups**, or lobbies, that are involved with the EU and active in seeking to influence EU policy development, but have no formal connection with the EU. There are numerous ways of classifying interest groups, such as according to type and number and whether they operate as national groups or Eurogroups. The majority of these groups represent business interests (e.g. ERT, UNICE) alongside a smaller number of non-business or more diffuse interests (e.g. trade unions, consumers' and environmental associations). There are multiple points of access to the EU policy process, including the **European Commission**, the **European Parliament** (EP), the Council and even the Courts. The EU system is very open to interest groups and, indeed, the European institutions consider interest group involvement to be essential in the development of legitimate and appropriate policies. The Commission has set up a database, CONECCS (Consultation, the European Commission and Civil Society), of around 1,000 NGOs working at EC level, covering approximately 100 branches of activity. Both the Commission and the EP have been seeking to regulate NGO activities in recent years in order to improve **transparency** and to establish minimum standards. (See also **lobbying**.)

NORDIC COUNCIL is the name of a body established in 1952 by the Nordic states as a loose association of intergovernmental co-operation. Despite its purely consultative character, the Nordic Council has achieved a high degree of co-operation and co-ordination in a wide range of policy fields. However, it failed, despite several initiatives, to secure an agreement on a Nordic economic union. After 1970 the Council created a limited institutional structure, with a small secretariat. In their membership applications to the European Communities (EC), **Denmark** and **Norway** made their continued membership of the Council an essential element of their submissions, a condition that was accepted by the EC. Denmark remained a member of the Council after joining the EC in 1973. It saw its role as one of liaison between the two organizations. Membership of both organizations did not create any severe policy problems for Denmark, and the Council's continued existence is currently in little doubt, despite the accession of **Finland** and **Sweden** to the European Union.

NORM PRICE is the term usually used to describe the price guaranteed to tobacco producers under the **Common Agricultural Policy**.

The **NORTH ATLANTIC CO-OPERATION COUNCIL** (NACC) was a body linking the **North Atlantic Treaty Organization** with the new democracies of **Central and Eastern Europe** and the **Commonwealth of Independent States**. It was established in 1991 as a framework for co-operation in defence and security to ensure stability throughout the continent of Europe. Its formation was criticized by some for duplicating and confusing the role of the Conference on Security and Co-operation in Europe, now the **Organization for Security and Co-operation in Europe**. The NACC was replaced by the **Euro-Atlantic Partnership Council** in 1997.

The **NORTH ATLANTIC FISHERIES ORGANIZATION** (NAFO) is a body that consists of all those states with a major fisheries interest in the North Atlantic. It deals with questions of fishing limits and zones, permissible quotas and catches, conservation of stocks and the types of equipment allowed. Given the existence of the **Common Fisheries Policy**, the Member States are represented in the organization by the **European Commission**.

The **NORTH ATLANTIC TREATY ORGANIZATION** (NATO) owes its existence to the Washington Treaty of 4 April 1949 that brought the **USA** and Canada together with 10 European countries (**Belgium, Denmark, France, Iceland, Italy, Luxembourg,** the **Netherlands, Norway, Portugal** and the **United Kingdom**) in a military arrangement for the collective defence of Western Europe. During the **Cold War** the membership of NATO was enlarged to include **Greece** and **Turkey** in 1952, the Federal Republic of **Germany** in 1955, and **Spain** in 1986. France, however, withdrew from the integrated military command structure in 1966 (although in 1996 it resumed participation in some of the military organs of NATO). Of the **Twenty-five** European Union (EU) Member States, **Austria, Cyprus, Finland, Ireland, Malta** and **Sweden** are not members of NATO.

NATO member states are committed to providing military forces according to their means; these forces are subject to the NATO chain of military command. An attack upon one state is regarded as an attack upon all, although the Treaty does not specify how the affected member state will receive assistance from its partners, who are only required to take such action as they deem necessary. The organization was not meant to be an agent of integration, but NATO and the other new international organizations of the late 1940s made an important contribution to integration by bringing Western European countries together in a series of institutional frameworks that obliged them to co-operate and liaise with each other on an intensive and continuous basis. After the end of the Cold War, there was some doubt over the future of NATO.

After 1990 it sought to redefine its role as a political and security alliance in association with the Conference on Security and Co-operation in Europe (now the **Organization for Security and Co-operation in Europe** – OSCE), and in 1992 it brought the former Communist states of Eastern Europe into its consultative processes through the formation of the **North Atlantic Co-operation Council** (since 1997 replaced by the **Euro–Atlantic Partnership Council** – EAPC). In 1994 the **Partnerships for Peace** programme was established under the aegis of NATO. This is open to EAPC and OSCE states and aims to promote political and military co-operation throughout Europe. By December 1997, 27 countries from **Central and Eastern Europe** and the former **USSR** had joined the initiative. Moreover, in March 1999 three Central and Eastern European countries – the **Czech Republic, Hungary** and **Poland** – joined NATO proper. At their Prague Summit in November 2002, NATO leaders agreed to extend membership invitations to up to seven more countries from the former Soviet bloc: **Bulgaria**, **Estonia**, **Latvia**, **Lithuania**, **Romania**, **Slovakia** and **Slovenia**. These countries joined NATO in 2004.

In general, relations between NATO and the European Communities (EC) and European Union (EU) have been close. NATO's protection permitted the EC to develop and consolidate themselves, while conversely the economic co-operation engendered by the EC contributed to a stronger Western Europe. Some states, especially France, have wished to see the **Western European Union** (WEU) reformed to become a European replacement for NATO. In establishing the **common foreign and security policy**, the **Treaty on European Union** re-emphasized the potential significance of WEU for the EU. The response of NATO was to build on regular joint NATO–WEU meetings and support the proposed improvement of WEU's operational capabilities. Fearful that such developments might undermine NATO, many Member States have insisted that NATO must remain the major European security organization. This has not prevented the establishment of either the **Eurocorps** in 1992 or, more recently and more controversially, a **European Rapid Reaction Force.**

NORWAY has been, in general, suspicious of close European relations that involve anything more than intergovernmental co-operation. It first applied to join the European Communities (EC) in 1962, doing so more out of necessity than enthusiasm for European integration. Indeed, there was considerable disquiet in the country over what membership might mean in terms of national sovereignty and the 'special problems' arising from the country's 'geographical location and economic structure', which the government had said would need to be resolved by the negotiations. Hence, **France**'s veto of the **United Kingdom**'s application in 1963 and again in 1967 was not wholly unwelcome. Opposition to membership increased after the resumption of negotiations in 1970, and the deep feelings aroused had widespread repercussions throughout Norway. In September 1972 a narrow majority (53%) voted against membership in a consultative referendum. Preparations for accession were halted and replaced by discussions on a **Free Trade Agreement**, which entered into force in 1973. Thereafter, EC membership disappeared from the Norwegian political agenda until 1988, when it re-emerged because of concerns over the possible effect of the **internal market**. Initially, the preference was for the **European Economic Area** (EEA), but Norway soon found itself following its neighbours in applying for membership in 1992. **Accession negotiations** were concluded in 1994, but once again membership was rejected in a referendum. Since then, Norway's relations have been based on full participation in the EEA as well as involvement in the **Schengen Agreement**. Future membership of the European Union has not, however, been ruled out.

NOUVELLES ÉQUIPES INTERNATIONALES was the name of a transnational association of Christian Democrat political parties formed in 1947. In 1965 it changed its name to the European Union of Christian Democrats, and in 1976 its members from Member States of the European Communities founded the European People's Party (see **Group of the European People's Party (Christian Democrats) and European Democrats**) as a transnational organization.

NOUVELLES FRONTIÈRES is the name of a French travel agency that challenged the price-fixing regulations of the French Civil Aviation Code in the **Court of Justice**. In April 1986 the Court ruled in favour of the company, declaring that air transport was not exempt from the **competition policy** of the European Communities, and that under the **Treaty of Rome** Member States were not permitted to approve air fares that resulted from agreements between airlines. This was the first major challenge to the cartel arrangements on air fares pursued by both governments and airlines. The Court also pointed out that responsibility for determining whether an air-fare agreement transgresses the Treaty rests with the **European Commission** and the national anti-trust authorities. The ruling gave the Commission greater powers, although subsequent progress on air transport liberalization was slow.

NUCLEAR ENERGY: See **Energy Policy**; **European Atomic Energy Community**; **European Fusion Development Agreement**; **Joint European Torus**

NUTS: See **Nomenclature of Territorial Units for Statistics**

O

OCTs: See **Overseas Countries and Territories**

OECD: See **Organisation for Economic Co-operation and Development**

OEEC: See **Organisation for European Economic Co-operation**

The **OFFICE FOR HARMONIZATION IN THE INTERNAL MARKET** (OHIM) is a decentralized European Communities agency responsible for the **harmonization** of intellectual property rights, **trademarks** and design rights across the Member States. It was established in 1994, and is located in Alicante, **Spain**.

The **OFFICE FOR OFFICIAL PUBLICATIONS OF THE EUROPEAN COMMUNITIES** (EUR-OP), which was formerly known by the acronym OOPEC, is based in **Luxembourg**. It is an agency of the **European Commission**, but provides services to, and is managed by, all European Communities (EC) **institutions**. It is responsible for the publication and dissemination of EC publications, including official reports and pamphlets. These are available directly from EUR-OP and from **Euro Info Centres** maintained throughout the European Union (EU). They are also lodged in several educational institutions throughout the EU, which have been recognized as depositories for EC publications and are known as **European Documentation Centres**.

OFFICE OF THE NORTHERN IRELAND EXECUTIVE IN BRUSSELS (ONIEB) was established in 2001 and is one of some 200 offices in Brussels that operate on behalf of regional and local authorities in the European Union (EU). The ONIEB was created, as part of the Belfast Agreement, as a means of enabling the newly devolved Northern Ireland executive to play a role in Europe. The functions of the ONIEB are essentially: to monitor the development by EU institutions of policies relevant to Northern Ireland; to provide up-to-date information to ministers and departments in Belfast; and to ensure that the interests of Northern Ireland are fully represented in policy developments by EU institutions. Moreover, the ONIEB seeks to raise the profile of Northern Ireland among European policy-makers and seeks to form inter-regional links with other regions in Europe. Technically the ONIEB forms part of the United Kingdom's Permanent Representation (UKREP) and works closely with it and both the **Scottish Executive** Office and the **National Assembly for Wales EU Office**.

The ***OFFICIAL JOURNAL OF THE EUROPEAN COMMUNITIES*** (OJ) is one of the principal publications of the **Office for Official Publications of the European Communities** (EUR-OP), covering all of the major European Communities (EC) **institutions**. It contains the details of all EC **legislation**. **Regulations** become law throughout the European Union (EU) as soon as they are published in the Journal. It also carries details of EC initiatives, and advertisements of staff vacancies. The OJ has three parts: the 'L' Series contains EC legislation, the 'C' Series draft legislation, information and notices, while the 'S' Series is a supplement comprising notices and advertisements for public works, supplies, services and research contracts. On the entry into force of the **Treaty of Nice**, the OJ became the *Official Journal of the EU*.

OHIM: See **Office for Harmonization in the Internal Market**

OJ: See *Official Journal of the European Communities*

OLAF: See **Anti-Fraud Office**

An **OMBUDSMAN**, a post created by the **Treaty on European Union**, is appointed by the **European Parliament** (EP) to deal with complaints of maladministration in European Communities **institutions** (with the exception of the **Court of Justice** and the **Court of First Instance**) and initiatives. Upon the receipt of complaints from citizens, business and other interests working in the European Union, the Ombudsman launches an inquiry to try to resolve any particular issue of concern. The first Ombudsman, who took office in September 1995, was Jacob Söderman of **Finland**; he remained in the post until March 2003. His successor was Nikiforos Diamandouros of **Greece**, who was elected by the EP in January 2003. Diamandouros assumed the post on 1 April 2003 and was re-elected in 2005; his term will run until 2009. The Ombudsman submits an annual report on his or her activities to the EP.

OMC: See **Open Method of Co-ordination**

ONIEB: See **Office of the Northern Ireland Executive in Brussels**

ONP stands for Open Network Provision, an initiative dating back to 1989 intended to harmonize the national regulations of the Member States regarding **telecommunications** services.

OOPEC: See **Office for Official Publications of the European Communities (EUR-OP)**

OPEN METHOD OF CO-ORDINATION (OMC) is associated with a relatively new policy method that essentially involves the comparison of national policies across the European Union (EU) and the dissemination of best practices in such areas as social policy and employment policy. This new instrument is expected to facilitate the exchange of ideas and experiences between the Member States and is intended to encourage greater policy and learning. It is hoped that, under this method, Member States will agree to and will apply non-binding EU guidelines to national and regional policies, while avoiding the necessity of enacting new EC **legislation**.

OPENNESS relates primarily to increasing calls from the 1990s onwards for the provision of greater information about European Union (EU) policy debates and the EU decision-making processes within the EU **institutions** and, in particular, the **Council of the European Union**. Openness is closely associated with the other concepts such as **transparency, legitimacy** and **accountability** that are familiar, recurrent themes of European **governance**. The EU institutions have promised greater openness in a serious effort both to reduce the criticisms of a '**democratic deficit**' and to enable the public to appreciate and understand much better the workings of the EU. The **Treaty of Amsterdam** included a chapter on transparency that gives 'any citizen ... a right of access to **European Parliament,** Council and **European Commission** documents'. Despite these aspirations, access remains rather restricted, especially to the workings of the Council. The launch of the **European Convention** in February 2002, following the meeting of the Laeken **European Council** of December 2001, must be recognized as a further means to draw the people of Europe closer to the EU.

OPET: See **Organization for the Promotion of Energy Technology**

OPINIONS are one of two kinds of non-binding pronouncement that may be issued by the **Council of the European Union** and the **European Commission**.

Like **recommendations** they do not constitute instructions, but merely express the preference of the European Communities, and may be disregarded by the Member States. (See also **Court of Justice**; **decisions**; **directives**; **law**; **legislation**; **regulations**; **resolutions**.)

OPTIMUM CURRENCY AREA is a term, attributed to the US economist Robert Mundell, which refers to a group of countries bound together by a system of fixed exchange rates. From 1970 such an area was an objective of the European Communities and was to be achieved through the establishment of **economic and monetary union**.

OPT-OUT is a term that came into common usage after the 1991 **Maastricht Summit**. It refers to a decision to allow a Member State the statutory right not to take part in any specific activity pursued by the European Union. Opt-outs are in fact exemptions from treaty provisions and have been granted to **Denmark** and the **United Kingdom** over **economic and monetary union**, and enabled the United Kingdom to remain outside the aspirations and all decisions pertaining to the Social Chapter of the **Treaty on European Union** until the new Labour administration abandoned this opt-out in 1997. Denmark, the United Kingdom and **Ireland** were granted various opt-out arrangements governing the **area of freedom**, **security and justice** established by the **Treaty of Amsterdam**. (See also **Charter of Fundamental Social Rights of Workers**.)

The **ORGANISATION FOR ECONOMIC CO-OPERATION AND DEVELOPMENT** (OECD) was established under US leadership in 1961 as a successor to the **Organisation for European Economic Co-operation**. The **USA** sought a collaborative body that might mitigate some of the feared adverse consequences of the division of Western Europe into the **European Economic Community** and the **European Free Trade Association**. The USA and Canada became full members of the new organization, and **Japan** joined in 1964. All the European Union Member States belong to OECD, which is a forum for the advanced industrial democracies, concerned not only with the effectiveness of the domestic economies of its members, but also with the broader and long-term problems of the international economic system. OECD membership increased in size with a spate of accessions in the mid-1990s (including Mexico in 1994, the **Czech Republic** in 1995 and **Hungary**, **Poland** and the Republic of Korea in 1996). Today OECD has 30 member countries and is based in Paris, where it maintains a substantial organization staffed by economic experts. It has often acted as a pioneer in developing economic concepts, for example on **competition policy** and labour markets, and its regular economic reports and surveys on the international and national economies are detailed and highly regarded. The recommendations of its reports are often implemented, although OECD cannot impose a policy upon any one state.

The **ORGANISATION FOR EUROPEAN ECONOMIC CO-OPERA-TION** (OEEC) was established in 1948 by 14 states, with the **USA** and Canada as associate members. It owed its existence to the fact that, in offering aid to Europe through the **Marshall Plan**, the USA had insisted that the European states must determine a method of allocating the aid in a way that was consistent with achieving the maximum economic effect throughout the Continent. The US offer was considered by a Committee for European Economic Co-opera-tion, which consisted of representatives of the interested European countries. The Committee was then reconstructed as the OEEC. Decisions by the OEEC Council of Ministers were to be binding on all members, but in practice the Council operated only on the basis of unanimous agreement. The OEEC administered the Marshall Aid programme, but with a substantial number of specialized boards and expert groups it outlived the programme, and went on, in the 1950s, to work for the liberalization of trade and the full convertibility of currencies. The OEEC's objective was not economic integration, but economic co-operation, an area where it was the first European body to work effectively. It provided both a base and useful lessons for subsequent developments in inte-gration. In 1961 the OEEC was transformed into the **Organisation for Economic Co-operation and Development.**

The **ORGANIZATION FOR SECURITY AND CO-OPERATION IN EUROPE** (OSCE) was originally known as the **Conference on Security and Co-operation in Europe** (CSCE), a series of European conferences on security, science and technology, economic, environmental and **human rights** issues. A meeting place for all European countries, the **USSR**, the **USA** and Canada, it first convened in Helsinki in July 1973. The conclusion of this first meeting was the Helsinki Final Act, which marked agreement in three main areas: economic co-operation, human rights and the exchange of information about military activities. Further meetings were held at regular intervals in Belgrade in 1977–78, Madrid in 1980–83, Vienna in 1986–89, Paris in 1990, Helsinki again in 1992, and Budapest in 1994, in addition to a number of more specialized sessions, primarily on arms control, disarmament and human rights. The CSCE quickly assumed considerable importance as the principal opportu-nity for dialogue between East and West during the **Cold War**; nevertheless, its significance as a pan-European forum could even be said to have increased after the ending of the Cold War.

Under the terms according to which the CSCE was established, and also at the insistence of the USSR, the European Communities (EC) were not allowed to have a common representation of their own at the first Helsinki meeting. However, the EC Member States collaborated closely with one another in one of the first successful applications of **European political co-operation**, and the Helsinki Final Act was signed by Aldo Moro of **Italy** (the holder of the presidency of the Council of Ministers – see **Council of the European Union** – at the time) 'for Italy, and in the name of the European Community'. At the 1990 Paris meeting, which concluded with the signing of the **Charter of Paris for a New Europe**, which endowed the CSCE with permanent institutions, the EC participated as a single entity, and not as separate states. In December 1994 the Budapest summit conference adopted the new name OSCE to indicate the organization's permanent nature and growing political role. The OSCE maintains a secretariat in Vienna and has 55 member states (if the European Union countries are counted separately), including all the former republics of the USSR. The abrupt rise in membership from 35 in 1990 to 55 by 1997 reflects the disintegration of the USSR and **Yugoslavia** in the early 1990s. The Federal Republic of Yugoslavia (now known as **Serbia and Montenegro**), which was suspended from the CSCE in 1992, was admitted to the OSCE in 2000.

The **ORGANIZATION FOR THE PROMOTION OF ENERGY TECHNOLOGY** (OPET) is a network of organizations already active in the promotion of relevant technology in various scientific and industrial areas. It was established, in conjunction with the THERMIE programme, in order to encourage the development of energy technology in Europe.

FRANÇOIS-XAVIER ORTOLI (1925–) served as one of the two French Commissioners on the **European Commission** from 1973 to 1984, and was its President from 1973 to 1977. Although he was a senior politician, serving as finance minister in **France** in the 1960s, his period of office in the Commission was troubled by the world-wide descent into economic recession of the mid-1970s. His inability to adopt coherent and determined policies led to a relatively unsuccessful presidency, as Ortoli preferred a cautious approach to issues, and failed to halt the decline in the momentum of integration occasioned by the economic problems of the 1970s. Unusually, he remained a member of the Commission as one of its Vice-Presidents under his two successors, **Roy Jenkins** and **Gaston Thorn**.

OSCE: See **Organization for Security and Co-operation in Europe**

OSTPOLITIK refers to the reorientation of the foreign policy of the Federal Republic of **Germany** (FRG – West Germany) after 1969 under the new left-of-centre Chancellor, **Willy Brandt**, which led to a series of treaties concluded by the FRG with the **USSR**, the German Democratic Republic (GDR – East Germany), **Poland**, and Czechoslovakia, and a Four Power agreement on Berlin. This change in policy was denounced by the Christian Democrats and their allies in Germany and caused a degree of concern in the West about Bonn's *rapprochement* with Moscow. To counter this, however, Brandt reinforced his support for European integration and strongly supported UK membership of the European Communities (EC). As a result of the agreement with East Germany, the latter's products gained access to the EC in such great numbers that East Germany was sometimes described as the silent member of the EC.

OUTER SEVEN was a phrase often used in the 1960s to describe the member states of the **European Free Trade Association**.

OUTERMOST REGIONS were formally acknowledged in the **Treaty on European Union** (TEU). There are seven such regions: four French overseas departments (Guadeloupe, French Guiana, Martinique and Réunion), the Azores, Madeira and the Canary Islands. All, by nature of their size, remoteness and climate, are dependent economically on a small number of export products. All the outermost regions are relatively depressed and receive substantial financial assistance through the European Union **budget**. The outermost regions are subject to a declaration drawn up at the time of the TEU, which acknowledges their major structural problems and the **Council of the European Union**, acting under the rules of **qualified majority voting**, can give these areas exemption from the application of the provisions of the common policies.

The **OVERSEAS COUNTRIES AND TERRITORIES** (OCTs) are colonies or former colonies constitutionally subject to European Union (EU) Member States and are the subject of Articles 182–187 of the **Treaty of Rome**. Mainly French possessions when the Treaty was signed in 1957, they were either overseas adjuncts to the metropolitan country or, in practice, colonies. A special convention annexed to the Treaty specified the details of the association. Products from OCTs would have access to the European Communities (EC) market on the same terms as those of the Member States, with a gradual removal of customs duties over five years. An Overseas Development Fund was established to finance development projects. After 1963 OCTs were absorbed into the broader EC agreements of the **Yaoundé Convention**, the **Lomé Convention** and the **Cotonou Agreement**. However, in 2001 a new **Association**

Agreement was adopted, which was to last until 2011, and which provided a new co-operation framework for EU–OCT relations. There were some 20 OCTs by the early 2000s, including seven that had the status of being an integral part of a Member State. All but seven were British or French territories; the others were linked to **Denmark** or the **Netherlands**.

OWN RESOURCES is a term that refers to the possession by the European Communities (EC) of financial resources that belong to it as of right and together form the **budget**. When the **European Economic Community** was established, its funding relied on the receipt of annual contributions from the Member States. With the 1970 **Treaty of Luxembourg**, the Member States agreed to move to a funding system of own resources, an independent source of income for the EC to spend as they wished within the limits of the obligations and decision-making criteria set down by the treaties. Own resources were to be phased in over a period of five years. The own resources of the EC collected for it by the Member States consist of **customs duties** on imports from third countries, levies on agricultural imports and the sugar and isoglucose levies, a contribution from the Member States based on each country's share of total gross national product (GNP) in the European Union and a proportion of the **value-added tax** levied by the Member States.

P

PADOA-SCHIOPPA REPORT is the name of a report commissioned by the **European Commission** and submitted in April 1987 by a committee headed by Tommaso Padoa-Schioppa (1940–), the Deputy Director-General of the Bank of **Italy**. The committee had been asked to evaluate the effect of the entry into the European Communities (EC) of **Portugal** and **Spain**, and of the commitment to an **internal market** upon the EC's economic system. The Report contained four major recommendations: the establishment of a common monetary policy; the promotion of cohesion; the completion on schedule of the internal market; and the development of a macroeconomic strategy. These steps, it argued, were necessary to promote economic development while preventing an aggravation of regional economic differences within the EC.

A **PARAGRAPH** is a sub-element of an **Article** in the **European treaties**. Paragraphs within an Article are usually numbered.

A **PART** is a main sub-division in a treaty of the European Communities. Parts may in turn be sub-divided into **Titles**. The **Treaty on European Union** does not contain Parts, but is divided instead into Titles.

PARTNERSHIP AND CO-OPERATION AGREEMENTS (PCAs) provide a framework for closer political, cultural and economic relations between the European Union (EU) and former republics of the **USSR**. In some cases, the agreements make reference to the possibility of eventual free trade with the EU. In all cases, emphasis is placed on the commitment of the contracting parties to **human rights** and democracy. PCAs have been concluded for a 10-year period with **Russia** (June 1994), **Ukraine** (June 1994) and **Moldova** (November 1994). Similar agreements were concluded with Belarus, Kazakhstan and Kyrgyzstan in 1995, with Georgia, Armenia and Azerbaijan in January 1996, with Uzbekistan in July 1996 and with Turkmenistan in 1998.

PARTNERSHIPS FOR PEACE (PfP) have been signed by more than 30 countries keen on developing their relationship with the **North Atlantic**

Treaty Organization (NATO). They allow for joint defence planning, joint military exercises and permanent high-level contacts. For countries in **Central and Eastern Europe**, PfPs, coupled with Membership Action Plans, became a preparatory step towards membership of NATO. By May 2004 all 10 of these countries had become NATO members.

PARTY GROUPS are the basic organizational feature of the **European Parliament** (EP). While **Members of the European Parliament** (MEPs) normally belong to national political parties, in the EP they band together in transnational party groups. The criteria for what constitutes a party group were originally laid down by the EP in 1979. If a proposed group contains MEPs elected from at least five Member States, then the minimum size required is 19 MEPs. A Member may not belong to more than one political group. Party groups cannot in theory be established if the proposed membership consists of MEPs from only one Member State. However, in the past, it has been possible for one-party groups to be created. The first example, following the 1994 EP elections, was the **Forza Europa Group**, which consisted exclusively of Italian MEPs. The President shall be notified in a statement when a political group is set up. This statement shall specify the name of the group, its members and its bureau. In each EP, a few MEPs have chosen to remain unaffiliated to any group, but in general groups are the basis of parliamentary procedure. They nominate and elect the President and Vice-President of the EP; all committee chairmanships and memberships are filled on a group basis (although some provision is made for the few independent MEPs), and seating in the EP is by party group. The groups also receive funding, in proportion to their size and the number of countries represented, to maintain a secretariat and their various activities. The **Court of Justice** has ruled that these funds cannot be used for electoral purposes.

An examination of the history of party groups in the EP reveals a considerable degree of fluidity and instability as groups (with the exception of the Socialists) have become subject to regular change as groups form, disband, amalgamate, constitute and reconstitute themselves. Consequently, the EP party groups can be said to be weakly institutionalized. There are currently seven political groups in the sixth elected parliament (2004–09), which comprises 732 deputies. These are, in order of size: the **Group of the European People's Party (Christian Democrats) and European Democrats** with 268 seats; **Group of the Party of European Socialists** (PSE) with 201 seats; **Group of the Alliance of Liberals and Democrats for Europe** (ALDE, new in 2004) with 88 seats; **Group of the Greens/European Free Alliance** (Verts/EFA) with 42 seats; the **Confederal Group of the European United Left/Nordic Green Left** (GUE/NGL) with 41 seats; the **Independence and Democracy Group** (new in 2004) with 36 seats; and lastly, the **Union for Europe of the Nations Group** (UEN/UPE) with 30 seats. The remaining MEPs sit as independents.

The fluidity within the EP can be illustrated by examining the evolution and fate of some of the more recent and well-known groups such as: the **Rainbow Group** (ARC); **Communists and Allies; Group for a Europe of Democracies and Diversities** (EDD); **Group of the European Democratic Alliance** (RDE); **Group of the European Liberal Democrats** (ELDR); and **Left Unity** (LU).

The 2004 **enlargement** of the European Union (EU), however, may destabilize the party group structure even more with the arrival of a host of new parties and MEPs. The real test for the party groups – and one that has not been accomplished to date – is the challenge to command loyalty and respect from EU citizens and to foster the idea and benefits of EU integration.

PARTY OF EUROPEAN SOCIALISTS: See **Group of the Party of European Socialists**

The **PASSERELLE CLAUSE** found in Article 42 of the **Treaty on European Union** allows the **Council of the European Union**, acting unanimously, to transfer policy competences from the intergovernmental pillar III to the supranational European Community pillar of the European Union. Any transfer must first be ratified by the Member States.

PATENTS are not necessarily exempt from the **competition policy** of the European Communities. The **European Commission** has the authority to decide whether a patent or trademark violates the rules of competition. The general principle of the non-exclusiveness of patents has been upheld by the **Court of Justice**. Conversely, the Commission has launched several initiatives to facilitate the registration and protection of patents. (See **Community Patent Convention; Office for Harmonization in the Internal Market**.)

CHRIS (CHRISTOPHER) PATTEN (1944–) of the **United Kingdom** was appointed to the **European Commission** in 1999 and served until 2004 in the **Prodi** Commission as Commissioner responsible for External Relations, Common Foreign and Security Policy, Delegations to Non-Member Countries and the Common Service for External Relations. Prior to taking up his post in the Commission, Patten was Governor of Hong Kong in 1992–97, at the time of the handover of the colony to the People's Republic of China. Previously he had been a Conservative Member of Parliament and had held several ministerial positions in the United Kingdom. He was elected to the position of Chancellor of Oxford University in March 2003. As part of the ongoing search for a successor to **Romano Prodi**, the United Kingdom government suggested Patten as a possible candidate in June 2004. President Chirac essentially vetoed this possibility when he argued that only individuals from Member States fully participating in the **eurozone** should be considered.

PCAs: See **Partnership and Co-operation Agreements**

PEOPLE'S EUROPE: See **Citizenship**; **Committee for a People's Europe**

PERMANENT MISSION is the name given to the diplomatic representation of a non-member state to the European Union.

PERMANENT REPRESENTATION is the name given to the large delegation which each Member State maintains in **Brussels**. It consists of both diplomats and administrative officials seconded from those national ministries whose work is affected by **decisions** of the European Union. Each delegation is headed by a Permanent Representative, who possesses senior ambassadorial status. Collectively, the Permanent Representatives meet at least weekly as the **Committee of Permanent Representatives** (COREPER).

PERMANENT STRUCTURED CO-OPERATION is a form of **enhanced co-operation** in the area of the **European security and defence policy** envisaged in the **Treaty establishing a Constitution for Europe**. It will involve the pooling of military means and capabilities and measures to enhance the availability, interoperability, flexibility and deployability of the armed forces of participating Member States.

The term **PERMISSIVE CONSENSUS** was coined by academics in the 1970s to describe the way in which European publics appeared to take for granted or readily accept the process of European integration. The permissive consensus has since been seriously challenged, as seen in: the rise of **Euro-scepticism**; the **ratification crises** surrounding the **Treaty on European Union**, the **Treaty of Nice** and, more recently, the **Treaty establishing a Constitution for Europe**; and the concerns expressed about the **legitimacy** of the European Union (EU). The degree to which a gap now exists between the political and economic elites and the wider populations of the old **Fifteen** and now **Twenty-Five** Member States cannot be disputed and has also been clearly displayed in the findings of **Eurobarometer** from 1992 onwards, and in the referenda on the euro in **Denmark** (2000) and **Sweden** (2003) and on the Treaty of Nice in **Ireland** (2001 and 2002). These have led to repeated calls for greater 'civic participation' in the EU project.

PESCA is a European Community initiative that was created to address the problems of areas particularly dependent on fishing. (See **Common Fisheries Policy**.) PESCA exists as an addition to the **Structural Funds** and has afforded these areas access to the Structural Funds for specific schemes aimed at lessening their dependence on fishing.

The **PETERSBERG TASKS** were originally set out in the Petersberg Declaration issued by foreign and defence ministers of the member states of the **Western European Union** (WEU) in June 1992. They cover humanitarian and rescue operations, peace-keeping activities and tasks for combat forces in crisis management, including peace-making. At the time, it was anticipated that the WEU would undertake these tasks. Since then, however, the emphasis has shifted to the European Union (EU), notably through the **Treaty of Amsterdam** and, more recently, the further development of the **common foreign and security policy** and the creation of a **European Rapid Reaction Force**. With the *de facto* transfer of many of the WEU's activities to the EU, the latter's responsibilities for and commitment to undertaking Petersberg tasks have increased.

PETITIONS may be referred to in the context of the right of citizens of the European Union (EU) to petition the **European Parliament** (EP) on any matter that falls within the EU's areas of authority, and that affects them directly. The right of petition was formalized by the **Treaty on European Union**, which empowered the EP to appoint an independent **Ombudsman** to receive and evaluate petitions and complaints. Where an allegation of maladministration is upheld by the Ombudsman, a report is submitted to both the institution concerned and the EP. The formalization of the right of petition was part of the attempt to develop a notion of EU **citizenship**.

PHARE, sometimes known as Operation PHARE, is the name originally given to the **Poland** and **Hungary** Assistance for Economic Restructuring programme, a system for co-ordinating economic aid set up by the **Organisation for Economic Co-operation and Development**, and co-ordinated by the European Communities. Established in 1989, it was subsequently extended to include **Albania**, **Bulgaria**, the **Czech Republic**, **Estonia**, **Latvia**, **Lithuania**, **Romania**, **Slovakia** and **Slovenia**. In March 1997 the **European Commission**

agreed to the extension of PHARE in order to provide specific assistance to the **applicant countries** of **Central and Eastern Europe**, to help these countries implement the reforms required to fulfil the criteria for European Union membership. Assistance was to focus on building democratic institutions and administrations and financing investment (especially in the areas of the environment, transport, product quality, working conditions and major infrastructure projects). Among the new projects funded were **Twinning**, the **Instrument for Structural Policies for Pre-Accession** (ISPA) and **SAPARD**. A Technical Assistance Information Exchange Office (TAIEX) was opened in 1996 as part of PHARE operations. Overall annual funding available under PHARE, SAPARD and ISPA in the period 1999–2003 amounted to €2,645m. This compares with an annual figure for PHARE during 1995–1999 of €730m. Assistance programmes similar to PHARE have been established for the former **USSR** (see **Technical Assistance to the Commonwealth of Independent States**) and the **Western Balkans** (see **CARDS**).

PHARMACEUTICALS have been a central concern of the **European Commission**. In pursuance of its **health and safety** policy, the Commission has been active in regulating pharmaceutical products, and a series of **directives** apply to their testing, patenting, production, marketing and labelling. Patenting in the use of brand names has also been held, in principle, to contravene **competition policy**, which has encouraged the growth of generic products that are often substantially cheaper than the branded product. In 1994 the **European Agency for the Evaluation of Medicinal Products** was established in London as a decentralized agency of the European Union responsible for overseeing the registration of human and veterinary medicinal products.

PILLAR is a term that has been applied to the notional structure of the European Union, which is held to consist of three pillars, the **European Council** being the only body capable of co-ordinating all three. The central pillar, the first pillar, is the European Communities (EC), where the **Community method** applies and the **European Commission**, **European Parliament** and the **Court of Justice** exercise their full powers. The two other pillars are **common foreign and security policy** (CFSP), pillar II, and **justice and home affairs** (JHA), pillar III. These are governed by principles of intergovernmental co-operation where the constitutional authority of the EC does not apply. The **Treaty of Amsterdam** amended the third pillar to the effect that it is now concerned with **police and judicial co-operation in criminal matters**. If the **Treaty establishing a Constitution for Europe** is ratified, the pillars will in effect be replaced by a more integrated structure, although the CFSP will retain many of its intergovernmental characteristics.

POCO: See **European Political Co-operation**

POLAND was an original beneficiary of the **PHARE** programme when it was launched in 1989. Subsequently, the new democratic government entered into negotiations for association with the European Communities, and a **Europe Agreement** was signed in December 1991. This was the first major step by **Poland** towards the ultimate objective of membership, and in April 1994 it submitted a formal application to join the European Union (EU). Three years later, the application received formal approval, although the **European Commission**'s report made clear that investment would be needed if the country was 'to comply with Community rules on agriculture, environment and transport', and that further administrative reform would be required for the application and enforcement of the *acquis communautaire*. **Accession negotiations** began in March 1998 and, despite some concerns within the EU about the capacity of the country to take on all the obligations of membership, were successfully concluded in December 2002. Six months later, in June 2003, 81.7% of those who participated in a national referendum (turn-out was 58.8%) voted in favour of EU membership. Poland therefore joined the EU on 1 May 2004 as its largest new member. Concerns that Poland might prove to be among the most difficult of the new members to integrate were borne out at the **European Council** meeting in December 2003 when the Polish and Spanish (see **Spain**) governments opposed changes to **qualified majority voting** rules, thereby preventing conclusion of the **intergovernmental conference** that had begun work three months earlier. This Polish/Spanish alliance came to an abrupt end with the election of a new Spanish government in the spring of 2004. The incoming socialist administration was more ready to reach agreement and effectively compelled the Polish government to do likewise. All Member States reached agreement on a treaty text in June 2004. Poland was one of a number of states that adopted a very tough bargaining stance towards the financing of the new budgetary package (2007-13), and was highly critical of the UK rebate.

POLICE AND JUDICIAL CO-OPERATION IN CRIMINAL MATTERS is the name given to Title VI of the **Treaty on European Union**. Originally known as **justice and home affairs**, this third pillar of the European Union was renamed by the **Treaty of Amsterdam**. The objective of police and judicial co-operation in criminal matters is to prevent and combat: problems of racism and xenophobia; terrorism; trafficking in human beings and crimes against children; drugs-trafficking; weapons-trafficking; and corruption and fraud. Through **Europol**, the European Police Office, there is scope for closer co-operation between national police forces and customs and judicial authorities, co-operation in the latter area also being provided for through **Eurojust**.

This co-operation may lead to closer **approximation** of rules on criminal matters in the Member States.

POLICY in the context of the European Communities (EC) refers to the collectivity of proposals, initiatives and **legislation** intended to achieve EC aims in specific fields of activity.

The **POLICY PLANNING AND EARLY WARNING UNIT** was set up as part of the reforms to the **common foreign and security policy** (CFSP) introduced by the **Treaty of Amsterdam** in 1999. Its main role is to monitor and analyse developments in areas relevant to the CFSP, provide assessments of and early warning reports on issues of concern to the European Union, and prepare papers on options for policies. The unit is staffed by personnel drawn from the Member States, the **European Commission**, the Secretariat-General of the **Council of the European Union**, and **Western European Union**.

The **POLITICAL AND SECURITY COMMITTEE** is the successor to the **Political Committee**. It was renamed and had its powers increased by the **Treaty of Nice**. Hence, acting under the responsibility of the **Council of the European Union**, the Committee exercises political control and strategic direction of crisis management operations undertaken by the European Union (EU). It may also be authorized to take specific implementing **decisions**. With the development of a more explicit defence dimension to the **common foreign and security policy**, the Committee has also provided support for the EU's embryonic military staff, which currently meets in an interim **Military Committee of the European Union**.

The **POLITICAL COMMITTEE** is the name of a body that has its origins in the committee of **Political Directors** originally charged with preparing the quarterly meetings of the Member State foreign ministers under **European political co-operation**. It was formally established by the **Treaty on European Union** as part of the **common foreign and security policy** (CFSP). The tasks of the Political Committee, which is composed of the Political Directors, are to monitor the international situation in areas covered by the CFSP, and to advise and submit proposals to the **European Council** on foreign and security policy. In conjunction with the Council presidency, the Committee also has responsibility for implementing policies decided upon according to the CFSP structure. The **Treaty of Nice** enhanced the committee's powers and renamed it the **Political and Security Committee**.

POLITICAL CO-OPERATION: See **Common Foreign and Security Policy**; **European Political Co-operation**

POLITICAL DIRECTORS, each of whom is appointed by a Member State as an aide to its foreign minister, are invariably senior diplomats. They formerly played an essential role in the operation of **European political co-operation**. Collectively, the Directors were responsible for the co-ordination and implementation of foreign policy initiatives, meeting monthly to review progress and urgent current issues. Under the **Single European Act**, the Directors were provided with their own secretariat in Brussels, and under the **Treaty on European Union**, they were formally constituted as a **Political Committee** with a major role in the **common foreign and security policy**. The responsibility for organizing the Directors belongs to the foreign ministry of the Member State currently holding the presidency of the **Council of the European Union**, and therefore rotates between the Political Directors, changing every six months. The division of labour between the Directors and the **Committee of Permanent Representatives** is under constant review. The immediate subordinate of the Political Director, responsible for routine business, is known as the European Correspondent.

POLITICAL UNION: See **European Union**; **Maastricht Summit**; **Treaty on European Union**

PORTUGAL originally had no prospect of becoming a member of the European Communities (EC) as long as it remained under an authoritarian regime. In 1962, along with other members of the **European Free Trade Association**, Portugal approached the EC, but without specifying the form of association it desired. Negotiations had not begun when the UK application for entry was vetoed by **France**, and Portugal's proposed schedule was abandoned. Discussions were not resumed until 1970, and a **Free Trade Agreement** was signed in July 1972. After the 1974 revolution, the new government expressed a desire for further co-operation with, and financial assistance from, the EC. A **protocol** to the free-trade agreement, providing for financial aid, was signed in September 1976; further protocols were signed in 1979 and 1980. Portugal formally applied for full membership in March 1977. Progress on the negotiations was slow. Officially commencing in October 1978, they did not begin in earnest until 1980. While there were some problems between the two sides, the slowness of the negotiations was perhaps due more to the simultaneous negotiations with **Spain**, about whose application there were more substantive concerns among some Member States. However, the two applications tended to be treated in conjunction with each other. The negotiations were concluded in March

1985, and Portugal joined the EC in January 1986. One of the poorest states in the European Union, it has benefited substantially from the **structural funds**, the **Cohesion Fund** and other aid programmes. Portugal has been well disposed towards the European Union, but in more recent times difficulties have arisen. In June 2005 the Portuguese government was requested to cut its budget deficit to fall in line with European Union (EU) rules on the **Stability and Growth Pact.** Portugal's economy has certainly been in trouble, running into recession in 2003 and recording only 1% growth the following year. Unemployment reached an eight-year high (some 7.5%) in 2005. The government of Prime Minister José Sócrates is determined to cut the deficit and is planning to limit public spending and raise **value added tax**. It will be interesting to see how such measures might impact on the planned referendum (which was postponed following events in France and the **Netherlands**) on the **Treaty establishing a Constitution for Europe**.

POTENTIAL CANDIDATE STATE, as opposed to **candidate state**, was the status assigned to the countries of the **Western Balkans** by the Feira Summit of the **European Council** in June 2000. The term has since been confirmed in the preambles to the **Stabilization and Association Agreements**. It is to be assumed that a potential candidate state becomes a candidate state once it is admitted to the accession process.

PPE: See **Group of the European People's Party (Christian Democrats) and European Democrats**

A **PRE-ACCESSION STRATEGY** to help prepare countries from **Central and Eastern Europe** for membership of the European Union was launched in 1994 by the **Essen Summit** of the **European Council**. The idea was to build on the existing relationship based on the **Europe Agreements** by intensifying co-operation and by outlining more precisely the steps necessary for meeting the obligations of membership, notably concerning adoption of the *acquis communautaire*. In 1998 the strategy was enhanced by the launch of **accession negotiations** and the conclusion of **Accession Partnerships**.

PREAMBLE refers to the opening recitals of a treaty. In the case of the European Communities (EC), the preambles to the **founding treaties** outline the aims and purposes of the EC. Preambles have often been referred to by the **Court of Justice** in defining EC **law**.

PREFERENTIAL TRADE AGREEMENTS signed by the European Communities (EC) with other countries are intended to lead, within a reasonable period of time, to the establishment of either a free-trade area or a customs union. This is a requirement that the **General Agreement on Tariffs and Trade** demanded of all preferential trade agreements. Those signed by the EC form part of the **common commercial policy** and fall into several categories: **Trade and Co-operation Agreements**; **Association Agreements** (see also **Europe Agreements** and **Stabilization and Association Agreements**); the several individual and collective agreements signed with states bordering the Mediterranean; the **Cotonou Agreement** (see also the **Lomé Convention**); and **Partnership and Co-operation Agreements**. In the overwhelming majority of cases, the agreements are not restricted to purely economic matters.

The **PRELIMINARY RULING** procedure is a key element of the legal system of the European Communities (EC). Under the procedure, a national court may refer a question about the meaning of an EC law to the **Court of Justice**. Once the Court issues its decision, it is applied to the relevant case by the national court.

PRESIDENCY: See **Council presidency**

PRICE-FIXING AGREEMENTS have been declared illegal by the **European Commission** on the grounds that they are contrary to the **competition policy** of the European Communities. The precedent was set in 1969 when the Commission successfully prosecuted the dyestuffs cartel that controlled some 80% of the European market at that time. Yet, price-fixing agreements remain an established fact of contemporary business activity across the European Union (EU). In recent years the European Commission has intensified its efforts to deter companies from engaging in such anti-competitive price-fixing arrangements. This resolve has seen a significant increase in the size of the fines imposed on companies that have deliberately sought to fix prices. In December 2002 the Member States agreed to radical reforms of the EU's anti-trust rules that are designed to make it easier for the Commission to act against price fixers (see **competition policy, cartels**). The new regime came into force in May 2004. Cartel-busting has been identified by **Neelie Kroes**, the Competition Commissioner in the **Barroso** Commission, as a particular focus of her term of office.

The **PRIVILEGES AND IMMUNITIES** of the European Communities (EC) were laid down in a **Protocol** of the 1965 **Merger Treaty**. It defines the privileges and immunities of all those who are members of, or who work for, EC **institutions**. It further establishes the rights of the Communities themselves within the territory of the Member States.

ROMANO PRODI (1939–), Prime Minister of **Italy** from 1996 to 1998, and one of the most successful incumbents of that office, was nominated as President of the **European Commission** following the resignation of **Jacques Santer** and his college of Commissioners in March 1999 over allegations of favouritism and failure to crack down on corruption. Once his appointment had been ratified by the **European Parliament**, Prodi's term of office began in September 1999. Charged with rebuilding the credibility of the Commission, he set about introducing a radical infrastructural reform. Prodi was also keen to re-establish the agenda-setting role of the Commission within the European Union. For many, his leadership has proved to be weak, however. He stepped down as President in November 2004. Although he ruled out returning to domestic politics in Italy once his term as Commission President expired, the continued presence in Italian politics of his bitter rival, **Silvio Berlusconi**, caused many on the left to encourage Prodi to lead them in the April 2006 legislative elections. Having achieved a narrow margin of victory in those elections, Prodi was widely expected to be appointed Prime Minister, in spite of Berlusconi's challenging the results of the election.

PRODUCTION QUOTAS can be imposed by the **European Commission** on the **coal** and **steel** industries. Under the powers it inherited from the High Authority of the **European Coal and Steel Community**, the Commission has the authority, if a state of **manifest crisis** is adopted, to impose quotas on individual companies. Severe production quotas were imposed upon steel companies in 1980, and were not abolished until June 1988. In the late 1980s, production quotas were also introduced into the **Common Agricultural Policy**.

PROPORTIONALITY, like **subsidiarity**, is a principle invoked to contain the accumulation of powers by the European Union (EU). In line with the principle of proportionality, the EU should not be taking any action that goes beyond the minimum necessary to achieve its objectives as laid down in the **European treaties**. Hence, proportionality is concerned with the scale and effect of any EU action.

A **PROTOCOL** is an additional element of a treaty. It either provides details of the implementation of treaty requirements or is too lengthy for inclusion in the treaty itself. However, protocols are equal in status to the main body of a treaty.

PROVISIONS is a term generally used in the context of the European Communities to describe the contents of the **European treaties**.

PSE: See **Group of the Party of European Socialists**

PUBLIC HEALTH: See **Health Policy**

PUBLIC PROCUREMENT, although referred to in the **Treaty of Rome**, has only recently become a major objective of European Communities **competition policy**. Since 1990, a series of **directives** have required all public contracts above a specific cost threshold to be open to competitive tender throughout the Member States. The threshold varies according to the product or service involved, but is otherwise the same throughout the European Union.

PUBLIC SERVICES do not enjoy the privileged status within the European Union that some Member States would like to see. Certainly their status often appears ambiguous. In principle, except where exemptions are approved, European Communities (EC) rules on **state aid** apply as much to public services as they do to commercial enterprises. That said, Article 16 of the **Treaty of Rome**, introduced by the **Treaty of Amsterdam**, draws particular attention to the role of 'services of general economic interest' and calls on the EC and the Member States to 'take care that such services operate on the basis of principles and conditions which enable them to fulfil their missions'.

Q

QMV: See **Qualified Majority Voting**

The **QUAD** comprises meetings between officials from the European Union, the **USA**, **Japan** and Canada, where multilateral trade issues are discussed. (See also **G-8**.)

QUAESTORS are five individuals elected from the ranks of the **Members of the European Parliament** (MEPs). They sit in an advisory capacity in the Bureau of the **European Parliament** and are responsible for financial and administrative matters affecting MEPs.

QUALIFIED MAJORITY VOTING (QMV) is one of the ways in which the **Council of the European Union** arrives at a decision on issues and proposals put before it. The vote is qualified in two ways. Firstly, a qualified majority must be substantially in excess of 50%: traditionally, it has been more than two-thirds. Secondly, it is qualified in that it is based on a weighted voting system, where each Member State has an indivisible block of votes at its disposal, the size of which is based roughly on the size of its population.

The **Treaty of Rome** envisaged that QMV would apply to most proposals after 1965. The achievement of this objective was prevented by the **empty chair crisis** and the **Luxembourg Compromise**. The possibilities for a greater use of QMV did not increase until the **Single European Act**. With the adoption of the **Treaty on European Union** and further **enlargement** of the European Union (EU), there was renewed pressure for an increase in the size of the minority that would be needed to obstruct a proposal, in the hope that this reform would speed up the process of integration. From January 1995, when the **General Affairs and External Relations Council** agreed on amendments to voting procedures in the Council which took into account the accession of three new Member States, the total number of votes was 87, weighted as follows: **France**, **Germany**, **Italy** and the **United Kingdom** had 10 votes each; **Spain**, eight votes; **Belgium**, **Greece**, the **Netherlands** and **Portugal**, five votes each; **Austria** and **Sweden**, four votes each; **Denmark, Finland** and **Ireland**, three votes each; and **Luxembourg**, two votes. A qualified majority was constituted by 62 votes, and thus 26 votes were sufficient for a blocking minority. However, as a result of pressure from Spain and the United Kingdom, the so-called **Ioannina compromise** of March 1994 meant that 23–25 opposing votes ensured the continued discussion of proposed **legislation** by the Council for a 'reasonable' period until a consensus was obtained.

QMV was extended by the **Treaty of Amsterdam** into a number of areas previously subject to unanimous decision. The **European Parliament** was also to have the right of co-decision in these areas (see **co-decision procedure**). As the EU expands, the use of qualified majority voting in a wider range of **decisions** is expected to minimize 'policy drag'. Under the terms of the **Treaty of Nice**, a further range of areas, mostly minor in nature and relating to appointments to various EU institutions (such as the **Court of Auditors**), became subject to QMV. By 2002 most areas under pillar I were determined by QMV, although there were some notable exceptions, including decisions in the area of **economic and monetary union**.

With EU **enlargement** imminent there was general acceptance in the Council in the late 1990s that the voting procedures would have to be altered. Agreement would not be easy, given political sensitivities. Not surprisingly therefore, the issue was postponed at the Amsterdam **summit meeting** and agreement was finally reached, after a great deal of acrimony, at the Nice summit in December 2000. The **Treaty of Nice** had two major impacts. First, it complicated decision-making by requiring a triple majority for a decision to be adopted by QMV. This comprises: firstly, a qualified majority of the weighted votes; secondly, a majority of the Member States (which is already implicit under the existing regime); and, lastly, a demographic majority of at least 62% of the EU's total population. In effect, this new formula ensures that numbers and percentages have become more important in determining voting in the Council. It also increases the leverage of the larger EU states.

Second, the Treaty of Nice reformulated the votes for an EU of **Fifteen** and agreed the anticipated vote allocations for the **candidate countries** in an EU of **Twenty-Five**. These were subsequently confirmed in the **Accession Treaty**. Hence, from 1 November 2004, the total number of votes in the Council was 321, weighted as follows: **France, Germany, Italy** and the **United Kingdom** have 29 votes each; **Spain** and **Poland**, 27 votes; the **Netherlands**, 13; **Belgium**, the **Czech Republic, Greece, Hungary** and **Portugal**, 12 votes each; **Austria** and **Sweden**, 10 votes each; **Denmark, Finland, Ireland, Lithuania** and **Slovakia**, seven votes each; **Cyprus, Estonia, Latvia, Luxembourg** and **Slovenia**, four votes; and **Malta**, three votes. A qualified majority can now be attained with 232 votes. Assuming **Romania** and **Bulgaria** join, they will be allocated 14 and 10 votes respectively. In the future, it may well be that the existing QMV system is replaced by a dual majority system comprising a majority of Member States representing a majority of the EU's population. This was certainly the approach advocated in the **draft Treaty establishing a Constitution for Europe** adopted in 2003 and agreed in the **Treaty establishing a Constitution for Europe**. Had ratification proceeded successfully, the voting arrangements would have been altered. It was expected that on 1 November 2009 the support of 55% of the Member States, representing 65% of the EU's population, would have been sufficient to reach a qualified majority. Moreover, the measure being adopted would also have had to command the support of at least 15 Member States. In certain areas of **justice and home affairs**, the common foreign and security policy, and economic and monetary policy where the Council does not act on the basis of a proposal from the Commission, a qualified majority would have required the support of 72% of the Member States, representing 65% of the EU's population.

The **QUALITY OF LIFE AND MANAGEMENT OF LIVING RESOURCES PROGRAMME** superseded existing programmes covering agricultural research (i.e. **FAIR**), biomedicine and health (BIOMED) and bio-technology (**BIOTECH**) in 1999. It supports research carried out by industry or educational establishments in Member States and non-member states in all areas of the life sciences, including infectious diseases, nutrition, environment and health, sustainable agriculture, ageing, public health and neurosciences.

QUANTITATIVE RESTRICTIONS: See **Quota Restrictions**

QUOTA RESTRICTIONS on internal trade in the European Communities (EC) were abolished by the **Six** by 1968. Later entrants to the EC were allowed a transitional period of between four and six years in which to complete the process of abolition. In external trade, quota restrictions have been removed by many of the international agreements that the EC have signed with other countries. They still exist, however, in certain areas such as agriculture and textiles, and for specified manufactured goods from some countries. For example, under the **Common Agricultural Policy**, milk quotas were introduced in 1984 as a means of stabilizing milk production.

R

RACE (Research and Development in Advanced Communications Technologies in Europe) was a major **European Commission** initiative launched in 1987 and aimed at ensuring that the European Communities remained in the forefront of developments in the **telecommunications** sector and continued to be competitive. It complemented the **European Strategic Programme for Research and Development in Information Technology** (ESPRIT) and other more specific **information technology** projects; it was replaced in 1994 by **ACTS**.

RAILWAYS have not been a prominent element of European Communities (EC) **transport policy**. While accepting that state **subsidies** are in conflict with **competition policy**, the EC have agreed to the public service function of railways, and policy has been designed to make the railways more competitive with other forms of transport. Infrastructure development has been at the centre of EC involvement in the railways, particularly within the context of efforts to develop **Trans-European Networks**.

RAINBOW GROUP (ARC) was one of the **party groups** in the **European Parliament** until 1994. It was formed after the 1984 **direct elections** as a disparate alliance between various small and mainly regionalist–nationalist parties and Green parties who, on account of their numerical weakness, were unable to create their own groups. It had little hierarchical organization and no coherent policy position, deficiencies that did not disappear in 1989, when the Greens left to form their own Green Group (see **Group of the Greens/European Free Alliance**).

RAPHAEL was a cultural programme that supported natural heritage activities, including co-operation between European Union museums, training for cultural heritage professionals, and the study, preservation and enhancement of European heritage. It was introduced in 1996 for five years, after which it was subsumed into the **Culture 2000** framework programme. (See also **Kaleidoscope**; **Ariane**.)

The **RAPID REACTION MECHANISM** (RRM) was created in February 2001 to ensure the swift deployment of civilian experts to crisis areas while negotiations on the structure and composition of a **European rapid reaction force** continued. The RRM was granted funds of €25m. for 2002; by 2005 the budget had risen to €30m. While the RRM is a very flexible instrument, the Council Regulation establishing it imposes a number of legal contraints, notably: the maximum duration of any RRM project is six months; the RRM cannot finance humanitarian assistance; and it can only finance an operation where other EC instruments cannot respond within the timeframe necessary.

RAPPORTEUR is the title given to the **Member of the European Parliament** (MEP) responsible for drafting and presenting a report to a committee and to the plenary session of the **European Parliament**.

RATIFICATION refers to the process of approval of a treaty (e.g. one of the **European treaties**, or an **Accession Treaty**, or an external relations agreement) by the Member States according to the rules and procedures established by their own constitutions. Treaties and agreements requiring ratification cannot come into force unless ratified by all the Member States. In the case of an **accession treaty** or an **association agreement**, ratification also involves the **European Parliament** giving its approval via the **assent procedure**.

RATIFICATION CRISES is the term given to the political crises that have followed the popular rejection of a Treaty. The first ratification crisis came after the Danish 'no' to the **Treaty on European Union** (TEU) in June 1992, a crisis that intensified when the French people only narrowly gave their support to the TEU in a referendum three months later. The Danish 'no' was later overturned by popular endorsement of the TEU in a further referendum in May 1993. A second ratification crisis occurred following the rejection by Irish voters of the **Treaty of Nice** in June 2001. The response was to hold a second referendum in the latter half of 2002, when the original result was overturned by a vote in favour of the Treaty. (See **Ireland**). A third crisis, and the most major to date, occurred when the **Treaty establishing a Constitution for Europe** was rejected by French and Dutch voters in the late spring of 2005.

RDE: See **Group of the European Democratic Alliance**

RECHAR was the acronym of a major initiative of the **European Coal and Steel Community** (ECSC), introduced in 1989 for the reconversion and redevelopment of coal-mining areas. The objectives were to provide occupational training for redundant workers, and economic diversification in areas severely affected by the contraction of the coal industry. RECHAR II funded projects from 1994 to 1999.

RECITE stands for Regions and Cities in Europe, a 1991 initiative launched as part of the objective of establishing greater social and economic cohesion in the territory of the European Communities. Its purpose was to encourage and provide support for co-operative networks of joint economic projects undertaken by regions and cities throughout the Member States. The original programme ran until 1995 before being replaced by RECITE II, which lasted until 2001.

RECOMMENDATIONS are one of two kinds of non-binding pronouncement that may be issued by the **Council of the European Union** and the **European Commission**. Like **opinions**, they do not constitute instructions, but merely express the preference of the European Communities (EC), and may be disregarded by the Member States. Recommendations made according to the provisions of the **Treaty of Paris** were slightly different, however: they were binding upon Member States as to the final result, but not the means of achieving it, and were thus more similar to EC **directives**. (See also **legislation**.)

REDISTRIBUTIVE POLICIES are those policies of the **European Communities** that primarily involve the redistribution of resources from the richer to the less-developed areas of the European Union as part of the process of promoting economic and social cohesion. Such policies are generally financed from the **structural funds**. Also included under the broad heading of redistributive policies are those policies that involve financial support being given to particular areas of production, for example, agriculture (via the **Common Agricultural Policy**) and fisheries (via the **Common Fisheries Policy**).

The **REFERENCE PRICE** is a key price in the **Common Agricultural Policy**. It is the average price calculated from the market prices for food and vegetables in each Member State. If the price of foodstuffs imported into the European Union is lower than the reference price, the imports incur a levy to raise their price to the same level.

REFERENDA on European Union (EU) issues play an increasingly important role in the European integration process. Countries joining the EU have tended to submit the terms of accession to their people for approval, while some

Member States have sought popular support, often in line with a constitutional requirement, for various of the more recent **European treaties** such as the **Treaty on European Union** (TEU) and the **Treaty of Nice**. In the case of referenda on accession to the EU, the outcome of a referendum has always been respected. The Norwegian government, for example, has been forced twice to abandon plans to join the European Communities and the EU following a 'no' vote. By contrast, where a Member State's electorate has rejected the TEU or the Treaty of Nice and therefore brought about a **ratification crisis**, a second referendum has so far been held. Nine of the 10 **candidate countries** that joined in May 2004 held a referendum on EU membership. In each case the outcome was positive. The EU is currently gearing up for what amounts to the most important series of referenda in its history on the issue of the **Treaty establishing a Constitution for Europe**, which was approved by the **European Council** in June 2004 and signed in November 2005. Some ten member states (the **Czech Republic, Denmark, France, Ireland, Luxembourg,** the **Netherlands, Poland, Portugal, Spain** and the **United Kingdom**) pledged in 2004 to hold a referendum on this issue and it was generally assumed, according to early opinion polls, that the treaty would be endorsed by the public where and when it was put to a referendum. However, events have taken a rather different course. The first of these referenda took place in Spain in February 2005, with the treaty being approved, but the rejections of the treaty in France and the Netherlands (two of the founding Member States of the EU) in the late spring of 2005 sent out a number of shockwaves that resonated throughout the entire European Union. The approval of the treaty in Luxembourg in July 2005 was welcome, but it could not conceal the immediate difficulties confronting European leaders. At best the French and Dutch results have postponed the ratification process by a couple of years, and at worst they have killed off the treaty altogether. All Member States need to endorse the Constitution, whether by referendum or by parliament or by both, in order for it to come into effect. The United Kingdom has opted to postpone its referendum for the time being.

REFERRALS: See **Court of Justice**

The **REFLECTION GROUP** consisted of representatives of the ministers of foreign affairs of the Member States and of the **European Parliament** and **European Commission**. It was responsible for preparing the agenda of the 1996 **intergovernmental conference** (IGC), which resulted in the **Treaty of Amsterdam**.

REFUGEE POLICY forms part of the European Union's **asylum policy** and is a relatively new area of competence of the European Union. Explicit reference to refugees in the **founding treaties** came with the **Treaty of Amsterdam** and the goal of creating an **area of freedom, security and justice**. This placed emphasis on adopting measures to ease the sharing of the burden of incoming refugees, and on proceeding in accordance with the 1951 Geneva Convention and the 1967 **Protocol** concerning refugees, as well as on consulting with the United Nations High Commissioner for Refugees.

REGIO is one of the European Communities statistical domains of the **New Cronos** database, which deals with European Union socio-economic statistics at regional (**Nomenclature of Territorial Units for Statistics – NUTS**) level.

REGIONAL FUND COMMITTEE: See **European Regional Development Fund**

REGIONAL POLICY was not specifically covered by the **Treaty of Rome**, although the **Preamble** refers to the need to reduce 'the differences existing between the various regions and the backwardness of the less favoured regions', while a special **protocol** stated that the Italian *Mezzogiorno* (the southern half of the country) was a European responsibility. Pressure for a regional policy grew in the late 1960s and early 1970s, firstly because of increasing pessimism about the rate of economic growth, and secondly because of **enlargement**, with the **United Kingdom** and **Ireland** joining **Italy** in insisting upon a regional policy. Although formally established in 1973, it did not acquire a high profile as a European Communities (EC) activity until the enlargements of the 1980s.

The **European Commission** has the responsibility of developing policy relating to the regions. The targets of EC regional policy are twofold: under-developed rural areas with low levels of agricultural modernization and high levels of unemployment or underemployment; and industrialized regions in rapid decline. To secure the modernization or renewal of these regions, EC policy has three strands. In addition to providing aid for the development of poorer regions, the Commission seeks to co-ordinate the regional policies of Member States and secure a co-ordinated approach to regional problems in all relevant EC policy concerns.

The principal element of regional policy is the financial programme, channelled primarily through the **European Regional Development Fund** (ERDF), which was established in 1975 and funded from the EC **budget**. The other **structural funds** of the EC are also required to maintain a strong regional focus in their own areas of concern. A number of further special regional programmes have been launched by the European Commission to deal with the problems of regions that are economically coherent, but divided politically between two or more Member States, and several attempts have been made to ensure that the poorer regions benefit from, and participate in, technological developments and programmes. To ensure co-ordination across all these investment activities, the Commission monitors and reviews the socio-economic state of the regions on a regular basis, and undertakes analyses of the regional impact of all EC policies. With respect to the regional policies of the Member States, the Commission is concerned to avoid duplication or waste of resources. Maximum limits have been established for the financial inducements that governments may offer to potential industrial investors in the poorer regions: the limits vary according to the nature of the particular regional problem. The resources of the structural funds have been directed more towards integrated programmes that link together various elements of a region's needs rather than isolated and discrete development projects. Financial resources are distributed under the terms of various agreements, or Community Support Frameworks (CSFs), between the Commission and the Member States. Regional policy was formally recognized in the **Single European Act**, which identified it as a major element in developing the socio-economic cohesion of the EC. Its centrality was further emphasized by the **Treaty on European Union**, particularly by the establishment of a **Cohesion Fund** and the commitment to **Trans-European Networks**.

REGIONAL POLICY COMMITTEE: See **European Regional Development Fund**

REGIONS: See **Cohesion Policy**; **Committee of the Regions**; **European Regional Development Fund**; **Nomenclature of Territorial Units for Statistics**; **Regional Policy**

REGULATIONS are one of three different types of **legal instrument** that the **European Commission** and **Council of the European Union** are empowered to issue. Regulations are the highest, most rigorous form of **legislation**. They are fairly detailed instructions, applicable throughout the European Union, and are directly binding upon all Member States. (See also **decisions**; **directives**; **law**; **opinions**; **recommendations**; **resolutions**.)

REGULATORY POLICIES are those policies of the European Communities based on regulations designed to achieve specific, and generally **internal market**-orientated, policies. Most prominent among them are **competition policy** and **environmental policy** and measures to promote **health and safety.**

RESEARCH AND DEVELOPMENT IN ADVANCED COMMUNICA-TIONS TECHNOLOGIES IN EUROPE: See **RACE**

RESEARCH FRAMEWORK PROGRAMMES are the principal means through which the European Union implements its **Research and Technological Development Policy**. Each programme consists of a variety of specific projects.

RESEARCH AND TECHNOLOGICAL DEVELOPMENT (RTD) POLICY and the application of new technologies, apart from the sponsoring of research in the nuclear area through the **European Atomic Energy Community** (EAEC or Euratom), received relatively little attention until the 1980s. It remained very much an issue for the various Member States. The lack of a European-level policy led to both duplication of effort and, often, missed opportunities. More importantly, high-level research is increasingly complex and costly. Observing that the majority of items such as microcomputers and video recorders were imported into the European Communities (EC), the **European Commission** intensified its efforts to encourage technological and collaborative research, to foster and promote research networks and teams at the European level in order to permit the EC to remain economically competitive.

The main objective of EC research and development policy is to amalgamate the many projects and individuals conducting research in the Member States into collaborative programmes that involve companies, universities and research institutes. The focus is not so much on basic research as on the development of new technologies that can more appropriately be co-ordinated at EC level, and that will provide products for existing and new markets. The **European Strategic Programme for Research in Information Technologies** (ESPRIT), adopted in 1984, marked a real turning point and was swiftly followed by the first framework for research and technological development. The **Single European Act** made science a Community responsibility. A second framework programme identifying several priority areas for research was adopted in 1987, and in 1988 a monitoring system was introduced in the form of Strategic Analysis, Forecasting and Evaluation in Matters of Research and Technology (MONITOR). The importance of research and development was confirmed by the **Treaty on European Union**, and further general framework programmes that extended the list of priority research areas were adopted in 1990, 1993 and 1998. In just over a decade the budgets for these programmes had grown substantially, from €3,250m. for the first programme to €13,215m. for the fourth (1994–98). Overall, the 1990s heralded the emergence and increasing salience of EU RTD policy and this ensured the inclusion of this theme on the agenda of a series of **European Council** summits. For example, the summit in Lisbon in March 2000 acknowledged that European research and development needed to develop before the European Union (EU) could legitimately claim to be the most competitive and dynamic knowledge-based economy in the world. Meanwhile, in 2001 a sixth framework programme was adopted for 2002–2006. This new programme, with some €15,000m. of funds, was much more ambitious in scope than its predecessors. It sought to integrate research in priority areas (through the creation of centres of excellence) and to create and structure a European Research Area. To maximize its impact, the Framework Programme has focused its attention on a limited number of research areas – technological, economic, social and cultural, among others. These will consider the quality of life; a user-friendly information society; competitive and sustainable growth; energy and the environment; improving human resource potential; and the promotion of innovation and growth of SMEs. (See also **BRITE-EURAM**; **BIOTECH**; **EUREKA**; **European Strategic Programme for Research and Development in Information Technology**; **Research and Development in Advanced Communications Technologies in Europe.**)

RESIDER is the acronym of a 1988 initiative by the **European Coal and Steel Community** to assist in the economic conversion and redevelopment of areas formerly heavily dependent upon the **steel** industry. It was later complemented by the **RECHAR** and RENAVAL programmes. RESIDER II superseded the programme, and ran from 1994 to 1999.

RESOLUTIONS are statements of principle adopted by the **Council of the European Union** on the recommendation of the **European Commission**. While indicating governments' agreement or willingness to act, they have no basis in the **founding treaties** of the European Communities and are not legally binding upon the Member States. (See also **opinions**; **recommendations**.)

RESTITUTIONS form an essential part of the **Common Agricultural Policy** (CAP). They are the export subsidies or refunds that allow European Union (EU) agricultural produce to be competitive on world markets, where prices are usually lower. EU exporters receive restitutions to make up the difference between what they must pay to CAP producers and the lower prices at which they must sell on the world markets. Restitutions have been one of the most controversial elements of the CAP, because in the past they have consumed up to 30% of the expenditure made through the Guarantee Section of the **European Agricultural Guidance and Guarantee Fund**. This figure has been reduced and currently stands at some 15% of expenditure.

REVENUE accrues to the European Communities (EC) from a variety of sources. Initially, the EC were financed by contributions from Member States based upon the gross national product (GNP) of each Member State. The **European Commission** argument that the EC should have their own sources of revenue was one of the contributing factors to the 1965 **empty chair crisis**. In 1970 the Member States agreed that a system of **own resources** should progressively replace that of national contributions, with the change to be completed by 1975. Today, the European Union (EU) has its own resources to finance its expenditure. These form the basis of the EU's own tax revenues which automatically accrue to it without the need for any subsequent decision by national authorities. In other words, while the own resources would be collected by the Member States, the revenue would belong as of right to the EC.

In terms of revenue, own resources consist of several elements. The first is levies and duties on imports, comprising customs duties on finished products and a levy on agricultural imports to raise their price to the level set by the **Common Agricultural Policy** (CAP). The second, which soon became the most important source of revenue, was a proportion of the **value–added tax** (VAT) imposed by the Member States. The VAT contributions that would accrue to the EC were set at a maximum of 1.0% of the final selling price of a common base of goods and services. By the early 1980s this revenue was proving insufficient to meet demands and, after much argument, the VAT maximum level was raised to 1.4% in 1986. This still proved to be insufficient, and annual deficits in the EC **budget** had to be covered by non–refundable contributions from the Member States. The reform of the Community's finances altered again in June 1988 when a new category of revenue, which is based on GNP and is derived from the application of a rate to the sum of the GNPs of all the Member States, was approved by the **European Council**. This new revenue source provided the necessary funds for the **Delors I** package in 1989. To contain the growth of the resources taken up by the Community, the European Council decision set an overall ceiling rising to 1.2% of total Community GNP in 1992. This figure was applied for both 1993 and 1994. From 1994 a new decision on the own resources raised the ceiling of the GNP contribution to 1.21% and, in stages, to 1.27% of GNP by 1999. During this period the uniform VAT rate was gradually reduced from 1.4% to 1% by 1999.

In terms of EU budgetary calculations and expectations **Gross National Income** (GNI) has widely replaced Gross National Product (GNP) in Commission documentation as an indicator of income. This alteration took effect in 2002. In order to maintain unchanged the cash value of the ceiling of EU revenue, referred to as the 'own resources ceiling,' it became necessary to recalculate it in percentage terms. It was established at 1.24 % of GNI instead of the previous 1.27 % of EU GNP. (By means of a definition GNI at market prices represents total primary income receivable by resident institutional units:

compensation of employees, taxes on production and imports less subsidies, property income (receivable less payable), operating surplus and mixed income. GNI equals GDP minus primary income payable by resident units to non-resident units plus primary income receivable by resident units from the rest of the world.)

Total revenue during the 1990s increased from ECU 47,000m. (**see ECU**) in 1990 to €93,000m. by 2002. With the prospect of **enlargement**, the estimated costs of admitting more Member States ranged from €4,000m. to €38,000m. for the CAP alone, plus an estimated €30,000m. for the **structural funds.** There was an expectation that total revenue would have to rise significantly. Reluctance on the part of Member States to increase contributions meant, however, that greater emphasis was placed on reforming policies. Hence, according to the budgetary perspective for 2000–06 agreed at the Berlin **European Council** in March 1999, revenue was set to remain at or below current levels. This summit reached a political consensus on the EU budget and own resources and the Council adopted a new own resources decision in September 2000 that became effective in January 2002. This saw further reduction of the VAT resource, which in 2004 stood at 0.50%, and a reduction of the GNI contribution to 1.24%. Agreement was reached on the next financial perspective (2007–13) at a meeting of the **European Council** in December 2005 and, significantly, saw a further diminution of the GNI contribution.

The 2006 budget is worth some €121 billion. Some 13% comes from customs duties, agricultural duties and sugar levies, while 14 % of the revenue stream emanates from a uniform percentage rate applied as part of all EU countries' VAT rates. A third stream, and the most important at 72%, is associated directly with a uniform rate that is applied to Gross National Income. Finally, around 1% stems from unspent amounts from the previous year.

The **RIGHT OF ESTABLISHMENT**, as laid down in the **Treaty of Rome**, confers on nationals of one Member State the right to set up business operations in another Member State. It is a key principle underpinning the **internal market** and the free movement of services.

The **RIGHT OF INITIATIVE** within the European Communities has traditionally been the preserve of the **European Commission**, it being the only institution that could formally initiate **legislation**. Since the **Treaty on European Union**, however, this is no longer technically the case. The **European Central Bank** has a right of initiative in certain areas concerning **economic and monetary union**, and Member States were to enjoy a right of initiative over measures concerning asylum, immigration and border controls until 2004. The right of initiative under the **common foreign and security**

policy and **police and judicial co-operation in criminal matters pillars** of the European Union is shared by the European Commission and the Member States. The **European Parliament** has no formal right of initiative, but can request that the European Commission submit a proposal under the **Treaty of Rome**.

ROAD TRANSPORT is the area of European Communities (EC) **transport policy** where the **European Commission** has been most active. Most initiatives have been concerned with conditions of employment and road safety. Rules covering, for example, training and minimum rest periods have existed since the 1970s, and the ensuing decade saw the introduction of a common standard for the weight and dimensions of commercial vehicles, maximum limits for the axle weights of articulated vehicles, and several **directives** concerning road safety. More recently, the focus of road transport measures has been the deregulation of national licensing and quota systems governing inter-state road freight. A transitional road freight system of *cabotage* (the right to ply for hire in another country) was agreed to in 1993 and was to begin by 1998, and a decision was taken to introduce a *vignette*, or freight licence, which would raise funds for distribution among the Member States most affected by road transport, to be fully operative by 1998.

ROMANIA concluded a trade and economic **co-operation agreement** with the European Communities in 1990, and a **Europe Agreement** was signed in 1993, coming into effect in 1995. Although Romania applied for membership of the European Union (EU) in the same year, the **European Commission** recommended in 1997 that **accession negotiations** be deferred, owing to the need primarily for further economic reform in Romania. Its report stated that 'a considerable amount of work is still needed on environment, transport, employment, social affairs, home affairs, justice, and agriculture, and substantial reform is essential to provide Romania with the structures it needs for effective application and enforcement of the full body of Community law'. Subsequent reports made similar calls for further reform so that Romania could meet all the **accession criteria**. All the same, in 1999, and following the Kosovo conflict, Romania was invited to start **accession negotiations**. Despite the public commitment of a new government elected in 2000 to speed up integration with the EU, progress in the negotiations was the slowest of all **candidate countries** involved. By the end of 2003, only 22 of the 31 negotiating chapters had been closed. As a consequence, Romania did not join the EU as part of the 2004 **enlargement**. By the end of that year, however, it had concluded the out-standing chapters. An **Accession Treaty** followed in April 2005 that envisaged Romania joining the EU alongside **Bulgaria** on 1 January 2007. However, concerns persisted about the country's preparedness for membership. With this in mind, it was agreed that accession could be delayed, through a decision by a qualified majority of the Member States, if Romania failed to address EU concerns, particularly regarding corruption, state aid policy and border controls.

The **ROYAUMONT PROCESS** was launched in 1995 as a European Union-sponsored effort to promote stability and good neighbourliness in the **Western Balkans**. It has since been subsumed within the **Stabilization and Association Process**.

RRF: See **European Rapid Reaction Force**

RRM: See **Rapid Reaction Mechanism**

RUSSIA's relations with the European Union (EU) are based on a **Partnership and Co-operation Agreement** (PCA) concluded in June 1994, which provides for closer political, cultural and economic relations and which entered into force in December 1997. This PCA followed an earlier agreement in 1993 on the establishment of regular political dialogue. This has led to annual summits between the President of the **European Commission**, the EU's **High Representative** and the Russian President. The PCA was complemented by the adoption in 1999 by the **Council of the European Union** of a **common strategy** on EU–Russia relations. The strategy places considerable emphasis on assisting with the promotion of political and economic stability within Russia and the development of a market-based economy, as well as addressing common challenges relating to the environment, crime and illegal immigration. To these ends, financial assistance has been made available under the **Technical Assistance to the Commonwealth of Independent States** programme, although there have been calls for such assistance and the PCA to be suspended over Russia's handling of the Chechnya conflict. The EU has generally resisted these. Nevertheless, the relationship – as a Commission report in 2004 highlighted – has not developed as positively as envisaged. There have been major disagreements over whether negotiations should be opened on upgrading the EU–Russia trade relationship to a free-trade area, over access in an enlarged EU for Russian citizens to the exclave of **Kaliningrad**, over **ratification** of the Kyoto Protocol, and over the extension of the PCA to the 10 **candidate countries** that joined the EU in 2004. Such differences threaten to undermine progress in achieving the strategic objective of EU–Russia relations as set out in St Petersburg in May 2003: a common economic space, a common space of freedom, security and justice, a common space of co-operation in the field of external security as well as a common space of research and education, including culture. A set of road maps for the development of these common spaces was adopted in May 2005 at an EU-Russia summit in Moscow.

S

SAA: See **Stabilization and Association Agreements**

SAFETY: See **Health and Safety**

SANCTIONS and their collective imposition against specific countries were accepted by the Member States as a valuable element of their collaboration on foreign policy under **European political co-operation**. European Communities (EC) sanctions have been applied on several occasions. However, it is debatable whether any had the desired effect upon the embargoed countries, or whether they were not much more than symbolic gestures of EC solidarity. In addition, not all Member States are willing to participate in a collective imposition of sanctions against a named country. The most infamous example in recent years involved the imposition of sanctions against **Austria** in 2000 following the inclusion of the far-right Freedom Party under Jörg Haider in the Austrian government. The sanctions were strongly resented in Austria and only helped to fuel anti-European Union feeling; they were lifted within six months.

JACQUES SANTER (1937–) was Prime Minister of **Luxembourg** in 1994 when he was chosen as President of the **European Commission** after a contentious debate among the national governments of Member States to find a successor to **Jacques Delors**. The **United Kingdom** had blocked the selection of Jean-Luc Dehaene, the Belgian Prime Minister at the time, even though his candidature was supported by the governments of the other 11 European Union Member States. Santer was the compromise candidate and took up his appointment on 9 January 1995. He pursued a less ambitious programme than his immediate predecessor, a programme that was encapsulated in his phrase 'to do less but to do it better'. He was also responsible for introducing a series of internal reform initiatives within the Commission that encountered varying degrees of resistance. However, Santer's term in office is more associated with the scandal and malpractice that led to the resignation of the entire College of Commissioners. The resignation followed a report that was highly critical of parts of the Commission and in particular of two Commissioners. When the two individuals concerned refused to accept the blame for their alleged malpractices, Santer and the entire body of Commissioners assumed collective responsibility and resigned in March 1999 before the almost certain prospect of being censured by the **European Parliament**. This was the first time that the College had resigned in the history of the Commission. Santer and his team, however, remained in charge of the Commission until a new College was appointed under his proposed successor, **Romano Prodi**, in the latter half of 1999. In 2002 Santer was appointed the Luxembourg government representative to the **European Convention**.

SAPARD is the acronym of the Special Accession Programme for Agriculture and Rural Development, a programme of the European Communities operating in the **candidate countries** of **Central and Eastern Europe** in order to prepare their agricultural sectors for membership of the European Union. Following the enlargement of May 2004, when 10 candidate countries became members, SAPARD continued with a budget of €225.2m. for Bulgaria and Romania in 2004. SAPARD came under the remit of DG Agriculture, and covered the period 2000 to 2006.

SCADPLUS is a European Communities system for accessing documentation relating to European Union **legislation**, official publications and articles. It is an Internet information service, produced by the **European Commission**, which includes the INFO 92 and SCAD databases. It is accessible through the Europa server.

The **SCHENGEN AGREEMENT** is the name of a document originally signed by five founder members of the European Communities in the town of Schengen, **Luxembourg**, on 14 June 1985. The Schengen Convention was signed in June 1990. Under the Agreement **Belgium**, **France**, the Federal Republic of **Germany**, Luxembourg and the **Netherlands** agreed in principle to work towards the formation of a border-free zone. The Agreement was implemented with effect from March 1995 by the original five signatories, along with **Portugal** and **Spain**. Frontier controls at airports on travellers between the countries were dismantled. However, France continued to impose border controls on countries other than Spain and Germany. **Italy**, **Austria**, **Greece**, **Denmark**, **Finland** and **Sweden** (along with non-member states **Norway** and **Iceland**) are signatories, but not full members. **Ireland** and the **United Kingdom** remained outside the Agreement.

Five years of negotiations were required before the Agreement was finalized in detail, but even then the increased worries of some Member States over drugs-trafficking and illegal immigration led to doubts about its value and created further delays in its **ratification** and implementation. Although the Schengen Agreement began as an international agreement outside the framework of the European Union (EU), it was incorporated into the **Treaty of Rome** and the **Treaty on European Union** following provisions contained in the **Treaty of Amsterdam** as part of moves to create a common area without frontiers. The United Kingdom and Ireland negotiated an **opt-out** and were allowed to retain jurisdiction over their borders and rules of asylum and immigration. Both states kept open the possibility of involvement, and in May 2000 the United Kingdom government secured agreement in the **Council of the European Union** that enabled the country to participate in substantial parts of the Schengen *acquis,* particularly in relation to the creation and operation of the **Schengen Information System** (SIS); Ireland did likewise. Currently both the United Kingdom and Ireland are partial members of Schengen. It should also be noted that two other non-EU states, Iceland and Norway, are closely associated with Schengen because of their involvement with the 1957 Nordic Passport Union, and also because of the lengthy land border between Norway and Sweden. Both non-EU states, however, remain uninvolved in decision-making within Schengen. **Switzerland** became the latest signatory to the Schengen Agreement when the Swiss electorate approved the move in a referendum in June 2005. The decision means that Switzerland will open its borders, and become part of Europe's passport-free zone, as well as share information with its EU colleagues on crime and on asylum applications. The vote brings engagement with the EU – and a potential application to join the EU – a step closer.

The **SCHENGEN INFORMATION SYSTEM** (SIS), also known as the European Information System (EIS), is a computer network based in Strasbourg that links the computer systems of immigration services and the police in signatory countries of the **Schengen Agreement**.

HELMUT SCHMIDT (1918–) was Chancellor of the Federal Republic of **Germany** (West Germany) from 1974 to 1982. During this period he exerted great influence on the operation of the European Communities (EC). Believing that many of the objectives and timetables set at previous **summit meetings** had been unrealistic, he was willing to support and advance initiatives for further integration only if they appeared to be both possible and practical. He was the principal supporter in the **European Council** of **Roy Jenkins'** proposal for a **European Monetary System**. At the same time, he firmly defended West

German interests in the EC, and was particularly concerned about the costing of proposed programmes and initiatives. He collaborated closely with President **Valéry Giscard d'Estaing** of **France** and, acting in conjunction, the two men were often able decisively to influence the direction and **decisions** taken by the European Council. However, Schmidt's more pragmatic approach and scepticism perhaps caused the EC to operate in a particular way, accumulating issues, such as the question of the **United Kingdom** budgetary contributions, which had to be dealt with in the 1980s.

GERHARD SCHRÖDER (1944–) became Chancellor of **Germany** in September 1998, when he headed a coalition government of Social Democrats and Greens that was returned to power in October 2002. Schröder's political career unfolded rather quickly within the left-of-centre Social Democratic Party (SPD) and he rose swiftly through the ranks. He was elected a member of parliament in 1980 and became the minister-president of Lower Saxony in 1990. Before becoming a politician he had pursued a successful career as a lawyer. His reputation as German Chancellor was decidedly mixed, and he was often portrayed as changing his mind or his policies to reflect prevailing opinion. On the foreign policy front he spoke out strongly against the war on Iraq during 2003, and refused any military assistance in that enterprise. This was a very popular move at home but helped to foster tensions with the United States of America (see **USA**). He sought to cultivate closer relations with President **Jacques Chirac** of France and **Russia**'s President Vladimir Putin, and sometimes found himself at odds with **United Kingdom** Prime Minister **Tony Blair**. On the domestic front he found it particularly difficult to push through a much-needed series of economic and social reforms and was not only attacked from all sides for trying to do so, but damaged both his reputation and the fortunes of his party for the foreseeable future. Schröder requested a dissolution of parliament and hoped that new elections in the autumn of 2005 would bolster his authority. Opinion polls indicated in June 2005 that the SPD would suffer a major defeat and the elections would pave the way instead for the return of the Christian Democrats and their allies. These predictions proved to be wrong as the SPD gradually clawed its way back in opinion polls over the summer. The elections in September 2005 brought a much narrower victory for the CDU/CSU and dented any possibility of the Christian Democrats forming a government in their own right. The CDU/CSU beat the SPD by only 1 percentage point. The arithmetic arising from the results was extremely complicated and left the CDU with no other real possibility but to push for a 'grand coalition' with the SPD. Negotiations were prolonged and difficult but both parties eventually settled to participate in Germany's only second ever post-war grand coalition, under the leadership of **Angela Merkel**.

ROBERT SCHUMAN (1886–1963) was foreign minister of **France** from 1948 to 1953. He imposed continuity in French policy towards Europe, which in part reflected his own cosmopolitan background. Born in **Luxembourg**, he spent his formative years in Lorraine, at the time part of the German Empire. He was a firm believer in European integration and an ultimate political federation, and was convinced that this could be secured only through a lasting reconciliation between France and **Germany**. He was persuaded of the practicality of **sectoral integration** by **Jean Monnet** and, with his declaration of the **Schuman Plan** in May 1950, began a new era of European developments. Schuman's pioneering role was acknowledged by the first meeting of the **European Economic Community**, when its Parliamentary Assembly (that is, the **European Parliament**) elected him as its first President, rejecting the nominee of the **Six** foreign ministers. In 1986, the centenary of Schuman's birth, the European Communities (EC) declared 9 May, the day in 1950 on which he made the speech that led to the creation of the EC, to be **Europe Day**.

The **SCHUMAN PLAN** named after **Robert Schuman**, was the original proposal for a consolidation of **coal** and **steel** resources that led to the **European Coal and Steel Community** (ECSC). In addition to the economic benefits, the Plan also argued that it would 'immediately provide for the establishment of common bases for economic development as a first step in the federation of Europe'; it went on to state explicitly that 'Europe must be organized on a federal basis'. The more specific political objective was to secure a *rapprochement* between **France** and the Federal Republic of **Germany** (FRG – West Germany); the Plan opened with the declaration 'the French government proposes that Franco-German coal and steel production should be placed under a common High Authority within the framework of an organization open to the participation of the other countries of Europe'. The Schuman Plan was first revealed at a press conference on 9 May 1950. It was immediately supported by West Germany and the **USA**. Only six countries entered the negotiations resulting in the **Treaty of Paris** of 18 April 1951, which formally established the ECSC.

The **SCIENTIFIC AND TECHNICAL RESEARCH COMMITTEE** (CREST) is an **advisory committee** to the **European Commission** composed of scientific experts. It is usually consulted on its opinions about proposals and funding for scientific research programmes. It meets on a regular basis, and also reviews progress reports on ongoing research programmes.

SCOTLAND EUROPA is an innovative alliance of public, private and civil society bodies networking Scotland in Europe. Its aim is to promote Scotland's interests to the key institutions of the European Union (EU) and to the regions of the EU and beyond. It is located in Scotland House alongside the EU Office of the **Scottish Executive**.

The **SCOTTISH EXECUTIVE** established a European Union (EU) Office in 1999 to support and promote both itself and its EU-related work and to help increase Scotland's influence in the EU. The office is co-located in Scotland House with **Scotland Europa** and provides a focal point for Scottish interests in the EU. The Office works closely with the United Kingdom's Permanent Representation, UKREP, which remains responsible for representing the views of the **United Kingdom** as a whole to the EU institutions, and alongside the **ONIEB** and the Welsh National Assembly Office.

SCREENING is an integral stage of the process leading to accession. In order to ensure as smooth a transition as possible into the European Union (EU) for the countries of **Central and Eastern Europe**, a 1995 **White Paper** drew up an initial list of European Communities **legislation** that had to be incorporated into the domestic legislation of all the applicant states before membership could be deemed possible. The negotiations on EU membership began formally in 1998 and have involved a careful examination of the compatibility of all existing legislation with current EU rules and the necessity of additional legislative action. This process conforms to a screening mechanism. It is conducted primarily by the **European Commission** and each of the **applicant countries**, which together analyse, sector by sector, the degrees of compatibility. The process has allowed outstanding measures to be identified and a timetable for their implementation to be drawn up.

SCRUTINY is the process whereby **national parliaments** monitor and try to influence **legislation** emanating from the European Union (EU). In the United Kingdom, for example, the procedure is centred on the 'scrutiny reserve', which prohibits a national minister from adopting any legislative proposal unless it has been examined by the House of Commons Select Committee on European Legislation. Scrutiny of the EU policy process and of the annual **budget** is performed by the **European Parliament** (EP). Members of the EP can put forward questions (orally and in writing) to both the **Council of the European Union** and the **European Commission**; they can, moreover, question individual Commissioners and national ministers in parliamentary committees. The EP also has the authority to draw up reports in particular policy areas and can pass **resolutions** on current themes. It can also hold public hearings and establish committees of inquiry. Ultimately, the EP can dismiss the Commission and can bring cases before the European courts.

SEA: See **Single European Act**

SEC DOCUMENTS are those produced by the **Secretariat-General** of the **European Commission**. Less formal than **COM Documents**, they consist of internal reports, discussion papers and draft **resolutions**.

SECRETARIAT-GENERAL is the name of the senior and central bureaucratic service of the **European Commission**. It sits alongside other services such as **Eurostat**, the European **Anti-Fraud Office** and the **European Community Humanitarian Office**. It is answerable to the President of the Commission, and is the major administrative link between the President and the various **Directorates-General** and other agencies. It comprises 450 officials and is headed by the Secretary-General of the Commission, the most senior official within the Commission, whose post should not be confused with that of the **Secretary-General of the Council of the European Union**. The Secretariat-General is a highly important part of the Commission's machinery and ensures that all parts of the Commission co-ordinate their activities, act in accordance with established procedures and liaise properly with the other **institutions**.

The **SECRETARY-GENERAL OF THE COUNCIL OF THE EUROPEAN UNION** heads the administration of the Council. The structure of the Secretariat-General was changed in the late 1990s to make the Secretary-General also the European Union's **High Representative** for the **common foreign and security policy**. The Secretary-General is appointed by the Council (although in reality he or she is selected by the **European Council** operating under unanimity). The appointment of **Javier Solana** in 1999 marked a significant departure from previous practice, since, for the first time, a politician was selected instead of the more customary senior diplomat. Solana is the fifth Secretary-General to date and heads the Secretariat-General. The Council's Secretariat-General is divided into nine Directorates-General, the largest of which is responsible for administration.

A **SECTION** is a subdivision of a **Chapter** within a European Communities treaty.

SECTORAL INTEGRATION was the major alternative to the federalist approach to integration. **Jean Monnet** was the main proponent of the more gradualist sectoral approach. The strategy was to integrate national economies in stages, by taking one economic sector at a time. The process would be accelerated by '**spillover**', and would eventually create such an interlocking of national economies that a common political structure for their direction would be required and inevitable. Ultimately, the **European Coal and Steel Community** was the only successful example of sectoral integration, following which the **Six** directed their efforts instead to the development of a **common market**.

SEDOC: See **EURES**

SEM 2000 stands for Sound and Efficient Management and was one of the first initiatives launched by the **European Commission** as headed by **Jacques Santer** in 1995. The main aim of this project was to ensure that the Commission complied with the basic principles of sound financial management, and that issues such as financial controls, internal audits, public procurement and evaluation of resource management were assessed.

SERBIA AND MONTENEGRO is how the Federal Republic of Yugoslavia (FRY) was renamed in early 2003. For much of the 1990s, the FRY underwent a process of disintegration, with Serbia, under Slobodan Milošević, being held responsible internationally for much of the ensuing conflict. After the departure from office of Milošević in October 2000, sanctions imposed by the European Union (EU) in the 1990s were lifted and the FRY was included in the EU's **stabilization and association process** and financial assistance programme for the **Western Balkans** (**CARDS**). Despite fears of the disintegration of the FRY, agreement was reached in 2002 on maintaining the republic and renaming the country Serbia and Montenegro. However, in April 2002 the coalition government in Montenegro collapsed, as a result of opposition to the agreement, although this was subsequently ratified by the Federal Assembly in May. Within Serbia, the assassination of the Prime Minister, Zoran Djindjic, in March 2003 reinforced concerns about organized crime and political stability in the country. Such concerns, along with continued instability in Kosovo, which remains under international civilian and military administration, initially prevented the EU from opening negotiations on a **Stabilization and Association Agreement** with Serbia and Montenegro. However, progress with political and economic reforms in 2004 led the Commission to propose such negotiations in April 2005 and these were later opened in the October. However, the negotiations were soon very much overshadowed by the possibility of Montenegrin independence – on which a referendum was scheduled for April 2006 – and the future of Kosovo, which is currently governed by an interim administration established by the **United Nations**. Talks on Kosovo's status began in early 2006 and could result in the province's independence.

The **SET-ASIDE SCHEME** was adopted by the **European Council** in Brussels in 1988 as a means of improving the effectiveness of the **Common Agricultural Policy** (CAP) through the elimination of surpluses of produce. Under the scheme, farmers receive financial compensation, on the condition that they undertake not to produce anything, leaving land uncultivated or destroying crops and livestock, on at least one-fifth of their arable land for five years. The idea of set-aside became a fundamental part of the **Ray MacSharry** CAP reform package endorsed by the Council in 1992.

SEVESO DIRECTIVES are the name given to European Communities **directives** first issued in 1982 on requirements relating to the accident risks of several industrial activities, and to the supervision and control of the transportation between Member States of hazardous waste. They are named after Seveso, the Italian site of a major chemicals accident in 1976.

SHIPPING has only recently been regulated by the European Communities (EC), despite the fact that some 95% of EC external trade is carried by sea, and land links between Member States on the geographical fringes of the European Union are relatively indirect. A common shipping policy was adopted in December 1986, consisting of four **regulations**. The first made sea transport subject to EC **competition policy**, from which it had been exempted in 1962; certain shipping consortia still remain exempt from competition rules. The second endorsed the right of EC ships to ply freely for trade within and beyond the EC. This was reinforced by a 1992 regulation on the liberalization of coastal shipping within the EC. The other two regulations dealt with discrimination. One permitted the **European Commission** to take anti-**dumping** measures against third parties: where the case is proved by a complaints investigation procedure, duties may be imposed upon vessels from the country concerned. The other regulation permitted the EC to retaliate against countries that reserved a proportion of the trade between themselves and the EC for their own vessels: the Commission is authorized to impose loading or discharging permits and quotas, and/or to levy duties. To maintain an adequate shipping fleet, the EC have, since the 1970s, had guidelines for state **subsidies** to shipping, in order to help it combat world competition, and proposals have been made for an EC system of vessel registration.

SIMMENTHAL SpA v COMMISSION is the title of an important case heard by the **Court of Justice**, which ruled that national governments must apply European Communities **law** in full, and that, where this is not done, individuals have the right to appeal to the Court.

SIMPLIFICATION relates to efforts to simplify **legislation** in order to make it much easier to comprehend, and to ensure greater effectiveness. The notion dates back to the 1985 **White Paper** on the Completion of the **Internal Market** and was explicitly dealt with at the December 1992 meeting of the **European Council** in Edinburgh. Since the 1980s the pursuit of a genuine single market based on the free movement of people, capital, services and goods has produced a substantial amount of European Communities **legislation**. Simplifying this is a necessity. A pilot programme (SLIM – Simpler Legislation for the Internal Market) was launched in 1996 and this could be extended to other areas. Simplification is also used to describe the process undertaken via the **Treaty of Amsterdam** to repeal or amend obsolete **articles** in the **founding treaties**. The **Treaty establishing a Constitution for Europe** should also be read as an attempt to simplify EU machinery and EU decision-making.

SINGLE CURRENCY: See **Euro**; **Economic and Monetary Union**

The **SINGLE EUROPEAN ACT** (SEA) was an important amendment of the **founding treaties** of the European Communities (EC) that came into force in July 1987 after **ratification** by the national legislatures of the Member States. The Act consists of 34 Articles, divided into four sections. The first section (Articles 1–3) constituted the objective of the SEA – 'making concrete progress towards European unity' – as well as legitimizing the status of the **European Council**. The second section (Articles 4–29) formed the greatest part of the SEA, dealing with the amendments to the founding treaties. The third section (Article 30) provided for a permanent secretariat for **European political co-operation** (EPC), while the final section (Articles 31–34) outlined the procedures necessary for the ratification and implementation of the Act.

The SEA had three main themes: the **internal market**, EPC and institutional reform. Its implications for the internal market were enormous. It obliged the EC to deal definitively with the whole range of national systems of **taxation** and law, national standards and **regulations** in a number of policy areas, and national social security and welfare systems. It specifically strengthened the role of the EC in several policy areas. It made the **European Commission** an equal partner in EPC, with the views of the **European Parliament** (EP) also needing to be taken into consideration; and it committed the EC to extending EPC to include collaboration on security policy issues. While its institutional reforms were limited, it provided for a more widespread use of **qualified majority voting** in the Council (see **Council of the European Union**), and required the latter to collaborate more with the EP in the legislative process according to a new **co-operation procedure**, whereby a rejection by the EP of a Council decision could be overturned only by unanimous agreement in the Council. A final amendment created a **Court of First Instance** to reduce the workload of the **Court of Justice**.

SINGLE MARKET: See **Internal Market**

SIS: See **Schengen Information System**

The **SIX**, or the Europe of the Six, is a popular way of referring to the membership of the European Communities from the **Schuman Plan** of 1950 until the first **enlargement** of 1973. It refers to the six founder members: **Belgium**, **France**, the Federal Republic of **Germany**, **Italy**, **Luxembourg** and the **Netherlands**.

SLOVAKIA applied for membership of the European Communities (EC) in early 1993, and subsequently signed a **Europe Agreement** in October of that year. This agreement superseded the earlier Europe Agreement signed between the EC and the former Czech and Slovak Federative Republic (Czechoslovakia) in 1991. The first Agreement had become obsolete in January 1993 with the creation of two separate states, the **Czech Republic** and Slovakia. Relations between Slovakia and the European Union (EU) can be divided into two periods. The early years of the new Slovak state under the authoritarian Prime Minister, Vladimír Meèiar, were characterized by a degree of friction between that country and the EU. The second period, since the election of a new Prime Minister, Mikuláš Dzurinda, in October 1998, has constituted nothing less than a complete transformation in relations and contacts with the EU.

Despite the Europe Agreement in force since the beginning of 1995, and Slovakia's application for EU membership, doubts about the country's potential membership persisted under the Meèiar regime because of reservations about the country's commitment to democracy. The **European Commission's** 1997 report on Slovakia's membership application stated that the country's institutions were unstable and that there were shortcomings in the functioning of its democracy, a situation which was 'all the more regrettable as the country would be capable of meeting the economic criteria [for membership] in the medium term'. Considerable improvements were made under Dzurinda's leadership, particularly with regard to minority rights, but Slovakia continued to struggle on the economic front. Unemployment in the early 2000s stood at some 20%. However, progress was made in the **accession negotiations**, which were opened in 2000. By the end of 2002 Slovakia had closed all negotiating chapters. A national referendum in May 2003 then endorsed membership (92.46% of those who participated voted in favour), and paved the way for Slovakia to join the EU on 1 May 2004. The Slovakian parliament ratified the **Treaty establishing a Constitution for Europe** by 116 votes to 27, with four abstentions, in May 2005.

SLOVENIA was the first of the former Yugoslav republics to declare independence, in 1991. The country was recognized by the European Communities in 1992. Slovenia is a small nation with some 2m. citizens and was clearly the most economically advanced of the former Yugoslav republics. Moreover, Slovenia found the transition from a socialist to a market economy easier than most. Nevertheless, relations with the European Union (EU) – primarily the conclusion of a **Europe Agreement** – were initially held up by difficulties with **Italy**, which demanded compensation for Italian nationals who had left territory now held by Slovenia in 1947. Once a compromise solution had been found and a Europe Agreement concluded in 1995, Slovenia applied for EU membership in June 1996. The country then received praise from the **European Commission** for its economic endeavours and political stability and, with strong political support from both **Austria** and **Germany**, opened **accession negotiations** with the EU in early 1998. These were successfully concluded just under five years later and, following the successful outcome of a referendum on EU membership held in March 2003, when 89.61% of the electorate voted in favour of accession, Slovenia joined the EU on 1 May 2004. Slovenia's parliament voted overwhelmingly (79 votes for and four against) to ratify the **Treaty establishing a Constitution for Europe** in February 2005. Slovenia is currently seeking membership of the **eurozone** from 1 January 2007.

The **'SLUICE-GATE' PRICE** is similar in its effect to the **threshold price**. It applies to pig meat and eggs and other poultry products. Imports of these products into the European Union are liable to a levy to raise them to the level of the sluice-gate price.

SMALL AND MEDIUM-SIZED ENTERPRISE TASK FORCE: See **SME Task Force**

SMALL AND MEDIUM-SIZED ENTERPRISES (SMEs) and their development in the **internal market** have been the subject of a number of European Communities policies. In 1996 the **European Commission** agreed new guidelines for state assistance for SMEs: aid for the acquisition of licences, patents, etc., would be allowed at the same level as aid for tangible investment. SMEs have been financially assisted to invest in new technologies. **Euro Info Centres** were established primarily as a source of information for SMEs. The third Multiannual Programme for SMEs began in 1997, and was intended to assist SMEs to create employment. The Commission has prioritized the simplification of the legislative, regulatory and administrative constraints on SMEs, and in 1997 a **European Council** meeting approved an action plan for the **European Investment Bank** to generate additional investments for SMEs. In November 1998 CREA, which is the French acronym for Risk Capital for Business Start-Ups, was launched to offer investment to small businesses.

The **SME TASK FORCE** was an agency directed by the **European Commission**. It offered help and advice to **small and medium-sized enterprises** (SMEs) on **competition policy** and the **internal market**. It was later subsumed into the former **Directorate-General** XXIII. (See also **European Business and Innovation Centre Network**; **European Private Equity and Venture Capital Association**.)

SMEs: See **Small and Medium-Sized Enterprises**

SNAKE was the name given to an agreement in 1972 by several European states to establish a European system of exchange rates within the broader Smithsonian Agreement, with only one-half of the permissible fluctuation range of the latter. It proved to be ineffectual as an instrument of exchange-rate control. Many countries were forced to leave it because of their inability to stay within the prescribed parameters. The Snake was effectively abandoned by the mid-1970s, and its failure disappointed the European Communities' hope that it would enable them to achieve **economic and monetary union**.

SOCIAL ACTION PROGRAMME is the name of a document adopted by the European Communities (EC) in 1974 as a response to the severe economic problems of the time. It was an attempt to counter criticisms that the EC had not fulfilled their obligation to develop a **social policy**. Under the programme, the Member States undertook to implement some 40 priority measures over the next three years in pursuance of the main principles of social policy: full and better employment, improved living and working conditions, and closer collaboration between employers and workers. Further social action programmes have included the 1995–97 medium-term programme, and the 1998–2000 Social Action Programme, whose priority areas were promoting jobs, skills and mobility, the changing world of work, and developing an inclusive society. Since the last programme, the EC have launched a 'Social Policy Agenda', which seeks to strengthen economic performance, create more and better jobs, and make the most of the opportunities offered by the knowledge-based society. It is based on a desire to ensure that economic, employment and social policies work together in a mutually reinforcing way.

SOCIAL CHAPTER: See **Charter of Fundamental Social Rights of Workers**

SOCIAL CHARTER: See **Charter of Fundamental Social Rights of Workers**

The **SOCIAL DIMENSION** is a concept that gained increasing significance from the second half of the 1980s onward. It was promoted by left-of-centre politicians, most notably by the then French President, **François Mitterrand**, Spanish Prime Minister, **Felipe González Márquez**, and the President of the **European Commission, Jacques Delors**. They argued for the development of a social dimension at the European Communities level to protect and advance matters relating to workers. This new policy commitment was regarded as an essential complement to the **internal market** programme, which essentially contained benefits for the business community. Social issues emerged as one of a series of policies that culminated in the 1989 **Charter of Fundamental Social Rights of Workers** and the **Social Protocol**, part of the **Treaty on European Union**.

SOCIAL DUMPING is a phrase that has been used to describe the process whereby, taking advantage of the greater freedoms available under the **internal market**, manufacturers relocate their production sites within the European Union from high- to low-wage areas.

SOCIAL FUND COMMITTEE: See **European Social Fund**

SOCIAL PARTNERS refers to the organizations that the **European Commission** is obliged to consult when it wishes to pursue policy proposals in the field of **social policy**. This social dialogue takes place between the Commission and the following three main organizations that represent the social partners: the **European Trade Union Confederation** (ETUC), the **Union of Industrial and Employers' Confederations of Europe** (UNICE) and the European Centre for Public Enterprise (CEEP). The Commission encourages and facilitates discussion with each of these groups in issues relating primarily to the labour market. In addition, the Commission is also obliged under the 1957

Treaty of Rome to consult with the **European Economic and Social Committee** on a range of policy issues.

SOCIAL POLICY in the context of the European Communities (EC) has a much narrower ambit than is usually implied by the phrase in the domestic context: it refers specifically to employment matters, education and vocational training, health and safety issues, equality matters and that part of social policy that relates to employer–worker relations. During the first decade of the EC's existence, social policy had a very low profile and priority. The **Treaty of Rome** contained very few references to a specific social policy. The provisions that did exist related to the free movement of workers and the freedom of establishment and creation of a then small **European Social Fund**. Social policy became much more important with the arrival of mass unemployment in the 1970s, and the EC adopted a **Social Action Programme** in 1974. From 1983, social policy had two priority areas: the training and employment of people aged 25 years or under, and the provision of training and employment in the most economically disadvantaged regions of the EC. Social policy is administered by the **European Commission** through the **European Social Fund** (ESF).

The **United Kingdom** under Prime Ministers **Margaret Thatcher** (1979– 90) and **John Major** (1990–97) strongly resisted the development of EC **competences** in the field of social policy and was highly critical of the 1989 **Charter of Fundamental Social Rights of Workers**; the country, moreover, gained an **opt-out** at Maastricht from the new social policy **protocol** that was annexed to the **Treaty on European Union** (TEU). The UK opt-out caused a great deal of confusion and effectively meant the existence of two distinct legal bases for social policy measures: the TEU itself and a separate agreement (the **Social Protocol**) from which the United Kingdom was exempt. This situation only came to an end when the government led by **Tony Blair** signed the Charter soon after coming to power in May 1997.

The **Treaty of Amsterdam** marked an important step forward in this particular policy area as it promoted a series of social policy priorities at European Union (EU) level, particularly in the area of employment which has now been designated as a Community objective (under Article 2) and a matter of common concern. The aim is to reach a 'high level of employment' throughout the EU and to this end the Community is charged with developing a 'co-ordinated strategy' for employment that should complement the activities of the Member States. A new title on employment (Articles 125–130) spells out Community priorities in this area and provides for the creation of an **Employment Committee**. Furthermore, Article 13 of the amended Treaty of Rome refers to the adoption of provisions on non-discrimination and enables the Council, acting unanimously, to take appropriate action to tackle any discrimination that is based on sex, race, ethnic origin, religion or belief, disability, age or sexual orientation. Now, as a result of changes introduced by the **Treaty of Amsterdam**, all social policy measures can be adopted on the basis of a new Chapter within the Treaty. This has effectively created a new legal base for equal opportunities and equal treatment of men and women at work under Article 141. Indeed, the Treaty of Rome now explicitly states that the Community must strive to eliminate all inequalities and to promote equality. As regards decision-making, the Council adopts **directives** by **qualified majority vote** and in conjunction with the **European Parliament** under the co-decision procedure in the following areas: workers' **health and safety**, working conditions, integration of persons excluded from the labour market, information and consultation of workers and equality between men and women. Unanimity prevails, however, in relation to the following areas: social security and social protection of workers, conditions of employment for third country nationals residing in the EU and financial contributions for promotion of employment and job creation. It should be noted also that certain matters have not been brought into Community competences. These include pay issues, the right of association, the right to strike and the right to impose lockouts. Since the Treaty of Amsterdam, the **Charter of Fundamental Rights** has been drawn up. It restates many of the principles and goals underpinning social policy, including the aim of combating social exclusion.

More and better jobs as well as equal opportunities are the key watchwords of European employment and social policy. The EU wants to make sure that no one gets left behind as it strives to become the world's most competitive and dynamic knowledge-based economy. The framework is a Social Policy Agenda designed to link economic, employment and social policies. The key strands of the agenda are: the **European Employment Strategy**; improving working conditions and standards; social inclusion and social protection; and equality of women and men.

An overriding objective is to cut unemployment and under-employment significantly by 2010. At present only 64% of people of working age are in employment. The aim is to raise this level to 70%. Specific objectives also apply to women and older workers. Achieving these goals implies creating 22 million jobs in the new EU of 25 by 2010, compared to the six million created in the 15-member EU between 1999 and 2003.

The EU has long sought to protect workers' rights by reaching agreement on common minimum rules on working conditions and health and safety at work. It has also sought to promote better relations and an improved dialogue between worker representatives and employers. More recently, the European Commission has been encouraging corporate social responsibility by promoting the concept that companies should include social and environmental concerns as an integral part of their business strategies.

Common EU rules establish the baseline standards in a wide range of areas. These include protection against specific health risks, such as noise or exposure to chemicals, or in specific circumstances, such as pregnancy or where workers are under 18. They also cover workers' rights. Equal pay for equal work, protection against sexual harassment and all forms of discrimination are fundamental tenets of the EU. The fight against discrimination and xenophobia has been stepped up through an action programme to combat discrimination covering the period 2001–06. Moreover, a Gender Equality Framework Strategy for the period 2001–05 sought to ensure that gender issues were taken into account in all EU policies.

Three agencies provide essential technical input into EU work on employment, carry out research on social policy matters and disseminate best practice. They are the **European Agency for Safety and Health at Work** in Bilbao; the **European Foundation for the Improvement of Living and Working Conditions** in Dublin; and the **European Monitoring Centre on Racism and Xenophobia** in Vienna.

The **SOCIAL PROTOCOL** was an agreement, stemming from the **Charter of Fundamental Social Rights of Workers** (aiming to promote employment, improve living and working conditions and combat exclusion), reached between 11 of the **Twelve** European Communities Member State governments at a meeting of the **European Council** in December 1991 at Maastricht. The only hesitant state was the United Kingdom. On account of the United Kingdom's negotiated **opt-out**, the agreement was annexed to the **Treaty on European Union** as a **protocol** and became part of the Treaty only when the **United Kingdom** finally signed up to the social charter in 1997.

SOCIALIST GROUP IN THE EUROPEAN PARLIAMENT: See **Group of the Party of European Socialists**

SOCRATES, a European Communities programme, was introduced in 1995 to bring language, education and learning programmes together in order to promote co-operation and the exchange of information between Member States with regard to education, as well as the mobility of students, especially in higher education. It has developed considerably since its creation. The current five-year programme, based in **Brussels**, combined a number of educational programmes, including **ERASMUS, GRUNDTVIG, LINGUA, MINERVA** and **COMENIUS**. €383m. was provided by the EU in 2006 to assist mobility and co-operation networks. Around half of these funds are earmarked specifically for ERASMUS. According to the Commission, nine out of ten universities in Europe participate in this programme, with some 165,000 mobility scholarships being awarded each year.

The Commission also encourages the mobility of teachers, and some 23,000 received money in 2006 to enable them to benefit from cross-border educational exchanges.

SOFT LAWS are rules of conduct which in principle have no legally binding force, but which nevertheless may have practical effects in aiding policy development. This broad definition encompasses not only international agreements but also texts issued by the European Union (EU) **institutions**. In terms of the **European Commission**, soft law is usually equated with the following: codes of conduct, frameworks, **resolutions**, communications, **declarations**, guidance notes and circulars. Although the concept of soft law remains a highly problematic one for lawyers, it is generally regarded by policy-makers as a useful instrument to encourage consistency in bureaucratic decision-making, to enable speedy resolution of issues that would otherwise demand **legislation** and to allow for regulation where no regulation would otherwise be possible. However, the use of soft law has its detractors, who emphasize the dangers and the undemocratic and illegitimate concerns arising from such informal policy-making. When soft law is utilized, parliaments are bypassed, which, as far as the public is concerned, leads to opaque decision-making, and the content of policies may often be vague, as well as possibly inconsistent with existing legislation. Moreover, it can be argued that because soft law is not legally binding, implementation must rest on the goodwill of those agreeing to it. Nevertheless, soft law is a fundamental part of EU policy-making (e.g. state aids – see also **subsidies**).

JAVIER SOLANA (1942–) became **Secretary-General of the Council of the European Union** and the European Union's first **High Representative** for the **common foreign and security policy** in October 1999. During his period in office, he was instrumental in overseeing the development of the **European security and defence policy**. He was also the author of the **European Security Strategy** adopted in late 2003. While in office he was also Secretary-General of the now essentially defunct **Western European Union**. Previously, Solana had been Secretary-General of the **North Atlantic Treaty Organization** (NATO) in 1995–99. During the earlier part of his career, Solana was a Socialist member of parliament and minister in **Spain**.

SOLEMN DECLARATION ON EUROPEAN UNION is the title of the general statement signed by the heads of government and foreign ministers at the conclusion of the meeting of the **European Council** held in Stuttgart, Federal Republic of **Germany**, in June 1983, which had discussed the **Genscher–Colombo Plan**. The Declaration reviewed the extent to which the potential of each institution of the European Communities (EC) had been implemented, and considered possibilities for their further co-ordination. It asserted a wish to work for further EC development as a nucleus of European union, to strengthen **European political co-operation** (EPC), to promote closer cultural co-operation, to launch a concerted action to deal with international problems of law and order, and to seek further **approximation** of the legislation of the Member States. It also indicated the purpose of the Council and its relationship to the EC **institutions**. More a statement of belief than a plan of action, it nevertheless contributed to the movement in favour of change that developed during the 1980s.

SOUTH AFRICA over the last two decades has witnessed a transformation in its relations with the European Union. For much of the 1980s it was the focus of sanctions adopted under **European Political Co-operation**, although a European Special Programme (ESP) was agreed in 1995 to assist the victims of apartheid. Later, once the apartheid regime collapsed, the ESP was renamed the European Programme for Reconstruction and Development. This committed €500m. to South Africa for the period 1996–99. Further financial assistance has since been agreed. In addition, a trade, development and co-operation agreement was concluded in 1999.

SOUTH AND CENTRAL AMERICA has not been, in general, the subject of a co-ordinated policy. However, the European Communities (EC) have concluded economic and trade co-operation agreements with most of the countries in this area, which enable the latter to benefit from the EC **Generalized System of Preferences**. The arrangements allow duty-free access into the EC for some of their manufactured products. Moreover, regular ministerial meetings have been held with the so-called 'Rio Group' (Brazil, Colombia, Mexico, Panama, Peru, Uruguay and Venezuela) since 1987. The San José dialogue exists as the institutional forum between the European Union (EU) and six countries of Central America. In 1998 the **European Commission** proposed negotiating mandates for the creation of a free-trade area with the countries of Mercosur (Argentina, Brazil, Paraguay and Uruguay) and Chile. This was followed by a first summit between heads of state and government of the EU, Latin America and the Caribbean at Rio in June 1999. At this a highly ambitious action plan with 54 priorities covering institutional dialogue, trade liberalization and investment was agreed. Such multilateral co-operation supplements existing bilateral co-operation between the EU and countries in the region.

SOUTH-EASTERN EUROPE is a term used by the European Union when referring to **Bulgaria**, **Romania** and the countries of the **Western Balkans** collectively. (See **Stability Pact for South-Eastern Europe**.)

The **SOVEREIGNTY** of the Member States has been significantly diminished by their acceptance of the principles of the **founding treaties** and their subsequent amendments. Encroachment on national sovereignty has further increased with the accumulation of the *acquis communautaire*. The net effect is that while the European Union (EU) may not be a sovereign body in the full political or legal sense, neither are the Member States. The question of sovereignty has remained a contentious issue within the EU.

SOVIET UNION: See **USSR**

PAUL-HENRI SPAAK (1899–1972), head of government or foreign minister of **Belgium** on several occasions after 1945, became popularly known as 'Mr Europe'. He was one of the principal conceivers of **Benelux**, was involved in the 1948 **Congress of Europe** and the subsequent **European Movement**, and took the first initiative in the developments that led to the creation of the **Council of Europe**. Elected as the first President of its Assembly, he resigned in 1951 because of his disillusionment over its inability to achieve concrete progress towards integration. He supported the **sectoral integration** approach of the 1950s, and it was he who led the initiative that resulted in a draft plan for a **European Political Community**. As Belgian foreign minister, he attended the 1955 **Messina Conference**, where he was charged with chairing a committee that would consider, develop and report on the proposals made at Messina. The Spaak Report was accepted by the **Six**, after which Spaak and his committee went on to draft the treaties for the **European Economic Community** and the **European Atomic Energy Community**.

SPAAK REPORT: See **Messina Conference**; **Paul-Henri Spaak**

SPACE POLICY has been barely considered by the European Communities (EC). While some of the Member States were involved in space research and development as early as the 1960s, the EC were slow in developing a collaborative approach to space, despite retaining links with the **European Space Agency** (ESA). A space policy document was produced by the **European Commission** in July 1988. It identified six 'action lines': the promotion of coordination and complementary action between space programmes and EC **research and technological development policy**; **telecommunications** and satellite technology; industrial development and the **internal market**; the development of observation of the Earth from space; the legal environment; and the development of space-related technology training programmes. Since 1988 the EC has collaborated more closely with ESA. The **Treaty establishing a**

Constitution for Europe envisages the EU adopting a more focused engagement, with space policy as part of its activities in the area of **research and technological development policy**.

SPAIN first approached the European Communities (EC) in 1962, with a request for an **association agreement** that would, in time, permit full membership. The request was renewed in 1964. Negotiations on a **preferential trade agreement** began in 1967, and an agreement was signed in 1970. Full membership could not be considered by the EC as long as Spain continued to be governed by an authoritarian regime. Discussions on a new agreement for a free-trade area were broken off by the EC in October 1975 in protest against executions in Spain that violated 'the principles of the rule of law and in particular the rights of the defence'. The new, democratic Spanish government that emerged after General Francisco Franco's death in November 1975 submitted an application for full membership in July 1977, and negotiations began in February 1979. The negotiations proved to be difficult, particularly where agriculture and fishing were concerned, but were eventually concluded in March 1985, and Spain joined the EC the following January. A beneficiary of EC **regional policy**, including the **Cohesion Fund**, and **social policy**, Spain has been a strong supporter of further economic and political integration, even though its determination to meet some of the economic and monetary criteria set by the EC placed enormous strains on the Spanish economy. Nevertheless, Spain successfully entered stage three of **economic and monetary union** in 1999. Under the premiership of the conservative José María Aznar (1996–2004) Spain's economic boom continued. Little known outside Spain prior to his first election victory and appointment as Prime Minister in 1996, he rapidly emerged as a leading figure on the European stage. His decision to support the **USA**-led invasion of Iraq in 2003 (see **Gulf War**) may have won both American and British plaudits, but it was not a popular move in Spain. His decision to stand down in 2004 may also have contributed to his determination to resist the proposals (which reduced Spain's position) outlined in the **Draft Constitution** on the new voting arrangements within the **Council of the European Union** after **enlargement**. This led to bitter recriminations from other European Union (EU) Member States and the entire episode not only marginalized Spain but also helped to ensure that the 2003 Rome **intergovernmental conference** collapsed without agreement. A change in government in April 2004, when José Luis Rodríguez Zapatero became Prime Minister, brought a more accommodating Spanish approach to the EU and a swift decision to settle any outstanding differences. This approach helped the EU leaders to agree a treaty text in June 2004. Spain was the first EU Member State to hold a referendum on the **Treaty establishing a Constitution for Europe** in February 2005 and a decisive majority (77%) approved the text. However, turnout was low, at just 42%.

SPECIAL COMMITTEE ON AGRICULTURE is the name of a specialist committee within the **Committee of Permanent Representatives** (COREPER). It is the only COREPER body that deals with all agricultural issues that come before the plenary Committee.

SPIERENBURG REPORT is the name of a document produced for the **European Commission** in 1979. A group of experts headed by the former **Netherlands** diplomat, Dirk Spierenburg, was asked to review the structure and organization of the European Communities. The Report recommended a rationalization of the Commission – including a reduction in the number of Commissioners – and of its system of personnel management. It was opposed by the Council of Ministers (see **Council of the European Union**), and was never implemented.

SPILLOVER was a term widely used in the 1950s to describe how **sectoral integration** would lead to full European union. It had two components. Functional spillover was based on the principle that modern economies were based on interrelated sectors. Once one economic sector had been integrated, this complexity would generate pressure for the integration of other sectors. Political spillover suggested that once European institutions had been established for one sector, economic interest groups would look to that political level for the realization of their demands, and the advantages provided would lead them also to press for further sectoral integration. The notion largely fell into disfavour after the late 1950s as an explanation of, and strategy for, integration.

ALTIERO SPINELLI (1907–86) was a life-long advocate of a federal United States of Europe. His views had first been expressed in the Ventotene Manifesto of 1941, which served as the basis of several documents prepared for international meetings of federalists and Resistance activists in 1944 and 1945. Spinelli drafted most of these documents, which envisaged a federal Europe with a written constitution, a judicial tribunal and a supranational government directly responsible to the people of Europe. Active in the federalist organizations of the late 1940s and 1950s, Spinelli, with his more populist approach, was out of tune with the élite-led economic approach to integration that came to dominate developments. He later served as a member of the **European Commission** from 1970 to 1976, but his greatest contribution to the European Communities (EC) came after 1979 when, as a **Member of the European Parliament**, he was the principal conceiver of the **draft Treaty establishing the European Union**, a document that influenced much of the later development of the EC and of the European Union itself.

SPORT was identified by the **Committee for a People's Europe** as an area where, because of the mass interest and loyalties it generates, the European Communities (EC) could seek to encourage a sense of European identity and awareness. The **European Commission** had already sought, on a modest scale, to involve the EC in sporting events, most prominently through its sponsorship since 1976 of the Sail for Europe Association, a group which has formed international crews of EC nationals to compete in round-the-world races and other sailing events. The Commission also sponsored the European Yacht Race in 1985, an event that now takes place on a biennial basis. Tennis and swimming championships have also been sponsored, along with a number of football, motor rally and walking events. The Eurathlon programme provides grants to sports projects. However, the EC does not have a coherent sports policy, and it is not officially identified as a major responsibility of any branch of the Commission, although the Commission proposed in 2001 that the year 2004 be declared European Year of Education through Sport. In 1997 the **European Parliament** passed a resolution requesting that a reference to sport be inserted into the **article** of the **Treaty of Rome** dealing with culture. This was not taken up, although the **Treaty establishing a Constitution for Europe** does envisage a greater role for the EU in promoting European sporting issues as well as developing the European dimension in sport. This is to be done by 'promoting fairness and openness in sporting competitions and co-operation between bodies responsible for sports, and by protecting the physical and moral integrity of sportspeople'.

The **STABILITY AND GROWTH PACT** emerged as an essential aspect of the third stage of plans for **economic and monetary union** (EMU). It was realized that if EMU were ultimately going to be successful, budgetary discipline across all **eurozone** members would have to be maintained after EMU had been launched in 1999. This demand was principally led by **Germany** and resulted in a **European Council** resolution (adopted at the Amsterdam European Council in 1997) and two subsequent Council regulations. The Pact established clear and detailed arrangements for the surveillance of budgetary positions, for the co-ordination of economic policies, and procedures for dealing with excessive deficits. All eurozone members pledged to pursue a budget close to balance or in surplus for the foreseeable future and to present both the **European Commission** and the **Council of the European Union** with annual reports on their economic situation.

The Stability and Growth Pact allows the Council to penalize any participating Member State that fails to take the necessary measures to end an excessive deficit. In the first instance the penalty is more likely to constitute a non-interest-bearing deposit with the European Union (EU), but it could be converted into a fine if the deficit is not corrected within two years. The Commission is charged with supervising the economic policies of the participating countries and with alerting the Member States to potential problems. To date, both **Ireland** and Germany have been rebuked by the Commission for failing to control their deficits. The situation with Germany, the prime architect of the pact, deteriorated further in 2003 as both Berlin and Paris watched their economies remain locked in recession or stagnation. For the third year in a row, both states breached one of the keystones of the pact – maintaining budget deficits at less than 3% of gross domestic product (GDP), the total value of goods and services the economy produces. With their economies stagnant, tax receipts are down, while public spending in terms of unemployment benefits have gone up. In November 2003 the Stability and Growth Pact was effectively suspended through the reluctance of **France** and Germany to accept the recommendations of the European Central Bank and the Commission to reduce their budget deficits to below 3% of GDP. According to the rules, both states were therefore liable to pay substantial fines. However, the **Economic and Financial Affairs Council of Ministers** (ECOFIN) disregarded the Commission's recommendation and granted the eurozone's two largest economies an extra year's grace. France and Germany therefore were allowed to break the 3% rule again in 2004. The pact has thus been severely undermined. Germany wishes to draw up additional EU fiscal rules that will lead to a 'better interpretation' – in other words, a less strict interpretation – of the pact, allowing more account to be taken of the economic situation, the impact of ageing on social security systems and the role played by public investment in modernizing the economy. The **United Kingdom** has consistently criticized the pact for its rigidity and has argued that countries should be allowed to run deficits in bad times provided they accumulate surpluses in good times.

Still, neither **Italy** and **Portugal** were able to keep within these more relaxed rules and were criticized by the European Commission in June 2005 for exceeding the acceptable levels. Both were struggling with rather stagnant economies. Accordingly, the Portuguese government announced plans to reduce its budget deficit in line with EU rules. To this end, Lisbon aims to increase **Value-Added Tax** (from 19% to 21%) and to introduce public spending cuts. It is hoped that these new measures will bring Portugal's deficit down to 2.8% of GDP by 2008, though they are certain to increase public disquiet that will culminate in renewed strikes.

The **STABILITY PACT FOR SOUTH-EASTERN EUROPE** was launched in June 1999 following the Kosovo conflict. It is designed to assist in the stabilization and reconstruction of the region, the European Union playing a lead role through its **Stabilization and Association Process** and the implementation of the **CARDS** programme of financial assistance.

STABILIZATION AND ASSOCIATION AGREEMENTS (SAAs) are the **association agreements** that the European Union (EU) has devised for countries in the **Western Balkans** as part of the **stabilization and association process**. The first was concluded with the Former Yugoslav Republic of **Macedonia** (FYROM) in 2001 and was soon followed by an agreement with **Croatia**. SAAs with **Albania** and the Federal Republic of Yugoslavia (renamed **Serbia and Montenegro** in 2003) were expected to follow. These, like the agreements with FYROM and Croatia, would be modelled very much on **Europe Agreements**, but would place a much greater emphasis on the pursuit of regional co-operation as a prerequisite for closer collaboration with the EU. They also confirm the associate country's status as potential candidate for EU membership (see **potential candidate state)**.

The **STABILIZATION AND ASSOCIATION PROCESS** (SAP) was launched by the European Union as its contribution to the **Stability Pact for South-Eastern Europe** following the Kosovo conflict in 1999. Its key elements are the **Stabilization and Association Agreements** and the **CARDS** programme of financial assistance.

STABILIZERS were introduced into the **Common Agricultural Policy** (CAP) in 1988. They are fixed ceilings, or upper limits, imposed on the production of several agricultural products. They involve production quotas, limits on both production and processing guarantees, and intervention ceilings, and have been supported by a system of **co-responsibility levies**. If the ceiling is exceeded, an automatic reduction in the level of price support provided by the CAP is triggered. The most significant effect, perhaps, has been upon cereal production.

The **STAFF** employed by the European Communities numbers some 28,000, and about two-thirds of these work for the **European Commission**. The total is substantially lower than staff employed by national bureaucracies. Formally, there are no quotas for each of the Member States; in practice, however, an unofficial system of national allocation is employed, to ensure that each Member State is adequately represented in all areas and at all levels of the administration. In principle, officials must be European Union (EU) nationals and adequately bilingual, and those appointed as translators or interpreters must be reasonably

proficient in two EU **languages** other than their own. Apart from these qualifications, most posts are filled by open competition, having been advertised in
the **Official Journal of the European Communities**. Usually, however, there
is an upper age limit, although this was to be phased out following a decision
made in 1998. In addition, several senior posts are filled by nomination from the
Member States.

STAGIAIRE is the name given to a short-term trainee, usually a recent
graduate, attached to a **European Commission** office. The position provides
the appointee with an apprenticeship and in-service training, but does not
guarantee subsequent employment with the European Communities.

STANDARDIZATION: See **CEN**; **CENELEC**

The **STANDING COMMITTEE ON EMPLOYMENT** was established in
1970 to act in an advisory capacity. In 1996 the **European Commission**
invited interested parties to consider how the Standing Committee could be
reformed in order to improve social dialogue. Two years later the Commission
presented a draft decision for reform to the **Council of the European Union**.
The document entitled 'Adapting and promoting the social dialogue at Community level' was adopted by the Council in March 1999. The newly revised
Committee was to serve as a European forum, in effect a tripartite dialogue,
between the Council, the Commission and European Union-level employer and
employee organizations (including the **European Trade Union Confederation**, the **Committee of Agricultural Organizations in the European
Union** (COPA), EUROCOMMERCE and the **Union of Industrial and
Employers' Confederations of Europe**) to discuss employment strategy.

STATE AID: See **Subsidies**

STATISTICAL OFFICE OF THE EUROPEAN COMMUNITIES: See
Eurostat

STEEL is subject to potentially stringent control by the **European Commission** because of the greater powers, covering investment, production, sales and
financial aid, which the latter inherited from the High Authority of the
European Coal and Steel Community (ECSC). In the 1950s and 1960s, the
ECSC policy of abolishing customs barriers encouraged an expansion of the
industry, although this was due in equal measure to increased world demand.

After 1973, there was a dramatic decline in demand for steel. Many companies were close to bankruptcy, a situation that necessitated large-scale government intervention. After the failure of an attempt to secure voluntary rationalization of the steel industry, a state of **manifest crisis** was declared in 1980, placing most steel production under compulsory European Communities control. Reduction targets were set for each Member State in a programme of rationalization. While the targets were largely met by 1985, the state of manifest crisis was not lifted until 1988. The steel industry became more financially secure, but at the cost of much lower output and the loss of a substantial part of the labour force. An aid programme (**RESIDER**) for the conversion of areas dependent on steel production was adopted in 1988. In 1996 a new code on steel aid was adopted by the European Commission, covering the period 1997–2002, stipulating the conditions whereby Member States could grant aid to steel companies: for research and development, environmental protection, or full or partial closure of capacity.

STOCKHOLM CONVENTION is the name of the document that in 1960 formally established the **European Free Trade Association**. The signatories accepted the economic aim of an elimination of tariffs on reciprocal trade in industrial goods, with special provisions for agriculture and fisheries. The Convention had no political implications.

STRASBOURG, France, is central to the theme of European unity because it is the home of the **Council of Europe**, and became the location of the plenary sessions of the **European Parliament** (EP) after 1958. Although the EP continues to meet in the city, many of its members would prefer it to be relocated in **Brussels**, where many EP committees meet. Any decision to move must be agreed by all European Union Member States and France is adamantly opposed to a move. Indeed, the **Treaty of Amsterdam**, by means of a **protocol** on the location of the **institutions**, effectively put an end to suggestions that the EP might relocate by confirming Strasbourg as its home and requiring that 12 plenary sessions be held in the city each year.

The **STRUCTURAL FUNDS** (see also the **Cohesion Fund**) form part of the **cohesion policy** of the European Union (EU). This is designed to reduce economic and regional disparities in the most disadvantaged parts of the EU and to promote economic and social cohesion. The structural funds refer to the four major **expenditure** funds of the European Communities (EC) that are intended to achieve these objectives: the **European Regional Development Fund** (ERDF) that was set up in 1975 and finances infrastructure, productive investment to create jobs, local development projects and assistance to SMEs; the **European Social Fund** (ESF) that was established in 1960 and is designed to help the workforce adapt to changes in the labour market; the Guidance section of the **European Agricultural Guidance and Guarantee Fund** (EAGGF) which dates from 1962 and finances rural development measures and provides assistance to farmers; and, lastly, the **Financial Instrument for Fisheries Guidance** (FIFG) which was created in 1992. In addition, there exists a special solidarity fund called the **Cohesion Fund** that aids projects relating to the environment and transport networks. The major beneficiary of this fund has been **Spain**. The funds are intended to support integrated rather than individual projects, and increasingly are expected to have a regional focus. They are allocated through Community Support Frameworks (CSFs) that are negotiated between the regions, the **European Commission** and the Member States. The financial assistance for these programmes is calculated on a multi-annual basis, with periods running from 1994 to 1999 and 2000 to 2006. To facilitate the provision of financial assistance to the most needy areas and to prepare the EU for **enlargement** (see **Agenda 2000**), the EU's structural policy was substantially reformed and now focuses on a number of objective areas. The declared aim of particular reform initiative was to concentrate aid where it was most needed; that is, on those regions that were falling furthest behind. Objective 1 areas are those regions which are lagging behind the rest of the EU in terms of development, i.e. regions in which gross national product (GNP) per head is less than 75% of the EU average. These objective 1 areas consume 70% of structural funds expenditure. Objective 2 areas are those areas with structural difficulties, such as areas undergoing economic change, rural areas in decline and areas dependent on fishing. The third objective area relates to the development of human resources outside those regions eligible for objective 1 aid.

In addition, there are currently four major structural funds initiatives. These are **INTERREG**, which seeks to stimulate cross-border, transnational and inter-regional co-operation; **LEADER**, which aims to foster rural development through the initiatives of local action groups; **EQUAL**, which provides assistance for the creation of new means to combat discrimination and inequalities in general; and **URBAN**, which promotes economic and social revitalization of cities and suburban areas in crisis.

As the **candidate states** moved closer to EU membership, it was decided to create two new funds to assist their progression for the period 2000–06. These funds (see **Agenda 2000**), namely the **Instrument for Structural Policies for Pre-Accession** and the Special Accession Programme for Agriculture and Rural Development (**SAPARD**), were designed to support infrastructure projects, industry, services, SMEs, agriculture and the environment. Negotiations commenced in 2004 in relation to the future size and priorities of the structural funds from 2007.

STRUCTURAL POLICY: See **Structural Funds**

STUTTGART DECLARATION: See **Solemn Declaration on European Union**

SUBSIDIARITY is a term that was first used in the context of the European Communities (EC) in the 1970s, but it only became politically contentious in the period preceding the signing of the **Treaty on European Union**. As defined by the **Treaty of Rome**, the term embodies the principles that the EC can act only when they possess the legal power to do so, that the EC should act only when an objective can be better achieved at the supranational level, and that the means employed by the EC when they do act should be proportional to the desired objective. It implies, therefore, that national powers are the norm, with EC action the exception. It remains, nevertheless, an ambiguous and controversial concept regarded by both those for and those against more intensive integration as supporting their own agenda. An attempt was made in a **protocol** introduced by the **Treaty of Amsterdam** to provide a clearer definition of subsidiarity. In the framework of the **intergovernmental conference** launched in February 2000, the **Committee of the Regions** asked for the principle of subsidiarity to be amended to formally recognize the role of the local and regional authorities. This did not happen at the Nice **summit meeting**. The **European Commission** produces on an annual basis a report (*Better Law-making*) that for the most part examines the application of the subsidiarity principle. The concept of subsidiarity was reaffirmed in the **Treaty establishing a Constitution for Europe**.

SUBSIDIES by the Member States to either private companies or public enterprises are, in general, not permitted if the effect is likely to be contrary to the **competition policy** of the European Communities (EC). **European Commission** guidelines permit subsidies for industries experiencing very severe economic difficulties, but in each instance the case should be demonstrated to be exceptional, the aid programme should be short-term only, and the objective should be the re-establishment of economic viability by a planned reduction in capacity. State aid is also permitted for natural disaster relief, depressed regions, and investment in new economic activities. In each instance, Member States must inform the Commission of their intentions. Where Member States have provided subsidies that do not conform to EC **regulations**, the Commission has the authority to demand their repayment and to levy fines on Member States. In a significant development in early 2002, the **Council of the European Union** queried the Commission's authority to decide on issues of whether state aid should or should not be granted. If this is deemed to be the correct interpretation of the **articles** on state aid in the **European Treaties**, it will have huge implications for developments in this area.

SUMMIT MEETINGS are gatherings of the heads of government of the Member States. During the first decade of the three European Communities only three summits were held by the **Six**. Three further *ad hoc* summits were held between 1972 and 1974. In 1974 it was agreed to institutionalize summits with the establishment of the **European Council**, which was to meet three times a year. This frequency was reduced to twice yearly in 1986. Provisions also exist for the convocation of extraordinary or emergency sessions. Most summit meetings deal primarily with routine business and general reviews; a few, however, have been highly significant for European developments. (See, for example, **Essen Summit**; **Fontainebleau Summit**; **Hague Summit**; **Maastricht Summit**; **Milan Summit**; **Tampere Summit**.) It has traditionally been the practice that summits have been held in the country holding the presidency of the **Council of the European Union**. Since the second half of 2003, however, all scheduled summit meetings of the European Council have been held in Brussels.

SUPRANATIONALISM is the condition whereby the structures and **decisions** of the European Communities are superior to and, some would claim, independent of national governments. Supranationalism is completely different from intergovernmental **co-operation**.

SUPREMACY OF EUROPEAN COMMUNITY LAW is a doctrine established by the **European Court of Justice** in 1964. The case that provided this landmark decision was *Costa v Enel* and, when this decision is taken together with the doctrine of **direct effect**, the conclusion to be reached is nothing less than a complete metamorphosis of the nature and scope of EC law. These two doctrines transform the EC into a powerful means to advance the **supranational** idea and to challenge existing national law.

The **SUSPENSION CLAUSE** was written into the **Treaty on European Union** by the **Treaty of Amsterdam**. Under this clause, some of the rights of a Member State (e.g. voting in the **Council of the European Union**) can be suspended if that particular Member State consistently or seriously contravenes the principles on which the European Union has been constructed, such as liberty, democracy, respect for **human rights** and the rule of law.

SUSTAINABILITY is the quality that may be ascribed to a form of economic growth that is self-maintaining without exhausting natural resources.

The **SUTHERLAND REPORT** dates from 1992 and was produced by a former Commissioner responsible for competition, Peter Sutherland, at the request of the **European Commission**. He was charged with producing a report on how the European Communities (EC) could develop a strategy to ensure that the **internal market** functioned properly and efficiently. The Report advocated a series of initiatives to achieve this goal. These included the necessity for greater **transparency** and much more monitoring and enforcement of EC **legislation** at the national level. It also placed an emphasis on **subsidiarity**. The Commission responded to the report by promising to pursue many of the suggestions, particularly with regard to national enforcement. In addition it promised to publish an annual report on the state of the single market and make more use of **Green Papers** to engage the wider public in suggestions on proposed legislation.

SWEDEN maintained a position of political and military neutrality after 1945, eschewing involvement in anything other than intergovernmental and economic co-operation. In 1961, it approached the European Communities (EC) for a form of economic association that did not imply full membership. Negotiations eventually began in 1970, and in 1971 Sweden ruled out full membership as being incompatible with its policy of **neutrality**. A **Free Trade Agreement** was signed in 1972. Following the EC decision to implement the **internal market** by 1992, Sweden accepted the need for a closer economic relationship with the EC. This was eventually achieved through the **European Economic Area**. Before this was concluded, however, Sweden revised its view on membership, and in 1991 submitted a formal application to join the EC. Negotiations were completed in 1994 and, following approval in a popular referendum, Sweden joined the European Union (EU) on 1 January 1995. Sweden's transition to membership of the EU has been smooth, but the EU remains, according to **Eurobarometer**, less popular in the country than in other Member States, and, like **Denmark** and the **United Kingdom**, Sweden opted not to enter **economic and monetary union** (EMU) in 1999. In a referendum held in September 2003 on joining EMU, a majority of those participating (56%) voted against replacing the krona with the **euro**.

SWITZERLAND has historically adopted a strict position of **neutrality**, but did, nevertheless, become a founder member of the **European Free Trade Association** (EFTA). It applied to the European Communities (EC) in 1961 for an economic association, but negotiations began only in 1970. A **Free Trade Agreement** was signed in 1972 and subsequently ratified by a national referendum. In 1989 Switzerland accepted the need for EFTA to seek a new and closer relationship with the EC, and subsequently began examining the question of EC membership. However, in a referendum in December 1992, the Swiss rejected participation in the **European Economic Area**, thus forcing the government to suspend the application for EC membership that had been submitted in the previous May. Since then, the Swiss have negotiated a series of sector-specific bilateral agreements with the European Union (EU) covering free movement of persons, air and land transport, agriculture, research, public procurement and the mutual recognition of conformity assessments; these were signed in June 1999 and entered into force two years later. In June 2002 negotiations on a further 10 bilateral agreements began. These are ongoing and cover services; pensions; trade in processed agricultural products; the environment; statistics; education, occupational training and youth; the media; taxation of savings; the fight against fraud; and co-operation in the fields of justice, police, asylum and migration. It remains to be seen whether these will provide the long-term basis for Switzerland's relations with the EU: official government policy is to seek EU membership. In 2001, however, the government advised the population against supporting a popular initiative to open negotiations. In the referendum, 77% of voters voted against the initiative. In 2005 Switzerland moved a step closer to the EU when its citizens voted in a referendum to join the **Schengen Agreement.** The decision means that Switzerland will open its borders and become part of Europe's passport-free zone, and that the Swiss authorities will also share information with their EU colleagues on crime and on asylum applications. Whether Switzerland will revive the 1992 membership application remains to be seen.

SYNERGY is the name of a programme introduced in 1997 to encourage international co-operation in the energy sector. It ended in 2002.

T

TAC: See **Total Allowable Catch**

TACIS: See **Technical Assistance to the Commonwealth of Independent States**

The **TAMPERE SUMMIT** of the **European Council** in November 1999 represents a highly significant event in the development of European Union (EU) policy governing **justice and home affairs** (JHA). It was the first time that an area of loose intergovernmental co-operation had been propelled to the top of the political agenda. The origins of this agenda date back to early 1999 and a joint letter from the German Chancellor, **Gerhard Schröder**, and the Finnish Prime Minister, Paavo Lipponen, which called for European action in three broad areas. These all related to the third pillar activities initiated by the **Treaty on European Union**, and covered **asylum** and **immigration policy**, the creation of a European **area of freedom, security and justice** and combating transnational crime. These became the main agenda items of the Tampere Summit, where the heads of state and government reached agreement on the need for a 'common asylum system'. Tampere highlighted the expanding nature and position of the European Council as an agenda-setter and a driving force for EU integration. It led directly to a further extension of the EU's scope *vis-à-vis* policy-making in the field of JHA and resulted in several new initiatives and new bodies being set up in 2000, such as **Eurojust** and a European Police College.

With regard to the **European Commission**, Tampere was the first occasion for the post-**Jacques Santer** Commission to present itself as a credible and potent force to the leaders of the Member States. However, the scandal surrounding the Santer regime and the growing determination of the European Council to control the policy agenda had already put the Commission on the defensive. The changing relationships amongst the EU **institutions** were epitomized by the European Council's rejection of the Commission's report on the restructuring of the EU institutions.

TARGET, or Trans-European Automated Real-time Gross Settlement Express Transfer, is a system of inter-bank payments established on 1 January 1999, the start of the third stage of **economic and monetary union**, to regulate transactions between the **European Central Bank** and commercial banks of the participating Member States. National central banks of non-participating Member States also have some access to the settlement system.

The **TARGET PRICE** is the basic price set annually for each commodity covered by the **Common Agricultural Policy**. The price support provided for farmers is calculated with reference to the target prices.

TARIC is the acronym for the Integrated Community Tariff established within the former CADDIA (Co-operation in Automation of Data and Documentation for Imports/Exports and Agriculture) structure in 1988. It is similar to the **common external tariff**, but contains additional provisions relating to preferences and quotas. The tariff is published annually in the **Official Journal of the European Communities**.

TARIFFS on intra-European Communities (EC) trade were removed by the **Six** by 1968, well within the time limit set by the **Treaty of Rome**. New Member States have been given a transitional period in which to remove their tariffs, although increasingly, acceding states already participate in free-trade arrangements with the EC. The EC **common external tariff** has been progressively reduced in line with decisions taken under the **General Agreement on Tariffs and Trade**, and now by the **World Trade Organization**.

TAX HARMONIZATION: See **Taxation**

TAXATION has, in general, been accepted by the European Communities (EC) as a policy field that is the province of the Member States and, normally, proposals relating to taxation that come before the **Council of the European Union** require unanimous approval. Despite the introduction of an **internal market** and **economic and monetary union**, a European Union (EU) policy on taxation is still absent and this reflects the political sensitivity of fiscal policy and explains why the principle of unanimous decision-making in this area was maintained in the **Single European Act** and beyond. The exceptions to the general rule are cases where national taxation policy is against EC **competition policy**, or where it discriminates against nationals of other Member States. By contrast, the EC has an interest in indirect taxation and is bound to work for the

harmonization of indirect taxation in order to enable the **internal market** to function properly. Currently, significant disparities exist in the levels of excise duty paid, for example, on alcohol and tobacco within the internal market. A code on corporate taxation was agreed in 1997 that would eliminate harmful tax competition between Member States. Proposals made in December 1998 for the harmonization of taxes in the Member States were rejected by the United Kingdom, which made it clear that a **veto** would be used to keep taxation within the realm of national governments. Such a position, shared by other Member States, was emphatically restated during the **intergovernmental conference** in 2000. Consequently, the **Treaty of Nice** failed to extend **qualified majority voting** to tax harmonization. Nevertheless, it should be noted that the adoption of a single currency is intensifying the pressure for a truly common rate of **value-added tax** (VAT) and for common rules in the area of corporate taxation in the EU. Moves in this direction continue to be strongly resisted by both the **United Kingdom** and **Ireland**.

TECHNICAL ASSISTANCE TO THE COMMONWEALTH OF INDEPENDENT STATES (TACIS) is an aid programme for the successor states of the **USSR**, often referred to as the **Commonwealth of Independent States**, and also Mongolia. Established in 1991, TACIS has as its objective to assess and aid economic reform and privatization in a range of economic sectors and to foster the development of democratic societies. In 1995 the **European Commission** extended the programme until 1999, when a revised programme to promote democracy and encourage investment was proposed. A **PHARE** and TACIS Information Centre was opened in Brussels in 1998 to offer advice on the programmes. In the period 1991–99, the European Communities provided more than €4,000m. in assistance under the TACIS programme. A further €3,138m. was allocated for the period 2000–06.

TED: See **Tenders Electronic Daily**

The **TELECOMMUNICATIONS** sector has been regarded by the **European Commission** as a growth industry in which the Member States must collaborate more closely in order to compete with their major world rivals. Several initiatives have been launched in the fields of **media policy**, information networks, common standards and the **harmonization** of technical rules, and the development of satellite transmissions. Moreover, telecommunications are targeted as part of efforts to develop **Trans-European Networks**. These initiatives, however, have yet to lead to an integrated policy. The push towards the creation of an **internal market** focused attention on the public monopolies, and, in particular, on telecommunications and energy. The former became a priority for the Commission (as identified in the Commission's 1987 **Green Paper** on the development of the common market for telecommunications services and equipment). This led to a 1988 directive that opened the telecommunications terminals market up to competition. This was supplemented by a **directive** relating to the liberalization of satellite telecommunications equipment and services that came into force in late 1994, but allowed for deferment until 1 January 1996. Telecommunications infrastructures in the European Union, which are operated mainly by state monopolies, also faced the arrival of competition. In 1993 the **Council of the European Union** decided to liberalize fully voice telephony services by January 1998 (although some states, such as **Ireland**, **Spain**, **Portugal** and **Greece**, were given **derogations** until 2003). Simultaneously, the Commission defined the concept of universal service, detailing the provision and quality of the service, the charging principles and the dispute settlement procedures.

TELEVISION: See **Media Policy**

TEMPUS stands for the Trans-European Mobility Scheme for University Studies, a European Communities programme introduced in 1990. Its objectives are to provide financial assistance for university education in, for the most part, the countries of the former **USSR** and the **Western Balkans**, and to facilitate courses taught in **Central and Eastern Europe** by European Union (EU) nationals, and student and staff exchanges with EU countries. Tempus has featured also as part of the programmes providing assistance for the economic and social reform of the countries of Central and Eastern Europe (see **PHARE**) and the territories of the former USSR (see **Technical Assistance to the Commonwealth of Independent States** – TACIS), where it operated as an EU aid scheme to assist the restructuring of higher education in these states and to facilitate their development towards a market economy. The Tempus programme is, as well as being open to the eligible countries under the **CARDS** and TACIS programmes, also open to all EU Member States, the EU **candidate countries**, and Australia, Canada, **Iceland**, **Japan**, **Liechtenstein**, New Zealand, **Norway**, **Switzerland** and the **USA**. Countries outside the EU are able to participate only through co-financing projects. From 1990 to 1999 Tempus/PHARE actions received €720.9m. and from 1993 to 1999 Tempus/ TACIS actions amounted to approximately €130.2m. The programmes were to continue in the period 2000–06. Tempus has facilitated joint European projects in higher education that have resulted in joint teaching actions, the development of new courses, the promotion of links between universities and the wider community and increasing the mobility of teachers and students. Some 120,000 teachers and 35,000 students from over 2,600 institutions from the G-24 states have directly benefited from the Tempus programme.

The **TEN** or the Europe of the Ten, are terms sometimes used to describe the membership of the European Communities (EC) between January 1981, when **Greece** became the 10th Member State, and January 1986, when EC membership rose to **Twelve**.

TENDERS ELECTRONIC DAILY (TED) is an electronic information service detailing those **public procurement** contracts awarded by national and local authorities where bidding for the contract is open to any supplier within the European Union. It is operated by the **Office for Official Publications of the European Communities.**

TENs: See **Trans-European Networks**

TEU: See **Treaty on European Union**

TEXTILES: See **Multi-Fibre Arrangement**

MARGARET THATCHER (1925–), now Baroness Thatcher of Kesteven, was Prime Minister of the **United Kingdom** from 1979 to 1990. Throughout much of the 1980s she was the most forceful personality on the **European Council**, even though she often adopted an isolated position. Her first major argument with the European Communities (EC) concerned the size of the United Kingdom's contribution to the EC **budget**, and the fact that the United Kingdom, one of the poorer Member States, was the second-largest net contributor to the budget. The issue appeared on every European Council agenda between 1979 and 1984, and was related to what she saw as the profligacy of the **Common Agricultural Policy**. The issue was resolved at the 1984 **Fontainebleau Summit** with the acceptance of an adjustment mechanism that gave the United Kingdom a rebate.

Thatcher supported many of the economic goals of the EC, including liberalization and the completion of the **internal market**. Her political vision, however, was one of willing and positive co-operation between sovereign states, and she resisted all demands for political, economic and monetary union. She was a strong critic of anything that would increase the powers of the **European Commission**, which she regarded as overly bureaucratic and unrepresentative. In 1988 she denounced it for attempting to construct what she described as an 'identikit European personality' and a 'European superstate exercising dominance from Brussels'. Her views brought her into constant conflict with both the Commission and the other 11 Member States. After resigning from the premiership, she continued her criticism of the European Union (EU), particularly over the **Treaty on European Union** and **economic and monetary union.** In her 2002 book *Statecraft* Thatcher called for the United Kingdom's withdrawal from the EU.

GASTON THORN (1928–), a former Prime Minister of **Luxembourg**, served as President of the **European Commission** from 1981 to 1985. Widely perceived as a less dynamic figure than his predecessor, **Roy Jenkins**, he failed to maintain the momentum of previous years, and his Commission struggled without much success to deal with the accumulation of unresolved issues facing the European Communities.

THRESHOLD PRICE is the name of the minimum price fixed for cereals, milk products and sugar within the **Common Agricultural Policy**. Cheaper imports into the European Union (EU) are subject to a levy to raise their price to the level of the threshold price which, unlike the **target price**, includes internal transportation costs from the port of entry into the EU.

TINDEMANS REPORT is the name of a document that originated at the 1974 **summit meeting** in Paris, where the heads of government commissioned Leo Tindemans, the Prime Minister of **Belgium**, to undertake a series of consultations in the national capitals examining what might be achievable by political co-operation. The Tindemans Report was published in 1976. It proposed a common foreign policy and defence collaboration, economic and monetary union, the development of regional and social policies, a common industrial policy and a strengthened **European Commission** elected by, and accountable to, a popularly elected European legislature. It also advanced the notion of a 'two-speed' Europe, suggesting that the goals of the European Communities (EC) might be more easily achieved if all Member States were not expected to proceed at the same rate in all policy areas. Despite remaining on the agenda of all its sessions until 1978, the Report was never discussed by the **European Council**. It did, however, serve as a basis for the several reviews of the EC that occurred in subsequent years.

A **TITLE** is a sub-division of a **Part** within a European Communities treaty. Titles can in turn be divided into **Chapters**. In the **Treaty on European Union**, titles form the main sub-division of the treaty.

TOBACCO is the name of a programme dedicated to research and information into the health and social effects of tobacco.

The **TOTAL ALLOWABLE CATCH** (TAC) is a central element of the **Common Fisheries Policy**. It relates to the conservation and management of fish stocks. TACs are overall quotas, fixed annually by the **Council of the European Union**, for each species of fish that is thought to be threatened by over-fishing. Within each overall quota for the European Union, each Member State is allocated its own quota. The documentation of catches and other surveillance measures are the responsibility of the Member States. The scheme is supervised by a team of inspectors who report directly to the **European Commission**, which has the authority to impose penalties for infringements of the TAC quotas.

TOURISM is a major industry in the European Union and an important growth area for employment. There was no coherent European Communities (EC) tourism policy by the early 2000s. **European Commission** efforts to gain Member State approval of a multi-annual programme for European tourism (Philoxenia) failed. The major emphasis since has been focused on tourism within the context of employment. The **Treaty establishing a Constitution for Europe** does, however, envisage EU action complementing that of the Member States in promoting the competitiveness of undertakings in the tourism sector.

TOURS DE TABLE refers to the procedure where each national delegation at a meeting of the **Council of the European Union** is allowed to make an opening statement on their views of a particular proposal or subject. In the enlarged European Union of 25 states, such interventions could be problematic in terms of time. For example, assuming each Member State took five minutes to make its statement, this would still mean that more than two hours would elapse before any discussions proper could commence.

TOWN TWINNING was launched by the **European Commission** in 1989. Through carefully targeted grants it seeks to foster and develop further existing links between the populations of the Member States. It aims to raise awareness of other European cultures and to promote an understanding, through meetings of twinned towns and municipalities, of what European integration has achieved to date and what challenges remain. The Commission's work under this programme is divided into two areas. Under 'Town Twinning' the Commission promotes exchanges between towns across the European Union and projects that involve towns in current Member States and in **applicant countries**. To this end it supports financially exchanges between citizens and towns that are twinned, conferences and meetings on European subjects, and training seminars for organizers of town-twinning schemes. The second area deals with the co-called 'golden stars of town twinning', which is essentially an annual award presented to the towns that are judged to have done the most in forging closer links between their respective citizens.

TRADE and its development between the Member States was the initial economic objective of the European Community (EC). By 1968 internal **tariff** barriers had been removed by the **Six**, and new Member States have been given a short transitional period in which to eliminate their tariffs. The process of free trade was not completed until the implementation of the **internal market**. The European Union has become the world's largest trader, accounting for some 20% of world trade. The European Communities have agreements of various kinds – **association agreements**, **free trade agreements** and **trade and co-operation agreements** – with over 120 countries, as well as some 30 multilateral arrangements.

TRADE AND CO-OPERATION AGREEMENTS take various forms and have been concluded with a variety of states, notably those in **Central and Eastern Europe** before the negotiation of **Europe Agreements**. Such trade and co-operation agreements form part of the **common commercial policy** and normally involve preferential access to the European Communities' **internal market** and the eventual establishment of an industrial free-trade area. This is supplemented by co-operation in areas of mutual interest, often focused on facilitating trade and the economic development of the signatory state.

TRADEMARKS are important as indicators of the origin and quality of goods, but companies have had to make separate applications in each Member State to secure protection for their trademarks. Since 1980 the **European Commission** has pursued a policy of **harmonization** that envisaged a common European Union trademark that would exist alongside the national ones. (See also **Community Patent Convention**; **Office for Harmonization in the Internal Market**.)

The **TRANSATLANTIC DECLARATION** is the name of a document signed in November 1990 by the European Communities (EC) and the **USA**. It was intended, given the common heritage and the close historical, political, cultural and economic links between Europe and the USA, to form the basis of greater collaboration and co-operation between the two. The Declaration affirmed their desire for a partnership with specific goals and aspirations. These included openly supporting democracy and the rule of law and advancing respect for **human rights** and individual liberties. The signatories of the declaration sought to safeguard peace and promote international stability; to pursue policies that were targeted at advancing economic growth (such as greater liberalization and **competition policy**) and maintaining low inflation; to promote market principles; to reject all manner of protectionism; and to provide adequate support, in co-operation with other states and organizations, for the emerging liberal democracies of **Central and Eastern Europe**. The Declaration envisaged close consultation between the EC and the US government on issues of mutual concern and common interest. For example, emphasis was placed on the need to strengthen the multilateral trading system and its organizations, on promoting liberalization and on pursuing bilateral dialogue in order to reduce and eventually eliminate other non-tariff barriers that impeded trade. Also within the Declaration, attention was focused on the need to develop joint scientific research projects in areas such as high-energy physics, space policy and environment protection, as well as on extending youth and student exchanges. To facilitate such co-operation and networking the Declaration set up a regular system of biannual summits and ministerial meetings. (See also **New Transatlantic Agenda**.)

TRANS-EUROPEAN MOBILITY SCHEME FOR UNIVERSITY STUDIES: See **TEMPUS**

TRANS-EUROPEAN NETWORKS or TENs is a concept introduced by the **Treaty on European Union**, which commits the European Union (EU) to developing such networks in energy, **telecommunications** and transport through the interconnection and opening-up of national networks. The assumption is that such networks will aid both the **internal market** and social and economic cohesion within the EU. The European Communities are expected to develop common projects and provide financial assistance through, for example, the **Cohesion Fund**, while Member States are expected to co-ordinate national infrastructure projects that are likely to have a trans-European effect. The priority transport projects for development include high-speed rail links, such as the British Maritime and Cork–Dublin–Belfast–Larne rail links, a rail and road tunnel through the Brenner pass in **Italy** and a motorway linking Lisbon and Valladolid (**Spain**). The TENs scheme has since been extended into **Central and Eastern Europe**, using financial assistance from the **PHARE** programme; projects include a motorway link between Berlin and Kiev.

TRANSPARENCY is a term now used widely in the context of the need for more **openness** in and easier public access to the working of the institutions of the European Union (EU). It is hoped that increased transparency and openness will improve the **legitimacy** and **accountability** of the EU.

TRANSPORT POLICY was slow to develop in the European Communities (EC), despite being identified as an objective by the **Treaty of Rome**. The vested interests of the Member States in the question of transport – for example, road haulage quotas and licences, customs documentation, **subsidies** for **railways** and **shipping**, and the protection of national airlines – meant that little progress was made towards a common transport policy until 1982. The catalyst was an action brought by the **European Parliament** in the **Court of Justice** against the Council of Ministers (see **Council of the European Union**) for failing to fulfil the requirements of the Treaty of Rome. The Court upheld the complaint, arguing that the Council had an obligatory duty to liberalize international transport within the EC and to make it open to carriers of all Member States, and recommended the establishment of a common transport policy. The Court ruling enabled the **European Commission** to act with more vigour. In 1983 the Commission formulated a list of policy objectives: a more effective integration of national transport policies; greater productivity and efficiency through reducing the number of bureaucratic constraints and the amount of documentation; greater competition within and between different modes of transport; and **harmonization** of rules relating to working conditions, health and safety, environmental protection and technical standards. However, because of the different problems and requirements of the various transport sectors, the Commission found it difficult to develop a common transport policy. Instead, it has sought common rules and harmonization within each major sector: **air transport**, inland waterways, railways, **road transport** and shipping. Common to all sectors is a programme of support for infrastructural developments and modernization. (See also *cabotage*; **Trans-European Networks**.)

The **TREATY ESTABLISHING A CONSTITUTION FOR EUROPE** was agreed in June 2004 and, assuming **ratification** is completed, will replace the **Treaty of Rome** and the **Treaty on European Union** (TEU) as the formal legal basis of the European Union (EU). Often referred to as a **Constitutional Treaty** or the **European Constitution**, the treaty emerged out of the deliberations of the **European Convention** that adopted the **draft Treaty establishing a Constitution for Europe** and the negotiations that took place in the subsequent **intergovernmental conference**.

The Treaty establishing a Constitution for Europe envisages a range of reforms to the EU and its institutions. These include abolishing the existing **pillar** structure and granting the EU **legal personality**. New posts of **Union Minister for Foreign Affairs** and **European Council President** are planned, as are a new system of **qualified majority voting** (QMV) and a revised range of **legal instruments**. Ratification of the treaty will also result in the **Charter of Fundamental Rights** being made legally binding, increased use of QMV, the extension and a renaming of the **co-decision procedure** as the 'ordinary legislative procedure', an eventual reduction in the size of the **Commission** and changes in the rotation of the **Council presidency**. The rules governing use of **enhanced co-operation** will also be eased, a **European Public Prosecutor's Office** may be created and, for the first time, a formal mechanism for **withdrawal** from the EU will exist.

Unlike the **Single European Act** or the **Treaty on European Union**, no significant expansion of the EU's policy competences will occur if the Treaty establishing a Constitution for Europe is ratified. All the same, the list of areas in which the EU enjoys a formal competence to act is increased, mainly in recognition of existing practice. Such areas include administrative co-operation, energy, **humanitarian assistance**, intellectual property, **public health**, **space**, **sport**, and **tourism**. One new area of competence is **civil protection**. In addition, the Treaty establishing a Constitution for Europe envisages reforms to the **common foreign and security policy**, the **European security and defence policy**, EU activities regarding **police and judicial co-operation in criminal matters** and the **area of freedom, security and justice**.

Whether the Treaty establishing a Constitution for Europe will enter into force was thrown into question in early summer 2005 when electorates in **France** and the **Netherlands** voted against its ratification. For some, such a dual rejection should have seen the ratification process abandoned. Instead, it was agreed that Member States could choose for themselves whether they wished to pause for 'reflection' as the **European Council** in June 2005 agreed or push ahead. **Cyprus**, **Luxembourg** and **Malta** took the latter route while others put on hold their ratification processes, pending clarification from the French and Dutch on how they intended to proceed. For states outside the EU seeking membership, the **ratification crisis** was worrying since it threatened to postpone or derail further **enlargement**. For others, there were concerns that it would lead to a period of introspection on the part of the EU as well as political weakness – two situations that the treaty had been designed to avoid. There were also concerns that the enlarged EU would not be able to function effectively without the reforms contained in the document. This led to suggestions that alternative mechanisms might be sought to allow key elements to enter into force. Any significant progress, it was widely held, would have to await the outcome of elections in France and the Netherlands in 2007.

TREATY ESTABLISHING THE EUROPEAN ATOMIC ENERGY COMMUNITY: See **Treaty of Rome**; **European Atomic Energy Community**

TREATY ESTABLISHING THE EUROPEAN COAL AND STEEL COMMUNITY: See **Treaty of Paris**

TREATY ESTABLISHING THE EUROPEAN COMMUNITY: See **Treaty of Rome**

TREATY ESTABLISHING THE EUROPEAN ECONOMIC COMMUNITY: See **Treaty of Rome**

TREATY OF ACCESSION: See **Accession Treaty**

The **TREATY OF AMSTERDAM** was agreed in June 1997 by the **Fifteen** heads of state and government of the European Union (EU). The Treaty was signed in October 1997 and, following **ratification** by the Member States, came into force on 1 May 1999. The measures it introduced were discussed during the 1996 **intergovernmental conference** (IGC) review of the **Treaty on European Union** (TEU), which sought to address changing circumstances in **Central and Eastern Europe**, and the new arrangements that would be required on **enlargement** of the EU. The IGC also highlighted measures introduced by the TEU that had not proved effective, particularly in relation to closing the gap between national governments and the people, regarding the way the EU was developing (see **democratic deficit**). The new Treaty therefore amended and updated the TEU. It also amended the **founding treaties**, removed many obsolete provisions and renumbered the **articles** of these treaties.

High priority was given in the Treaty of Amsterdam to measures that combat high unemployment, extend citizens' rights and improve democratic **accountability** and participation in the institutions of the EU. In future, governments were to co-ordinate their employment strategies and a new **Employment Committee** was to be established to oversee the co-ordination process. Greater efforts were to be encouraged in the battle against discrimination on grounds of sex, race, ethnic origin, religion or belief, age, disability or sexual orientation. Member States were also required to address gender inequality, and protect citizens against misuse of data stored in **institutions** of the European Communities (EC). New and continued efforts in the fields of public health, the environment and sustainable development, and consumer protection were also to be encouraged. The **protocol** on social policy (see **Charter of Fundamental Social Rights**

of Workers) was incorporated into the revised **Treaty of Rome**, following the decision of the UK Labour government to sign the Charter in 1997.

The **pillar**-based system brought in by the TEU was kept, although much of the province of the **justice and home affairs** pillar was transferred to the Treaty of Rome, thereby coming under the first, or Community pillar, leaving the third pillar to deal primarily with **police and judicial co-operation in criminal matters**.

In an attempt to improve public accountability, the Treaty introduced measures to ensure greater **openness** and **transparency** by improving public access to documents originating from the institutions of the EC, and to the voting results of legislative **decisions** taken by the **Council of the European Union**. Moreover, in an attempt to counter criticisms that a democratic deficit exists within the institutions of the EU, members of **national parliaments** were to become more involved in the decision-making processes of the EU through **COSAC** (the Conference of European Affairs Committees). This group was to be encouraged to voice its opinions in specific policy areas such as fundamental rights and freedoms, justice and security, and **subsidiarity**. National parliaments were also to be given more time to debate EU issues, as the Treaty provided for a six-week interval between the tabling of legislative proposals and their placement on the Council agenda, thereby improving democratic participation.

Institutional reforms also featured in the Treaty (see Council of the European Union; **European Commission**; **European Parliament** – EP), not only to improve democracy but for practical reasons as the EU prepared for expansion. The number of **Members of the European Parliament** (MEPs) elected to the EP was to be limited to 700, and decision-making procedures were simplified. **Qualified majority voting** was extended, although unanimity was required for constitutional matters and certain policy areas, such as taxation. The authority of the Commission's President was also enhanced prior to a review of that institution before enlargement.

Moreover, membership of the EU was made more explicitly conditional. This means that successful applicants have to agree to abide by the principles of **human rights** and fundamental freedoms, liberty and democracy in relation to their citizens, as set down by the EU, or face suspension of certain membership rights, including the right to vote.

The Treaty also focused on creating a safer and stronger Europe by introducing new internal security measures, as well as measures that were intended to promote greater co-operation in foreign policy. A timetable was set within which a series of common **immigration** and **asylum** rules was to be established. Improved co-operation between national police forces and the legal systems of the Member States was also required, as was incorporation of the **Schengen Agreement** *acquis* into the treaties (although the **United Kingdom** and

Ireland were allowed an **opt-out**). Strict anti-fraud measures were to be introduced. The position of the **Court of Auditors** was to be enhanced to assist in fraud prevention, and greater co-operation between customs authorities in the Member States was to be developed. A stronger Europe in the world was also considered to be a priority, given the EU's failure to agree on a united policy during the 1990–91 hostilities in the Gulf, or in relation to the break-up of, and civil war in, the former **Yugoslavia**. The Secretary-General of the Council was to become the **High Representative** of the **common foreign and security policy**. A new unit charged with early warning, planning and analysis in EU foreign affairs was also to be created. Closer co-operation between the EU and **Western European Union** (WEU) was called for, and the possibility of the integration of WEU into the EU was raised, but the **North Atlantic Treaty Organization** (NATO) was still seen by the EU to be the main security organization for Europe.

Despite its innovations and reforms, the Treaty failed to introduce the institutional reforms necessary to prepare the EU for enlargement. Hence, even before it entered into force on 1 May 1999, preparations were being made for a further IGC that would lead to the **Treaty of Nice** in 2001.

The **TREATY OF BRUSSELS** was signed in March 1948 by the governments of the **United Kingdom**, **France** and the **Benelux** countries. It was modelled on the 1947 **Treaty of Dunkirk** and as such was an agreement on mutual military assistance against military attack from either **Germany** or, more likely, the **USSR**. It also sought to foster greater economic, social and cultural issues between the five states. The Treaty was a precursor to the **North Atlantic Treaty Organization** (NATO) in 1949 and **Western European Union** in 1954. The Treaty was largely the creation of Ernest Bevin, the United Kingdom's Foreign Secretary. This initiative was endorsed warmly by the **USA** and by many Europeans who hoped that it promised greater UK involvement in the construction of a new European order. However, the Treaty was rendered almost meaningless with the creation of NATO under US hegemony in 1949.

TREATY OF DUNKIRK was the name of a document signed in 1947 by **France** and the **United Kingdom**. Although the pact called for bilateral economic assistance and co-operation, its justification was primarily military: a guarantee of mutual aid in the event of any future German aggression. It was superseded by the **Treaty of Brussels** in 1948.

TREATY OF FRIENDSHIP is the name of the pact, also known as the Elysée Treaty, signed by **France** and the Federal Republic of **Germany** (West

Germany) on 22 January 1963. It was the only tangible result of the **Fouchet Plan** for greater political co-operation and integration, and provided for institutional co-operation between the two states in the four policy areas of defence, foreign affairs, education and culture. Strongly criticized at the time by the other members of the European Communities (EC), it became the basis of a considerable degree of liaison and regularized co-operation between the two states, and of a powerful Franco-German axis within the EC.

TREATY OF LUXEMBOURG is the name of a document signed by the Member States in April 1970. An amendment to the **Treaty of Rome**, it incorporated the new budgetary system of **own resources** into the structure of the European Communities.

The **TREATY OF NICE** was agreed in December 2000 and signed in February 2001. The **ratification** process took longer than expected after the process was thrown into doubt when in June 2001 the Irish people rejected the treaty in a referendum. As had been the case following the **ratification crisis** in 1992, when the Danish people rejected the **Treaty on European Union** (TEU), a second referendum was scheduled. This took place in October 2002 and on this occasion the Treaty was endorsed by 63% of those who voted. The Treaty was then successfully channelled through both Irish houses of parliament before finally coming into force on 1 February 2003.

The essential purpose of the Treaty was explained in its preamble: to prepare the European Union (EU) for **enlargement**. It did this by introducing a series of staged reforms to the **institutions**, notably by: reducing the size of the **European Commission** to a maximum of one national from each Member State; re-weighting votes within the **Council of the European Union**, essentially to the advantage of the larger Member States; and re-allocating seats in the **European Parliament** (EP). Moreover, Council votes and EP seats were provisionally allocated to the **candidate countries** (albeit with the exception of **Turkey**), as were seats on the **Committee of the Regions** and the **Economic and Social Committee**. The **Court of Justice** and **Court of First Instance** were also to undergo some reform: innovations included **Grand Chambers** and **Judicial Panels** in an attempt to enable the courts to deal with an already large case-load. The existence and activities of **Eurojust**, established to enable Member States to co-operate in the area of cross-border crime, were also formally recognized.

Beyond institutional reform, the Treaty of Nice introduced changes to the **common foreign and security policy** (CFSP), allowing for **enhanced co-operation** and essentially excising from the TEU references to **Western European Union**, a move that coincided with the establishment of the CFSP.

More generally, enhanced co-operation was to be facilitated by reducing the number of Member States needed to begin a project. Likewise, decision-making generally was also facilitated through the extension of **qualified majority voting** to more than 40 provisions, although unanimity was still retained for the most sensitive areas (e.g. tax **harmonization**).

Unlike earlier treaties such as the **Single European Act** and the **Treaty of Amsterdam**, the Treaty of Nice did little in the way of increasing the competences of the European Union and European Communities (EC). Little was included beyond a slight extension of the treaty-making powers of the EC to include services and the insertion into the **Treaty of Rome** of a new **title** on economic, financial and technical co-operation with third countries. However, when adopting the Treaty, the Member States set in motion a process that could lead to significant increases in the activities of the EU. Equally, it could lead to limits being placed on them. The process in question was the debate on the future of Europe, which was later expanded in the **Laeken Declaration** and provided with a forum for expression in the **European Convention** launched in February 2002. Its conclusions informed a further **intergovernmental conference** that began work in October 2003.

TREATY OF PARIS is the commonly used name of the document, signed on 18 April 1951 and designated to remain in force for 50 years, which established the **European Coal and Steel Community**. This **founding treaty** committed the signatories to contribute to economic expansion through 'the development of employment and the improvement of the standard of living in the participating countries through the institution, in harmony with the general economy of the Member States, of a common market'. Later entrants to the European Communities and European Union had to accept the terms and obligations of the Treaty, although after 2002 new members would no longer have to, as the Treaty of Paris expired in July 2002.

TREATY OF ROME is the commonly used name of the document that established the **European Economic Community** (EEC). Signed on 25 March 1957, it is the most important of the **founding treaties** of the European Communities. It was concluded for an unlimited period of time and committed the signatories, 'by establishing a **common market** and progressively approximating the economic policies of Member States, to promote throughout the Community a harmonious development of economic activities, a continuous and balanced expansion, an increase in stability, an accelerated raising of the standard of living, and closer relations between the States belonging to it'. The greater part of the Treaty lists the actions and common policies to which the Member States committed themselves, and the institutions of the new body. The

Treaty has been amended on several occasions since 1957, most significantly by the **Single European Act**, the **Treaty on European Union**, the **Treaty of Amsterdam** (which renumbered the Treaty's **articles**) and the **Treaty of Nice**. If the **Treaty establishing a Constitution for Europe** is ratified, it will replace the Treaty of Rome. The **European Atomic Energy Community** was established by a separate document, also often referred to as the Treaty of Rome, which was signed at the same time.

TREATY OF ROME (EURATOM): See **European Atomic Energy Community**; **Treaty of Rome**

TREATY OF WESTMINSTER: See **Council of Europe**

The **TREATY ON EUROPEAN UNION** (TEU) is one of the main **European treaties**. Agreed at the **Maastricht Summit** of the **European Council** in December 1991 and later signed by representatives of the Member States of the European Communities (EC) on 7 February 1992, it formally established the European Union (EU), basing it on three **pillars**: the existing EC as the first pillar and two new pillars of intergovernmental co-operation covering a **common foreign and security policy** (CFSP), and **justice and home affairs**. In doing so, the TEU also brought about a significant revision of the **Treaty of Rome**, thereby increasing the powers of the EC. The Member States, with the exception of the United Kingdom, agreed to further integration in social affairs in the form of a Social Chapter (see **Charter of Fundamental Social Rights of Workers**). Substantial institutional reforms to the EC were also introduced, as was the notion of EU **citizenship**. More significantly, the TEU laid down a detailed timetable and established **convergence criteria** for **economic and monetary union** (EMU), which was to be established by 1999 at the latest. Not all Member States wished to be tied to the goal of EMU, however. Hence special **opt-outs** were agreed for **Denmark** and the **United Kingdom**, the latter also gaining an opt-out from the Social Chapter. The opt-out did not assuage the concerns of the Danish people, however, who rejected the TEU in a referendum in June 1992. This led to a **ratification crisis** and the granting of further concessions to Denmark. In May 1993, the Danish people approved the TEU and it entered into force on 1 November 1993.

The Treaty was formally reviewed by an **intergovernmental conference** in 1996. The conference debated the measures required to address the shortfalls of the TEU, with the place of the EU in the world and its position *vis-à-vis* **enlargement** featuring prominently in debates. Measures required to move forward to a 'People's Europe' were also discussed and introduced via the

Treaty of Amsterdam, which was signed in October 1997. Amendments to the TEU made in the Treaty of Amsterdam were soon to be followed by further revision via the **Treaty of Nice**. If the **Treaty establishing a Constitution for Europe** is ratified, it will replace the TEU.

TREVI stands for *Terrorisme, Radicalisme, Extrémisme, Violence Internationale*. It was established in 1975 as a forum for intergovernmental co-operation by the Member States on matters relating to internal security, organized crime, terrorism and drugs-trafficking. It also worked for the co-ordination of **asylum policy** and **immigration policy**. Its twice-yearly meetings of justice and home affairs ministers were held in secret. A more structured approach towards these policy areas was accepted as a consequence of the decision to establish an **internal market**, and in the late 1980s several more specialized subgroups were established within the **TREVI** framework. It formed the basis of the more formal **justice and home affairs** pillar of the European Union that was established by the **Treaty on European Union**.

JEAN-CLAUDE TRICHET (1942–) became the second president of the European Central Bank in July 2003. Trichet was well-equipped for this post and was recognized as a leading authority in monetary and banking matters. His academic and professional backgrounds are steeped in the knowledge and experience of the banking sector. After obtaining a degree in economics from the University of Paris, he studied at the prestigious Ecole Nationale d'Administration before pursuing a career in the French civil service, where he spent most of his time in the Treasury. In 1987 he became director of the Treasury Department and an alternate governor of the International Monetary Fund as well as an alternate member of the World Bank. In 1993 he started his first term as governor of the Bank of France and also in this year became governor of the World Bank. The choice of Trichet as ECB president was made in 1998, as part of a Franco-German deal to share power, and Trichet might possibly have taken over even earlier had he not become embroiled in an investigation of France's Crédit Lyonnais. Trichet was cleared of any wrongdoing in June 2003 and was subsequently endorsed by all the eurozone governments.

TROIKA is a term that refers to the grouping that represents the European Union internationally as part of the **common foreign and security policy** (CFSP) and, previously, **European Political Co-operation**. Originally it comprised the Member State occupying the presidency of the **Council of the European Union**, its immediate predecessor and scheduled successor. The idea was that such a combination would achieve consistency in the activities and efforts of the European Communities and greater success in the attainment of their aims. Since the **Treaty of Amsterdam**, however, the Member State holding the presidency of the Council is accompanied by the **High Representative** for the CFSP and the member of the **European Commission** responsible for external relations.

TUNISIA: See **Maghreb States**

TURKEY, recognized by the European Communities (EC) as a European state, submitted an application for association in July 1959. Negotiations began in 1962 and concluded with an **Association Agreement** in 1963. This specified a transitional period of 22 years, commencing in 1970, that was designed to lead to a **customs union**. Further developments were delayed by EC opposition to the Turkish military coup of September 1980. Talks were resumed in 1983, after the re-establishment of civilian government, and in 1987 Turkey submitted an application for full membership. The application did not progress within the EC because of fears over Turkey's weak economy, doubts about its suitability in terms of democracy and **human rights**, and concern over the continuing partition of **Cyprus**. However, in March 1995 an agreement on a customs union was signed and came into force in December 1995, following ratification by the **European Parliament**. In spite of persisting doubts over Turkey's progress in the economic, political and human rights fields and over the Cyprus issue, Turkey's eligibility for accession to the European Union was confirmed in 1997: the country would be judged according to the same criteria as the other **applicant countries**. As a result, a number of measures were proposed by the **European Commission** in 1997 to assist the country in preparing for accession by extending its relations with the EC beyond the customs union. Turkey was not, however, invited to participate in the accession process launched in 1998. This led to a further souring of relations before the **European Council** at Helsinki in December 1999 decided to recognize Turkey, alongside the applicant countries from **Central and Eastern Europe**, as a **candidate state**. At the same time, Turkey was invited to become part of the accession process. However, **accession negotiations** did not begin. Instead, further progress with economic and political reforms was deemed necessary before they could be opened. In 2002, the **European Council** agreed to address the question of whether to open accession negotiations in December 2004. This it duly did, scheduling the formal opening of negotiations for 3 October 2005.

Before the negotiations opened, there was considerable discussion as to the desired outcome. While no Member State government was willing to oppose the possibility of Turkey joining the EU, several were sympathetic to ideas of a 'privileged partnership' ultimately being offered instead. In some Member States there was evident popular disquiet at the prospect of Turkish membership. This led to promises of a referendum in **France**, while some opposition politicians campaigned openly against Turkey being allowed to accede to the EU. How concerns will impact on the negotiations remains to be seen. What is clear is that the negotiations will take many years to complete. In June 2005 the Commission indicated that Turkey was unlikely to join the EU before 2014.

TV WITHOUT FRONTIERS: See **Cultural Policy; Media Policy**

TWELVE, or the Europe of the Twelve, are terms sometimes used to describe the membership of the European Communities after 1986, when the accession of **Portugal** and **Spain** increased the number of Member States from **Ten** to **Twelve**, and before 1995, when the accession of **Austria**, **Finland** and **Sweden** made the number **Fifteen**.

TWENTY-FIVE, or Europe of the Twenty-Five, is a term used to describe the membership of the European Union after May 2004, when **Cyprus**, the **Czech Republic**, **Estonia**, **Hungary**, **Latvia**, **Lithuania**, **Malta**, **Poland**, **Slovakia** and **Slovenia** joined the existing **Fifteen** Member States.

TWENTY-SEVEN, or Europe of the Twenty-Seven, is a term sometimes used to describe the anticipated membership of the European Union after 2007, when **Bulgaria** and **Romania** are scheduled to join the **Twenty-Five** existing Member States.

TWINNING is a programme directed at assisting the process of administrative reform in **candidate countries** in **Central and Eastern Europe**. The focus of the project is the development of the administrative capacity in these countries to implement effectively the *acquis communautaire*.

TWO-SPEED EUROPE is a more limited variant of **multi-speed Europe**.

U

UEN: See **Union for Europe of the Nations Group**

UK: See **United Kingdom**

UKRAINE gained its independence from the **USSR** in 1991. It has since concluded a **Partnership and Co-operation Agreement** (PCA) with the European Union (EU), which entered into force in 1998, and hopes to see this eventually replaced with an **association agreement**. It is also a recipient of financial assistance from the EU under the **Technical Assistance to the Commonwealth of Independent States** programme, and in 1999 was the focus of an EU **common strategy**. This is designed to support the democratic and economic transition process in Ukraine; ensure co-operation in meeting common challenges in the areas of stability and security in Europe, the environment, energy and nuclear safety; assist Ukraine's integration into the European and world economies; and enhance co-operation in the field of **justice and home affairs**. To date, Ukraine's relations with the EU have not developed much beyond the PCA, despite the Ukrainian government's wish for a more advanced form of relationship. However, with **enlargement** in 2004 meaning that Ukraine would share a border with the EU, further developments in relations can be expected. These are likely to occur within the framework of the EU's **Wider Europe – New Neighbourhood** policy. The new westward-looking Ukrainian government, under Viktor Yushchenko's presidency, has expressed strong interest in EU membership sometime in the future.

UNANIMITY applies to certain types of decision taken by the **Council of the European Union**. Its use is laid down in the **founding treaties**. Policies that are subject to unanimity require the agreement of all Member States before a proposal can be adopted. For much of the early history of the European Communities (EC), especially following the **Luxembourg Compromise**, unanimity was essential. Since the **Single European Act**, there has been a general shift away from unanimity towards greater use of **decisions** being taken under

qualified majority voting (QMV). The **Treaty on European Union**, the **Treaty of Amsterdam** and the **Treaty of Nice** have extended the use of QMV and currently far fewer decisions are subject to unanimous agreement in the Council. In contrast to pillar I (the EC), where voting by QMV is now almost the rule, areas under pillar II on the **common foreign and security policy** and those under pillar III on **police and judicial co-operation in criminal matters** are still subject to unanimity. However, even with QMV, the Council prefers to reach unanimous agreements where possible.

UNICE: See **Union of Industrial and Employers' Confederations of Europe**

UNIFORM ELECTORAL PROCEDURE relates to the method of elections to the **European Parliament** (EP). The idea that some form of uniform electoral procedure based on direct universal suffrage should be used across all Member States dates back to the **Treaty of Paris** and can be found also in Article 190 of the **Treaty of Rome**. However, despite treaty commitments there has been little progress towards any uniform procedure. Elections in the Member States and rules pertaining to them were decided at the national level. Elections to the EP first occurred in June 1979 but the procedures varied from state to state. Most countries opted for some form of proportional representation, while the **United Kingdom** maintained its 'first past the post' system that was used in elections to Parliament. The United Kingdom (with the exception of Northern Ireland, which was deemed a three-member constituency where the **Members of the European Parliament** (MEPs) are elected under the single transferable vote procedure) maintained this system until the Labour government introduced legislation to use proportional representation in the European elections of June 1999. Currently there is no single electoral procedure throughout the Member States, and voting continues to take place on different days (e.g. Thursday in the United Kingdom, Sunday in **France** and **Germany** and both Sunday and Monday in **Italy**).

The **UNION FOR EUROPE OF THE NATIONS GROUP** (UEN/UPE) is one of the **party groups** in the **European Parliament** (EP). It was formed in mid-1995 by the merger of the **Forza Europa** Group and the Gaullist **European Democratic Alliance**. This centre-right-leaning group later split and a separate and more Eurosceptic **Group for a Europe of Democracies and Diversities** (EDD) was established after the 1999 EP elections. In 2002 UEN had 21 members in the EP. After the 2004 elections it increased its representation in the parliament by securing 27 deputies. The UEN remains a multinational party comprising (at April 2006): Italian (9 deputies); Irish (4 deputies); Danish (1 deputy); Polish (10 deputies); Latvian (4 deputies); and Lithuanian (2 deputies) members and observers.

A **UNION MINISTER FOR FOREIGN AFFAIRS** is envisaged in the **Treaty establishing a Constitution for Europe** and will replace the **High Representative** for the **common foreign and security policy** (CFSP). The post-holder will be appointed by the **European Council** to chair meetings of the Council of Ministers (see **Council of the European Union**) dealing with foreign affairs and will also be a vice-president of the **European Commission**. The main responsibilities of the minister will be the conduct and development of the CFSP and the **European security and defence policy**. Assistance in fulfilling these tasks will come from a **European External Action Service**. The creation of this 'double-hatted' post is designed to provide greater coherence and prominence to the EU's role in international affairs.

The **UNION OF INDUSTRIAL AND EMPLOYERS' CONFEDERATIONS OF EUROPE** (UNICE) is a transnational federation of employers' associations. It is one of the earliest (founded in 1958) and most influential of the pressure groups (see **interest groups**; **lobbying**) operating in Brussels. UNICE represents the interests of industry as a whole, and is a confederation comprising national federations of major business associations from across Europe. For example, it includes the Confederation of British Industry and the Irish Business and Employers Confederation, as well as groups from the largest states such as the German Confederation for Industry (*Bundesverband der Deutschen Industrie*) and the smallest states such as the **Malta** Confederation of Industry. In 2006 there were 39 members from 33 countries, including the **European Union** countries, the **European Economic Area** countries, and some central and Eastern European countries. UNICE plays both an informal and a formal role in European public affairs. On an informal level, UNICE meets **European Commission** officials on an almost daily basis, and on a more formal level is frequently asked for its views on policy initiatives. UNICE's priorities centre on market liberalization and deregulation. It remains much more unenthusiastic, however, about initiatives in the area of social policy. UNICE has as one of its objectives the promotion and elaboration 'of an industrial policy in a European spirit', which is qualified by the statement that it 'should mainly consist in taking into consideration the industrial imperatives in the various policies of the European Communities and not become an instrument of intervention'. UNICE has therefore tended to oppose measures such as the proposed **Company Law Statute**, which threatened to place restraints upon its members, although on occasions its impact on the European Communities has been weakened by differences of interest between both its economic and its national components. UNICE operates as one of the Commission's **social partners** alongside the **European Trade Union Confederation**. UNICE's activities can be grouped under six key headings. These strive to release entrepreneurial energy; to boost innovation; to unleash the **internal market** of 25+; to improve the functioning of the labour market; to make environmental policy more effective and efficient and to foster international trade and investment.

UNION OF SOVIET SOCIALIST REPUBLICS: See **USSR**

The **UNITED KINGDOM**, in terms of its resistance to European integration, has been widely regarded as one of the most problematic members of the European Communities (EC), and later of the European Union (EU). In 1945 British prestige in Europe was very high, and in many states there was an expectation and hope that the United Kingdom would take the lead in developing European integration. However, British policy was to seek nothing more than intergovernmental co-operation, and the United Kingdom avoided involvement in any partnership that might diminish its own sovereignty and affect its relations with the **USA** and the Commonwealth. Europe was seen as an important issue, but it ranked behind both of these. Consequently, the United Kingdom dismissed the European initiatives contained within the **European Coal and Steel Community**, the **European Economic Community** (EEC) and the **European Atomic Energy Community**. The United Kingdom finally applied for membership of the EEC in 1961 and again in 1967, but both applications were effectively vetoed by **France** under President **Charles de Gaulle**. Negotiations recommenced in 1970, and the United Kingdom became a member of the European Communities (EC) in January 1973. Both major political parties, however, were divided over the merits of membership.

After 1973, the United Kingdom was often seen as only a partial member of the EC. It demanded and obtained a renegotiation of its terms of entry in 1975, and waged a campaign until 1984 for a reduction of what it regarded as its excessive contribution to the EC **budget**. Although the United Kingdom was at the forefront of plans for the **internal market**, its Prime Minister, **Margaret Thatcher**, grew increasingly hostile to the process of European integration by the late 1980s, and was particularly opposed to plans towards **economic and monetary union** (EMU). The United Kingdom has frequently maintained a position of complete isolation in the **European Council** and the Council of Ministers (now the **Council of the European Union**). For example, the United Kingdom declined full membership of the **European Monetary System** until October 1990: even then, as a result of speculative pressure on sterling, it withdrew from the **exchange-rate mechanism** in September 1992. The United Kingdom also negotiated exemptions, or **opt-outs**, from parts of the **Treaty on European Union**, most notably from the Social Chapter (see **Charter of Fundamental Social Rights of Workers**), and from the **Treaty of Amsterdam**, which incorporated the **Schengen Agreement**. However, the Labour government, which came to power in 1997, agreed to sign the Social Chapter shortly after coming into office, and hence the **protocol** on social policy was incorporated by the Treaty of Amsterdam into the revised **Treaty of Rome**. Although often hostile to moves towards political integration, the United Kingdom has been a strong advocate of economic reform, supporting **freedom of movement** and the internal market. It refused, however, to join EMU, which came into operation in January 1999. The United Kingdom strongly supported **European political co-operation** and its replacement, the **common foreign and security policy**, and it has a reasonably good record of compliance with EC **legislation**. The government led by **Tony Blair** has been very pro-active in pushing EU integration (e.g. promoting a **European rapid reaction force**), but in general the United Kingdom has adapted less easily to EU membership than most other EU Member States. Public opinion in the country remains highly divided as to the desirability of membership of the EU and of joining EMU and adopting the **euro**. The UK government has also pledged to hold a referendum on the **European Constitution** and this was originally scheduled to take place in 2006. Opinion in the country was certainly divided, although most opinion polls predicted that any referendum on the **Treaty establishing a Constitution for Europe** would be rejected. This outcome seemed even more likely following events in France and the **Netherlands,** and in June 2005 the UK government announced that it would shelve any such referendum, at least for the time being. The UK took up the presidency of the European Council in the latter half of 2005, at a more troubled time than had been expected, and found itself trying to advance its arguments for more liberalization and economic reform while also having to deal with the issue of the budget, the reform of the agricultural policy and the future direction and priorities of the EU itself. All were particularly controversial and getting agreement was going to be extremely difficult. This presidency sought to make the single market work better, but in retrospect never managed to escape the more pressing issues outlined above. They dominated the UK's discussions with all the other Member States as all participants prepared for the crunch meeting to determine the budget in December 2005. Agreement on securing the commencement of **accession negotiations** with Turkey is clearly one of the highpoints of the UK presidency, alongside the deal on the budget. Both were achieved after much internal bickering and disagreements, and this disharmony may be the lasting memory of this particular presidency for some time to come.

The **UNITED KINGDOM BUDGET REBATE** or the 'British Budgetary Question' (BBQ) resurfaced as a major and controversial issue in discussions over the future financing of the EU at a **European Council** summit in **Luxembourg** in June 2005. The issue had lain dormant for a number of years, but is now a major point of disagreement between the Member States. The **United Kingdom** (UK) rebate was negotiated by Prime Minister **Margaret Thatcher** after a long battle (and 'handbagging') at practically every European Council summit meeting between 1979 and 1984. In the end a deal was reached, essentially between **François Mitterrand**, **Helmut Kohl** and Margaret Thatcher, at the **Fontainebleau Summit** in 1984 to settle the BBQ and to allow the EU time to pursue the **single market** programme. The UK's annual rebate is roughly worth about £3 billion, but it was only designed or agreed to as a temporary measure. The rebate was intended to make up the shortfall between what the UK paid into the EU **budget** and what it received back. The UK argued that the difference was significant because some 60% of the EU budget went towards the **Common Agricultural Policy**, a fund from which the UK was not a major recipient. Another issue that should be factored into understanding the UK arguments for the rebate was the much weaker economic position of the UK in the 1980s. The actuality and desirability of the UK rebate has appeared sporadically on the EU agenda over the course of the last 20 years – particularly whenever the Member States have been considering the overall composition of the budget. It surfaced in March 1999 at the Berlin summit of the **European Council** and emerged again in the deliberations for the next financial period that runs from 2007 to 2013. Other Member States, such as **Germany** and the **Netherlands**, also expressed an interest in achieving their own rebate. President **Jacques Chirac** has long questioned the need for the UK rebate, but **Tony Blair** stated that he was unwilling to consider its curtailment unless major reforms were made to how agriculture was financed. This stance opened up an immediate battle with **France**, the largest recipient of CAP spending, and relations between Chirac and Blair took an extremely frosty turn for most of the UK presidency. An agreement on the budget was finally reached in December 2005, whereby the UK gave back some of its rebate in return for the promise of a wholesale review of the CAP in 2008.

The **UNITED NATIONS** (UN) is one arena where **European political co-operation** and the **common foreign and security policy** have been, generally, applied successfully. The permanent representatives to the UN of the European Union (EU) Member States continue to meet regularly, to ensure that the Member States vote together in as many divisions within the UN General Assembly as possible. In addition, the foreign minister of the Member State currently holding the presidency of the **Council of the European**

Union addresses the opening session of the UN each September on behalf of the EU.

UNITED STATES OF AMERICA: See **USA**

UPE: See **Union For Europe of the Nations Group**

URBAN is the acronym of a 1994 initiative intended to promote the proliferation of innovative ideas and actions by means of their exchange between cities in the European Union, and to develop co-operative networks for the exchange of experience. Funded via the **European Regional Development Fund**, the current initiative, URBAN II, covers the period 2000 until 2006. In the United Kingdom, Northern Ireland is a recipient of URBAN II funding, which is designed to assist urban regeneration of inner North Belfast.

URUGUAY ROUND is the name of a series of talks within the **General Agreement on Tariffs and Trade** (GATT). They began in 1986 and were initially due to be completed by the end of 1990. They were hindered by several disagreements over various aspects of the attempt to extend GATT rules beyond manufactured products to a variety of other areas, including services and intellectual copyright, and were eventually blocked by an impasse between the **USA** and the European Communities (EC), primarily over agriculture (with **France** being the most vocal defender of the EC agricultural policy regime). Risking collapse on several occasions, the Round was eventually concluded in 1994, after France had agreed to accept the inclusion of agriculture in the agreement, resulting in a World Trade Agreement, leading to the creation of a **World Trade Organization**.

The **US–EC DECLARATION** of 20 November 1990 was an attempt to place the relationship between the **USA** and the European Communities (EC) on a more regularized base. Its major element was an agreement on the need for a framework within which consultations could be held on political and economic issues of interest to both sides, and since 1991 regular biannual meetings have been held. (See **Transatlantic Declaration**.)

The **USA** (United States of America) made a major contribution to the development of European integration in the form of its strong involvement in European affairs after 1945, especially its provision of economic assistance (see **Marshall Plan**) and a defensive shield (see **North Atlantic Treaty Organization**), with the benefit of which the Western European states had the time to consider and explore ways of closer collaboration. Itself a federation, the USA encouraged efforts at integration until the 1960s, and did not seem to be averse to the notion of political union. After the 1960s, relations between the European Communities (EC) and the USA became more strained. While to some extent this has been due to political arguments over foreign and defence policy, the major point of difference has been economic. As the EC grew to be a more integrated economic entity, a conflict of interest developed with the USA, which was both a major economic rival and the EC's most important trading partner. Threats of action and retaliation from across the Atlantic, which reached their peak during the **Uruguay Round**, became commonplace, but disputes have usually been resolved eventually by some form of compromise. (See **bananas**.)

During the 1990s, relations between the EC and the USA were institutionalized via a number of initiatives. The **Transatlantic Declaration** of 1990 provided a basis for greater collaboration and co-operation, and was followed in 1995 by the launch of a New **Transatlantic Agenda**. As a consequence of this, in May 1998 a Transatlantic Economic Partnership was initiated. In its draft Action Plan for the Partnership, the **European Commission** proposed that the European Union (EU) and the USA stimulate trade liberalization at world-wide level. Efforts to achieve such a goal have often been hindered by EU–US trade disputes. Equally, relations have often been soured as a consequence of major differences over, for example, the Middle East and the war in Iraq. Annual summits nevertheless provide opportunities to stress the extent to which the EU and the USA do co-operate in an ever wider range of areas, including for example sharing information on competition policy cases.

The **USSR** (Union of Soviet Socialist Republics) was the major European military power after 1945 and unwittingly influenced the development of integration in Western Europe by arousing fears about its own power and intentions. Its actions in Eastern Europe between 1945 and 1948 persuaded many Western states of the virtues of collaboration, at least in the form of a collective security system, and led them to urge greater involvement of the **USA** in Europe. The USSR remained hostile to Western European integration on both economic and political grounds, and only in 1988 did it declare a willingness to enter into discussions with the European Communities on a possible trading agreement. Since then, the USSR has disintegrated, with most of the successor states becoming part of the **Commonwealth of Independent States** and concluding **Partnership and Co-operation Agreements** with the European Union (EU). The three Baltic States – **Estonia**, **Latvia** and **Lithuania** – are the main exceptions, having concluded **Europe Agreements** and having now gained EU membership, which all three countries applied for in 1995.

V

V: See **Group of the Greens/European Free Alliance**

VAL DUCHESSE is a château on the outskirts of **Brussels** variously associated with the European Communities and the European Union. It was at Val Duchesse that the **Spaak Report** was drawn up in 1955–56. More recently, in 1985, the château gave its name to the process of social dialogue between the employers represented by the **Union of Industrial and Employers' Confederations of Europe** (UNICE), employees represented by the **European Trade Union Confederation** (ETUC), and the European Centre of Public Enterprises.

VALUE-ADDED TAX (VAT) is the second most important source of **revenue** for the European Communities (EC), and represented 14.4% of the total revenue in 2005. (The most important source of revenue is based on gross national income (GNI) and accounts for around 73% of total EU revenue.) Traditional **own resources** (TOR) are the third most important and comprise customs duties, agricultural duties and sugar levies. These own resources are levied on economic operators and collected by Member States on behalf of the EU, and make up just under 12% of the budget.

In 1967 two **directives** obliged all Member States that had not already done so to introduce a system of VAT as the third major element of indirect taxation by 1970. New members have also had to introduce a VAT system. With the introduction of own resources to fund the budget, the EC was to receive up to a maximum of 1.0% of the VAT collected by the Member States. In 1986 this was increased to 1.4%. By 2000 the percentage had been reduced to 1.0% and fell back further, to 0.75%, in 2002; it was reduced further, to 0.50%, in 2004.

A second dimension to VAT is the issue of **harmonization**. As part of the **internal market** programme, an attempt to introduce a greater degree of harmonization was made by Francis Cockfield in his **White Paper** (see **internal market**). This was only partially successful, and the Member States continued to contribute moderately different VAT rates. In 1992, however, formal agreement was reached on a minimum standard rate of 15%. This was subsequently confirmed in 1996 when informal agreement was also reached on a maximum rate of 25%. Certain goods remain 'zero-rated' or appear on a special list subject to 'reduced rates' of VAT. Clearly, full harmonization is far from having been achieved. Moreover, the determination of several Member States to make certain that the harmonization of VAT rates specifically, and indirect taxes in general, continues to be subject to voting by **unanimity** looks likely to ensure that it remains an elusive goal.

VAN GEND EN LOOS is the shortened name of a case, *Van Gend en Loos v Nederlandse Administratie der Belastingen*, that was heard by the **Court of Justice** in 1962. The Court ruled that European Communities **law** was a new legal order, directly applicable in the Member States, and that individuals were required to be aware of this.

VARIABLE GEOMETRY is a phrase that was coined by **Jacques Delors** in the early 1980s and used widely to refer to the possibility of common policies being developed and implemented at different rates by the Member States, depending upon their degree of commitment to each policy. Reminiscent of the notion of a **two-speed Europe** raised by the 1976 **Tindemans Report**, it met with strong criticism from countries wary of political union. All the same, it has come to characterize aspects of the European Union's activities, notably **economic and monetary union** and the **area of freedom, security and justice** where certain Member States enjoy **opt-outs**.

VAT: See **Value-Added Tax**

GÜNTHER VERHEUGEN (1944–) was born in Bad Kreuznach, **Germany**, and initially trained as a journalist before studying history, sociology and politics in Cologne and Bonn in the later 1960s. He worked as a civil servant in the Federal Ministry of the Interior and then the Federal Foreign Office before being elected as a deputy for the Social Democratic Party in 1983. Thereafter he took a keen interest in foreign affairs, serving as a member of the Foreign Affairs committee from 1983 (and also chaired the parliament's European Union Special committee in 1992) until he was appointed as Minister of State in the Foreign Office in 1998. He was appointed to the **Prodi** Commission in September 1999 and served his term as the Commissioner for Enlargement. He quickly emerged as a highly competent individual and was re-appointed (as one of only three commissioners from the Prodi team) to the new **Barroso** Commission by the German government in 2004. In November 2004 he assumed responsibility for the Enterprise and Industry portfolio and was also made one of the five vice-presidents of the Commission. His portfolio is largely a new departure for someone who has specialized and is more familiar with foreign affairs. It will be interesting to see how he handles this portfolio, particularly given Germany's increasing dissatisfaction with Brussels **regulations**.

VERs: See **Voluntary Export Restraints**

VETO refers to the option available to each Member State in the **Council of the European Union** to reject proposals put before it. Thanks to the **Luxembourg Compromise**, the option to veto survived almost unscathed until the mid-1980s. Since then, and thanks mainly to the increased use and acceptance of **qualified majority voting**, the use of the veto is essentially restricted to areas (e.g. tax **harmonization**, the admission of new Member States, treaty reform) where **unanimity** is still required under the treaties. In practice, the veto is rarely used.

A **VISA POLICY** was established by the **Treaty on European Union** (TEU), which declared the aim of developing such a policy, applicable throughout the European Union, for nationals from third countries. The TEU demanded the establishment of a common format for all visas before January 1996, by which time visa policy decisions would require only a **qualified majority vote** in the **Council of the European Union**. The visa policy does not prevent Member States from pursuing their own policies with regard to internal security and the maintenance of law and order. The **Treaty of Amsterdam** was also concerned that there should be greater co-operation over visa policies.

The **VISEGRAD GROUP** originally consisted of **Czechoslovakia, Hungary** and **Poland** when it was created in 1991–92 as a mechanism for the three states to support each other in efforts to pursue closer integration with Western European organizations, notably the European Communities. In 1993 membership rose to four countries when the **Czech Republic** and **Slovakia** replaced the now-disbanded Czechoslovakia. Among the activities of the Visegrad group was the establishment of the **Central European Free Trade Association** (CEFTA). The extension of CEFTA to include other countries from **Central and Eastern Europe** and Slovakia's slower progress towards European Union membership during the mid-1990s led to the effective demise of the Visegrad Group. Bilateral co-operation between the members has nevertheless continued.

VOLUNTARY EXPORT RESTRAINTS (VERs) are bilateral agreements reached by the European Communities (EC) with other countries, whereby the latter voluntarily agree to limit exports of particular products to the European Union. The restraints are not in fact truly voluntary, but have been accepted by the exporting countries in preference to other restrictions that might be imposed. The best-known VERs have related to trade in **steel** and cars. The **European Commission** has a mandate to negotiate VERs on behalf of the EC.

The **WARSAW PACT** was the name of the **Cold War** alliance of Eastern European countries led by the **USSR** that regarded itself as a mutual defence organization against the ambitions of the **North Atlantic Treaty Organization** (NATO). It derived its name from the Warsaw Treaty of Friendship, Co-operation and Mutual Assistance that was signed by the USSR, **Albania, Bulgaria**, Czechoslovakia, **Hungary, Poland** and **Romania** in May 1955. The Warsaw Pact was dissolved in 1991 following the fragmentation of the USSR.

WATER and its pollution are major European Communities (EC) concerns, and a number of **European Commission directives** have been aimed at improving the quality and protection of water in all its aspects. High standards have been set for the quality of both drinking and bathing water, and Member States risk punitive action if they do not meet the required standards within stipulated deadlines. Further directives relate to fish habitats and the discharge of pollutants. The EC have also signed several international conventions designed to reduce the level of water pollution. (See also **environmental policy**.)

The **WERNER REPORT** is the name of a 1970 plan for **economic and monetary union** (EMU) prepared by a committee, headed by Pierre Werner (1913–2000), then Prime Minister of **Luxembourg**, which was appointed by the 1969 **Hague Summit**. The Report emphasized the need for the European Communities to proceed simultaneously in co-ordinating and harmonizing economic policy, narrowing exchange-rate margins, integrating capital markets and establishing a common currency and a **European Central Bank**. It presented a three-stage programme for the implementation of full EMU by 1980, the deadline imposed by its remit. Although its views were accepted in a modified format by the Council of Ministers (see **Council of the European Union**), the economic difficulties of the 1970s led to the programme's abandonment. The question of full EMU was not considered again fully until **Jacques Delors** was appointed by the Council in 1988 to consider the EMU question, and this led directly on this occasion to a specific title on EMU being inserted into the **Treaty of Rome** by the **Treaty on European Union**.

WEST GERMANY: See **Germany**

The **WESTERN BALKANS**, as far as the European Union (EU) is concerned, comprises **Albania**, **Bosnia-Herzegovina**, **Croatia**, the Former Yugoslav Republic of **Macedonia** and **Serbia and Montenegro**. Currently they are involved in a **stabilization and association process** with the EU. The EU continues to support political stabilization and economic development in this region, and provided some €483m. in 2006 to the above countries (through the **CARDS** programme) to anchor the democratization process and promote economic growth.

WESTERN ECONOMIC SUMMITS: See **G-8**

WESTERN EUROPEAN UNION (WEU) originated in the 1948 **Treaty of Brussels** and was designed to promote co-operation in the fields of defence and security. After the collapse of the **European Defence Community** (EDC) proposals in 1954, the Treaty was used to establish a body 'to promote the unity and to encourage the progressive integration of Europe', which included the Federal Republic of **Germany** (West Germany) and **Italy** in addition to the original five signatories (**Belgium**, **France**, **Luxembourg**, the **Netherlands** and the **United Kingdom**). WEU had little infrastructure, and was only occasionally activated in the 1950s. Its military functions were more or less immediately absorbed by the **North Atlantic Treaty Organization** (NATO) after 1949, and it ceded its social and cultural responsibilities to the **Council of Europe** in 1960, in effect becoming moribund. Some attempts to revive it were made in the 1960s and 1970s, but it was not until 1984, partly as a result of the growing *rapprochement* between the **USA** and the **USSR** that it was reactivated as a body that could provide a distinctive Western European voice on defence and security issues.

In 1987 it adopted a programme that called for the creation of a 'cohesive European defence identity', strengthening conventional capabilities while retaining nuclear potential, improving consultation and co-operative mechanisms, and establishing a common system of monitoring obligations. The **Treaty on European Union** made WEU an integral part of the European Union (EU), identifying it as a *de facto* constituent of the pillar of **common foreign and security policy** (CFSP). The EU was to 'foster closer institutional relations with the WEU with a view to the possibility of the integration of the WEU into the Union'. WEU moved its headquarters to Brussels, granted observer status to other Western European countries, and engaged in discussions on closer ties with countries from **Central and Eastern Europe**. Consequently, by 2002,

28 countries enjoyed one of four different types of status with regard to WEU. These ranged from membership through associate membership and observer status to associate partner. All EU Member States, with the exception of **Austria**, **Denmark**, **Finland**, **Ireland** and **Sweden**, which hold observer status, are full members of WEU.

The pursuit of closer co-operation between the Member States of the EU and WEU was further encouraged by the **Treaty of Amsterdam**. Moreover, the **Treaty of Nice** paved the way for the *de facto* incorporation of WEU into the EU by reducing the status of WEU and establishing a **European security and defence policy**. The Treaty effectively removed various references to WEU from the TEU, with the most visible representation of the incorporation of WEU into the EU being **Javier Solana**'s new dual roles as both Secretary-General of WEU and the **Secretary-General of the Council of the European Union**.

WEU: See **Western European Union**

WHITE PAPER is the term used to describe a **European Commission** document setting out proposed legislative initiatives, such as, for example, the 2001 White Paper on **Governance** or the 2006 White Paper on a **European Communication Policy**. In some cases they follow a **Green Paper**, which is used by the Commission to launch a full-scale public discussion on a proposal. The document produced in 1985 by Francis Cockfield for the European Commission on the measures required to implement the **internal market** by 1992 is still the most widely known example. Entitled *Completing the Internal Market*, it listed some 300 separate measures that would need to be taken, for each of which a target date and a timetable were set. The measures related to the removal of physical, technical and fiscal barriers to a single market. To facilitate their implementation, appropriate provisions were incorporated into the 1987 **Single European Act** and, by 1992, most of the measures had been introduced. When a White Paper has been endorsed enthusiastically by the **Council of the European Union**, it becomes the action programme for the European Union in that specific policy area.

WIDENING involves extending the membership of the European Union (EU) through the process of **enlargement**. For much of the history of the EU, widening has been subordinate to **deepening**.

The **WIDER EUROPE – NEW NEIGHBOURHOOD** initiative was launched by the European Union (EU) in 2003 in order to place relations with regions bordering on the EU of **Twenty-five** on a new footing. See **European Neighbourhood Policy**

HAROLD WILSON (1916–95), later Baron Wilson of Rievaulx, was Prime Minister of the **United Kingdom** from 1964 to 1970 and again from 1974 to 1976. He submitted the second UK application to join the European Communities (EC) in 1967, reversing Labour Party policy. However, after 1970 he attacked the terms of entry negotiated by the Conservative government, and upon his return to office in 1974 sought their renegotiation. Talks with the EC were completed in January 1975, and the new terms were subsequently endorsed in a referendum on whether the United Kingdom should remain in the EC, held in June 1975. The result showed a clear majority in favour of continued membership (67.2%). However, the renegotiations and referendum deepened the divisions within the Labour Party over EC membership, and became one of the reasons why **Roy Jenkins** and others subsequently left the party.

WINE LAKE, like **butter mountain**, is a term, usually of derision, that has been employed to symbolize the consequences of the price guarantee and intervention elements of the **Common Agricultural Policy**. It referred to the large surplus stocks of wine created by over-production.

WITHDRAWAL from the EU has rarely been seriously contemplated by any Member State, although **Greenland**, as part of **Denmark**, did withdraw in 1985. With increasing evidence of **Euroscepticism** and concerns among some Member States over the future path of integration, the **Treaty establishing a Constitution for Europe** includes a dedicated withdrawal clause. This will allow a Member State to withdraw from the EU provided it notifies the **European Council** of its intention. An agreement setting out the arrangements for withdrawal is then to be concluded by the Council, acting by a two-thirds majority and after obtaining the assent of the **European Parliament**. Withdrawal will take place two years at the latest after the notification to withdraw has been received by the European Council.

WITHDRAWAL PRICES: See **Common Fisheries Policy**

WOMEN'S RIGHTS have become an important European Communities (EC) concern, based initially upon Article 141 of the **Treaty of Rome**. The Article, as amended by the **Treaty of Amsterdam**, committed the Member

States to ensuring that 'the principle of equal pay for male and female workers for equal work or work of equal value is applied'. Various **directives** require the Member States to amend their laws to exclude any form of sex discrimination and to ensure equality in training, appointments, promotion and pay. Workers who believe they are the victims of discrimination have the right to take their case to a tribunal without fear of dismissal: the **Court of Justice** can act as the final arbiter as to whether national laws conflict with EC rules. Discrimination in social security systems was banned in 1978, and in 1986 it was decreed that discrimination in occupational pension schemes had to end by 1993. In 1997 the **Council of the European Union** adopted a directive on sex-discrimination cases, whereby the plaintiff and defendant were to share the burden of proof. The **European Commission** has also launched a number of special action schemes. In May 1998 the European Union's first conference on women's employment was held in Belfast. (See also **Equal Opportunities**.)

WORKER PARTICIPATION: See **Charter of Fundamental Social Rights of Workers**; **Fifth Directive**; **Workers' Rights**

WORKERS' RIGHTS were referred to in the **Treaty of Rome**, which obliged the Member States to promote the improvement of living and working conditions for workers and required Member States to collaborate on a number of questions relating to employment. Most European Communities activity has been devoted to improving working conditions through the implementation of several **directives** on occupational **health and safety** (see **European Foundation for the Improvement of Living and Working Conditions**; **Mines Safety and Health Commission**). Other directives relate to the principle of **freedom of movement**. Restrictions on free movement can be applied by the Member States only on grounds of a risk to public order, safety or health, or where jobs are in a particular sector of public administration. Persistent efforts by the **European Commission** to establish worker participation in company decision-making (see **Fifth Directive**) first achieved success when all the Member States except the **United Kingdom** decided to implement the **Charter of Fundamental Social Rights of Workers**; the United Kingdom eventually signed up to the Charter in 1997 after the election of a Labour government. Workers' rights are also prominent in the **Charter of Fundamental Rights** proclaimed in December 2000.

The **WORKING TIME DIRECTIVE** (WTD) aims to protect the health and safety of workers against the adverse effects of working long hours without adequate breaks. It also addresses disrupted working patterns and sets a maximum working week of 48 hours within any four-month period. Guidelines relating to daily rest times, weekly rest periods, minimum holiday entitlements and night-shift working are also included. Certain categories of workers, including those employed in oil extraction and transport, and junior doctors in training are excluded from the **directive** at present.

The 1993 Working Time Directive has a treaty basis under Article 138 of the **Treaty of Rome**, which was incorporated into the Treaty as part of the **Single European Act** in 1986. Approval of measures is by **qualified majority voting**. The **United Kingdom** opposed the directive and was successful in obtaining an **opt-out**. This allows Member States not to apply the limit to working hours under certain conditions. Following the adoption of the **Charter of Fundamental Social Rights of Workers** by the Labour government in 1997, however, the Working Time Directive became effective in the United Kingdom in September 1998. (See also **health and safety**.) The original Working Time Directive (93/104/EC) covered all sectors of activity except transport, activities at sea and the activities of doctors who are training. The provisions of the WTD did not apply if other European Union (EU) law contained more specific provisions in a particular field or if national laws contained provisions that were more favourable to workers.

It provided for: a maximum 48-hour working week averaged over a reference period; a minimum daily rest period of 11 consecutive hours a day; a rest break where the working day is longer than six hours; a minimum rest period of one day a week; and a statutory right to annual paid holiday of four weeks; night working must not exceed eight hours a night on average. Normal hours of work for night workers must not exceed an average of eight hours in any 24-hour period. Workers are entitled to a free medical examination before being employed on night work and at regular intervals thereafter. Anyone suffering from health problems connected with night work must be transferred, wherever possible, to day work. The issue of the WTD remains highly topical and controversial. In 2000 the scope of the WTD was extended to include some previously excluded professions (doctors in training, transport workers, activities at sea) to cover some 5m. people. In 2003 the **Commission** issued a Communication on the review of the directive which analyses the opt-outs and derogations in Member States, and summarizes recent case law concerning the definition of working time. This consultation period ran until the end of March 2004 and fed into a new Commission proposal that still contained an opt-out, but one that made it more difficult for employers to press staff against their will to work for any longer than 48 hours. The sensitivities that working hours still cause for some Member States, including especially the United Kingdom but also **Germany, Malta, Poland, Slovakia** and **Slovenia,** became apparent in the spring of 2005 when the **European Parliament** voted in its first reading of the proposal to phase-out the opt-out over a three year period. The **ETUC** strongly supports the ending of the opt-out as do some of the UK's main trade unions, but **Tony Blair** has consistently resisted any such moves and has sought to garner enough support in other Member States to form at least a blocking minority in the Council. This strategy is working for the moment: the UK government won the first round of the battle on the European working time directive in June 2005, when the Council voted to maintain the opt-out.

The **WORLD TRADE ORGANIZATION** (WTO) was established on 1 January 1995 as the successor to the **General Agreement on Tariffs and Trade** (GATT). The origins of both GATT and the WTO can be traced back to the late 1940s and efforts to liberalize international trade by reducing the levels of tariffs. By the 1990s the agenda of international discourse on trade issues had widened considerably with a series of policy issues requiring consideration at a multilateral level. These included **competition policy, environmental policy** and approaches to labour market deregulation. GATT had been a fruitful exercise, but was limited in its scope and for this reason it was decided to establish a new organization that became the WTO, which, in 2002, comprised 144 member countries. The WTO has a much broader scope than GATT. Whereas GATT regulated trade in merchandise goods, the WTO also covers trade in services, such as telecommunications and banking. The highest body of the WTO is the Ministerial Conference. This meets every two years and, among other things, elects the organization's chief executive – the director-general – and oversees the work of the General Council. The General Council is in charge of the day-to-day running of the WTO and is made up of ambassadors from Member States who also serve on various subsidiary and specialist committees. The WTO has a crucial role to play in ensuring, promoting and protecting trade liberalization. It serves as a forum to settle disputes – these have occurred between the European Union and the **USA** over such issues as **bananas**, hormone-treated beef and hush kits (noise reduction devices) for aircraft – and may operate as the ideal body for settling cases on competition policy that involve European and North American companies. Despite the apparent logic of such an international forum to resolve disputes, there has been growing unease and dissatisfaction among sections of the public about the democratic credentials of this body. Four main criticisms abound. These are: firstly, that the WTO is too powerful; secondly, the belief that the WTO only serves the needs of the rich states and is largely indifferent to the needs of the economically less advanced states; thirdly, that the WTO is indifferent to the impact of free trade on workers' rights, child labour, the environment and health; and lastly, that this organization lacks democratic **accountability**. This discontent was, in the early 2000s, manifest in street protests and a series of violent confrontations between protesters and the police at meetings of the WTO in response to the perceived threat of **globalization**. In September 2002 the former Thai deputy prime minister, Dr Supachai Panitchpakdi, began a three-year term as Director-General and was charged with pursuing the **Doha Round**. He was the first WTO head to come from a developing nation. As a respected economist, he played a key role in leading Thailand out of the Asian currency crisis. In September 2003 the world trade talks in Cancún, Mexico, collapsed after four days of wrangling over farm subsidies and access to markets. Many commentators maintain that the failure to reach agreement will hit the poorest nations hardest. Pessimism intensified when the WTO announced that there was little hope of restarting the collapsed world trade talks in December of that year because both the developing countries and the rich nations seemed unable to agree on the scope of trade negotiations and the need to reduce agricultural subsidies. Nevertheless, agreement was attained in Geneva in August 2004 when talks achieved consensus on a framework agreement on opening up global trade. The United States and the European Union will reduce agricultural subsidies, while developing nations will cut tariffs on manufactured goods. In December 2005 Saudi Arabia became the 149th member of the WTO, and membership negotiations with Viet Nam were in the final stages in April 2006. Russia continues to seek admission, but must first convince the EU and US that it has reformed business practices. In September 2005 Frenchman Pascal Lamy became the fifth Director-General of the WTO, beginning a new four-year term.

WTO: See **World Trade Organization**

XYZ

YAOUNDÉ CONVENTION is the name of an agreement signed in 1963 and renegotiated in 1969. Named after the capital of Cameroon, the Convention provided for the former colonial territories of the Member States to be associated with the **European Economic Community**. Eighteen countries, known collectively as the Associated African States and Madagascar, were signatories of the Convention. They were permitted duty-free access to the European Communities for most of their products on a non-reciprocal basis and were eligible for grants from the **European Development Fund** and loans from the **European Investment Bank**. The Yaoundé Convention was superseded in 1975 by the **Lomé Convention**.

YOUTH FOR EUROPE is the name of a programme established in 1987 to promote a sense of European identity and understanding among young people. It is a scheme enabling young people not engaged in higher education to spend at least one week in another European Union country. Participants are expected to have already received some instruction about socio-cultural aspects of the country they wish to visit. The scheme is modelled on the successful bilateral youth exchange programme between **France** and the Federal Republic of **Germany** (West Germany), which began in the 1950s. Youth for Europe was renewed in 1991 for three years, and was subsequently extended until 1999. It was replaced by the **Youth Programme** in 2000.

The **YOUTH PROGRAMME** superseded **Youth for Europe** in 2000, and targets young people aged between 15 and 25 years. The programme was to run until 2006 and was given financial resources of €520m. in order to contribute to the education of young people, particularly through exchange activities and European voluntary service. The scheme involves 31 countries: the 25 European Union Member States, plus Iceland, Liechtenstein, Norway, Bulgaria, Romania and Turkey. The programme focuses particularly on promoting co-operation in youth-related matters. The programme incorporates the **European Voluntary Service** programme and runs a Euro-Med partnership programme. The 2001 **White Paper** on Youth was the result of a wide-ranging consultation at national and European level, and seeks to engineer new mechanisms and ways to counter young people's strong disaffection with the traditional forms of participation in public life. At its core it calls on young Europeans to become active citizens.

YOUTH TRAINING: See **European Social Fund**; **Social Policy**

YUGOSLAVIA's disintegration in the 1990s was associated, as far as the European Union (EU) was concerned, with the early failure of efforts to develop an effective **common foreign and security policy** (CFSP). From the outset of the conflict in the Balkans (see **Western Balkans**), the European Communities (EC) were involved in efforts to try to avert war and the disintegration of the Yugoslav federation. Initially, the EC offered the prospect of an **association agreement**, but this failed to prevent the secession of **Slovenia** and **Croatia** in 1991. Indeed, under pressure from **Germany**, the EC effectively sealed the fate of Yugoslavia by recognizing the two countries. Soon after, **Bosnia-Herzegovina** was recognized, although Greek objections delayed recognition of the Former Yugoslav Republic of **Macedonia** until 1995. All that was now left of Yugoslavia was Serbia and Montenegro, which existed as the Federal Republic of Yugoslavia until adopting the name **Serbia and Montenegro** in 2003. In the meantime, the EC sought to avert further conflict in Bosnia by sponsoring a Conference on Yugoslavia in August 1992 and seeking a new mandate for sanctions from the **United Nations**. Sanctions and renewed attempts to broker cease-fires failed to have much impact, and a plan for a confederal solution in 1993 had to be abandoned for lack of support within Bosnia. The plan was replaced by a proposal to, in effect, divide the new state, but this too was eventually rejected by the Bosnian Serbs in 1994. Soon the **USA** became more deeply involved and, with the backing of the **North Atlantic Treaty Organization**, secured a peace deal at Dayton in November 1995.

Post-Dayton, the role of the EU in the reconstruction of the former Yugoslavia was initially focused on the **Royaumont Process** aimed at promoting stability and good neighbourliness between the successor states, and the administration of Mostar, a city divided between Croats and Muslims. In 1997 proposals on closer ties with the EU were put forward. In what was referred to as the 'regional approach', the EU required that the successor states co-operate with one another and commit themselves to respect minority and **human rights** as well as democratic principles as preconditions for financial aid and better trade access to the EU market. Following the Kosovo conflict in 1999, the need to promote stability in the region – now referred to as the **Western Balkans** and incorporating **Albania** – led to the creation of the **stabilization and association process**. As part of this process countries of the former Yugoslavia gained the status of **potential candidate state** as well as access to a new programme of financial assistance: **CARDS**.

The Politics of Series

This new series from Routledge provides a fresh perspective on various political issues world-wide. Subjects including **Terrorism, Oil, Migration, the Environment, Water** and **Religion** are analysed in detail, with statistics and maps providing a thorough examination of the topic.

Each book comprises an A-Z glossary of key terms specific to the subject, as well as relevant organizations, individuals and events.

A selection of 8-10 chapters in essay format, each around 5,000 words in length, written by a group of acknowledged experts from around the world provide in-depth comment on some of the issues most relevant to each title.

Key Features:
- This mixture of analytical and statistical information is a unique aspect of this series, and provides the reader with a comprehensive overview of the subject matter
- Information can now be found on each of these topics in these one-stop resources
- This series provides the only detailed examination of politics relating to specific subjects currently available.

For more information on this series, including a full list of titles, please contact reference@routledge.co.uk

Routledge
Taylor & Francis Group